Web Engineered Applications for Evolving Organizations:
Emerging Knowledge

Ghazi I. Alkhatib
Princess Sumaya University for Technology, Jordan

Senior Editorial Director:	Kristin Klinger
Director of Book Publications:	Julia Mosemann
Editorial Director:	Lindsay Johnston
Acquisitions Editor:	Erika Carter
Development Editor:	Mike Killian
Production Coordinator:	Jamie Snavely
Typesetters:	Keith Glazewski, Natalie Pronio and Milan Vracarich, Jr.
Cover Design:	Nick Newcomer

Published in the United States of America by
Information Science Reference (an imprint of IGI Global)
701 E. Chocolate Avenue
Hershey PA 17033
Tel: 717-533-8845
Fax: 717-533-8661
E-mail: cust@igi-global.com
Web site: http://www.igi-global.com/reference

Library of Congress Cataloging-in-Publication Data

Web engineered applications for evolving organizations : emerging knowledge /
Ghazi I. Alkhatib, editor.
     p. cm.
  Includes bibliographical references and index.
  Summary: "This book explores integrated approaches to IT and Web
engineering, offering solutions and best practices for knowledge exchange
within organizations"--Provided by publisher.
  ISBN 978-1-60960-523-0 (hardcover) -- ISBN 978-1-60960-524-7 (ebook) 1.
Web site development. 2. Organizational change. I. Alkhatib, Ghazi, 1947-
TK5105.888.W37243 2011
006.7068--dc22
                              2011009995

British Cataloguing in Publication Data
A Cataloguing in Publication record for this book is available from the British Library.

All work contributed to this book is new, previously-unpublished material. The views expressed in this book are those of the authors, but not necessarily of the publisher.

Table of Contents

Section 2

Section 3

Detailed Table of Contents

Section 1

Chapter 1

Stefan Stieglitz, University of Potsdam, Germany
Christoph Fuchß, Virtimo Webbased Applications, Germany

Mobile phones and PDAs can be utilized as ad-hoc mobile messaging communication devices for near field communication by using Bluetooth technology and mobile ad-hoc networks (MANET). Until now known MANET concepts rely on stationary networks. Liability and stability of the connection in near field communication-based networks are pivotal ans require sophisticated and complex mechanisms. However, these mechanisms often do not reflect the application's particularities such as memory or interface restrictions. This contribution provides an approach for an ad-hoc messaging network (AMNET), which uses simple store-and-forward message passing to spread data asynchronously. This approach focuses primarily on application-specific needs that can be covered by simple message passing mechanisms. In this chapter, we will describe a network based on the AMNET approach. Results are derived by scenario analysis to provide insights into speeding up the network setup process and enable the use of AMNETs - even with a limited number of participants - by introducing a hybrid infrastructure and by adding mobile nodes.

Chapter 2

P. Mariño, University of Vigo, Spain
F. P. Fontán, University of Vigo, Spain
M. A. Domínguez, University of Vigo, Spain
S. Otero, University of Vigo, Spain

Biological research in agriculture needs a lot of specialized electronic sensors in order to fulfill different goals, like as: climate monitoring, soil and fruit assessment, control of insects and diseases, chemical pollutants, identification and control of weeds, crop tracking, and so on. That research must be supported by consistent biological models able to simulate diverse environmental conditions, in order to predict the right human actions before risky biological damage could be irreversible. In this chapter an experimental distributed network based on climatic and biological wireless sensors is described, for providing real measurements in order to validate different biological models used for viticulture applications. Firstly is introduced the rationale of zoning in Galicia's territory. Then the experimental network for field automatic data acquisition is presented. Following, the design of the wireless network is explained in detail. Finally future developments and conclusions are stated.

Chapter 3

Faïza Najjar, National School of Comp. Science, Tunisia
Hassenet Slimani, Faculty of Sciences, Tunisia

Mobile query processing is, actually, a very active research field. Range and nearest neighbor queries are common types of queries in spatial databases and location based services (LBS). In this chapter, we focus on finding nearest neighbors of a query point within a certain distance range. An example of query, frequently met in LBS, is "Find all the nearest gas stations within 2 miles neighborhood of his/her current location". We propose two approaches for answering such queries. Both are based on a recent indexing technique called N-tree. The first one is a branch and bound approach, whereas the second, called 'neighborhoods scanning', is based on a variant of N-tree, Leaves-Linked N-tree (LLN-tree). LLN-tree is an index tree structure that avoids visiting multiple paths during range search. Both techniques are presented, illustrated and evaluated. Experiments show that the latter approach outperforms the former in response time and disk access as well.

Chapter 4

Michael Decker, University of Karlsruhe, Germany

Workflow management systems (WfMS) are a special class of information systems (IS) which support the automated enactment of business processes. Meanwhile there are WfMS which allow the execution of tasks using mobile computers like PDA with the ability of wireless data transmission. However, the employment of workflow systems as well as mobile technologies comes along with special security challenges. One way to tackle these challenges is the employment of location-aware access control to enforce rules that describe from which locations a user is allowed to perform which activities. The data model behind access control in termed Access Control Model (ACM). There are special ACM for mobile information systems (IS) as well as for WfMS, but no one that addresses mobile as well as workflow specific aspects. In the chapter we therefore discuss the specific constraints such a model should be able to express and introduce an appropriate ACM. A special focus is on location constraints for individual workflow instances.

Chapter 5

Wolfgang Woerndl, Technische Universitaet Muenchen, Germany
Michele Brocco, Technische Universitaet Muenchen, Germany
Robert Eigner, Technische Universitaet Muenchen, Germany

We give an overview of ideas for integrating context in recommender systems in general and specifically in various mobile application domains. Our main case study is an approach for vehicular ad-hoc networks (VANETs). The system recommends gas stations based on driver preferences, ratings of other users and context information such as the current location and fuel level of a car. We explain the main design issues behind our recommender. Our approach first filters items based on preferences and context, and then takes ratings of other users and additional information into account, which can be relayed from car to car in a VANET. We also outline other mobile scenarios for contextualized recommender systems: a system for recommending mobile applications based on user context, an approach to find relevant resources in mobile semantic personal information management, and a decentralized recommender system for personal digital assistants (PDAs) that has been successfully applied in a real world mobile city guide.

Section 2

Chapter 6

L. Robert, Government Arts College, India
R. Nadarajan, PSG College of Technology, India

There has been an unparalleled explosion of textual information flow over the internet through electronic mail, web browsing, digital library and information retrieval systems, etc. Since there is a persistent increase in the amount of data that needs to be transmitted or archived, the importance of data compression is likely to increase in the near future. Virtually, all modern compression methods are adaptive models and generate variable-bit-length codes that must be decoded sequentially from beginning to end. If there is any error during transmission, the entire file cannot be retrieved safely. In this chapter we propose few fault-tolerant methods of text compression that facilitate decoding to begin with any part of compressed file not necessarily from the beginning. If any sequence of one or more bytes is changed during transmission of compressed file due to various reasons, the remaining data can be retrieved safely. These algorithms also support reversible decompression.

Chapter 7

Raoudha Ben Djemaa, MIRACL, Tunisie
Ikram Amous, MIRACL, Tunisie
Abdelmajid Ben Hamadou, MIRACL, Tunisie

This chapter proposes a generator for adaptive Web applications called GIWA. GIWA's objective is to facilitate the automatic execution of the design and the generation of Adaptable Web Applications (AWA). Characteristically, the effort in this work has to be pursued with special attention to both issues applied to AWA: adaptability and adaptivity. The architecture of GIWA is based on three levels: the semantic level, the conceptual level and the generation one. Using GIWA, designers specifies, at the semantic level the features of Web application. The conceptual level focuses on the creation of diagrams in WA-UML language; the extended UML by our new concepts and new design elements for adaptation. At the generation level, GIWA acquires all information about users' preferences and their access condition. Consequently, the generated pages are adaptable to all these information. An evaluation and a validation of GIWA are given in this chapter to prove our adaptation.

Chapter 8

In this data-centric world, as web services and service oriented architectures gain momentum and become a standard for data usage, there will be a need for tools to automate data retrieval. In this chapter we propose a tool that automates the generation of joins in a transparent and integrated fashion in heterogeneous large databases as well as web services. This tool reads metadata information and automatically displays a join path and a SQL join query. This tool will be extremely useful for performing joins to help in the retrieval of information in large databases as well as web services.

Chapter 9

Grids are increasingly being used in applications, one of which is e-learning. As most of business and academic institutions (universities) and training centres around the world have adopted this technology in order to create, deliver and manage their learning materials through the Web, the subject has become the focus of investigate. Still, collaboration between these institutions and centres is limited. Existing technologies such as grid, Web services and agents are promising better results. In this chapter the authors support building our architecture Regionally Distributed Architecture for Dynamic e-Learning Environment (RDADeLE) by combining those technologies via Java Agent Development Framework (JADE). By describing these agents in details, they prove that agents can be implemented to work well to extend the autonomy and interoperability for learning objects as data grid.

Chapter 10

The routing problems can be divided into two major classes. They are 1) Unicast routing and 2) Multicast routing. The Unicast routing problem is as follows. Given a source node sr, a destination node dn, a set of QoS constraints qc and an optimization goal (optional), find the best feasible path from sr to dn, which satisfies qc. The Multicast routing problem is as follows. Given a source node sr, a set st of destination nodes, a set of constraints cts and an optimization goal (optional), find the best feasible path covering sr and all nodes in st, which satisfies cts. This chapter presents two such Unicast QoS based algorithms called as Source Routing and the proposed Heuristic Routing. A Client Server based model has been generated to study the performance of the two algorithms with respect to the message overhead, response time and path delay. The Experiments and the results are analyzed.

Section 3

The rapid growth of the World Wide Web has complicated the process of Web browsing by providing an overwhelming wealth of choices for the end user. To alleviate this burden, intelligent tools can do much of the drudge-work of looking ahead, searching and performing a preliminary evaluation of the end pages on the user's behalf, anticipating the user's needs and providing the user with more information with which to make fewer, more informed decisions. However, to accomplish this task, the tools need some form of representation of the interests of the user. This chapter describes the SWAMI system: SWAMI stands for Searching the Web with Agents having Mobility and Intelligence. SWAMI is a prototype that uses a multi-agent system to represent the interests of a user dynamically, and take advantage of the active nature of agents to provide a platform for look-ahead evaluation, page searching, and link swapping. The collection of agents is organized hierarchically according to the apparent interests of the user, which are discovered on-the-fly through multistage clustering. Results from initial testing show that such a system is able to follow the multiple changing interests of a user accurately, and that it is capable of acting fruitfully on these interests to provide a user with useful navigational suggestions.

Web cache systems enhance Web services by reducing the client side latency. To deploy an effective Web cache, study about traffic characteristics is indispensable. Various reported results show the evidences of long range dependence (LRD) in the data stream and rank distribution of the documents in Web traffic. This chapter analyzes Web cache traffic properties such as LRD and rank distribution based on the traces collected from NLANR (National Laboratory of Applied Network Research) cache servers. Traces are processed to investigate the performance of Web cache servers and traffic patterns. Statistical tools are utilized to measure the strengths of the LRD and popularity. The Hurst parameter, which is a measure of the LRD is estimated using various statistical methods. It is observed that presence of LRD in the trace is feeble and has practically no influence on the Web cache performance.

This chapter identifies and measures correlations between compliance with usability guidelines and the popularity of a Web site. A sample of e-learning Web sites was reviewed and their usability scored using a Web-based evaluation system developed during the study. This usability score was then tested against five different ranking systems using Spearman's Rank correlation. The results of these tests show a strong correlation between compliance with usability guidelines and Web site popularity. The five ranking systems also showed positive correlations to each-other and to the usability of the sites. The conclusion drawn from these results is that compliance with usability guidelines could be a way to achieve higher Web site popularity and visitor numbers.

Chapter 14

This chapter describes an Integrated Web Services Brokering System (IWB) to support the automated discovery and application integration of Web Services. In contrast to more static broker approaches that deal with specific data servers, our approach creates a dynamic knowledge base from Web Service interface specifications. This assists with brokering of requests to multiple data providers even when those providers have not implemented a community standard interface or have implemented different versions of a community standard interface. A specific context we illustrate here is the domain of meteorological and oceanographic (MetOc) Web Services. Our approach includes the use of specific domain ontologies and has evaluated the use of case-based classification in the IWB to support automated Web Services discovery. It was also demonstrated that the mediation approach could be extended to OGC Web Coverage Services.

Section 4

Chapter 15

This chapter focuses on the adoption and adaptation of methodologies drawn from research in psychology for the evaluation of user response as a manifestation of the mental processes of perception, cognition and emotion. We present robust alternative conceptualizations of evaluative methodologies, which allow the surfacing of views, feelings and opinions of individual users producing a richer, more informative texture for user centered evaluation of software. This differs from more usual user questionnaire systems such as the Questionnaire of User Interface Satisfaction (QUIS). We present two different example methodologies so that the reader can firstly, review the methods as a theoretical exercise and secondly, applying similar adaptation principles, derive methods appropriate to their own research or practical context.

Techniques and tools that enable website developers without formal training in human-computer interaction to conduct their own usability evaluations would radically advance the integration of usability engineering in website development. This chapter presents experiences from usability evaluations conducted by developers in an empirical study of means to support non-experts in identifying usability problems. A group of software developers who were novices in usability engineering analyzed a usability test session with the task of identifying usability problems experienced by the user. When doing this, they employed a simple one-page conceptual tool that supports identification of usability problems. The non-experts were able to conduct a well-organized usability evaluation and identify a reasonable amount of usability problems with a performance that was comparable to usability experts.

Developing usable products becomes more and more important for software developers. Developing web applications it's more challenging than developing desktop applications due to the various users that will interact with the final product. Satisfying users' expectations becomes a very difficult task, as usability proves to be a very complex goal to achieve in the context of increased productivity targets in software engineering process. The present chapter focuses on the idea of rethinking the concept of usability moving from the traditional view of usability expressed in the internal characteristics of the product towards usability understood as deriving from the quality of interactions between humans, their work and the web design product. Usability is not only an add-on or a final result in the design process but it is embedded as a main concern within the design process itself. In order to build usable products, a great attention should be oriented to users and their needs, and this can be a very challenging task for software developer teams. In this chapter we will describe an interdisciplinary approach, based on applying social sciences techniques and methods that can be helpful in overcoming the difficulties in understanding the users. We will provide a short description of the proposed methods, a guide in applying these methods and a framework that integrates each of the proposed methods into the corresponding step of the web product development life cycle. The chapter ends with the presentation of two case studies showing the applicability of the proposed solution in real design contexts.

Chapter 18

Christopher Power, University of York, UK
André Pimenta Freire, University of York, UK
Helen Petrie, University of York, UK

This chapter presents methodologies and techniques for performing accessibility evaluations on web applications. These methodologies are discussed in the context of performing them within a web engineering process, be it a traditional, unified or agile process. In this chapter the case is made that website commissioners and web engineers cannot afford to overlook accessible practices as they risk alienating an increasingly large user base who may require accessible web features.

Chapter 19

Dimitris Spiliotopoulos, University of Athens, Greece
Georgios Kouroupetroglou, University of Athens, Greece
Pepi Stavropoulou, University of Athens, Greece

This chapter presents the state-of-the-art in usability issues and methodologies for VoiceWeb interfaces. It undertakes a theoretical perspective to the usability methodology and provides a framework description for creating and testing usable content and applications for conversational interfaces. The methodologies and their uses are discussed as well as certain technical issues that are of specific importance for each type of system. Moreover, it discusses the hands-on approaches for applying usability methodologies in a spoken dialogue web application environment, including methodological and design issues, resource management, implementation using existing technologies for usability evaluation in several stages of the design and deployment. Finally, the challenging usability issues and parameters of the emerging advanced speech-enabled web interfaces are presented.

Preface

INTRODUCTION

This is the fourth sequel of volumes on the series of Advances in Information Technology and Web Engineering titled: Web Engineering Applications for Evolving Organizations: Emerging Knowledge based on revised and extended articles published in Volume 4, 2009, and highlights the importance of knowledge in the new evolving organization in the next decade. In this introduction, two disciplines related to the theme of the book are explained: Software engineering and knowledge systems. In the second section, the characteristics of the knowledge-based evolving organization are explained. The latter two sections highlight recent technology platforms for Web-based applications and related latest application domains, respectively.

SCOPING THE WEB ENGINEERING DISCIPLINE

Looking back at the articles published in the first four volumes, perhaps it is time to go back and reflect on the scope of software engineering before we start highlighting issues related to the theme of this volume.

The field of Web Engineering has been defined in several ways. Here are two definitions: (1) The application of systematic, disciplined and quantifiable approaches to the cost-effective development and evolution of high-quality solutions in the World Wide Web. (webengineering.org), and (2) Web Engineering covers the realization of solutions within the World Wide Web, its applications and its advancement, in particular its approaches, methods, models, principles and tools, which are based on the information and communication technologies of the Internet. (iswe-ev.de)

In an article that reviewed 11 books on Web Engineering highlighted the following common themes and contents (Pröll and Reich, 2010):

- Web Engineering Process
- Formulation and Planning Analysis
- Modeling of Web Applications
- Design Modeling for Web Applications
- Testing of Web Applications
- Web Science extensions
- Semantic Web

An analysis of a Web Engineering maturity model shows the concentration on application development processes and user analysis (Deshpande, 2003).

In a keynote presentation, the author presented 8 levels of Web application types (www.icwe2004. org/speakers.html):

- **Document centric:** Static homepages, company Web sites
- **Interactive:** Virtual exhibition, news sited, and travel planning
- **Transactional:** online banking, online shopping, booking systems
- **Workflow-based:** E-government, B2B solutions, and patient workflow
- **Collaboration:** Chat room, e-learning, and virtual shared workspace
- **Portal-oriented:** community portals, online shopping mall, and business portals
- **Ubiquitous:** Customized services, location-aware services, and device independent delivery
- **Knowledge-based:** recommender system, syndication, and management information system

Clearly, previous discussions may lead readers to believe that the concentration of Web Engineering field is on Web-base application development, such as Web site design and E-business and E-government applications. However, research in the field during the past four years expounded other areas, such as Web search mechanisms, email filtering, Web-based cooperative learning, practices of open software development, agent technologies, and social networks. Therefore, researches and practitioners need to look at Web engineering field as encompassing other areas beside Web site application development. This nullifies the notion that Web engineering is purely a subset of software engineering.

The discussion on Web engineering will not be complete without mentioning two other related fields found in the literature when searching for Web engineering, namely Web science and GeoWeb. To shed some light on these two fields, a sample curriculum and conference themes are provided below.

A sample curriculum for Web science follows (wiki.websciencetrust.org/w/Curriculum_topics):

- History of the Web
  - Forerunners (Otlet, Wells, Bush, Engelbart, Nelson) - information systems, concepts, early computer systems
  - Hypertext Community - information systems
  - Internet history - DARPA, IP, TCP, FTP, WAIS, GOPHER
  - W3C History - See W3C timeline
- Building the Web
  - Web Architecture (HTTP, HTML, URI, XML, XSLT, JavaScript, AJAX)
  - Key Algorithms
  - Community Inclusion- Incentives for Innovation - Openness / universality
  - Decentralization
  - Governance
  - Standards
- The Web in Society
  - E-commerce
  - IP / copyright
  - Privacy
  - Co-evolution of society and web

- - Culture and technology
  - Systems theory
  - Social structures and processes
  - Groups and identity
  - Commercial structures and economics
  - Globalization
  - Social capital and power inequality
  - Collective intelligence
- Deploying the Web - Operational sing Web Science for a World of International Commerce
  - Business Strategy
  - Information systems (basics of)
  - Cloud computing infrastructure
  - Policy
  - Regulation and security
  - Sector-specific info
  - Online markets
  - Design vs evolution
  - International context - developed and developing world
  - Profit vs common good
  - Software / hardware context (speeds etc)
- Analyzing the Web
  - Methodologies (build around case studies)
  - Uncertainties and critical thinking
  - Graph theory
  - Power laws
  - Statistics / regression analysis
  - Networks - game theory, social network analysis, ANT
  - Web mining
- Understanding Web Users: Surveys and Qualitative

The 2011 GEOWEB conference program will focus exclusively on Smart World Applications and their value within the following industry areas (geowebconference.org/program/theme-areas): Smart Grids and Utilities, Air Traffic Management, Urban Infrastructure and, Transportation, Business and Consumer, Public Safety and Security, and Environment and Climate Change

The following figure attempts at showing the relationship among the fields of computer science (CS), software engineering (SE), Web engineering (WE), Web science (WS), and GEOWEB (GW).

The overlapping between disciplines is explained as follows:

- **Between CS and SE:** programming courses such as Java and XML
- **Between SE and WE:** Principles of SE, HTML, development environments such as Expression and Dreamweaver
- **Between WE1 and WS:** Web site development and application life cycle management for Web-based application development

Figure 1. Relationship among Computer Science (CS), Software Engineering (SE), Web Engineering (WE) (WE1: Web site development, WE2: other Web-based Applications), Web Science (WS), and GE-OWEB (GW)

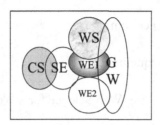

- **Between GW and WS, WE:** the methodologies and techniques employed by latter disciplines in developing applications of GW, as listed above.

KNOWLEDGE MANAGEMENT SYSTEMS (KMS) AND KNOWLEDGE-BASED SYSTEMS (KBS)

KBS is a branch of Artificial Intelligence (AI) and its corresponding application of Expert System (ES). Knowledge is represented as facts or symbols. Facts are quantifiable numbers and symbols are beliefs expressed in degrees/levels or probabilities. Knowledge could be automatically extracted from databases that stores historic facts related to a specific domain such as approving credit card applications, or manually from an expert in the domain field. Knowledge in the KMS, on the other side, is classified as tacit and explicit knowledge. KMS deals with the capturing, coding, storing, distributing, and use of structured and unstructured knowledge. Part of the KMS may be used as input to the KBS following a period of use. Therefore, we introduce the principle of validation and verification of KMS to ensure that knowledge stored in KMS continues to be valid.

Knowledge is validated during the following stages as follows: (1) Capturing: knowledge is validate against the source which could be either internal (employees of all levels) or external (suppliers and customers), (2) Coding: during this step, new knowledge is validated for proper coding for retrieval, and is checked against existing knowledge to discover any inconsistencies to be removed or explained, (3) Distribution: validation is done to ensure that knowledge is accessed at the right time, with the right format, and by the right people, (4) Knowledge verification is done at the last stage to ensure that it is used for the right decision. A feedback is requested from the user to decide whether to keep the knowledge as stored, be modified, or be removed from knowledge base.

For the purpose of building the evolving knowledge-based organization, the KMS is adapted.

Characteristics of the Knowledge-based Evolving Organization

The 11th European Conference on Knowledge Management ECKM 2010 lists the following selected sample topics for its program:

- Knowledge creation and sharing mechanisms
- Knowledge sharing between different groups in an organization

- Sharing and co-operation in Communities of Practice
- KM and innovation
- Content management systems
- Establishing Innovation networks
- KM performance criteria
- Knowledge Ontologies
- KM towards stakeholders needs
- KM and the Web and e-Business
- Km and eBusiness models
- KM sharing between individuals vs groups

In addition, The 7th International Conference on Knowledge Management, October 2010 lists the following sample topics:

- Social Networking and Online Communities
- Communication, Collaboration and Knowledge Sharing
- Knowledge Discovery
- Risk Knowledge Management

Another study suggested that utilization and processing of knowledge in the real-time enterprise is accomplished through human machine intelligence and organic sense making coupled with attention/ motivating/commitment and creativity/ innovation. In a sense, the enterprise's business environment drives the KM system through radical and discontinuous change rather than the use of information and communication technologies.

In another paper, authors cited three types of knowledge management initiatives in organization (Bold emphasis are added by author) (Alavi and Leidner, 2001)

*(1) the coding and sharing of best practices. For example, an insurance company was faced with the commoditization of its market and declining profits. The company found that applying the best decision making expertise via a new underwriting process **supported by a knowledge management system** enabled it to move into profitable niche markets and, hence, increasing income, (2) the creation of corporate knowledge directories, also referred to as the mapping of internal expertise. Because much **knowledge in an organization remains uncodified, mapping the internal expertise is a potentially useful application of knowledge management**. One survey found that 74% of respondents believed that their organization's best knowledge **was inaccessible** and 68% thought that **mistakes were reproduced several times**. Such perception of the failure to apply existing knowledge is an incentive for mapping internal expertise, and (3) the creation of knowledge networks. For example, when Chrysler reorganized from functional to platform-based organizational units, they realized quickly that unless the **suspension specialists could communicate easily with each other across platform types**, expertise would deteriorate. Chrysler formed Tech Cul, bringing **people together virtually and face-to-face** to exchange and build their collective knowledge in each of the specialty areas. In this case, the knowledge management effort was less focused on mapping expertise or benchmarking than it was on **bringing the experts together** so that important knowledge was shared and amplified. Providing online forums for communication and discussion may form knowledge networks. Buckman Laboratories uses an **online interactive forum***

*where user comments are threaded in conversational sequence and indexed by topic, author, and date. This has reportedly enabled Buckman to respond to the changing basis of competition that has evolved from merely selling products to solving customers' chemical treatment problems. In another case, Ford found that just by sharing knowledge, the **development time for cars** was reduced from 36 to 24 months, and through **knowledge sharing with dealers**, the delivery delay reduced from 50 to 15 days.*

Discussion on KM will not be complete without discussing organizational learning (OL). In his paper, the author links OL to knowledge. Organizational learning calls for continuous assessment of performance, both successes and failures. This activity ensures that learning takes place to support continuous improvement. After-action reviews and retrospects are tools that facilitate evaluation of knowledge by asking teams to discuss activities and project openly and honestly. Knowledge is a critical asset in every learning organization. Because learning is both a product of knowledge and its source, a learning organization recognizes that the two are inextricably linked and manages them accordingly. Knowledge leads to OL, and OL feedbacks to knowledge for improvements. The units of knowledge production are both individual-based and team-based. Learning organizations implies that while knowledge is created in the minds of individuals, knowledge development thrives in a rich web of social contact among individuals, groups, and organizations. A learning organization provides creative opportunities for this knowledge to be developed and shared with others through interpersonal contact and access to documentation (Serrat, 2009a).

Based on the selected reviews of previous research, the ensuing section presents several characteristics of knowledge-based organizations.

First: Ability to capture knowledge from different sources, i.e. internal and external. Employees of all levels should be given the proper and convenient venues to contribute to knowledge bases without revealing privacy information. External groups, such as customers, suppliers, and strategic partners should also have the same arrangement.

Second: Incorporate knowledge creation and capturing in all of its processes. Organizations should allow a knowledge layer to be on top of all its processes. This would include activities looking for new innovative ideas, lessoned learned, and others similar activities. This activity will provide input to the next characteristic.

Third: Effective knowledge sharing mechanisms. The following is a suggested list of areas for knowledge sharing:

- E-practices for idea management
- Best practice
- Lessons learned
- Special Interest Groups
- Expert or Expertise Directory
- Lead Tracking System for customer relationship management (CRM)
- Collaborative Systems (patents, and trademarks)
- E-Learning Systems

Fourth: Organization must learn as teams first and then as individuals by supporting triple loop organization learning through team organization structure. A model for knowledge base build up life cycle based on the three learning loops: single, double, triple is presented below as developed by the author.

Figure 2. Knowledge base build-up life cycle (KBBLC). (SLL, DLL, TLL: single, double and triple loop learning, respectively)

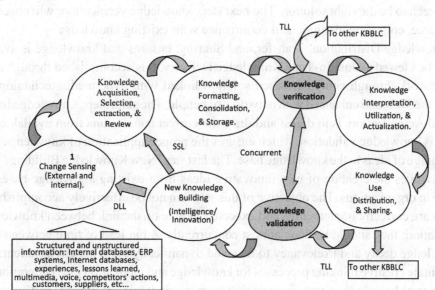

The suggested model is depicted in Figure 2.

The underlying assumptions behind this model are as follows:

- All knowledge used and created are integrated and made available; it acts as a supportive system for all activities.
- Single-Loop Learning and Double-Loop Learning are included in the model. SSL operated in functional silos, while DLL crosses boundaries of different processes belonging to one functional area or several functional areas in an organization. The Duetro Learning or Triple Loop Learning (TLL) is the link between different knowledge base build-up life cycles. The mean of implementing the latter one is through team organization, where each KBBLC is treated as a team with intra- and inter- communication is permitted to share knowledge.
- The model incorporated the steps of knowledge verification (KR) (identifying the knowledge right) and knowledge validation (KL) (adding the right knowledge) similar to the same concepts used in software engineering and as stated in the above discussion.

The steps of the KBBLC are explained in the following paragraphs. The objective in the first step, Change Sensing (externally and internally), is to obtain continuous input and feedback from external and internal environments, and have a continuous flow of new ideas, learning from organization's experience and from the experiences of best practices of other organizations. This step will provide durability and sustainability of organization's KMS. It will help the organization to become flexible enough not only to respond, but also to anticipate internal and external changes competitively. The second step, Knowledge Acquisition, Selection and Review, makes scanning of all available knowledge to decide on what to preserve for the next step. The media for the third step, Knowledge Formatting, Consolidation, and Storage, is proposed to be a hybrid model of the different tools currently used to preserve knowledge: that is a multimedia of computer-based approach and human-centered approach. The basic problem with the first one is the content-rich, context-poor of stored knowledge. In human-centered approach, knowledge is volatile and its storage is linked to the wills of those people involved. A mix between people and technology is seen to be the right solution. The next step, knowledge verification, will check knowledge against the source, collection medium, and congruence with existing knowledge.

Step 5, Knowledge Distribution, Transfer, and Sharing, ensures that knowledge is available when needed. It can be viewed as Just-In-Time Knowledge Delivery. It is accomplished through an integrated knowledge network through computer-based solution linked with hypermedia technology and made available over the Web, and enhanced with networks of people. The sixth step, Knowledge Interpretation, Utilization and Actualization, is to digest and draw the correct conclusions from available knowledge. The next step is knowledge validation, which ensures the proper application of knowledge to guarantee continuous storage of ideas to the knowledge base. The last step, New Knowledge Building / Intelligence/ Innovation, involves the creation of new innovative ideas from existing knowledge bases through its intelligent use in organizations. The objective of this step can not be effectively accomplished unless all previous steps are correctly implemented and executed. A note on the link between knowledge verification and validation: they should be done almost concurrently. A big lead of time between the two may result in knowledge decay and irrelevancy to new and dynamically evolving environment.

Fifth: Facilitate creative thinking processes for knowledge and innovation idea generation. This could be based on current knowledge bases or stemming from the dynamics of internal and external environments. One author explains the relationship between creativity and innovation.

One article defines the relationship between creativity and innovation "creativity is the mental and social process—fuelled by conscious or unconscious insight—of generating ideas, concepts, and associations. Innovation is the successful exploitation of new ideas: it is a profitable outcome of the creative process, which involves generating and applying in a specific context products, services, procedures, and processes that are desirable and viable. Naturally, people who create and people who innovate can have different attributes and perspectives. It follows, then, that innovation begins with creativity." (Serrat, 2009b)

A suggested method is for organizations to adapt creative thinking processes and personal/team profiles. The latter one could be based on measure such as Myers Briggs Type Indicator (MBTI) (myersbrings.org) or Herrmann Brain Dominance Instrument (HBDI.com). By reviewing both sites, the author believes that the latter one is more suited to creativity thinking and team communication. In this part, the author presents an approach to integrate creative thinking process and HBDI.

Creative thinking steps include: interest, preparation, incubation, illumination, verification, application, validation, and storage. The definitions of the four brain quadrants as used by HBDI are as follow: quadrant A (QA): Logical, factual, rational, critical, analytical, quantitative, authoritarian, and mathematical, quadrant B (QB): Technical reader, data collector, conservative, controlled, sequential, articulate, dominant, and detailed, quadrant C (QC): Musical, spiritual, symbolic, talkative, emotional, intuitive, (regarding people), and reader (personal), and quadrant D (QD): Intuitive (regarding solutions), simultaneous, imaginative, synthesizer, holistic, artistic, and spatial. Measure of HBDI may be applied to individuals, teams, and organizations. Any of these three measurements, individually or collectively, may show strength in one or more of these quadrants. Strength of measure is low, intermediate, strong, and very strong, ranked from the middle of the circle outwards. Each individual, team, or/and organization has a profile that depicts the strength in one or more of these quadrants: higher measures are the ones away from the center of the circle. The figure below depicts an explanation of the four quadrants of the brain and a sample team profiles. The little circles inside depicts team member's profiles.

Figure 3. (a) The four quadrant explained, and (b) Team with balance profiles on the left and team with strong profiles in QA and QB on the right

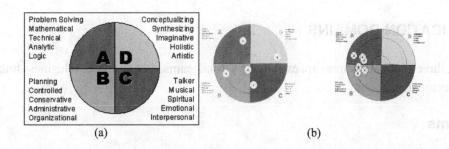

(a)   (b)

The paper again added the verification and validation steps as used in software engineering: verification will ensure that the correct procedure is followed in the adaptation of new knowledge, while validation will ensure that new knowledge do achieve intended outcomes and provide the justification to continue the use of such new knowledge. In each of the creative thinking steps, specific type of people who are strong in one or more of these quadrants is required. To start with, all four types of quadrants are required for interest and preparation steps. For incubation and illumination, however, people strong in QD and QC are required to carry on the task of adopting new ideas. People who are strong in QC are needed to convince people who are strong in AQ and QB, who normally will object to change unless they are gently brought into the wagon, perhaps through information meeting at lunch or sports activity. Individuals who are extremely strong in one quadrant should not be put at top management or as team leaders, since such HBDI characteristic would hamper progress towards adapting new knowledge. The paper suggests that the team leader should be alternated according to the step involved in creative thinking: steps 1 and 2 for QA and QB, steps 3 and 4 for QC and QD, steps 5 for QA and QB, step 6 for QB and QA, step 7 QA and QD, step 8 for QB. Figure 4 shows the steps of creative thinking and the relationship to the four quadrants.

In one reported case, for example, a software development team consisted of member profiles that are mainly strong in QA and QB and weak in QC and QD, while the team leader had a strong QD. Team members were waiting for instructions from the team leader, while the team leader was expecting members to perform independently. The team was dissolved and the project failed. Therefore, HBDI and creative thinking should assist in building effective communication channels among the following groups:

Figure 4. Steps in creative thinking and role of the four quadrants for each step (appearing letter in quadrants indicates importance)

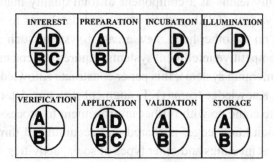

team members, team members and team leader, and inter-teams. In addition, it will create an atmosphere conducive to creative thinking processes.

NEW APPLICATION DOMAINS

In this section, three application areas are explained: virtual teams, data analytics (Business Intelligence), and Web content management.

Virtual Teams

Virtual Communities (VC) may consist of organizations, teams, and social groups. A VC indicates an organizational or community structure that is flexible enough to optimize individual and group performance under new and changing conditions. A VC should create a sense of sharing experiences, perspective, support, and trust between people working toward similar goals or solving problems together. Some of the issues related to the operations of VC:

- What are metrics for community Web site performance?
- Risk assessment and management, configuration control and management project plan.

The following discussion present a framework for virtual teams on demand (VTonD) using the HBDI principle as explained above. In addition, the framework distinguishes between three types of teams: quality, knowledge, and innovation, supporting SLL, DLL, and TLL, respectively. The three types of teams generate quality ideas, knowledge ideas, and innovation ideas, respectively.

The objective of "VTonD" is to establish a mechanism by which team construction is performed based on team function by employing HBDI technique.

Team Types/Functions

Previous research in the area of linking HBDI to organization and team innovation [Leonard & Straus, 1997] makes a very strong case for the use of the HBDI (Herrmann Brain Dominance Instrument) and whole brain concepts to foster creativity and innovation, build and manage productive teams, and communicate more effectively. This article provides a holistic approach to teams functions and structure in organizations and develops idea generation life cycle of the different types/functions of teams

Three types of teams or team functions are identified: Quality, Knowledge, and Innovation. Most organizations establish quality teams as a component of total quality management program. Quality teams (QT) generate quality ideas (QI) based on structured databases to improve process efficiency and reduce costs. Recently, on the other hand, new areas of systems such as knowledge management systems and strategic and competitive intelligent systems required the construction of different types of teams. As a result to these emerging systems, this paper constructs Knowledge and innovation teams as extensions to quality teams. Knowledge teams (KT) augment structure databases with unstructured and semi-structure information to come up with further improvement to processes.

Knowledge, including tacit knowledge, is shared and accumulated through social exchanges and informal organization, such as meetings and other types of social activities. IBM's project "Knowledge

Figure 5. Virtual Teams on demand: Individual and team profiles and team construction (Bold lines on the top left circle indicate profiles) (Note: the position of the little circle indicates the strength of the quadrant)

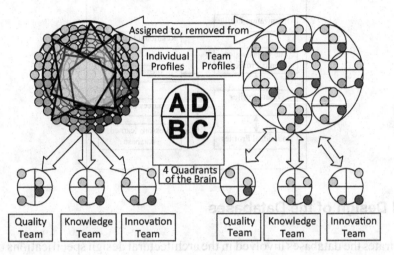

Socialization" is an example of how tacit knowledge could be shared through story telling. (http://www. IBM.com) An article reported the results of a study that highlighted the importance of humanistic and entertainment approaches to facilitate tacit knowledge sharing and elicitation (Desouza, 2003). This is an important point because it will impact the identification of the relevant candidate quadrant of HBDI to KT function as well as the inter-team communication link, namely quadrant C. KTs generate knowledge ideas (KI), such as improving customer care, after sales customer satisfaction, and meeting management.

At the final level, innovation teams (IT) uses the same information/knowledge as KT, in addition to external information/knowledge, as well as sharing ideas among processes and organizations. Normally, it dwells in depth on current process assumptions and will lead to fundamental changes in these processes. Innovation teams generate innovation ideas (I^2) that will lead to maintaining and/or improving the competitive advantage and devising new strategic directions for organizations operating in the global economy, such as new product development, new market penetration, new quality checks, and innovative advertising campaign. When discussing types of teams, we refer to team types as team functions also. This is needed to support the notion of one team generating all three types of ideas.

Pictorial Representation of the VTonD

The first step is to store individual and team profiles using HBDI techniques. Once these profiles are stored, team membership selection, composition, and transfer should be conducted dynamically so that team and individual satisfaction and performance should be maximized. Figure 5 demonstrates the profiles of members and teams. New teams will be constructed based on the major intended function: quality, knowledge, innovation, or a combination of the three. Members will be transferred from one team to the other to bring harmony and complementary functions to teams. In addition to team membership, leaders of teams should be selected based on the map between team function, members' profile, and team's profile.

Figure 6. Architectural design of the creative thinking framework. (Single and two-sided arrows represent one-to-many and many-to-many relationship, respectively

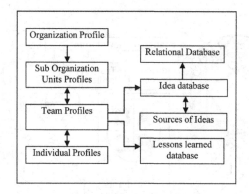

Architectural Design of the Databases

Figure 6 demonstrates the databases involved in the architectural design specifications of the framework. Based on the figure, here is a sample list of use case scenarios:

- create the profiles of the organization, organization sub-units (such as marketing, production, accounting, and purchasing departments}, teams, and individuals
- update the above database of profiles, if needed
- Verify and validate ideas
- Store/update ideas and lessons learned
- Remove profiles from teams and individuals
- Update relational database from ideas database
- Add an individual profile to a team
- Remove an individual profile from a team
- Recompose team profile
- List team profiles
- List team members profiles
- List ideas and lessons learned generated by respective teams

WEB ANALYTICS WITH AN APPLICATION IN BUSINESS INTELLIGENCE (BI)

According to Thomas Davenport, analytics represent a subset of business intelligence. While BI can answer questions such as "what happened; how many, how often, where; where exactly is the problem; what actions are needed", analytics can answer "why is this happening; what if these trends continue; what will happen next; what is the best that can happen". From this perspective, we can asses a Web Analytics Maturity Model could borrow from the TDWI model. (www.tdwi.org)

This section contains discussions of Web analytics maturity model and BI maturity model. Then it presents an application for BI in human resource appraisal.

Web Analytics Maturity Model (Hamel, 2009)

Overview: Jim Sterne, dubbed as the "godfather of web analytics", was pushing for online marketing as early as 1994. In his "E-Metrics: Business metrics for the new economy" paper published in 2000 he mentioned that "while all e-business managers clearly recognize the tremendous value of e-customer analytics, most lack the staff, technical resources, and expertise to harness and put to effective use the flood of raw data produced by their Web systems". A decade later, we can only admit this statement remains true.

The Web Analytics Maturity Model (WAMM) is adapted and derived from proven models in fields such as business intelligence and process optimization, or inspired from models proposed by industry analysts and leaders. Based on the critical success factors contributing to the "use of analytics to make better decisions and extract maximum value from business processes", those are applied to a five level multi-dimensional capability maturity model.

The proposed model presents five maturity states:

- Analytically impaired
- Analytically initiated
- Analytically operational
- Analytically integrated
- Analytical competitor

The six key process areas, or success factor dimensions, are:

- Management, Governance and Adoption
- Objectives definition
- Scoping
- The Analytics Team and Expertise
- The Continuous Improvement Process and Analysis Methodology
- Technology and Data Integration

Those maturity levels and key process areas defines common features and attributes as well as key practices that will significantly increase the likelihood of success and positive return of a web analytics program.

BI Maturity Model

Wayne Eckerson is the creator of The DataWarehouse Institute (TDWI) BI Maturity assessment tool, Director of Research and author of "Performance Dashboards: Measuring, Monitoring and Managing Your Business". The TDWI model main purpose is to "gauge where your datawarehousing initiative is now and where it should go next". Each of the six stages is defined by a number of characteristics: scope, analytic structure, executive perceptions, types of analytics, stewardship, funding, technology platform, as well as change management and administration.

The TWDI model addresses the business intelligence maturity, a term coined by Gartner analyst Dresner in 1989 as the "set of concepts and methods to improve business decision making by using fact-based support systems".

1. **Prenatal – Management Reporting:** Standard set of generic reports distributed without discrimination for actual needs. Inflexible and hard to modify, users tend to bypass the established solution.
2. **Infant – Spreadmarts:** Individual, disconnected spreadsheets and desktop solutions with their own set of data, metrics and rules that are not aligned with the organization. Although they offer a low cost and locally controlled solution, they prevent management from getting a clear and consistent picture of the organization.
3. **Child – Data Marts:** All knowledge workers are empowered with timely information and insight. Data is shared and standardized at the department level, offering a standard set of application, business data and metrics.
4. **Teenager – Data Warehouse:** Definitions, rules and dimensions are standardized across the organization and deeper analysis is available through interactive reporting and analysis. Queries crosses functional boundaries and the data warehouse becomes a tactical tool to improve process efficiency across the whole value chain, contributing to a fact-based decision making culture.
5. **Adult – Enterprise Data Warehouse:** There is now a single version of the truth, data becomes an asset as important as people, equipment and cash. Scorecards and dashboards contribute to align every worker with the corporate strategy. ROI becomes positive and new, unexpected ways of using this knowledge emerge as a competitive asset.
6. **Sage – BI Services:** Data is open to customers and suppliers, extending the value chain beyond the corporate boundaries. Knowledge workers don't have to switch context to analyze data since the data, information and insight is embedded into operational applications and contribute to decision engines (think of fraud detection, behavioral targeting, and automated applications). Business Intelligence becomes ubiquitous and value increase exponentially.

BI Application to Human Resources Appraisal System

On company has an HR appraisal system in traditional Entity Relationship Diagram (ERD) database system running of Microsoft SQL Server. A suggestion was made to migrate this application to a BI platform. Two alternatives were considered: IBM's Cognos as a third party software and using native facilities of MS SQL Services. The latter alternative was selected for ease of transformation from the current platform to the new one. The following steps were followed based on the standard method of Extract, Transform, and Load (ETL) for creating HR appraisal mart for BI platform:

1. **Extract:** data and relationships were selected from the traditional ERD and transformed into a star schema where all relations are linked to the fact table at the middle of the star. The fact table represented the key fields to be linked to the corresponding relations containing detailed information.
2. **Transform:** data in the traditional ERD were linked to data in the star schema and any inconsistencies in data definitions were removed.
3. **Load:** two years of data were loaded from the traditional database to the new star schema database. A pivot table-like spreadsheet appears for presentation of multilevel selected facts in columns and

rows and with results of evaluation in the body of the sheet. This will allow a drill down capability as well.

Now the company can display different facts and generate reports quickly based on the tables. HR manager can look for trends and exceptions in these reports and make decisions to remedy the situation. Also, the HR mart is considered as a repository of employees skills where weaknesses and strengths can be identified. Plan can be devised for training needs and incentives.

Web Content Management (WCM)

Introduction (en.wikipedia.org)

A web content management system (WCMS) is a software system which provides website authoring, collaboration and administration tools designed to allow users with little knowledge of web programming languages or markup languages to create and manage the site's content with relative ease. A rich WCMS provides the foundation for collaboration, offering users the ability to manage documents and output for multiple author editing and participation. Most systems use a database to store content, metadata, or artifacts that might be needed by the system. Content is frequently, but not universally, stored as XML, to facilitate, reuse, and enable flexible presentation options

A presentation layer displays the content to Web-site visitors based on a set of templates. The templates are sometimes XSLT files. Most systems use server side caching to improve performance. This works best when the WCMS is not changed often but visits happen on a regular basis. Administration is typically done through browser-based interfaces, but some systems require the use of a fat client.

Unlike Web-site builders, a WCMS allows non-technical users to make changes to a website with little training. A WCMS typically requires an experienced coder to set up and add features, but is primarily a Web-site *maintenance* tool for non-technical administrators

A presentation layer displays the content to Web-site visitors based on a set of templates. The templates are sometimes XSLT files. Most systems use server side caching to improve performance. This works best when the WCMS is not changed often but visits happen on a regular basis. Administration is typically done through browser-based interfaces, but some systems require the use of a fat client.

Unlike Web-site builders, a WCMS allows non-technical users to make changes to a website with little training. A WCMS typically requires an experienced coder to set up and add features, but is primarily a Web-site *maintenance* tool for non-technical administrators

The Gartner Maturity Model for Web Content Management (WCMMM) (MacComascaigh, 2008)

Introduction: WCMMM outlines a model for assessing the state of an organization's Web content management (WCM) solution. CIOs and other IT leaders responsible for the strategic success of their organization's WCM strategy can use this model to articulate what they would like to achieve with their WCM solution, and to assess the level of change required to make that happen.

The Gartner Maturity Model for WCM Explained: A maturity model for WCM is a tabular representation of solution areas, such as Web authoring, workflow and solution architecture, together with a rating of how "mature" or developed that solution area is and can become. It is a framework with which to assess the value of your current WCM implementation and how it suits your business or organizational needs.

Level 1 - Initial: This level features no standardized processes. Instead, different approaches are still applied on a case-by-case basis. This level is characterized by a lack of auditing, reporting and controls. Links between key business objectives and aspects of the WCM solution are being formed, but have yet to be converted into metrics. Formal executive sponsorship for these links is not yet evident. In most cases, the need for executive sponsorship is under-estimated.

Level 2 - Developing: The business objectives that can be addressed using a WCM solution are documented. Due to a lack of formal training, different individuals perform similar tasks using their own procedures. Platform diversity is being replaced by standardization. However, there is no formal communication of standard processes, and what documentation exists is weak. There is much reliance on the knowledge of individuals, so errors are likely.

Level 3 - Defined: Program definition for the WCM solution is complete. Procedures have been identified — for the authoring and publication of content, for example. These procedures are standardized, documented and communicated through training. Procedures are unsophisticated and formalized from existing practices. It is left to individuals to follow these procedures, and deviations are unlikely to be detected. Web sites still exhibit inconsistencies, and multi-site management is cumbersome. Governance is included as part of the overall strategy but remains difficult. Executive awareness is achieved. Solid progress from this level requires more formal executive sponsorship. WCM program goals are linked well to business objectives.

Level 4 - Managed: Tracking is in place to monitor the progress of the WCM solution against selected business objectives. It is possible to monitor and measure compliance with procedures, and to take action where processes are not working effectively. Processes are under constant improvement and constitute good practice. Automation and tools are used in a limited or fragmented manner. Executives in charge of the change management strategy champion the WCM solution internally, and communicate the benefits of that strategy to the whole organization. Full user adoption has typically not yet been achieved. Only one WCM interface is exposed to users, while repositories from other vendors can be accessed for legacy purposes either through federated search or back-end integration.

Level 5 - Optimized: Processes are refined into best practices, based on the results of continuous improvement and maturity modeling with other parts of the business. IT is used in an integrated way to automate the workflow, providing tools to improve quality and effectiveness, and making the enterprise quicker to adapt. Agility, scalability and effectiveness are broadly associated with the successful WCM solution. Benefits of the WCM strategy are realized and communicated to the organization as part of the continuing change management effort. User adoption is typically complete. The solution architecture is homogeneous and optimized. Migrations to this platform are complete, and cost reductions due to this strategy have been identified and communicated.

CURRENT TECHNOLOGIES FOR WEB BASED APPLICATIONS

This section discusses two technologies: Cloud computing (CC), and Internet Protocol Multimedia Subsystem (IMS), in addition to one new software development platform, namely Application Life Cycle Management (ALM) tools.

Cloud Computing (CC)

In compliance with Software as a Service (SaaS), Data as a Service (DaaS), Infrastructure as a Service (IaaS), and Platform as a Service (PaaS) models, cloud computing (CC) has recently emerged as a new computing paradigm for creating a shared and highly scalable (a.k.a elasticity) computing infrastructure from physical and virtual resources to deliver seamless and on-demand provisioning of software, hardware, and data as services. Cloud computing has all the necessary attributes and potential to support a global outsourcing environment with lower infrastructure costs, lower energy costs from eliminating hardware boxes, and improved scalability to provide computing resources to meet demand in an unpredictable global market. Current CC can be viewed as a global delivery continuum, where many organizations will originally evolve from initial business process outsourcing (BPO) environments, explore SaaS delivery to optimize that environment, and ultimately experiment with SaaS applications that are deployed in a Cloud "plug-in" model.

Cloud will revolutionize the delivery of technology. In the very near-term, it's adoption will likely be impacted as many firms, and CC will surely be at the forefront of new investment plans for organizations seeking more computing power for their money.

Speaking at the Microsoft Azure Transitioning the Cloud conference, held at the Burlington Hotel, Dublin, Ulf Avrin, senior partner at Tellus International Limited, told the conference he believes that up to 67% of cloud adaptation over the next two years is likely and such an adaptation would represent a huge shift in the way organizations do business.

In two separate surveys, cloud computing and mobile application development, were listed as the top two job security in IT. That's where the IT jobs are expected to be, according to 2,000 IT professionals recently surveyed by IBM. In another survey, when asked about the top technology trends affecting application development, survey participants reported innovations in cloud computing/virtualization and mobile as the most disruptive technologies currently influencing development projects across the enterprise.

Topics in cloud computing includes the following, as compiled by the author may include:

Technologies of CC:

- Tools and platforms
- Virtualization
- Standards for CC software development
- Security challenges and issues in CC
- Evaluating global cloud computing research test beds, such as HP, Microsoft, VMware, Oracle, IBM, Intel, Google, Amazon, and Yahoo
- Searching mechanisms of resources and applications
- Cloud interoperability: status, challenges, and guidelines
- Comparing cloud computing and Web services architectures

Software development issues in CC:

- Use of Software product line development practices
- Open source software development
- Construction of virtual teams and organizations
- Applications in global environments

- Applicability of software development models, such as agile methods, model driven architecture, and CMMI.
- Software agent deployment
- Software development management of cloud computing projects

Applications and management issues in CC

- Performance evaluation of cloud computing applications, customer satisfaction, and total cost of ownership studies
- Applying business process re-engineering/improvement for migrating to cloud computing
- Role of social media and computing for global adaptation and dissemination
- IT governance of people, processes, and technology.
- Managing relationships with outsourced companied
- Cases of best practices, industry reports on experiences and patterns, and strategies for cloud computing adaptation
- egovenment applications to achieve global competitiveness: epratices and eservices in CC
- Cloud computing best practices

Internet Protocol Multimedia Subsystem (IMS)

Introduction

IMS was originally defined by an industry forum called 3G.IP, formed in 1999. 3G.IP developed the initial IMS architecture, which was brought to the 3rd Generation Partnership Project. (El-Sayed, 2006), IMS or IP Multimedia Subsystem has become the de facto standard for Next Generation Networks architecture. It will help facilitate the development and offering of many advanced multimedia applications, such as VoIP, Video, Presence and Location-based applications, Multi-player Gaming, Instant Messaging, and so on.

In (en.wikipedia.org), IMS is explained in as simple as possible way.

"The IP multimedia Subsystem (IMS) is a network functional architecture that is seen as a promising solution for facilitating multimedia service creation and deployment, as well as supporting interoperability and network convergence. IMS allows network operators to play a central role in traffic distribution, therefore being more than "bit pipes" IMS refers to a functional architecture for multimedia service delivery, based upon Internet protocols. Its aim is to merge Internet and cellular worlds, in order to enable rich multimedia communications. It is specified in the 3rd Generation Partnership Project. IMS is an end-to-end architecture that must support several kinds of equipments. In addition, IMS is intended to be "access agnostic", which means that service delivery should be independent of the underlying access technology. Thus, the use of open Internet Protocols is specified in IMS for better interoperability. IMS supports roaming between different networks (3GPP Release 6). It allows the network operator to play a central role in service delivery, and bundle attractive services with their basic access offer. Moreover, IMS should support the creation and deployment of innovative services by operators or third parties and therefore create new business perspectives. The faster development of IMS services should reduce the time to market and stimulate innovation. The combination of several services in one session, the single sign on and unified billing are expected to raise customer's interest and increase the revenue opportunities. In IMS the operator is aware of the actual services the customer is using. Therefore, appropriate billing schemes can be developed IMS is also designed to allow substantial network infrastructure and management savings, therefore improving cost effectiveness. It should decrease the investment threshold for new service deployment thanks to a uniform service delivery platform.

Future possible services on IMS networks are, for instance, Push to Talk over Cellular (PoC), Instant Messaging (IM), mobile gaming or a combination of several existing services (e.g. combination of IM and multiplayer gaming). IMS is intended to enable the deployment of "better and richer" services. It should enable the delivery of real-time IP based communications. It should make the integration of real-time, near real-time and non real time applications easier. It should enable the delivery of simultaneous conversational services in a single session. It should be access agnostic, i.e. allow a user to access its services by any supported media.

Although IMS was originally created for mobile applications by 3GPP and 3GPP2, its use is more widespread as fixed line providers are also being forced to find ways of integrating mobile or mobile associated technologies into their portfolios. As a result the use of IMS, IP multimedia subsystem is crossing the frontiers of mobile, wireless and fixed line technologies. Indeed there is very little within IMS that is wireless or mobile specific, and as a result there are no barriers to its use in any telecommunications environment.

IMS itself is not a technology, but rather it is an architecture. It is based on Internet standards which are currently the major way to deliver services on new networks. However one of the key enablers for the architecture is the Session Initiation Protocol (SIP), a protocol that has been devised for establishing, managing and terminating sessions on IP networks. The overall IMS architecture uses a number of components to enable multimedia based sessions between two or more end devices.

One of the elements is a presence server that handles the user status, and this is a key element for applications such as Push to talk over Cellular (PoC) where the presence, or user status is key to enabling one user to be able to talk to another. .With users now needing to activate many sessions using different applications and often concurrently, IMS provides a common IP interface so that signaling, traffic, and application development are greatly simplified. In addition to this IMS architecture means that subscribers can connect to a network using multiple mobile and fixed devices and technologies. With a variety of new applications from Push to talk over Cellular (PoC), gaming, video and more becoming available, it will be necessary to be able to integrate them seamlessly for users to be able to gain the most from these new applications. It also has advantages for operators as well. Apart from enabling them to maximize their revenues, functions including billing and "access approval" can be unified across the applications on the network, thereby considerably simplifying this area."

Quality of Service (QoS) Management Principle (Bertrand, 2007)

Two strategies are usually associated for providing a good level of QoS in packet networks. The first involves avoiding congestion phenomena. This can be done by implementing Connection Admission Control (CAC), resource reservation or simply by over-dimensioning the network (over-provisioning). A famous example of a QoS framework based on resource reservation is "Integrated Services" (IntServ) [34]. This strategy can also be used in Multiprotocol label switching (MPLS) networks using the Resource ReserVation Protocol (RSVP). The second method focuses on managing congestion. It usually relies on traffic differentiation for providing better QoS to most important flows.

We can distinguish between two types of QoS management schemes. The first aims at providing guaranteed QoS while the other is focused on Relative QoS. QoS guarantees like delay or loss rate bounds can be provided by resource reservation schemes. Relative QoS can be implemented by traffic differentiation. The end-to-end model adopted in IMS introduces several technical challenges, for example concerning QoS, privacy and billing. The main technological issue is related to interoperability. IMS mixes the points of view of IP, wireline telephony and mobile network operators. Moreover, it introduces new networking paradigms and provides specifications, not implementation-ready solutions. Finally, it uses some recent protocols like Diameter that have not been widely deployed. For all these reasons, interoperability may be difficult to achieve in IMS networks. One of the main motivations for IMS is to enable the delivery of real time multimedia services using IP related technologies, but IMS has to manage the different access related constraints imposed by heterogeneous access technologies (e.g. handover in radio access networks). In particular, this makes the establishment of end-to-end QoS guarantees quite difficult.

IMS architecture (_____, IMS, IP Multimedia Subsystem tutorial)

IMS provides a unified architecture which can be divided into three layers:

- Transport and Endpoint Layer
- Session Control Layer
- Application Server Layer

IMS Transport and Endpoint Layer: This layer initiates and terminates the Session Initiation Protocol (SIP) signaling, setting up sessions and providing bearer services including the conversion from analogue or digital formats to packets. It also provides the media gateways for converting the VoIP data to the IMS format.

IMS Session Control Layer: This layer contains what is termed the Call Session Control Function (CSCF) which provides the endpoints for the registration and routing for the SIP signaling messages, enabling them to be routed to the correct application servers. The CSCF also enables QoS to be guaranteed. It achieves this by communicating with the transport and endpoint layer. The layer also includes other elements including the Home Subscriber Server (HSS) that maintains the user profiles including their registration details as well as preferences and the like. It includes the presence server essential to many interactive applications such as PoC. A further element of the session Control Layer is the Media Gateway Control.

Application Server Layer: The control of the end services required by the user is undertaken by the Application Server Layer. The IMS architecture and Session Initiation Protocol (SIP) signaling has been designed to be flexible and in this way it is possible to support a variety of telephony and non-telephony servers concurrently. Within this layer there is a wide variety of different servers that are supported. This includes a Telephony Application Server (TAS), IP Multimedia - Service Switching Function (IM-SSF), Supplemental Telephony Application Server, Non-Telephony Application Server, Open Service Access - Gateway (OSA-GW), etc

Charging

IMS uses a unified billing/charging interface for all services with potential for savings by using common billing for all services. Offline charging is applied to users who pay for their services periodically (e.g., at the end of the month). Online charging, also known as credit-based charging, is used for real-time credit control of postpaid services. Both may be applied to the same session (en.wikipedia.org/wiki)
Potential integration of future IMS based services/applications with IPTV (Ahmad, 2009).

- New IPTV architecture scenarios provide foundation for support of tomorrows IMS IPTV services
- Link IPTV Control and OSS with mobile network trends
- Potential for savings with common billing for all services
- Unified IPTV Control and OSS with mobile network trends
- IPTV Evolution envisages IMS, Web, hybrid services for comprehensive content delivery
- Web and hybrid broadcast services will be integrated with IMS for comprehensive content delivery anytime, anywhere, any screen
- Ability to respond to mobile Internet trends, Web services, and profit centers

Current Research in IMS

Sample research from (Al-Begain, 2010):

- Energy-aware cooperative management of the cellular access network of the operators that offer service over the same area to identify amount of energy to be saves by using all network in high traffic condition.
- Enabling rapid creation of content, such as advertising and general data for consumption in mobile augmented reality based on the Image Apace mirror world services.
- A continuous quantity factor in the condition formula search using the data processing system called Cellular Data Systems which is based on Incrementally Modular Abstraction Hierarchy. It is used for effective development of core business applications that deals with objects that express continuous quantity factor.
- The Geobashing architecture for location-based mobile massive multiplayer online games.
- An analysis of the digital forensic examination of mobile phones.
- Media Share to leverage the end users' viewing and interactive television experience using IPTV development and delivery platform over IMS.
- A hierarchical semantic overlay system for semantic search and service matchmaking.
- Real time video adaptation in next generation networks.
- An IMS-based testbed fro fleet management services
- A heuristic buffer management scheme on Android to enhance video quality on digital handheld devices.
- A novel scalable architecture for efficient QoS to cater IMS services for handheld devices base on Android.
- Using Long Term Evolution (LTE) capacity and service continuity in multi radio environments.

Application Life Cycle Management (ALM)

ALM is the new software development environment for managing software development employing Agile Methods in particular and other methodologies, such Capability Maturity Model Integration (CMMI) designed by the Software Engineering Institute of Carnegie Mellon University. Several ALM exists in the market, such as IBM Jazz and Microsoft Visual Studio Team System (VSTS).

Both Gartner Group (GG) and Forrester Research published reports on ALMs. (Duggan, Light, and Murphy, 2008, West, et. al., 2010) In its report, GG put IBM ALM ahead of Microsoft VSTS ALM. However, the latter tool is the only one that provides two different templates for each of CMMI and AM. Therefore, this introduction opted to present Microsoft ALM.

The discussions below present overview of the Microsoft VSTS ALM. With Visual Studio Team System and the integrated process templates, teams can deliver predictable results, continuously improve and adapt, and effectively collaborate and communicate with team members and stakeholders. Visual Studio Team System includes Microsoft Solutions Framework (MSF) for Agile Software Development and MSF for CMMI Process Improvement. In addition, partner organizations offer processes including SCRUM, and Rational Unified Process (RUP) for Visual Studio Team system. These templates can be used as is, or customized to perform individual development processes. The list below include suggested outline for a presentation on VSTS (en.wikipedia.org/wiki):

FOUNDATIONAL PRINCIPLES

The following are the eight foundational principles, which form the backbone for the other models and disciplines of MSF:

- Foster open communication
- Work towards a shared vision
- Empower team members
- Establish clear accountability and shared responsibility
- Focus on delivering business value
- Stay agile, expect change
- Invest in quality
- Learn from all experiences

MSF MODELS

MSF consists of two models:

- MSF Team Model. This describes the role of various team members in a software development project. The members of this team would be:
  - Product Management: Mainly deals with customers and define project requirements, also ensures that customer expectations are met
  - Program Management: Maintains project development and delivery to the customer

    ◦   Architecture: Responsible for solution design, making sure the solution design optimally satisfies all needs and expectations

    ◦   Development: Develops according to the specifications

    ◦   Test: Tests and assures product quality

    ◦   Release/Operations: Ensures smooth deployment and operations of the software

    ◦   User Experience: Supports issues of the users

One person may be assigned to perform multiple roles. MSF also has suggestions on how to combine responsibilities such as the developer should not be assigned to any other role.

MSF Governance Model

This model describes the different stages in processing for a project. The MSF Governance Model has five overlapping tracks of activity, each with a defined quality goal. These tracks of activity define what needs to be accomplished and leave how they are accomplished to the team selected methodology. For instance, these tracks can be small in scope and performed quickly to be consistent with an agile methodology, or can be serialized and elongated to be consistent with a Waterfall methodology.

- Envision: think about what needs to be accomplished and identify constraints
- Plan: plan and design a solution to meet the needs and expectations within those constraints
- Build: build the solution
- Stabilize: validate that the solution that meets the needs and expectations
- Deploy: deploy the solution

MSF Project Management Process

- Integrate planning and conduct change control
- Define and manage the scope of the project
- Prepare a budget and manage costs
- Prepare and track schedules
- Ensure that right resources are allocated to the project
- Manage contracts and vendors and procure project resources
- Facilitate team and external communications
- Facilitate the risk management process
- Document and monitor the team's quality management process

MSF for Agile Software Development Methodology

The MSF for Agile Software Development (MSF4ASD) is intended to be a light weight, iterative and adaptable process. The MSF4ASD uses the principles of the agile development approach formulated by the Agile Alliance. The MSF4ASD provides a process guidance which focuses on the people and changes. It includes learning opportunities by using iterations and evaluations in each iteration.

MSF for Capability Maturity Model Integration Process Improvement Methodology

The MSF for Capability Maturity Model Integration Process Improvement (MSF4CMMI) has more artifacts, more processes, more signoffs on milestones, more planning, and is intended for projects that require a higher degree of formality and ceremony.

The MSF4CMMI is a formal methodology for software engineering. Capability Maturity Model was created at the Software Engineering Institute of Carnegie Mellon University, and is a process improvement approach that provides organizations with the essential elements of continuous process improvement resulting in a reduced Software Development Life Cycle (SDLC), improved ability to meet the cost and schedule targets, building products of high quality. The MSF4CMMI has extended the MSF4ASD guidance with additional formality, reviews, verification and audit. This leads to a Software Engineering Process (SEP) that relies on process and conformance to process rather than relying purely on trust and the ability of the individual team members. The MSF4CMMI has more mandatory documents and reports than the agile version, and this more formal development process reduces risk on large software projects and provides a measurable status. One of the benefits of using the CMMI process is the standard evaluation by which one can compare the ability to develop software in other organizations.

Lab Components for MS VSTS

For education and training purposes of future students and professionals, the list below contains the components for establishing a laboratory with VSTS.

- Visual Studio Team System 2010 Team Foundation Server Workgroup Edition
- Microsoft Visual Studio Team Suite 2010 which includes: Microsoft Visual Studio Team Architecture, Microsoft Visual Studio Team Development, Microsoft Visual Studio Team Test (includes Microsoft Test and Lab Manager), Microsoft Visual Studio Team Architecture, Microsoft Visual Studio Team Development, Microsoft Visual Studio Team Test (includes Microsoft Test and Lab Manager), Microsoft Visual Studio Team Test Essentials (includes Microsoft Test and Lab Manager), Microsoft Visual Studio Team Lab Management, and Microsoft Visual Studio Team Foundation Server
- Visual Studio Team System 2010 Test Edition
- Visual Studio Team System 2010 Test Load Agent
- MSF for Capability Maturity Model Integration Process Improvement methodology
- MSF for Agile Software Development methodology

Further research recommendations

- Agile methods and VSTS
- Capability Maturity Model Integration (CMMI) and VSTS
- Global software development in VSTS
- ISO implementation in VSTS
- Other model-based and agile methods and VSTS
- Comparative analysis of agile vs. CMMI software development: a case study

- Evaluating Usability of VSTS
- Developing distributed service oriented architecture in VSTS
- Testing approaching in VSTS
- Customization of VSTS for different methodologies
- Business intelligent and VSTS
- Comparing VSTS and UML standards

Ghazi Alkhatib
Princess Sumaya University for Technology, Jordan

REFERENCES

Ahmad, K. (2009), "IMS Based IPTV: Today and Tomorrow," PowerPoint Presentation. www.bloobble. com/broadband-presentation. Accessed Feb 3, 2011.

Alavi, M., & Leidner, D. E. (2001). "Review: Knowledge Management and Knowledge Management System: Conceptual Foundation and Research Issues," March 2001 . *Management Information Systems Quarterly, 25*(1), 107–136. doi:10.2307/3250961

Al-Begain, K. (Ed.). (2010) "Proceedings of the 4th International Conference on Next Generation Mobile Applications, Services, and Technologies," Amman, Jordan at Princess Sumaya University for Technology, 27-29 July 2010 and sponsored by IEEE Communication Society.

Bertrand, G. (2007), "The IP Multimedia Subsystem in Next Generation Networks," May 30, 2007, http://www.rennes.enst-bretagne.fr/~gbertran/files/IMS_an_overview.pdf.

Deshpande, Y. (2003), Web Engineering and The BarBar Web, PowerPoint presentation, file://WebEngAdvacesBook/EnggTheBaBarWebsemifinaMaturitymodel.ppt#256,1,Web Engineering and The BaBar Web, 30 April 2003.

Desouza, K. C. (2003). Facilitating Tacit Knowledge Exchange . *Communications of the ACM, 46*(6), 85–88. doi:10.1145/777313.777317

Duggan, J., Light, M., & Murphy, T. E. (2008) "MarketScope for Application Life Cycle Management," Gartner RAS Core Research Note G00162941, 17 December 2008.

El-Sayed, M. (2006), IP Multimedia Subsystem summary tutorial, Advanced Network Modeling & Optimization Group at Bell Labs Research, Lucent Technologies, Holmdel, USATutorial 4 - IP Multimedia Subsystem

Hamel, S. (2009), "The Web Analytics Maturity Model: A strategic approach based on business maturity and critical success factors." October 2009. Available from http://immeria.net.

Leonard, D. and Straus, S. (1997) "Putting your company's whole brain to work," The Harvard Business Review Julty/August, 1997.

MacComascaigh, M. (2008), "Introduction to the Gartner Maturity Model for Web Content Management," Publication Date: 11 April 2008/ID Number: G00156759 Page 5 of 7 © 2008 Gartner, Inc. and/or its Affiliates

Pröll, B., & Reich, S. (2010),"An Analysis of Textbooks for Web Engineering," in WECU-2010, 1st Educators' Day on Web Engineering Curricula, Proceedings of the 1st Educators' Day on Web Engineering Curricula, Vienna, Austria, July 6, 2010. http://sunsite.informatik.rwth-aachen.de/Publications/CEUR-WS/Vol-607.

Serrat, O., (2009a), "Building a Learning Organization, Knowledge Management," Center, Regional and Sustainable Development Department, Asian Development Bank (oserrat@adb.org). May 2009.

Serrat, O., (2009b) "Harnessing Creativity and Innovation in the Workplace, Knowledge," Management Center, Regional and Sustainable Development Department, Asian Development Bank (oserrat@adb.org). September 2009.

West, D., Hammond, J. S, Gerush, M., and Rose, S., (2010) "Customer needs new vendor strategies, and agile approaches drive ALM to the next level: The time is right for ALM 2.0+," October 19, 2010.

Section 1

Chapter 1
Message–Based Routing in Mobile Networks

Stefan Stieglitz
University of Potsdam, Germany

Christoph Fuchß
Virtimo Webbased Applications, Germany

ABSTRACT

Mobile phones and PDAs can be utilized as ad-hoc mobile messaging communication devices for near field communication by using Bluetooth technology and mobile ad-hoc networks (MANET). Until now known MANET concepts rely on stationary networks. Liability and stability of the connection in near field communication-based networks are pivotal ans require sophisticated and complex mechanisms. However, these mechanisms often do not reflect the application's particularities such as memory or interface restrictions

This contribution provides an approach for an ad-hoc messaging network (AMNET), which uses simple store-and-forward message passing to spread data asynchronously. This approach focuses primarily on application-specific needs that can be covered by simple message passing mechanisms. In this paper, we will describe a network based on the AMNET approach. Results are derived by scenario analysis to provide insights into speeding up the network setup process and enable the use of AMNETs - even with a limited number of participants - by introducing a hybrid infrastructure and by adding mobile nodes.

INTRODUCTION

Nowadays, simple mobile phones as well as smart phones, provide multiple communication interfaces which enable users a wide spectrum of interconnectedness for various applications. However in most cases, the underlying networks depend on infrastructures that are bound to stationary devices, such as access points, cellular mobile radios, or providers who regulate access to the

DOI: 10.4018/978-1-60960-523-0.ch001

Internet and to the traffic control. In our research, we concentrate on a new "message-based" approach. This allows data exchange between mobile devices without the need for a centralized service unit. Data exchange mechanisms are based on the Bluetooth standards and follow store-and-forward principles. By categorizing the transferred data into personalized or anonymous messages, it is possible to analyze the different requirements in ad-hoc messaging networks (AMNETs) regarding security, stability, and flexibility (Fuchß et al., 2006). This contribution is embedded in research on routing problems (Zhen et al., 2003) between nodes on mobile ad-hoc networks, e.g. common MANETs or mesh-networks (Macker et al., 1998). On this basis, we will present the AMNET concept and provide empirical research in this field of ad-hoc networking based on Bluetooth connectivity.

Furthermore, we will test the concept in a simulation and investigate the message transfer behavior in AMNETs. For this reason, we set up an environment that allows numeric simulations of message transfers. Therefore, we are able to track the influence of additional stationary nodes that are statically connected. This structure represents a hybrid network of mobile and stationary nodes which speed up message transfer compared to scenarios containing only mobile nodes. This is the most important factor concerning a potential use of AMNET technology in reality. This contribution ends with the description of the simulation results and final conclusions.

ROUTING IN MOBILE NETWORKS

In this section, we describe the AMNET approach, based on the IEEE 802.15 Bluetooth standards for wireless local networks (e.g. personal area networks). We will concentrate on the issue of addressing and routing messages in the first step. Second, we will discuss the potentials and possible applications for AMNETs.

In recent years, a growing number of research has been conducted on routing in MANETs (Artail et al. 2008, Chin et al., 2002; Royer et al., 1999; Xu et al., 2003), particularly with regard to the limitations of routing protocols (Ni et al., 1999). Some reactive and proactive routing algorithms are provided with respect to different situations. Common protocols show specific vulnerabilities according to scalability, mobility, and network utilization. In growing networks, both methods run out of control because scalability is not suitable and depends on the network's structure. According to Broch et al. (Broch et al., 1998), the main factors that delay the effectiveness of the algorithms in scaling networks are unpredictable mobility, network load, and complex topology. Networks with fast moving nodes often change their topology. These "vivid" networks rely on mechanisms to find routes that are too complex to grant enduring topologies (Chlamtac et al., 2003).

These highly dynamic MANETs, which contain a large number of network nodes, are based on ad-hoc routing protocols (Ni et al., 1999; Woo et al., 2001). In practice, a trade-off between stability and the maintenance of bandwidth overhead limits the effectiveness of those settings in growing scenarios. Especially reactive algorithms tend to be unusable within huge networks, and reactive routing algorithms do not tend to scale well in large settings (Xiaoyan et al., 2002; Yu-Chee et al., 2002).

Promising improvements have been suggested by Hass et al., combining proactive and reactive paradigms to a hybrid routing algorithm, such as the "Zone Routing Protocol (ZRP)" (Haas et al., 2002), which proves efficient in various environments. With respect to a remarkable increasing complexity of the cutting-edge MANET routing algorithms (which are the main obstacle for implementing and using them in practice), we follow an approach of a different direction: To keep routing as simple as possible, one should consider messages as the point of interest and deny the ambition to bring all internet features to mobile networks.

Table 1. Comparison AMNET – MANET

MANET	AMNET
Routing Properties	
Real Time Message Routing	Time-delayed Message Exchange
Directed Message Addressing	Message Exchange With Multicast Patterns
Source-Destination Addressing	Optional Addressing or Category-based Message Filtering
Proactive/Reactive Routing Protocols	Store-and-Forward Principle
Non-optimal Performance in Dynamic Networks	Inherently Based on Dynamic Networking Properties
Single Route per Message	Multiple Routes per Message
Network Properties	
Scaling Issues	Focuses on Localized Communication (Scaling is Subject to Further Research)
Providing End-to-End Connection Infrastructure	Loose Coupling of Nodes
Consistency of Nodes and Relations (e.g. routing tables)	No Network-Based Addressing Mechanisms
Network Properties Mostly Application-Transparent	Applications According to Network Properties (Anonymous, Profile-Based, Personalized)
Deterministic and Reliable Routing	Fish-Eye Routing (Pei et al., 2000b)

AMNET concentrates on mechanisms to provide a best-fit solution for certain applications' needs in vivid network environments.

AMNET CONCEPT

The term AMNET (ad-hoc messaging network) describes a virtual network infrastructure which does not provide any guaranteed reliability for attached network services. Although such limitation does not meet the requirements for a vast number of applications, several scenarios with lower demands regarding transport reliability would benefit from the AMNET approach.

AMNET is based on an ad-hoc store-and-forward procedure for data message transfer. Message forwarding in AMNETs is not subject to time constraints or real-time message routing respectively. This reflects AMNET's store-and-forward character. As a consequence, message routing and forwarding is significantly less complex than in traditional MANET scenarios.

Bluetooth is AMNET's currently employed wireless networking standard because it is widely available in mobile phones and small computers such as PDAs, and consequently carries potential for a dense network of AMNET-enabled nodes. Other wireless network technologies, e.g. IEEE 802.11 techniques, may be used for the set up of AMNETs as well. However, until now there are no implementations on these devices.

As we focus on mobile devices for spontaneous data transmission without a formal infrastructure, message exchange cannot rely on multi-hop end-to-end connections between the involved nodes. This strongly reduces, if not eliminates, the route maintenance complexity compared to mesh networks. Table 1 compares the AMNET and MANET approaches regarding routing and network capabilities.

The differences between MANET and AMNET approaches towards routing as well as network properties provide answers to typical ad-hoc network problems by forming a network infrastructure, which is tailored for a specific class of applications. The most important differences

Table 2. Message Structure in AMNETs

General Header	Message ID	Application ID	Hop Count	Sending Time
Application Header	Category	Addressing	Validity	
Application Data	Payload			

between the generally accepted transfer of classic ISO-OSI layer compositions for mobile networks is the fallback to the network's particularities even on the application layer. For example, the application's ability to determine the relevance of a message also depends on the sender's and receiver's positions and the time difference between posting a message and entering this "orbit of relevance", an atmosphere, in which transferred data loses relevance because of growing time leaks and space.

AMNET IMPLEMENTATION

A prototype for mobile phones has been implemented to exchange messages via Bluetooth. In accordance with typical layer models, as known from the ISO-OSI layering, the architecture has been designed with a programmable Bluetooth interface, along with a message repository for data storage. The differences between the layer model based on the ISO-OSI principles and the prototype implementation can be seen in the way the applications access the data: It is of interest to determine the scope (in space and time) of a message. Configurable message filters control the access of applications towards the repository content. Message properties, set by the various applications by means of message filters, allow for certain message exchange rules between the mobile devices. Apart from that, the applications have direct connection to the message exchange process itself.

The mentioned reference implementation is Java-based and uses the Java Platform 2, Micro Edition. For interaction with the device's Blue-

tooth stack, we use the Java API for Bluetooth (JSR-82). Along with this prototype, a program interface has been implemented that allows to simulate numerous mobile devices moving within a simulated environment. This provides a test bed for message exchange and routing behavior.

AMNET PROTOCOLS

Messages are the central objects in AMNETs. The message format varies among the layers in the AMNET architecture.

Table 2 shows the general structure of messages transmitted between AMNET nodes. The message header ("General Header") is followed by application-specific fields ("Application Header") and, finally, by the application-specific message payload itself. The different parts of a message are handled by different components of the AMNET architecture. The general header is analyzed by the message repository; the evaluation of the application header takes place in the application-specific filter connected to the repository, and the message data are passed through to the application. The following steps are performed when a message is received via the network link:

This process is described in Table 3: Newly received messages are added to the message repository. Rejected messages are ignored from further processing within the actual component. That means that messages rejected by the application-specific filter are not passed on to the application but still exist in the message repository. Thus, such messages still will be passed on to other nodes within range even when they are not relevant to the nodes' own applications. This

Table 3. Actions on Message Receiving

Repository	1. Message ID exist in repository? Reject! 2. Application ID not installed? Reject! 3. Pass to application-specific filter based on application ID
Application-Specific Filter	1. Validity parameters invalid according to application settings? Reject! 2. If application supports addressing: Address does not match application instance? Reject! 3. If category filtering is enabled: Category does not match application category? Reject!
Application	1. Application-specific handling

is part of the AMNET store-and-forward concept. Nodes store messages for a maximum amount of time and deliver them to close-range nodes, with storage time and maximum hop count as limiting factors. This prevents messages to live forever within the network and congestion can be reduced. Messages can be identified by sender address, message payload, message authentication code (MAC), and hop count, among others. This establishes a multicast-like procedure in order to synchronize message repositories of nodes within a certain distance.

Repository organization and message storing are key areas within the AMNET concept. Since the main platform envisioned for AMNET consists of mobile phones and other small digital devices with considerably limited storage and computation capabilities, the repository handling has to be carefully designed, along with message caching and efficient storage techniques. Corresponding to existing approaches for data management in explicitly resource-limited systems, a filtering system has been implemented (Ni et al., 1999; Pei et al., 2000), which can also be used and extended by applications for various message filtering purposes.

Devices for AMNET

The AMNET approach inherently requires a large number of AMNET-enabled devices in order to provide effective message transfers. With a growing density of AMNET nodes, message delivery speed and reliability increase consider-

ably. It should be noted that real-life Bluetooth implementations in mobile devices often do not implement all properties required in the Bluetooth standard, and specifically do not allow multiple simultaneous Bluetooth connections (Fuchß et al., 2006; Leopold et al., 2003), which stresses the need for a high AMNET node density. There are some restrictions to the devices the application has to handle.

A serious problem for the attempt of message propagation without user interaction is the device-specific implementation of Bluetooth security activities. Many operating systems, e.g. Symbian, do not allow programs to listen for incoming Bluetooth connections without asking for approval each time. In this environment, a quiet and transparent passing through is not possible.

Additionally, standard mobile phones pose considerable limitations to J2ME applications. Especially low-end consumer devices do not accept applications that use more than 512kB of memory. This is because of the CDLC specifications and has been empirically shown by Huopaniemi et al. (2003).

As Handy & Timmermann (2006) point out, power demand of Bluetooth technology can be rated as "low" as well as "high" depending on the observer's point of view. In the ad-hoc network domain, Bluetooth is often classified as a technology that consumes low power, e.g. compared to WLAN. From a sensor network researcher's point of view, Bluetooth may have a power consumption that is too high (Leopold et al., 2003). However, Bluetooth power or energy consumption, on the one hand, depends on many technology-specific parameters, and therefore varies according to the selection of these parameters. On the other hand, there are manufacturer-dependent differences and measurement results for the Bluetooth device of a specific manufacturer which cannot simply be transferred to devices of other manufacturers.

Based on Linsky (2001) who presents time-slot-based equations for the energy consumption of synchronous Bluetooth connections and for the page state, Handy & Timmermann (2006) extended their system of equations in order to include all Bluetooth states. They present analytical results for the following states: page, page scan, inquiry, and inquiry scan. These equations can serve as a tool for a manufacturer-independent evaluation of the energy consumption of Bluetooth technology in general and of Bluetooth-based communication protocols such as scatternet formation protocols. Handy & Timmermann (2006) elaborate a system of equations that enables developers to evaluate Bluetooth power consumption independent of a specific device manufacturer. With these equations, communication protocols using Bluetooth can be compared objectively. Therefore, manufacturer-dependent results and time-slot-based energy consumption values can be measured and integrated into these equations.

This approach can be used to obtain more information about power consumption of AMNETs in a real environment.

A Prototype Simulation

As mentioned above, the number of participating users represents a critical factor concerning the success of AMNETs. Only a sufficient amount of network nodes guarantees the successful deployment of applications that deliver messages by diffusion. The common impact of network externalities has been discussed on the basis of various technologies with regard to the introduction of new standards (Ebner et al., 2004).[1]

One main factor to accelerate technology diffusion is to reach a critical mass of users (Ebner et al. 2004). The typical network effects (Witt, 1997) may apply in AMNETs as well. Problems result in the initial (phase) if only very few users participate. Previous research on positive external effects assumes a small increase of benefit for every user when new participants join even throughout the starting phase (Witt, 1997). This is not the case with AMNETs where a certain fixed quantity of existing nodes is mandatory for the message transfer. To reach an initial critical quantity of nodes, stationary connected network participants could be implemented.

To analyze network effects within AMNETs, we implemented a simulation environment which is capable of displaying a varying number of mobile nodes. The dynamically designed round-based model provides information about the number of rounds necessary until a message is spread to a certain quota of mobile nodes. In round zero, one node at random receives a message which is to be transferred to other nodes in its simulated radio range. The following parameters and data describe our simulation environment:

- Simulated area: 6 * 4 km urban area (Berlin Center, Germany)
- Pseudo-realistic urban landscape using street maps
- Participants walk on streets and open spaces
- Pace rate of the simulated nodes matches walking speed, which is up to 3 km/h
- Radio range of participants is restricted to 10 m (according to Bluetooth standards)
- Round-based simulation: One step of simulation equals one second.
- Connection to other devices is only established after 5 rounds of mutual visibility (according to tests regarding Bluetooth discovery times (Fuchß et al., 2006))
- Up to 3 message transfers per node per round

- Different patterns of movement can be assigned to network participants
- The virtual environment can be replenished by mutually connected stationary nodes.

SIMULATION RESULTS

AMNET nodes in the simulation start with an empty repository. In this numeric, round-based simulation, the nodes are moved according to different patterns. If two nodes meet for longer than 5 simulation rounds (which is comparable to up to 20 seconds for the Bluetooth initiation process), the message repositories will be synchronized for each message until the nodes lose connection. Additionally, in some test runs, we added permanently connected stationary nodes (infrastructure nodes). These nodes are capable to synchronize messages with mobile nodes in the vicinity. After receiving a message from a stationary node, the message will be forwarded to all other stationary nodes into the same or another network segment. To research the effects of stationary network participants, their quantity was varied in different simulation runs, and the speed of message distribution is documented.

Figure 1 shows the distribution of the initial message in the network in relation to the number of rounds. The light dotted line represents the progression without stationary nodes, while the other line shows the message distribution in an environment with five additional randomly positioned stationary units.

However, we performed a multitude of simulations running with varying parameters. Our analyses show that the number of nodes determines the acceleration of message distribution. Moreover, stationary nodes speed up the message transfer regardless of the quantity of mobile nodes. The 'geographical' positions of the stationary nodes are important. If stationary nodes are close to each other and mobile nodes are spread widely, the accelerating effect of networks of message

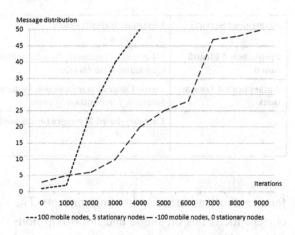

Figure 1. Results with 100 mobile nodes

transfers is less significant. Stationary nodes are especially effective when only few mobile nodes are involved. With an increasing number of mobile nodes, stationary ones lose significance. On the basis of our simulation results, it is possible to calculate the optimal quantity of stationary nodes in proportion to a varying quantity of mobile nodes.

APPLICATIONS IN AMNETS

Use Cases

Applications which utilize the described AMNET network fall into three categories based on their levels of authentication and authorization. These levels range from complete anonymity to verified authorship and addressees. As long as identifications and authorizations are not part of the AMNET platform itself, it can be supported by the application-specific filters. An authorization scheme may support this function. Additionally, addressing can be achieved through application-specific filters that check for an ID or address specific to the application instance. The address types may range from category-based messages to specifically addressed messages with different hop ranges. Table 4 shows applications with dif-

Table 4. Applications within AMNETs

Anonymous Services	Electronic Bulletin Board	Location-Centric Advertisement	Client-Server-Architecture
Profile-based Identification	E-Learning, Community-based Applications (Reputation Systems etc.)	File-Sharing	General Network Applications, Portals
Authenticated Transactions	Traffic Congestion Information Systems, Emergency Information Systems	E-Payment	VPN, Business Transactions
	Category-based Messages (multi-hop)	Messages with Specific Addressee(s) (single-hop)	Messages with Specific Addressee(s) (multi-hop)

ferent authorization and addressing concepts. The current focus lies on single and multi-hop non-addressed but category-based messages (marked gray in Table 4) since the addressed scenario has been subject to comprehensive research (Wang et al., 2002). The described store-and-forward mechanism with hop count limitations can be easily used to control the message distribution range.

The authentication and personalization levels are implemented on top of the AMNET data structures, with various implications for the AMNET network protocol. The existing prototype implementation is sufficient for illustrating the basic functionality and operation of AMNETs but requires further development for enhanced studies, mainly in the area of applications.

Sample Applications

The described concept of AMNET–based message transfer can be used to run several applications such as an electronic bulletin board, community features, mobile learning scenarios or to realize traffic notification services.

Electronic Bulletin Board – Category-based routing and anonymous messaging.

An electronic bulletin board can be used to send messages addressed to all individuals in a specific area (non-personal messages). Receiving posts from bulletin boards can be restricted by defining different categories which one can subscribe to. For example, an electronic bulletin board can be used to signalize specific interests

or offers to other people nearby. By supporting multiple node hops, messages can be sent to a wide range of individuals. Limiting the number of valid hops can be used as an instrument to control the range of the local area in which this message can be received. The diffusion of messages can be accelerated by the use of stationary nodes as our simulations show.

Community Features – Combining who-is-online lists with position-based information.

Community services such as configuring a personal profile using who-is-online lists or complex reputation systems can be provided by mobile ad-hoc networks, e.g. for virtual communities (Lattemann et al., 2007, Stieglitz, 2008). Generating social network effects can be used as one key element to increase diffusion of the described standard (Tscherning and Mathiassen, 2010). Taking part in a virtual community with one's own, self-administrated, personalized user profile enables AMNET applications to offer many services by sharing profile information via ad-hoc message propagation: e.g. to meet people with special interests or to be informed if someone from the who-is-online list is in the current local area.

An Environment for Ubiquitous, Pervasive, Mobile E-Learning

To meet the requirements for ubiquitous e-learning (Ogata et al., 2003), a technical solution for the exchange of learning content can be found in ad-hoc messaging. Hence, AMNETs are applicable to exchange messages and learning objects among participants. This process does not even require any user interaction. A connection could be established and information could be shared automatically (Fuchß et al., 2006). With the combination of decentralized synchronization processes and fixed synchronization points (static AMNET nodes) a platform can be created that covers all issues for modern mobile e-learning environments, which was already shown by the authors in an applied AMNET project (Stieglitz et al., 2007).

Car Traffic Notification Service

Imagine a pseudo-intelligent in-car warning system, which recognizes an arising traffic jam due to accumulating state messages in the direct environment from many other nodes. This information can be forwarded to all nodes taking part in the traffic and thus the driver can be warned in time. First approaches can be seen in the project FleetNet (Franz et al., 2001), which relies on a commercial infrastructure to be built especially for this system.

AMNET can contribute to this scenario by providing the loose coupling of nodes and adopting a sophisticated filter system that aggregates all messages and generates warnings to the driver.

Security Issues

Systems that share data in an unknown network environment must address in-depth security problems which are known from a range of common internet applications. This includes authorization, authentication, trusted data transmission and other issues that are needed to guarantee secure transactions in personal messaging sequences.

A new concept to implement security functions in a distributed mobile network is the web-of-trust approach. Web-of-trust[2] is a popular topic in current research and allows security services in distributed network environments without centralized online trust authorities that imple-

ment those duties and responsibilities in common network settings (Balfanz et al., 2002; Michiardi & Molva, 2001; Haiyun et al., 2002). As Pirzada and McDonald (2004) describe it, depending on a central trust authority is an impractical requirement for mobile ad-hoc networks. They present a model for trust-based communication in ad-hoc networks that also demonstrate that a central trust authority is a superfluous requirement.

A web-of-trust model can handle different types of nodes that act unexpectedly. Deficient nodes have to be bypassed, malicious nodes have to be isolated while warning other nodes nearby, and selfish nodes have to be limited in their actions. Thus, a powerful model has to cover a range of nodes' misbehavior and consider their direct impact on security aspects.

Since security issues are not the main focus in the field of AMNET research at this point, there is no proof of concept implementation yet. This is part of further development and has to be integrated when the AMNET concept is used in applications and products.

CONCLUSION

Our research in the field of AMNET suggests that beneficial message communication can be introduced for an ad-hoc network that serves many specialized applications. These applications need to be designed to rely on asynchronous message passing, thus called time-shifted. AMNETs allow a fast diffusion of messages in dense networks within a given number of hops.

In contrast to some other technologies, this architecture requires a critical mass of nodes to be successful. It is a particularity of AMNETs that a certain number of participants are needed to gain a benefit from passing messages to others. As our study shows, stationary nodes can help to overcome these problems and reduce the barrier for setting up an AMNET system.

Within the scope of further research, new AM-NET prototypes will be developed. The presented simulation environment will be expanded in order to gain more information and to increase the efficiency in AMNETs using hybrid networks that consist of stationary and mobile nodes.

ACKNOWLEDGMENT

This article is a revised and extended version of the contribution "A Concept for Mobile Ad-hoc Messaging Networks (AMNET)" published in volume 4, issue 1, of *The International Journal of Technology and Web Engineering* (JITWE). We gratefully thank Dr. Lattemann and Mr. Stöckel for being co-authors in this manuscript.

REFERENCES

Artail, H., Safa, H., Mershad, K., Abou-Atme, Z., & Sulieman, N. (2008). COACS: A Cooperative and Adaptive Caching System for MANETs. *IEEE Transactions on Mobile Computing, 7*(8), 961–977. doi:10.1109/TMC.2008.18

Balfanz, D., Smetters, D. K., Stewart, P., & Wong, H. C. (2002). Talking to strangers: authentification in ad-hoc wireless networks. Proceedings of the Network and Distributed System Security Symposium.

Broch, J., Maltz, D. A., Johnson, D. B., Hu, Y.-C., & Jetcheva, J. (1998). A performance comparison of multi-hop wireless ad hoc network routing protocols. Proceedings of the 4th annual ACM / IEEE international conference on Mobile computing and networking, ACM Press, Dallas, Texas, United States, 85-97.

Chin, K.-W., Judge, J., Williams, A., & Kermode, R. (2002). Implementation experience with MANET routing protocols. *SIGCOMM Comput. Commun. Rev, 32*(5), 49–59. doi:10.1145/774749.774758

Chlamtac, I., Conti, M., & Liu, J. J.-N. (2003). Mobile ad hoc networking: imperatives and challenges. *Ad Hoc Networks, 1*(1), 13–64. doi:10.1016/S1570-8705(03)00013-1

Ebner, G., Köhler, T., Lattemann, C., Preissl, B., & Rentmeister, J. (2004). *Rahmenbedingungen für eine Breitbandoffensive in Deutschland, Research study for Deutsche Telekom AG*. DIW-Berlin.

Franz, W., Eberhardt, R., & Luckenbach, T. (2001). FleetNet - Internet on the Road. Proceedings of the 8th World Congress on Intelligent Transportation Systems, ITS 2001, Sydney, Australia.

Fuchß, C., Stieglitz, S., & Hillmann, O. (2006). Ad-hoc Messaging Network in a Mobile Environment. Proceedings of the International Conference of Internet Technology and Secured Transactions, London.

Haas, Z. J., Pearlman, M. R., & Samar, P. (2003). *The Zone Routing Protocol (ZRP) for Ad Hoc Networks*. IETF.

Haiyun, L., Zerfos, P., Jiejun, K., Songwu, L., & Lixia, Z. (2002). Self-securing ad hoc wireless networks. Proceedings of the 7th International Symposion on Computers and Communications, 567-574.

Handy, M., & Timmermann, D. (2006). Time-Slot-Based Analysis of Bluetooth Energy Consumption for Page and Inquiry States. Proceedings of the 9th Euromicro Conference on Digital System Design (DSD 2006), 65-66.

Huopaniemi, J., Patel, M., Riggs, R., Taivalsaari, A., Uotila, A., & Peursem, J. v. (2003). *Programming Wireless Devices with Java (TM)*. Platform Addison Wesley Professional.

Lattemann, C., & Stieglitz, S. (2007). Online Communities for Customer Relationship Management on Financial Stock Markets - A Case Study from a German Stock Exchange, Proceedings of Americas Conference on Information Systems (AMCIS 2007), Colorado, USA.

Leopold, M., Dydensborg, M. B., & Bonnet, P. (2003). Bluetooth and sensor networks: a reality check. Proceedings of the 1st international conference on Embedded networked sensor systems.

Linsky, J. (2001). Bluetooth and power consumption: issues and answers. *R.F. Design*, 74–95.

Macker, J. P., & Corson, M. S. (1998). Mobile ad hoc networking and the IETF. *ACM Mobile Computing and Communications Review*, *2*(1), 9–14. doi:10.1145/584007.584015

Michiardi, P., & Molva, R. (2001). CORE: A Collaborative Reputation Mechanism to enforce node cooperation in Mobile Ad hoc Networks, IFIP Conference Proceedings, Vol. 228, 107-121.

Ni, S.-Y., Tseng, Y.-C., Chen, Y.-S., & Sheu, J.-P. (1999). The broadcast storm problem in a mobile ad hoc network. Proceedings of the 5th annual ACM/IEEE international conference on Mobile computing and networking, ACM Press, Seattle, Washington, USA, 151-162.

Ogata, H., & Yano, Y. (2000). Supporting Knowledge Awareness for Ubiquitous CSCL. *E-learning*, 2362–2369.

Pei, G., Gerla, M., & Chen, T.-W. (2000). Fisheye state routing: a routing scheme for ad hoc wireless networks. Proceedings of the IEEE Internations Conference on Communications, 70-74.

Pirzada, A. A., & McDonald, C. (2004). Establishing trust in pure ad-hoc networks. Proceedings of the 27th conference on Australian computer science, 26.

Royer, E. M., & Toh, C.-K. (1999). *A Review of Current Routing Protocols for Ad Hoc Mobile Wireless Networks*. IEEE Personal Communications.

Stieglitz, S. (2008). *Steuerung Virtueller Communities*. Wiesbaden: Gabler.

Stieglitz, S., Fuchß, C., Hillmann, O., & Lattemann, C. (2007). Mobile Learning by Using Ad Hoc Messaging Network. Proceedings of the International Conference on Interactive Mobile and Computer Aided Learning, Amman, Jordan.

Tscherning, H., Mathiassen, L. (2010). Early Adoption of Mobile Devices: A Social Network Perspective, Journal of Information Technology Theory and Application (JITTA). 11(1), Article 3.

Wang, K., & Li, B. (2002). Efficient and Guaranteed Service Coverage in Partionable Mobile Ad-hoc Networks. IEEE INFOCOM, 1089-1098.

Witt, U. (1997). "Lock-in" vs. "critical masses" - Industrial change under network externalities. *International Journal of Industrial Organization*, *15*(6), 753–773. doi:10.1016/S0167-7187(97)00010-6

Woo, S.-C. M., & Singh, S. (2001). Scalable routing protocol for ad hoc networks. *Wireless Networks*, *7*(5), 513–529. doi:10.1023/A:1016726711167

Xiaoyan, H., Kaixin, X., & Gerla, M. (2002). Scalable routing protocols for mobile ad hoc networks. *Network IEEE*, *16*(4), 11–21. doi:10.1109/MNET.2002.1020231

Xu, K., Hong, X., & Gerla, M. (2003). Landmark routing in ad hoc networks with mobile backbones. *Journal of Parallel and Distributed Computing*, *63*(2), 110–122. doi:10.1016/S0743-7315(02)00058-8

Yu-Chee, T., Sze-Yao, N., Yuh-Shyan, C., & Jang-Ping, S. (2002). The Broadcast Storm Problem in a Mobile Ad Hoc Network. *Wireless Networks*, *8*(2-3), 153–167.

Zhen, B., Park, J., & Kim, Y. (2003). Scatternet formation of Bluetooth ad networks. Proceedings of the 36th Annual Hawaii International Conference on System Sciences, Hawaii, USA.

ENDNOTES

[1] A discussion concerning well-known problems in networking environments, e.g. free-rider behavior, tippiness effects or the existence of malign nodes is not included here.

[2] First mentioned in PGP software.

Chapter 2
Viticulture Zoning by an Experimental WSN

P. Mariño
University of Vigo, Spain

F. P. Fontán
University of Vigo, Spain

M. A. Domínguez
University of Vigo, Spain

S. Otero
University of Vigo, Spain

ABSTRACT

Biological research in agriculture needs a lot of specialized electronic sensors in order to fulfill different goals, like as: climate monitoring, soil and fruit assessment, control of insects and diseases, chemical pollutants, identification and control of weeds, crop tracking, and so on. That research must be supported by consistent biological models able to simulate diverse environmental conditions, in order to predict the right human actions before risky biological damage could be irreversible. In this paper an experimental distributed network based on climatic and biological wireless sensors is described, for providing real measurements in order to validate different biological models used for viticulture applications. Firstly is introduced the rationale of zoning in Galicia's territory. Then the experimental network for field automatic data acquisition is presented. Following, the design of the wireless network is explained in detail. Finally future developments and conclusions are stated.

INTRODUCTION

The experimental wireless network is deployed in a peninsula surrounded by two large sea arms called "rias" in Spanish language. In that peninsula, located in the northwest of Spain (near the northern border of Portugal), on the autonomous region called Galicia, the vineyards have four main productive zones called: Meaño, Cambados, Ribadumia and Meis (Figure 1).

Currently differences in productivity and quality of grapes are broadly related with relative heights and sea proximity from each of four zones but nevertheless more rigorous biological

Figure 1. Peninsula photograph

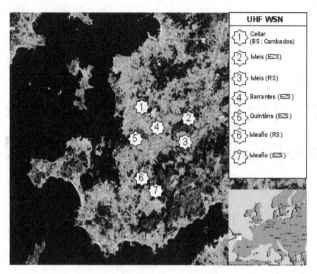

and climatic research (Perry, 2002; Gail, 2007) must be done, in order to provide accurate biological models for ecological simulations applied to viticulture. The relevant pests of vineyards to be detected by such models are: Botrytis Cinerea (noble rot), Plasmopara Viticola (downy mildew) and Uncinula Necator (powdery mildew). For that reason multidisciplinary work must be done among electronic engineers, biologists and ecologists.

Each zone has an electronic zonal station (EZS), in order to bring differences (microclimates), in measurements like: temperature, relative humidity, leave humidity, soil temperature, solar radiation, rain gauge (tipping bucket), and other biological sensors. A data logger and a radio modem is included in each EZS in order to sense, process and transmit the data, enabling the development of an automatic wireless sensor network (WSN), which nodes (the EZSs) are accessible from a wide area. These wireless communication capabilities allow that data could be remotely monitored. The implementation of a warehousing approach, allows the data to be stored in a centralized database that is responsible for query processing. The stored data will be used for biological and ecological models.

This article is an extended version of reference (Mariño et al., 2008a) written by the authors. It is organized in eight parts including this introduction. Part II gives an overview about zoning in viticulture. Part III describes the Data Acquisition System. Part IV outlines the global data management. Part V provides a state-of-the-art in wireless sensor networks. Part VI details the implementation of experimental WSN. Finally, Parts VII and VIII present the future developments and conclusions.

RATIONALE ON ZONING AND PRODUCTION RESULTS

Previous work about climate and viticulture (zoning) in Galicia has been reported for a period of 1971-2000, based on data from 52 meteorological stations spreaded over the vineyard's 10,000 hectares within a whole territory of 29,434 square kilometres (Queijeiro, 2006).

In the Galicia's territory the main climatic features are (Figure 1):

- Presence of wet winds from Atlantic Ocean (direction West-East)

- A North-South highland barrier easing the precipitation over the inner land (1km of maximum altitude) and the Miño River at 50 km from coast
- A stepping relief with depressed zones alternated higher ones towards the East
- Atlantic and Mediterranean winds with dynamic results heavily dependent of: distance to the sea, slope direction and altitude. For this reason is possible to found climates whether oceanic or Mediterranean (several microclimates in the region)

To identify and characterize microclimates for viticulture in the world were proposed several bioclimatic indexes, that are a final account over a growing cycle of six or seven months (time for grapes in the vineyard). The proponents of the six indexes what could identify about 36 different climates for viticulture in the world (Tonietto, 2004), called to their system "Multicriteria Climatic Classification" (MCC).

In the Table 1 a simplified version of the MCC system is shown, where only three main bioclimatic indexes are used: Huglin´s Heliothermic

Index (HI), Drought Index (DI) and Nocturnal Freshness Index (FI). Those three indexes were computed from several climatic and biological parameters:

HI:

$$\sum [(Tmed - 10{\circ}C) + (Tmax - 10{\circ}C)/2]*d$$

DI:

$$\sum (Wo + P - Tv - Es)$$

FI:

$$(Tmed - min(Sept.)$$

The eight variables in the equations are the following:

- *Tmax*, *Tmin*, *Tmed*: maximum, minimum and mean temperatures respectively
- *d*: correction coefficient for the period of diurnal light given the considered latitude (40°-50° N)

Table 1. MCC key for describing climates in viticulture

Index	Class	Abbreviation	Interval
HI	Very hot	HI + 3	HI > 3000
	Hot	HI + 2	2400 < HI ≤ 3000
	Warm	HI + 1	2100 < HI ≤ 2400
	Mild	HI - 1	1800 < HI ≤ 2100
	Fresh	HI - 2	1500 < HI ≤ 1800
	Very fresh	HI - 3	HI ≤ 1500
FI	Very fresh nights	FI + 2	FI ≤ 12
	Fresh nights	FI + 1	12 < FI ≤ 14
	Mild nights	FI - 1	14 < FI ≤ 18
	Hot nights	FI - 2	FI > 18
DI	Very dry	DI + 2	DI ≤ -100
	Moderate dry	DI + 1	-100 < DI ≤ 50
	Sub damp	DI - 1	50 < DI ≤ 150
	Damp	DI - 2	DI > 150

- *Wo*: soil humidity in the starting of grapes's growing cycle
- *P*: monthly precipitation
- *Tv*: potential transpiration
- *Es*: direct evaporation from soil

In the Table 2 are shown the Galicia's microclimates for viticulture compared from other places in the world, based on the MCC system (Blanco-Ward, 2007). It is very interesting to point out that over the territory of Galicia (29,434 square kilometres) were founded more than 1/3 (13) of all microclimates for viticulture in the world (36).

Also there can be seen the Galicia's five "*Origin Denomination*" (OD) or areas with excellent conditions for high quality wine production. In fact

there is a production of white grapes about 50,000 Tons/year under the mentioned five OD's called: Rias Baixas, Ribeiro, Ribeira Sacra, Valdeorras and Monterrei. From them, only the Rias Baixas OD/Albariño provides near 600 trademarks to the Spanish's white wine market. In the world of commercial wine market is worth to say that this Rias Baixas OD has some trademarks in the Parker's index upper than WA 93 (eRobertParker, 2008), an internationally well known high quality rating.

DATA ACQUISITION SYSTEM

The electronic zonal stations (EZSs) are connected with the base station (BS) by the UHF band (not

Table 2. Galicia's microclimates for viticulture compared from other places in the world (based on the MCC system)

MCC System	%	Meteorological stations	Kind of wine growing	Similar zones for viticulture in the world
HI-2 DI-1 FI+1	2	Betanzos	Wines of Earth	Napier (New Zealand)
HI-2 DI-1 FI+2	10	Mabegondo, Arbo, Xinzo, Marroxo, Maceda	Marginal	Tours, Nantes, Colmar (France)
HI-1 DI-2 FI+1	2	Herbón	Marginal	Pau (France)
HI-1 DI-1 FI+1	12	Ames, Salcedo, Lourizán, Rosal, Currás, Ribadumia,	Origin denomination	Cognac, Burdeos, Toulouse (France)
HI-1 DI-1 FI-1	8	Cambados, Vilagarcía, Vilariño, Padriñán	Origin denomination	----------------
HI-1 DI-2 FI+2	4	Caldas, Brollón	Marginal	Macon (France)
HI+1 DI-1 FI+1	13	Monçao, Frieira, Ponteareas, Páramos, Ourense, Peares, Sequeiros	Origin denomination	Módena, Treviso (Italy)
HI+1 DI-1 FI+2	17	Arnoia, Prado, Quinza, Vilamartín, Pumares, Barbantes, Fontefiz, Coles, Pinguela, Montefurado	Origin denomination	Bei Jing (China)
HI-1 DI-1 FI+2	17	Leiros, Mesiego, Belesar, Verín, Coles, Conchada, Bóveda, Castro C., Petarelas	Origin denomination	Perugia (Italy), Bratislava (Eslovaquia)
HI+2 DI-1 FI+1	4	Castrelo, Velle	Origin denomination	Yi Couniy (China)
HI-3 DI-1 FI+2	2	Castro Caldelas (800m)	No wine growing	Vancouver (Canada)
HI-1 DI+1 FI+2	8	Larouco, Villafranca, Ponferrada, Carucedo	Origin denomination	Viseu (Portugal), Valladolid (Spain)
HI-2 DI+1 FI+2	2	Castelo da Pena (740m)	No wine growing	Summerland (Canada)

licensed) between 869.4MHz to 869.65MHz, and the BS is also connected through Internet to the Data Base (DB), the biological and ecological models (BEMs), and to the Web access (Figure 2). Each zonal station comprises an UHF radio modem that transmits the sensors information to the BS through a data call. A powering solar panel (PSP) is located near each EZS for feeding its circuits. In order to reduce costs, the BS makes a call to all the EZSs every 24 hours by means of a polling procedure (Mariño et al., 2008b). During these calls the EZSs send all the information that has been stored on that period. Therefore the BS periodically executes the reading data process and later database storage of the received information, through an Ethernet local area network.

Data from Sensors

An electronic zonal station (EZS) is the basic acquisition equipment of the distributed system, which carries out the data registration (measurements and processing), and the communication with the base station (BS). In this way, each EZS comprises an automatic measurement unit with data transfer capability. The data acquisition process is made inside the EZS by the sensors and the data logger. Each EZS comprises the following sensors: temperature, relative humidity, leave humidity, soil temperature, solar radiation, rain gauge (tipping bucket), and other biological

and ecological features depending on running models (Poza et al., 2006).

All that sensors are integrated in the data logger. The data logger is the EZS nucleus; it captures the data from each sensor, automates the measurements, synchronizes the data and manages the communications. The data transmission is carried out by means of the data logger and the UHF radio modem connected to it. Next, the data captured by the EZS is sent to the database (DB), through the base station (BS), where they are saved. The communication process setting, through the UHF radio modem connected to the data logger, allows the control and programming of several tasks as well as the acquisition of stored data.

The data captured by the data logger are organized in registers. The registers comprise the sensor outputs as well as the time and date. These registers are then sent to the storage system where they are saved for a future access. The data logger is programmed for capturing and storing the sensors information each minute. Due to the limited capacity of the storage system integrated in the data logger, the data can only be stored during a day (24 hours). Figure 3 illustrates the data logger, the storage system, the UHF radio modem and connections with the sensors and electrical supply. All these elements are placed inside a box which protects them from the weather conditions. This box and all the sensors are fixed to a metallic base located at the site (Figure 4).

Figure 2. Network architecture and database interfaces

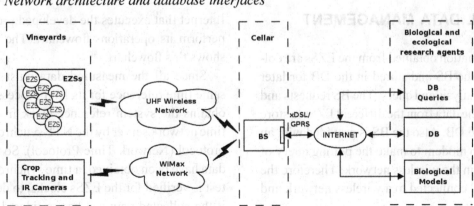

Figure 3. EZS data acquisition and communications system assembled in the protection box

Figure 4. Final assembly and EZS installation

GLOBAL DATA MANAGEMENT

The information obtained from the EZSs are collected by the BS and stored in the DB for later process, analysis and query. The BS requests and compiles the data from the different EZSs to store them in the DB. Also the BS is provided with an UHF radio modem to make the polling query of each EZS in the wireless network. Therefore the BS is a PC connected to a wireless network and

Internet that executes the developed program to perform its operations flowchart. The Figure 5 shows this flowchart.

Since all the measured data must have the same time reference for its later process, the BS obtains the system reference clock from a real time network server by the NTP synchronization protocol (Network Time Protocol). So after the data have been obtained, a time synchronization test is verified for the EZSs clocks, to determine if the collected data can be considered valid. If

Figure 5. BS operations flowchart

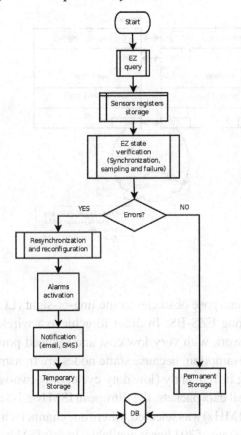

this is the case, the information is stored directly in the DB. Otherwise the problem is corrected (if it is possible), it is notified by e-mail and/or a message, and finally the data and the error information are stored. In this way is possible to know exactly when and what type of errors took place and, depending on this information data can be corrected.

The data from the EZSs are centralized in a relational database. This DB presents one interface with the BS through which all the system information is introduced, and three interfaces to access this information: general data access, access to interesting data to analyze viticulture features, and query of data for providing models (Figure 5). The interface between BS-DB and queries-DB are executed directly by means of ODBC (Open Database Connectivity).

The general data access will directly take place through an Internet accessible Web page. Whereas for queries related to the analysis of viticulture features and models, the access is made through specific views for each type of study (Mariño et al., 2008c). Figure 6 shows an example of the EZS data management. This picture illustrates the structure of communications among equipments, interfaces and layers.

STATE-OF-THE-ART IN WSN'S

Past decade has been very fruitful in the development and application of several standards for mobile, nomadic and fixed wireless networks related with sensors (Akyildiz et al., 2002; Niculescu, 2005; Demirkol et al., 2006). Some specific problems about this kind of networks have been well studied, like: energy efficiency due to collisions, overemitting-receiving, control of packets and idle listening; scalability and changes adaptation in network size, node density and topology; communication paradigms like node-centric, data-centric and position-centric; and many others.

Nevertheless this great researching effort over wireless networks for sensors, there is no any accepted MAC for them, because this kind of sensor networks has a very big dependence of the application. Recent surveys about the most advanced wireless networks like MANETs (Conti et al., 2007a and b) show poor real results in front of expected ones, because the great complexity involved in simulated MAC protocols (Egea-López el al., 2006), on big programming tools, was not after validated with implementation, integration and experimentation over real equipment (chips, microcircuits, modems, antennas, and others). In this way, a particular field of application, called ``wireless sensor networks'' (WSN) is proposed for environmental monitoring, industry (Hodgkinson, 2008) and precision agriculture, among other sectors of activity. The WSNs are featured

Figure 6. Communication example between equipments, interfaces and layers

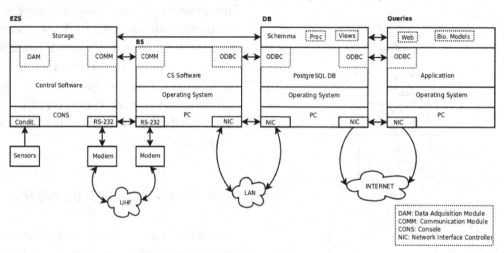

by a stronger interdisciplinary collaboration for creative projects, and a change in the communication paradigm from node-centric to data-centric one, because the main point is the transfer of data from the application field, and not the communication between all the network nodes.

The Wireless Sensor Network (WSN)

Several comparatives among general wireless standards like ZigBee (Prophet, 2004; Wheeler, 2007), Ultra Wide Band (UWB) (Oppermann et al., 2004), Bluetooth (Willig et al., 2005) and WiFi (Kunz, 2006) have been made in order to evaluate some examples of application included industrial wireless sensors (Mariño et al., 2007). Also, more specific WSN applications could be found about environmental research like: hydrology (Moore et al., 2000), fire monitoring (Ruiz et al., 2005), deep ice (Guizzo, 2005), climate monitoring (Gall and Parsons, 2006) and others (Cutler, 2005).

Given the hilly nature of the vineyard zones, the coverage challenges for linking the EZSs with the BS were founded in power, data speed and acceptable error ratio. For example, in the Meis zone the coverage area was over 5 km, with difference in heights about 200 m, very prone

to interpose obstacles in the line-of-sight (LOS) among EZS-BS. In order to achieve a wireless network with very low cost and reduced power consumption, because static nodes are transmitting infrequently (low duty cycle) only two-way small data packets, the European ISM band (868-870 MHz) was selected, where one channel with a data rate of 20 kbps is available. In this ISM band the used radio modems for linking EZS-BS, have the following features: 10-500 mW of transmitting power, 25 kHz of channel spacing, half-duplex communication, 10% duty cycle and 36 seconds of maximum emission time (must be controlled by the data logger). To avoid an obstacle in the LOS between the BS and the EZS, a repeater station (RS) is inserted with other ISM radio modem and a directive antenna, linking the EZS (2.1 km) with the BS (5.17 km). Figure 7 shows an illustrative example of measured rain series carried out between EZS-RS-BS in the Meis zone.

IMPLEMENTATION OF THE WSN IN THE UHF BAND

The wireless network has been implemented using dataloggers from Campbell (CR200 series) linked

Figure 7. Measured rain plot

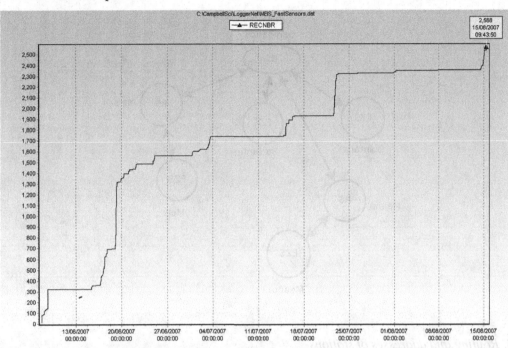

by radio modems (Satelline 3AS). Those radios are working in the UHF band (869.400-869.650 MHz) that is unlicensed in Spain. Power emission is limited until 500mW and the binary ratio is about 19,200 bps for a 25 kHz half-duplex channel. Without obstacles (LOS) the coverage can be more than 5 km at maximum allowed power (Satel Co., 2004).

One of the advantages of those radio modems is the capability of routing data packets among them, making more or less complex networks of nodes depending on the wireless applications. For configuring this kind of networks an unique address is assigned to each radio modem, and all possible routes must be declared on the node where the polling procedure is controlled (BS). Therefore this network configuration is only valid for centralised architectures, where a central station makes periodically the queries to all nodes of the wireless network (Mariño, 2003).

Each EZS is made by a data logger and its corresponding radio modem both connected by a

serial port with a binary rate of 9,600 bps (RS232). In the most cases dedicated repeaters are not necessary given that whatever radio modem, how has been said, can be a repeater. Where NLOS must be supported then a radio modem will be used only as a dedicated repeater (RS). In the Figure 8 is shown the current designed WSN, where four EZS's are linked with the BS, with two of them through one repeater (RS) each one. The Table 3 specifies the routing map for the BS, and the Table 4 justifies the relative positions and heights involved in the EZS's coverage.

The assignment of network addresses is the same of the data loggers CR200. Those data loggers are linked using the proprietary protocol from Campbell called PakBus, which frames are composed following the Figure 9. The starting configuration of routes and available wireless nodes is made in the BS. For each available EZS an unique address is assigned included the repeater address, if any, linked to its route. How has been said, a routing map is stored in the BS

Figure 8. WSN configuration

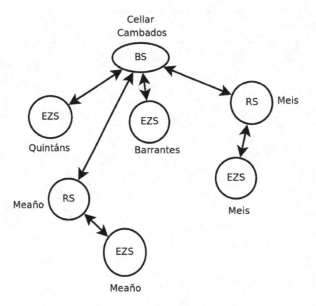

Table 3. Routing and addresses of stations

WSN	Address	Route	Hops
Cellar (BS: Cambados)	1	---	---
Meis (EZS)	2	3-2	2
Meis (RS)	3	3	1
Barrantes (EZS)	4	4	1
Quintáns (EZS)	5	5	1
Meaño (RS)	6	7	1
Meaño (EZS)	7	6-7	2

Table 4. Location of EZSs, Repeaters (RS) and BS

UHF WSN	Length (Km)	Area (m2)	Altitude (m)	Latitude (N)	Longitude (W)
Cellar (BS) Cambados	--	--	50	42°31'11.60"	8°47'33.28"
Meis (RS)	5.17	--	202	42°29'31.69"	8°44'13.13"
Meis (EZS)	2.1	15000	176	42°30'28.33"	8°43'31.3"
Barrantes(EZS)	2.6	5300	13	42°30'17.98"	8°46'5.36"
Quintáns(EZS)	3.31	4000	34	42°29'28.35"	8°48'14.53"
Meaño (RS)	7.64	--	135	42°27'3.42"	8°47'40.89"
Meaño (EZS)	8.61	5000	20	42°26'36.27"	8°47'8.99"

Figure 9. Pakbus frame

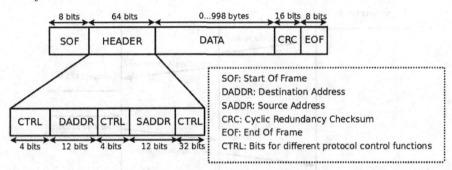

radio modem (Table 3). All EZS's and repeaters (RS) know the routing configuration when a frame comes through them, in order to send correctly the back data packet as response to a first query from the BS

The PakBus frames used by the EZS's are composed by a Start-Of-Frame (SOF), a header, the body of message, a Cyclic-Redundance-Check (CRC) and an End-Of-Frame (EOF). The header includes the destination address and the origin one. Using those data the configuring task of radio modems is possible, because the EZS's can know to whom send the information in a transparent way. For accomplishing the configuration task of radio modems, an offset and a length are setting to indicate where must get the corresponding address inside the received frame from the serial port.

This task only can be correctly executed if no fragmentation is assured over the frames from data logger, easing a correct location by radio modems of the message destination address. In that way must be avoided the received frames from diverse network nodes, could exceed the maximum allowed limit per frame in the radio modems. In the implemented WSN this limit is 1 KB, because an overhead is imposed to the frames by routing protocol of the radio modems. The configuration software of data loggers allows limiting the maximum size of sending frame, assuring no fragmentation in that way. It is worth to say that if a fragmentation occurs data will be lost, or even worse, a communication blocking is present because only the first fragment of the

frame would be correctly received, given that radio modems would routing erroneously the remainder fragments (Figure 10).

The routing of frames is possible through the unique network addresses and inner tables of routing stored in the radio modems. Although the routing tables are only firstly configured in the BS, the intermediate wireless nodes hold actualised their own tables because the routing information is included in the frames sent by all radio modems. When the BS receives new data from the serial port, the radio modem gets the address network from received data. If that address is in their routing tables, this information is added at the beginning of the new frame to send close the original encapsulated frame and checking codes (CRC), and send it to the following hop in the route. Each radio modem receiving this message learns from headers the routes, and actualises correctly their own tables for getting aware of routing back messages.

The queries from the BS are implemented by a Campbell software tool called Loggernet. This tool discharges periodically data from data loggers (EZS's) configured in its database. For each data logger is configured an unique address and a station name with which data are stored. The Loggernet tool allows registering a lot of communication parameters such as: binary rate of serial port, starting of serial port, marking of numbers for communications by GSM modems, etc. One of parameters with great interest is the time between retransmissions. This time should

Figure 10. EZS data flow

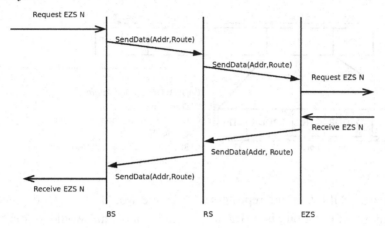

be great enough to allow that a data query could arrive to the destination data logger and return with requested data. Depending on network topology and the number of hops until destination, this elapsed time could be higher than a second.

It is very important that the computer, where the Loggernet program of data discharges is executed, had a dependable time reference. For that reason the NTP protocol is used (Mohl, 2008), synchronizing the computer time through Internet with servers offering stable and dependable time references. Each time that the BS queries an EZS, it checks the time differences and if are relevant an adjustment is made in order to get a temporal coherence among data from all EZS's.

FUTURE DEVELOPMENTS

Experimental work over the implemented WSN is being made in the following lines:

- Addition of new climatic and biological sensors to the EZSs.
- Change of UHF proprietary modems for new RF modular technologies integrated by the authors, in order to enhance the WSN's capabilities.

- Deployment of new EZS over different vineyard zones for providing more spatial resolution to biological and ecological models.
- Design of a wireless broadband (20 Mbps) network in order to provide crop tracking by real time images, and infrared cameras (zonal isotherm maps), by WiMax (IEEE 802.16) equipment (Ghosh et al., 2005; Livingston and Franke, 2006; Yeh et al., 2008) over the 5 GHz ISM band.
- Integrate those images in the global data management system, for giving to the biological and ecological researchers, new knowledge for future enhancement of models.
- Propagation simulations with geographical data for the WSN deployment (Fontán and Mariño, 2008).

CONCLUSION

The authors have developed an experimental distributed network based on the WSN paradigm for wireless sensors. This WSN is based on the European ISM band for providing a low cost and low power consumption network, bringing real measurements to validate different biological and ecological models used for viticulture applications.

Also a global data management system is designed to integrate consistently the measured data in the models. New developments in the experimental wireless network are being tested to add real time images and infrared cameras information, by means of broadband network standards.

ACKNOWLEDGMENT

This work has been sponsored by an R&D project from the Research General Directorate of the Galician Autonomous Government (Xunta de Galicia, northwest of Spain), Ref. PGIDITO6TIC052E. The authors want to thank the staff from MARTÍN CÓDAX CELLAR enterprise, for the kind permission to deploy the experimental wireless network in their properties and facilities.

REFERENCES

Akyildiz, I. F., Su, W., Sankarasubramaniam, Y., and Cayirci, E. (2002). Wireless sensor networks: a survey. *Computer Networks*, No. 38, Vol. 4, pp. 393-422.

Blanco-Ward, D., Garcia Queijeiro, J.M. And Jones, G.V. (2007). Spatial climate variability and viticulture in the Miño river valley of Spain. *Vitis,* No. 46, Vol.2, pp. 63-70.

Conti, M. and Giordano, S. (2007a). Multihop ad hoc networking: The reality. In *Communications Magazine, IEEE*, Vol. 45, pp. 88-95, Toronto, Ont., Canada.

Conti, M. and Giordano, S. (2007b). Multihop ad hoc networking: The theory. In *Communications Magazine, IEEE*, Vol. 45, pp. 78-86, Toronto, Ont., Canada.

Cutler, T. (2005). Case study: wireless, serial and etherner link for enviromental project. *The Industrial Ethernet Book*, pp. 37-40.

Demirkol, I., Ersoy, C., and Alagoz, F. (2006). MAC protocols for wireless sensor networks: a survey. *IEEE Communications Magazine*, No. 44, Vol. 4, pp. 115-121.

Egea-López, E., Vales-Alonso, J., Martinez-Sala, A., Pavon-Mariño, P., and Garcia-Haro, J. (2006). Simulation scalability issues in wireless sensor networks. *IEEE Communications Magazine*, pp. 64-73.

eRobertParker, LLC. (2008). http://www.erobert-parker.com.

Fontán, F., and Mariño, P. (2008). *Modeling the Wireless Propagation Channel*. John Wiley & Sons.

Gail, W. B. (2007). Climate control. *IEEE Spectrum*, No. 44, Vol. 5, pp. 20-25.

Gall, R., and Parsons, D. (2006). It's hurricane season: do you know where your storm is?. *IEEE Spectrum*, pp. 25–30.

Ghosh, A., Wolter, D. R., Andrews, J. G., and Chen, R. (2005). Broadband wireless access with wimax/802.16: current performance benchmarks and future potential. *IEEE Communications Magazine*, No. 43, Vol. 2, pp. 129-136.

Guizzo, E. (2005). Into deep ice [ice monitoring]. *IEEE Spectrum*, No. 42, Vol. 12, pp. 28–35.

Hodgkinson, G. (2008). Industrial wireless standards: what's really going on at ISA?, *The Industrial Ethernet Book*, pp. 28–29.

Kunz, M. (2006). Wireless lan planning is a science, not an art! *The Industrial Ethernet Book*, pp. 32–34.

Livingston, M. and Franke, R. (2006). Choosing a 802.16 radio for use in a wimax application. *Embedded Systems Europe*, pp. 31-34.

Mariño, P. (2003). *Enterprise-wide communications: standards, networks and services.* 2nd ed., Ed. Rama (Madrid, Spain).

Mariño, P., Domínguez, M.A., et al. (2007). *Industrial communications: basic principles (Vol. I), Distributed systems and Applications (Vol. II),* In Spanish. UNED, Madrid (Spain).

Mariño, P., Fontán, F., Domínguez, M.A., and Otero, S. (2008a). Experimental wireless sensor network for viticulture research. In *IADIS International Conference Wireless Applications and Computing (WAC 2008),* pp. 38-44, Netherlands.

Mariño, P., Machado, F., Fontán, F., and Otero, S. (2008b). Hybrid distributed instrumentation network for integrating meteorological sensors applied to modeling RF propagation impairments. *IEEE Transactions on Instrumentation and Measurement,* vol. 57, no. 7, pp. 1410-1421.

Mariño, P., Domínguez, M.A., Otero, S., and Merino, M. (2008c). University-enterprise technology transfer for education and training about industrial processes. In *International 2008 Conference on Human Systems Interactions (HIS 2008),* pp. 40-43, Krakow (Poland).

Mohl, D. (2008). IEEE1588: Precise time synch for realtime automation applications, *The Industrial Ethernet Book,* pp. 12–16.

Moore, R. J., Jones, D. A., Cox, D. R., and Isham, V. S. (2000). Design of the hyrex raingauge network. *Hydrology and Earth System Sciences,* No. 4, pp. 521-530.

Niculescu, D. (2005). Communication paradigms for sensor networks. *IEEE Communications Magazine,* No. 43, Vol. 3, pp. 116-122.

Oppermann, I., Stoica, L., Rabbachin, A., Shelby, Z., and Haapola, J. (2004). UWB wireless sensor networks: UWEN - a practical example. *IEEE Communications Magazine,* No. 42, Vol. 12.

Perry, T. S. (2002). Capturing climate change. *IEEE Spectrum,* No. 39, Vol. 1, pp. 58-65.

Poza, F., Mariño, P., Otero, S., and Machado, F. (2006). Programmable electronic instrument for condition monitoring of in-service power transformers. *IEEE Transactions on Instrumentation and Measurement,* No. 55, Vol. 2, pp. 625-634.

Prophet, G. (2004). Is zigbee ready for the big time? *EDN Europe.*

Queijeiro, J.M., Blanco, D., and Álvarez, C. (2006). Climatic zoning and viticulture in Galicia (North West Spain). *Terroirs viticoles 2006,* Vol. 1, pp. 34-39, Burdeos, France.

Ruiz, L. B., Braga, T. R. M., Silva, F. A., Assuncao, H. P., Nogueira, J. M. S., and Loureiro, A. A. F. (2005). On the design of a self-managed wireless sensor network. *IEEE Communications Magazine,* No. 43, Vol. 8, pp. 95-102.

Satel Co. (2004). Satelline-3AS/d 869 and Epic. *Radio Modem User Guide,* version 2.5, Finland.

Tonietto, J. and Carbonneau, A. (2004). A multi-criteria climatic classification system for grape-growing regions worldwide. *Agricultural and Forest Meteorology,* No. 124, pp. 81-97.

Wheeler, A. (2007). Commercial applications of wireless sensor networks using zigbee. In *Communications Magazine, IEEE,* volume 45, pp. 70-77, Toronto, Ont., Canada.

Willig, A., Matheus, K., and Wolisz, A. (2005). Wireless technology in industrial networks. *Proceedings of the IEEE,* No. 93, Vol. 6, pp. 1130-1151.

Yeh, S., Talwar, S., Lee, S-Ch., and Kim, H. (2008). WiMAX Femtocells: a perspective on network architecture, capacity and coverage. *IEEE Communications Magazine,* pp. 58-65.

This work was previously published in the International Journal of Information Technology and Web Engineering 4(1), edited by Ghazi I. Alkhatib, and Ernesto Damiani, pp. 14-30, copyright 2009 by IGI Publishing (an imprint of IGI Global).

Chapter 3
A Linked Neighboring Leaves N-Tree to Support Distance Range Search

Faïza Najjar
National School of Comp. Science, Tunisia

Hassenet Slimani
Faculty of Sciences, Tunisia

ABSTRACT

Mobile query processing is, actually, a very active research field. Range and nearest neighbor queries are common types of queries in spatial databases and location based services (LBS). In this paper, we focus on finding nearest neighbors of a query point within a certain distance range. An example of query, frequently met in LBS, is "Find all the nearest gas stations within 2 miles neighborhood of his/her current location". We propose two approaches for answering such queries. Both are based on a recent indexing technique called N-tree. The first one is a branch and bound approach, whereas the second, called 'neighborhoods scanning', is based on a variant of N-tree, Leaves-Linked N-tree (LLN-tree). LLN-tree is an index tree structure that avoids visiting multiple paths during range search. Both techniques are presented, illustrated and evaluated. Experiments show that the latter approach outperforms the former in response time and disk access as well.

INTRODUCTION

Given a set of objects S = {s_1, s_2,...s_n}, having certain properties/attributes, if the properties' domain supports comparison operations, the range search problem is to find all objects in S that satisfy any range query.

It's obvious that such a type of a query allows investigating correlation between attributes of the considered system and events occurring within it. Hence, it's met in a wide range of research areas such as computational geometry (de Berg, 2000), database applications, geographical information systems and computer graphics (Hjaltason, 2003; Samet, 2007).

Yet, the problem of multidimensional/multiattribute/orthogonal range search has gained a lot of investigation from researchers in centralized databases (Papadopolous, 2005; Ind, Iss; Alstrup, 2000) and distributed databases as well (Andrzejak, 2002; Li, 2003; Ratnasamy, 2003; Marzolla, 2006; Bharambe, 2004). An example of an orthogonal search query in a centralized database context is: "Select ID, NAME from STUDENTS where HOURS BETWEEN 75 AND 90 AND GPA BETWEEN 2.5 AND 3.0". For a distributed context like a sensor network, an example of query is: "List all events that have temperatures between 50 Fa and 60 Fa, and light levels between 10 and 20 in a monitoring system for the growth of marine micro-organisms" (Li, 2003).

Proposed solutions include balanced binary trees for the one dimensional form, kd-tree for higher dimensional form, its embedding for specific systems, multi attribute trees, doubly chained trees, distributed Hash Table... etc.

The temporal aspect of range queries is dealt with in (Shi, 2005). In this work, the focus was on designing efficient indexing structures allowing fast retrieval of objects whose attributes fall within a set of ranges during a given period of time.

In spatial databases, a range may reduce to a distance range/interval as in the query 'Find data objects situated within the range/ interval *[5k,10km]* from a certain query point *q*'. It, also, may reduce to a window/ a 2-d rectangle as in 'Find data objects situated in the box *[x1, x2]*[y1, y2]*'. Solutions are, also, essentially based on tree-like indexing structures (Jim).

In this article, we are interested, within a spatial context, in combining the following two issues: a distance range problem and nearest neighbors search. 'Find nearest neighbors situated within the distance range *[md, Md]* from a query point' is the query model which expresses our issue.

In the literature, we find a lot of work concerning nearest neighbors search, objects ranking and range search in spatial databases (Brabec , 1999; Hjaltason, 1995; Xu, 2004). Most of the proposed

solutions are based on branch and bound algorithms based on hierarchical indexing structures. When used for nearest neighbor search, indices like R-trees (Papadopolous, 2005), kd-trees and quad-trees (de Berg, 2000) do not need to pre-compute the solution (e.g. Voronoi Diagram), hence they are called object-based indexing structures whereas solution based indexing structure like D-tree (Xu, 2004). Actually, R-tree had shown many limitations in nearest neighbor search, compared to solution based indices, because of overlapping between MBRs and subsequent backtracking in the search algorithm. This was shown in (Xu, 2004) and in a previous work (Najjar, 2006). The quad-tree has a fixed partitioning scheme which splits a 2d space into four equal sub squares. This splitting makes a deficiency in indexing sparse clouds of points and non-uniformly distributed datasets.

In (Najjar, 2006), we proposed an efficient solution based indexing structure, called *N-tree*, to efficiently process nearest neighbor queries. We focus on extending it, in this article, to support distance range search in the context of nearest neighbor queries. We develop two approaches for answering range nearest neighbor queries with different properties and advantages. The first approach, called branch and bound, visits index nodes which are expected to be candidate by the pruning strategy. The second approach, called jumping neighborhoods scan, explores neighborhoods of the query point's nearest neighbor to find sites falling within the query range. This exploration is done due to a leaves-linked version of the index.

The main contributions of this article can be summarized as follows:

- We proposed in (Slimani, 2008) an adapted branch and bound approach for a solution based index to process distance range queries in a spatial context;
- We propose, as an extension to (Slimani, 2008), a linked leaves index tree that allows

scanning and reconstruction of the whole space search, then we develop the algorithm to scan the neighboring regions of a query point based on a pertinent selection of links that it follows;

- Both approaches are computationally compared and experimentally evaluated. Results show that neighborhoods scanning approach notably outperforms branch and bound approach.

The remainder of the article is organized as follows: First, we state the distance range search and give an overview of the indexing structure N-tree. Then, we detail the branch and bound approach through a presentation of the resolving algorithm, its basis, illustrations and discussion. Further, we detail, in the same way, the jumping neighborhoods scanning approach. Then, we focus, in an evaluation section, on comparison of both approaches through illustrations, computational cost and experimental evaluation. Finally, we conclude by a summary and a glance at future work.

PROBLEM STATEMENT AND OVERVIEW OF N-TREE INDEXING STRUCTURE

Hypotheses and Problem Statement

A distance range query, over static objects, submitted by a mobile client (a traveler) is for example "find the closest restaurants within a 2 miles neighborhood" – implicitly from my current position on a particular region.

Obviously, to process such a query, there are several assumptions that could be taken: the client is considered static during processing such a query (the classic range query in spatial databases), he/she is considered moving on a given trajectory (continuous range query), the mode in which the client accesses data on the server is the classic client/server (use of N-tree as a disk index) or the periodic broadcasting (use of N-tree as an air index).

We are interested in distance range queries over a spatial tessellation which is the Voronoi diagram of a set of points in a planar Euclidean space. The mobile issuer of the query is supposed static during the processing of the query and data is accessed in classic client/server access mode.

Formally, the problem can be stated as follows: Given a set, S, of N sites (points of interest such as hotels, gas stations...) $S = \{s_1, s_2, ...s_N\}$, in a planar Euclidean space, find in S the nearest neighbors to a query point q whose distances from q are in the range *[md, Md]* where *md* is the *lower_bound* and *Md* is the *upper_bound*.

Overview of N-Tree Data Structure

The N-tree (neighbors' tree) is a solution based index for nearest neighbor search; it is, to the best of our knowledge, the unique index devised to index sites of a Voronoi diagram based on their neighborhoods and whose properties are derived from that famous computational geometry structure. N-tree is a balanced binary search tree. It recursively partitions the space, consisting of a set of sorted sites according to x-coordinates or to y-coordinates, into two complementary subspaces containing almost the same number of sites until all the sites of the partitioned space are on the partitioning frontier. The frontier separating the two subspaces is defined to be the set of neighboring edges which are edges of the Delaunay Triangualtion(DT-- The dual of the VD). It is represented by two subsets of sites: the left subspace bordering sites (LSF—Left Sites of the Frontier) and the right subspace bordering sites (RSF—Right Sites of the Frontier).

An internal N-tree node corresponds to a step of partitioning and it's represented by a frontier between the two induced subspaces. Its basic structure includes, then, two components: LSF and

Figure 1. Voronoi diagram of 30 sites (dashed) and corresponding DT (bold)

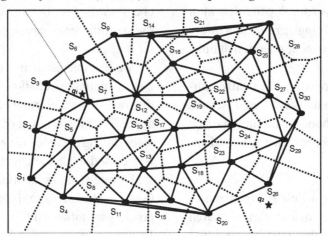

Figure 2. The corresponding N-tree index of figure 1

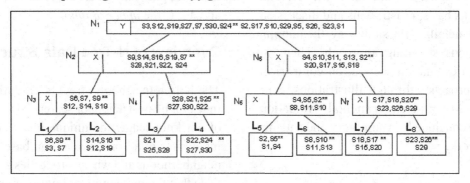

RSF (separated, in Figure 2, by two stars), plus, links to its Left Child (LC) and its Right Child (RC). A leaf is a region of neighboring sites split into two subsets LSF and RSF. Figure 1 and Figure 2 show, respectively, the VD of randomly generated 30 sites and the corresponding N-tree index.

The nearest neighbor query processing based on N-tree starts from the root of the index and then, recursively at each node, suggests the sub-region containing the query point q. The search is directed to the corresponding child on internal node: it follows the left subtree when the minimum distance between q and all the frontal sites is reached in LSF or it follows the right subtree when the minimum distance between q and all the frontal sites is reached in RSF. At a leaf level where we have all the sites of the partitioned space, the nearest site is immediately located.

N-TREE BASED BRANCH AND BOUND APPROACH FOR DISTANCE RANGE QUERY PROCESSING

Overall Idea

Given a range of distance values, a range query must find all the sites that lie within the range. Like range search with object-based indexing structures, this approach consists in a recursive processing which starts from root node and, then, decides to explore its left child or its right child depending on a pruning strategy. The outline of the processing is shown by *Procedure 1 : rangeSearch()*.

It starts by calculating for Current Node N (*CN*- applying at first call to index root node) its left range $LR=[mL, ML]$ (i.e. the interval whose lower (resp. upper) bound is the minimum (resp. maximum) distance between the query point and current node left frontal sites) and its Right Range $(RR =[mR,MR])$. During this computation, any new site falling within the range is added to the result vector Q. (line 2 in Procedure 1)

The procedure enumerates four alternatives to be considered during each call (lines 3-15 in procedure 1) and which correspond to the position of CN's ranges compared to the query range. Notice that there are two worst cases, in which both of the left child and the right child must be visited. In the other two cases, only one child is visited and, here, a pruning strategy is applied. This strategy is based on a property of N-tree which's explained in the next subsection.

An N-Tree Property

The pruning strategy for processing distance range queries is based on inherent properties of N-tree, expressed as follows:

1. The right child for the current node should not be visited when the minimum distance between q and all the frontal sites is reached in left frontal sites (i.e. $mL < mR$) while the query range is strictly below the right range (i.e. $Md < mR$) (lines 4-6 in the procedure).

2. Symmetrically, the left child for the current node should not be visited when the minimum distance between q and all the frontal sites is reached in right frontal sites (i.e. $mR < mL$) while the query range is strictly below the left range (i.e. $Md < mL$) (lines 10-12 in the procedure).

Property Proof

Let's consider the first item in the above-stated property.

For each node of N-tree, if $(mL < mR)$ and $(Md < mR)$, this means that the sites on the right of the frontier (RSF sites) are too far from q to fall within the range. Meanwhile, all the sites in the right subtree are on the right of actual RSF

Procedure 1. rangeSearch algorithm

```
      Procedure  rangeSearch(CN, q, md, Md, Q)
      Input:
      CN: the current node   /*Initialized to the root node*/
      q : the query point.
      [md, Md]: the query range   /*minimal distance-Maximal distance*/
      Output:
      Q: the result set for the distance range query
1     begin
2     Calculate for CN its Left Range LR =[mL, ML] (i.e. the interval with lower (resp. upper )
      bound  distance between q and current node left frontal sites)  and its Right Range (RR
      =[mR,MR]). Add to the result vector
      Q any new site falling within the range.
3     if the current node is not a leaf then
              /*Decide whether to visit its left child (LC) or its Right Child (RC).*/
4             if (mL < mR) then
5                     if (Md < mR) then
6                             rangeSearch(LC, q, md, Md, Q)
7                     else{
8                             rangeSearch(LC, q, md, Md, Q)
9                             rangeSearch(RC, q, md, Md, Q)}
10            else
11                    if (Md < mL) then
12                            rangeSearch(RC, q, md, Md, Q)
13                    else{
14                            rangeSearch(RC, q, md, Md, Q)
15                            rangeSearch(LC, q, md, Md, Q)}
16    end
```

Figure 3. Nearest neighbors within the range [0, 90] for q2 = {(S26, S23, S20)}

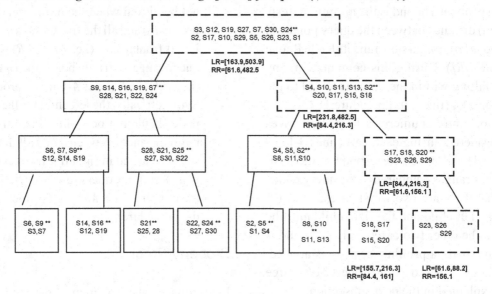

sites and, so, could not be closer to q than RSF sites. We assure, due to VD properties inherited by N-tree indexing structure, that all sites of the right subtree could not fall in the range. Hence, the right child must not be visited. The same reasoning can be made to prune the left subtree in range search when $(mR < mL)$ and $(Md<mL)$.

Examples and Discussions

In this section, we're going to discuss some executions of the first approach for range search. We are going to present three examples of distance range query processing over the VD of Figure 1 where two query points q_1 and q_1 are represented by stars.

In the following illustrations, we present the visited nodes by procedure *rangeSearch()* in fine-dashed boxes and the result set in its caption as a set of sites within the given range pairs (site identifier, q's distance to this site).

Figure 3 illustrates an example of range query for the query point q_2 and a query range [0, 90]; the regular nearest neighbor is the site S26. Observe that, the nodes explored (bold dashed lines in Figure 3) correspond to the path of near-

est neighbor localization for q_2 and the left leaf node of the extreme right of N-tree. It shows an efficient pruning strategy.

In Figure 4 and Figure 5, we vary the distance range for q_1. In these two figures, we see the controversial impact of query range on the number of visited nodes (7); sometimes almost all the tree is explored!

The number of RN-tree nodes visited depends on the query range and ranges of visited nodes, especially the root node. As we see in Figure 3 the range where $Md < min(mL, mR)$ at root node is a particular value of input. This value allows pruning the half of the whole index since it allows pruning the left subtree for the root node if $(mR < mL)$ or pruning the right subtree for the root node if $(mR > mL)$.

Generally, for a range query, widely encountered in LBSs, having the form *'Find nearest neighbors within distance d–implicitly from my actual position'*, our algorithm can propose to the user nearest neighbors within a threshold $th= min(mL,mR)$ at root node instead of d. This allows guaranteeing an interesting level of performance. It, also, makes the proposed solution reactive towards user input. Obviously, this reactiveness

Figure 4. Nearest neighbors within the range [0, 100] for q1= {S3, S5, S6, S7}

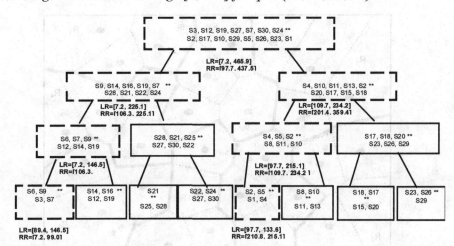

Figure 5. Nearest neighbors within the range [100,250] for q1 {S1, S2, S4, S8, S9, S10, S11, S12, S13, S14, S16, S17, S19}

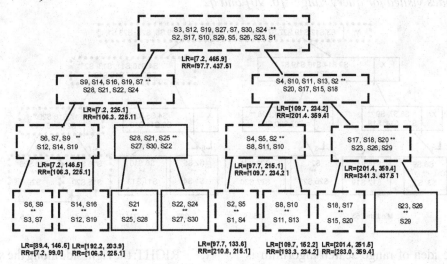

can be shaped differently through finding out different strategies to calculate a specific range values allowing interesting performances.

N-TREE BASED NEIGHBORHOODS SCANNING APPROACH

A leaf node in N-tree corresponds to a cluster of VD neighboring cells representing a *region*

of the precalculated solution space (Cf. Figure 6). Together, all regions constitute a higher level partitioning over the VD tessellation and they are still neighboring regions iff they share at least one Voronoi edge (or Delaunay edge). The Figure 6 shows the final level of partitioning induced by N-tree over the VD. There are 8 regions: R1-R8 corresponding respectively to the 8 leaves of the corresponding N-tree shown in Figure 2. Figure 7 will show the final construction of a variant of N-tree, where the leaves are linked with neighborhood properties.

Figure 6. Final level partitioning induced by N-tree over the VD in Figure 1

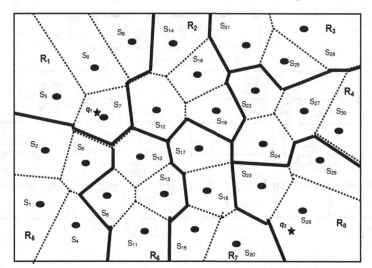

Figure 7. Nodes visited for query range=[0, 90] and q2

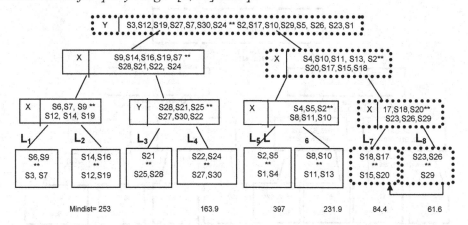

The basic idea of range search algorithm is to retrieve, at first, the nearest neighbor, and then to use the neighboring regions by following neighborhood links around the regular nearest neighbor of the query point q. We focus to check as few nodes as possible.

Introducing the Idea

A region/a leaf Lj is linked to another leaf Li as a neighbor according to the following cases:

1. RIGHT: the right side along the x dimension (RX-neighbor) if all Lj sites have greater x-coordinates than all Li sites.

2. LEFT: the left side along the x dimension (LX-neighbor) if all Lj sites have lower x-coordinates than all Li sites.

3. DOWN: the right side along the y dimension (RY-neighbor) if all Lj sites have greater y-coordinates than all Li sites.

4. UP: the left side along the y dimension (LY-neighbor) if all Lj sites have lower y-coordinates than all Li sites.

Procedure 2. findNeighbors(CL)

```
Procedure FindNeighbors(CL)
Input:
   CL: the Current Leaf in the extend N-tree.
Output
   CL with its neighbors fixed in vector 'neighbLeaves'.
Begin
   /*Searching for RX neighbors ?*/
1    ancest = findAncestor(CL, X, R, bordSTS)
     if (ancestor != null) then
3    seekNeighbLs(CL, ancest.RC, X, R, bordSTS,neighbLeaves)

     /* Searching for RY neighbors?*/
4    ancestor =findAncestor(CL,Y, R,bordSTS);
     if (ancestor != null) then
6    seekNeighbLs(CL, ancest.RC, Y, R, bordSTS,neighbLeaves)
End.
```

We define a direction to be a combination of the splitting dimension (X or Y) and the regarded side (left or right). In Figure 6, the region R2 has three neighbors: R3 (as RX), R4 (as RX) and R1 (as LX).

Furthermore a leaf node L will be added an attribute which's a vector of its neighboring leaves: L.neighbors.

Given a query point q, N-tree based Nearest Neighbor search ends by reaching the leaf node containing the nearest site to q, corresponding to the nearest neighbor region (NNR) in the final partitioning. The basic idea is to follow neighborhood regions through linked leaves in order to retrieve all the sites lying within a distance range from q. Actually, following neighborhoods links from the NNL corresponds to an expanding scanning of NNR neighborhoods; this is the basis of N-tree based neighborhoods scanning approach for both nearest neighbor and distance range search.

Construction of the Linked Leaves N-tree—LLN-tree

LLN-tree is primarily a N-tree augmented with an auxiliary data structure. We need to link each index leaf node to all of its neighboring leaf nodes.

We go through these steps :

1. The linking procedure visits all leaves starting from the index extreme left leaf (which actually corresponds to an extreme left region in the VD) and in the order they appear at leaves levels in the index. In Figure 8, the extreme left leaf is L1 and leaves will be visited in the order L1, L2, L3, …, Lm

2. For each leaf (CL), the Procedure 2, find-Neighbors(), determines its neighbors according to the two directions : RX and RY. The neighbor regions according the other directions (LX and LY) are deduced directly through the searching of RX and RY in the corresponding neighbor regions. For each right direction D, it starts, through the call of the function findAncestor(), by looking for the ancestor node for the CL from which an eventual neighboring leaf according to direction D might be sought. Then, the call of the procedure seekNeighbLeaves() allows finding neighboring leaves of CL according to the direction D in the ancestor right child-rooted subtree. These leaves are added incrementally to vector 'neighbLeaves' containing neighbors of CL.

Figure 8. Nodes visited for query range [0,100]

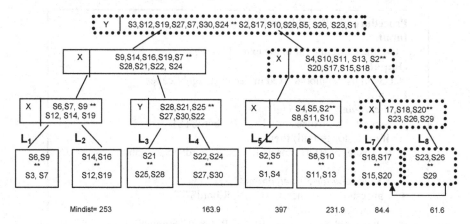

Mindist= 253   163.9   397   231.9   84.4   61.6

Function 1. findAncestor(CL,D,R,bordSTS)

```
Function findAncestor(CL, D, side, bordSTS)
Input :
CL : Current leaf in the extend N-tree
D: X or Y dimension
side : right or left.
Output
The ancestor node returned.
bordSTS : the bordering neighboring sites of CL in its ancestor
Begin
1    child =CL
     fnode = CL.father;
3    while (fnode != null)
     {
4       if (fnode.dim = D & child.side = left)
        {
           Retrieve from the frontier edges bordSTS of CL
           return fnode
        }
        else
        {
7          child = node
8          fnode = fnode.father
        }
     }
     return fnode
End.
```

i.   In Function 1, the FindAncestor() algorithm is sketched to retrieve the CL's ancestor; it allows finding RX (resp. RY) neighboring region of CL. The ancestor is found by going upward the index from CL's father until reaching the first node having an X-dimensional resp. a Y-dimensional) splitting and for which the

CL is in the left subtree (in worst cases it might be the root node or null). The findAncestor() also returns the bordering sites of the neighboring leaf in order to prune the search space as early as possible. For example in Figure 7, for the leaf L2 with searching RX, findAncestor() will return the node N2 as the ancestor and {S21, S22, S24} as bordering sites.

ii. To seek neighboring leaves for CL according to a given direction. The procedure seekNeighbLeaves() (see Procedure 3) goes downward the ancestor Right Child-rooted subtree to identify the leaves containing these bordering sites and link them to CL as neighboring leaves. The seekNeighbLeaves() uses the minimum bounding rectangle of the bordering sites set [min_x,max_x]*[min_y,max_y] to localize leaves containing these sites through relative position of the MBR and limits of reached node ([LMaxx, RMaxx] for an x-dimensional node or [LMaxy,RMiny] for a y-dimensional node). Finally, for each CL with RX (resp. RY) linked to an identified neighbor leaf (NL), CL is recorded as LX (resp. LY) in NL.

To illustrate the procedure findNeighbors, let's take the previous example (Cf. Figure 2). For example, we want to look for the neighbors of the leaf L2 according to RX. findAncestor() goes upward the index from L2 until finding the first ancestor having an X-dimensional splitting and for which L2 is in the left subtree. The ancestor of the leaf L2 is identified by his grandfather(N2) and returns bordSTs={S21, S22, S24}. Then, the procedure seekNeighbLeaves() goes down the right child-rooted subtree. The current node (N3) contains only S21 (in LSF) and S22 (in RSF) so we have to explore both the left and right children.

The L3 contains S21 so it is an RX neighbor of L2 with bordering sites {S21}. Consequently, LX of L3 is recorded to be L2. For the right child of N3 we retrieve L4 as neighbor leaf to L2 in RX with neighbor bordering sites {S22, S24}. Symmetrically, L2 is recorded as LX-neighbor for both of L3 and L4 resp. with bordering sites {S14,S16} and {S16,S19} resp. (Cf. Figure 7)

This variant of N-tree obtained through the neighboring linking procedure is called **LLN-tree** (Leaves- Linked N-tree).

Range Search Based on LLN-Tree

Introducing Neighborhoods Scanning

LLN-tree based range search processing consists in neighborhoods scanning. To search for all sites within a given distance range *[md,Md]*, the first step in LLN-tree is to follow a path from the root to a leaf to find the regular nearest neighbor (1-NN) and returns the nearest neighbor leaf/region (NNL). And then, the second step finds all candidate neighbor sites within the range in order to discard unnecessary links to neighbor regions/leaves:

We compute for the NNL the minimum distance between its sites and the query point, *mindist*. If *mindist* is less than *Md*, NNL is not out range, and, therefore, we continue to follow its neighboring links to scan progressively the neighborhoods for possible candidate sites falling within the range. We decide to expand the neighborhoods scanning to a neighboring leaf whenever it is not already visited and the *mindist* to its bordering sites is less or equal to Md.

As it's noticed when applying this scanning on Voronoi regions, neighborhoods scanning according to the underlying linking of leaves does grow in a manner that guarantees a constant increasing distance between visited regions' sites and *q*. Now let's sum up the search algorithm.

Procedure 3. seekNeighbLeaves () algorithm

```
Procedure 3.  seekNeighbLeaves(CL, CN, Dim, bordSTS, neighbLeaves)
Input:
  CL: Current leaf; CN: current node;
  Dim: X or Y dimension
Output
    bordSTS : the bordering neighboring sites of CL
    neighbLeaves: the set of neighboring leaf nodes
Begin
   if (CN is not a leaf) {
       if (CN.dim = Y)
       {
           if (bordSTS.maxy<CN.lMaxy)
               seekNeighbLs(CL, CN.LC, Dim, bordSTS, neighbLeaves)
           else
               if (bordSTS.miny > CN.rMiny)
                       seekNeighbLs(CL,CN.RC, Dim, bordSTS, neighbLeaves)
               else
               {
                   LBS= Left Bordering frontier sites of  CN
                   RNS= Right Bordering sites  of CN
                   seekNeighbLs(CL,CN.LC, Dim, LBS,neighbLeaves)
                   seekNeighbLs(CL,CN.RC, Dim, RBS, neighbLeaves)
               }
       }
     else {//CN.dim=X
         if (bordSTS.maxx < CN.lMaxx)
                 seekNeighbLs(CL,CN.LC, Dim, bordSTS,neighbLeaves)
         else
             if(bordSTS.minx > this.rMinx)
                 seekNeighbLs(CL,CN.RC, LFDim, bordSTS, neighbLeaves)
             else
             {
                 LBS=Bordering sites to the Left of the CN's frontier.
                 RNS= Bordering sites to the right of the CN's frontier.
                 seekNeighbLs(CL,CN.LC,LFDim, LBS,neighbLeaves)
                 seekNeighbLs(CL,CN.RC, LFDim, RBS, neighbLeaves)
             }
    }
   else {//CN is a leaf which contains at least one bordering site.
   {
       A neighborhood having CN as leaf, right as direction and  bordSTS as bordering sites is
       added to neighboring leaves of CL.
       Symmetrically, a neighborhood having CL as leaf,  left as direction and 'mirrored
       bordSTS' as bordering sites is added to neighboring leaves of CN.
   }
   End
```

Range Search Algorithm

It's a two-phased algorithm:

Step 1: *NNL ←searchNN(rootNode, q):* search of N-tree leaf containing the 1st Nearest Neighbor of q.

Step 2: *rangeSearch2(NNL,q, md, Md,Res):* rangeSearch2() (Cf. Procedure 3) has as inputs : parameters of the range query (*q,md,Md*), the current leaf (CL) applying at first call to NNL and the result set (Res) obtained incrementally through recursive expanding of neighborhoods scanning. Its processing can be summarized in these steps :

1. checkSites(q,d1, d2, res) returns the minimum distance (mindist) between the NNL's sites and the query point *q*. If a site falls within the query range it's immediately added to the result set of the query range.

2. If mindist is greater than Md, then the CL is out of range and, therefore neighborhoods scanning stops. The result set for the range query is empty.

3. If mindist is less than Md, the CL might contain sites lying within the range or be under range and its neighboring leaves might intersect the query range. To avoid searching in all linked neighbor leaves, we use the bordering neighboring sites added at each neighboring link. They are the sites of the corresponding neighboring leaf that share at least one VD edge with CL sites. Actually, for each neighboring leaf L of CL which are not yet visited, the procedure rangesearch2(), calculates the bordering minimum distance (bord_mindist) between bordering sites and q. If bord_mindist is greater than Md, the corresponding linking is discarded and may be pruned out.

4. In the worst case all neighborhoods should be visited. This is done through calculating for each neighboring leaf the mindist between *q* and its bordering sites. to procedure expandNS().(Lines 16-30)

Illustrations and Discussion of Neighborhoods Scanning Approach

In this section, we're going to discuss some executions of the second approach for range search. We are going to present three samples of distance range query processing over the VD of Figure 7 where two query points q_1 and q_2 are represented by stars.

In the following illustrations, we present nodes visited by procedure *rangeSearch2()* in fine-dotted boxes and use the original NTree for the sake of simple presentation. Actually links between leaves guide the search.

In Figure 7, we show the nodes visited for a query point *q2* and query range [0, 90]; the bold dashed nodes shows the explored nodes and path to retrieve the nearest neighbors within 90's distance; therefore only pertinent nodes are visited. The answer for this query is : {S23, S26, S20}. For the moment the same number as for branch and bound (5 visited nodes).

In Figure 8, we show the nodes visited for the query point *q2* and the range [0, 100]. Observe that only one link (LX) to a neighboring region is followed after finding the 1-NN(=S26) whereas the link according LY is discarded due that the distances from q2 to the bordering neighbor sites are out of range. Consequently, the number of visited nodes is equal to 5 (v.s. 7 in branch and bound).

In Figure 9, starting from the leaf L_8, all neighborhood links are visited to determine nearest neighbors of *q2* within the distance range [100, 250]. Therefore, the number of visited nodes is 7 versus 11 in branch and bound).

Actually, a leaf/a region is out of range when all of its sites have greater distances than the query range upper bound. Adding some redundancy in the index through the bordering sites with each neighboring leaf allows predicting efficiently if all sites of a neighbour may intersect the query range or not.

Figure 9. Nodes visited for query range=[100, 250] and the query point q2.

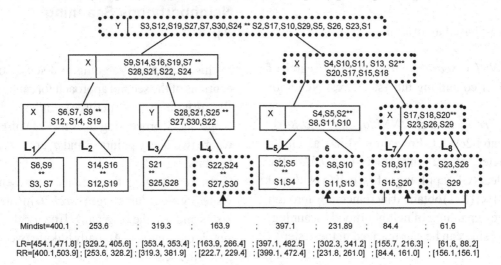

Mindist=400.1 ; 253.6 ; 319.3 ; 163.9 ; 397.1 ; 231.89 ; 84.4 ; 61.6

LR=[454.1,471.8] ; [329.2, 405.6] ; [353.4, 353.4] ; [163.9, 266.4] ; [397.1, 482.5] ; [302.3, 341.2] ; [155.7, 216.3] ; [61.6, 88.2]
RR=[400.1,503.9] ; [253.6, 328.2] ; [319.3, 381.9] ; [222.7, 229.4] ; [399.1, 472.4] ; [231.8, 261.0] ; [84.4, 161.0] ; [156.1,156.1]

EVALUATION

Experimental Evaluation

Let's N be the dataset size i.e. the total number of sites in the search space in Voronoi diagram. We are going to compare both range search approaches in terms of average response time (ART) as function of N, then in terms of average number of visited index nodes (MVN).

We randomly generate N sites (within a square 7000*7000), and we build the solution space represented by the VD and then we construct the corresponding index tree (N-tree and LLN-Tree). Next, we evaluate the average response time for range queries issued for 100000 randomly generated query points and thus for several ranges. Experiments are carried out with a machine having a processor with a frequency of 1.6 GHz and central memory of 1GB.

The Figure 10 and the Figure 11 show clearly that range algorithm based on LLN-tree improves as the range increases for both the response time and the number of visited nodes. Neighborhoods scanning based range search has better perfor-

Figure 10. Query response time for N=2000

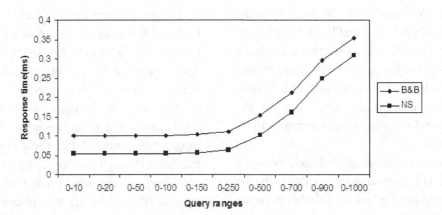

Figure 11. Visited nodes in LNN-tree for N=2000

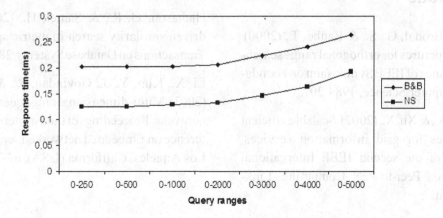

mance compared to branch & bound based range search. NS is twice as fast (in msec.) as B&B.

Figure 12 and Figure 13 illustrates the average running time of range queries and the number of visited nodes in LNN-tree for 10,000 sites in Voronoi diagram, versus several ranges. The neighborhood scanning range query processing clearly achieves about up to two of magnitude better performance than the B&B.

SUMMARY AND CONCLUSION

In this article, we described and provided efficient algorithms for the extension of N-tree, LLN-tree,

to support both regular nearest neighbor and range queries. The objective of this article is to tackle the distance range problem with an efficient solution-based indexing structure, N-tree, and two appropriate processing strategies.

The first approach is an N-tree based branch & bound solution similar to classic solutions already used for object-based indices.

The second approach, called neighborhoods scan, is based on neighborhoods progressive scanning starting from the "nearest neighbor region" of the query point. We devised an algorithm that allows neighborhoods scanning from any point in a 2D Voronoi diagram tessellation based on linking of index leaves. Then we devised a range search

Figure 12. Query Response time for N=10000

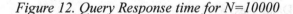

Figure 13. Visited nodes in LNN-tree for N=10000

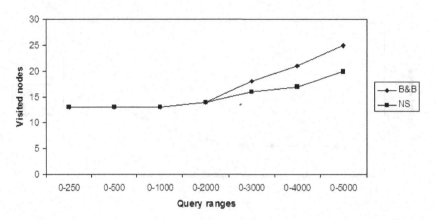

algorithm based on this linking. The algorithm visits leaves which intersect the query range.

The experimentations affirm that neighborhoods scanning approach is substantially better performing than branch and bound approach. This is due to its fast range search algorithm and to its lower number of visited index nodes – indicator of disk access.

Furthermore, the proposed neighborhoods scanning algorithm over a VD tessellation seems to be very suitable to of k-nearest neighbors search.

Finally, work remains for a variety of related directions, like multi-dimensional range queries (e.g. window), and continuous queries for network distance.

REFERENCES

Alstrup, S., Brodal, G., S., & Rauhe, T., (2000). New data structures for orthogonal range searching. Proceedings of IEEE Symposium on Foundations of Computer Science, 198 - 207.

Andrzejak, A., & Xu, X., (2002). Scalable,efficient range queries for grid information services. Proceeding of the second IEEE International Conference on Peer-to-Peer Computing, Linkping, Sweden.

Bharambe, A.R., Agrawal, M., & Seshan, S., (2004). Mercury: Supporting scalable multiattribute range queries, in: Proceedings of ACM SIGCOMM, Portland, OR(USA).

Brabec, F., & Samet, H., (1999). Visualizing and animating search operations on quadtrees on the worldwide web. Proceedings of the nineteenth annual symposium on Computational geometry. San Diego, California (USA), 374 -375.

de Berg, M., van Kreveled, M., Overmars, M., & Scwartzkof, O., (2000). Computational Geometry – Algorithms and Applications. Springer-Verlag.

Hjaltason, G., R., & Samet, H. (1995). Ranking in spatial databases. Proceedings of the 4th International Symposium on Advances in Spatial Databases, 83-95.

Hjaltason, G. R., & Samet, H., (2003). Index-driven similarity search in metric spaces. ACM Transactions on Database Systems, 28(4),517–580.

Li, X., Kim, Y., J., Govindan, R., & Hong, W., (2003). Multi-dimensional range queries in sensor networks. Proceedings of the 1st international conference on Embedded networked sensor systems, Los Angeles, California (USA), 63-75.

Marzolla, M., & Mordacchini, M., (2006). Tree vector indexes: efficient range queries for dynamic content on peer-to-peer networks. Proceedings of the 14th Euromicro International Conference on Parallel, Distributed, and Network-Based Processing, 457 – 464.

Najjar F., & Slimani H., (2006). The N-Tree: an Indexing Technique for Nearest Neighbor Queries. Proceedings of the IEEE International Conference on Computer Systems and Applications, 460- 467.

Okabe, A., Boots, B., Sugihara, K., & Chiu, S. N., (2000). Spatial Tesselations: Concepts and Applications of Voronoi Diagrams, Wiley.

Papadopoulos, A.N., & Manolopoulos, Y., (2005). Nearest Neighbor Search: a Database Perspective. Springer.

Ratnasamy, S., Hellerstein, J. M., & Shenker, S., (2003). Range queries over DHTs. Intel Research Technical Report, IRB-TR-03-011.

Samet, H., (2007). K-nearest neighbor finding using maxnearestdist. IEEE Transactions On Pattern Analysis and Machine Intelligence.

Shi, J., & JaJa, J., (2005). A new framework for addressing temporal range queries and some preliminary results. Theoretical Computer Science, 332 , 109 – 121.

Slimani, H., Najjar, F., & Slimani, Y., (2008). N-tree based nearest neighbors search within distance range queries. Proceedings on Wireless and Application Computing (part of MCCSIS 2008), 53-60.

Xu, J., Zheng, B., Lee, W. C., & Lee, D. L., (2004). The D-Tree: an Index Structure for Planar Point Queries in Location-Based Wireless Services. IEEE TKDE, 16(12),1–17.

Chapter 4
Location–Aware Access Control for Mobile Workflow Systems

Michael Decker
University of Karlsruhe, Germany

ABSTRACT

Workflow management systems (WfMS) are a special class of information systems (IS) which support the automated enactment of business processes. Meanwhile there are WfMS which allow the execution of tasks using mobile computers like PDA with the ability of wireless data transmission. However, the employment of workflow systems as well as mobile technologies comes along with special security challenges. One way to tackle these challenges is the employment of location-aware access control to enforce rules that describe from which locations a user is allowed to perform which activities. The data model behind access control in termed Access Control Model (ACM). There are special ACM for mobile information systems as well as for WfMS, but no one that addresses mobile as well as workflow specific aspects. In the article we therefore discuss the specific constraints such a model should be able to express and introduce an appropriate ACM. A special focus is on location constraints for individual workflow instances.

INTRODUCTION

Mobile technologies subsume portable computers like notebooks, PDA, smartphones and wireless data transmission based on standards like GPRS, EDGE, WiFi or UMTS. Such technologies pro-

vide the potential for many hitherto unthinkable applications since they enable access to computer technology almost anywhere and anytime. However, the development of mobile information systems (MIS) entails some specific challenges such as limited accumulator lifetime, unreliable data transmission, small displays and limited means for data input. A further challenge considered as

DOI: 10.4018/978-1-60960-523-0.ch004

a very serious one by many experts are security-related issues (e.g., Ernest-Jones (2006)): Security concerns arise because due to their portability mobile computers often get lost or stolen so un-authorized people can gain access to confidential data or even services. Mobile computers are often used in environments like public and highly fre-quented places where unauthorized people could take a look over the user's shoulder to learn about confidential data (so called "shoulder surfing" or "shoulder sniffing"). Also, since users consider mobile computers as personal device they often use their business devices (provided by their em-ployer) also for private matters and are following the company's security policy (e.g., prohibition to install software) to a lower degree than this would be the case for a stationary computer.

There are various approaches to tackle the specific security challenges that come along with mobile computing:

- Wireless data communication can be en-crypted to thwart eavesdropping and ma-nipulation of transmitted data
- Sensitive data can be stored in encrypted form on the mobile device
- There are even devices that have a built-in finger print reader because prompting for passwords as means for authentication is not appropriate for all mobile scenarios.

And besides these preventive measures there are even some approaches that can be taken after a mobile device got lost:

- The so called "kill pill" is an special com-mand message which is sent to a mobile device to triggers the deletion of sensible data that might be stored on that device
- The "Equipment Identity Register" (EIR) in GSM-networks is a database that stores a list of devices reported as stolen or lost so the network access can be denied for those devices.

In the paper at hand we focus on the employ-ment of so called *Access Control Models (ACM)* as further preventive approach to tackle specific security problems of MIS. ACM are special models to formulate which users of an information system are allowed to perform particular operations (e.g., read, write, append, delete, execute) on particular resources under the protection of an information system (e.g., data objects, services). For example, an instance of such a model could state that user Alice is allowed to perform the operation "read" on the resource "address database". Meanwhile there are ACM that were developed to express location-related access restrictions. Using such models policies like the following can be formu-lated: "An employee is only allowed to access a particular resource while staying at the premises of his company". Beside location-aware ACM there are also ACM to express workflow-specific rules. However, as far as we know there are no ACM that are location-aware as well as process-aware. There are several mobile workflow systems but they don't have a special ACM. Our work therefore concentrates on the development of an ACM that is able to express specific constraints for mobile workflow systems.

At the end of the paper we will also explain how ACM can address another mobile-specific problem, namely usability issues due to the con-strained user interface for data output (tiny display of poor quality) and input (often no fully-fledged keyboard but just a few buttons, no pointer device like a "mouse").

The remainder of this article is structured as follows: in the next section we cover workflow systems and approaches how to adapt them to support mobile users. The section after this is devoted to an overview about ACM in general and location-aware respective workflow-aware ACM in particular. Following this we give a short introduction to the relevant aspects of location determination and the location model. In the subsequent section we first describe an example workflow process before we introduce our ACM;

this description uses Petri nets as graphical notation, but we also mention some other notations that were used for the depiction of mobile workflows. The last section summarizes the contents of the article and gives an outlook to further work.

WORKFLOW SYSTEMS

Business Processes and Workflow Systems

A *business process* is an ordered set of activities to reach a certain goal within an organization, e.g., the fulfilment of a customer's order or inquiry. If a business process is automated by an IS, we talk about a workflow. Automation means that the IS schedules the individual activities of a process according to specified rules and routes the required documents and data to the particular person. *Workflow management systems (WfMS)* support not only the enactment of the workflow, but also the definition of processes types and the monitoring of individual process instances (Oberweis, 2005). Nowadays the definition of processes is typically supported by special graphical tools that employ some kind of flowchart-like notation, e.g., the *Business Process Modeling Notation (BPMN)*. Process definitions are not "hard-coded" but configured so it is easy to alter them if required. The actors of a workflow typically use some kind of workflow-client application that presents a list of activities to be performed (work list) and to invoke the necessary forms and applications (e.g., word-processing software, viewer for electronic document). Processes with many instances and well-defined rules for the order of activities and whose data can be represented in digital form are good candidates to be implemented with a WfMS. Often mentioned examples for workflows are approval processes (e.g., approval for vacation and overtime, purchase orders, claims for travel expenses), processes found in insurance companies (e.g., application for insurance coverage, insurance claim) or handling of customer inquiries ("trouble tickets", complaints, quote requests, orders).

MOBILE WORKFLOW SYSTEMS

The availability of mobile technologies enabled the realization of *mobile workflow management systems (mWfMS)*, e.g., Exotica/FMDC (Alonso et al., 1996) or WHAM (Jing et al., 2000). These are WfMS with special support for mobile actors, i.e., actors that use mobile computers to perform their activities. Examples for mobile workflows are processes with actors that work in the field, e.g., traveling salesmen, delivery services, maintenance engineers, messengers, gas or water meter readers. But in our work we also consider processes with activities that aren't necessarily performed in situations without access to conventional IS as candidates for mobile workflow systems, because this way dead times on journeys (waiting at airport or railway station, evening in hotel, transportation time itself) can be utilized in a productive manner and the backlog of waiting work when returning to the office can be reduced or avoided at all.

However, the implementation of mWfMS requires some special measurements to deal with mobile-specific challenges (see also Jing (2000)): in mobile scenarios we cannot assume that the workflow client is connected with the workflow server all the time. It is therefore necessary to implement some kind of "offline" support, i.e., the workflow client should be able to prefetch activities and the pertinent data. When assigning activities to different actors the workflow engine should also consider the location of the individual actors, e.g., assign an activity that has to be performed at a certain location to the actor with the shortest travel path. More sophisticated approaches even consider the order of activities to assign groups of consecutive activities from the same workflow instance to a mobile actor.

Another technique to support mobile workflows is that the workflow enactment (i.e., the scheduling of individual activities) is partly performed on mobile clients. This implies that more than one workflow engine might be responsible for the execution of a particular workflow instance, which is also denoted by the term "distributed workflows". This approach was first devised for the realization of cross-organizational business workflows like those to be found in supply chains. A system realizing this approach for mobile workflows is "Commune" (Davis et al., 2006) where parts of the workflow called "mini workflow" can be executed autonomously on the mobile clients. In this way it is possible to perform several activities of one workflow instance on a mobile device that has no connection to the backend system.

Stormer & Knorr (2001) developed the AWA/PDA-system, an mWfMS that is based on software agents. Agents in this sense are software components that act on behalf of a user and dispose over a certain degree of intelligence. In their approach an activity is represented by an agent instance that is migrated to the mobile device of the respective actor. Because agents are autonomous, the actor can perform the activity even without having connectivity.

Domingos et al. (1999) describe an mWFMS that uses messaging channels based on the concept of asynchronous communication for the communication with the mobile computers. Asynchronous communication is better suited than conventional synchronous communication for mobile scenarios because wireless data communication is relatively prone to drop-outs. When the central planer assigns a job to a mobile workflow team then the respective mobile client has to periodically send a confirmation message; if the confirmation message isn't received then the job can be assigned to another team.

In literature there can also be found a second generation of mWfMS. In contrast to the systems discussed so far these system employ techniques from the domain of "Service Oriented Architectures" (SOA, see Erl (2006)). Systems following the SOA paradigm typically make use of the

XML-based technologies like webservices. An example of an mWfMS belonging to this second generation is the one described by Pajunen & Chande (2007): for this system a BPEL engine executable on mobile computers was developed. "BPEL" stands for "Business Process Execution Language" and has the purpose to describe the order in which individual webservices have to be invoked. A further mobile-specific feature of this system is the support for protocols like SMS, MMS and Bluetooth. "Sliver" (Hackmann et al., 2006) is another example for a workflow system which provides a BPEL engine for mobile computers and supports mobile-specific protocols. Developing a mobile BPEL engine represents a considerable challenge, because usual BPEL engines are rather heavy-weight components.

ACCESS CONTROL MODELS

Overview

Access Control Models (ACM) are formal models which are used by an access control monitor to decide if a subject's request to perform a certain operation (e.g., read, write, delete, append, change metadata, execute) on an object (e.g., object in file system, database record, web service) should be granted or denied (Benantar, 2006). Together with other models (e.g., inference control models and data flow models, see Denning & Denning (1979)) they constitute so called *security models*. However, since ACM are the most popular type of security models many authors use the term security model when they actually mean ACM.

To show how ACM are related to other security concepts we depict in Figure 1 a diagram called the "security stack": the purpose of security models is to formulate security policies, i.e., statements in natural languages that define what is deemed as security by a particular organization, e.g., laws or best practises. Models are needed as formal representation of the policy in a machine-readable

Figure 1. The "Security Stack"

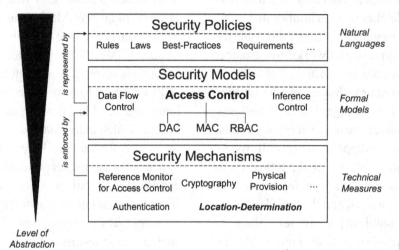

form and in some cases to prove that a model instance has desirable properties. But to actually enforce what is stated by a model we need technical measures like encryption of data or physical provisions like locking away a computer. For many cases of access control authentication of the user is required as prerequisite. The distinctive feature of location-aware access control is that the user's location is evaluated as further piece of information to decide whether the user's request is granted or denied. In Figure 1 it is also shown that when we go from the bottom to the top of the security stack the level of abstraction increases.

An appropriate example to introduce and exemplify the concept of an ACM is Lampson's "Access Control Matrix" (Lampson, 1974): in this matrix the rows represent the subjects (e.g., human user or computer program) and each column an object (e.g., file, database table). Each element of the matrix enumerates the operations that the respective subject is allowed to perform on the respective object. The matrix is an incarnation for "Discretionary Access Control" (DAC), i.e., an ACM where the owner (in most cases the creator) of an object can grant and revoke the rights to perform certain operations to individual subjects. For example, if Alice creates a file it is at her discretion to grant the permission to perform

the operation "read" and/or "write" to Bob or Claire.

Another approach for access control is "Mandatory Access Control" (MAC) with the Bell-LaPadula-Model as best-known incarnation (Bell & LaPadula, 1976; Bell, 2005): for this we have to assign a security label to each subject and to each object in the system. It is necessary that there exists an order on the set of security labels. A commonly used set of security labels is "Top Secret", "Secret", "Confidential" and "Unclassified", whereas "Top Secret" is the strongest and "Unclassified" the weakest level. So if we assign the label (or clearance) "Secret" to a subject, the respective user can read objects that have the label (classification) "Secret" or below, but not objects that are classified as "Top Secret". Because of these multiple levels MAC is also called *multilevel security*. MAC-rules are system-wide rules that intent to retain mistakes made by users in their DAC configuration. The origin of MAC lies in the military domain but meanwhile there are also implementations available that come from the commercial domain, e.g., SELinux (Security Enhanced Linux), AppArmor for Linux, or "Label Based Access Control" (LBAC) for IBM's database management system "DB2".

The third approach for ACM is "Role Based Access Control" (RBAC, see Ferraiolo et al., (2007)) which is also the most popular one for business applications: the basic idea is to assign permissions to roles which in turn are assigned to subjects rather than assigning all the permissions directly to subjects. A role is a collection of all the permissions necessary to perform a certain job within an organization, e.g., there might be roles like "manager", "accountant", "secretary" or "travelling salesman". This greatly reduces the effort necessary for the administration of an ACM, because if someone enters the organization we just have to assign him the appropriate roles for his job rather than many individual permissions. RBAC further allows the definition of inheritance relationships between these roles, so a role like "senior developer" could inherit all the permissions assigned to the role "junior developer"; this is called "hierarchical RBAC". "Constrained RBAC" allows the definition of set of roles, that cannot be assigned to a user at the same time (static constraint) or that can be used by one user within one session (dynamic constraint). RBAC emerged in the 1990s and was standardized by the NIST in 2004, so it is a rather young approach when compared to DAC and MAC which were already devised in the early 1970s.

Location-Aware Access Control Models

Most location-aware ACM to be found in literature are extensions of RBAC. The basic notion is to disable roles for individual subjects only if they stay at particular locations. For example, the role "nurse" should only be active if the respective user is currently located in a hospital ward. Rules for location-aware access control can stem from several considerations: access to functions provided by mWfMS can be restricted to locations where it is necessary or plausible to perform that activity, e.g., it's only reasonable for a user to perform the activity "lab results" if he currently stays at the lab. The administrator of an mWfMS might also forbid the access from places that are deemed as "insecure", e.g., public places where a mobile device could get stolen/lost or someone could peek at the display to see confidential data. Also it might be an organization's policy not to allow data access from foreign countries because they have to fear industrial espionage or they are obliged not to transfer person-related data abroad.

There are already some location-aware ACM: The SRBAC-Model (Spatial RBAC) by Hansen and Oleshchuck (2003) is motivated by applications in hospital scenarios. In this model the permissions assigned to a role depend on the location of the user. The LRBAC-model by Ray et al. (2006) is able not only to express that a given role should only be activatable at certain locations, but also consider the location where a user can acquire a role; e.g., the role "conference delegate" can only be assigned to a user when he is present at that conference. LoT-RBAC (Location and Time-based RBAC) by Chandran & Joshi (2005) considers not only location but also time to restrict roles, so a role could be only enabled from 6 a.m. till 5 p.m. The model comprehends also a location model which distinguishes between a schema and an instance level and considers possible containments of locations. Damiani et al. (2007) propose GEO-RBAC, an expressive extension of RBAC with a location-model based on the *Geographic Markup Language (GML)*. It offers also role schemas to define common properties that are shared by different role instances and there is also a XML-grammar for representations of its instances. STRBAC (Spatio-Temporal RBAC) by Kumar & Newman (2006) considers not only location but also time as constraints for enabling permissions that are bound to roles.

An example for a location-aware ACM that is not based on RBAC but on MAC is proposed by Ray & Kumar (2006): the basic notion of their model is that security levels are assigned to particular locations, e.g., a room in a building is classified as "top secret" whereas a public place is "unclassified". Operations on objects can only be performed when the object's security level isn't higher as the level of the user's current location, e.g., it is not allowed to read a "secret" document in a building that is classified only for "confidential".

All the location-aware ACM mentioned in this section so far are generic ones, i.e., they were not developed with a special application domain in mind. The model proposed later in the paper at hand is a non-generic model, because it is especially tailored for WfMS. Another example for a non-generic but location-aware ACM can be found in Decker (2009d): this model is for database management systems (DBMS) and based on MAC. The basic principle is that individual table rows can "remember" the location where they were created, so it can be prevented that these rows are accessed (e.g., read, updated, deleted) when the mobile actor is not at the same location.

It is important to mention that all the location-aware ACM discussed in this section are process-agnostic. For a more complete overview on location-aware ACM we refer the reader to the survey article by Decker (2009b).

Workflow-Aware Access Control Models

An aspect addressed by many workflow-specific ACM is that a user is not allowed to perform a certain activity for a given workflow instance depending on other activities he already performed. For example, Alice has the permission to perform the activities "submit proposal" and "review proposal", but she is not allowed to perform both activities for the same workflow instance, i.e., she is not allowed to write a review for her own proposal. This principle is called "Separation of Duties" (SoD) and aims at reducing the danger of fraud or omission by distributing the responsibilities for a workflow amongst several actors (Sandhu, 1991).

The opposite case is called "Binding of Duties" (BoD). BoD rules express that if a particular actor performed an activity within a workflow instance he is also obliged to perform certain other activities. For example, if Alice entered a client's inquiry she received by phone into the workflow system she is also obliged to perform the last activity "inform client by phone" because the organization supports the "one face to the customer" policy. For many approval workflows it is also reasonable that the person who initiated the workflow is obliged to perform the activity "receive decision". Given the case of a workflow for the publication process of a research article we could demand that the reviewer who was chosen by the workflow system for the initial review has also to perform subsequent review iterations, because he already knows the respective article.

The principle of BoD was the original source of idea for the ACM to be introduced later in this article: instead of binding particular activities of a workflow to certain actors for a mobile workflow system it should also be possible to bind activities to locations. Referring to an example from the housing industry it could be reasonable to demand that the location where the activity "report damaged facility" was performed is the only location where the subsequent activity "repair" for that workflow instance can be performed.

In the remainder of this subsection we cover some ACM that were developed especially for WfMS: An early example is "WAM", the "Workflow Authorization Model" by Atluri & Huang (1996): it focuses on the synchronization of workflow with authorization flow, i.e., the necessary permissions to perform a certain task are granted to the user when he starts the tasks and are revoked immediately after. Another ACM for WfMS is W-RBAC (Wainer et al., 2003). It is also able to express constraints with regard to an organization's structure, e.g., the activity "approve reimbursement of travel expenses" should be performed by an actor that comes from the same department as the originator of that workflow. Further, W-RBAC supports "reciprocal separation of duties" which means that SoD can be enforced on an intra-instance level: if Alice performed the activity "approve proposal" for a workflow started by Bob then Bob won't be allowed to approve any proposal from Alice. Bertino et al. (1999) developed another ACM along with a formal language to express policies according to their model. Their work also covers an algorithm to check the consistency of constraints. This ACM is also capable of evaluating the hierarchy of roles and there might be a refined role-order for individual activities. Another feature is that the number of times an actor invokes an activity type within a workflow can be restricted. Bussler (1995) proposes a model, where permission might depend on the content of a workflow instance. For example, if the instances deal with processing of insurance claims then the decision which actor is allowed to make the final decision depends on the amount of the damage, so if the amount is not higher than 10,000 USD an ordinary clerk is allowed to make the decision, but for higher amounts an executive has to perform this activity.

LOCATION

Locating Techniques

For the determination of the mobile's user position there are many locating techniques available, see Küpper (2007) or Hightower & Borriello (2001) for an overview. One classification approach is to distinguish between self-locating and remote-locating techniques: For self-locating the location-determination is performed by the mobile device. The well-known "Global Positioning System" (GPS) is an example for self-locating: Based on the signals emitted by at least four satellites the mobile device can calculate its position. Remote-locating means that the location-determination is performed by a locating network and not on the device. An example for such a system is the Cell-ID-approach (also called "Cell of Origin") in cellular networks for mobile telephony like GSM

or UMTS: the network knows which base-station is currently used by the mobile device and returns the position of that base station as estimation for the user's position. Since GPS and Cell-ID don't work well for indoor locating there are also systems especially developed to work within buildings, e.g., the remote locating system "Active Badge" (Want et al., 1992), the self-locating system CRICKET (Priyantha, Chakraborty and Balakrishnan, 2000) or various WiFi-based systems (see Wallbaum & Diepolder (2005) for an overview).

The most obvious deployment scenario for an mWfMS would be that mobile devices with the workflow clients access the workflow engine which is hosted on a stationary backend server. To enforce the ACM an appropriate control module has to be integrated into the workflow engine. So if self-locating is employed, the mobile client has to provide the location information to the workflow engine. However, in this case the mobile device could "invent" arbitrary location information and forward it to the server. If the assumption is made that the user of the mobile device is able to manipulate the location calculation or the device is captured by a malicious attacker (maybe after it was lost or stolen), then we cannot guarantee the enforcement of the ACM. The manipulation of a location system is called "Location Spoofing". However there are special approaches for self-locating that cannot be manipulated by the possessor of the device, see Mundt (2006) for an example: he describes an approach that employs a special tamper-proof hardware module that encapsulates the GPS receiver and a precise clock. Using remote-locating is preferable for this scenario because then it's harder to forge the location determination since this would require breaking into the locating network. However, if an ACM is employed as usability support, we don't have to consider the trustworthiness of the location determination. It is also thinkable to combine a self- and a remote locating technology, e.g., GPS and Cell-ID. Cell-ID is more trustworthy from the workflow engines point of view but also less precise than GPS, but the workflow engine could check if the position reported by the mobile device actually lies in the cell obtained by the Cell-ID method.

There are other techniques to validate the location claim of a mobile device: e.g., Sastry, Shankar & Wagner (2003) proposed a protocol that is based on the measurement of the time needed by the mobile device to reflect a message containing an unpredictable bit-sequence. The system "CyberLocator" described by Denning & MacDoran (1996) takes advantage of the fact that the signals broadcasted by the GPS satellites are altered by different disturbing factors (e.g., ionospheric effect, weather conditions like rainfall, atmospheric effect), so for each location there is an individual "radio fingerprint". This radio fingerprint has to be provided by the mobile devices and is compared to the radio fingerprint for that location which is provided by trusted reference stations. To prevent a so called "rerouting attack" (the mobile device isn't at the alleged location but receives the fingerprint by a colluding device that stays at that location) it is required that the radio fingerprint is forwarded with a delay not greater than 5 ms. For an overview on different approaches to prevent or at least detect location spoofing we refer the reader to the survey article by Decker (2009a).

Location Model

A "location model" is a special data model to describe spatial data, e.g., the coordinates/boundaries of different locations and the relation between them (Becker & Dürr, 2005).

For the ACM presented later in this paper the following simple location model is sufficient: a location is just a non-empty area (e.g., polygon, circle) within the reference space. Locations can have a class, e.g., "city", "country" or "room". Examples for location instances of class "city" are "Amsterdam" or "Munich". As long as two locations don't belong to the same class they may

overlap. One location may also contain another one, e.g., the location "Netherlands" contains the location "Amsterdam". We don't demand that all location instances of a given class cover the whole reference space, i.e., the instances of a given location class are non-exhaustive.

But besides these geometric locations there are also "placeholder locations". Such a placeholder location is just a term for a kind of location that will differ from user to user. To resolve the actual geometric location behind a placeholder location at runtime there are "placeholder definitions". As example we consider a placeholder location called "personal residence": For user Alice this placeholder location is mapped to a polygon that covers her bungalow in Amsterdam, but for Bob this placeholder location is mapped to the rectangle that represents the ground of his house in Berlin. Using these placeholder locations more general location-aware ACM can be formulated. Another placeholder location could be "personal sales district": For Alice this is a region in Netherlands while for Bob it is a region in Eastern Germany. Further examples would be "personal office" or "personal department".

ACCESS CONTROL MODEL FOR MOBILE WORKFLOWS

Scenario

In the scenario we assume there is a multinational company that operates several local branches in the two neighbouring countries Germany and the Netherlands in Europe. One local branch in each country is the national head quarter for that country. The considered workflow deals with mobile workers that have to visit a customer's home to do some kind of maintenance work (e.g., repairing a central heating system or a machine): an employee with role "dispatcher" receives a call from a customer and creates a new workflow instance or "job" in the mWfMS and assigns it

Figure 2. Example Workflow

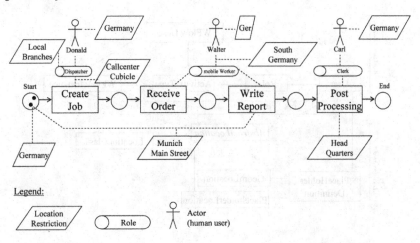

Legend:

Location Restriction   Role   Actor (human user)

to a mobile worker (activity type "create job"). Another employee with role "mobile worker" receives such a job (activity type "receive order") and drives to the target location where the job has to be performed. After completing the job he enters a report (activity type "write report"), e.g., what had to be repaired or which spare parts he had to use so later the bill can be prepared or if a further visit it necessary. This report should be written at the target location, because if it is written later then the technician might forget details (or forget to write the report at all). The reports are forwarded to the head quarter of the respective country where an employee with role "clerk" performs the activity type "post processing" (e.g., writing a bill, statistical evaluations, surveying customer's satisfaction and replenishment of spare parts). Another role in the scenario is "manager": he is allowed to perform all mentioned activity types.

The process together with roles and actors (except role "manager") is depicted in a diagram based on Petri nets in Figure 2. The circles ("places") represent the states a process can have (e.g., not started, first step completed, process finished) and the rectangles ("transitions") are activities that have to be performed (or "fired") so the process goes to a different stage. All the places with solid arcs pointing to a given transition are called "pre-set" of that transition; in analogy to

this, the "post-set" of a given transition is the set of all places that are target of a solid arc starting at that transition (Peterson, 1977). Parallelograms attached to elements of the model represent the location constraints and will be discussed below. In the place "Start" there are two tokens representing different jobs (workflow instances or cases), e.g., two different houses to visit. If all the places in the pre-set of a given transition contain at least one token then that transition is "activated" and may "fire". When firing, the transition removes one token from each place in its pre-set and adds one token to each place in its post-set. For the simple example in Figure 2 this means that the token "moves" from the place directly before the transition to the place directly after the transition.

Basic Model

The proposed ACM is depicted in Figure 3 as UML class diagram, in which the cardinality "*" (asterisk) stands for "0..N" and "+" (plus) for "1..N". We first explain the workflow-specific entities in the upper half: A workflow description consists of several types of activities with a partial order. The partial order defines in which order the activities can or have to be performed, if there are optional activities or activities that can be performed simultaneously, but for the sake of

Figure 3. Access Control Model for mobile Workflows

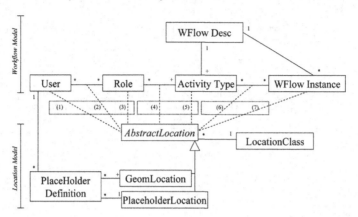

clarity we don't consider this partial order in our model. Based on a workflow description several workflow instances can be created, e.g., for our scenario one instance could be "repair facility in street S1 in city C1" and another instance would be "repair facility in street S2 in city C2". The model follows the basic notion of RBAC: the activity types which can be performed by a user depend on the roles he has, it is not allowed to directly assign activity types to users.

In the lower part of the diagram the location model as described above is represented. An *AbstractLocation* is either a *GeometricLocation* or a *PlaceHolderLocation*. For *PlaceHolderLocations* there are instances of class *PlaceHolderDefinition* to define to which *GeometricLocation* a given *PlaceholderLocation* should be mapped for an individual user. An *AbstractLocation* is associated to exactly one instance of class *LocationClass*, so each location whether it is a *GeometricLocation* or a *PlaceHolderLocation*, can be considered as instance of a distinct *LocationClass*. This modeling approach of having a schema layer of location classes can also be found in the LoT-RBAC model by Chandran & Joshi (2005) already mentioned above or in the *Geographic Markup Language (GML)*, see Burggraf (2006). The *Geometric-Location* that resolves a *PlaceHolderLocation* has to be of the same class as the *PlaceHolderLocation*, of course.

Types of Location Constraints

As depicted in Figure 3 we identified seven different points in the workflow model where it should be possible to assign location constraints. A *location constraint* is a statement that can disable the component of the ACM when the mobile user is not at a particular location. We will discuss the meaning of each type of location constraint in the following and exemplify them by referring to the scenario with the on-site maintenance work depicted in Figure 2:

Restriction 1: If a location constraint is assigned to a user this means that the user can work with the mWfMS only at particular locations. In the scenario all employees of the company that are *not* at executive level can only access the mWfMS when they are inside the country where they usually work, e.g., user Donald is restricted to "Germany". This type of constraint could also be used to confine the area where an intern is allowed to use the system (e.g., to the department of the organization where she has to work).

Restriction 2: If a location constraint is assigned to the association between a user and a role this means that the user can play that role only in particular locations (but the assignment of other roles is not affected by this). The role "mobile worker" is assigned to Walter with a location constraint to southern Germany because that's the region where he lives and works. Other mobile workers get that role restricted to northern Germany or southern and northern Netherlands.

Restriction 3: A location constraint assigned to a role means that the respective role can only be activated at a particular location. In the example the role "dispatcher" has a location constraint so it can be only activated while the user is at any of the company's local branches in both Germany and Netherlands. For a hospital scenario we could think of a role "nurse" that can only be activated while staying at the premises of the hospital.

Restriction 4: These location constraints express that certain roles can perform an activity type only at certain locations. In the scenario the activity "create job" can only be performed at a call-center cubicle by role "dispatcher", but the same activity is also assigned to the manager without any location constraints.

Restriction 5: A location constraint assigned directly to an activity type means that this activity can only be performed on particular locations allowed by the constraints. In our scenario this is the case for "post processing" which can only be performed at one of the company's headquarters in Germany or Netherlands. A location constraint at this level can also be used to enforce license-restrictions if the mWfMS is provided by an "Application Service Provider" who charges fees based on the size of the region where the system can be used. Location constraints for activity types represent the strictest form of location constraints because even if all other entities in the model don't have any location constraints the respective activity type cannot be performed outside the designated area.

Restriction 6: The association between activity type and workflow instance represents an activity instance for a particular workflow instance. If we assign a location constraint to this association we can express that certain activities for a given workflow instance are restricted to particular locations. In our scenario the activity "write report" is restricted to the target location of the

respective workflow instance, e.g., "Main Street no 3 in Munich". In figure 2 this is depicted by the location constraint attached to the line between the workflow instance token and the activity type.

Restriction 7: A location constraint assigned to a workflow instance means that *all* activities of that instance have to be performed at particular locations. In our scenario we use this to enforce that the whole processing for one workflow instance is done within the country, e.g., to prevent misunderstandings because of different languages. It could also be the company's policy not to transfer person-related data (e.g., the data for a workflow of type "job application") across national borders. In figure 2 this is depicted by attaching a location constraint directly to a token.

As hinted by the three dotted boxes in figure 3 we can further classify the seven location constraints: Restrictions 1 to 3 are at *user-role-level* (and thus are workflow-agnostic), restrictions 4 and 5 are at *workflow description level* (or *workflow schema level)*, and restrictions 6 and 7 at *workflow instance level*.

Since we can assign location constraints at different levels, it may be necessary to calculate the intersection of several locations to obtain the region where a particular user is allowed to perform a particular activity type for a particular workflow instance indeed. Example: Donald has the role "dispatcher" to perform the task "create job". He is allowed to use the MIS only in Germany and the "create job" activity is assigned to the "dispatcher" role with a location constraint to the company's call centre cubicles. If we calculate the intersection of "call center cubicles" and "Germany", this results in all the company's call center cubicles in Germany. The problem is that there might be empty intersections, so that there is no eligible location for the execution of an activity; this is addressed in Decker (2008b). Another problem is that there might be no employee who is allowed to perform the activity when considering all locations constraints (Hewett & Kijsanayothin, 2009).

There are $2^7=128$ different combinations of these seven types of locations constraints. It is unlikely for a real-world scenario that all seven types of constraints are employed. A security administrator of an mWfMS using our ACM has the choice to employ that subset of constraint types (or maybe just a single constraint type) that is most natural to express the security policy of the corresponding organization.

Location Constraints at Instance Level

The most interesting location constraints are those at workflow instance level (type 6 and 7), because they have to be obtained at runtime of a workflow instance and cannot be assigned in advance at administration time. We identified several ways how location constraints at workflow instance level can be acquired:

Manual setting: The creator of the workflow instances specifies that some or all activities should be restricted to certain locations. For example, when a user starts a workflow instance for the processing of a possibly confidential document (e.g., research report has to be reviewed, spell-checked, layouted, translated) he could require that no activity of the workflow is performed in countries where industrial espionage has to be feared. It could also be reasonable that all or some of the actors involved in a workflow have the permission to alter the location constraint. The actors who have that right can be specified over a certain permission assigned to their role. There could be even a dedicated activity type "set location constraint".

Location-binding Rules: Employing rules is another way to retrieve location constraints for individual instances automatically. If we consider as example a workflow where a salesman has to visit a customer at his premises several times a rule could enforce that if the activity type "write customer note" is executed for the first time at location *L1* within a workflow instance, this implies

that further executions of this activity within the same process instance are restricted to *L1*. Such a rule is termed "self-binding rule" since it only imposes location constraints for the same activity-type. But there are also rules where the location of an activity type implies location constraints for other activity types, e.g., the location where the activity type "take customer order" is the location where the activity types "write customer report" and "post-inspection" have to be performed; such rules are called "non-self-binding-rule".

A rule refers to a location class to be able to generate the appropriate location constraint, i.e., the location class is needed to obtain the location object that describes "the same location" at the right level of granularity. For example, if an activity is performed at a certain house in Amsterdam and the self-binding rule points to the location class "city", then the respective activity is bound to the location "Amsterdam" for the given workflow instance; if the rule points to location class "country" then the runtime system will try to retrieve a location instance of that class (i.e., a country like Netherlands or Germany) which contains the current position of the user.

Automatic setting: Another way of setting location constraints automatically is the employment of automatic workflow activities. In this case arbitrary programming logic can be employed to calculate a location constraint so this approach isn't limited to the expressiveness of the location-binding rules provided by the ACM. Referring to the maintenance scenario introduced above there could be an automatic activity (i.e., activity performed solely by computer) looking up the calling customer's address in a CRM-database and setting the location constraint for the activity "receive order" to a rectangular location (e.g., of size 1km x 1km) enclosing that address.

To exemplify these concepts further another process is shown in Figure 4. It is basically the same process as the one shown in Figure 2, but without the role constraint and static constraints. Again, the arrows with dotted lines do not influ-

Figure 4. Mobile workflow with annotations for location constraints at instance level

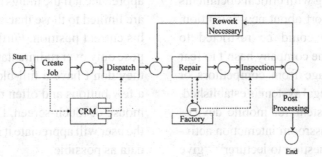

ence the control flow; the purpose of these arrows is to assign location constraints to the process graph. After the job is created in the company's workflow system a *Customer Relationship Management (CRM)* system decides which local branch is responsible for the activity "Dispatch", i.e., to assign a mobile technician for the on-site visit at the customer's premises. The CRM system stores the addresses of all customers and is therefore able to decide which local branch is in the least distance to that customer and therefore responsible for dispatching a service technician; this is the "automatic setting" mechanism for the retrieval of location constraints during runtime mentioned above. After the actual repair of the machine at the customer's site the next activity is "inspection": during an inspection a senior technician (the inspector) of the company visits the customer's factory to check if the repair work was thoroughly done. If the inspector approves the work then the next activity is "post processing"; however, if the inspector is not satisfied with the work then the transition "Rework Necessary" will fire, so the activity "Repair" will be performed again. The cycle "Repair", "Inspection" and "Rework necessary" may occur several times.

To ensure that the two activities "Repair" and "Inspection" are performed at the same factory site we employ a "Location-binding Rule", which is depicted as a circle holding an equal sign ("="). Attached to that circle is a box with the lettering "Factory", which denotes the location class to specify the granularity of the rule. The dotted

arrow starting at activity "Repair" and pointing towards the rule triggers the rule, so the location where this activity is performed determines where the targets of that rule have to be performed. The target of the rules can be found by following the arrows which start at the rule and point to activities in the form of transitions. In the example these activities are "Repair" and "Inspection". Activity "Repair" was also the trigger of the rule, so we have a self-binding rule for the case of repeated execution of that activity.

Further Examples

We'd like to give some more examples for location constraints at instance-level:

- Some activities of a workflow dealing with the treatment of a patient in a hospital should be restricted to the patient's room, e.g., "prescribe medicine", "write on-bed memo", "record vital data" or "administer medicine".
- The activity "enter x-ray results" should be restricted to the x-ray-lab in the part of the hospital where the patient has his bed.
- Serving guests in a restaurant can also be supported by an mWfMS; here activities like "take order for drinks", "take order for main course" and "cash up" should be restricted to the respective table and "prepare meal" to the kitchen.

- Workflows dealing with critical documents (e.g., internal report about new invention, financial figures) could be restricted to countries where the company hasn't to fear industrial espionage from competitors or where a reliable legal system is established.
- An e-learning system for mobile devices should restrict classroom interaction activities like "send question to lecturer", "give realtime feedback" or "answer classroom quiz" to the teaching room of the respective course so students who are absent cannot disturb the lesson.

All examples for location-aware ACM given so far aimed at protecting the MIS from security threats or handling errors. But we also can envision scenarios where our ACM can be employed "the other way round" to guarantee the privacy of mobile users, which is another serious problem that comes along with the employment of MIS (Decker, 2008a): for this approach the providers of location-based services (e.g., navigation service, advertising service, tourist guides, friend-finder) are modeled as "users". "Activity types" are permissions an LBS might need to provide its service but which could constitute a privacy infringement, e.g., "send SMS/MMS message once/x-times" (since unsolicited push-messages could be regarded as annoying Spam) or "query location with precision of x meters once/continuously". Using roles the user can group permissions to a collection of LBS, e.g., a role "vacation services" can be restricted to his holiday destination or role "work" could be restricted to his employer's premises.

Access Control Models as Approach for Context-Awareness

Another major challenge that comes along with the employment of MIS is usability: mobile devices have only a small display, which often is only able to provide images of poor quality with regard to contrast or color-depth; so the mobile user will

appreciate it if the things displayed on the display are limited to those that are actually necessary in his current position. Further mobile devices dispose only over rudimentary means for data input: they don't have a full-blown keyboard but only a few buttons and often no pointer-device like a mouse or touch-screen. Due to these constraints the user will appreciate it if he has to enter as little data as possible.

Such access rules can also be "misused" to improve the usability of a MIS by using the ACM to only present data to the user that is of relevance for him at his current location, e.g., in a list of customers only those could be listed which have their premises at a location in proximity to the user's current location. Such interaction support is termed "context-awareness" in mobile computing (Dourish, 2003).

Further Approaches for Graphical Modelling of Mobile Workflows

In this paper we used a notation based on Petri nets to model location constraints for mobile workflows. However, there are some other graphical notations for mobile workflows which will be mentioned in this subsection.

In Decker et al. (2010) the „Business Process Modeling Notation" (BPMN) is used to draw mobile workflows. The BPMN is also extended to be able to depict several types of location constraints. Activity diagrams from the *Unified Modeling Language (UML)* have also been used to model mobile workflows with location constraints (Decker, 2009c). The advantage of BPMN and UML is that these notations offer an explicit mechanism to define custom extensions. UML also offers class diagrams which can be used to define the necessary location model. Hewett & Kijsanayothin (2009) also used UML activity diagrams with location constraints assigned to individual activities; however, their approach only has simple static constraints, no explicit location model, and is more concerned to determine model configuration where it could happen that there is no mobile user who could perform a given activity under consideration of all location constraints. Baumeister et al. (2003) also used UML activity diagrams to model mobility in processes. However, this approach is concerned with the representing how mobile objects are moved by individual activities during a process.

CONCLUSION: SUMMARY AND OUTLOOK

In the article we motivated an *Access Control Model (ACM)* that is capable of expressing workflow-specific location constraints. This is a novel approach since so far no ACM that supports both mobility and workflows is available. We identified seven points in the model where location constraint could be assigned to. Each type of location constraint was discussed and exemplified by examples.

Our model focused on the most salient context parameter of mobile information systems, namely location. But it would be interesting to integrate further types of relevant context information like the features of the currently used mobile device, the resources in proximity or the security level of the wireless data connection. It would also be a worthwhile task to develop a software tool that enables a user-friendly administration of security policies according to our ACM, because currently there are almost no works available concerning special tools for working with location-aware ACM.

REFERENCES

Alonso, G., Günthör, R., Kamath, M., Agrawal, D., El Abbadi, A., & Mohan, C. (1996). Exotica/FMDC: A Workflow management System for Mobile and Disconnected Clients. *Distributed and Parallel Databases, 4*(3), 229–247. doi:10.1007/BF00140951

Atluri, V., & Huang, W. (1996). An Authorization Model for Workflows. Proceedings of the 4th European Symposium on Research in Computer Security (ESORICS), London, U.K. (pp. 44-64). Berlin, Germany: Springer.

Baumeister, H., Koch, N., Kosiuczenko, P., & Wirsing, M. (2003). *Extending Activity Diagrams to Model Mobile Systems. Proceedings of NetObjectDays 2002 (NOD), revised papers, Erfurt, Germany* (pp. 278–293). Berlin, Germany: Springer.

Becker, C., & Dürr, F. (2005). On Location Models for Ubiquitous Computing. *Personal and Ubiquitous Computing, 9*(1), 20–31. doi:10.1007/s00779-004-0270-2

Bell, D. E. (2005). Looking back at the Bell-LaPadula Model. *Proceedings of the 21st Annual Computer Security Applications Conference (ACSAC 2005)*, Tucson, USA (pp. 337-351). Los Alamitos, USA: IEEE Computer Society.

Bell, D. E., & LaPadula, J. (1976). *Secure Computer System: Unified Exposition and Multics Interpretation. Technical Report of MITRE Corporation.* Bradford, MA, USA: MITRE Corporation.

Benantar, M. (2006). *Access Control Systems. Security, Identity Management and Trust Models.* New York, USA et al.: Springer.

Bertino, E., Ferrari, E., & Atluri, V. (1999). The Specification and Enforcement of Authorization Constraints in Workflow Management Systems. ACM Transactions on Information and System Security. 2(1), 1999, 65-104.

Burggraf, D. S. (2006). Geographic Markup Language. *Data Science Journal, 5,* 187–204. doi:10.2481/dsj.5.178

Bussler, C. (1995). Access Control in Workflow-Management Systems. *Post-Workshop Proceedings of IT-Sicherheit*, Vienna, Austria, (pp. 165-179). Munich, Germany: Oldenbourg-Verlag.

Chandran, S. M., & Joshi, J. B. D. (2005). LoT-RBAC: A Location and Time-Based RBAC Model. *Proceedings of the 6th International Conference on Web Information Systems Engineering (WISE '05)*. New York, USA (pp. 361-375), Berlin, Germany: Springer.

Damiani, M. L., Bertino, E., & Perlasca, P. (2007). Data Security in Location-Aware Applications: An Approach Based on RBAC. *International Journal of Information and Computer Security.*, *1*(1/2), 5–38. doi:10.1504/IJICS.2007.012243

Davis, J., Sow, D., Bourges-Waldegg, D., Guo, C., Hoertnagl, C., Stolze, M., et al. (2006). Supporting Mobile Business Workflow with Commune. Proceedings of the 7th IEEE Workshop on Mobile Computing System & Applications (WMCSA), Washington, DC, USA, (pp. 10-18). Los Alamitos, USA: IEEE Computer Society.

Decker, M. (2008a). An Access-Control Model for Mobile Computing with Spatial Constraints - Location-aware Role-based Access Control with a Method for Consistency Checks. *Proceedings of the International Conference on e-Business (ICE-B 2008)*, Porto, Portugal (pp. 185-190), Sétubal, Portugal: INSTICC Press.

Decker, M. (2008d). Location Privacy — An Overview. *Proceedings of the International Conference on Mobile Business (ICMB 08)*, Barcelona, Spain. Los Alamitos, USA: IEEE Computer Society.

Decker, M. (2009a). Prevention of Location-Spoofing. A Survey on Different Methods to Prevent the Manipulation of Locating-Technologies. *Proceedings of the International Conference on e-Business (ICE-B)*. Milan, Italy (pp. 109-114). Sétubal, Portugal: INSTICC Press.

Decker, M. (2009b). Location-Aware Access Control: An Overview. In *Proceedings of Informatics 2009 – Special Session on Wireless Applications and Computing (WAC '09), Carvoeiro, Portugal* (pp. 75–82). Lisbon, Portugal: IADIS.

Decker, M. (2009c). Modelling Location-Aware Access Control Constraints for Mobile Workflows with UML Activity Diagrams. *The Third International Conference on Mobile Ubiquitous Computing, Systems, Services and Technologies (UbiComm 2009),* Sliema, Malta (pp. 263-268). Los Alamitos, USA: IEEE Computer Society.

Decker, M. (2009c). Mandatory and Location-Aware Access Control for Relational Databases. *Proceedings of the International Conference on Communication Infrastructure, Systems and Applications in Europe (EuropeComm 2009)*, London, U.K. (pp. 217-228). Berlin, Germany: Springer.

Decker, M., Che, H., Oberweis, A., Stürzel, P., & Vogel, M. (2010). Modeling Mobile Workflows with BPMN. *Proceedings of the Ninth International Conference on Mobile Business (ICMB 2010)/Ninth Global Mobility Roundtable (GMR 2010)*, Athens, Greece (pp. 272-279). Los Alamitos, USA: IEEE Computer Society.

Denning, D., & MacDoran, P. (1996). Location-Based Authentication: Grounding Cyberspace for Better Security. *Computer Fraud & Security*, (2): 12–16. doi:10.1016/S1361-3723(97)82613-9

Denning, D. E., & Denning, P. J. (1979). Data Security. *ACM Computing Surveys*, *11*(3), 227–249. doi:10.1145/356778.356782

Domingos, H., Martins, J. L., Preguica, N., & Duarte, S. M. (1999). A Workflow-Architecture to Manage Mobile Collaborative Work. *Proceedings of Encontro Portugues de Computacao Movel (EPCM '99)*, Tomar, Portugal.

Dourish, P. (2003). What we talk about when we talk about context. *Personal and Ubiquitous Computing*, *8*(1), 19–30. doi:10.1007/s00779-003-0253-8

Erl, T. (2006). *Service-oriented architecture: concepts, technology, and design.* Upper Saddle River, NJ, USA: Prentice Hall PTR.

Ernest-Jones, T. (2006). Pinning down a security policy for mobile data. *Network Security*, (6): 8–12. doi:10.1016/S1353-4858(06)70399-3

Ferraiolo, D. F., Kuhn, D. R., & Chandramouli, R. (2007). *Role-Based Access Control* (2nd ed.). Boston, USA: Artech House.

Hackmann, G., Haitjema, M., Gill, C., & Roman, G.-C. (2006). Sliver: A BPEL Workflow Process Execution Engine for Mobile Devices. *Proceedings of the 4th International Conference on Service Oriented Computing (ICSOC 2006)*, Chicago, IL, USA (pp. 503-508). Berlin, Germany: Springer.

Hansen, F., & Oleshchuk, V. (2003). SRBAC: A Spatial Role-Based Access Control Model for Mobile Systems. *Proceedings of the 7th Nordic Workshop on Secure IT Systems (NORDSEC '03)*. Gjovik, Norway (pp. 129-141). Trondheim, Norway: NTNU.

Hewett, R., & Kijsanayothin, P. (2009). Location Contexts in Role-based Security Policy Enforcement. *Proceedings of the 2009 International Conference on Security and Management*. Las Vegas, USA (pp. 13-16). Las Vegas, USA: CSREA Press.

Hightower, J., & Boriello, G. (2001). Location Systems for Ubiquitous Computing. *IEEE Computer*, *34*(8), 57–66.

Jing, J., Huff, K., Hurwitz, B., Sinha, H., Robinson, B., & Feblowitz, M. (2000). WHAM. Supporting Mobile Workforce and Applications in Workflow Environments. Proceedings of 10th International Workshop on Research Issues in Data Engineering (RIDE), San Diego, California, USA (pp. 31-38). Los Alamitos, USA: IEEE Computer Society.

Kumar, M., & Newman, R. E. (2006). STRBAC — An Approach Towards Spatio-Temporal Role-Based Access Control. *Proceedings of the Conference on Communication, Network, and Information Security (CNIS)* (pp. 150-155). Calgary, AB, Canada: ACTA Press.

Küpper, A. (2007). *Location-based Services. Fundamentals and Operation (reprint)*. Chichester, U.K.: Wiley & Sons.

Lampson, B. (1974). Protection. *Operating Systems Review*, *8*(1), 18–24. doi:10.1145/775265.775268

Mundt, T. (2006). Two Methods of Authenticated Positioning. Proceedings of the International Workshop on Quality of Service & Security for Wireless and Mobile Networks (Q2SWinet). Terromolinos, Spain (pp. 25-32). Boston, MA, USA: ACM Press.

Nissanka, B. Priyantha, N.B., Chakraborty, A., Balakrishnan, H. (2000). The Cricket location-support system. Proceedings of the 6th Annual International Conference on Mobile Computing and Networking (MobiCom 2000), Boston, MA, USA (pp. 32-43). Boston, MA, USA: ACM Press.

Oberweis, A. (2005). Person-to-Application Processes. Workflow-Management (Chapter 2). In M. Dumas, W. v.d. Aalst, & A. Hofstede (Eds.), *Process-Aware Information Systems — Bridging People and Software Through Process Technology* (pp. 21-36). Hoboken, USA: Wiley Interscience.

Pajunen, L., & Chande, S. (2007). Developing Workflow Engine for Mobile Devices. *Proceedings of the 11th IEEE International Enterprise Distributed Object Computing Conference (EDOC 2007)*, Annapolis, Maryland, USA (pp. 279-286). Los Alamitos, USA: IEEE Computer Society.

Peterson, J. L. (1977). Petri Nets. *ACM Computing Surveys*, *9*(3), 223–252. doi:10.1145/356698.356702

Ray, I., & Kumar, M. (2006). Towards a Location-based Mandatory Access Control Model. *Computers & Security*, *25*(1), 36–44. doi:10.1016/j.cose.2005.06.007

Ray, I., Kumar, M., & Yu, L. (2006). LRBAC: A Location-Aware Role-Based Access Control Model. *Proceedings of the Second International Conference on Information Systems Security (ICISS '06)*, Kolkata, India (pp. 147-161). Berlin, Germany: Springer.

Sandhu, R. (1991). Separation of Duties in Computerized Information Systems. *Database Security IV: Status and Prospects - Results of the IFIP WG 11.3 Workshop on Database Security*, Halifax, U.K. (pp. 179-189). Amsterdam, Netherlands: North-Holland Publishing.

Sastry, N., Shankar, U., & Wagner, D. (2003). Secure Verification of Location Claims. *Proceedings of the Conference on Wireless Security (WiSe)*, San Diego, California, USA (pp. 1-10). Boston, MA, USA: ACM Press.

Stormer, H., & Knorr, K. (2001). PDA- and Agent-based Execution of Workflow Tasks. Proceedings of Informatik 2001, Vienna, Austria, (pp. 968-973). Bonn, Germany: Gesellschaft für Informatik (GI).

Wainer, J., Barthelmess, P., & Kumar, A. (2003). W-RBAC — A Workflow Security Model Incorporating Controlled Overriding of Constraints. *International Journal of Cooperative Information Systems*, *12*(4), 455–485. doi:10.1142/S0218843003000814

Wallbaum, M., & Diepolder, S. (2005). Benchmarking Wireless LAN Location Systems. *Proceedings of the Second IEEE International Workshop on Mobile Commerce and Services (WMCS '05)*, Munich, Germany (pp. 42-51). Los Alamitos, USA: IEEE Computer Society.

Want, R., Hopper, A., Falcao, M., & Gibbons, J. (1992). The active badge location system. [TOIS]. *ACM Transactions on Information Systems*, *19*(1), 91–102. doi:10.1145/128756.128759

Chapter 5
Context–Aware Recommender Systems in Vehicular Networks and Other Mobile Domains

Wolfgang Woerndl
Technische Universitaet Muenchen, Germany

Michele Brocco
Technische Universitaet Muenchen, Germany

Robert Eigner
Technische Universitaet Muenchen, Germany

ABSTRACT

We give an overview of ideas for integrating context in recommender systems in general and specifically in various mobile application domains. Our main case study is an approach for vehicular ad-hoc networks (VANETs). The system recommends gas stations based on driver preferences, ratings of other users and context information such as the current location and fuel level of a car. We explain the main design issues behind our recommender. Our approach first filters items based on preferences and context, and then takes ratings of other users and additional information into account, which can be relayed from car to car in a VANET. We also outline other mobile scenarios for contextualized recommender systems: a system for recommending mobile applications based on user context, an approach to find relevant resources in mobile semantic personal information management, and a decentralized recommender system for personal digital assistants (PDAs) that has been successfully applied in a real world mobile city guide.

1. INTRODUCTION

The ever-growing networking of devices and services lead to an increasing availability of

DOI: 10.4018/978-1-60960-523-0.ch005

information not only in desktop computing settings, but also in pervasive domains. The sheer volume of available data makes it more and more difficult for users in general to find and access relevant information. Personalization of content is a technique to reduce the omnipresent information overload by customizing information according to user needs and preferences. Often, recommender systems using collaborative or content-based filtering are applied. Another promising and possibly complementary approach is to utilize context. This is especially true in mobile settings. For example, a user travelling in a car needs access to the current traffic situation on her route, the weather report at her destination or a recommendation for restaurants, gas stations or other points-of-interests (POIs) in her vicinity. So, the main characteristic of the mobile application domain is the availability of context information and it is evident to exploit this information for user assistance. This applies to car-to-car networking, for example, where recent efforts make it possible to detect and exchange warnings about hazardous road conditions among other pieces of information. These vehicular ad-hoc networks (VANETs) can also serve as an infrastructure for driver information systems. Thus, input data for context-aware recommender systems can be obtained by exchanging data over the network with other cars or access points and can be used to tailor the recommendations.

As the integration of context into recommender systems has not been investigated thoroughly up to now (Anand & Mobasher, 2005), it is the overall goal of this work is to investigate context-awareness in personalization and recommender systems in mobile scenarios. Its use is illustrated by presenting a context-aware gas station recommender in VANETs and other mobile and context-aware recommender systems. The rest of this article is organized as follows. First, we give some background on what context is and how it can be modeled, and introduce recommender systems in Section 2. We also discuss some general ideas to contextualize recommenders. In 3 we present our gas station recommender system for VANETs in detail. The approach uses a hybrid, multidimensional recommender system which takes contextual information in addition to user ratings and item metadata into account, most

notably the current fuel level. In Section 4, we outline some other mobile application scenarios for context-aware recommender systems we are currently working on. Finally, we conclude with a short summary and outlook.

2. INTEGRATING CONTEXT INTO RECOMMENDER SYSTEMS

In this section we provide some background on context and recommender systems, present some ideas to integrate context into recommender systems and outline selected related work.

2.1 Context: Definition and Model

Recommender and personalization systems are often not tailored towards the context of users, i.e. they return the same results regardless of the current situation of the user. One of the reasons is that it is first of all hard to arrive at a consensus of what defines context and how to model it (Anand & Mobasher, 2005). In our work we follow the context definition by Dey, Salber & Abowd (2001): Context is "any information that can be used to characterize the situation of entities (i.e. whether a person, place or subject) that are considered relevant to the interaction between a user and an application, including the user and the application themselves" (p. 11). This means, context is very dynamic and transient. For example in our mobile domain, a context model could include location, movement, lighting condition or current availability of network bandwidth of mobile devices. Which context attributes are actually modeled and used in systems is largely dependent on the requirements of the application domains. In comparison to (user) context, a user model (or user profile) that is used in most personalization systems is rather static and somewhat longer lasting and includes demographic data or user preferences or interests, for example.

As far as context modeling is concerned, several approaches for representing context information have been developed (Strang & Linnhoff-Popien, 2004). Key-value pairs can be used as a simple data structure. Markup scheme models consist of hierarchically organized mark-up tags with attributes and content. An example is W3C's standard "Composite Capabilities/Preference Profile (CC/PP)" (W3C, 2004) for representing device capabilities. Object oriented or graphical models, e.g. using the Unified Modeling Language (UML), provide more powerful means to represent context types and describing attributes. In addition, ontologies are a very promising instrument for modeling contextual information due to their high and formal expressiveness and the possibilities for applying ontology reasoning techniques. Ontology-based models can thereby represent complex relationships between (context) concepts.

2.2 Recommender Systems

A recommender system tries to predict the relevance of information items for a user. This is traditionally based on information about the user, meta data associated with items and/or implicit or explicit ratings for items made by a group of users. The standard data model can be summarized as follows (Anand & Mobasher, 2005): Given is a set of n items $I = \{i_j: 1 \leq j \leq n\}$, and a set of m users $U = \{u_k: 1 \leq k \leq m\}$. Each user is described by a t-dimensional vector of attributes, which is also called (user) profile. So the profile contains attribute-value pairs such as "language = english" to express a language the user speaks. The items have meta data associated, in form of a s-dimensional vector (item description). For example, an item may be a particular restaurant (in a restaurant guide application), and the item description may contain "location = (longitude, latitude)", and also the price range and opening hours of a restaurant to be utilized in a tourist guide. Thus, items and users are technically modeled in the same way with respect to data structures.

In addition, often users' ratings of items are used. Technically, a rating is a function r: U x I → S that maps a user instance (and therefore the values of the user profile attributes) and an item instance (or the values of the corresponding item meta data attributes) to some appropriate mapping result-space S, e.g. a rating value in [0, 1]. In other words, a rating $r_{i,s}$ expresses how much a user u_j likes an item i_s. The goal of the personalization process is to recommend items i_j to an active user u_a that would be of interest to the user. (Woerndl & Schlichter, 2008).

The process of recommender systems can be roughly grouped into two categories, individual and collaborative approaches. Individual filters make predictions for an active user based on her profile and information about the item set. Therefore, individual filters are often characterized as content-based systems. Collaborative filters take also other users into account. The two steps of collaborative filtering (CF) in its basic form can be summarized as:

1. Finding similar users, based on past ratings (neighborhood creation)
2. Suggesting items that similar users liked

Neighborhood creation means selecting users that are similar to the active user. In most approaches, similar users are users that rated items in a similar way as the active user in the past. This user-user similarity usually is calculated by using Pearson correlation, cosine-based approach or other likewise metrics (Adomavicius & Tuzhilin, 2005). Subsequently, a set S of n users who are most similar to the active user is computed. For predicting the ratings of some items for the active user, the mean average of ratings given by the users in S for an item is determined. This average can be weighted according to the actual user similarity of a user to the active user and also adjusted if some users are always giving higher-than-average (or lower) ratings. Finally, a set of items with the highest predicted ratings is presented to the active user as recommendations.

One variant of CF is the so-called "item-item" collaborative filtering; the users' ratings are first used to compute the similarity between items. The result is an item-item matrix. This matrix and the ratings vector of the active user are then evaluated to make recommendations. The advantage of this approach in comparison to the explained standard collaborative filtering method is that after pre-computing the item-item matrix, the generation of a set of recommended items is much less computationally expensive.

In individual or content-based recommender systems, the approach is to generate recommendations based on the analysis of items previously rated by the active user and generating a user profile based on the meta data of these items. The profile is then used to predict a rating for previously unseen items. Thus only one row of the user-item matrix is used, the ratings of the active user. Matching between items can be done in different ways, for example by identifying and applying rules (Woerndl & Schlichter, 2008).

Different recommender approaches have different characteristics. For example, a disadvantage of CF is that recommendations for new users are hard to generate because no ratings exist (the so called cold start problem). Hybrid recommender systems combine different approaches with the goal of utilizing the strengths of one algorithm while avoiding its weaknesses by applying a second approach (Burke, 2002). Combination strategies include "weighted", i.e. the scores of several recommendation techniques are combined, or "cascading", i.e. one recommender refines the recommendations given by another, among others.

2.3 Introducing Context into Recommender Systems

In mobile scenarios, the process of giving a recommendation becomes very dynamic. The quality

and validity of a recommendation depends on context. Therefore, context information has to be incorporated into the data model and recommendation process of recommender systems. Adomavicius & Tuzhilin (2010) provide a recent overview on integrating context in recommender systems in general.

2.3.1 Data Model

As far as the context model is concerned (chapter 2.1.), most available contextualized recommender systems only use a rather simple model as yet, such as attribute-value pairs. More formally, the context C can be described as a vector of context attributes, analogous to the user profile and the item meta data. The similarity or identity of context values is not as clear as with users or items and it may depend on the actual application domain. For example, for a tourist guide the "same" context might be constituted by a range of GPS coordinates. The integration of context extends the domain of the rating function to U x I x C. In other words, context adds another dimension to the item-user matrix, as introduced by Adomavicius, Sankaranarayanan, Sen & Tuzhilin (2005). This is also of importance with regard to the sparseness of ratings, because R may only be defined for a small part of possible contexts, e.g. ratings may be valid in one particular context only.

2.3.2 Recommendation Process

Context can be integrated in the recommendation process based on three principle methods (Adomavicius & Tuzhilin, 2010). First, contextual information can be used to select among the input data and build a data set for the specific context. This is called contextual pre-filtering or contextualization of recommendation input. Then, ratings can be predicted using any traditional non-contextual recommender system on the selected data. The second method is to initially ignore context information, apply any traditional recommender and filter the resulting set of recommendations (contextual post-filtering or contextualization of recommendation output). Finally, contextual information can be used directly in the modeling technique as part of the rating prediction (contextual modeling or contextualization of recommendation function) (Adomavicius & Tuzhilin, 2010).

The general idea of contextual modeling in the collaborative filtering process is to weight the ratings according to context similarity with the current context. For example, if one user A rated restaurants when having lunch, and another user B rated the restaurant when dining in the evening, the current time – noon or evening – when the active user asks for a recommendation plays a significant role when determining the neighborhood of similar users. Therefore, a contextualized CF algorithm should store a snapshot of the current context with every rating made.

As for the ratings prediction (step 2 in the general CF process, chapter 2.2), the option is to apply a higher weight to ratings that were made in a similar context in comparison to the current context of the active user, analogous to applying weights to user similarity. For instance, we assume {A, B} as the set of users who are similar to the active user. User A rated an item as "0.2" on a scale from 0 to 1 in a context c1, the other user gave a rating "0.8" in context c2. A contextualized CF algorithm would compare the current context of the active user to c1 and c2 and then compute the predicted rating according to the context similarity, e.g. "0.7" if the current context of the active user is similar to c2.

There are different approaches to realize a contextualized content-based recommender. In a rule based system, context conditions can trigger certain rules. An example will be given in Section 4: recommending mobile application based on point-of-interests in the current vicinity of a user (PoiAppRecommender, see below in chapter 4.1.2). If the item space is formalized as a graph,

the context can be used to determine starting nodes or edge weights to compute related items in the graph. An example is our recommender for semantic personal information management (chapter 4.2.2).

When integrating context, one option is to combine several algorithms to one hybrid context-aware recommender system to reduce the mentioned complexity of the user-item-context matrix. Thereby, a first algorithm would operate on two dimensions and compute an intermediary result set of items by taking only user and context attributes into account. In a second step, the results are further filtered and ranked by considering the 3rd dimension, for example by utilizing item meta data (Woerndl & Schlichter, 2008). This results in a cascading hybrid recommender system. Realizations of these general ideas have been implemented in our recommender examples that will be explained in Sections 3 and 4.

2.4 Related Work

There is quite a lot of work going on with regard to context-aware applications and personalization research in general. Baldauf, Dustdar & Rosenberg (2007) present a overview on context-aware systems in general. Ricci (2010) provides a recent overview on mobile recommender systems. Some recommender approaches consider some kind of context information as part of their user and/or item models, but only a few take contexts explicitly as a separate entity in the model into account. In the following we discuss three approaches that are related to our ideas more closely.

Chen (2005) presents a context-aware collaborative filtering system based on past experiences of users. The goal is to assist users with mobile devices. For example, it could recommend activities customized for Bob for the given weather, location, and travelling companion(s), based on what other people like Bob have done in a similar context (Chen, 2005). To incorporate context into the recommendation process, the approach weights the current context of the active user against the context of each rating with respect to their relevance in order to locate ratings given in a similar context, as explained above. One major problem of this approach is the availability of ratings in comparable contexts. The sparseness of ratings is an issue in collaborative filtering in general and further aggravated when integrating context.

Adomavicius, Sankaranarayanan, Sen & Tuzhilin (2005) enhance the user-item data model to a multidimensional setting where additional dimensions constitute different context attributes such as location and time. They propose a reduction-based approach with the goal to reduce the dimensions, ideally to $n = 2$. Then, traditional recommender techniques can be used to generate item lists. To our knowledge, the approach has not been applied to a pervasive setting similar to ours.

The proposed approach by Horvitz, Koch & Subramani (2007) uses gas station recommendation for cars as an application example, similar to a system that we explain in Section 3. Unlike our or the other discussed approaches, their system is based on Bayes networks and thus uses statistical methods to filter items. Their system needs training data to be able to calculate probabilities, which may lead to cold start problems in a practical application.

3. A GAS STATION RECOMMENDER FOR VEHICULAR AD-HOC NETWORKS

In this section we explain our gas station recommender for vehicular ad-hoc networks (VANETs). The main goals were to evaluate and select suitable recommender system techniques for VANETs, and to investigate the role of context. The example of the gas station recommender was chosen because context information such as fuel level is very important in this scenario.

3.1 VANETs and the Network-on-Wheels (NoW) Project

With the cheap availability of wireless technologies, VANETs have recently become a major field of research for industry and academia alike. The core idea is to decrease the number and severity of accidents by means of active safety applications that support the driver in fulfilling her task. A large number of vehicles are already equipped with sensors necessary to determine their current driving situation. If a dangerous situation is detected, it can be reported to other vehicles in the vicinity. Thus, an extension of the driver's horizon of perception beyond what is visible locally is possible, with human or technical sensors.

While the reduction of accidents is the primary goal, business models developed in the project showed that applications in VANETs suffer from direct network effects meaning that the value of application increases with rising network density. Furthermore, no value and functionality may be obtained when the network density is below a certain threshold. For these reasons, a second class of applications has to be developed that offer an immediate benefit to potential customers: the so-called deployment applications (Eigner & Linsmeier, 2006). These applications are taken from the domains of entertainment, information access and increased driving comfort, and can be functional without networking but just by point-to-point communication. A recommender system suggesting items such as restaurants or gas stations is an example for a deployment application. VANETs can provide context and additional information to improve recommender system in various ways and thus benefiting the driver:

- The increasing use of digital technologies in the automotive domain leads to an availability of more and new context data that has not been available before. Therefore, recommendations can be adapted to the current context of the user. In our application scenario of vehicular ad-hoc networks, context attributes are the current location of the car, driving speed, fuel level, road conditions etc.

- VANETs tap into new information sources: Remote data such as ratings from other users that recommendation systems are highly dependent on. This information can be transmitted via the wireless link. As already described in Section 2.2, the systems are now able to determine similar users and items in an ad-hoc manner.

- VANETs open new fields of applications: While before all decisions of an application had to be made based on local knowledge, they give access to distributed sources of knowledge and to collaboration techniques.

The goal of the Network-on-Wheels (NoW) project (see http://www.network-on-wheels.de) is to investigate all problems of VANETs including technical issues. NoW is funded by the German ministry for education with a mission to specify car-to-car-communication protocols as an input to standardization bodies along with an implementation of these protocols and applications utilizing them. The NoW project started in June 2004 with BMW, Daimler, Volkswagen, NEC, several German universities and other partners. The system developed in this project serves as a technical basis for our work.

In the next section, we explain the design issues regarding the integration of context into our recommender system for VANETs.

3.2 Data Sources

To comply with the requirements of context-aware recommendation systems, a large set of data is needed. Depending on the type of recommender, the required data can vary. As explained in Section 2, collaborative recommender systems use information about other people's preferences or ratings of items, while content-based filters utilize metadata associated with items. In addition, for every context-aware recommender system the key to effectiveness is to acquire the context information needed to generate context-dependent recommendations. In more detail, the data sources for our specific recommender are:

- User profile: driver preferences, e.g. whether she prefers a specific gas station chain, or gas stations with adjacent restaurants
- Item descriptions: in our example, the list of gas stations, with geo coordinates and additional information, e.g. if a restaurant is present
- Context information: in (newer) vehicles, a variety of sensors are built in that can be used to acquire context, e.g. the fuel level and the remaining driving range
- Ratings of other users and the current price of gas at particular gas stations which can be obtained by using the NoW communication system between cars and also between a car and an infrastructure hot spot (Woerndl & Eigner, 2007)

In theory, our idea could be realized with a centralized server that stores all the information about points-of-interest. However, we feel that a decentralized approach has some merits because recent information about local POIs can be exchanged from car to car in the local area. So far, we use context information – most notably the current fuel level – on the node itself (the car), but it would be also possible to customize the recommender according to the context of nearby cars, e.g. the driving speeds. The POI data was initially created using a database available on the Internet, but it is also envisioned that drivers can extend the data set by providing information about (local) POIs themselves.

Figure 1. Architecture

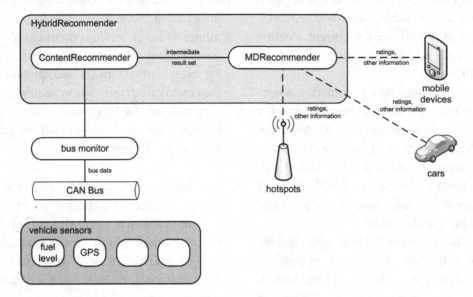

3.3 Recommendation Process

The proposed gas station recommender analyzes the available data and generates a list of recommended items. From a high level perspective, our recommendation process can be summarized as follows:

1. Retrieve context information from the vehicle bus, e.g. the current fuel level, and also the current GPS position and/or route information from a in-car navigation device
2. Analyze context data: search for gas stations in the vicinity and within the fuel range
3. Filter preferences: eliminate all items that are not matching the driver's preference, e.g. particular gas station chains
4. Search for cars and infrastructure hot spots in the vicinity for additional information, in particular ratings of other users and current gas prices of (near-by) stations
5. Multidimensional collaborative filter: filter and rank the pre-selected items according to the ratings of other users and current price information

6. Optionally: The user selects a gas station and is guided to it through the navigation system. After filling up, the driver can manually enter price information and a rating for the gas station, judging the cleanliness of restrooms or food selection, for example

In step 4, if a list of current gas station prices exists, it can be accessed and used for the recommendation. Since such a list may not be available, the idea is to exchange data about near-by gas stations (or other point-of-interests) between cars. If there are no or too few ratings available, the system is still able to generate recommendations using the context and preference filters. If in any step, the number of selected gas stations falls below a configurable threshold, the constraints are relaxed according to context hierarchies (see chapter 3.5). In this case, the system will suggest gas stations that do not fully comply with the driver's preference if there are no other options.

In terms of recommender systems, our approach is a cascading hybrid recommender, because it combines several algorithms consecutively. Thus our system is an implementation of the general idea of a contextualized hybrid recommender as explained in chapter 2.3.2.

3.4 Architecture

Figure 1 shows the architecture of our recommender. The system consists of two main components, the ContentRecommender, which realizes the preference and context filter (step 2 and 3), and the MDRecommender for step 4 and 5.

The ContentRecommender manages the (static) list of gas stations and generates an intermediate list of suggested items based on car context and user preferences. By first applying the ContentRecommender it is possible to filter out inappropriate items, e.g. a gas station that is beyond the current fuel range even if it has the lowest price and is rated highly by other users.

The pre-filtered items then serve as input for MDRecommender that takes ratings and additional information from other users or infrastructure hotspots into account. We have incorporated some general ideas of the multidimensional recommender (Adomavicius, Sankaranarayanan, Sen & Tuzhilin, 2005) (see Section 2) in the MDRecommender component. Context attributes are modeled as dimensions in addition to users and items in the recommender data model. Thus, different algorithms can be used to make recommendation utilizing different dimensions. The MDRecommender does not distinguish between new and already rated items. Therefore, the system generates similar item lists in comparable contexts, while traditional recommender systems are usually tailored towards recommending new items to the user.

3.5 Context Hierarchies

The basic idea behind context-awareness in both individual and collaborative recommender techniques is to put a higher weight on items or ratings that correspond to the current context attributes (see chapter 2.3). Therefore, it is important to choose the right granularity in the context model. This is done in our approach by defining different levels of context in a hierarchy. If the ContentRecommender generates too few items as result set, the system moves up in the context hierarchy.

A practical example for the context attribute "location" is the following. A driver who drives from southern Germany to northern Italy through Austria may formulate a preference for Austrian gas stations because the gas price is generally lower in this country than both Germany and Italy. Thereby, price is just one example; preference can also include quality of service, cleanliness or safety standards. In this case, the exact GPS position of a gas station (low level in the hierarchy) is less important than the actual country (higher level location information). In addition, price as dominating criterion may be overridden by other user preferences. The implementation of the context hierarchy has to be done for every context attribute. Since hierarchical structures can be easily modeled with ontologies, they serve as a good use case for ontological context models (see chapter 2.1).

3.6 Implementation

The implementation of the prototype application was done in the Java programming language. For the management of the data, we realized a Storage subsystem that is able to persistently store data in either a file format, or in a MySQL database. The system design allows for the easy integration of other recommender modules. Therefore, it is possible to replace the ContentRecommender with another component, for example, and also modify the sequence of recommender modules in the hybrid approach.

The task of a BusMonitor component is to provide access to the car bus data using triggers. A trigger analyzes the context data and starts a recommender module when a certain situation occurs. Examples are the LocationBasedTrigger that implements the location context hierarchy (see 3.5), and the FuelLevelTrigger. The Fuel-LevelTrigger monitors the fuel level until it goes below a threshold and the gas station recommendation module is started. This threshold can be configured by the user on system startup. Our framework allows for new triggers to provide (high level) access to additional context information that can be exploited by new recommender modules.

For the connection with cars, hotspots and other mobile devices we implemented a simple peer-to-peer system. The peers monitor the availability of other peers at regular intervals and update the information. We developed a XML format for the exchange of ratings and fuel prices. The data about gas stations that is exchanged between cars includes a time stamp, allowing the system to distinguish between older and newer prices, and to maintain a list of prices.

With regard to the collaborative filtering part of our recommender, we have integrated the publicly available Taste library (see http://taste.sourceforge.net) since collaborative filtering algorithms are independent from the actual application domain. Taste provides a set of components which can be used to construct a customized recommender system from a selection of state-of-the-art collaborative filtering algorithms (Lemire & Maclachlan, 2005).

3.7 Simulation and Evaluation

Evaluating context-aware recommender systems is difficult in principle, because every recommendation is only valid in a particular context. In addition, standard data sets do not have associated context information. Therefore, standard recommender evaluation methods like mean average errors of precision and recall metrics (Herlocker, Konstan, Terveen & Riedl, 2004) cannot easily be applied. Therefore, we decided to implement a simulation environment in order to test the approach with real world data. As item set, the simulation uses a geo-coded list of 2300 gas stations in Germany. The simulation was done using

Figure 2. Simulation visualization

a driving log that was recorded within the NoW project. The log consists of all car bus data accrued on a trip in Munich. The visualization (Figure 2) is based on a Google Earth map.

After starting the simulation, the movement of the car and the position of gas stations are shown on the map (Figure 2). The simulation also displays a list of recommended items in a separate window (Figure 3). Top rated gas stations are highlighted on top, while other options are shown below. The secondary options are gas stations that passed the preference filter but could not be ranked according to the collaborative filter, because there were no ratings for these items. The tests showed that our recommender delivers reasonable and meaningful results in our (few) test cases, for example no gas stations beyond the current fuel range were recommended. The implementation also proved that it is possible to analyze the accumulated data in real time because the simulation on a standard PC took less time than the driving

Figure 3. List of recommended gas stations

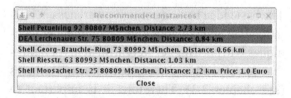

time of actual car in the driving log. Hence, while the simulation indicated the feasibility and applicability of our ideas in general, further simulation results, especially with more cars simultaneously, are needed: up to now, only transmission of data between the monitored car and a non-moving car has been simulated.

4. OTHER MOBILE SCENARIOS FOR CONTEXT-AWARE RECOMMENDER SYSTEMS

After describing our gas station recommender for VANETs in detail, we outline other context-aware recommender systems in different mobile application domains we are currently working on in this section.

4.1 Recommending Mobile Applications

4.1.1 Project Background

This recommender system is integrated in a framework supporting the development of mobile applications (Woerndl, Schueller & Wojtech, 2007). Part of the framework is a deployment server where developers of mobile applications can register their services and end users can browse and search for relevant and interesting gadgets, e.g. a mobile tourist guide for the city the user is currently traveling in. Typically, the applications consist of client modules that interact with servers to provide the service. One problem for users is to find interesting and – with regard to their current context – relevant applications on their mobile device.

4.1.2 Recommender System

The (hybrid) recommender system developed in this scenario recommends mobile applications to users derived from what other users have installed

and rated positively in a similar context (location, currently used type of device, etc.) (Woerndl, Schueller & Wojtech, 2007). Users can choose between several content-based and collaborative filtering components:

- LocationAppRecommender: recommends applications that were used in a similar location by other users
- CFAppRecommender: applies existing collaborative filtering algorithms to generate results using the already mentioned Taste library (Lemire and Maclachlan, 2005)
- PoiAppRecommender

The PoiAppRecommender does not recommend point-of-interests (POIs) but recommends mobile applications based on POIs in the vicinity of the user using triggers. An administrator can select among types of point-of-interests (such as restaurant, museum or train station) and specify the distance to an actual POI within which an application is recommended. This is done when registering the application with the deployment server mentioned in chapter 4.1.1.

When making a recommendation, the system then retrieves the current user position (using a GPS-enabled mobile device), determines POIs in the vicinity and generates a recommendation based on this context information. For example, an administrator can specify that her mobile train table application shall be recommended when the user is near a train station. After applying the trigger rules, our approach uses collaborative filtering to rank found items according to user ratings of applications in a second step. User ratings are collected implicitly by automatically recording when a user installs an application within our framework. It is also optionally possible for users to explicitly rate applications after usage. The ratings are stored together with context information (time, location, used device etc.) to capture the situation when a rating was made. These context-based ratings can then be utilized by the CFAppRecommender to recommend applications.

We have designed and implemented the recommender in the explained framework for the development of mobile applications. The recommender consists of a thin-client JME (Java Micro Edition) program and a server application. We are currently improving the components of our framework and then testing the system in practice with real world end-user applications.

4.2 Mobile Semantic Personal Information Management

4.2.1 Project Background

Personal information management (PIM) is intended to support the activities people perform to organize their daily lives through the acquisition, maintenance, retrieval, and sharing of information. One approach to deal with PIM is the Semantic Desktop. Users can assign meta data to all data objects that she uses on her computer. Thereby, relations between resources can be defined with the goal to integrate desktop applications and enhance finding relevant information. Semantic Desktop approaches rely on ontologies to formalize the relationships between resources and define a concept hierarchy that can be utilized for information retrieval (Sauermann et al., 2006). Supporting PIM on mobile devices, e.g. field staff members meeting customers, seems to be particularly important, because of the limitations of mobile devices in network bandwidth, storage capacities, displays and input capabilities. Yet most of current PIM research is not geared towards mobile and ubiquitous information access. Therefore, the goal of this subproject is to support the user in mobile personal information management using Semantic Desktop ideas which allows for interoperability with existing, desktop PC based, approaches.

4.2.2 Recommender System

We have designed and implemented SeMoDesk which is a realization of the Semantic Desktop for personal digital assistants (PDAs) running Microsoft Windows Mobile (Woerndl & Woehrl, 2008). Users can define, manage and browse a personal ontology to structure their personal information space across different applications. To do so, SeMoDesk assists as much as possible, for example calls or short messages on the mobile device are integrated automatically. Figure 4, left, shows the top level ontology of concepts in SeMoDesk. Users can browse their information space, and display all resources such as messages, document or appointments that are associated with a particular project, for example, with one tap on the touchscreen of the mobile device. However, browsing the ontology is not enough because only direct relationships between concepts and resources can be retrieved.

Therefore, we have designed a context-aware recommendation function to improve information access (Woerndl & Hristov, 2009). The recommender consists of the following two steps:

1. Finding current resources (Figure 4, left), i.e. resources that are of interest for the user right now
2. Recommending other items, starting from the instances found in step 1

In step one, users have the option to manually select concepts or resources. In addition, the system proposes items in this first step based on the current context: date, time and location. As a result, the system displays a list of resources which are of current interest to the user (Figure 4, middle). This list may already contain relevant resources, but serves as possible starting nodes for the more advanced search in step two. The user can select one node and start the recommendation

Figure 4. SeMoDesk screenshots

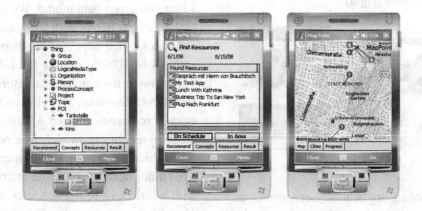

process: the system traverses the graph of concepts and resources and analyzes every node according to an evaluation function using configurable heuristics. For example, if the recommender finds a path between the starting node and a particular project resource via "related" edges, this project is considered relevant in the current context. The details of this recommendation process are explained in (Woerndl & Hristov, 2009). As a result of the recommendation process, the system displays several resources and also information why these results are suggested, i.e. the path from the starting node to the result entry.

The personal ontology can also be utilized to recommend additional resources, items that are not explicitly managed by the user. The application scenario is that users are looking for points-of-interests (POIs) in the current geographic vicinity to perform certain tasks. For this purpose, we have extended the ontology by a POI concept with subconcepts such as "cinema", "restaurants", "shop" etc. The user can then relate tasks or any other resources to POI types. SeMoDesk offers a feature to show information about relevant POIs on a map (Figure 4, right), together with the location of upcoming appointments. This recommender is a content-based non-collaborative approach, because only the model of the active user is utilized.

4.3 Decentralized Recommender for PDAs

4.3.1 Project Background

The goal of this project is to realize a decentralized recommender system on PDAs without a centralized server. Decentralized recommenders offer advantages with regard to user privacy (Kobsa, 2007). Most importantly, users exercise more control about their data and might feel more comfortable to submit ratings and use the system, because ratings and other personal information are stored locally on the client-side. For the recommendation process, the basic idea is to utilize item-item collaborative filtering (see chapter 2.2). Each PDA – respectively user – maintains an item-item matrix and synchronizes the information with other PDAs. Note that the item-item matrix only retains item similarities based on user ratings, but the user's ratings are kept on her own PDA only. The main research question was to investigate whether it is feasible to realize such a recommender on a PDA in a meaningful application scenario, since this has not really been tried before, to the best of our knowledge. One of the questions is the storage requirement for the item-item matrix, because PDAs usually offer only limited storage capacity.

Figure 5. Scenario with shared display (left), and mobile user interface (right)

One envisioned application scenario is an exposition where attendants share common interests and want to exchange information and ratings about items such as exposition stalls, news, products etc. Other end-user scenarios are imaginable. One of our ideas is to combine item-item collaborative filtering with group recommendations. Users can rate items on their PDAs, exchange information about item similarity with other users passing by in the mobile scenario, and receive personalized recommendations on her (private) PDAs. In addition, a shared display is used to recommend items to (small) groups of people (Figure 5, left). In this case, the context is the current group of users with their PDAs in front of the shared display. This leads to very dynamic recommendations, while the item similarities change only gradually.

4.3.2 Recommender System

Our recommender builds on previous work on a "personal" recommender system by Miller, Konstan and Riedl (2004) in the PocketLens project. PocketLens introduces a collaborative filtering algorithm based on item-item collaborative filtering (see chapter 2.2), along with five peer-to-peer architectures for finding neighbors. We have extended the PocketLens algorithm with several improvements and implemented it on PDAs. The first refinement was to optimize the storage of item similarity in the item-item matrix

by eliminating duplicate entries and thus attaining a more compact data model. We have tested the scalability on PDAs with the standard MovieLens data set (see http://www.grouplens.org/) that consists of 100000 ratings for 1682 movies by 943 users (Herlocker, Konstan, Borchers & Riedl, 1999). As a first step, our refinement reduced the storage requirement from 45 mega bytes to 32 mega bytes. In our model, it is possible to further reduce the storage requirement by adapting what a duplicate entry in the matrix constitutes, with a little loss of the accuracy of predictions. Thereby, the corresponding item-item matrix from the MovieLens data set can stored using only 19 mega bytes, which is more easily feasible on a state-of-the-art PDA. Other improvements include the introduction of versioned rating vectors. By doing so, users can alter ratings and item-item matrices can be updated accordingly later on. The group recommendations of the touchscreen interface were calculated by combining the rating vectors of currently active user and utilizing the item-item matrix of the touchscreen peer. The item-item matrices on different peers (touchscreen display and user PDAs) may vary, depending on which peers have exchanged information. It is important to note that the shared display in our approach is not a server, but a peer storing an item-item matrix, just like any of the user PDAs.

The approach was evaluated in a (small) experiment with 13 participants and an item set of 63 pictures. A 32 inch touchscreen monitor was used as shared display (Figure 5, left). Figure 5, right shows the user interface on the mobile device which was designed to be very simple and straight-forward to use. The test proved that our system ran smoothly and provided comprehensive recommendations. We conducted a survey among the participants. The study showed that users found the system beneficial and envisaged its usage in various application domains such as collaborative shopping or museum visits. With regard to privacy, users found the shared display somewhat worrying – which is not the main feature

Figure 6. Screenshots of the mobile city guide with the explicit rating process

of our recommender and can be omitted in a real life application –, while recognizing the overall advantage of managing their personal ratings on their own mobile devices.

4.3.3 Applying the Recommender System in a Mobile City Guide

We have applied the explained decentralized PDA recommender systems in a real world mobile city guide. This application was developed by voxcity s.r.o. and jomedia s.r.o. (see http://www.voxcity.de). The idea is to rent out a mobile device with GPS positioning capabilities to support tourists. These devices do have a network connection; therefore a decentralized model for recommending POIs is needed. The model (item-item matrices) is updated with ratings of other users when a device is returned to the renting station. The guide is currently available for the Czech city of Prague. The mobile application plays audio, video, pictures and (HTML) text of tourist attractions based on the current position.

The city guide application has been extended with options to rate point-of-interest (POI) information and recommend new items based on the decentralized, item-based collaborative filtering (chapter 4.3.2). The city guide application and the explicit rating process when viewing a POI are illustrated in Figure 6 (Moegele 2010). We also use implicit ratings that are derived from the usage of audio files. To be able to compare recommendations based on explicit and implicit ratings, we developed two distinct models: one

based on explicit and one on implicit user ratings. The system generates recommendations by alternating the two models. Additionally, the collaborative filter and a contextual filter based the current distance from a POI were integrated in the implementation of a score model. This recommender combines the prediction values of the collaborative recommendation and the distance values of the context based filter in a linear way.

A preliminary user study indicated that users liked the application and felt that the mobile guide selected sights according to her interests/ratings. Users were willing to provide ratings to get better recommendations. In a second, larger, field study we investigated the recommendation quality of our different recommenders. During this field study, five devices with the recommendation methods were distributed among the rental stations in Prague. 128 persons – regular tourists from various countries – were using the devices and generated 1739 data sets. The results of the analysis show a slightly better average user rating of the implicit ratings in comparison to the explicit ratings. The user ratings of the collaborative recommendations indicate improvement in recommendation quality in comparison to the location-based filter (Moegele 2010).

5. CONCLUSION

In this article we have explained some ideas for integrating context in recommender systems in general and specifically in various mobile applications domains. Our main case study is an approach for vehicular ad-hoc networks. Recommending gas stations is an example, the system could possibly be applied to recommend other item types as well, for instance other point-of-interests such as restaurants or sights, or suggesting music based on context attributes like time of the day or current driving speed. Our approach takes the current context in a car into consideration and proposes context hierarchies that could be used for other personalization services as well. The system is a hybrid recommender and combines different strategies. By doing so, collaborative filtering using ratings of other users can be utilized on the one hand, but on the other hand, the context and preference filtering can generate appropriate items even if none or few ratings are available. Additionally, using the VANET transmission, missing metadata about items (e.g. fuel price) as well as user ratings and items themselves can be exchanged. In addition to the VANET recommender, we outlined several other mobile application scenarios and the proposed recommender systems we have realized and are currently working. Next steps include refinement of the recommender algorithms and more empirical analysis of the characteristics of different recommenders in our very different application domains.

ACKNOWLEDGEMENT

Parts of this work were performed within the scope of the Network-On-Wheels (NoW) research project supported by the Federal German Ministry for Education and Research (BMBF) under contract no. 01AK064.

REFERENCES

W3C (2004). *Composite Capability/ Preference Profiles (CC/PP)*, W3C Recommendation January 2004, Retrieved November 02, 2008, from http://www.w3.org/TR/ CCPP-struct-vocab/.

Adomavicius, G., Sankaranarayanan, R., Sen, S., & Tuzhilin, A. (2005). Incorporating contextual information in recommender systems using a multidimensional approach. *ACM Transactions on Information Systems*, *23*, 103–145. doi:10.1145/1055709.1055714

Adomavicius, G., & Tuzhilin, A. (2005). Towards the Next Generation of Recommender Systems: A Survey of the State-of-the-Art and Possible Extensions. *IEEE Transactions on Knowledge and Data Engineering*, *17*(6). doi:10.1109/TKDE.2005.99

Adomavicius, G., & Tuzhilin, A. (2010). Context-Aware Recommender Systems. In Ricci, F., Rokach, L., Shapira, B., & Kantor, P. B. (Eds.), *Recommender Systems Handbook: A Complete Guide for Research Scientists and Practitioners*. Berlin, Heidelberg: Springer.

Anand, S. S., & Mobasher, B. (2005). Intelligent techniques for web personalization. *Proceedings of the 2nd Workshop on Intelligent Techniques in Web Personalization (ITWP 2003)*, Springer LNAI 3169, Acapulco, Mexico.

Baldauf, M., Dustdar, S., & Rosenberg, F. (2007). A survey on context-aware systems. *In Ad Hoc and Ubiquitous Computing*, Vol. 2, 263-277.

Burke, R. (2002). Hybrid recommender systems: Survey and experiments. *User Modeling and User-Adapted Interaction*, *12*, 331–370. doi:10.1023/A:1021240730564

Chen, A. (2005). Context-aware collaborative filtering system: predicting the user's preferences in ubiquitous computing. *Proceedings of the 1st International Workshop Location- and Context-Awareness (LoCA 2005)*, Springer LNCS 3479, Oberpfaffenhofen, Germany.

Dey, A. K., Salber, D., & Abowd, G. D. (2001). A conceptual framework and a toolkit for supporting the rapid prototyping of context-aware-applications. *Human-Computer Interaction*, *16*, 97–166. doi:10.1207/S15327051HCI16234_02

Eigner, R., & Linsmeier, W. (2006). Design criteria for wireless payment applications in vehicular ad-hoc networks. *Proceedings of the IADIS International Conference e-Commerce*, Barcelona, Spain.

Herlocker, J., Konstan, J. A., Terveen, L. G., & Riedl, J. T. (2004). Evaluating collaborative filtering recommender systems. *ACM Transactions on Information Systems, 22*, 5–53. doi:10.1145/963770.963772

Herlocker, J. L., Konstan, J. A., Borchers, A., & Riedl, J. (1999). An algorithmic framework for performing collaborative filtering. *Proceedings of the 22nd Annual international ACM SIGIR Conference on Research and Development in information Retrieval*, Berkeley, CA.

Horvitz, E., Koch, P., & Subramani, M. (2007). Mobile opportunistic planning: Methods and models. *Proceedings of the 11th Conference on User Modeling (UM 2007)*, Springer LNCS 4511, Corfu, Greece.

Kobsa, A. (2007). Privacy-Enhanced Personalization. *Communications of the ACM, 50*(8), 24–33. doi:10.1145/1278201.1278202

Lemire, D., & Maclachlan, A. (2005). Slope one predictors for online rating-based collaborative filtering. *Proceedings of the SIAM Conference on Data Mining (SDM 2005)*, Newport Beach, USA.

Miller, B. N., Konstan, J. A., & Riedl, J. T. (2004). PocketLens: Toward a Personal Recommender System. *ACM Transactions on Information Systems, 22*(3), 437–476. doi:10.1145/1010614.1010618

Moegele, K. (2010). *Evaluating the Recommendation Quality of a Mobile Recommender System*. Munich, Germany: Guided Research, Institut fuer Informatik, Technische Universitaet Muenchen.

Ricci, F. (2010). (to appear). Mobile Recommender Systems. *International Journal of Information Technology and Tourism*.

Sauermann, L., et al. (2006). Semantic Desktop 2.0: The Gnowsis Experience. *Proceedings 5th International Semantic Web Conference*, Springer LNCS 4273.

Strang, T., & Linnhoff-Popien, C. (2004). A Context Modeling Survey, *Proceedings UbiComp 1st International Workshop on Advanced Context Modelling, Reasoning and Management*, Nottingham, UK.

Woerndl, W., & Eigner, R. (2007). Context-aware, collaborative applications for inter-networked cars. *Proceedings of the 5th IEEE International Workshop on Distributed and Mobile Collaboration (DMC 2007)*, Paris, France, IEEE.

Woerndl, W., & Groh, G. (2007). Utilizing physical and social context to improve recommender systems. *Proceedings of the IEEE Workshop on Web Personalization and Recommender Systems (WPRS), International Conference on Web Intelligence (WI 2007)*, Silicon Valley, USA, IEEE.

Woerndl, W., & Hristov, A. (2009). Recommending Resources in Mobile Personal Information Management. *Proc. Third International Conference on Digital Society (ICDS2009)*, Cancun, Mexico.

Woerndl, W., & Schlichter, J. (2008). Contextualized Recommender Systems: Data Model and Recommendation Process. In Pazos-Arias, J., Delgado Kloos, C., & Lopez Nores, M. (Eds.), *Personalization of Interactive Multimedia Services: A Research and Development Perspective*. Hauppauge, NY: Nova Publishers.

Woerndl, W., Schueller, C., & Wojtech, R. (2007). A Hybrid Recommender System for Context-aware Recommendations of Mobile Applications. *Proceedings IEEE 3rd International Workshop on Web Personalisation, Recommender Systems and Intelligent User Interfaces (WPRSIUI'07)*, Istanbul, Turkey.

Woerndl, W., & Woehrl, M. (2008), SeMoDesk: Towards a Mobile Semantic Desktop. *Proceedings Personal Information Management (PIM) Workshop*, CHI 2008 Conference, Florence, Italy.

Section 2

Chapter 6
Fault–Tolerant Text Data Compression Algorithms

L. Robert
Government Arts College, India

R. Nadarajan
PSG College of Technology, India

ABSTRACT

There has been an unparalleled explosion of textual information flow over the internet through electronic mail, web browsing, digital library and information retrieval systems, etc. Since there is a persistent increase in the amount of data that needs to be transmitted or archived, the importance of data compression is likely to increase in the near future. Virtually, all modern compression methods are adaptive models and generate variable-bit-length codes that must be decoded sequentially from beginning to end. If there is any error during transmission, the entire file cannot be retrieved safely. In this article we propose few fault-tolerant methods of text compression that facilitate decoding to begin with any part of compressed file not necessarily from the beginning. If any sequence of one or more bytes is changed during transmission of compressed file due to various reasons, the remaining data can be retrieved safely. These algorithms also support reversible decompression.

INTRODUCTION

The data compression field has always been an important part of computer science and it is becoming increasingly popular and important today. Although computers become faster and data storage becomes less expensive and more efficient, the increased importance of usage of data necessitates the use of at least a small measure of data compression due to vast storage and transmission requirements. The question in many applications is no longer whether to compress data, but what compression method should be applied. Many modern compression methods are adaptive models and generate variable-bit-length codes (Maxime & Thierry, 1999). The Huffman algorithm (Huffman, 1952; Knuth, 1985) uses the notion of variable length prefix code for replacing characters of the text. The code depends on the input text, and more precisely on the frequencies of characters in the text. The most frequent characters are given shortest code words, while the least frequent symbols correspond to the longest code words. The basic idea of Arithmetic Coding (Moffat, Alistair, Witten, & Neal, 1998) is to consider symbols as digits of a numeration system, and texts as decimal parts of numbers between 0 and 1. The length of the interval attributed to a digit is made proportional to the frequency of the digit in the text. Ziv and Lempel (1977) designed a compression method using encoding segments. These segments of the original text are stored in a dictionary that is built during the compression process. In this model where portions of the text are replaced by pointers on previous occurrences, the Ziv-Lempel compression can be proved to be asymptotically optimal. LZW (Welch, 1984) is another popular variant of Ziv-Lempel compression which eliminates a second field of a token. Chu (2002) describes a method derived from LZ family called LZAC. The objective of LZAC is to improve the compression ratios of the LZ77 family still retaining the family's key characteristics: simple, universal, fast in decoding, and economical in memory. LZAC presents new ideas of composite fixed-variable-length coding and offset difference coding. Albert Apostolico (2005, 2006) describes variants of classical data compression paradigms by Ziv, Lempel and Welch. The phrases used for compression are strings of intermittently solid and "don't care" characters produced in a deterministic fashion, by certain autocorrelations of the source string generated by the very mechanics of parsing. Joaquin Adiego et al. (2004) describe a new LZ based approach called LZCS in which the main idea is the replacement of frequently repeated subtrees by a backward reference to their first occurrence.

Michael Burrows and David Wheeler (1994) released the details of a transformation function that opens the door to some revolutionary new compression techniques. The Burrows-Wheeler Transformation (BWT) transforms a block of data into a format that is extremely well suited for compression. It takes a block of data and re-arranges it using a sorting algorithm. The resulting output block contains exactly the same data elements that it started with, differing only in their ordering. The transformation is reversible. M. Hosang (2002) describes a variant of BWT, character elimination algorithm for lossless data compression intended for use on files with non-uniform character distributions. This algorithm takes advantage of the relatively small distances between character occurrences after the removal of less frequent characters.

J. Cleary and I. Witten (1984) developed Prediction by Partial Matching (PPM) which is an adaptive statistical data compression technique based on context modeling and prediction. PPM models use a set of previous symbols in the un-compressed symbol stream to predict the next symbol in the stream. PPM is capable of very high compression rates, encoding English text in as little as 2.2 b/character. Moffat (1990) describes a variant of PPM which encodes and decodes at over 4 kB/s on a small workstation and operates within a few hundred kilobytes of data space, but still obtaining compression of about 2.4 b/character for English text. Eibe Frank et al. (2000) describe text categorization using compression models. Text categorization is the assignment of natural language texts to predefined categories based on their content. It has been observed that compression seems to provide a very promising approach to categorization.

Drinic and Kirovski (2002) present PPMexe - a set of compression mechanisms for executables that explore their syntax and semantics to achieve superior compression rates. The fundamental principle of PPMexe is the generic paradigm of prediction by partial matching. They combine

PPM with two pre-processing steps: instruction rescheduling to improve prediction rates and partitioning of a binary program into streams with high auto-correlation. Weifeng Sun et al. (2003) describe a dictionary based multi-corpora text compression system. They introduce a text compression system StarZip together with its transform engine StarNT. This achieves a superior compression ratio than almost all the other recent efforts based on BWT and PPM. The main idea is to recode each English word with a representation of no more than three symbols. This transform not only maintains most of the original context information at the world level, but also provides some kind of artificial but strong context.

Jeehong Yang, et al. (2007) describe a dictionary-based English text compression algorithm Star Word Ending (StarWE) which is a variant of StarNT. StarWE borrows techniques such as EOL coding, punctuation mark modeling, and n-gram matching. The main difference between StarWE and StarNT is in the division of the external dictionary; StarWE divides it by word endings so that the compressor would be able to obtain some of the tag information. Jan Lansky et al. (2007) describe a method focused on compression of dictionaries of words or syllables. Dictionary is used by many compression methods. Some of them put the dictionary into the compressed message. In such cases the improvements in dictionary compression can improve the performance of the compression methods.

Przemyslaw Skibinski (2005) describes a basic idea of preprocessing to transform the text into some intermediate form, which can be used as an input for any existing general-purpose compressor and compressed more efficiently. Dictionary-based preprocessing is based on the notion of replacing whole words with shorter codes. The dictionary of words is usually static (for a given language) and given in advance. This method presents dictionary-based preprocessing technique and its implementation called TWRT (Two-level Word Replacing Transformation). The preprocessor uses several dictionaries and divides files into various kinds. The first level dictionaries (small dictionaries) are specific for some kind of data (e.g., programming language, references). The second level dictionaries (large dictionaries) are specific for natural language (e.g., English, Russian, French). Before ordinary preprocessing, TWRT uses "faster dictionaries detection" mechanism, which chooses the best combination of the dictionaries, one small and one large.

Conventional compression techniques exploit general redundancy features in data to compress them. For example, Huffman or Lempel-Ziv techniques compresses data by statistical modeling or string matching while the Burrows-Wheeler Transform simply sorts data by context to improve compressibility. On the other hand, data can often be compressed better by exploiting their specific features as described by Kiem-Phong Vo (2007). For example, columns or fields in a database table tend to be sparse, but not rows. Techniques have been developed to either group related table columns or compute dependency among them to transform data and enhance compressibility.

In all these models, random access to large data sets can be provided only by dividing the data into smaller files or blocks and compressing each chunk separately. Even if an application is sophisticated enough to decompress separate blocks of data, it still must begin decompressing each block at the beginning of that block. There is a simple text compression trick that allows random access; it employs the unused high order bit in ASCII characters to indicate that the preceding space character has been removed. This technique in effect removes all single spaces and reduces runs of consecutive spaces to half length, compressing typical text by 15 percent (Robert & Nadarajan, 1999). Another simple approach is to encode common words as one byte using the fixed dictionary of the most frequently used words. But schemes such as these are not for general purpose and have limited usefulness. Byte Pair Encoding scheme-BPE (Gage, 1997) is a universal com-

Box 1.

```
1   Read file into buffer
2   Initialize Pairtable
3   Code = 128
4   do
    {
5       Find the most frequent byte pair in buffer
6       If there is no such pair, break
7       Add the pair to the Pairtable
8       Replace all such pair with the Code
9   Code ++
10  }while (Code <= 255)
11  Write Pairtable and buffer into the output file
```

Box 2.

A	B	A	B	C	A	B	C	D	C	D	A	B	C	D	B	C	D	B	C
65	66	65	66	67	65	66	67	68	67	68	65	66	67	68	66	67	68	66	67

pression algorithm that supports random access in the compressed file for all types of data. The global substitution process of BPE produces a uniform data format that allows decompression to begin anywhere in the data. Using BPE, data from anywhere in a compressed block can be immediately decompressed without having to start at the beginning of the block. This can provide a very fast access for some applications. It is like being able to grab a volume of an encyclopedia off the shelf and open it to the exact page one wants without having to flip through all the earlier pages in the volume.

BPE Algorithm

The ASCII character set uses only bytes from 0 to 127. This method uses 128 to 255 for replacing the most frequently occurring pairs of adjacent bytes. The BPE operates by finding the most frequently occurring pairs of adjacent bytes in the text and replacing all instances of such pairs with a code from 128 to 255. To begin with the compressor finds a pair that appears large number of times compared with other pairs in the input file and replaces the pair with a byte code 128 wherever the byte appears. Again another such pair is found and replaced by 129. This process is repeated until there is no frequent pair or all codes from 128 to 255 are exhausted. The algorithm records the details of the replacements in a table, which is stored as a header in the compressed file. The following algorithm illustrates the process of compression.

Compression

See Box 1.

The Process of compression is illustrated by the following example. Consider the following line of text and their ASCII values. (See Box 2.)

Box 3.

```
1    Initialize a stack
2    Read first byte, assign a name count
3    If( count>128) Then
     {
4        Read and store Pair table in buffer
5        While(stack not empty OR not EOF)
         {
6            If stack empty, read byte from file
                      else Pop byte from stack.
7            If byte is a Pair code, Push pair on to stack
                      else write byte to output file
         }
     }
```

As the pair (66,67) is occurring more times than the other pairs, out of (65,66)(66,65)(66,67)(67,65) (67,68)(68,67)(68,65) and (68,66), the pair (66,67) is selected for replacement by the code 128.

65 66 65 128 65 128 68 67 68 65 128 68 128 68 128

Replace the most frequently appearing pair (65, 128) by the code 129

65 66 129 129 68 67 68 129 68 128 68 128

At this stage, the compressed file will be

130 66 67 65 128 65 66 129 129 68 67 68
    129 68 128 68 128
Input bytes = 20, Output bytes = 17.

The resulted file starts with a byte represents the next free paircode and is followed by a pairtable and compressed text.

Decompression

The decompression process, first reads the pair table from the input stream, and stores the table

in a buffer. The decoder then processes each byte of compressed data, maintaining a small-stack of partially expanded bytes. The next byte to be processed is popped from the stack, or if the stack is empty, read from the input file. If the byte is a pair code, the pair of bytes is looked up in the table and pushed onto the stack; otherwise, the byte is putout as a normal character. The algorithm in Box 3 illustrates the process of decompression.

Analysis

Time complexity of an algorithm concerns determining an expression of the number of steps needed, as a function of the problem size. As the step count measure is somewhat coarse, one does not aim at obtaining an exact step count. Instead, one attempts only to get asymptotic bounds on the step count. Asymptotic analysis makes use of the O (Big Oh) notation. The performance evaluation of an algorithm is obtained by totaling the number of occurrences of each operation when running the algorithm. The performance of an algorithm is evaluated as a function of the input size N and is to be considered modulo a multiplicative constant. Let us now estimate the amount of work that BPE will do, so that we can make comparisons with other methods. When these kinds of random access compression algorithms are studied, it soon becomes clear that the total amount of work done is closely related to the number of replacements of sequence of bytes by a code in the source file. So, to analyze the behavior of these random access compression algorithms, we shall use the count of replacements as our measure of the work done. All these algorithms are assumed to take an input file of size N Bytes. Considering the BPE algorithm, in the worst possible case, there can be at most 128 pair replacements. In the best possible case, when the file consists of bytes without any repetition, even a single replacement may not take place. If a pair i appears p_i times, then the total number of replacements is calculated as

$$\sum_{i=1}^{128} p_i.$$

Since, at least three occurrences are required to replace a pair, minimum value of p_i is 3. If a file consists of a repetition of only one byte, then a maximum value of p_i is $N/2^i$. So, minimum number of replacements is termed as 3+3+ ... +3(128 times) =384, which can be denoted as O(1). The maximum number of replacements is termed as $N/2 + N/4 + N/6 + \ldots\ldots N/2^{128} = N(1) = N$. This can be denoted as O(N) which is linear complexity.

DESIGN OF NEW RANDOM ACCESS TEXT COMPRESSION ALGORITHMS

BPE+ Algorithm

The main key of the BPE algorithm for text file compression is that the bytes 128 to 255 are used for replacing the most frequently occurring pairs of bytes. All the text files are not using all the bytes from 0 to 127. Particularly the control characters from 0 to 31, except end of line bytes, are very rarely used. So, this improved version of

BPE uses those unused bytes from 0 to 127 along with 128 to 255, for replacing the most frequently occurring pair of bytes. Two tables are maintained here for recording information about replacements. One table with a maximum size of 128x2, keeps the pairs that are replaced by codes 128 to 255. The second table is for keeping the replacements using unused bytes. Let us name it as UNUSED table. It is of size nx3, where n is the number of unused bytes in the input file.

Compression

The algorithm starts with finding all unused bytes from 0 to 127 and stores them in the 0th column of the UNUSED table. Then, it finds the most frequently occurring pairs and replaces with code 128 through 255, and store the information about these replacements in the pair table. The pair table is written into the output file. Then, the algorithm starts replacing the most frequently occurring pairs, if any, by the unused bytes that are collected in the first column of UNUSED table. It records the replacements by the unused byte in the UNUSED table. This process continues until there is no pair for replacement or all the unused bytes are used for replacements. The algorithm in Box 4 illustrates this compression process.

Decompression

In this method, the decompression is performed in two stages. The compressed code is decompressed by using the table UNUSED in the first stage. The algorithm finds the code stored in UNUSED[i][0] and replaces the code stored with the pair stored in UNUSED[i][1] and UNUSED[i][2]. In the second stage, the resulted file from the first stage is again decompressed using the PAIR table. That is, the algorithm finds all the codes from 128 to 255 from the given file, and replaces those codes by the pair stored in PAIR[$code$-128][0] and PAIR[$code$-128][1]. The algorithm in Box 5 illustrates this process.

Box 4.

```
1    Read file into buffer
2    Find the unused bytes from 0 to 127 and store them in
     UNUSED[i][0],i varies from 0 to nb-1, where nb is number of unused bytes
3    Construct the Pair table and replace the most frequently
     occurring pairs as per BPE
4    Write the Pair table in to the output file
5    index = 0
6    While (index < nb )
     {
7         Code = UNUSED[index][0]
8         Find the most frequently occurring pair
9         If there is no such pair, Break
10        Add the pair to UNUSED[index][1],UNUSED[index][2]
11        Replace all such pairs by Code
12        index++
     }
13   Write index to the output file
14   Write UNUSED table to the output file
15   Write buffer to the output file
```

Box 5.

```
1        Read and Store PAIR table into the Buffer
2        Read and Store UNUSED table into the Buffer
3        Initialize Stack
4        While (Stack not Empty OR Not EOF(input file))
         {
5            If Stack Empty, read a Byte from input file
             else Pop Byte from Stack
6            If Byte is in UNUSED[i]0] for any i from 0 to nb-1 then
7            Push the pair UNUSED[i][2], UNUSED[i][1] into stack
             else Write Byte on output file FILE1
         }
8        Initialize Stack
9        While (Stack not Empty OR Not EOF(FILE1))
         {
10           If Stack Empty, read Byte from FILE1
             else Pop Byte from Stack
11           If Byte is in PAIR table then
             Push the pair into stack
             else Write Byte on output file FILE2
         }
```

Analysis

Let the number of unused bytes from 0 to 127 in a given file of N bytes be *m*. The range of *m* is from 0 to 127. If the value of m is zero, then all the bytes from 0 to 127 are used in the input file. If the value of *m* is 127 only one out of 128 possible bytes is used in the input file. The total number of pair codes generated in this algorithm is 128+*m*. So, at most there can be 128+*m* most frequently appearing pairs replaced. If a pair *i* appears p_i times, the total number of replacements is calculated as

$$\sum_{i=1}^{128+m} p_i.$$

Since, at least three occurrences are required to replace a pair; minimum value of p_i is 3. If a file consists of a repetition of only one byte, a maximum value of p_i is $N/2^i$. So, minimum number of replacements is termed as 3+3+ … +3(128+127 times)=765, which can be denoted as O(1). The maximum number of replacements is termed as $N/2 + N/4 + N/6 + \ldots\ldots N/2^{128+127} = N(1) = N$. This can be denoted as O(N) which is linear complexity.

BPE++ ALGORITHM

The BPE+ algorithm uses the bytes from 128 to 255, and unused bytes from 0 to 127, for replacing the most frequently occurring pairs of bytes. After compression, because of the successive replacements we find some of the bytes that are used in the file before compression become unused after the compression. For example, see Box 6.

Here the byte 65 becomes unused after the replacements. So, by using those bytes as codes, again the process of replacing the most frequently occurring pair is done. This process is repeated until all bytes (0-255) are there in the resulted file or there is no frequently occurring pair in the input file.

Compression

In this algorithm, compression process involves many stages. At the first stage of the compression, the algorithm finds the most frequently occurring pairs and is replaced by the bytes from 128 to 255. In the second stage, it finds all the unused bytes in the resulted file of stage-1, and replaces the most frequently occurring pairs by those unused bytes. At the third stage, the algorithm finds the unused bytes after stage-2, and replaces the most frequently occurring pair by those unused byte. Like this, the process is continued until, either there is no frequently occurring pair or there is no unused byte in the resulting file from the previous stage. At each stage, the UNUSED table is constructed and written to the output file. The total number of stages is written as a first byte in the compressed file. The algorithm in Box 7 illustrates this process.

Decompression

This algorithm just performs the reverse process of compression. The decompression is performed at multi stages as done in compression. If there are

Box 6.

A	B	A	B	C	D	B
65	66	65	66	67	68	66
128 128	67	68	66			

n stages at the time of compression, decompression also involves n stages. Firstly, the algorithm reads the *n* UNUSED tables, and a PAIR table, from the header of the compressed file. Then it processes the nth stage UNUSED table, by finding all codes stored in the table location UNUSED[*i*][0] in the compressed file and replaces the found codes with the respective pairs UNUSED[*i*][1], UNUSED[*i*][2]. The algorithm does the same process for n-1, n-2...1 stages. At each stage the input is the output of the previous stage. At last, the algorithm finds the bytes from 128 to 255 and the found bytes are replaced by the respective pairs from the PAIR table. The algorithm in Box 8 illustrates this process

Analysis

There are many stages in this algorithm. Let total number of stages be L. Assume there are m_i unused bytes found in stage i. Since the first stage in this algorithm is BPE, $m_0 = 128$. The maximum value of m_i in any stage after first may be 255. If p_{ij} is a number of occurrences of a pair j in stage i, then the total number of replacements in all the stages is termed as

Box 7.

```
1    Read file into the Buffer
2    Construct the PAIR table and replace the most-frequently
     occurring pairs as per BPE
3    Write the PAIR table into the Output file
4    Over = 0
5    do
     {
6        Find the unused bytes, if any, and store into
         UNUSED[i][0],i varies from 0 to nb-1, where nb is
         the number of unused bytes.
7        If (nb==0) then break
8        index = 0
9        While( index<nb )
         {
10       Code=UNUSED[index][0]
11       Find the most frequently appearing pair in the buffer
12       If there is no such pair then {Over=1; Break}
13       Add pair to the UNUSED[Index][1] and UNUSED[Index][2]
14       Replace all such pairs by Code
15       Index++
         }
16   Write Index into the Output file
17   Write UNUSED table into the Output file
18   If(Over==1) then Break
19   }While(True)
20   Write the Buffer into the output file
```

Box 8.

```
1    Read and Store Pair table in a Buffer
2    Read number of stages from input file, Let it be n.
3    Read the set of n UNUSED tables and
     Store it in a 3D array named as Stage
     Stage[0][][] <--- 0th stage table
     Stage[1][][] <--- 1st stage table
     :
     Stage[n-1][][] <--- (n-1)th stage table
4    st = n-1
5    Copy the input file to the file FILE1
6    Initialize Stack
7    do
     {
8        While( Stack not Empty OR not EOF(FILE1))
         {
9            If Stack is Empty, Read byte from FILE1
                    else Pop byte from stack
10           If byte is in Stage[st][i][0] for any i then
                    Push the pair Stage[st][i][2],Stage[st][i][1]
                    into stack
                        else Write Byte into file FILE2
         }
11       Copy the file from FILE2 to FILE1.
12       st--, Initialize Stack
13   } While ( st >= 0 )
     //FILE1 is decompressed using PAIR table //
14   initialize Stack
15   While (Stack Not Empty OR Not EOF(FILE1))
     {
16       If Stack is Empty, Read byte from FILE1
                    else Pop byte from stack
17       If byte is in PAIR table then
                    Push the pair into Stack
                    else Write Byte on Output File
     }
```

$$\sum_{i=0}^{L-1} \sum_{j=1}^{m_i} p_{ij}.$$

Since, at least three occurrences are required to replace a pair; minimum value of p_i is 3. So, minimum number of replacements is termed as $384+3(m_1 + m_2 + \dots m_L)$, which can be denoted as O(1). If a file consists of a repetition of only one byte, then a maximum value of p_i is $N/2^{i*m_i+j}$. Thus the maximum number of replacements is in O(N) which is linear complexity.

Box 9.

```
1    Read File into the buffer
2    Code = 128
3    Do
     {
4        Find a most frequent Triplet in the Buffer
5        If No such Triplet, then Break
6        Add Triplet into a TRIPLET table
7        Replace all such Triplet by Code
8        Code++
9    } While( Code <= 255)
10   Write Code into the Output file
11   Write TRIPLET table into the Output file
12   While (Code<=255)
     {
13       Find the most frequent byte pair in buffer
14       If No such pair then Break
15       Add pair to a PAIR table
16       Replace all such pair with the Code
17       Code ++
     }
18   Write Code into the Output file
19   Write PAIR table into the Output file
20   Write buffer into the Output file
```

Byte Triplet Encoding (BTE) Algorithm

In this version of the algorithm, an attempt is made to replace most frequently occurring adjacent triplets, by the code from 128 to 255. The idea of replacing triplets is evolved from the fact that most of the English words have prefixes and suffixes with length 3. Example: ing, ted, sed, ies, dis, etc. While replacing, if there are no more adjacent triplets, then the algorithm replaces the most frequently occurring pairs. The details of replacements are recorded in two tables.

Compression

The algorithm starts by replacing the most frequently occurring triplets by the codes 128 through 255. If there are no more triplets, and still there exist some bytes from 128-255 to use, the algorithm starts finding and replacing most frequently appearing pairs. The following algorithm illustrates this process (Box 9). This algorithm can be further improved by using the unused bytes also as code for replacing Triplets and Pairs.

Decompression

In this method, the decompression process consists of two stages, replacing pair codes by a pair of bytes, and replacing tri codes by triplets. Firstly, the algorithm finds all pair codes and are replaced by the pair of bytes by using the PAIR table. Then the algorithm starts finding tricodes, which are replaced by the triplets by using the TRIPLET table. The algorithm in Box 10 illustrates this process.

Analysis

There are two stages in this algorithm. There are 128 byte codes from 128 to 255 used for replacement. At first, most frequently appearing triplets are replaced. In the second stage, if any byte code is spared then the most frequently appearing pairs are replaced. Let there are T number of frequently appearing triplets. Let there are P number of frequently appearing pairs. The range of T and P is from 0 to 128. If a triplet i appears t_i times and

pair j appears p_j times, then the total number of replacements are

$$\sum_{i=1}^{T} t_i + \sum_{j=1}^{P} p_j$$

Since, at least three occurrences are required to replace a triplet or a pair, minimum value of t_i and p_j is 3. So, minimum number of replacements is termed as $128*3 = 384$, which can be denoted as O(1). If a file consists of a repetition of only one byte, a maximum value of t_i is $N/3^i$. The maximum number of replacements is termed as $N/3 + N/9 + N/27 + \ldots\ldots N/3^{128} = N(1/2) = N/2$. This can be

Box 10.

```
1      Code = the first Byte of the Input file
2      Read the TRIPLET table and Store in a Buffer
3      Initialize Stack
4      If ( Code!=255 ) then
   {
5          Read and Store the PAIR table in a Buffer
6          While (Stack not Empty OR Not EOF(input) )
           {
7              If Stack empty, Read byte from input file
                   Else Pop Byte from Stack
8              If Byte is a Pair code then
                   Push the pair onto stack
                   Else Write the Byte to the file FILE1
           }
   }
   else Copy the Input file to file FILE1
9      Initialize Stack
10     While (Stack not Empty OR Not EOF(FILE1))
       {
11         If Stack empty, Read byte from FILE1
           else Pop Byte from Stack
12         If Byte is a TRI code then
                   Push the respective Triplet onto stack
           else Write the Byte to the output file
       }
```

denoted as O(N) which is linear complexity. If T =0 then this algorithm behaves like BPE.

Byte Quad Encoding (BQE) Algorithm

Most of the English words are four-lettered or consist of four-lettered prefixes and suffixes like sion, tion, sing, etc. So, in a text file, there may be an excessive repetition of four consecutive bytes. This algorithm starts finding those most frequently occurring four bytes, which are replaced by the code from 128 to 255. After replacing all the frequent adjacent four bytes, if any code from 128 to 255 remains unused, the algorithm starts finding the frequent adjacent triplets for replacement. After the replacement of triplets, if there are bytes from 128 to 255 that are unused (that is if the number of frequent quads and triplets replaced are less than 128) then the algorithm starts replacing the frequently appearing pairs by remaining codes. This algorithm significantly improves the compression ratio. This algorithm uses three tables for recording the replacements. A PAIR table, and a TRI table are used for storing the replacements of pairs and triplets respectively. Other than these tables, another table namely Q-table is used to store the most frequently appearing quadruplets.

Compression

In this method, the Compression starts by replacing most frequently appearing Quads, Triplets, and then pairs by the codes from 128 through 255. For each substitution, the details are to be entered into their respective tables. (See Box 11.)

Decompression

The decompression process consists of three stages viz., replacing pair codes by pair of bytes using PAIR table, replacing tri code by triplets using TRI-table, and replacing quad codes by quad of bytes using Q-table. The algorithm in Box 12 illustrates this process.

Analysis

There are three stages in this algorithm. There are only 128 byte codes from 128 to 255 used

Box 11.

```
1    Read File into the buffer
2    Code = 128
3    Do
     {
4        Find the most frequent Quad in Buffer
5        If No such Quads, Then Break
6        Add Quad into Q-table
7        Replace all such Quads by Code
8        Code++
9    }While( Code <= 255)
10   Write Code into the Output file
11   Write Q-table into the Output file
     While(Code<=255)
12   {
13       Find the frequent Triplet in Buffer
14       If No such Triplet, then Break
15       Add Triplet into a TRI-table
16       Replace all such Triplets by Code
17       Code++
     }
18   Write Code into the Output file
19   Write TRI-table into the Output file
20   While (Code<=255)
     {
21       Find the frequent byte pair in buffer
22       If No such pair then Break
23       Add pair to a PAIR-table
24       Replace all such pair with the Code
25       Code ++
     }
26   Write Code into the Output file
27   Write PAIR-table into the Output file
28   Write buffer into the Output file
```

Box 12.

```
1    Read the first Byte of Input file and Let it be QuadN
2    Read the Q-table and Store in a Buffer
3    Initialize Stack
4    If( QuadN!=255) then
     {
5        Read a Byte and assign to TriN
6        Read and Store the TRI-table in a Buffer
7        if (TriN !=255)
         {
8            Read a Byte and assign to PairN
9            Read and Store the PAIR-table in a Buffer
10           While (Stack not Empty OR Not EOF(input) )
             {
11               If Stack empty, Read byte from input file
                 else Pop Byte from Stack
12               If Byte is a Pair code then
                 Push the pair onto stack
                 else Write the Byte to the output file
             }
13           copy the output file to the inputfile
         }
14       Initialize Stack
15       While (Stack not Empty OR Not EOF(input) )
         {
16           If Stack empty, Read byte from input file
             else Pop Byte from Stack
17           If Byte is a TRI code then
                 Push the respective Triplet onto stack
             else Write the Byte to the output file
         }
18       Copy the output file to input file
     }
19       Initialize Stack
20       While (Stack not Empty OR Not EOF(input) )
         {
21           If Stack empty, Read byte from input file
             else Pop Byte from Stack
22           If Byte is a QUAD code then
                 Push the respective quad of bytes onto stack
             else Write the Byte to the output file
         }
```

for replacement. To begin with, most frequently appearing quadruplets are replaced. In the second and third stages, if any byte code is spared, the most frequently appearing triplets and then pairs are replaced. Let there are Q number of frequently appearing quadruplets, T number of frequently appearing triplets and P number of frequently appearing pairs. The range of Q, T and P is from 0 to 128. If a quadruplet i appears q_i times, triplet j appears t_j times and pair k appears p_k times, then the total number of replacements is

$$\sum_{i=1}^{Q} q_i + \sum_{j=1}^{T} t_j + \sum_{k=1}^{P} p_k.$$

Since at least three occurrences are required to replace a quadruplet, triplet or a pair, minimum value of q_i, t_i and p_j is 3. So, minimum number of replacements is termed as $128*3 = 384$, which can be denoted as $O(1)$. If a file consists of a repetition of only one byte, a maximum value of q_i is $N/4^i$. The maximum number of replacements is termed as $N/4 + N/16 + N/64 + \ldots\ldots N/3^{128} = N(1/3) = N/3$. This can also be denoted as $O(N)$ which is linear complexity. If $Q=0$, this algorithm behaves like BTE and if $Q=0$ and $T=0$, this algorithm behaves like BPE.

Box 13.

BQE+ Algorithm

This algorithm simply combines the concept of BPE++ algorithm and BQE algorithm. The BQE uses bytes from 128 to 255 for replacements. This algorithm starts with BQE, for the given file. The resulted file is further processed here. BQE+ finds all unused bytes in the resulted file and finds all frequent pairs and is replaced by those unused bytes. This process is repeated until all bytes are used in the resulted file or there are no more pairs to replace. Mostly, this algorithm gives better compression ratio compared with all the algorithms analyzed here.

Compression

In this method, the input file to be compressed has to be given to the BQE; the resulted file is given as input to the algorithm seen in Box 13.

Decompression

The decompression is done in two major stages. In the first stage the compressed file is decompressed by using the algorithm in Box 14, which replaces

```
1    Read the resulted file into the buffer
2    do
     {
3        Collect all unused bytes from the buffer
4        For each unused byte
         {
5            Find the most frequently appearing pair in the buffer
6            Replace the frequently appearing pair by an unused byte
7            Store the details of the replacement into UNUSED table
         }
8        Write UNUSED table into the output file
9    } While(if there is an unused Byte in the Buffer)
10   Write the Buffer into the output file
```

Box 14.

```
1   Read number of stages from input file, assign to n.
2   Read the set of n UNUSED tables and
        Store it in a 3'D array named as STAGE
        STAGE[O][][] ← Oth stage table
        STAGE[1][][] ← 1st stage table
        :
        STAGE[n-1][][] ← (n-1)th stage table
3   st = n-1
4   Copy the input file to the file FILE1
5   Initialize Stack
6   Do
    {
7       While( Stack not Empty OR not EOF(FILE1))
        {
8           If Stack is Empty, Read byte from FILE1
            else Pop byte from stack
9           If byte is in STAGE[st][i][O] Then
                Push the pair STAGE[st][i][2],STAGE[st][i][1]into stack
            else Write Byte into file FILE2
        }

10  copy the file from FILE2 to FILE1
11      st--
12 }While (st >= 0)
```

the pair codes by the pair of bytes by using the UNUSED tables.

In the second stage the FILE1 is given as input to the decompression algorithm of BQE. The outcome of the BQE decompression algorithm is a decompressed file.

Analysis

Initially, there are 128 byte codes from 128 to 255 used for replacement of most frequently appearing quadruplets, triplets and pairs. Then, the resulted file is fed into many stages in this algorithm. Let total number of stages be L. Assume there are m_i unused bytes found in stage i. The range of m_i is from 0 to 255. Let p_{ij} is a number of occurrences

of a pair j in stage i, then total number of replacements in all the stages is termed as

$$\sum_{i=0}^{L-1} \sum_{j=1}^{m_i} p_{ij}.$$

Since, at least three occurrences are required to replace a pair; minimum value of p_i is 3. So, minimum number of replacements is termed as $384+3(m_0 + m_1 +.... m_{L-1})$, which can be denoted as $0(1)$. If a file consists of a repetition of only one byte, then a maximum value of p_i is $N_0 / 2^{i*m_i+j}$. Here N_0 is a size of a resulted file from BQE. Since N_0 is always less than N, the maximum number of replacements in this algorithm is also in O(N) which is a linear complexity. If L=0 then this algorithm behaves like BQE.

Byte Word Encoding (BWE)

There are two stages in this algorithm. In the first stage, most frequently appearing words of any size are replaced by the byte codes 128 through 255. There are two variations of this first stage. Dictionary of most frequently used words (Pike, 1981) may be maintained according to the decreasing order of frequency in natural English text. The first 128 words from the list are found in the input file and are replaced by the codes 128 through 255. Another variation is, the dictionary of most frequently appearing words may be created every time at the time of compression. In the second case, the dictionary needs to be added along with coded file. The second stage is the resulted file which is fed into BPE++ for further compression. The number of replacements is in O(N), which is a linear complexity.

Implementation Issues

The major issue in these types of random access algorithms is searching for the most frequently used pairs, triplets and quadruplets. This requires more scans on the input file. But, all these algorithms provide very fast decompression. To reduce the scanning time, the input file should be brought to a buffer in main memory. If the file is too large, divide the file into smaller blocks and compress each chunk separately. Even though more scans are required on these types of algorithms, each time after the replacement text size is reduced considerably. For higher orders the reduction in the text size will also be high each time. It is necessary to keep all different pairs, triplets, and quadruplets appearing in the input file along with their counts to select a most frequently appearing pair, triplet or quadruplet. In a typical text file there exist a large number of different pairs, triplets and quadruplets. Hashing seems to be the single best technique for keeping all these. Hash size restricts the number of different pairs, triplets and quadruplets that can be kept with their counts.

So, the compression ratio may differ with a Hash table size. From the experimented results, one can infer that if an input file contains more repetitive data, the compression time is minimal. The file with less repetitive data requires more time to compress, because of keeping lots of pairs, triplets and quadruplets. So, the compression time differs with the nature of an input file.

Experimental Results

The Table 1 contains sample experimental results showing the behavior of the BPE and developed algorithms on different types of texts. Table 2 provides the average compression time in Hundredths of a Second, taken by each algorithms. The algorithms were run on a machine with 433 MHz processor speed, 128K of Cache, and 640K of main memory. From the experimental table, one can infer that, if an input file has more repetitions then the compression time is minimal and if an input file has very less repetitions, then compression time is more. The compression time is proportional to the searching and replacement

Table 1. Compression ratio

Source Texts Sizes in Bytes	File1 17,465	File2 11,915	File3 8,331	File4 10,400	File5 8,120
BPE	9116 48%	5377 55%	3778 55%	119 99%	7906 3%
BPE+	8320 53%	4541 62%	3378 60%	119 99%	7907 3%
BPE++	8094 54%	4156 65%	2874 66%	120 99%	7908 3%
BTE	9333 47%	5045 58%	3499 59%	102 100%	7911 3%
BQE	9529 46%	5034 58%	3482 59%	88 100%	8012 2%
BQE+	7857 56%	4164 65%	2865 66%	89 100%	7914 3%
BWE	7360 58%	4146 65%	2997 64%	177 98%	8035 1%

Table 2. Average compression time in hundredth of seconds

Source Texts Sizes in Bytes	File1 17,465	File2 11,915	File3 8,331	File4 10,400	File5 8,120
BPE	38	14	17	6	27
BPE+	39	16	17	5	33
BPE++	39	27	22	5	22
BTE	39	27	16	5	16
BQE	56	47	17	3	5
BQE+	56	49	22	6	27
BWE	51	40	26	7	32

process. The decompression time taken by all the algorithms on these source file is less than a single hundredth of a second. These algorithms are very fast in decompression.

The source files are

File1 - DOS 6.22 Help File -Networks.txt
File2 - Sample XML file
File3 - Sample C Source file
File4 - A file containing a repetition of abc...z ABC...Z
File5 - Random text file generated using rand( ) function

CONCLUSION

Six new algorithms based on BPE have been developed. These algorithms compress typical text files approximately to half of their original size, but of course the actual amount of compression depends on the data being compressed. The behavior of the compression algorithms are exhibited through the experimental table. Considering the time taken for compression, all the improved algorithms are taking some more milli seconds than BPE. Most of the time is spent on searching for the most frequently occurring Pairs, Triplets and Quadruplets. But decompression is very fast in all

these algorithms. Some more work is necessary to improve the searching process in these algorithms, which can reduce the compression time further. The major strength of these algorithms is high reliability. Unlike modern compression algorithms, if a byte of an input to the decompressor is corrupted by transmission errors, only a similar fraction of output bytes are affected. Thus Random Access Data Compression algorithms are more suitable to real time mission-critical and data transmission applications. These algorithms are also used for managing compressed data base file. Based on these, separate area on managing compressed data bases may be evolved.

This article is an extension to the paper published in ITNG-2006 conference proceedings titled "New Algorithms for Random Access Text Compression", IEEE Computer Society Press, pp. 104-111.

REFERENCES

Apostolico, A., & Choi, Y.W. (2006). Textual Compression by Collapsible Tries. *Data Compression Conference* (p. 437). IEEE Computer Society Press.

Apostolico, A. (2005). Lempel-Ziv-Welch Parses with Refillable Gaps. *Data Compression Conference* (pp. 338-347). IEEE Computer Society Press.

Burrows, M., & Wheeler, D. (1994). *A Block sorting lossless data compression algorithms.* Technical report 124. Palo Alto, CA, USA: Digital Equipment Corporation.

Chu, A. (2002). LZAC Lossless Data Compression. *Data Compression Conference* (p. 449). IEEE Computer Society Press.

Cleary, J., & Witten, J. (1984). Data Compression using adaptive coding and partial string matching. *IEEE Transactions on Communications* (pp. 396-402).

Cormack, G.V., & Horspool, R.N.S. (1984). Algorithms for adaptive Huffman codes. *Inf. Process Lett., 18*(3), 159-165.

Salomon, D. (2000). *Data Compression-The Complete Reference*. New York: Springer.

Eibe, F., Chang, C., & Witten, I.H. (2000). Text Categorization Using Compression Models. *Data Compression Conference* (p. 555). IEEE Computer Society Press.

Gallager, R.G. (1978). Variations on a theme by Huffman. *IEEE trans. Inf. Theory, 24*(6), 668-674.

Hosang, M. (2002). A Character Elimination Algorithm for Lossless Data Compression. *Data Compression Conference* (p. 457). IEEE Computer Society Press.

Huffman, D.A. (1952). A method for the construction of minimum redundancy codes. *Proceedings of the I.R.E., 40*(9), 1098-1101.

Lansky, J., & Zemliicka, M. (2007). Compression of a Set of Strings. *Data Compression Conference* (p. 390). IEEE Computer Society Press.

Yang, J., & Savari, S.A. (2007). Dictionary–based English text compression using word endings. *Data Compression Conference* (p. 410). IEEE Computer Society Press.

Adiego, J., Navarro, G., & de la Fuente, P. (2004). Lempel-Ziv Compression of Structured Text. *Data Compression Conference* (p. 112), IEEE Computer Society Press.

Kiem-Phong, V. (2007). Compression as Data Transformation. *Data Compression Conference* (p. 403). IEEE Computer Society Press.

Knuth, D.E. (1985). Dynamic Huffman Coding. *Journal of Algorithms, 6,* 163-180.

Crochemore, M., & Lecroq, T. (1999). *Text Data Compression Algorithms, 12,* 1-22. CRC press.

Alistair, M., Neal, R., & Witten, I.H. (1998). Arithmetic Coding Revisited. *ACM Transactions on Information Systems, 16*(3), 256-294.

Gage, P. (1997). Random Access Data Compression. *The C/C++ Users Journal*, 23-28.

Pike, J. (1981). Text Compression using a 4 bit coding scheme. *The Computer Journal, 24*(4), 324-330.

Skibinski, P. (2005). Two-Level Directory based Compression. *Data Compression Conference* (p. 481). IEEE Computer Society Press.

Robert, L., & Nadarajan, R. (1999). *New Algorithms for Random Access Text Compression*. M.Phil.Thesis, Bharthiar University, India.

Welch, T.A. (1984). A technique for high performance Data Compression. *IEEE Computer, 17*(6), 8-19.

Welch, T.A. (1984). A technique for High performance Data Compression. *IEEE Computer Journal, 17*(6). 8-19.

Weifeng, S., Zhang, N., & Mukherjee, A. (2003). A Dictionary-Based Multi-Corpora Text Compression System. *Data Compression Conference* (p. 448). IEEE Computer Society Press.

Ziv, J., & Lempel, A. (1977). A universal algorithm for sequential Data Compression. *IEEE transaction on Information Theory* (pp. 337-342).

This work was previously published in International Journal of Information Technology and Web Engineering 4(2), edited by Ghazi I. Alkhatib, and Ernesto Damiani, pp. 1-19, copyright 2009 by IGI Publishing (an imprint of IGI Global).

Chapter 7
Adaptability and Adaptivity in the Generation of Web Applications

Raoudha Ben Djemaa
MIRACL, Tunisie

Ikram Amous
MIRACL, Tunisie

Abdelmajid Ben Hamadou
MIRACL, Tunisie

ABSTRACT

This article proposes a generator for adaptive Web applications called GIWA. GIWA's objective is to facilitate the automatic execution of the design and the generation of Adaptable Web Applications (AWA). Characteristically, the effort in this work has to be pursued with special attention to both issues applied to AWA: adaptability and adaptivity. The architecture of GIWA is based on three levels: the semantic level, the conceptual level and the generation one. Using GIWA, designers specifies, at the semantic level the features of Web application. The conceptual level focuses on the creation of diagrams in WA-UML language; the extended UML by our new concepts and new design elements for adaptation. At the generation level, GIWA acquires all information about users' preferences and their access condition. Consequently, the generated pages are adaptable to all these information. An evaluation and a validation of GIWA are given in this article to prove our adaptation.

INTRODUCTION

The growing demand for data-driven Web applications has led to the need for a structured and controlled approach to the engineering of such applications. Both designers and developers need a framework that in all stages of the engineering process allows them to specify the relevant aspects of the application. The engineering becomes even more complicated when we include notions of adaptation. Here, we address both adaptations during the presentation generation, for example to reflect user preferences or platform used, as well as adaptation inside the generated presentation.

The need for adaptation arises from different aspects of the interaction between users and Web applications. Users' categories which deal with these systems are increasingly heterogeneous due to their different interests, preferences, and the use of number of devices (PC, WebTV, PDA, WAP phone, etc...). User's preferences and interests can be deduced from his and browsing history.

Adaptive Web engineering is meant to provide a systematic and disciplined approach for designing, generating and maintaining adaptive Web applications (Cingil, 2000). For this reason, recently several models and methodologies have been proposed for supporting the development of adaptive Web applications. The main goal of such models is to help designers to reason in a structured way about aspects that are specific to hypermedia, such as links, structure and navigation, and to express adaptation in the design process. Moreover, such models and methodologies should help engineers to manage the overall complexity of Web development which requires a variety of activities, such as organizing the structure, choosing the contents and the presentation modality, some of them involving automated generation of Web page (Brusilovsky, 1998). So, methodologies usually provide guidelines for performing such activities and suitable models for expressing the results of such operations.

In our previous works (Ben Djemaa, 2006a; 2006b, 2006c; Ben Djemaa, 2007; Ben Djemaa, 2008) we have presented a methodology for AWA which guides the designer through different steps of the design process, each of them yielding a specific model that is being interpreted by the GIWA tools. The GIWA methodology is based on several following steps: requirement analysis, conceptual design, adaptation design and generation.

The requirement analysis step (Ben Djemaa, 2005) represents the application domain. This step expresses the purpose and the subjects of the Web application through the functionality model

and defines the target audience through the audience model. The result of these two models is a set of audience classes together with an informal description of their functional space. In GIWA, the functional space is determined by a semi automatic algorithm called AGCA.

In the Conceptual Design step (Ben Djemaa, 2008), the functional space for each audience class is represented using traditional conceptual modeling: use case diagram, sequence diagram, class diagram, etc. In GIWA, conceptual model is represented in a specific notation called Web Adaptive Unified Modelling Language (WA-UML) (Ben Djemaa, 2008). This new notation increases the expressivity of UML while adding labels and graphic annotations to UML diagrams. This extension of UML defines a set of stereotypes and constraints, which make possible the design of conceptual model. These models are translated and exported in XML files in a data repository.

The adaptation design level (Ben Djemaa, 2007) is based on the profile model, which takes into account the user's devices capabilities (hardware and software), Users' preferences presentation (desired layout, navigation patterns, etc.) and personal information (eg. Age, sex, language, etc...).

In this article we concentrate on the generation level. At this level the designer is invited to instantiate previous models using the specific interfaces offered by GIWA. Only the aspects related to the two first levels (requirement analysis and conceptual design) are instantiated by the designer. Information related to the devices' capabilities are dynamically captured by the system (using Logs files) and then stored in the profile model. At the end of the step of instantiation, the GIWA deployment can be launched.

Characteristically, the effort in this work has to be pursued with special attention to both issues applied to AWA: adaptability and adaptivity. Adaptability can be defined as the facility of an application to be configurable according to a set of decisions taken by the user, which usually define his preferences and/or background. Whereas adaptivity denotes the capacity of the application to alter the profile model according to the user's behaviour during the application run and adapt dynamically to the current state of the user model to any user.

The article is structured as follows. In Section 2 we provide an overview of related works. In section 3 we present an overview of the different models of GIWA. Section 4 presents the architecture of GIWA and some examples of interfaces which illustrated the prototype. In section 5 we present our experimental design and the carrying out of the experiment using the design. Finally, section 6 concludes the article and suggests future research directions.

RELATED WORKS

For a long time, Web application engineering has been synonymous with ad hoc development and not supports a systematic process. Aspects like adaptation and generation process complicate the design process of Web application engineering and bring its complexity beyond the level that is easily handled by a single human developer. Therefore, to support a systematic development process, a strong methodology (supported by a suite of tools) can help to keep the design process at a practical level. Recently, different approaches for modeling and engineering adaptive hypermedia system have emerged. Approved hypermedia design principles, such as those defined in OOHDM (Schwabe, 1998) or in RMM (Isakowitz, 1995; Isakowitz, 1998) have been enhanced with the notions of adaptation and personalization in a further extension of OOHDM (Rossi, 2001) or the RMM-based Hera methodology (Frasincar, 2001; Frasincar, Houben, 2002). UWE (Koch, 2000, 2001) included a design methodology for adaptive hypermedia applications (AHDM) and a develop-

ment process for such applications (AHDP). In the AMACONT project authors have introduced a component-based XML document format (Fiala, 2003). This project enables to compose adaptive Web applications by the aggregation of reusable document components.

All these methodologies were originally designed for Adaptive Hypermedia Application (AHA) and do not deal comfortably with Adaptive Web Application (AWA). These methodologies are very much data-driven or implementation oriented and do not covers the lifecycle of adaptive Web applications. Still, most solutions have been originally developed for a manual hypermedia design process and are not particularly well-suited in the context of automated hypermedia design.

Methodologies like RMM, UWE or AMACONT are not specifically targeted to support dynamic adaptation. For these methodologies, personalization means that the application acknowledges the user's situation and its information delivery are adapted. They may be able to solve adaptability problems to some extent but they do not address the real problem of adaptivity relating to the devices' capability (hardware and/or software). On the other hand, most of the currently existing methodologies lack a profile model that would allow for the design of truly adaptive Web applications. In fact, this model can play a significant role in such applications: our aim is to include this aspect in the personalization of the hypermedia presentations that get generated. Generating adaptive presentations requires a clean separation of concerns, as is advocated in (Frasincar, 2002).

OVERVIEW OF GIWA MODELS

In GIWA, Web applications data are defined by different models such functionalities model, audience model and profile model.

The Functionalities Model

Met with the increasing needs of Web applications users, we propose a functionalities model, gathering users' informational and functional needs. In this model, functionalities are classified into three functional classes: Static Informational (SI), Dynamic Informational (DI) and Professional (P) ones. The Static Informational functional class gathers all functionalities enabling the users to have access to the system to acquire static information being in a specific URL Web page. This class translates the set of the static informational users' needs. Using hypertext and hypermedia links, the user is capable to exploit a functionality of information's consultation.

The Dynamic Informational functional class regroups all functionalities enabling the users to have access to the system to acquire dynamic information. This class translates the set of the dynamic informational users' needs. Using techniques of research by a search engine, the user is capable to exploit a research functionality of information.

The Professional functional class is devoted to the representation of the users' functional needs. Indeed, Web applications are based on technologies which make their contents dynamic, enabling, thus, the user to modify the applicative state of the server by carrying out a set of functionalities.

Each of these functional classes, represented above, will be decomposed by the designer into a set of elementary functionalities representing both informational and functional needs. These functionalities, describing every functional class, are three:

- Static Informational Functionality (SIF) displaying a static Web page being in a specific URL.
- Dynamic Informational Functionality (DIF) displaying a dynamic Web page constructed from one (or several) "SELECT" server query (s). It is about a selection from the

database without affecting the applicative server's state.

- Profession Functionality (PF) displaying a dynamic Web page constructed from one (or several) server query: UPDATE, ADD or DELETE. The execution of this functionality affects the applicative server's state.

At the lowest level of the Functionalities Model, the concept "Functional Space" provides each actor with a list of authorized functionalities.

In Figure 1 we present the Functionalities' meta-model (using the UML notation). This figure illustrates the inheritance and composition links existing between the concepts constituting the Functionalities Model (Functional Class, Functionality and Functional Space). We notice that the Informational Functionality class executes link (hypertext and hypermedia link classes) and the Informational Functionality class uses a query of consultation (Query research class) which makes it possible to select and to organize the presented information. In this case, the Query class is composed of several classes representing various clauses of a simple query like in SQL. In this meta-model we present:

- The SQL Select clause by a Projection class which defines the expected structure of the query result;
- The SQL From clause by the Source class which introduces the collections from which the result is built;
- The Where clause by the Selection class which specifies a predicate allowing to filter the collections;

A query produces a result modelled by a Result class. A relation of dependence exists between the classes Query and Result: any modification made to a query has a direct influence on the result. In addition, the Profession functional class uses another type of query which updates the database system (Query Updating class). It also implements

Figure 1. Representation of the meta-model of the model of the functionalities

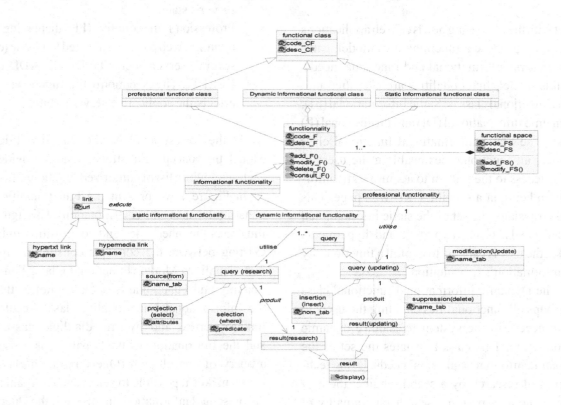

the composition of the classes representing the following clauses: The Insert clause represented by the class Insertion; the Delete clause represented by the class Delete and the Update clause represented by the class Modification.

In our approach, the Functionalities Model implementation is carried out in two stages. During the first stage, the designer is invited to define the first three levels of the model. The fourth level, relating to the functional space of the actors, is approached only after having defined the list of the actors involved in the application. However, this list is defined in the following section.

The Audience Model

The goal of this model is to define the actors' list of a Web application. Indeed, for this type of application, besides the human users (defines as of the physical actor) that exploits the Web system,

we can distinguish services (representing roles played by the human users) or systems (devices, data processing system, Web service,...). In this context, to take account these distinctions, we propose three categories of actors classified as follows: physical actor, logical actor and system actor.

Physical actor represents a human user (or human user group) who visits the application Web. This actor interacts with the system to search or consult information (to execute an informational functionality) and possibly to modify the state of the system (to execute a professional functionality). For example, in the case of an application of library in line; Subscribers and Visitors are some physical actors.

Logical actor represents a role played by a human user (or a human user group) to assure the maintenance of the Web application. This actor assures all actions and functionalities that participate

Figure 2. Meta-model of the audience model

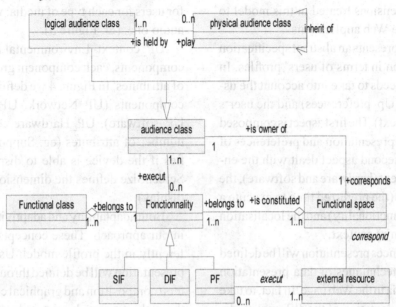

in the configuration and the administration of the system (to execute a professional functionality). For example, in the case of a Web application of a library the Webmaster and the Bookseller are some logical actors.

System Actor represents a computer system, an access device or a Web service, etc. These systems are connected generally to the application to provide news to the system or to update data. It is the external sources that will be charged automatically in the system.

In our approach, we have proposed an algorithm which generates the list of these different actors of the Web application starting from the concept of Functionality. We have presented in (Ben Djemaa, 2007), the process of operations of this algorithm.

The hierarchy of actors generated by this algorithm cannot describe a model for users because the definite actors are not all human actors. Therefore, in the goal to define an audience model (that leans logically on the human users), we propose to differentiate the human users by the concept "audience class" to inhuman one (systems) and, therefore to distinguish between "logical audience class" and "physical audience class".

By definition, an audience class is a potential user group which belongs to the application target audience and which has the same informational and functional needs. These classes are not necessarily disjoined (a user can belong to several classes of audience).

In Figure 2 we present the meta-model of our audience model. This figure illustrates the inheritance and composition links existing between the concepts constituting the Functionalities Model (Functional Class, Functionality and Functional Space).

To evaluate the audience model, we have proposed in (Ben Djemaa, 2005) an EPMA (Evaluation Process of the Audience Model) which evaluates the result generated by the algorithm of actor generation. This process is based on several mathematical symbols and formulas follow to check the distribution of the informational and functional needs between the actors for the application.

Profile Model

In our approach we proposed a new model specific for adaptive Web application called Profile

Model (Ben Abdallah, 2008). In Figure 3 we show the different dimensions treated in this model to generate adaptive Web applications.

This model represents an abstract specification of the presentation in terms of users' profiles. In fact, this model needs to take into account the users' preferences (Up_preferences) and the user's context (UP_context). The first aspect is composed of preferences of presentation and preferences of navigation. The second aspect dealt with the environmental context (hardware and software), the temporal context (the preferred time to execute a FIS, FID or FM functionality) and the localisation (GPS information's) context.

Users' preferences presentation will be defined through specific techniques of data presentation and different media in the Web page. In fact, to take into account the adaptation of the different media in a Web application we have defined a model of

media adaptation which presents preferred choices for users for each type of media: visual, video and audio one. (cf. Figure 5).

UP_context_Environmental has a number of components, each component grouping a number of attributes. In Figure 4 we defined three profiles components (UP_Network, UP_Hardware and UP_software). UP_Hardware component has a number of attributes (eg. Support_image specifies if the device is able to display images and ScreenSize defines the dimensions of the device display).

Both adaptability and adaptivity are considered in our approach. These concepts are treated differently in the profile model. Users' preferences presentation will be defined through specific charters (composition and graphical charters). Each of these charters can be choice by the user after the generation of his Web application (adaptability)

Figure 3. Profile model

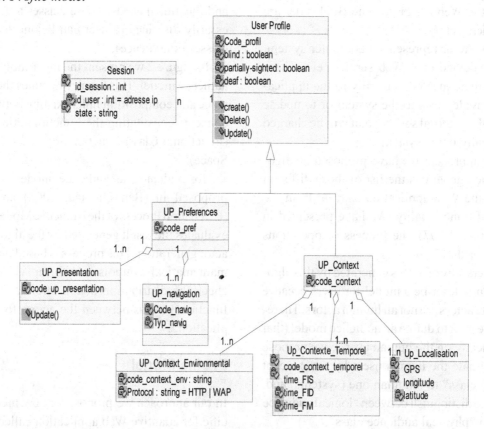

Figure 4. Environnemental context / user profile

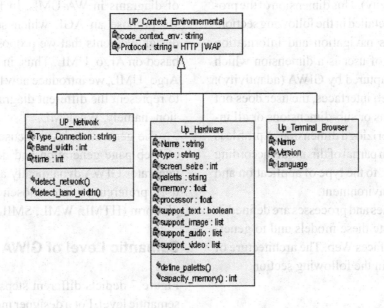

Figure 5. Model of media adaptation in GIWA

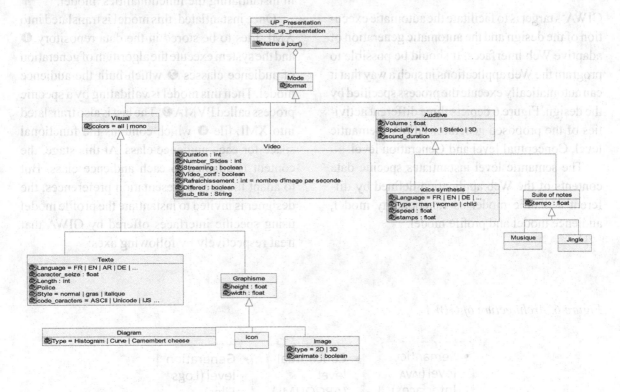

and he can also modify some information at his system use (adaptivity). This dimension of the profile model will be detailed in the following section. Users' preferences navigation and information about the context of user is a dimension which is automatically captured by GIWA (adaptivity).

To generate Web interfaces, the user does not need all dimensions or sub-dimensions or all information characterizing a dimension. A profile is thus an instantiation partial of this model according to the user's needs, to the type of application and to the execution environment.

Different engines and processes are defined in GIWA to instantiate these models and to generate adaptable interfaces Web. The architecture of GIWA is detailed in the following section.

ARCHITECTURE OF GIWA

GIWA's target is to facilitate the automatic execution of the design and the automatic generation of adaptive Web interfaces. It should be possible to program the Web applications in such a way that it can automatically execute the process specified by the design. Figure 6 depicts three different activities of the proposed generator GIWA: Semantic level, Conceptual level and Generation level.

The semantic level instantiates specific data contents of the Web application defined by different semantic model us functionality model, audience model and profile model.

The conceptual level focuses on the creation of diagrams in WA-UML. In fact, in this level we propose an AGL which supports the new design elements that we proposed. This AGL is based on Argo_UML. Thus, in this extension of Argo_UML, we introduce new types of diagrams to represent the different diagrams of our extension, namely, WA-UML.

The generation level focuses on the process of Web page generation and describes how the generator GIWA dynamically adjusts to varying user preferences into chosen implementation platform (HTML, WML, SMIL, etc.).

Semantic Level of GIWA

Figure 7 depicts different steps of GIWA in the semantic level. For a designer modelling an adaptive Web application using GIWA consists firstly, in instantiating the functionalities' model.

Once instantiated, this model is translated into XML files to be stored in the data repository ❶ and the system execute the algorithm of generation of audience classes ❷ which built the audience model. Then this model is validating by a specific process called PVMA ❸. The last is also translated into XML file ❹ which contains the functional space for each audience class. At this stage, the content is adapted to each audience class. But to adapt the user's presentation preferences, the designer is invited to instantiate the profile model using specific interfaces offered by GIWA that treat respectively by following axes:

Figure 6. Architecture of GIWA

- Personal information about the user like name, age, sex, language.
- Users' presentation preferences defined in by two charters called composition and graphical charters (defined in the model of media adaptation (cf. Figure 4)).

After instantiation, the profile model is exported in XSL files in the data repository ❺. At this stage GIWA treat the aspect of adaptability which appears through the choice of a graphical charter and through the composition of page after generated users' application. Figure 8 presents some interfaces of GIWA to instantiated the functionality model, the audience model and the profile model.

Figure 7. The semantic level of GIWA

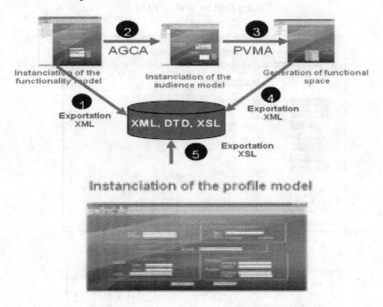

Figure 8. Interfaces of the semantic level in GIWA

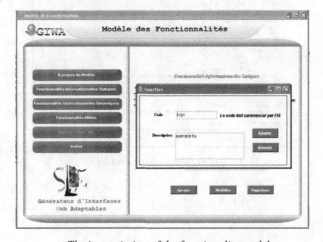

The instantiation of the functionality model

continued on following page

Figure 8. continued

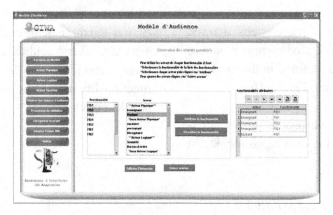

The application of the PVMA

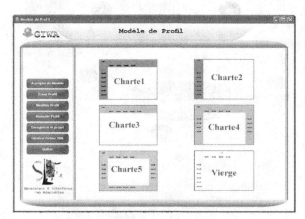

Composition charter of GIWA

XML file of the audience model

Figure 9. Conceptual level of GIWA

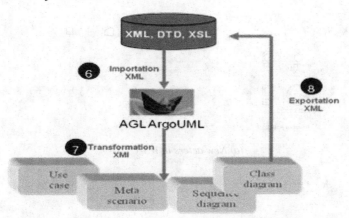

Conceptual Level

In the Conceptual level, the functional space for each audience class is represented using different conceptual modeling (use case diagram, sequence diagram, class diagram, etc) which are represented in WA-UML (Ben Djemaa 2006c; Djemaa, 2008). While this article is not solely devoted to the conceptual issue, we do want to shortly demonstrate how the functional space for each user, is modeling. In fact, diagram and meta-model of WA-UML are detailed in our work in (Ben Djemaa, 2008).

In this article we propose an AGL which supports the new design elements that we proposed in WA-UML. The last is based on Argo_UML because it permits to guide the user in the use of the UML notation through a mechanism of critiques and help messages. In addition, the source code of Argo_UML is available on the Web making it possible to analyze its inner workings. Thus, in this extension of Argo_UML, we introduce new types of diagrams to represent the different diagrams of our extension. In Figure 9 we present the different steps of the conceptual level in GIWA.

The XML files generated by the semantic level are extracted from the data repository ❻ to be imported into the AGL supporting the new design elements that we proposed.

This AGL is based on Argo_UML. So, in our use of Argo_UML, we introduce new types of diagrams to represent the new diagrams of our extension WA-UML (Ben Djemaa, 2008). In these diagrams, the user can add, displace and copy the different design elements as well as replace faces and publish their properties as used in Argo_UML. Figure 10 shows some examples of new icons of WA-UML presented by Argo_UML.

All conceptual diagram of WA-UML can be described with the new AGL based on Argo_UML ❼. The last diagram is translated in XML files ❽.

In Figure 11 we present some diagrams of GIWA at the conceptual level. Us an example we present conceptual diagrams related to E-commerce application.

Generation Level

The previous sections dealt with the engineering process of GIWA. This section focuses on the process of generation of adaptive Web applications and describes how the system is dynamically adjusted to varying audience classes.

The generation level focuses on the process of Web page generation and describes how the generator GIWA dynamically adjusts to varying user preferences into chosen implementation platform (HTML, WML, SMIL, etc.). The target of this step is to facilitate the automatic generation of

Figure 10. New icons in WA-UML

(a) New actors in WA-UML

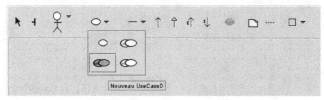

(b) New use cases in WA-UML

(c) New classes in WA-UML

Figure 11. Examples of WA-UML diagrams

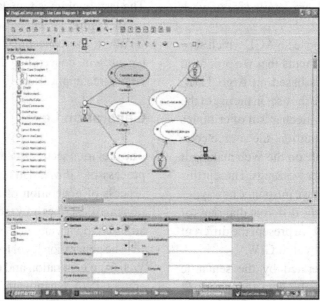

An example of WA-UML use case diagram

continued on following page

Figure 11. continued

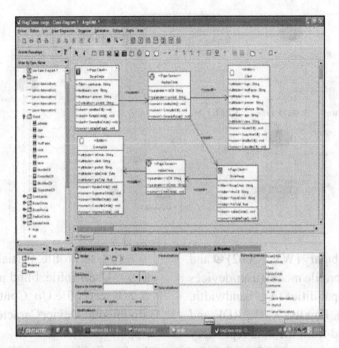

An example of WA-UML class diagram

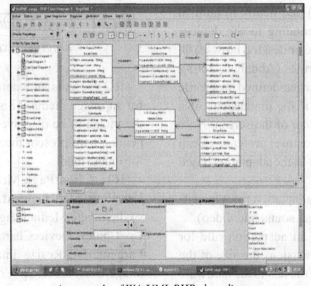

An example of WA-UML PHP class diagram

adaptive Web interfaces. It should be possible to program the Web applications in such a way that it can automatically execute the process specified by the design. The tool is based on a collection of engines, which interpret the models provided by the designer during the generation process. (cf. Figure 12).

According to the user/devices profile (refers aspect of adaptivity) is captured by the GIWA using data from logs files to be stored on the server ac-

Figure 12. Generation level of GIWA

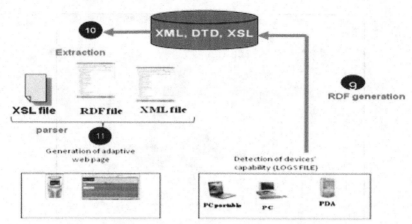

cording to a RDF vocabulary (W3C, 2002) ❾ and then to instantiate the profile model (user/devices profile) by specific capabilities (e.g. bandwidth, display resolution,…). Finally, XML, RDF and XSL files are extracted from the data repository ❿ and they are sent to the PARSER in order to apply some adaptation rules for each media (text, image, sound and video) and finally to publish the HTML page corresponding to the devices user (PC, PDA, cell phone or desktop browse) ⓫.

In adaptation media rules (Abdallah, 2008), we use the media properties defined in profile model, e.g. we can test if the dimensions of a particular image fit the size of the screen. Note that the adaptation based on user preferences can be treated in the same way as the adaptation based on device capabilities.

We proposed several adaptation rules for different Medias (text, image, sound and video).

R1 is an example of an adaptation rule for text media. This rule dimensions the size of the screen to adapt the size of the text to the hardware device or to user who is partially-sighted person or blind person. In appendix 1 we present the rest of adaptation rules for text media.

R1: ClientPage.Media.Texte.size_caracter >

$$\sqrt{\frac{height\_screen * width\_screen}{length\_text}})$$

$\wedge$ ($\neg$ UserProfile. partially-sighted person $\vee \neg$ UserProfile. blind person)
$\wedge$(UserProfile.Up_Context.Up_Context_Environmental.DeviceCaracteristic.Up_Hardware.support_text))
$\rightarrow t_1$ Resize_text(ClientPage.Media.Text.size_caracter, E(

$$\sqrt{\frac{height\_screen * width\_screen}{length\_text}}))$$

R 2 presents an example of adaptation rules for an image media. This rule adapts the size of the image to be displayed by the device. In appendix 2 we present the rest of adaptation rules for image media.

R2: ClientPage.Media.image.Hauteur > UserProfile.Up_Context.Up_Hardware.hauteur $\vee$ ClientPage.Media.image.largeur > UserProfile. Up_Context.DeviceCharacteristic.Up_Hardware. Largeur $\rightarrow t2$ Resize_image(ClientPage.Media. image,UserProfile.Up_Context.Up_Context_Environmental.Up_Hardware.hauteur,UserProfile. Up_Context.Up_Context_Environmental.DeviceCharacteristic .Up_Hardware.largeur)

R 3 presents an example of adaptation rules for sound media. This rule deletes the sound in the Web page where the device doesn't support it or where the user is a deaf person. In appendix 3

Figure 13. Simulation of GIWA using PC

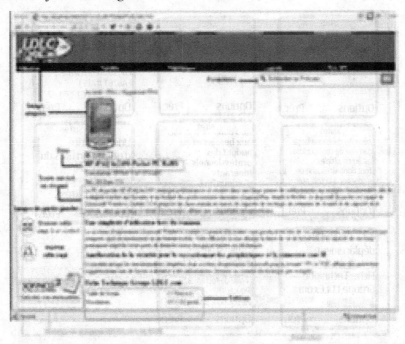

we present the rest of adaptation rules for sound media.

R3: UserProfile.deaf ∨ ¬ UserProfile. Up_Context.Up_Context_Environmental.DeviceCharacteristic .Up_Hardware.support_sound ∨ ClientPage.Media.audio.sound.jingle →t3 delete_sound(ClientPage.Media.audio).

R 4 presents an example of adaptation rules for video media. This rule is applied to substitute a video by an image if the device is enabling to display this video. In appendix 4 we present the rest of adaptation rules for video media.

r18:¬UserProfile.Up_Context.Up_Context_Environmental.DeviceCharacteristic .Up_Hardware.support_Video ∧UserProfile. Up_Context.Up_Context_Environmental.Up_Hardware.support_image →t18Convert_video_to_image(ClientPage.Media.video,UserProfile. Up_preference.Up_presentation.Charte.Modalite.Visual.graphic.format,number_image:1 default)

In Figure 13 we present the simulation of GIWA for a user who connected with a PC.

In Figure 14 we present other interfaces of GIWA related to user who connected to the system using cell phone (Nokia SDK 5100).

EXPERIMENTATION AND EVALUATION

Evaluating systems is a difficult task, and it becomes even more difficult when the system is adaptive. It is of crucial importance to be able to distinguish the adaptive features of the system from the general usability of the designed tool.

The evaluation of our GIWA system was designed to address the goals of the system, namely to help users to design and generate adaptive web applications. So firstly, we wanted to measure the usability of GIWA and testing the ability of the process, during its three levels (i.e. semantic, conceptual and generation), to design and generate adaptive interfaces. Secondly, we were also interested in subjects' own evaluation of how well the adaptive system worked compared to the non-

Figure 14. Simulation of GIWA using cell phone (Nokia SDK 5100)

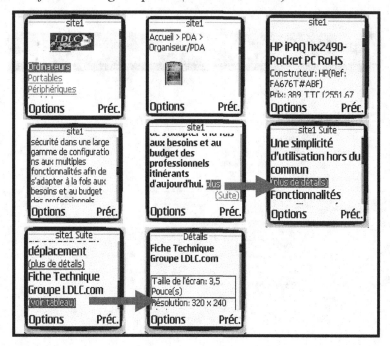

adaptive one, and whether they felt in control of the adaptive parts of the system. A last difficulty in making studies of adaptive systems is in the procedure of the study.

Design of the Experiment

The study was done in the laboratory of MIRACL. Subjects were videotaped, and the computer screen was recorded on the same videotape. The subjects' actions were tracked using DRUM (Diagnostic Recorder for Usability Measurement) and descriptive statistics of task completion time, actions performed inefficient use of the system, and others could be easily computed using this tool. There were 8 subjects in the study, 3 female and 5 male, all employed at the laboratory that had developed and used the target domain SDP. All had experience with World Wide Web (WWW) and hypermedia development. Subjects spent in total, approximately three hours in carrying out the steps of the experiment, out of which two hour

was spent testing the three level of GIWA. The rest of the time was used for questions on the subject's background, a small diagnostic test of their understanding of certain concepts in the on-line manual before using our system and after using our system, and finally answering some questions about their preferences regarding GIWA and the adaptive versus the non-adaptive system. Details of the steps of the experiment are presented below.

Each of the subjects followed three steps in this experiment, related to each level of GIWA. We proposed for them an example of web application related to the "teaching gate" of our institute. The two first steps related to the semantic and the conceptual level that were designed to test the explanations provided by the system rather than test the usefulness of the system as such. These two steps also served as a means to introduce subjects to the development of Web applications. The third step concerned the generation level that was realized for both of the two devices: the PC and the cell phone.

In the first step, a subject was given a set of functionalities related to the "teaching gate" with different types (FIS, FID, and FM), and was asked to use the generator to complete the following three tasks:

- **Task 1:** Instantiate the functionality model by adding, for each functionality, the code and the description, and generate the XML file for this model.
- **Task 2:** Apply the AGAC (Algorithm of Generation of Audience Classes).
- **Task 3:** Apply the PVMA and generate the XML file of the audience model.

In the second step the subject was given the XML file generated by the first step and asked to use the ArgoWA-UML to complete the following three tasks:

- **Task 4:** Import the XMI File related to the semantic level and created the use cases of the application.
- **Task 5:** create the sequence and classes diagrams with the new icons of WA-UML.
- **Task 6:** choose a Web language (PHP, JSP, ASP) and generated the technical class diagram.

In the third of the three above mentioned steps the subject was given the XML file generated by the second step and asked to use firstly a Pc and secondly, a cell phone, to complete the following three tasks:

- **Task 7:** connected to GIWA by taping: http://localhost:8080/GIWA/index.html (for PC) http://localhost:8080/GIWA/index.wml (for cell phone).
- **Task 8:** create an account and then choose a profile or create a new profile.
- **Task 9:** choose the XML file related to the conceptual model of the application "teach-

ing gate" and generated the results by PC and cell phone.

The design goal of these nine tasks (1 to 9) was to oblige the users to actively use all the commands provided, while at the same time expose their own patterns of command sequences when performing the various tasks.

Results of Carrying out the Experiment

Usability of the System

Our results are divided into those concerning:

- Some remarks concerning the task completion time, where we can see a weak tendency that users spend some time to achieve the first task.
- The actions in ArgoWA-UML that the subjects have to do (clicking on icons, making menu-choices, clicking on association, etc) to build WA-UML conceptual diagrams are less than the action of building UML diagrams. Thus, this confirms the result that conceptual level of GIWA is a semi automatic one.
- Adaptive Web pages generated by cell telephone are more interesting than those generated by a PC for most of users.
- The subjects' satisfaction with the system, where they compare the result (page generated) and their preferences described at the semantic level.
- The passage between the three levels of GIWA was not too clear by some of users.
- Combination of design and generation in GIWA is approved by users.

User Satisfaction

After the subjects had used the two variants of GIWA, we asked them to provide their viewpoints on various aspects of the generator. We did this through ten questions, and they were also asked to freely comment on various aspects of the system. For the ten questions the subjects put a cross on a scale grading from 1 to 7 - the interpretation of the scales can be seen from the statements left and right of the Table 1.

In the evaluation column of the Table 1 we present the interpretation of the scales which can be seen from the statements left and right. The x-axes represents the number of user for each scale, the y-axes represents the different interpretation of user for each question.

In Table 1 we see the result of the queries on how the subjects perceived the adaptive system in using GIWA. As we can see, the subjects preferred the adaptive system (mean 5.25); they also like the combination of design and generation in GIWA (mean 5.25); and they felt that the system made good adaptations to their needs (mean 4.75). Also, they claimed that they saw when the system changed the inferred task (mean 4.75).

Evaluating adaptive systems is often done through comparing a non-adaptive version of the system to an adaptive system. Our study is no exception from this approach. Still, an adaptive system should preferably be designed in such a way that the adaptivity is only one instrument in the repertoire of design techniques that together will form the tool that in its whole meets the users' needs and individual differences.

There are few studies of adaptive systems in general and even fewer of adaptive hypermedia. In the studies of adaptive hypermedia by (Boyle 1994; Kaplan 1993) the main evaluation criterion is task completion time. This should obviously be one important criterion by which some systems should be evaluated. In our case, though, the goal of the adaptive hypermedia system is to generate the right needs according to the user's preferences. The time spent in retrieving information is not as relevant as is the quality of the search and the result. Apart from task completion time, Boyle and al. also measured reading comprehension through

a diagnostic test put to the subjects after having used their system. Kaplan and al. measured how many nodes the users visited - in their case the more nodes the users visited the better.

CONCLUSION

The research described in this article targets the support of automated generation Web interfaces in the context of adaptive Web application. Specifically, for Web applications involving various functionalities (informational or professional one), the implementation requires a structured approach.

This article develops a generator called GIWA supporting both design aspect and generation one. The architecture of GIWA is based on three levels: the semantic level, the conceptual level and the generation level.

The primary focus of the GIWA is to provide engineering support for adaptive Web applications that automatically generate hypermedia presentations in response for each ad hoc user's requirements. GIWA guides the designer through the different steps of the generation process, each of them yielding a specific model that is being interpreted by the GIWA tools to achieve the objective of automatic presentation generation.

In GIWA, we have distinguished two kinds of adaptation: adaptability (implemented at the semantic level) and adaptivity (implemented at the generation level). Adaptability is based on information about user preferences presentation (a.g. font color, page layout etc.) and user preferences navigation stored in the profile model before browsing starts. Adaptivity is considered in GIWA to provide a system which is able to automatically adapt a given presentation to the user device capabilities (hardware and software configuration). Information about device capabilities are captured from Logs Files and stored then in the profile model. The prototype of GIWA has been built by different engines and equipments. The prototype uses java interfaces to instanti-

Table 1.

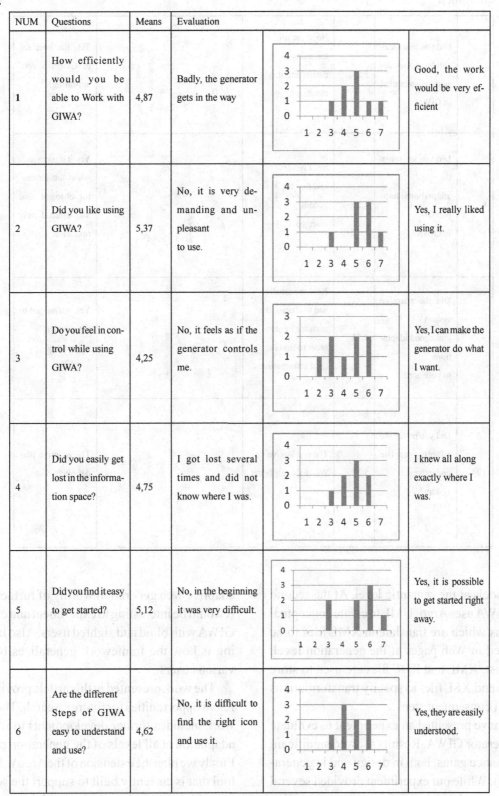

NUM	Questions	Means	Evaluation		
1	How efficiently would you be able to Work with GIWA?	4,87	Badly, the generator gets in the way		Good, the work would be very efficient
2	Did you like using GIWA?	5,37	No, it is very demanding and unpleasant to use.		Yes, I really liked using it.
3	Do you feel in control while using GIWA?	4,25	No, it feels as if the generator controls me.		Yes, I can make the generator do what I want.
4	Did you easily get lost in the information space?	4,75	I got lost several times and did not know where I was.		I knew all along exactly where I was.
5	Did you find it easy to get started?	5,12	No, in the beginning it was very difficult.		Yes, it is possible to get started right away.
6	Are the different Steps of GIWA easy to understand and use?	4,62	No, it is difficult to find the right icon and use it.		Yes, they are easily understood.

continued on following page

Table 1. continued

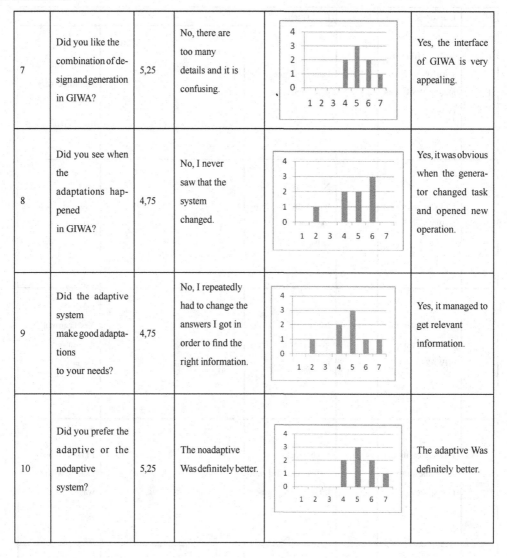

7	Did you like the combination of design and generation in GIWA?	5,25	No, there are too many details and it is confusing.		Yes, the interface of GIWA is very appealing.
8	Did you see when the adaptations happened in GIWA?	4,75	No, I never saw that the system changed.		Yes, it was obvious when the generator changed task and opened new operation.
9	Did the adaptive system make good adaptations to your needs?	4,75	No, I repeatedly had to change the answers I got in order to find the right information.		Yes, it managed to get relevant information.
10	Did you prefer the adaptive or the nodaptive system?	5,25	The noadaptive Was definitely better.		The adaptive Was definitely better.

ated models at the semantic level. At the second level GIWA uses Argo_UML to create conceptual diagrams which are translate in XML files to be generated in Web pages at the generation level. In the last, XML and RDF files are used to store the data and XSL files to specify transformations between consequent steps.

We have presented an experiment to evaluate our generator GIWA. Results showed significant performance gains, both in design and in generation step. While our experiment provided several revealing results, there are many issues regarding adaptive web generation worthy of further study. It would be interesting to experiment and evaluate GIWA with blind and sighted users. Also interesting is how the framework generalizes between various users.

The work presented in this article provides different opportunities for future research. The future work includes further developments to facilitate adaptation at all levels of the generation process. Firstly we plan the extension of the ArgoWA-UML tool that is currently built to support the semi automatic transition from design models to a running implementation of adaptive Web applications. Secondly we plan to extend adaptivity in GIWA in order to dynamically elaborate and modify both the functional space and the navigation patterns, learning from the user's behaviour.

ACKNOWLEDGMENT

The authors would like to thank Ben Abdallah Fatma, who helped in the design and the development of a part of media adaptation.

REFERENCES

Abdallah, F., Amous, I., Ben Djemaa, R., & Ben Hamadou, A. (2008). Génération d'Interfaces Web Adaptable au Contexte et aux Préférences des Utilisateurs. Les huitième journées scientifiques des jeunes chercheurs en Génie Electrique et Informatique (GEI'2008) (pp. 103-112), Sousse, Tunisie.

Ben Djemaa, R., Amous I., & Ben Hamadou, A. (2005, September). Towards an approach for adaptive Web applications' requirements engineering. The 7th International conference on Information integration and Web-based Application and Services (IIWAS05) (pp. 19-21). Kuala Lumpur.

Ben Djemaa, R., Amous I., & Ben Hamadou A. (2006a, May). Design and implementation of adaptive Web application. *In 8th International Conference on Enterprise Information Systems ICEIS'06 (pp. 23- 27), Paphos Cyprus.*

Ben Djemaa, R., Amous I., & Ben Hamadou A. (2006b, February). GIWA: A generator for adaptive Web applications. In *Proceedings of the Advanced International Conference on Telecommunications and International Conference on Internet and Web Applications and Services (AICT/ICIW 2006) IEEE (pp. 23-25), Guadeloupe, French Carabeen.*

Ben Djemaa, R., Amous I., & Ben Hamadou A. (2006c). Use case and meta-scenarios for modelling Adaptive Web Applications. In *proceeding of IEEE 1st International Conference on Digital Information Management (ICDIM).* 06-08 December, 2006. Christ College, Bangalore, India, pp. 283-288.

Ben Djemaa, R., Amous I., & Ben Hamadou A. (2007, May). Adaptable and adaptive Web applications: From design to generation. *International Review on Computers and Software (IRECOS), 2(3), 198-207.*

Ben Djemaa, R., Amous I., & Ben Hamadou, A. (2008, April/June). Extending a conceptual modeling language for adaptive Web applications. *International Journal of Intelligent Information Technologies (IJIIT), 4(2), 37-56.*

Boyle, C., & Antonio, O. (1994). MetaDoc: *An Adaptive Hypertext Reading System. User Models and User Adapted Interaction,* (UMUAI), 4, 1-19.

Brusilovsky, P. (1998). Methods and Techniques of Adaptive Hypermedia. In P. Brusilovsky, A. Kobsa, & J. Vassileva (Eds.), *Adaptive Hypertext and Hypermedia* (pp. 1-43). Kluwer Academic Publishers.

Cingil, I., Dogac, A., & Azgin, A. (2000). A broader approach to personalization. Communication of the ACM, 43(8), 136-141.

Fiala, Z., Hinz,, M., Meissner K., & Wehneer, F. (2003). A component-based component architecture for adaptive dynamic Web documents. *Journal of Web engineering, 2(1), 58-73.*

Fons, J., Pelechano, V., Pastor, O., Albert, M., & Valderas, P. (2003). *Extending an OO Method to Develop Web Applications.* The Twelfth International World Wide Web Conference (pp. 20-24), Budapest, Hungary.

Frasincar, F., & Houben, G.-J. (2002). Hypermedia presentation adaptation on the semantic Web. In P. de Bra, P. Brusilovsky, & R. Conejo (Eds.),

Proceedings of the 2nd International Conference on Adaptive Hypermedia and Adaptive Web-Based Systems (AH 2002) (pp. 133-142), Malaga, Spain.

Frasincar, F., Houben, G.-J., & Vdovjak, R. *(2001)*. An RMM-Based Methodology for Hypermedia Presentation Design. *In Proceedings of the 5th East European Conference on Advances in Databases and Information Systems (ADBIS 2001), LNCS 2151 (pp.* 323-337), Vilnius, Lithuania.

Isakowitz, T., Stohr, A., & Balasubramanian, E. (1995). RMM: A methodology for structured hypermedia design. *Communications of the ACM, 38*(8), 34-44.

Isakowitz, T., Kamis, A., & Koufaris, M. (1998). *The Extended RMM Methodology for Web Publishing.* Center for Research on Information Systems.

Kapla, C., Justine, F., & James, C. (1993). Adaptive Hypertext Navigation Based On User Goals and Context. *User Modeling and User-Adapted Interaction, 3*, 193-220.

Koch, N. (2000). Software Engineering for Adaptative Hypermedia Systems-Reference Model, Modelling Techniques and Development Process. Ph.D Thesis, Fakultät der Mathematik und Informatik, Ludwig-Maximilians Universität München.

Koch, N. (2001). The Authoring Process of the UMLbased Web Engineering Approach. 1*st International Workshop on Web-Oriented Software Technology. The Tenth International Conference on the World Wide Web,* Hong Kong.

Rossi, G., Schwabe, D., & Guimaraes, R. (2001) Designing Personalized Web applications. *The Tenth International Conference on the World Wide Web, Hong Kong.*

Schwabe, D., & Rossi, G. (1998*).* Developing hypermedia applications using OOHDM. *In Proceedings of Workshop on Hypermedia development Process, Methods and Models* (pp. 85-94).

Villanova-Oliver, M., Gensel, J., Martin, H., & Erb, C. (2002). *Design and generation of adaptable Web information systems with KIWIS.* In Proceedings of the 3rd IEEE Conference on Information Technology TCC-2002, Las Vegas, USA World Wide Web Consortium.

Argo UML. http://www.tigris.org. eXtensible Stylesheet Language, XSL Specification – version 1.0, W3C Recommendation. Retrieved October 15, 2001 from http://www.w3.org/TR/xsl/ World Wide Web Consortium, 2002.

RDF Vocabulary Description Language 1.0: RDF Schema, W3C Working Draft. Retrieved April 30, 2002 from http://www.w3.org/TR/rdf-schemadix.

APPENDIX A: ADAPTATION RULES FOR TEXT MEDIA

R5: (ClientPage.Media.Text.color $\not\subset$ UserProfile.Up_preference.Up_presentation.Charte.Modalite. Visual.colors) $\vee$ (ClientPage.Media.Text.color $\notin$ UserProfile.Up_Context.Up_Context_Environmental. DeviceCharacteristic.Up_Hardware.palette) $\rightarrow$ t5 Modify_color(ClientPage.Media.Text.color, color)

R6 : ClientPage.Media.Text.police$\neq$UserProfile.Up_preference.Up_presentation.Charte.Modalite. Visual.Text.police $\wedge$ (UserProfile.partially-sighted person $\vee$ UserProfile.blind_man $\vee$ UserProfile. Up_Context.Up_Context_Environmental.DeviceCharacteristic.Up_Hardware.support_Text$\wedge$UserProfile. Up_Context.Up_Context_Environmental.DeviceCharacteristic.Up_Hardware.support_image)$\rightarrow$t6 Convert_text_to_image(ClientPage.Media.Text)

APPENDIX B: ADAPTATION RULES FOR IMAGE MEDIA

R7: (ClientPage.Media.image.color $\not\subset$ UserProfile.Up_preference.Up_presentation.Charte.Modalite.Visual.colors) $\vee$ (ClientPage.Media.image.color $\notin$ UserProfile.Up_Context.Up_Context_Environmental.DeviceCharacteristic . Up_Hardware.palette)$\rightarrow$t7 color_image(ClientPage.Media.image.color, color)

R8: UserProfile.Up_Context.Up_Context_Environmental.Protocole_de_transfert="HTTP" $\wedge$ ClientPage.Media.image.size_File > UserProfile.Up_Context.Up_Context_Environmental.DeviceCharacteristic.Up_Hardware.memory $\rightarrow$ t8 $\wedge/\vee$ t_{10} $\vee/\wedge$ t_{13} convert_gif (ClientPage.Media.image)

R9:$\neg$UserProfile.Up_Context.Up_Context_Environmental.DeviceCharacteristic .Up_Hardware.support_image $\wedge \neg$ UserProfile.Up_Context.Up_Context_Environmental.DeviceCharacteristic .Up_Hardware.support_Text $\wedge$ UserProfile.blind_man $\rightarrow$t9 Delete (ClientPage.Media.image

APPENDIX C: ADAPTATION RULES OF SOUND MEDIA

R10: UserProfile.mal_entendant $\vee \neg$ UserProfile.Up_Context.Up_Context_Environmental.DeviceCharacteristic .Up_Hardware.support_sound $\vee$ $\exists$ClientPage.Media.audio.sound.jingle $\rightarrow$t10 Delete_sound(ClientPage.Media.audio).

R11: ClientPage.Media.audio.size_File > UserProfile.Up_Context.Up_Context_Environmental. DeviceCharacteristic .Up_Hardware.memory $\rightarrow$t11 Stereo_to_mono(ClientPage.Media..audio) $\wedge / \vee$ Reduct_sampling(ClientPage.Media..audio) $\wedge/\vee$ Convert_sound(ClientPage.Media..audio, UserProfile. Up_preference. Up_presentation. Charte .Modalite.auditive.format)

APPENDIX D: ADAPTATION RULES OF VIDEO MEDIA

R12: $\neg$ UserProfile.Up_Context.Up_Context_Environmental.DeviceCharacteristic .Up_Hardware. support_Video$\wedge\neg$UserProfile.Up_Context.Up_Context_Environmental.DeviceCharacteristic .Up_Hardware.support_image $\wedge \neg$ UserProfile.Up_Context.Up_Context_Environmental.DeviceCharacteristic. Up_Hardware.support_sound $\rightarrow$t12 Delete_video(ClientPage.Media.video)

This work was previously published in the International Journal of Information Technology and Web Engineering 4(2), edited by Ghazi I. Alkhatib, and Ernesto Damiani, pp. 20-44, copyright 2009 by IGI Publishing (an imprint of IGI Global).

Chapter 8
Automating the Generation of Joins in Large Databases and Web Services

Sikha Bagui
The University of West Florida, USA

Adam Loggins
Zilliant Inc., USA

ABSTRACT

In this data-centric world, as web services and service oriented architectures gain momentum and become a standard for data usage, there will be a need for tools to automate data retrieval. In this paper we propose a tool that automates the generation of joins in a transparent and integrated fashion in heterogeneous large databases as well as web services. This tool reads metadata information and automatically displays a join path and a SQL join query. This tool will be extremely useful for performing joins to help in the retrieval of information in large databases as well as web services.

INTRODUCTION AND RELATED WORKS

As we are working with more and more data, the sizes of databases are getting larger and larger. As businesses are going global, web services are becoming a standard for sharing data (Srivastava et al., 2006; Resende and Feng, 2007). Enterprises are moving towards service oriented

DOI: 10.4018/978-1-60960-523-0.ch008

architectures where several large databases may be layered behind web services, hence databases are having to become adaptable with loosely-coupled, heterogeneous systems (Srivastava et al., 2006) too. In such scenarios of web services and service oriented architectures, which may be dealing with several loosely coupled heterogeneous distributed large databases, it is no longer humanly possible to have handy all the information on all the tables and primary keys in all the large databases. Although considerable work is being done on the challenges associated with web services addressing the problem of multiple web services to carry out particular tasks (Florescu et. al., 2003; Ouzzani and Bouguettaya, 2004), most of this work is targeted towards work-flow of applications, rather than coordinating how data can be retrieved from multiple large databases in web services via SQL (Srivastava et al., 2006). In this paper we try to address one aspect of this problem of retrieving data from multiple heterogeneous large databases using SQL. Specifically, we present a tool that automatically formulates joins by reading the metadata of databases in the context of very large distributed databases or in the context of web services which may employ the use of several large heterogeneous distributed databases.

Let us look at an example of a query presented to a web service:

Suppose a health insurance company needs to verify the salary, health, and travel patterns of a person before determining the amount of health insurance he/she needs to pay. In a web service, this will require joining of several tables. And, of course, no one person will have knowledge of all the primary key/foreign key relationships between the tables to join in the web services.

When databases were smaller, it was possible to have knowledge of most of the tables and primary key/foreign key relationships in databases, and SQL join queries could easily be built by joining tables in databases. But, in large databases layered behind web services, it will not be possible to have knowledge of all the database schemas.

The join operation, originally defined in the relational data model (Codd 1970, 1972), is a fundamental relational database operation, facilitating the retrieval of information from two relations (tables). Writing efficient joins is simple for small databases since few relations are involved and one has knowledge of the complete database schema. But, writing efficient joins is

a challenge in large database scenarios and web services where it may not be possible to have a complete picture of the database schema and it's relations and relationships.

Since joins are one of the most time-consuming and data-intensive operations in relational query processing, joins have been studied extensively in the literature. Mishra and Eich (1992) present a very comprehensive study of works that have been done on joins. Query optimization issues in joins have been discussed by many, for example, Kim et al. (1985), Perrizo et al. (1989), Segev (1986), Swami and Gupta (1988), Yoo and Lafortune(1989), and Yu et al (1985, 1987). More recent works have also focused on devising strategies for distributed join processing, for example, works by Scheuermann and Chong (1995), Rao and March (2004), Michael, et al (2007), Ramesh et al. (2009), Frey et al. (2009), and Zhao et al (2010).

Scheuermann and Chong (1995) introduced an algorithm for join processing in distributed databases that makes use of bipartite graphs. Bipartitie graphs are tuples that can be joined, hence reducing the state of the relations. Rao and March (1997) developed a genetic algorithm-based solution which considers design decisions, communications and local processing costs to determine efficient join processing plans. Michael et al. (2007) showed how to improve performance of distributed joins with the use of Bloom filter based algorithms. However, the authors mention that the full potential of bloom filters has not yet been exploited, especially in the case of multi-joins where the data is distributed among several sites. Ramesh et al. (2009) also worked algorithms for distributed joins using bloom filters. Frey et al. (2009) worked on a distributed join execution mechanism that leveraged modern networking facilities to run joins of arbitrary size in distributed main memory rather than on disk. Zao, et. al (2010) studied the distributed resource allocation problem for synchronous fork and join processing network, with the goal of achieving the maximum total utility of output streams.

These works have to be extended in the context of databases for web services and service oriented architectures. Srivastava, et. al (2006) addresses the problem of query optimization over web services on a much broader scale.

In this paper we present a tool that we have developed that will: (i) read the meta data of databases, that is, search the database model or schema and discover the relationships between the tables using table indexes defined in the database catalogs; (ii) find efficient join paths between the tables to be joined; and, (iii) generate a SQL join query (in ANSI SQL standard).

This rest of the paper is organized as follows: Section two briefly describes relational databases with respect to the join operation; section three presents an architectural overview of our tool; section four presents the configuration details of our tool; section five describes how we tested our tool and presents some results; and section six presents the conclusion. Some relevant code portions are presented in the appendices.

RELATIONAL DATABASES AND THE JOIN OPERATION

In relational databases, data is stored in the form of tables or relations. Each table has information on a particular subject or concept and is composed of a group of "related" attributes. The attributes in a table are all "related" in the sense that they describe the subject or concept of the table. For example, there could be a table called Employee, with attributes emp_lastName, emp_midName, emp_firstName, emp_ssn, emp_birthdate, city, state, homePhone, cellPhone, deptnum, etc. All these attributes describe an Employee. Likewise, there could be another table called Department, with attributes, dept_Name, dept_Number, dept_manager, dept_location, etc. Here again, all these attributes describe a Department. Now, if we want information that is partly in the Employee table and partly in the Department table, for example, if

we want to know which employee is working for a department located in LA, we have to perform a "join" of the Employee table and the Department table on some common attribute (usually the primary key field of one table and the foreign key field of the other table). In this case we would perform this join with a simple SQL query where Employee.deptnum = Department.dept_Number.

Usually, when a join query is composed, one has to determine which tables contain the information needed to answer the query, and has to join those tables by the key fields. This is possible if there are few tables and one has a conceptual idea of the databases. But how do we compose joins when there are hundreds of tables (possibly even distributed), with an unknown (large number) of attributes per table in a database – the scenario for web services. Moreover, the conceptual schema of the databases could be constantly evolving or changing.

So, the join operation is used to combine related tuples from two relations into single tuples that are stored in a resulting new relation. The desired relationship between the tuples or some attributes in the tuples is specified in terms of the join condition. In its simplest form, the join of two tables or relations, R and S is written as:

$$R \bowtie_{r(a) \ominus s(b)} S$$

where $r(a) \ominus s(b)$ defines the join condition; a and b are the attributes, usually the key fields of the respective tables R and S (usually indexed); and $\ominus$ defines the join condition that must hold true between the attributes a and b of R and S, respectively. The $\ominus$ operation can be any one of the following: $=, \neq, >, <, \geq$ or $\leq$. The join condition also includes multiple simple conditions of the form shown above connected with the logical connective AND (Earp and Bagui (2000), Elmasri and Navathe (2007)):

condition AND condition AND condition

AN ARCHITECTURAL OVERVIEW OF OUR TOOL

We developed a tool that extracts configuration information from system tables in databases in web services. The primary keys of the tables in the databases are extracted. Primary key/foreign key relationships are determined. A list of table indexes is also constructed – this information is also obtained from the metadata of the databases. This information is then stored in an XML configuration document. A Java interface is then used to activate a GUI that takes, as input parameters, the names of tables that need to be joined. Then, a search routine is called that generates the table's neighbor nodes (tables) – that is, information on which table is linked to which table. From here, join paths are generated, from where a valid join path is then selected, and the final product is a SQL join query generated from the valid join path.

Below we present the algorithm of our tool.

Algorithm of our tool

Input: Activate GUI, input parameters, that is, the names of the tables that have the final information that is required (tables to be joined).

Output: SQL Query.

Method:

1. For all the metadata in the required database catalogs in web services
   a. Read the primary keys of the tables
   b. Check for primary key/foreign key relationships and generate primary key/foreign key relationship table
2. Call Search Routine
3. Generate join paths
4. Generate SQL query

Figure 1. Architectural overview of our tool

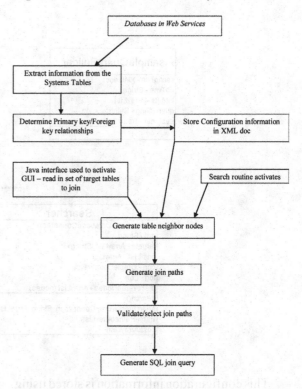

Figure 1 presents the architectural overview of our tool.

TOOL CONFIGURATION DETAILS

The UML class diagram of the tool is presented in Figure 2.

The first step is to extract the list of tables in the database from the information available in the Systems Table of the databases. This is done using the following SQL query:

```
SELECT table_name
FROM System_tables
WHERE table_type = 'TABLE'
```

The next step is to determine the primary key/ foreign key relationships between the tables and indexes used for the relationships. This is done using the SQL queries shown in Box 1.

Figure 2. UML for tool

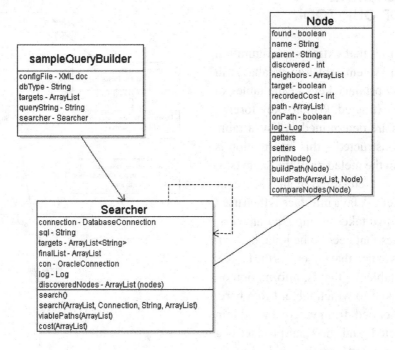

This configuration information is stored using an XML document, presented in appendix 1. The XML document creates a table of the form:

Table(localTable, localColumn, foreignTable, foreignColumn)

Then, a search routine, as can be seen from UML diagram (Figure 2), reads, as input parameters, a list of table names to find relationships between, and searches for the relationships between the tables by looking up the primary key/foreign key relationships between the tables. The code of the Searcher class is presented in appen-

Box 1.

```
SELECT DISTINCT scr.PKTABLE_NAME AS localTable,          scr.PKCOLUMN_NAME AS
localCol,
        scr.FKTABLE_NAME AS foriegnTable,
        scr.FKCOLUMN_NAME AS foriegnCol,
        scr.FK_NAME AS key
FROM System_CROSSREFERENCE scr
WHERE scr.PKTABLE_NAME = '-tablename-'
And,
SELECT DISTINCT scr.PKCOLUMN_NAME AS localCol,
        scr.FKCOLUMN_NAME AS foriegnCol
FROM System_CROSSREFERENCE scr
WHERE scr.PKTABLE_NAME = '-tablename-'
AND scr.FKTABLE_NAME = '-tablename2-'
```

Figure 3. Are these tables linked?

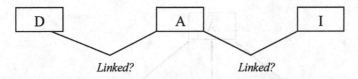

dix 2. The sampleQueryBuilder class develops the GUI. This class takes in the database type (in this case, hypersonic) as the input parameter, the XML configuration file (presented in appendix 1), the table names, and calls the Searcher class, which then creates the nodes.

The Search Routine

The search routine reads, as input parameters, a list of table names to find relationship between, and searches for relationships between the tables. Below we present the algorithm of our search routine.

Algorithm of Search Routine

Until all targets are found

a. Read in the tables to be joined
b. Determine the relationships between the tables
c. For all tables
    i.   Find all neighbors
        ▪ *If targets are found stop else find neighbors of new tables*

For example, let us assume that we have the following tables in a database schema:

{A, B, C, D, E, F, G, H, I, J, K, L}

And assume that you do not know the primary key/foreign key relationships between the tables.

Now, we need information that is partly in table A, partly in table D and partly in table I. That is, we want to see if tables A and D can be joined and if tables A and I can be joined. We need to determine if the following links, as shown in Figure 3, exist.

The algorithm takes the first table: A, and finds all its neighbors. A's neighbors are all the tables that A links to. Now suppose for example, it was found that A's neighbors are B, C, and D, that is, A links to B, C, and D, as in Figure 4.

Figure 4. Neighbors of Table A

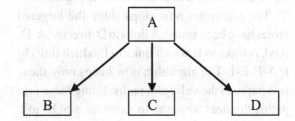

Figure 5. Primary key/Foreign key relationships

TableA(<u>PrimaryKeyOfA</u>, AttributeA1, AttributeA2)

TableB(<u>PrimaryKeyOfB</u>, AttributeB1, PrimaryKeyOfA)

TableC(<u>PrimaryKeyOfC</u>, AttributeC1, PrimaryKeyOfA)

TableD(<u>PrimaryKeyOfD</u>, AttributeD1, PrimaryKeyOfA)

Figure 6. Neighbors of Tables B, C, and D

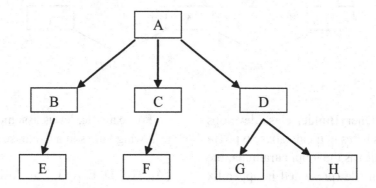

That is, A's primary key is in tables B, C and D as the foreign key, as shown in Figure 5.

So, one of the targeted links have been found, A-D. But, all the targeted links have not been found, so the algorithm keeps running until all the targeted links have been found. So now, the algorithm stores the links A-B, A-C, A-D, as shown in Figure 4.

Next the routine finds the neighbors of tables B, C, and D. Now suppose for example, B's neighbor is E, C's neighbor is F and D's neighbor is G and H. So now we have found the following links A-B, A-C, A-D, A-B-E, A-C-F, A-D-G, A-D-H, as shown in Figure 6.

Next search routine finds the neighbors of E, F, G and H. Now suppose that E links to I and J, and F links to K and L, as shown in Figure 7.

The algorithm now stops since the targeted tables have been found: A links to D directly: A-D. And, A links to B which links to E which links to I: A-B-E-I. The algorithm now keeps only these two paths as the valid join paths. Using these join paths, the next step was to generate a SQL join query.

Generating the SQL Query

Our algorithm to create the SQL join query goes down the shortest join path first. The shortest path is A-B-E-I. So, the joins will be in the form shown in Box 2.

As shown in Figure 8.

TESTING THE TOOL

We tested our tool using the hypersonic database and the Java Business Process Management (JBPM) in the context of web services. The hypersonic database (HSQLDB), freely available on the web at http://www.hsqldb.org/, is a leading SQL relational database engine written in Java. The HSQLDB database engine offers both in-memory and disk-based tables and supports embedded and server nodes.

The JBPM data model, available at http://www.jboss.com/products/jbpm, is a business friendly open source piece of software with an architecture that will run standalone or can be embedded with any Java application. JBPM (or JBOSS JBPM) presently has a fully-formed table schema of 38 tables with multi-table relationships. Figure 9 shows a snapshot of a portion of the complicated multi-table schema of the JBPM data model. These tables house data that record the state of a process as it progresses through its life cycle. The JBPM_ProcessInstance table, for, example, stores the process instance id along with start and end dates; the JBPM_ProcessDefinition table stores the various definitions that are present for use by the application along with their versions.

Figure 7. Neighbors of Tables E, F, G, and H

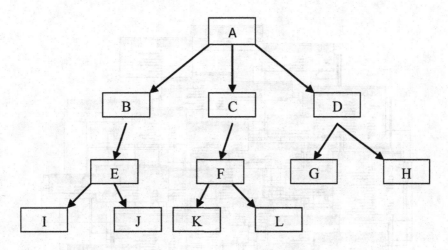

Box 2.

```
        Table A            INNER JOIN        Table
B                  ON            A.X = B.X
        Table B            INNER JOIN        Table
E                  ON            B.X = E.X
        Table E            INNER JOIN        Table
I                  ON            E.X = I.X
        Table A            INNER JOIN         Table
D                  ON            A.X = D.X
```

Figure 8. Join paths

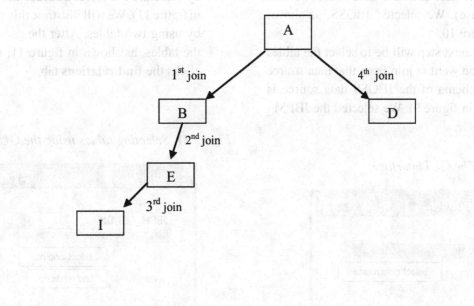

Figure 9. Schema of the JBPM data model

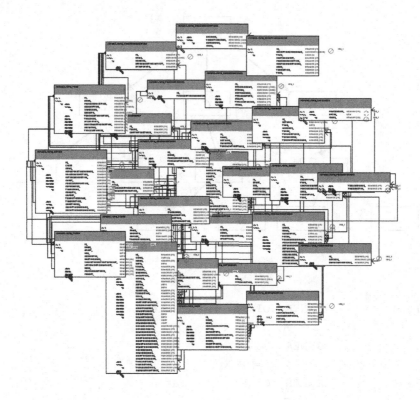

Running the Application

Step 1: From the GUI interface (shown in figure 10), the user selects a data source (of the database). We selected JBOSS, as shown in figure 10.

Step 2: The next step will be to select the tables that you want to join from that data source (the schema of the JBOSS data source is given in figure 9). We selected the JBPM_ ACTION and JBPM_BYTEBLOCK tables. This was an arbitrary selection, and the user can select any table or any number of tables by selecting the **select another** tab (shown in figure 11). We will illustrate this software by using two tables. After the user selects the tables, as shown in figure 11, the user clicks the **find relations** tab.

Figure 11. Selecting tables using the GUI

Figure 10. The GUI interface

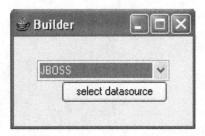

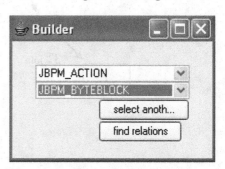

Figure 12. The join path

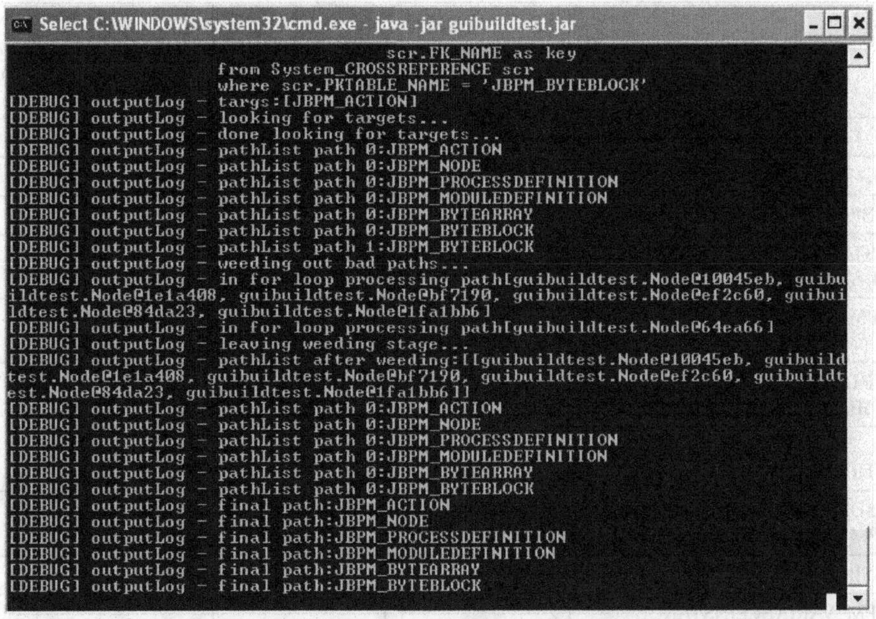

Step 3: Once you click **find relations**, you will get join path displayed in Figure 12.

From Figure 12's output screen we can see that there is join path from the JBPM_ACTION table to the JBPM_NODE table to the JBPM_PROCESS-DEFINITION table to the JBPM_MODULEDEF-INITION table to the JBPM_BYTEARRAY table to the JBPM_BYTEBLOCK table.

This join path generates the ANSI SQL join query shown in Figure 13.

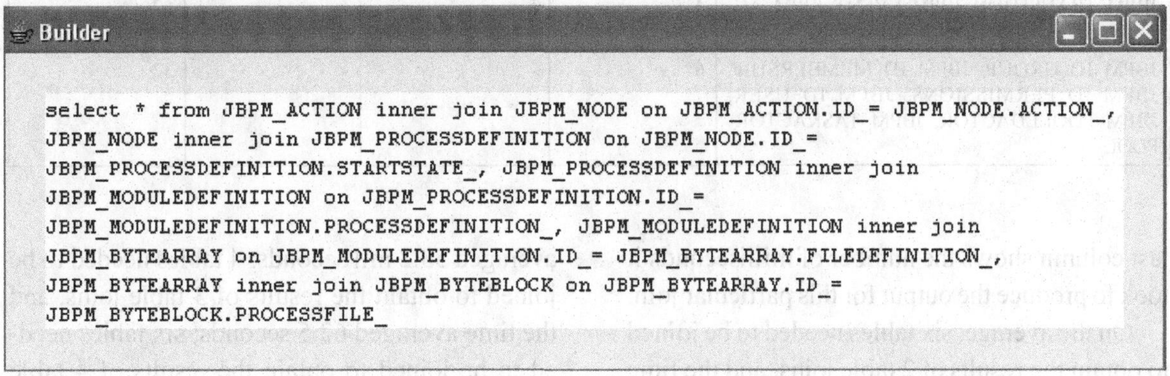

RESULTS

Using the large database, JBPM, we ran several tests to test our software. We present the results of some of the test runs in Table 1. The first column shows the tables that needed to be joined. The second column shows the number of tables that the algorithm needed for the output. The third column shows the resulting number of 2-table joins that the algorithm required for the output. And the

Figure 13. ANSI SQL join query generated

```
select * from JBPM_ACTION inner join JBPM_NODE on JBPM_ACTION.ID_ = JBPM_NODE.ACTION_,
JBPM_NODE inner join JBPM_PROCESSDEFINITION on JBPM_NODE.ID_ =
JBPM_PROCESSDEFINITION.STARTSTATE_, JBPM_PROCESSDEFINITION inner join
JBPM_MODULEDEFINITION on JBPM_PROCESSDEFINITION.ID_ =
JBPM_MODULEDEFINITION.PROCESSDEFINITION_, JBPM_MODULEDEFINITION inner join
JBPM_BYTEARRAY on JBPM_MODULEDEFINITION.ID_ = JBPM_BYTEARRAY.FILEDEFINITION_,
JBPM_BYTEARRAY inner join JBPM_BYTEBLOCK on JBPM_BYTEARRAY.ID_ =
JBPM_BYTEBLOCK.PROCESSFILE_
```

Table 1.

Tables to be joined	Number of tables to be joined	Number of 2-table joins required	Total Number of different tables joined to get result	Number of mil seconds it took to build the query
JBPM_ACTION, JBPM_BYTEARRAY	2	4	8	94
JBPM_ACTION, JBPM_RUNTIMEACTION	2	2	4	32
JBPM_NODE, JBPM_ACTION, JBPM_EVENT	3	2	4	47
JBPM_TASKINSTANCE, JBPM_SWIMLANEIN-STANCE, JBPM_SWIMLANE	3	4	8	47
JBPM_LOG, JBPM_COMMENT, JBPM_PROCES-SINSTANCE	3	4	8	31
JBPM_VARIABLEINSTANCE, JBPM_LOG, JBPM_TOKEN, JBPM_TOKENVARIABLEMAP	4	3	6	31
JBPM_ACTION, JBPM_PROCESSDEFINITION, JBPM_TRANSITION	3	2	4	47
JBPM_PROCESSDEFINITION, JBPM_VARIABLE-INSTANCE, JBPM_PROCESSINSTANCE	3	2	4	94
JBPM_PROCESSINSTANCE, JBPM_NODE	2	2	4	78
JBPM_LOG, JBPM_VARIABLEINSTANCE	2	1	2	31
JBPM_VARIABLEINSTANCE, JBPM_PROCESS-DEFINITION	2	2	4	47
JBPM_ID_PERMISSIONS, JBPM_ID_GROUP	2	-	-	16
JBPM_POOLEDACTOR, JBPM_PROCESSIN-STANCE	2	3	6	62
JBPM_TIMER, JBPM_TASK	2	2	4	31
JBPM_ACTION, JBPM_PROCESSINSTANCE	2	3	6	125
JBPM_PROCESSDEFINITION, JBPM_RUNTIME-ACTION	2	2	4	47
JBPM_PROCESSINSTANCE, JBPM_COMMENT	2	2	4	47
JBPM_SWIMLANE, JBPM_DELEGATION	2	1	2	140
JBPM_ACTION, JBPM_EVENT, JBPM_LOG, JBPM_SWIMLANE, JBPM_SWIMLANEIN-STANCE	5	5	6	204
JBPM_PROCESSDEFINITION, JBPM_PROCES-SINSTANCE, JBPM_NODE, JBPM_TOKEN, JBPM_TASKINSTANCE	5	5	6	266
JBPM_TRANSITION, JBPM_EVENT, JBPM_AC-TION, JBPM_LOG	4	5	6	62
JBPM_ID_GROUP, JBPM_ID_MEMBERSHIP, JBPM_ID_PERMISSIONS, JBPM_ID_USER, JBPM_POOLEDACTOR, JBPM_TASKACTOR-POOL	6	-	-	32

last column shows the number of milliseconds it took to produce the output for this particular join.

On the average, six tables needed to be joined to obtain the results of 2 table joins, and the time averaged 53.2 mil seconds; 4 tables needed to be joined to obtain the results of 3 table joins, and the time averaged 62.5 seconds; six tables needed to be joined to obtain the results of 4 table

Figure 14. Number of mil seconds to build a SQL join query for 2 tables

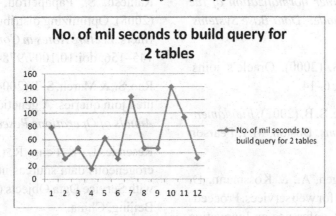

Figure 15. Number of mil seconds to build a SQL join query for 3 tables

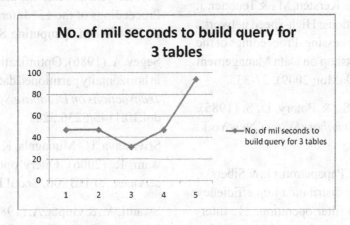

joins, and the time averaged 46.5 mil seconds; six tables needed to be joined to obtain the results of 5 table joins, and the time averaged 235mil seconds.

Figure 14 presents a graphical representation of the number of milliseconds it took to build a query for two table joins, and figure 15 presents a graphical representation of the number of milliseconds it took to build a query for three table joins.

CONCLUSION

This tool will generate join paths and a SQL join query from large databases as well as large databases in web services. The user only needs to know which tables he/she wants to join, but does not have to know the join path needed to join them (the primary key/foreign key relationships between the tables). The software finds the join path between the tables selected, and displays a SQL join query. This software is a very important step forward in the process of retrieving information efficiently from large databases as well as large databases used in Web Services and Service Oriented Architectures.

REFERENCES

Codd, E. (1970). A relational model for large shared data banks. *CACM, 13*, 6.

Codd, E. (1972). *Further normalization of the data base relational model. Data Base Systems.* Prentice Hall.

Earp, R., & Bagui, S. (2000). Oracle's joins. *Oracle Internals, 2*(3), 6–14.

Elmasri, R., & Navathe, S. B. (2007). *Fundamentals of Database Systems.* Boston, MA: Pearson Education.

Florescu, D., Grunhagen, A., & Kossmann, D. (2003). XL: A platform for web services. Proceedings of First Biennial Conference on Innovative Data Systems Research (CIDR).

Frey, P., Gonclaves, R., Kersten, M., & Teubner, J. (2009). Spinning relations: High-speed networks for distributed join processing. Proceedings of the 5th International Workshop on Data Management on New Hardware (DaMon 2009), 27-33.

Kim, W., Reiner, D. S., & Batory, D. S. (1985). *Query Processing in Database System.* New York: Springer-Verlag.

Michael, L., Nejdl, W., Papapetrou, O., & Siberski, W. (2007). Improving distributed join efficiency with extended bloom filter operation. 21st International Conference on Advanced Networking and Applications.

Mishra, P., & Eich, M. H. (1992). Join processing in relational databases. *ACM Computing Surveys, 24*(1), 63–113. doi:10.1145/128762.128764

Ouzzani, M., & Bouguettaya. (2004). A. Efficient access to web services. *IEEE Internet Computing, 8*(2), 34–44. doi:10.1109/MIC.2004.1273484

Perrizo, W., Lin, J. Y. Y., & Hoffman, W. (1989). Algorithms for distributed query processing in broadcast local area networks. *IEEE Transactions on Knowledge and Data Engineering, 1*(2), 215–225. doi:10.1109/69.87961

Ramesh, S., Papapetrou, O., & Siberski, W. (2008). Optimizing distributed joins with bloom filters. *Lecture Notes in Computer Science, 5375,* 145–156. doi:10.1007/978-3-540-89737-8_15

Rao, S., & March, S. T. (2004). Optimizing distributed join queries: A genetic algorithm approach. *Annals of Operations Research, 71*(0), 199–228.

Resende, L., & Feng, R. (2007). Handling heterogeneous data sources in a SOA environment with Service Data Objects (SDO). SIGMOD'07, Beijing, China.

Scheuermann, P., & Chong, E. I. (1995). Distributed join processing using bipartite graphs. Proceedings of the 15th International Conference on Distributed Computing Systems, 385.

Segev, A. (1986). Optimization of join operations in horizontally partitioned database systems. *ACM Transactions on Database Systems, 11*(1), 48–80. doi:10.1145/5236.5241

Srivastava, U., Munagala, K., Widom, J., & Motwani, R. (2006). Query optimization over web services. VLDB '06, Seoul Korea.

Swami, A., & Gupta, A. (1988). Optimizing large join query. Proceedings of SIGMOD, 8-17.

Yoo, H., & Lafortune, S. (1989). An intelligent search method for query optimization by semi-joins. *IEEE Transactions on Knowledge and Data Engineering, 1*(2), 226–237. doi:10.1109/69.87962

Yu, C. T., Chang, C. C., Templeton, M., Brill, D., & Lund E. (1985). Query processing in a fragmented relational database system: Mermaid. IEEE Trans. Software Eng. SE-11 8, 795-810.

Yu, C. T., Guh, K. C., Zhang, W., Templeton, M., Brill, D., & Chen, A. L. P. (1987). Algorithms to process distributed queries in fast local networks. *IEEE Transactions on Computers, C-36,* 10, 1153–1164. doi:10.1109/TC.1987.1676856

Zhao, H., Xia, C. H., Liu, Z., & Towsley, D. (2010).
*Distributed resource allocation for synchronous
fork and join processing networks*. SIGMETRICS.

APPENDIX A

Storing the Configuration Information Using an XML Document

```xml
<?xml version="1.0" encoding="UTF-8"?>
<!--
    Document : configDoc.xml
    Author   : Owner
-->
<config>
        <datasource id="TEST1">
                <driver>org.postgresql.Driver</driver>
                <url>jdbc:postgresql://localhost:5432/TEST1</url>
                <username>postgres</username>
                <password>****</password>
            <type>postgres</type>
        </datasource>
        <datasource id="school">
                <driver>oracle.jdbc.driver.OracleDriver</driver>
                    <url>jdbc:oracle:thin:@unix.cslab.uwf.
edu:1521:STUDENT_COURSE</url>
                    <username></username>
                    <password></password>
        </datasource>
      <datasource id="JBOSS">
      <driver>org.hsqldb.jdbcDriver</driver>
                    <url>jdbc:hsqldb:E:\Graduate_Project\guibuildTest\hy-
personic\localDB</url>
                    <username>sa</username>
                    <password></password>
                    <type>hypersonic</type>
        </datasource>
        <DBType id="oracle">
          <query id="tables">
                select table_name
                from ALL_IND_COLUMNS
            </query>
              <query id="table_relation">
                select con.table_name as localtable,
                    concol.column_name as localColumn,
                    icol.TABLE_NAME as foreignTable,
                    icol.Column_name as foreignColumn,
                    con.Constraint_name as key
                from all_constraints con,
```

```
                    all_ind_columns icol,
                    all_cons_columns concol
                where con.constraint_type = 'R'
                and con.R_constrant_name = icol.Index_Name
                and con.constraint_name = concol.Constraint_Name
          </query>
  </DBType>
  <DBType id="hypersonic">
     <query id="tables">
            select table_name
            from System_tables
            where table_type = 'TABLE'
     </query>
     <query id="table_relation">
            select distinct scr.PKTABLE_NAME as localTable,
                          scr.PKCOLUMN_NAME as localCol,
                          scr.FKTABLE_NAME as foriegnTable,
                          scr.FKCOLUMN_NAME as foriegnCol,
                          scr.FK_NAME as key
            from System_CROSSREFERENCE scr
            where scr.PKTABLE_NAME = '-tablename-'
     </query>
  </DBType>
  <DBType id="postgres">
     <query id="tables">
     select distinct tabs.tablename as table_name
     from pg_catalog.pg_tables tabs
     where tabs.schemaname = 'public'
     </query>
     <query id="table_relation">
     select localTab.tablename as localTable,
           locCol.column_name as localColumn,
           refTab.tablename as foriegnTable,
           refCol.column_name as foriegnColumn,
           keys.FK as key
     from pg_catalog.pg_indexes localTab,
          constraint_column locCol,cvs
          constraint_column refCol,
          pg_catalog.pg_indexes refTab,
          (select locTab.conname as localTabIndex,
                 refTab.conname as foriegnTabIndex,
                 con.conname as FK
          from pg_catalog.pg_constraint con,
               pg_catalog.pg_constraint locTab,
```

```
                              pg_catalog.pg_constraint refTab
                    where con.contype = 'f'
                    and con.conrelid = locTab.conrelid
                    and con.confrelid = refTab.conrelid) keys
            where localTab.indexname = keys.localTabIndex
            and refTab.indexname = keys.foriegnTabIndex
            and locCol.constraint_name = keys.localTabIndex
            and refCol.constraint_name = keys.foriegnTabIndex
            and localTab.tablename = locCol.table_name
            and refTab.tablename = refCol.table_name
            </query>
    </config>
```

APPENDIX B

Code for Searcher Class

```java
/* Searcher.java
*/
package guibuildtest;
import java.sql.*;
import org.w3c.dom.*;
import javax.xml.parsers.*;
import org.apache.commons.jxpath.*;
import java.util.*;
import java.io.*;
/** @author Owner
 */
public class Searcher {
    ArrayList targets;
    String tarDB;
    String searchQuery;
    ArrayList finalList;
    Connection con;
    String sql;
    /** Creates a new instance of Searcher
     */
    public Searcher(ArrayList tList, String DBType, Connection conn, String
sqlR) {
        tarDB = DBType;
        targets = tList;
        finalList = new ArrayList();
        con = conn;
```

```
        sql = sqlR;
    }


    public ArrayList search()
    {
        for(int i=0; i<targets.size(); i++)
        {
            //take the tableName to search
            String tblName = (String)targets.get(i);
            //make a stmt
            try{
                Statement stmt = con.createStatement();
                String runnableSQL = sql.replaceAll("-tablename-", tblName);
                ResultSet rs = stmt.executeQuery(runnableSQL);
            }
            catch(Exception e)
            {

            }
        }
        return finalList;
    }}
```

Chapter 9
Multi–Agent Based Dynamic E–Learning Environment

Saleh Al-Zahrani
De Montfort University, UK

Aladdin Ayesh
De Montfort University, UK

Hussein Zedan
De Montfort University, UK

ABSTRACT

Grids are increasingly being used in applications, one of which is e-learning. As most of business and academic institutions (universities) and training centres around the world have adopted this technology in order to create, deliver and manage their learning materials through the Web, the subject has become the focus of investigate. Still, collaboration between these institutions and centres is limited. Existing technologies such as grid, Web services and agents are promising better results. In this article the authors support building our architecture Regionally Distributed Architecture for Dynamic e-Learning Environment (RDADeLE) by combining those technologies via Java Agent DEvelopment Framework (JADE). By describing these agents in details, they prove that agents can be implemented to work well to extend the autonomy and interoperability for learning objects as data grid.

INTRODUCTION

E-learning has been increasingly used by both academic institutions and businesses for learning and training activities. Various types of e-learning platforms and tools have been introduced in many different education institutions and private training centres. Many technologies include web services (Rodriguez, Anido-Rifon, & Iglesias, 2003), grid computing and data grid technology (Yang & Ho, 2005) and agent technology (Sousa, Silva, Teixeira, & Filho, 2006) have been integrated into e-learning environments to enhance the architecture.

Web services have emerged as a paradigm of distributed computing, and have been proposed as an intermediary framework for the integration of standard compliant e-learning platforms in order to eventually embrace advantage of the benefits offered by their technology (Rodriguez et al., 2003).

Data grid technology is another supporting technology for e-learning services in order to make learning materials such as Learning Objects (LO) sharable by learners in different sites (Yang & Ho, 2005). In data grid, replication services can be used to enhance the performance in reliability, scalability and fault tolerance (Chervenak et al., n.d.) (Guy, Kunszt, Laure, Stockinger, & Stockinger, Edinburgh, Scotland, July 2002.).

Agents can provide both useful abstraction at data grid environment and very dynamic and robust services. Using the agents' essential powers is strongly recommended in grid environments.

MAG (Mobile Agents Technology for Grid Computing Environments) is developed by Federal University of Maranh˜ao, Brazil. The aim of the project is developing free software infrastructure based on mobile agents technology that allows the resolution of computationally intensive problems in computer grids. MagCat extends MAG to handle applications that manipulates huge amount of data. Although the multi-agent system MagCat has its search agent (known as SearchAgent) which is responsible for performing queries in distributed metadata repositories, this agent does not analyse the result of its search (Sousa et al., 2006).

These technologies have not been adopted cooperatively and collaboratively to support e-learning services. Agent and data grid architectures seem different from each other. As a matter of fact, we can learn from one in order to improve the other (Thompson, 2004). E-learning services are composed of many components which are part of distributed systems. These components and the system as a whole are designed to be cooperative. Grid and agent communities are pursuing the development of such distributed systems (Foster,

Jennings, & Kesselman, 2004). In our architecture, we intend to support e-learning services using these technologies.

The organisation of the article is as follows. First, in section II we present a background which includes grid computing and agent and information management. In section III we present an overview of our architecture Regionally Distributed Architecture for Dynamic e-Learning Environment (RDADeLE). This includes descriptions of architecture components and regional grid structure. In section IV, we introduce agents' specifications. This includes MAS-based e-learning, agent architecture, and agents formalisation. In section V, we introduce the implementation which includes the platform, registries and multi-agent systems, and case study. Finally, in section VI we conclude the article and future work.

BACKGROUND

The following is background about the technologies mentioned in the previous section in order to present an introduction and definitions. Those technologies are adopted to be embedded in our model to produce a dynamic e-learning environment. Those technologies include grid computing, agent and its role in data management, and finally learning objects.

Grid Computing

Grid computing provides an environment where a widely distributed scientific and academic community shares its resources across different administrative and organisational domains. The purpose of grid computing is to solve large-scale computing and data-intensive applications and collaborate in a wide variety of disciplines. Grid computing, therefore, enables the creation of a virtual environment which facilitates physical resources across different administrative domains in order to be beneficial; these resources are then abstracted into computing or storage units that can be transparently accessed and shared by large numbers of remote users.

Data grid is concerned with massive datasets and remotely separated storage units organised in a virtual environment. As a result of the increase of learning materials (Learning objects) and the need for huge masses of information to be archived and shared among academic institutions and training centres, data grids become an indispensable technology in learning fields. E-learning platforms and systems have been adopted, developed and published. These platforms and systems are based on client-server, peer-to-peer and web service architectures (Pankratius & Vossen, 2003).

Based on some papers written in grid fields, there are few extant data grid topologies which have been implemented as case studies or prototypes.

One of these topologies is the tree type (Lamehamedi, Shentu, Szymanski, & Deelman, 2003). The European Organisation for Nuclear Research (CERN) has adopted tree topology in its data grid. The CERN project is implemented as a tree topology consisting of three levels; the root (called Tier 0), intermediate (called Tier 1), and user (called Tier 2) levels (Nuclear Research (CERN), 2006). Another architecture which produced a platform using a Sharable Content Object (SCO) repository is based on data grid technology. This platform integrates the technology of data grids and Shareable Courseware Reference Model (SCORM) (Yang & Ho, 2005). Although this architecture uses Globus Toolkit middleware to accomplish learning processes it, does not exploit agent technology in its architecture.

There are two known Data Grid Management System (DGMS) middleware responsible for controlling and managing data grid within the grid environment. The _rst middleware is Storage Resource Broker (SRB). San Diego Supercomputer Center (SDSC) develops this middleware which supports shared collections that can be distributed across multiple organisations and

heterogeneous storage systems (Center, 2005). The second middleware is OGSA-DAI (Open Grid Services Architecture-Data Access and Integration). OGSA-DAI is a middleware product that allows data resources, such as relational or XML databases, to be accessed via web services (Team, 2007).

Agent and Information Management

Agents have many different definitions, one of which is that they are any entities that perceive their environment through sensors and act on that environment based on their own reasoning capability. Examples include human, robotic and software agents (Russell & Norvig, 1995). Agent technology has been exploited heavily on the web through applications in many fields including industry, business, education and training. One of the most famous agent applications is video games, which have become a large part of many people's lives. Applying agent technology in video games has many aspects. One of the obvious benefits of video games is the elimination of risk to human life involved in any real-world application. They also make an excellent testbed for techniques in artificial intelligence (Laird & Lent, 2000).

Information management has an important role in any enterprise system. The Internet and World Wide Web (WWW) refer to massive distributed datasets. If we want these datasets and data to be beneficial, we have to organise them in such way that they can be managed. One of the most well-known methods of managing information is by using agent technology. In the context of information management, the types of agents depend on their purposes and functions. There are three types of agent (Stathis, Bruijn, & Macedo, 2002). The first type is a personal service agent whose purpose is to model the interactions of community members with personal devices, the second type is a location service agent whose purpose is to models the interactions of community members with shared devices placed in specific community locations, and the third type is a memory service agent which models how the information content is stored and disseminated to people or locations. Agent technology has been exploited in e-learning environments for many reasons, especially for integration with other technologies to build more robust, scalable and e_cient systems. Many e-learning architectures have been proposed using integration between agent technologies and web services (Hussain, 27-28 Aug. 2005). Although this architecture integrates agent and web services technologies, it does not exploit data grid technology.

Agent-Based Grid

There are many projects which have been built based on grid, web service, and agent technologies. Those projects were built according to the user and organisation needs. At the same time those projects were produced based on different approaches and techniques. Yet there are some issues not resolved in those projects and at the same time the aim of using agents technology in our model is different from them. These differences will be detailed in the next chapter. The projects include ChinaGrid and ESESGrid (Engineering Structure Experiment and Simulation Grid).

ChinaGrid (Hai Jin and Li Qi, 2005) project is based on Open Grid System Architecture (OGSA) ChinaGrid is designed as four levels architecture. The levels are physical resources level, common support platform level, application support platform level, and applications level. The first level is physical resources level which takes care of all kinds of physical resources, such as computational resources, storage resources. The second level is common support platform level, which its kernel component is ChinaGrid Support Platform (CGSP). It provides the virtualization for the physical resources level and expands from the core of Globus Toolkits. The third level is application support platform level, which provides

the common Problem Solving Environment (PSE) to support the different requirements in various research domains. Application professionals and developers use this level to deploy grid-enabled applications. Finally, the fourth level is applications level, which is the general user interfaces for applications over ChinaGrid, so all requests to ChinaGrid are sent through this level. This level is designed for application users and researchers who need know their application specific knowledge.

ESESGrid (Wang Li, Wang Cong, Long Hao, and Di Rui-Hua, 2008) is designed to share resources for engineering structure researchers in and collaborative work environment. ESESGrid data acquisition system is based on open, common standards and compatible with the relevant norms of WSRF and WS-Notification to build distributed heterogeneous and dynamic resource management in engineering structure research. The structure is composed of four layers. There are local site, agent layer, grid core service layer, and client side. The first layer local site gets real-time experiment data from the experiment centre. The second layer is agent layer, which all agents are responsible for the real-time experimental data management and access. The third layer is grid core service layer. It supports the integration and share of heterogeneous resources. The forth layer is client side which is a means for administrators and common users to use the system.

RDADeLE

RDADeLE architecture was designed to achieve and fulfil objectives and aims designed for agent-based e-learning environment needs. These aims include:

1. Dynamic e-learning environment. This aim is achieved by using active components, agents here, which are responsible for most activities in the environment.

Figure 1. RDADeLE overview

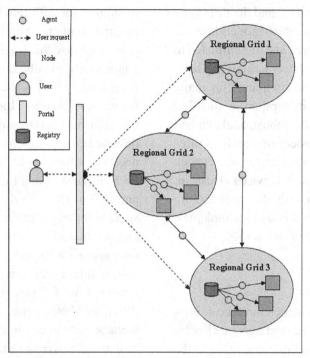

2. More coherent e-learning environment by using multi-agent system technology. Agents within multi-agent system have infrastructure specifying communication and interaction protocols. These protocols support the coherence in RDADeLE.

3. Scalable environment: the number of students, members of learning centres, grid services, and other RDADeLE components are increasing. This why scalable environment is required in order to accommodate all components (agents in our architecture).

4. Interoperable environment: environments in general and e-learning environments in particular are not using the same standards to communicate. Interoperability in e-learning environments plays a big role in communication between components in the same environment or between different environments.

RDADeLE is our architecture, which is different from other and above architectures mentioned in the previous section in many ways. The following is the main difference:

1. RDADeLE is divided into a number of regional grids in which each region has its own components as shown in Figure 1 (Al-Zahrani, Ayesh, & Zedan, 2008). These regional grids have been adopted in RDADeLE for many reasons. It is recommended that massive number of data (data grid) divided into smaller number of segments in order to reduce problems or congestions may occur. Another reason is that such a divided regional grid gives members of each regional grid flexible way to customise the regional grid according to the characteristics of members and environment. Yet another reason is that for any reason if a single regional grid is disconnected from the RDADeLE that will not affect other regional grid in particular and the whole system in general.

2. The multi-agent system is embedded in the RDADeLE. Mulit-agent system has many

Figure 2. Architecture of regional grid node of RDADeLE

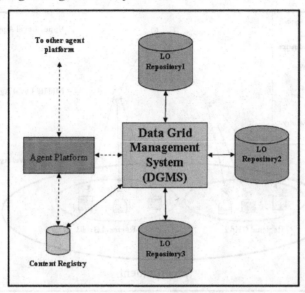

features which strengthen of RDADeLE. These features include coherence, interoperability, and scalability.

3. There are three layers in RDADeLE: learner (user) interface layer, agents' layer, grid service layer. The first layer is the learner interface which is considered as a means for entities outside RDADeLE to communicate to it. The second layer is the agent layer which is the core part of the RDADeLE. There are three types of agent in this layer administrative agent (AA), regional agent (RA), and sensor agent (SA). More details will be provided later in this chapter. Finally the third layer is the grid layer which is data grid management system. This layer is responsible for connecting between learning objects (LOs) repositories in the same regional grid.

Architectural Components

Figure 1 shows an overview of our architecture (RDADeLE) which consists of agents providing the internal structure. These agents are triggered when the state of e-learning environment is changed and when a request is initiated by a user. The user in our architecture refers to an end user or a requester representative. Dotted lines show the request path which travels to regional grids in order to search for LOs. The path also shows the results returned to the user. The portal is a thin client which provides a user interface. The portal is a means to enable the user to send a request and receive a response to and from the system. Using data grid and thin client (portal) enables learners, employees and the general public to search for and collect information about (LOs), learning units (LUs), courses and degree plans from nodes all over e-learning environment. The solid lines show the interaction between system components within each regional grid and between grids themselves. On the one hand, the role of agents within each regional grid is both to help users to search and retrieve LOs and update each regional registry. On the other hand, agents traveling between regional grids are responsible for controlling the data passing between them according to assigned constrains which are part of the regional grids' properties.

The square shapes represent nodes. Nodes represent the locations of servers which provide

Figure 3. Hierarchical agent organisation of MAS-based e-learning

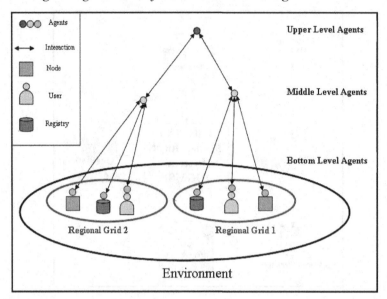

grid services. Grid services include providing educational materials (i.e. Learning Objects LOs). Each regional grid has one or more server which represents one or more academic institution or training centre.

Regional Grid Structure

Regional grids each represent one or more educational institutions and training centres. What concerns us is the grid services provided by these sites. Grid services in our architecture will make repositories of LOs and their metadata available to requesters. Each repository represents an institution or training centre as shown in Figure 3.

Reasons for using grid computing in our architecture (particularly data grid) include the following. Data grid provides an optimal organised platform for massive and remote separated storage units (LOs) in a virtual environment. These LOs are needed to be archived and shared among academic institutions and training centres.

Our purpose in distributing the registries in our architecture is based on an approach which will be explained in this section. There are two approaches which could be adopted in our ar-

chitecture. The first is to create a central global registry. The content of this global registry is the contents of all registries in each regional grid. Users can discover all LOs in all regional grids via the global registry. At the same time, registries in each regional grid are used to discover only that grid's LOs. Users can access global and regional registries to discover LOs. The second approach is based on assigning one regional registry for each regional grid. In this approach there is no central registry with which to discover LOs. Instead, regional registries are used to discover regional LOs. If any regional grid has been disconnected from the global grid other active regional grids will not be affected. In RDADeLE, members (users) of academic institutions or training centres represent the active entities, while the regional grids support the infrastructure:

A member may dynamically connect (join) and disconnect (leave) from RDADeLE.

- Regional grid is supposed always to be connected to RDADeLE.
- Each regional grid has one registry which publishes all LOs of institutions connected to it.

- A registry of a particular regional grid is updated according to the number of LOs repositories which connect or disconnect from the regional grid.
- Each regional grid has its own constraints which are considered part of its properties. Information is passing between regional grids according to these constrains.

Reasons for dividing our architecture into regional grids (regional segments) include the following. Such a division helps produce a sound structure. This gives the designer a flexible approach of constraint-based segments. The other reason is that regional grids could include one or more countries which have common cultural or demographic properties. This will ease the way for any institution or training centre to connect to the regional grid with the similar properties. Yet another reason that dividing our architecture provides a exible constraint setting for particular regional grids, which is useful in utilising each regional grid in particular and the whole global grid in general.

AGENTS' SPECIFICATION

We intend to create dynamic e-learning environment which depends on data grid and multi-agent technologies. In our architecture, services are distributed since each regional data grid has its own registry. However, requests from portal could be massive which affects services to be a bottleneck. Using distributed agents in this context will help in resolving part of this problem. Agents in our architecture have been designed to be intelligent and autonomous. In order to make agents autonomous and have flexible behaviours, they have to be reactive and social. Reactivity means that agents can perceive their environment, and respond in a timely fashion. Agents perceive the learning environment through the requesters (learners or students) and service providers

(institutions). On the other hand, social means that agents are capable of interacting and communicating with other agents and humans. Agents in our architecture from social context satisfy these features in interaction with requesters and in communication with each other. In this section we will present some details of three titles: MAS-based E-learning, Agent Architecture, and Agents Formalisation.

MAS-Based E-Learning

The primary concern of the MAS-based e-learning environment is the interaction of agents themselves and their relationships with their environment. These relationships are created in order to introduce dynamic e-learning environments. Controlling and organising agents' behaviours are another feature in producing a dynamic e-learning environment. The multi-agent platform in Figure 4 (Lee, 2006) plays a major role in relationships between regional grids themselves and between components within each regional grid. The main role of multi-agent systems in regional grids is to build a dynamic, intelligent and collaborative environment.

The multi-agent structure used here is hierarchical (i.e. layered). This approach is ideal for solving large-scale, complex problems. Hierarchical structures have been adopted and studied in many fields of research including scientific computing and business processing. The basic idea of hierarchical structure is that a complex system can be divided into subsystems; the overall behaviour of the system is figured out by its subsystems which perform sub-functions (Simon, 1960). Hierarchical layered MAS has three layers, the upper, middle and bottom levels, as shown in Figure 5.

Agents need to get behavioural instructions, whether from their higher level agents in the hierarchical structure or from other environment components (e.g. learners), and get support from agents in lower-level agents to perform their tasks.

Figure 4. Screen shot of sensor agent

Figure 5. Screen shot of regional agent

In our model, RDADeLE corresponds to the upper level agents (administrative agents). These agents are responsible for controlling and managing other agents at lower levels, who in turn are responsible for regional grids communicating with each other. Regional grids correspond to middle level agents, which are responsible for supporting activities within regional grids. Regional grid components correspond to bottom level agents which are con-

sidered to be sensors of the environment. Table 1 presents Agents Category:

Agent Architecture

Agent architecture is essentially a map of the internals of an agent. Agent architecture includes agent data structure, the operations that may be performed on these data structures, and control

Table 1. Agent catagory

Agent Name	Agent Category	Agent Level
Sensor	Sensor	Bottom Level
Regional	Regional	Middle Level
Administrative	Administrative	Top Level

flow between these data structures. There are many agents' architectures which have been adopted in many applications. These architectures include Logic-Based architecture, Reactive architecture, Belief-Desire-Intention architecture (BDI), Layered architecture, and Deliberative architecture. Subsumption architecture is arguably the best-known reactive agent architecture in which agent decision making is achieved through the interaction of a number of behaviours. Most of the agents in the e-learning environment are subsumption agents. This type of agents is behaviour-based architecture which decomposes complicated intelligent behaviours into many simple behaviours, which in turn organised into layers (Weiss, 1999).

There are two models of agents which could be compared. The first one is that there is only one type of layered architecture which substitutes to do different functions. This type of agent is suitable for homogenous systems. The other type of agent is behaviour-based agents. In our architecture, we intend to adopt behaviour-based agents which are capable of achieve intelligent behaviour. This type of agent suitable for heterogeneous systems.

Agents Formalisation

Based on what we have mentioned, there are three types of agents. The first one is the administrative agents, the second one is the regional agents, and the third one is the sensors agents.

The administrative agents are described as a tuple as follows:

$$AA = < cr, e, a, c > \tag{1}$$

Figure 6. Screen shot of another regional agent

Figure 7. Screen shot of registration of grid service

where:

- cr is a control request.
- e is an entity.
- a is an action.
- c is a constraint (policy).

Administrative agent: This kind of agent works as an information service for the system. It collects and preserves information about the system which includes registered regional grids, registered sensors (learners or users). Also it is responsible for authentication and registering of regional grids. This information helps in searching for grid services (learning objects). The agent is described as <cr, e, a> where cr: is control request, e: entity, and a: action. The control request (cr) includes creating and terminating other agents (regional agents and sensor agents). The entity (e) is either regional agents or sensor agents. Actions (a) which are performed include authentication services, registering and deregistering regional grids, creating grid model.

The second type is the regional agents which again can be described as a tuple as follows:

$$RA = < Rg, l, s, a > \qquad (2)$$

where:

- Rg is a regional grid.
- l is a learning object.
- s is a service.
- a is an action.

Regional agent: This agent type works on behalf of regional grid. Grid services through this agent are presented to help learners to search for desired learning objects. According the constraints the desired learning objects are delivered the learners. The agent is described as <rg, l, s, a, c> where rg: is regional grid, l: learning objects, s: service (grid), a: action, and c: is constraint. The regional grid (rg) is a unique name and the learning object is the description of the desired learning object. The service (s) here is a special agent represents a grid service which is published in regional registry (yellow pages) to be discovered in order to retrieve desired learning object (l). Some actions are performed by this type of agent with cooperation with other agents. Those actions include searching for desired learning

Figure 8. Screen shot of administrative agent

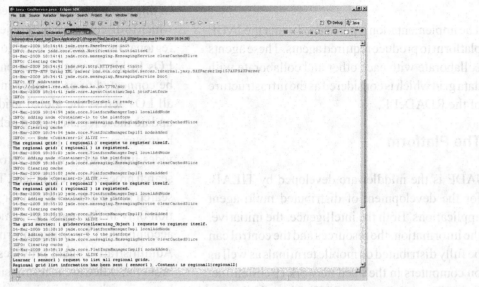

objects, updating regional grid data by authorised staff, and applying constraints to deliver learning objects.

The third type is the sensors agents which can also be described as a tuple as follows:

$$SA = <e, r, st, p>$$ (3)

where:

- e is an entity.
- r is a request.
- st is a state.
- p is a perception.

Sensor agent: This agent works on behalf of learners (users). The agent is described as <e, r, st, p> where e: is entity which is here a learner, r: is request from learner which include searching for learning objects. st: is state of learner which include some properties like unique name, number, institution belongs to, and regional grid belongs to. p: is perception.

In our model, the highest level agents are responsible for monitoring the environment. This means that the primary role of these agents is controlling both the behaviours of a whole environ-

ment and the data passing between regional grids according to assigned constrains. The middle level agents are intermediate ones which are responsible for controlling the behaviour of a regional zone that includes a number of low-level agents.

In a regional grid, possible requests can be represented as a set

$$R = \{r0, r1, r2,...\}$$ (4)

For each user request, there exists constraints which forms a set of constrains:

$$C = \{c0, c1, c2,...\}$$ (5)

Once the agent perceives the request, it executes an action. Agent capabilities can be represented by a set of actions:

$$A = \{a0, a1, a2,...\}$$ (6)

This process of agent action generation can be represented as a function:

$$action : R \ X \ C \rightarrow A \ (or \ an = action \ (rn, cn))$$ (7)

IMPLEMENTATION

The implementation is performed under the JADE platform to produce required agents. These agents collaborate with each other and collaborate with data grid which is considered as the infrastructure of the RDADeLE.

The Platform

JADE is the middleware developed by TILAB[1] for the development of distributed multi-agent applications. Both the intelligence, the initiative, the information, the resources and the control can be fully distributed on mobile terminals as well as on computers in the fixed network (Bellifemine, Caire, Poggi, & Rimassa, 2003). This middleware has some features within its platform. These features include heterogeneous entities communication, security, and Interoperability with other agents. JADE is an ideal platform to implement our model in order to present concepts and objectives of our research. In (Chmiel, Gawinecki, Kaczmarek, Szymczak, & Paprzycki, 2005), authors have proven some features of JADE platform. These features include efficiency, effective, and scalability. The features are limited by standard limitations of Java programming language and other factors which include processor speed, amount of available memory and speed of network connection. Experiments with thousands of agents and thousands of ACL messages had been implemented effectively. Hence, these features of JADE platform are needed in our model in order to present concepts and objectives of our research, and we see this platform is suitable to implement part of our model.

Registries and Multi-Agent Systems

As we have mentioned before in this article, we have adopted the second approach of registries distribution. This approach is based on assign-ing one regional registry for each regional grid. In this approach there is no central registry with which to discover learning objects (LOs). Instead, regional registries are used to discover regional LOs. In this approach, all regional registries should be connected to each other in order to discover all LOs across the global grid. Agents in MAS update these registries and help to communicate between registries. However, this approach provides information service in order to handle the search process more efficient. This means that the search process will search for required information only in the registries which have it. This is accomplished by using information service the Administrative agent provides in the system. A broker middleware is responsible for connection between regional registries and universal Description, Discovery and Integration (UDDI) in order.

Implementation Scenarios

The implementation is limited to the role of agents in our architecture. As we mentioned earlier, the following includes three types of agents and their roles in the implementation:

1. **Sensor (user):** This agent represents a learner or a user who sends a query. The query includes LOs, universities or institution connected to the global grid, and a degree (major).
2. **Regional:** This agent represents a regional grid. The role of this type of agents is to connect LOs registry of a particular regional grid to the global grid in order to make it available to be queried. Regional grids need to be registered using Administrative to be authenticated and connected to the global grid.
3. **Administrative:** This type of agent has two roles. The first one is to supply authentication and authorisation services for different regional grids to be connected to the global grid. The second role is to function as an

Figure 9. Illustrates the chart of processes of agents in our model

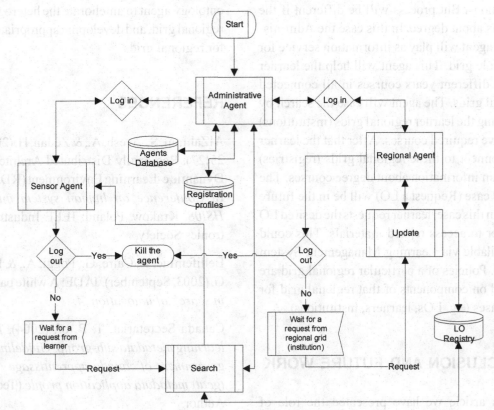

information service for the whole global grid to ease the search process and make it more efficient.

The cooperation of the developed multi-agent system begins when Administrative agent has been initiated. First, a regional agent is initiated to be authenticated and authorised using initiated Administrative agent in order to connect regional grid to the global grid. This means that a particular regional grid has been connected to the global grid which implies that registry of that regional grid has been connected to the whole system in order to be available for learners to be queried. The agent Administrative is responsible for registering and authentication of regional grids. It the same time, Administrative agent plays as information service which includes information about all connected regional grids all over global grid. Second, a learner agent is initiated to represent

a learner. The learner should be authenticated by authentication and authorisation agent in order to access to (LOs) via OGSA. At this time, learner may search for LO, connected institutions, and degree. On the other hand, authorised persons (staff) should be authenticated by Administrative agent in order to update and amend regional and institution registries. According to a learner request and the portal, a query could be:

• About LOs, institutions, and degree.
• Request a LO.

In the first case, a Sensor agent send a query about a LO. The search process will be initiated to search for the required LO. The required LO is determined by a field and subject from learner. The search process looks for all LO and their locations from all registries of connected regional grid and bring back search result to the learner.

The same process will occur if the query about institutions. But process will be different if the query is about degree. In this case the Administrative agent will play as information service for the whole grid. This agent will help the learner to find different years courses in all connected regional grids. The agent will ease the search by providing the learner regional grids (institutions) that have required courses. After that the learner will connect to these regional grids (registries) to obtain information about degree courses. The second case (Request a LO) will be in the future work. In this case, learner requests the desired LO in order to access related materials. This could be available via Learning Management System (LMS). Policies of a particular regional grid are applied on components of that regional grid for both cases (e.g. LOs, learners, institutions).

CONCLUSION AND FUTURE WORK

In this article we have presented the role of multi-agent system in Regionally Distributed Architecture for Dynamic e-Learning Environment (RDADeLE). This article, mainly describes in details the role of agents in regional data grids; the agent role is based on multi-agent systems using JADE to guarantee autonomy, interoperability, and reliability in the whole system. We began the article by highlighting two factors: grid computing and agent technology. Secondly, we presented an overview of our architecture Regionally Distributed Architecture for Dynamic e-Learning Environment (RDADeLE), its components, and regional grid structure. Then, we presented agents' specifications. Finally, we introduced the implementation. Implementation performance was analysed, and some practical applications and further experiments remain to be performed in the future. The next steps of our project are incorporating OGSA-DI in order to produce grid services, ameliorating the performance of the whole project in general and refining search result in particular, developing an ontology agent to ameliorate the heterogeneity of regional grid, and developing appropriate policies for regional grids.

REFERENCES

AlZahrani, S., Ayesh, A., & Zedan, H. (2008, May 25{27). Regionally Distributed Architecture for Dynamic e-Learning Environment (RDADeLE). In *Conference on human system interaction HSI08*, Krakow, Poland: IEEE Industrial Electronics Society.

Bellifemine, F., Caire, G., Poggi, A., & Rimassa, G. (2003, September). JADE: A white paper. EXP *in search of innovation, 4.*

Canada Secretariat, T. B. of. (2004). *Imrc - e-learning metadata sub-group: Guidelines for the government of canada apprentissage / training (gcat) metadata application profile* (Tech. Rep.). Author.

Center, S. D. S. (2005). *SRB the sdsc Storage Resource Broker* (Tech. Rep.). University of California, San Diego.

Chervenak, A. L., Deelman, E., Foster, I. T., Guy, L., Hoschek, W., Iamnitchi, A., et al. (n.d.). Giggle: a framework for constructing scalable replica location services. In *Proceedings of ieee supercomputing conference, 2002* (pp. 1-17). IEEE Computer Society.

Chmiel, K., Gawinecki, M., Kaczmarek, P., Szymczak, M., & Paprzycki, M. (2005). Efficiency of JADE agent platform. *Scientific Programming, 13*(2), 159-172.

Educational Communications, A. for, & Technology, B. (2000). *Connecting learning objects to instructional design theory: A definition, metaphor and taxonomy* (Tech. Rep.). Author.

Foster, I. T., Jennings, N. R., & Kesselman, C. (2004). Brain meets brawn: Why grid and agents need each other. In *Aamas* (pp. 8-15). IEEE Computer Society. Available from http://csdl.computer.org/comp/proceedings/aamas/2004/2092/01/20920008abs.htm

Guy, L., Kunszt, P., Laure, E., Stockinger, H., & Stockinger, K. (Edinburgh, Scotland, July 2002.). *replica management in data grids* (Tech. Rep.). Global Grid Forum Informational Document, GGF5.

Hussain, M., & Khan, N. (2005, August 27-28). Service-oriented e-learning architecture using web service-based intelligent agents. *First International Conference on Information and Communication Technologies, 2005, ICICT,* (pp. 137-143).

Koper, R. (2001). *Modeling units of study from a pedagogical metamodel behind eml* (Tech. Rep.). Open University of the Netherlands.

Laird, J., & Lent, M. V. (2000). Human-level AI's killer application: Interactive computer games. *The AI Magazine, 22*(2), 15-25.

Lamehamedi, H., Shentu, Z., Szymanski, B. K., & Deelman, E. (2003, April 22-26). Simulation of dynamic data replication strategies in data grids. In *Proceedings of 17th international parallel and distributed processing symposium (IPDPS-2003)* (pp. 100-100). Los Alamitos, CA: IEEE Computer Society.

Lee, J. (2006). *Design collaboration as a framework for building intelligent environments.* Unpublished doctoral dissertation, University of Illinois.

McClelland, M. (2003). *Metadata standards for educational resources, 36*(11), 107-109. Available from http://dx.doi.org/10.1109/MC.2003.1244540

Nuclear Research (CERN), E. O. for. (2006). *Global grid service for lhc computing succeeds in gigabyte-per-second challenge* (Tech. Rep.). Author.

Pankratius, V., & Vossen, G. (2003, October). Towards E-learning grids: Using grid computing in electronic learning. In *Proc. ieee workshop on knowledge grid and grid intelligence, ieee/wic international conference on web intelligence / intelligent agent technology* (pp. 4-15). Halifax, Nova Scotia, Canada: Saint Mary's University. Available from citeseer.ist.psu.edu/pankratius-03towards.html

Polsani, P. (2003, February). Use and abuse of reusable learning objects. *Journal of Digital Information, 3*(4). Available from http://jodi.ecs.soton.ac.uk/Articles/v03/i04/Polsani

Project, T. U. (2005). *Open elearning standards. how learning design can be used* (Tech. Rep.). Author.

Rodriguez, J. S., Anido-Rifon, L. E., & Iglesias, M. J. F. (2003). How can the web services paradigm improve the E-learning? In *The 3rd ieee international conference on advanced learning technologies, 2003, proceedings. icalt '03* (p. 479). IEEE Computer Society. Available from http://csdl.computer.org/comp/proceedings/icalt/2003/1967/00/19670479abs.htm

Russell, S., & Norvig, P. (1995). *Artificial intelligence: A modern approach.* Prentice Hall.

Simon, H. A. (1960). *The new science of management decision.* New York: Harper and Brothers.

Sousa, B. B. de, Silva, F. J. da Silva e, Teixeira, M. M., & Filho, G. C. (2006). Magcat: An agent-based metadata service for data grids. In *Ccgrid* (p. 6). IEEE Computer Society. Available from http://doi.ieeecomputersociety.org/10.1109/CC-GRID.2006.153

Stathis, K., Bruijn, O. de, & Macedo, S. (2002). Living memory: agent-based information management for connected local communities. *Interacting with Computers, 14*(6), 663-688. Available from http://dx.doi.org/10.1016/S0953-5438(02)00014-0

Steinacker, A., Ghavam, A., & Steinmetz, R. (2001, January). Standards: Metadata standards for Web-based resources. *IEEE MultiMedia, 8*(1), 70-76. Available from http://dlib.computer.org/mu/books/mu2001/pdf/u1070.pdf

Team, T. O.-D. P. (2007). *The ogsa-dai project* (Tech. Rep.). The OGSA-DAI Project.

Thompson, C. W. (2004). Agents, grids, and middleware. *IEEE Internet Computing, 8* (5), 97-99. Available from http://doi.ieeecomputersociety.org/10.1109/MIC.2004.32

Weiss, G. (Ed.). (1999). *Multiagent systems - A modern approach to distributed artificial intelligence.* Cambridge, MA, USA: The MIT Press.

Yang, C.-T., & Ho, H.-C. (2005, 29 March-1 April). A shareable e-learning platform using data grid technology. In *The 2005 ieee international conference on e-technology, e-commerce and e-service, 2005. eee '05. Proceedings* (pp. 592-595). IEEE Computer Society.

Hai, J., & Li, Q. (2005). ChinaGrid and its impact to science and education in China. *Collaborative Computing: Networking, Applications and Worksharing, 2005 International Conference on,* 9. URL: http://ieeexplore.ieee.org/stamp/stamp.jsp?arnumber=1651208&isnumber=34623

Wang, L., Wang, C., Long, H., & Di, R-H. (2008, August). An Adaptive MAS-Based Data Acquisition Model in ESESGrid. *ChinaGrid Annual Conference, ChinaGrid '08,* (pp.218-222, 20-22).

ENDNOTE

[1] Telecom Italia Lab is the R&D branch of the Telecom Italia Group and is responsible for promoting technological innovation by scouting new technologies, carrying out and assessing feasibility studies, and developing prototypes and emulators of new services and products. Telecom Italia has conceived and developed JADE, and originated the Open Source Community in February 2000.

This work was previously published in the International Journal of Information Technology and Web Engineering 4(2), edited by Ghazi I. Alkhatib, and Ernesto Damiani, pp. 61-77, copyright 2009 by IGI Publishing (an imprint of IGI Global).

Chapter 10
Analysis of Quality of Service Routing Algorithms

E. George Dharma Prakash Raj
Bharathidasan University, India

Sinthu Janita Prakash
Cauvery College for Women, India

S. V. Kasmir Raja
SRM University, India

ABSTRACT

The routing problems can be divided into two major classes. They are 1) Unicast routing and 2) Multicast routing. The Unicast routing problem is as follows. Given a source node sr, a destination node dn, a set of QoS constraints qc and an optimization goal (optional), find the best feasible path from sr to dn, which satisfies qc. The Multicast routing problem is as follows. Given a source node sr, a set st of destination nodes, a set of constraints cts and an optimization goal (optional), find the best feasible path covering sr and all nodes in st, which satisfies cts. This article presents two such Unicast QoS based algorithms called as Source Routing and the proposed Heuristic Routing. A Client Server based model has been generated to study the performance of the two algorithms with respect to the message overhead, response time and path delay. The Experiments and the results are analyzed.

INTRODUCTION AND RELATED WORK

The Internet Community today needs multimedia communication than the traditional, well known Internet Protocol (IP) infrastructure. IP has proven to be very effective since no privileged service classes are considered, but it is not adequate for the introduction of "Quality of Service" (QoS). QoS communications on the internet are high speed connections and the goal of QoS routing is to find routes that satisfy the requirements of individual flows and to provide quality multimedia communications.

In Computer communication networks, data packets are forwarded between different nodes. Multiple paths may exist from the start node to the destination node. Due to the different qualities of links and traffic load variations, different paths may have different performance related Quality of Service properties, such as delay, response time, overhead, etc. Finding a path that satisfies some given QoS constraints is the base of QoS routing (Chen & Nahrstedt, 1998; Zhang, Sanchez, Salkewicz, & Crawley, 1996).

The routing problems can be divided into two major classes. They are 1. unicast routing and 2. multicast routing. The unicast routing problem is as follows. Given a source node sr, a destination node dn, a set of QoS constraints qc and an optimization goal (optional), find the best feasible path from sr to dn, which satisfies qc (Zheng, Tian, Liu, & Dou, 2004. (Koundinya, Negi, & Sastry, 2004). The multicast routing problem is as follows (Yuan & Liu, 2001; Moen, & Pullen, 2007; Moen, & Pullen, 2005; Moen, Pullen, & Zhao, 2004; Simon, & Pullen, 2003; Moen & Pullen, 2003). Given a source node sr, a set st of destination nodes, a set of constraints cts and an optimization goal (optional), find the best feasible path covering sr and all nodes in st, which satisfies cts.

This article presents two such unicast QoS based algorithms called as Source Routing and the proposed Heuristic Routing. A Client Server based model has been generated to study the performance of the two algorithms with respect to the message overhead, response time and path delay. The Experiments and the results are analyzed.

SOURCE ROUTING

Source routing is a method of transferring a packet through a network in which the path is already determined by the source. The information about the packet is stored in the packet itself in source routing. Whenever a packet arrives at a switch-

ing device, the decision to forward it to the next node is not needed since they are all stored in the packet itself. The device simply looks at the packet header in the packet in order to determine the port on which it should forward the packet. Source routing denotes that the source knows about the topology of the network, and hence can specify a path (Ye Tian, 2002).

HEURISTIC ROUTING

Heuristic routing is a Routing method in which the data, such as path delay, response time and message overhead, extracted from incoming packets during specific time intervals and with different loads are used to determine the optimum routing for transmitting data back to the source. A heuristic routing scheme called as the Label Based Probing is proposed in this work (Yuan & Liu, 2001; Kweon & Shin, 1999; Chen & Nahrstedt, 1998).

In this routing, the source is not expected to have all the information about how to get from the source to the destination. It is sufficient for the source to know only about how to get to the next node, and so on until the destination is reached. The processing in the nodes in between the source and the destination in this case is more complicated. It has only the address of the destination rather than a complete specification of the route by the source node.

The working of the Label based distributed routing algorithm is as follows. When a connection request arrives at the source node, a certain number of "l" labels are generated and a probe packet with the "l" labels is sent to the destination in search of paths that satisfy the QoS constraints. Each probe packet carries one or more labels. Whenever an intermediate node receives a probe packet, it does the following. It searches the routing table and finds the next node that can establish connections for the request. Then it calculates the number of labels to be distributed for each of the next nodes, and finally sends a probe packet with the labels to each of the next nodes. A probe fails if there is no outgoing link that can satisfy the QoS requirement. When a probe packet reaches the destination, a path that can satisfy the QoS requirement is found. The algorithm controls the messaging overhead by manipulating the number of labels. Since intermediate nodes only distribute the labels but not generate any new labels, the maximum number of probe packets at any time is bounded by number of labels. Since each probe packet probes a path, the maximum number of paths probed is also bounded by the number of labels. Connecting a label based routing and forward reservation is simple. Whenever a connection request arrives at the source, the source node immediately sends a reservation packet with "l" labels to the destination. The reservation packet goes through the network and reserves resources along the path. A reservation packet fails when there is no available resource to support the QoS requirement. When the reservation packet reaches the destination, the destination sends an accept packet to inform the source and the intermediate nodes that this connection has been established. When the accept packet reaches the source, the source can start sending data. Once the source finishes sending data, it sends a release packet to release the resources along the path for the connection.

THE NETWORK

A point to point communication network is represented as a directed, connected, simple network $N = (V;E)$, where V is a set of nodes and E is a set of directed links. A node i is assumed to have the local state about all outgoing links. The state information of link(i,j) includes three parameters. They are given as follows.

1. delay (i,j) is the delay of the link, including propagation delay and the queuing delay.
2. bandwidth (i,j) is the unused bandwidth of the link and

3. cost (i,j) which can a hop count or a function of the link utilization.

The delay, bandwidth, and cost of a path $P = i - j - ... k - l$ are defined as follows:

*   delay(P) = delay(i,j) +...+.... delay (k,l)
*   bandwidth(P)={bandwidth(i,j)+...+... bandwidth(k,l)}
*   cost(P) = cost(i,j) + ...+..... cost(k,l)

SOURCE QoS ROUTING ALGORITHM

The flowchart for the Source Routing method used for the Client Server model is given in Figure 1.

The algorithm followed in the client server model for Source QoS Routing algorithm is as follows.

1. The client router first tries to find two paths, one that is going out of the server and the other ,a path that is coming into the server. This is found in this model using the Dijsktra's Shortest Path Algorithm. There is a need to find two paths since the QoS requirements may be different for each direction. For example, the server might be a multimedia file that responds to requests from the client that denotes that the incoming path needs more bandwidth allocated to it than its outgoing line. The outgoing and incoming paths could be formed by different links since traffic and resource conditions are not the same usually in both directions.
2. If any one of the path (outgoing or incoming) is not found, then the client is informed and the connection process stops.
3. Otherwise, the client router immediately issues an unused ID that is randomly generated to the connection and makes an entry in the routing table. This is done in order to

161

Figure 1. Flowchart for source QoS routing algorithm

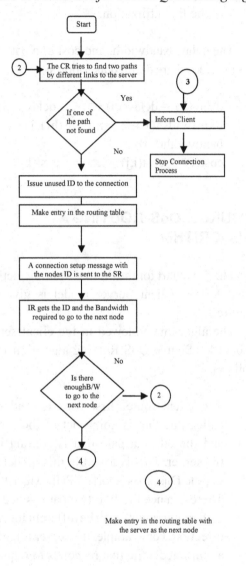

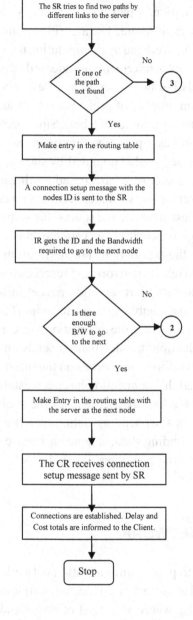

record where packets are to be forwarded and the amount of bandwidth allocated to it.

4. A message relating to the connection setup with the IDs of the nodes that form the outgoing path and the QoS constraints for both directions is then sent along the path to the server. This is done in order to reserve and allocate bandwidth for this connection.

5. The Intermediate routers are nodes, other than the client and server routers, in an outgoing or incoming path. When a connection setup message arrives, the intermediate node gets the ID and the bandwidth required for the next node.

6. If there is enough bandwidth along the outgoing path to the next node, an entry is made in the routing table. Also, the appropriate

delay and the cost of the connection setup message are updated, and the message is forwarded.

7. When a connection setup message is received by the server, the previous node makes an entry in the routing table with the server as the next node in the path.

8. Next, the server performs a source based search for a path that meets the incoming bandwidth availability. If successful, it issues an ID that is randomly generated to the connection going in the opposite direction. A routing table entry is done for the second time.

9. A connection setup message with the incoming path, total delay and cost information present in the old message is sent back to the client router.

10. If enough bandwidth is available, the client router finally receives the connection setup message generated by the server router.

11. This indicates that both the client side and the server side connections are ready and that the client can be informed of the delay and cost totals.

SOURCE QoS ROUTING: ADVANTAGES AND DISADVANTAGES

The source routing is simple in a way that it transforms a distributed problem into a centralized one. The methodology of source routing is that the source node calculates the entire path locally by maintaining a complete reserved global state. This actually avoids the distributed computing problems such as deadlock detection problem. Many source routing algorithms are very simple and easy to implement, evaluate, debug and upgrade.

The source routing has some disadvantages also. The global state maintained at every node has to be updated frequently. This is done to adjust to the dynamics of network parameters such as

bandwidth and delay. It makes the communication overhead to a great extent for relatively large scale networks. The computation overhead at the source is also excessively high. This is the problem in the case of multicast routing or when multiple constraints are involved. Finally, the source routing has the scalability problem. It is not practical for any single node to have access to the detailed state information about all nodes and all links in a large network.

HEURISTIC QoS ROUTING ALGORITHM

The proposed Heuristic QoS Routing algorithm uses Label based probing method. A short note on probes is given below before proposing the algorithm for Heuristic QoS Routing.

Probes are nothing but routing messages. The basic idea of probing is as follows. Several probes are sent from the start node to the destination node. Each probe is forwarded independently according to some QoS metrics. At the destination node, every received probe represents a possible route. From the set of the received probes, the one that satisfies the given QoS constraints is selected. Furthermore, since multiple probes are used for one routing request, more than one path can be explored.

The flowchart for the proposed Heuristic QoS Routing method is given in ..

The algorithm followed in the Client Server model for Heuristic QoS Routing is as follows.

1. A request message is sent to the server when a connection request arrives at the client.

2. When the server receives the request message, it issues a certain number of n labels and sends probes, containing the labels, to the client router again.

3. In order to search for good paths in terms of delay and cost, y labels are colored yellow and g labels are colored green. Yellow labels

Figure 2. Flowchart for heuristic QoS routing algorithm

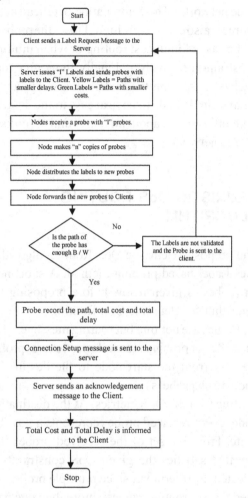

prefer paths with smaller delays, while green labels prefer paths with smaller costs.

4. Whenever a node receives a probe pr with N(pr) labels, it makes at most N(pr) copies of pr. It also distributes the labels among the new probes, and forwards them along the selected outgoing paths towards the client.

5. The Probes can travel only along the paths that satisfy the bandwidth constraint. If a probe arrives at a node whose outgoing paths cannot give the requested bandwidth, its label(s) are not validated, and the probe is sent to the client.

6. Each probe records the path, total cost, and total delay of the path it explores. This is

done since it can choose the best valid path when the client receives all labels.

7. Once a path has been selected, a connection setup message is sent to the server. The message sent in Heuristic Routing is different from those used in Source Routing in the sense that it reserves and allocates bandwidth for an incoming connection, and at the same time the message travels in the outgoing path also.

8. When the connection setup message is received by the server, it replies with an acknowledgment message depending on the result.

9. Finally, when the client receives the acknowledgement for connection, the total delay and cost of the incoming path in the client is informed.

HEURISTIC QoS ROUTING ALGORITHM: ADVANTAGES

In this routing, the computation of paths is in a distributed manner among the intermediate nodes between the source and the destination. This makes the routing response time shorter and makes the algorithm more scalable. The searching of multiple paths in parallel for a feasible one is made in this algorithm, which increases the chance of success. Most of the existing Heuristic routing algorithms require each node to maintain a global network state based on which the routing decision is made on a hop by hop manner

EXPERIMENTS AND EVALUATIONS

A Client Server model is developed using VC++ for Source and Heuristic QoS routing Algorithms. The model has been designed in such a manner that it is very easy to use and at the same time very efficient also. The source is assumed as

Figure 3. The network topology

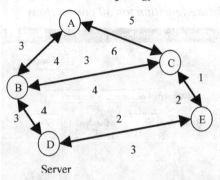

Server

the Client and the destination as the Server. The connections were made based on the network topology as given below in Figure 3.

Experiments were conducted to compare the performance of the Source Routing and label based QoS routing algorithms based on three metrics namely the average message overhead, the average response time and the average path delay. When the Number of requests and the bandwidth are given as input, the three metrics are evaluated based on the following definitions.

1. Average message overhead = total number of routing messages sent / cr,

2. Average response time = time to handle all requests (accept or reject) / cr,

3. Average path delay = total cost of all established connection paths / ecp and where cr is the total number of connection requests and ecp is the number of established connection paths.

The Figure 4 shows the working of the QoS based Source Routing Algorithm. The figure depicts the working of the client server model when the connection requests are given as 10 and the bandwidth is given as 256. The corresponding values of the response time, message overhead and the path delay are computed and are displayed in the figure.

The Figure 5 shows the working of the client server model developed for the QoS based Source QoS Routing Algorithm for 30 requests. In the model developed, when the connection request is given as 30 and the bandwidth is given as 512 respectively, the response time, the message overhead and the path delay are computed and are shown in the figure.

The Figure 6 shows the working of the client server model developed for the QoS based Heu-

Figure 4. The client server model for the QoS based source routing with 10 requests

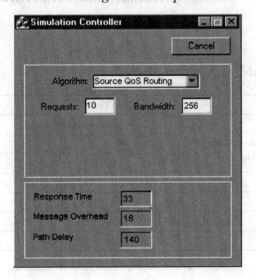

Figure 5. The Client Server model for the QoS based Source Routing with 30 requests

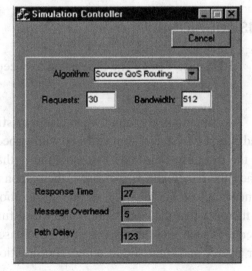

Figure 6. The Client Server model for QoS based Heuristic Algorithm for 20 connections

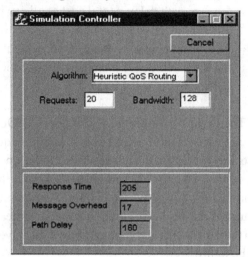

Figure 7. The Client Server model for QoS based Heuristic Algorithm for 30 connections

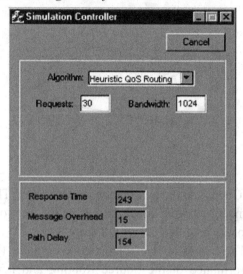

ristic QoS Routing Algorithm for 20 connections. In the figure when the connection request is given as 20 and the bandwidth is given as 128 respectively, the response time, the message overhead and the path delay are computed and are shown in the figure.

Figure 7 displays the computed result of response time, message overhead and path delay when the connection request is given as 30 and the bandwidth is given as 1024 for the QoS based Heuristic Routing Algorithm.

DISCUSSIONS

1. **Response Time** (The time taken to accept or reject a connection)

Two situations are found when the Heuristic and Source based algorithms are used with respect to the response time. The first situation is that when the bandwidth is increased, the response time shoots up initially. The second observation is that as when the bandwidth is increased further, it is seen that the response time decreases for Source and Heuristic Routing. The situation

that affects the Heuristic Routings response time is that the probes carrying the labels may have to travel along difficult paths and take longer times to reach the destination. The table given below shows the complete list of readings when 10, 20 and 30 connection requests are done for Heuristic and Source Routing with respect to the Response Time. The corresponding graphs for each of the connections as given in Table 1 are given in Figures 8, 9 and 10 respectively.

2. **Message Overhead** (Number of messages)

Table 1. Response time

Average Bandwidth (kbps)	Response Time (ms)					
	Connection Requests					
	10		20		30	
	S	H	S	H	S	H
64	4	32	3	72	2	81
128	14	174	31	205	32	189
256	33	202	31	188	33	205
512	20	248	22	221	27	231
1024	19	220	25	264	22	243

Figure 8. Response Time for 10 connections

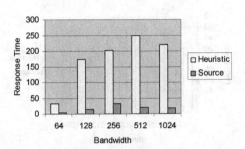

Figure 9. Response Time for 20 connections

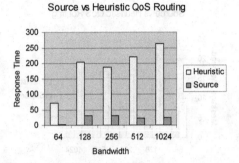

As presented in Table 2, the average message overhead of source based routing is always lower than Heuristic routing. This is because the labels in a Heuristic Routing algorithm may travel along multiple paths instead of the single path produced by the Source Routing algorithm. The table below shows the complete list of readings taken from the Client Server model that is developed for 10,

20 and 30 connection requests with respect to the Message Overhead. The corresponding graphs for each of the connections are also given below.

3. **Path Delay** (Total cost of all established connection paths)

Figure 10. Response Time for 30 connections

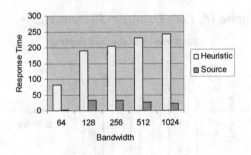

Table 2. Message overhead

Message Overhead (Number of messages)						
Average Bandwidth (kbps)	Connection Requests					
	10		20		30	
	S	H	S	H	S	H
64	12	17	4	9	2	4
128	13	24	7	17	4	10
256	16	26	8	16	5	11
512	16	28	7	17	5	13
1024	16	27	6	21	4	15

Figure 11. Message overhead for 10 connections

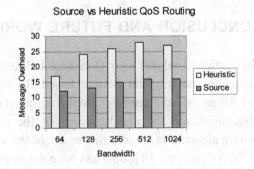

Table 3. Path Delay

Path Delay (ms)						
Average Bandwidth (kbps)	Connection Requests					
	10		20		30	
	S	H	S	H	S	H
64	121	106	89	121	81	126
128	112	148	125	160	121	148
256	140	158	143	143	129	141
512	138	157	134	153	123	148
1024	148	153	138	155	126	154

Figure 12. Message Overhead for 20 connections

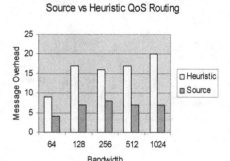

Figure 13. Message Overhead for 30 connections

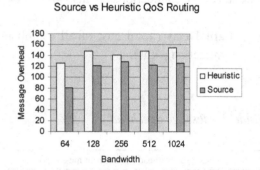

Table 3 shows that whenever Souce Routing manages to find a path that satisfies the bandwidth requirement, it produces paths of slightly lower delay than the Heuristic Routing algorithm.

The readings in Tables 2 and 3 show that there is a sudden increase in the average response time and average path delay when the average bandwidth is increased from 64 to 128 kbps. The main reason for this is that, when the bandwidth request is set to 64 kbps, only a few requests are accepted initally, but when the average bandwidth is set to 128 kbps, there are more path possibilities , which results in a increased response time and path delay.

The Graphical representations with respect to Path Delay for the complete list of readings found in Table 3 are given in Figure 14, 15 and 16 respectively.

Figure 14. Path Delay for 10 connections

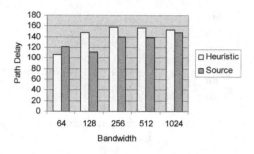

Figure 15. Path Delay for 20 connections

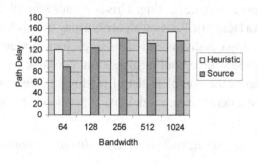

Figure 16. Path Delay for 30 connections

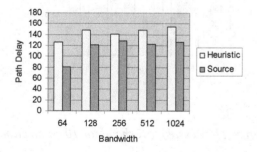

CONCLUSION AND FUTURE WORK

This article analyses two QoS based Routing Algorithm namely the Source based Routing and the proposed Heuristic based Routing. The advantages and the disadvantages of the two routing algorithms are also discussed. Moreover a Client Server based model has been developed using VC++ for computing three important metrics such the Response Time, Message Overhead and Path Delay. These metrics are computed whenever the connection requests and the bandwidth values are given by the user in the developed model. The Tables and graphs have been shown and discussions regarding the performance of the two Algorithms for the three metrics are done. It is found that the proposed Heuristic Routing performs better than the Source Routing. As a future work the client server model that has been developed can be used for computing more metrics such as QoS Ratio and Mobility Ratio.

REFERENCES

Chen & Nahrstedt (1998). An overview of Quality of Service routing for the next generation high-speed networks: Problems and solutions. *IEEE Network, Special issue on Transmission and Distribution of Digital Video, 12*, 64-79.

Chen, S., & Nahrstedt, K. (1998). Quality of Service routing in high-speed networks based on selective probing. *Proceedings of Annual Conference on Local Area Networks.* Boston, MA.

Koundinya, A.K, Negi, A., & Sastry, V.N. (2004). Unicast Routing Algorithm with Multiple Quality-of-Service Parameters *2004 International Symposium on Parallel Architectures, Algorithms and Networks (ISPAN'04)* (p. 520).

Kweon, S. K., & Shin, K. G. (1999). *Distributed QoS routing using bounded flooding.* Technical Report CSE-TR388-99, University of Michigan.
Moen, D.M., & Pullen, J.M. (2003). Enabling Real-Time Distributed Virtual Simulation over the Internet Using Host-based Overlay Multicast.

Workshop on Distributed Simulation and Real Time Applications, Proceedings of the IEEE/ACM Distributed Simulation-Real Time Applications Symposium.

Moen, D.M., & Pullen, J.M. (2005). Performance Evaluation of the XMSF Overlay Multicast Prototype. *Simulation Interoperability Workshop.*

Moen, D.M., & Pullen, J.M. (2007). *Private Overlay Multicast for the Defense Threat Reduction Agency Collaboration Center (DCC).* George Mason University Network Research Laboratories.

Moen, D.M., Pullen, J.M., & Zhao, F. (2004). Implementation of Host-based Overlay Multicast to Support of Web Based Services for RT-DVS. *Proceedings of the Eighth IEEE Distributed Simulation--Real Time Applications Workshop.*

Simon, R., & Pullen, J.M. (2003). Agents for enhanced end-host multicasting in distributed simulation systems. *Networking and Simulations Lab Technology Report.*

Tian Y. (2002). *QoS Routing – Source Routing – Problems and Solutions.* MSc Thesis, New Jersey Institute of Technology.

Yuan, X., & Liu, X. (2001). Heuristic algorithms for multi-constrained quality of service routing. *Proceedings of INFOCOM.*

Zhang, Z., Sanchez, C., Salkewicz, B., & Crawley, E. (1996). *QoS Path First Routing (QOSPF).* Internet draft.

Zheng, X.Y., Tian, J., Liu, Z.F., & Dou, W.H. (2004). A limited path unicast QoS routing algorithm. *Ninth IEEE Symposium on Computers and Communications 2004, 2 (ISCC''04)* (pp. 870-875).

This work was previously published in the International Journal of Information Technology and Web Engineering 4(2), edited by Ghazi I. Alkhatib, and Ernesto Damiani, pp. 78-89, copyright 2009 by IGI Publishing (an imprint of IGI Global).

Section 3

Chapter 11
SWAMI:
A Multiagent, Active Representation of a User's Browsing Interests

Mark Kilfoil
University of New Brunswick, Canada

Ali Ghorbani
University of New Brunswick, Canada

ABSTRACT

The rapid growth of the World Wide Web has complicated the process of Web browsing by providing an overwhelming wealth of choices for the end user. To alleviate this burden, intelligent tools can do much of the drudge-work of looking ahead, searching and performing a preliminary evaluation of the end pages on the user's behalf, anticipating the user's needs and providing the user with more information with which to make fewer, more informed decisions. However, to accomplish this task, the tools need some form of representation of the interests of the user. This article describes the SWAMI system: SWAMI stands for Searching the Web with Agents having Mobility and Intelligence. SWAMI is a prototype that uses a multi-agent system to represent the interests of a user dynamically, and take advantage of the active nature of agents to provide a platform for look-ahead evaluation, page searching, and link swapping. The collection of agents is organized hierarchically according to the apparent interests of the user, which are discovered on-the-fly through multi-stage clustering. Results from initial testing show that such a system is able to follow the multiple changing interests of a user accurately, and that it is capable of acting fruitfully on these interests to provide a user with useful navigational suggestions.

INTRODUCTION

It was once possible, it is said, for one person to have read all the books that were in existence.

DOI: 10.4018/978-1-60960-523-0.ch011

Soon, however, that became impossible, but it was possible to index and house all the books organized by a generally acceptable set of topics. That too, is becoming rapidly unmanageable, so people turn to the opinions of people, organizations, and tools that they trust in order to determine which books they should read.

The Web has undergone a similar growth pattern, at a far greater pace. Today, we are presented with a cornucopia of information, but it has become increasingly hard to navigate and find information related to our interests. It has become necessary to find people, organizations and tools that will assist us in navigation because we can no longer read it all ourselves.

Tools have been developed to assist us. Search engines offer one-step navigation aids in response to particular immediate information needs, but provide little in the way of ongoing assistance. Personalized, adaptive Web systems reorganize information contained within a single site to achieve local assistance, but do not offer a user any cross-site benefits.

Server-side approaches such as these only have a limited shared experience with a user, and thus they have only a narrow amount of advice they can offer. Client-side approaches are closer to the concept of a "personal assistant," someone who knows your information history, patterns and needs and can provide ongoing assistance. However, they also observe the Web from a limited perspective.

The SWAMI system was devised to bridge the gap between client-side and service-side solutions and create an intelligent, natural, personalized assistant for user browsing. It uses the user's own behaviour as an input to an intelligent, innovative multi-agent system which takes the drudgery out of Web navigation by reading ahead of the user, leveraging existing tools, interacting with intelligent Web sites, and sharing browsing suggestions socially.

In this article, we introduce the SWAMI system. First, we describe the domain of the problem in more detail and other approaches with their limitations. Next, we outline the high-level architecture of the full SWAMI system and how it functions. The results gathered from the currently implemented subset of the SWAMI system are discussed next. Finally, we present a summary of the benefits and drawbacks of the SWAMI approach and discuss future directions for research.

RELATED WORK

The Web is a relatively new phenomenon, and has elevated certain problems to a critical level. In this section, the two most prominent problems of Web navigation and Web personalization are discussed, and a short summary of current solutions is presented.

Web Navigation

Because of its large size, dynamic nature and inconsistent structure, the Web is difficult to navigate. "Traditional," direct navigation approaches depend on an evaluation of the relevance of the currently viewed page as the best indicator of the value of pages pointed to by the current page. This approach relies upon the benevolence of the creator of the link (Kleinberg, 1999), and the hope that by following a series of related links the user will end up at another cluster of useful pages. This "hope" is described as the "small world" phenomenon, which suggests that a highly complex but interacting system will, over time, evolve paths of a limited number of hops between any two related pages.

When the user has discovered a page of lessening interest to them than a previous page, they return backward to an appropriately interesting (although already viewed) page and go forward from a link on that page (if there is one) until all links from that page have been exhausted, retreating back up another level. This navigation strategy is implicitly promoted by the linear nature of Web navigation tools, such as the "back" button of a Web browser.

The traditional strategy closely resembles a depth-first graph search, where leaf nodes are represented by pages of less interest. Effectively, however, the user must go "one page too far" in such a scheme, and travel deeper and deeper distances from the original page they were browsing into possibly uninteresting areas. Due to the highly connective nature of the Web, this suggests that the user will spend more time in distant pages than in pages more closely connected to the original. This, intuitively, is the opposite of the desired result, as pages directly connected to the current page are most likely to be the most relevant pages to it (Lieberman, 1995).

Search Engines

An alternative approach is to use a search engine, which, in effect, reconstructs the connection graph of the Web, reconnecting all the distant pages together into a single layer. In this way, more relevant pages become more likely at an earlier stage of browsing. In the case of Yahoo (Yahoo!, 2004), this rearrangement is done explicitly through a hierarchical, soft categorization of Web site links. By contrast, Google builds a response page (effectively the top-level of a tree or entrance to a graph) dynamically around a set of initial keywords in a query.

Once the user has selected a link from a search engine, however, they are out of the arena of that technology, and browsing returns to a traditional strategy. Thus, this technology produces only a one-shot or one-level navigational benefit, not ongoing navigational support.

In addition, the criteria for the evaluation of results are very specific: the keywords of the request are the only measure of relevance to the user that the system can use, although there are additional measures of the relative importance of a page (some partially dependant of the particular request made). In other words, the result evaluation does not take into account the full nature of the user, such as prior information or additional interests.

Personalized, Adaptive Web Sites

Adaptive Web sites take a highly personalized approach. They use knowledge about the specific user to modify both the presentation of individual pages (Kobsa, Koenemann, & Pohol, 2001) and/or the navigation from one page to another (Brusilovsky, 1996). In this way, they can be seen to either add additional links between pages of relevance to the user or do a similar rearranging of the graph to the search engine, although beyond just a single level of rearrangement and navigational support. These links may come from a mining of a large set of pages within a scope (Kleinberg, 1999), from an online search and evaluation scheme (Lieberman, 1995) from an external knowledge of the structure of the domain (De Bra & Ruiter, 2001; Freitag, Joachims, & Mitchell, 1995), from other, similar users through collaborative recommendation (Cosley, Lawrence, & Pennock, 2002; Lieberman, Van Dyke, & Vivacqua, 1999; Mobasher, Dai, & Tao, 2002) or through some combination of these techniques (Balabanovic & Shoham, 1997).

Prominent examples of adaptive Web systems include WebWatcher (Joachims, Freitag, & Mitchell, 1997), AHAM (Lieberman, 1995), IfWeb (Asnicar & Tasso, 1997) and AVANTI (Fink, Kobsa, & Nill, 1997). Each of these systems provides server-side adaptive navigation or presentation based on perceived user characteristics.

Server-side solutions for adaptive Web sites also offer the possibility of collaborative recommendations, where knowledge about groups of users can be used to make suggestions to individuals who are members of a group. Groups might be arbitrarily chosen—such as the group of a person and his friends—or created through observations of common patterns of behaviour or common attributes.

Server-side solutions, however, are generally limited to a single Web site or set of close Web sites, something to which the search engine approach is not limited. Privacy concerns, however, keep users from wanting information to be shared between Web sites, particularly when personal information is being collected.

User Modelling

A user model is a representation of the user's information needs. It is used to search for new information and evaluate it. Information needs can be broadly classified into three types: short-term, long-term and periodic. Short-term needs are specific and require immediate and direct response, but their significance sharply descends in time and can be quickly forgotten. Long-term needs are more general, but always have at least some value and should rarely be forgotten. Periodic needs are a compromise between both of these, having periods of high intensity interspersed with gaps of very low intensity, but should not be forgotten often.

There are two methods of discovering a user's desired information needs: explicitly asking them to describe what they need and implicitly learning what those needs are based on behaviour. The former approach is favoured by solutions like search engines with only short-term needs in mind, and the latter approach is preferred in most other cases which use long-term needs.

Needs are not static—they change over time. Thus, a model of a user should also change to meet the current needs. Godoy and Amandi (2002) present a general architecture for discovering and maintaining a user profile in agent terms. This architecture suggests that users have multiple interests of varying levels of detail, and organizes these topics in terms of a hierarchy. It is also recognized in this architecture that user interests are not static, but tend to both change and recur over time. In their architecture, they suggest an explicit "temporal context" might be used to modify the strength of suggestions about particular topics at a given time.

Continual learning techniques are necessary for ongoing navigational support to keep up-to-date when implicit user model building is used. This approach has proven to be effective in many cases (Chan, 1999; Pazzani & Billsus, 1997; Schwab, Pohl, & Koychev, 2000).

ARCHITECTURE

SWAMI is a full system for providing ongoing navigational support to an end-user. The architecture covers everything from a front-end client to components responsible for representing the user's needs to components for multiple ways to interact with sites, other tools, and other users.

This section describes the high-level architecture of SWAMI, including several of the design considerations which distinguish this work from others.

Design Considerations

The design process of the SWAMI system was guided by several considerations. These include:

1. **The system should not require the user to explicitly state their needs.** The system must be capable of learning the user's needs from observation.
2. **A user may have multiple different needs.** Many systems consider the user needs to be all related to some degree. In SWAMI, it was felt that this was an unrealistic assumption, so a model that allows for multiple competing needs was developed.
3. **A user may have several related needs ("sub-interests") within the context of a general need.** Topic hierarchies and ontologies have been proposed and used in adaptive Web agent systems before (Chen & Chen, 2002; Godoy & Amandi, 2000). When combined with the previous design goal this naturally leads to multiple, independent hierarchies.

Figure 1. A high level view of the SWAMI system

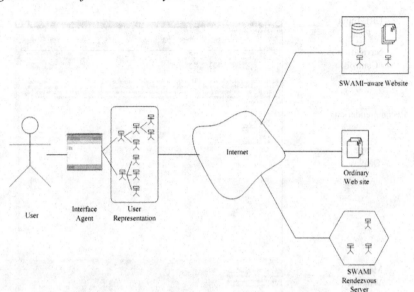

4. **A user's needs change over time.** In particular, needs may be short term, long term or periodic.

5. **Recent, active interests are most important.** The system should put the most attention to supporting the greatest needs and the current needs.

6. **The system should be capable of evaluating a page based on the user's needs.** The needs in the hierarchies representing a user are each described by a weighted vector of keywords that can be used to evaluate a potential page. Each need can also refine its evaluation based on its parent need, having its expertise further specialized.

7. **The system should be able to search for pages that might be of interest to the user.** It is not enough to merely be able to model a user's needs, but allow those needs to actively work on the user's behalf.

8. **Like-minded users should share recommendations.** A user shares interests with the communities to which they belong, and the SWAMI system is designed to take advantage of that idea. Elements of a user's

representation can rub virtual shoulders with those from other users in a common location called a "rendezvous server."

9. **A Web site knows itself best.** The SWAMI architecture allows for interaction with expert agents which can be consulted for local, specialized recommendations, taking advantage of any hidden context they might have.

High-Level Architecture

SWAMI stands for "Searching the Web with Agents having Mobility and Intelligence." At the heart of SWAMI is a multi-agent system in which agents representing a front-end interface, the user's needs and page searchers. It is implemented using a (custom) multi-agent system (see Figure 1).

A user browses Web pages using the front-end interface, which passes the page to the multi-agent system representing the user's needs. The Web page is analysed and migrates to the most appropriate representative. At all times, the needs representation may be engaging search compo-

Figure 2. A screenshot of the browser with integrated SWAMI

URL Input Field

Navigation Controls

Recommendations

Page Display

Message Window

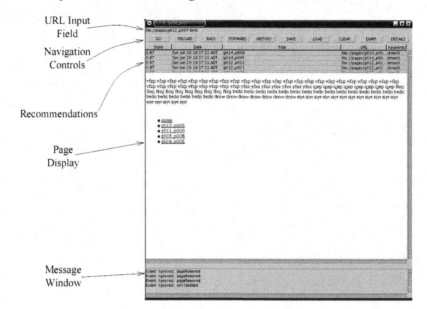

nents to push recommendations back to the interface agent for the user to view.

The Front-End Interface

The user interacts with the system using the SWAMI interface agent (shown in Figure 2). This is currently integrated into a simple Web browser, allowing the user to interact with search and evaluations results, and allow the system to observe user activity.

This browser has basic features of a typical browser:

- it has a URL input field, so that a user may enter a URL and jump immediately to any page;
- it has history, and the user can navigate backward/forward through history;
- a link on any displayed page can be followed by clicking on it.

In addition, several specialized features have been added:

- there is a table of current page recommendations for the user to select from, if desired
- the current analysis of any page can be displayed
- each of the agents working for the user can be inspected using the agent browser
- the state of all agents can be saved and loaded, allowing the user to take a snapshot of the system
- a message window at the bottom tells the user the current activity, including which agent won the bid for the current page, if a new agent has been created, retired or removed, and when a search has been conducted. (This was primarily used for monitoring activity during testing.)

Representation of User Needs

The user's needs are represented by a hierarchically-arranged collection of agents. Each representation agent represents a cluster of pages the user has viewed. Agents are organized into hierarchies referred to as "corporations," within which each

Figure 3. User interests can be characterized as belonging to orthogonally separate groups with differing levels of specialized interests within each group

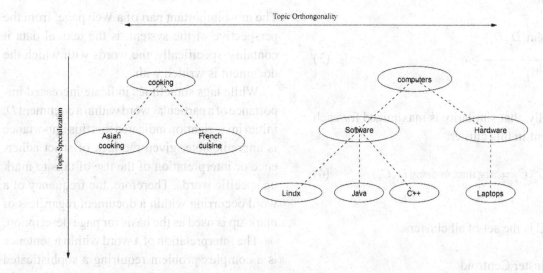

represent an informal topic hierarchy devised from the agents themselves. Each corporation can be considered to represent a category of interest, where each agent is a specific topic within that category. (See Figure 3).

A similar approach to Godoy and Amandi (2002) has been taken in SWAMI, but with a significant difference: where in Godoy and Amandi (2002) an externally organized hierarchy was created, pages placed in that hierarchy, and the user's interests being taken from a subset of that hierarchy, in SWAMI the hierarchy is developed entirely from scratch, allowing it to be a customized size to reflect the user's interests.

General Overview

The hierarchies of agents are self-organized using an online, dynamic self-clustering technique. As pages are viewed by the user, an agent collects pages that are similar to the pages it has already gathered. The agent continually checks the compactness of its cluster, and if it is too loose (beyond a threshold), it will attempt to split the collection of pages up into tighter subgroups. If it is successful, it creates (or "hires") new agents to represent

the subgroups. These agents are positioned below the original agent, so that incoming pages are first examined by the original agent, and then may be passed down to the more specialized sub-agents, and so on, until the best match has been made.

Initially, the interface agent collects all pages until a distinct group is discovered, forming the first representation agent. If no current agent is representative of a given page, the interface agent holds on to it until a new group manifests itself.

Definitions

In order to describe things more formally, a few definitions are needed, particularly with respect the notions surrounding clustering. Note that each agent represents a cluster of pages.

a. Document Cluster

A *document cluster C* is a collection of documents that all share an acceptable level of similarity:

$$C = D_1, D_2, \ldots, D_n \tag{1}$$

$$\forall D_i, D_j \in C, \mathrm{sim}(D_i, D_j) \geq \sigma \tag{2}$$

or at least the average similarity is above a threshold:

$$\frac{\sum\limits_{\forall D_i, D_j \in C} sim(D_i, D_j)}{|C|} \geq \sigma \qquad (3)$$

Ideally, that similarity is maximized for each document in this cluster:

$$\forall D_i \in C_x, C_x = \underset{\forall C_j \in \mathbf{C}}{\arg\max}\, avgsim(D_i, C_j) \qquad (4)$$

where $\mathbf{C}$ is the set of all clusters.

b.   Cluster Centroid

To save time, a cluster may be represented by a set of features in much the same way as a document. This creates a "virtual" document (referred to as a *centroid*), which is the point with the most similarity (or least distance) from all other pages within the cluster:

$$\forall D \in C, D_{centroid} = \underset{\forall D_j, D_i \in C, D_j \neq D_i}{\arg\max}\, avgsim(D_i, D_j) \qquad (5)$$

Since each page is represented as a collection of terms, the ideal centroid may be described as the average of all pages, $\overline{D}$:

$$\overline{D} = \left\{ \frac{\sum\limits_{\forall D_i \in C} D_i \bullet w_1}{|C|}, \ldots, \frac{\sum\limits_{\forall D_i \in C} D_i \bullet w_n}{|C|} \right\} \qquad (6)$$

The set of all clusters being considered at a particular time is denoted by $\mathbf{C}$.

To denote that a document D is being considered in the context of a cluster C, the notation D_C is used.

Page Representation

The most important part of a Web page, from the perspective of the system, is the textual data it contains; specifically, the words with which the document is written with.

While tags sometimes indicate increased importance of a particular word within a document D, initial investigation indicated that this importance is unpredictable, given the lack of strict adherence or interpretation of the use of tags to mark up specific words. Therefore, the frequency of a word occurring within a document regardless of mark-up is used as the basis for page description.

The interpretation of a word within a sentence is a complex problem requiring a sophisticated language-specific model. To increase the throughput of the system's analysis of Web pages and allow the system to be (largely) language-agnostic, sentence structure and punctuation is ignored for the processing of pages.

Thus, the basic representation is the well-known *bag-of-words* model. This representation collects all the unique words from a document and notes the frequency of each. The procedure for collecting these words involves eliminating HTML from the input, separating text from punctuation, reducing words to word stems, using the well-known Porter stemming algorithm (Porter, 1980), and removing arbitrarily uninteresting words listed in a stop list.

Once the words have been extracted from a document, it is necessary to determine which words are significant descriptors of the page, to extract the features from the words.

Features are terms which for which a sufficient weight has been calculated. For this purpose, the well-known TFIDF measurement was considered but has been modified to better suit the hierarchical context. In a hierarchical cluster, the terms of the parent cluster are already significant and have already been taken into account to form the parent cluster. To distinguish a child cluster and properly focus and specialize its terms, it is necessary to change the weighting scheme of the terms to take into account the fact that words from the parent are going to be present in all of the child cluster's pages.

The modified TFIDF-based calculation is as follows:

$$w_t = f_t \times \left(\frac{DF_{C_C}(t)}{N_{C_C}} \right) \times \left(\frac{N_{C_P}}{DF_{C_P}(t)} \right) \quad (7)$$

where $DF_{C_C}(t)$ is the document frequency of the term in the child cluster, C_p refers to the parent of cluster C, $DF_{C_P}(t)$ is the document frequency of the term in the parent cluster, N_c is the number of pages in the child cluster (including the candidate page), and N_c is the number of pages in the parent cluster.

If the cluster has no parent, the last term would result in a zero error, so the following truncated formula is used:

$$w_t = f_t \times \left(\frac{DF_{C_C}(t)}{N_{C_C}} \right) \quad (8)$$

Note that this formula is nearly the opposite of the TFIDF formula. In TFIDF, a term is considered less important if it occurs in more documents of a group, because the intent is to find terms that uniquely describe the page. In this case, terms that are common to more pages better describe the cluster, and are thus more important to the cluster. Those terms that are common to the cluster which are shared with the parent, however, are not as important to distinguish this cluster, because, by definition of being a subcluster of the parent, all of the parent's terms are already found throughout the cluster; in other words, no new information is learned about a cluster by those words it inherits from its parent.

Document Comparison

Now that documents have been represented as a collection of weighted features, it is easier to compare documents against each other for similarity. A number of similarity measures were considered for this role, however, most are computation-intensive, and do not significantly improve upon the basic cosine similarity algorithm. The cosine method treats the features of documents as vectors in a multidimensional space, and calculates the angle between the vectors. As the angle decreases, the similarity between the two documents increases.

Note that in order for two documents to be properly compared, the feature weights need to be recalculated within the same context.

Placement

The placement of new pages is directly based on the ability to compare two pages discussed above.

To determine whether a document D should be part of a cluster C, we can calculate the similarity between the document in the context of the cluster (D_C) and the cluster's centroid, $\overline{D}_C$:

$$\text{sim}(D_C, C) = \text{sim}(D_C, \overline{D_C}) \quad (9)$$

The best cluster $\hat{C}$ for a given document D is therefore the cluster that maximizes the similarity:

$$\hat{C} = \arg \max_{C \in \mathbf{C}} \text{sim}(D_C, C) \quad (10)$$

Formally:

1. Given a set of existing clusters **C** and a new document D, for each cluster C_i recalculate the term weights of document D, producing a candidate document D_{C_i}.

2. For each candidate document D_{C_i}, calculate the similarity of the candidate to its cluster C_i: $\text{score}(D_{Ci}) = \text{sim}(D_{C_i}, \overline{D_{C_i}})$

3. A clear winning cluster $\hat{C}$ is discovered by finding a cluster for which the document score is better than every other cluster, and for which the score is greater than a given minimal similarity threshold (ε=0.6):

$$C_i, \hat{C} \in \mathbf{C}, \forall C_i \neq \hat{C},$$
$$\text{score}(D_{\hat{C}}) > \text{score}(D_{C_i}), \text{score}(D_{\hat{C}}) > \varepsilon \qquad (11)$$

4. If there is a single winning cluster $\hat{C}$, the page is given to that cluster.

5. If there is a tie for the winning cluster or there is no clear winner, the page is held back in the "general area" until such time as it can be awarded to a clear winner.

Hierarchical Placement

When hierarchical clusters are involved, a distant descendant of a cluster may be the winning cluster. The simple placement algorithm can be extended by searching through all of the children for the best possible match. This can be accomplished by changing the score function of the cluster to return the best score between the cluster and its children:

$$\text{score}(D_C) = \max\left(\text{sim}(D_C, \overline{D_C}), \max_{\forall C' \in C_C} \text{score}(D_{C'})\right) \qquad (12)$$

Redistribution

As subclusters can change periodically, pages should be moved from a more general cluster to a more specific one whenever possible. The process of redistribution is the same as placement; the only difference being that the winning cluster must not only surpass all other clusters and the minimal similarity threshold, but also must be a better fit than the current cluster containing the page.

Splitting

Since pages are added incrementally and are held back if there is no clear winner, it is possible that a number of pages in a given cluster actually form a subcluster. The clustering program (in this case, an agent) must periodically examine the cluster it represents in order to discover these subclusters.

In order to find these subclusters, the following definition is used: given a set of documents **D**, a subcluster is defined as a group of documents within that set for which the following holds:

1. the documents that best match/have the best similarity to a given document D' is denoted as the set $B \subseteq \mathbf{D}$;

2. all best match sets for each document within a given subcluster C are also contained within the subcluster;

3. all best match similarity scores are above a minimum similarity score.

If the set of documents **D** is viewed as a weighted graph, such that each vertex represents a document within that set, and each edge is weighted with the similarity score between the documents on its vertices, then the clusters are those distinct, non-overlapping subgraphs.

Given the pages $\mathbf{D}=\{A,B,C,D,E,F\}$ in the example in Figure 4, two subsets, $\{A,B,C\}$ and $\{D,E,F\}$ can be found.

Formally:

1. For all documents $D_i, D_j \in \mathbf{D}, D_i \neq D_j$, calculate the similarity score to be placed in the half-filled matrix M. That is, each entry $M[i][j]$ contains $\text{sim}(D_i, D_j)$.

2. Initiate a set of clusters **C**.

3. For each document D_i:
   a. If $\exists C \in \mathbf{C}$ such that $D_i \in C$, skip to the next document.
   b. Otherwise, find the set of best matching pages, B; that is, those pages that have the best c. similarity scores with the

Figure 4. A graph representation of the largest disjoint set algorithm

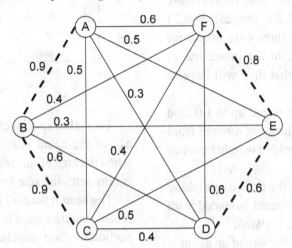

given document. Together, this forms a potential cluster *C'*.

c.   If any document in *B* is contained in any cluster of **C**, this cluster is invalid.

d.   For each document *D'* in *B*, repeat from step 3(b) until no new pages are discovered.

4.   If the cluster is not of a sufficient size, the cluster is invalid.

5.   If the cluster has not been invalidated, add the new cluster to the set of clusters.

6.   Repeat from step 3.

Hierarchical Profile Agents

The representation of the user's needs is carried by Hierarchical Profile Agents. These agents are motivated by continued survival to organize Web pages on behalf of a user and find new pages related to those viewed. The current status of an agent is a measurement called "wealth."

Wealth Calculation

Each agent has a measurement of "wealth," which reflects the importance and relevance to the user of the cluster the agent represents. Equation 13 shows the formula used to calculate wealth. This combines the agent's size (*sizeActivity*), the suc-

cess the agent has had in finding new pages for the user (*search*), the success the agent has had in having found pages accepted by the user (*acceptance*) and a history momentum which allows an agent to rest on its laurels briefly (*wealth(t-1)*).

$$
\begin{aligned}
wealth(t) = \ &\alpha \times sizeActivity \\
&+ \beta \times search \\
&+ \phi \times acceptance \\
&+ \gamma \times wealth(t-1)
\end{aligned}
\tag{13}
$$

In this formula, α, β, ϕ and γ are arbitrary weights describing the relative importance of each factor. Useful values of each of these factors were discovered experimentally. A value of 0.25 was initially used, and was modified as the relative rates of change of each of the components were observed. The goal in this was to achieve an acceptable balance between the sustaining of active agents and the decay of inactive agents, while remaining sensitive enough to allow changes in the system to happen in a reasonable time frame. That is, the functioning of the system for each of the main points (agents increasing and decreasing in importance, agents splitting, agents retiring, agents rehiring and agents being removed) could be observed within a short number of page views.

After several iterations, the values were assigned as follows: α=0.50, β=0.25, φ=0.24 and γ=0.01. While these values were useful for demonstrating the system, in the future use of the system it is expected that they will have to be less sensitive.

Note that all of the factors add up to 1.0, and each of the component values has a range from between 0.0 and 1.0; this yields a weight between 0.0 and 1.0.

The agent's *sizeActivity* is a time-diminishing measure of the size of the agent balanced with how recently the agent was updated.

First, a few definitions: the *size* of an agent is calculated as the number of pages the agent holds and the total number of pages held by its children:

$$size(A) = |\,pages(A)\,| + \sum_{\forall c \in children(A)} size(c) \qquad (14)$$

The *age* of an agent is the number of pages it has bid on since its birth. The *recency* of activity is the difference between the current age and the age when a page was last added:

$$recency(A) = age(A) - \max_{\forall p \in pages(A)} addAge(p) \qquad (15)$$

The general *sizeActivity* equation is:

$$sizeActivity(A) = \frac{f1 + f2}{2} \qquad (16)$$

where *f1* and *f2* are defined in Equations 17 and 18:

$$f1 = \begin{cases} 1.0 & size(A) > age(A) \\ \dfrac{size(A)}{age(A)} & otherwise \end{cases} \qquad (17)$$

$$f2 = \begin{cases} 1.0 & size(A) = recency(A) = 0 \\ 0.0 & recency(A) \geq size(A) \\ 1.0 - \dfrac{recency(A)}{size(A)} & otherwise \end{cases} \qquad (18)$$

Two other special conditions apply: when the age of the agent is 0, the *sizeActivity* is 0, and when the size of the agent is zero but the *recency* is non-zero, the *sizeActivity* is 0.

The search success is a measure of how good recent searches have been, calculated as the proportion of good searches to all searches:

$$search(A) = \frac{\displaystyle\sum_{\forall r \in \mathbf{R}_{good}} \left(\frac{score(r)}{age(A) - birthAge(r) + 2} \right)}{\displaystyle\sum_{\forall r \in \mathbf{R}} \left(\frac{score(r)}{age(A) - birthAge(r) + 2} \right)} \qquad (19)$$

where $\mathbf{R}$ is the set of all pending recommendations, r is an individual recommendation, $birthAge(r)$ is the age of the agent when the recommendation was created, and $\mathbf{R}_{good}$ is the set of all good searches:

$$\mathbf{R}_{good} \subseteq \mathbf{R} \,\big\|\, \forall r \in \mathbf{R}_{good}, score(r) \geq \rho$$

The threshold ρ is arbitrarily set to 0.5 in the prototype.

Acceptance is a measure of how many recommendations were followed by the user, calculated as the proportion of recommendations followed relative to the number of recommendations made:

$$acceptance(A) = \frac{|\mathbf{R}_A|}{|\mathbf{R}|} \qquad (20)$$

where $\mathbf{R}_A \subseteq \mathbf{R}$, and all recommendations in $\mathbf{R}_A$ were followed by the user at some point.

Each of these formulae was created to arbitrarily represent elements believed to be of importance to an agent. They are all designed to diminish with a lack of activity over time.

Retirement

When an agent's wealth is reduced below a threshold, the agent is removed from the hierarchy and moved into a holding area ("retired"). In this way, agents which are not producing useful assistance are prunes from the hierarchy. However, to represent periodic interests, these agents are not immediately deleted. Rather, they remain in the *holding area*, continuing to decay, until one of two conditions is satisfied: either they are the best representative for a new page viewed by the user, or they represent a newly discovered subcluster better than a blank agent. In the first case, they become the head of a new corporation; in the second case they are simply added into the hierarchy at the appropriate point. This also allows subclusters to migrate to the most appropriate place; for example, a "Mexican cooking" agent might be retired from beneath the general "cooking" agent, but later be rehired under a "Mexican culture" agent. (Note that agents are not labelled in this way; this is merely for illustration purposes.)

Life Cycle of an Agent

A hierarchical profile agent goes through the following steps in its life-cycle:

1. **Birth**: When a profile agent is first created, it is being created to take over the control of one or more pages. From this initial page collection it calculates its features to be used for page comparisons. The wealth of an agent after it has been initially created is the minimum wealth, 0.0.

2. **Page bidding.** Each time a user views a page, a profile agent is called to bid on that page. If the page is already owned by the agent or the page matches one of the agent's recommendations, the value of the bid is 1.0 (perfect match). Otherwise, the value of a bid is simply the comparison between the page in the context of the agent's pages and the agent's features; in this case, the agent's age increases by one, and its wealth is recalculated. Bids from all children agents C_C are also collected and returned.

3. **Page acceptance.** If a profile agent is the winner of a bid for a page, it will be given the page to own. If the page is one of the agent's recommendations, that recommendation is marked as "accepted." When a page is added, the agent is marked as increasingly "dirty." When the dirtiness surpasses a threshold δ (currently in the system, this is 2), the agent's features are recalculated to match the possibly shifting centroid of its cluster. A page might not be accepted directly by an agent, but might be delivered to the appropriate winner of the bid.

4. **Page distribution.** If a page has been accepted by a child agent, that agent may have recalculated its features and pages owned by the parent agent might more appropriately fit with the child agent. Thus, the parent agent asks all of its child agents for a comparison score. Note that this is different from a bid, in that it does not increase the age of any agents. If there is a clear winner for a page, it is redistributed down the branch that won to the appropriate child agent. This allows a limited reconfiguration of the hierarchy, so that pages flow downward to the most specific agent for the page topics.

5. **Wealth recalculation.** If pages have been accepted or redistributed there will possibly be changes in the wealth of agents along the way.

6. **Subcluster search, or "splitting."** At the core of the hierarchical structure is the ability of a cluster to contain one or more subclusters. An agent will search through its pages to attempt to find one or more maximal subclusters. For each of these subclusters a new child agent is created.

7. **Searching.** After a page has been accepted and the wealth recalculated, the agent may initiate a search if its wealth exceeds the threshold. The profile agent creates a new search agent of the appropriate type and starts that search agent in a separate thread. When that thread completes, the search agent will notify the profile agent that it has finished searching, and the profile agent will retrieve the list of recommendations from the search agent (if there are any) and destroy the search agent.

8. **Recommendation gathering.** At any time, the recommendations found for a particular profile agent may be requested. If the agent has not yet searched or is in the middle of searching, it may not have any recommendations. When the recommendations are requested of a hierarchical profile agent, it in turn requests all the recommendations from all of its children and collects them all in a list. If more than one agent has a recommendation for a particular page, the best recommendation is used.

9. **Retirement.** After an agent's wealth has been recalculated, the agent may be deemed no longer relevant to the profile if its wealth falls below a particular threshold, η. When this happens, it will be removed from its current place ("retired") and put into the holding area. The *holding area* is a special area maintained by the interface agent. This allows agents that performed well to exist longer, in case the topics that they represent are repeated in the future.

When in the holding area, an agent may not create any child agents nor create any search agents. It continues to make bids on incoming pages and therefore, to age. If it should win a bid from an incoming page, it will be reinstated from retirement and added as the head of a new corporation. This reflects the situation of a recurring interest, where the user had drifted away from an interest for a period, but has now returned to it.

If an agent fails to win any bids, its wealth will gradually decrease over time. Once its wealth has fallen below a second threshold, τ, it is permanently removed from the system.

Note that there is a "grace period" of 5 age units during which time an agent is not considered for retirement. This allows an agent to establish itself.

This stage allows interests that are no longer significant to fade away.

When a hierarchical profile agent is retired, all of the children agents become children of the agent's parent agent. If the agent has no parent, that is, it is the head of a corporation, all of the child agents become heads of new corporations under the interface agent.

While retired, a hierarchical profile agent may not create any new children.

10. **Reinstatement from reserve.** If an agent that has been retired is successful on a new page bid, it may be returned to active service by the interface agent. In this way, interests that recur are represented.

With hierarchical profile agents, new agents may be added beneath existing agents (as opposed to the simple profile agents, where new agents can only be created as new corporations). Whenever a hierarchical profile agent discovers that it has need of a new agent, it may request from the interface agent that an agent be retrieved from the holding area and used instead of creating a new agent from scratch. This allows the older agent a new lease on life, and the parent benefits from the existing knowledge of the older agent.

11. **Death.** If an agent falls below a lower threshold τ of wealth, the agent is removed from the system. This only applies if the agent is already retired (and therefore has no children).

Search Components

When a representation agent reaches a sufficient level of wealth and experience, it can create search agents to work for it. Search agents take criteria from the representation agent (the set of word features the representation agent has used to form its cluster, for example) and attempts to find and evaluate pages on its behalf.

Four types of search agents have been considered for the system: agents who search the links from existing pages, agents which leverage search engines as a source of potential recommendations, agents which consult with local topic experts for recommendations, and agents which consult with other search agents.

Link-Following Search Agent

The link-following search agent follows links from pages the user has already viewed and evaluates them based on its criteria. The agent, in a way, acts like a user in its pattern of browsing, following a similar depth-first pattern as discussed earlier.

Search-Engine Based Search Agents

The search-engine based search agent can submit different combinations of word features to a search engine and evaluate the results. In this way, it can take advantage of the massive database of knowledge available to a search engine, but provide the personalization that the search engine lacks.

Topic Expert Consulting Search Agents

The topic expert consulting search agents are mobile agents which can travel to SWAMI-aware Web sites and interact with topic expert agents representing the Web page owner. These topic expert agents may have access to information that cannot be gathered from simply browsing the pages, and may be in a better position to provide recommendations. For example, the topic expert agents may know about arbitrary groupings of pages that do not have labels on the pages themselves.

Collaborative Search Agents

The collaborative search agent seeks to take advantage of the browsing behaviour of people with similar interests. It travels to a host (referred to as the "rendezvous server") where it can interact with agents representing other people. There, they can swap recommendations based on how similar the agents are to each other. Another type of agent, the rendezvous hosts, remain in the rendezvous server at all times, interacting with all the visiting search agents and collecting all recommendations that they have. The rendezvous host becomes a "memory" for the rendezvous server, so that not all interactions between agents need to be synchronized.

SUMMARY

In order to provide personalized, ongoing, cross-Web site browsing navigation support to end-users, the SWAMI system was developed.

The SWAMI system contains a custom agent implementation written in Java. The majority of the agents form "corporations" representing user interests demonstrated from normal browsing behaviour, and map to clusters. An incremental, distributed clustering scheme is used to achieve this, and each agent is capable of independently initiating searches for other interesting Web pages on behalf of the end-user.

A number of parameters control the agent's life cycle, including the balance of importance between agent size, agent searching, agent recommendation success and momentum. Other parameters include the retirement threshold and the death threshold of wealth. Parameters governing the clustering include the minimum number of pages an agent must see in order to search for clusters (the minimum dirtiness threshold).

EVALUATION

An initial evaluation of the SWAMI system consisted of developing a prototype and determining if it was capable of detecting multiple, different interests by observing browsing behaviour, and of then acting on behalf of the test user to search out and evaluate new potential pages of interest.

To perform this evaluation, test data was generated that represents a web of pages that are interconnected and that have localized coherence. From this test data, numerous trial runs were conducted in order to demonstrate that all of the key events expected of the system were observed, and that the system was behaving as expected. Four typical example runs are highlighted here.

Because the test data was generated offline and never made available to a search engine, no examination of the search-engine-based search method could be attempted, without implementing a specialized search engine, which was beyond the scope of this initial research.

Test Methodology

The SWAMI system was tested with a test end-user by selecting a random start page and then having that end user follow links according to one of five typical user motivations, derived from the earlier observations about browsing behaviour:

1. **Continued interest.** Links might be chosen to represent a continued interest in an existing topic. The links followed for this motivation were links to pages within groups from which other pages had been visited in this session.
2. **Changing interest.** Links might be chosen to represent a break in the interests of the user. These links were chosen at random from the page being viewed or their URLs were entered directly into the input area.
3. **Returning interest.** Links might be chosen that represent a return to a past interest. Often, these links were chosen to be relevant to an agent that had been retired but not yet deleted from the system, to demonstrate that such an agent would be returned to active service.
4. **Intense and specialized interest.** Links might be chosen to represent a deepening and possibly specialized interest within an existing topic. These links were chosen from the best recommendations provided by the system.
5. **Shallow interest.** Links might be chosen to represent the seeking behaviour of a user, wherein links are essentially chosen at random.

Test runs were continued until it had demonstrated a particular feature. In total, 25 test runs were complete.

For each test run, the following events were observed:

*   when an agent is created;
*   when an agent splits; this is distinct from the previous event in that it concentrates on the effect of the change on the parent, rather than the details of the new child agent;
*   the bids for each page from each agent in the system;
*   the wealth of each agent after each bid
*   when a search was conducted, and the results it found;
*   when an agent is retired;
*   when an agent is reinstated;
*   when an agent is deleted permanently;

To summarize the results, two charts were devised: the *page group activity* chart and the *agent activity* chart. The time scale on both of these charts is in terms of page views by the user.

The *page group activity* chart shows the activity of the user in terms of the pre-generated page group to which each page the user chose belonged. Note that pages within the same pre-generated page group share a high similarity, while pages between groups tend to have a much lower similarity, so a steady line indicates a consistent interest that the system should recognize.

The *agent activity* chart shows the wealth of all of the agents in the system over the same period. As agents accumulate pages and become more certain about the topics they represent, their wealth should increase; as the topics they represent fall out of favour, the wealth should decrease. The identification of subtopics can also be seen in the creation of child agents, which is shown as a sudden start of a weight track on the chart. When agents are removed, their weight track disappears.

These two charts, when taken together, show the inputs and outputs of the system, and the better they correspond, the better the system is tracking the user and acting on their behalf.

Results

The following sections describe the results from two particular trial runs in detail. These trial runs were chosen to clearly illustrate the performance of the system, but are typical of the results.

It should be noted that the system uses a particular naming scheme for all agents within the system. All agents begin with the prefix "Charlie" and have a suffix indicating their parentage. In the case of the topmost agent, the Interface Agent, no suffix is used. The first child of the Interface Agent is called "Charlie_0"; the second child of this agent would be called "Charlie_0_1", and so on.

To describe the life-cycle of an agent, a chart showing the agents' wealth over time is used. This chart is calibrated in absolute terms, meaning that while an individual's age is calculated relative to when they were born, it has been adjusted to the appropriate real outside age relative to the age of the Interface Agent. The age also describes the number of unique pages viewed. Where a line begins on the graph indicates when an agent was born; if the line ends prematurely, that agent was removed from the system.

The lower threshold for an active agent's wealth before being retired is 0.2; only the Interface Agent

cannot be retired. If their wealth continues to drop, an agent will be removed when it falls below 0.15.

Pages within a particular group are known to be similar to each other, and thus represent a topic. This is used both to train the system and to interpret its results.

Also, as the agents search, they discover pages in other page groups that are relevant to the topic, thus forming a virtual topic group based on the user's demonstrated interests.

Example 1: Interest Shifts

This example demonstrates SWAMI's ability to follow a user's changing interests and react accordingly. The page groups that the user visited can be seen in Figure 5. On the weight track in Figure 6, five agents (in addition to the Interface Agent) are shown.

Each agent was created when the system detected a cluster of similar pages. The set of pages initially chosen all came from pre-generated group 40, followed by a number of pages selected from group 38. Charlie_0 was created when the subset of pages from group 40 were detected as distinct, at age 4. At age 11, a second agent (Charlie_1) was created to take control of the second subcluster discovered (for group 38). Note that while the pages were chosen from the pre-generated group, the system itself has no knowledge of these groups.

Between ages 14-36, links were followed semi-randomly from existing pages, but not corresponding to any previous page. These pages were similar enough to existing agents that Charlie_0 rose in wealth during this time period, and Charlie_1 maintained a high wealth. Concentration by the user on a single pre-generated page group again from age 36-43 resulted in the creation of a new agent, Charlie_2, to handle a newly-discovered cluster formed out of those pages. Another agent, Charlie_3 was created at the same time, as the new pages highlighted some previous cluster in the previous pages.

Figure 5. The page groups visited by the user on the first example test run

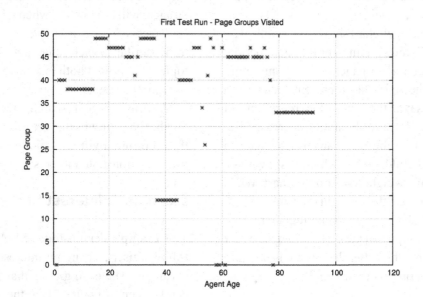

Between ages 53 and 77, recommendations made by Charlie_0 were followed, resulting in that agent's consistent wealth, while other agents diminished. At age 77, a new topic was focused on, and a new agent, Charlie_4 was created in response.

Note that when the user concentrated on a particular topic, the system responded by creating a new agent to handle this new topic when it detected it. As the user drifted away from that topic (by not visiting again), the agents that had been responsible for it waned in wealth.

Figure 6. Agent activity from the first example test run

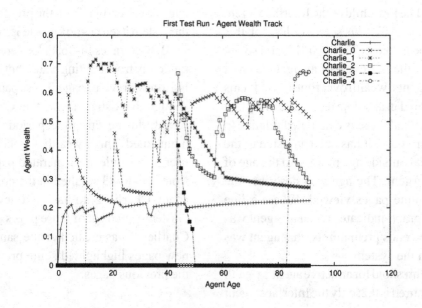

Figure 7. The page groups visited by the user on the second example test run

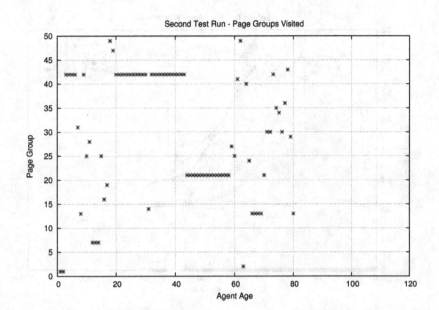

The longevity of both Charlie_0 and Charlie_1 indicate long-term interests. Charlie_0, in particular, has received a lot of attention from having suggestions followed.

Charlie_2 and Charlie_3 accurately map to short-term interests. In the case of Charlie_3, no recommended pages from that agent were viewed, leading it to degrade in wealth very quickly and disappear within about 5 page views. Charlie_2 was a short-term interest which the user paid a little attention to.

Finally, Charlie_4 is a new interest to which the user is paying attention and good recommendations have been found. The system responds quickly to the newly discovered cluster, and it becomes the most influential among them.

This example has shown that the system creates new agents to handle new user interests, and the wealth of those agents reflects the ongoing interest in the topic they represent.

Example 2: Interest Specialization

In stark contrast to the previous example, this example demonstrates the creation of specialized agents for sub-topics discovered within the context of a larger topic. While the page group activity shown in Figure 7 seems to be chaotic (particularly after age 57), the corresponding location on Figure 8 shows relatively stable behaviour.

Charlie_0 represents a long-term interest (page group 42) which was concentrated on for a considerable period. Two sub-topics were detected from within this one, represented by Charlie_0_0 and Charlie_0_1. The second of these was pursued momentary, but was forgotten for a period. Note that Charlie_0_1 was retired but brought back instantaneously when the user returned to that topic. At that point, it actually triggered a split, creating the very short term topic represented by Charlie_0_1_0.

At approximately age 45, the system has detected that the user has decided to view another topic intensely for which good suggestions could be found. This is represented by Charlie_1, whose

Figure 8. Results from the second example test run

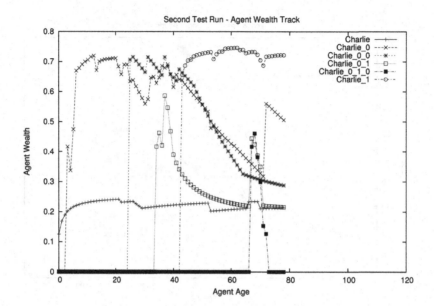

continued strength is due to its suggestions being followed. The return of a peak in Charlie_0 at approximately age 72 was due to following a link on a page suggested by Charlie_1 which led off to an older topic.

The relative stability of the wealth track of Charlie_1 after age 45 despite the apparent randomness of the page group activity for the same time period is due to the agent having found pages within multiple groups which are similar to the topic at hand. In this way, it has created a virtual group of pages centred around the user's interests.

CONCLUSION

This article describes a framework for a multi-agent system for providing personalized Web page recommendations to users. The SWAMI framework features a sophisticated user model using a social multi-agent system with a cost-driven and time-variable interaction model organized into hierarchies of related topics. Agents representing particular topical interests in this system can

search for recommendations for the user with one of multiple strategies. Among those search strategies is the ability of the search agents to become mobile. Mobile search agents can travel to particular, SWAMI-aware Web sites and interact with local topic experts, or they can travel to SWAMI "rendezvous servers," where they can interact with user-independent collaborative recommendation agents and with other search agents representing users.

Key features of this framework include local representation of a user's interests (allowing the system to "learn once, apply everywhere"), the integration of local, site-based and collaborative recommendations, and an active user profile representation which takes into account short-term, long-term and recurring interests, as well as the specialization of interests.

This holistic approach to Web search represents a more realistic solution to the problem of Web search than site-specific or user-agnostic approaches.

Several trial runs were performed, from which typical examples were chosen to examine in detail.

These trial runs demonstrate that the agents do grow to mirror the user activities and change over time to reflect changes in the user intentions. Short-term, long-term and recurring interests have been detected by the system, as well as specialization to accommodate a particularly important interest. Recommendations could be gathered successfully by using a link-search algorithm, by consulting with site experts or through interacting with a community. Recommendations in the community were successfully distributed between members of that community.

Future Work

This research has proved promising, but there are several additional questions raised throughout the work that would make interesting follow-up research. These questions include:

- **Parameter setting.** There are a large number of parameters within this system, including: minimum similarity thresholds; minimum agent wealth before retirement; minimum agent wealth before deletion; the relative weights of each component in the agent wealth calculation; the minimum number of pages required before an agent considers splitting; the minimum number of pages that must remain in a cluster after all others have been allocated to sub-clusters; and so on. These parameters are currently established through observation and arbitrary decision. However, in some cases, these parameters do not always work correctly. It seems natural that these parameters might either be adjusted by evidence or even determined entirely by evidence within the system. In addition, it may also be beneficial to allow parameters to be tuned according to user tastes.
- **Agent hierarchy/structure reorganization.** As agents are retired and rehired, the hierarchical structure of the agents is re-organized, allowing multiple independent but similar specializations the possibility of converging in one branch. This specialization will only occur, however, when interest in a particular sub-agent has waned significantly. There seems to be a natural role for a "headhunter" agent or something similar which can help facilitate reorganizations of the agent structure without the need of a diminished interest.
- **Open agent structure.** The agents are currently arranged in a strictly hierarchical manner, with each agent having at most one parent and any number of children. This structure, while convenient, is artificial; information often does not follow a strictly hierarchical structure, instead having more of an open graph structure. One possible modification of the SWAMI architecture is to modify the concept of "parent" and "child" agents into the more general "ancestor" and "descendant" roles, or even into the most general "sibling" role. Such a structural change would be capable of modelling much more subtle interactions within the data, but each agent would have a larger web of information from which to discover patterns.
- **Page comparison.** Several page comparison mechanisms were examined before selecting the cosine similarity measure. In particular, several variations on the Jaccard measure were strong contenders. Only a few of the measures examined take into account structural or positional information about the term on a page. Alternative methods of page comparison might improve the identification of page clusters and the ability for pages to reach the appropriate agent. Pages are also currently viewed only as the collection of terms that physically occur within the body of the document (in their stemmed forms). The system might be significantly improved if a facil-

ity such as WordNet could be included to search for other words based on common relationships such as antonym or synonym, although at a cost of complication and processing time.

- **Incremental calculation.** When a page is added to a new cluster, it affects the centroid of that cluster, which may shift the set of features enough that some of the pages that had been part of the cluster may no longer fit properly within it, or might fit more appropriately within a sub-cluster. Thus, every time a page is added to a cluster, a significant amount of re-calculation is potentially performed, significantly impacting performance. If it could be possible to calculate only the effect itself on the cluster instead of calculating everything, or to calculate a predictor that can indicate whether a full recalculation should be done, this would significantly improve the speed of the system.

- **Local expert agents.** Only one form of the local expert agent was examined in the process of this thesis, but several are possible. In particular, it might be possible for the local experts to reorganize themselves to reflect the kind of requests that are being made, making the local experts adaptive to usage.

- **Rendezvous agents environment.** The rendezvous server implemented here is basically functional, but it does not have any sophisticated mechanisms for creating new rendezvous host agents. Currently, if no host agents are discovered to serve a particular incoming search agent, a new host agent is created. Also, there is little attempt to guarantee that two host agents do not end up covering the same material; in fact, in the evaluation of the rendezvous server, there were in fact two host agents that had a difference of only two pages.

- **Remote search environment locating.** The current system looks for a remote search environment (whether rendezvous server or local expert environment) on the local machine, at a known port. To make the system more generally useful, a mechanism for identifying these remote environments is necessary.

- **Choosing search methods.** In the current system, the method of searching is hardwired into the particular incarnation of the executable. It is desirable that multiple search methods be available simultaneously to the system. It is also desirable to allow the agents to choose which method is appropriate, perhaps under the direction or suggestion of the user. This includes preferences, perhaps, for different remote search environments for different topics. It is expected that the search methods would complement each other well: local expert agents allow specialized exploration in a particular local environment; link search agents allow easy exploration between local page environments; rendezvous servers link individuals together into communities, allow transfer of recommendations between users; and the search-engine-leveraging search agents allow disconnected local environments to be connected.

- **User control and manipulation of agents.** It has been speculated that if users were able to tag or name the agents working for them, they would be able to further judge the recommendations provided by those agents. Other controls might also be useful, such as the ability to freeze an agent from changing (thus always providing the same kind of judgement without fear of being retired), arbitrarily remove an agent (to prune the system), or arbitrarily reward an agent for a particularly useful suggestion.

- **Page re-occurrence.** The system currently takes a simplified view of pages: they are unchanging entities, so when a page has been viewed once, it need never be viewed again. The interface tracks the list of pages that have been viewed so far this session, and simply does not process those pages that have already been seen. This simplification works for a large number of pages, but a significant portion of the Web changes constantly. If these changing pages could be identified, the system could automatically scan the pages to see if they have changed enough to be revisited by the user.

- **User profile persistence.** Currently, the system is only designed to work for the duration of a single session. The ability to save the state of the system was experimented with early in the development, but it was vulnerable to incompatibilities introduced by code changes. For such a system to be generally useful, however, it must have a way to store a user's profile between sessions. In a similar way, the rendezvous server should have the ability to persistently store the community it represents.

- **Wealth as accumulated value.** The system calculates the wealth of an agent as an instantaneous value based on the performance and other history of the agent. An alternative view is to treat wealth more like the real economic concept, in that it is something acquired for success and paid out to perform actions or to simply "live." The instantaneous system was implemented to give some measure of control and confidence that the system would have a continuing downward trend if no beneficial activity took place. A more open economy also requires additional controls to ensure that it changes appropriately and maintains a good balance.

- **Earlier detection of groups.** To circumvent the "cascading group" problem, the system requires that a small number of pages be left behind in a parent agent before

a child agent can be created. In particular, the interface agent, which is not capable of searching itself, will not create any corporations if there are not a sufficient number of pages that remain after the corporation has been created. This leads to the system apparently not able to find a group until after the user has left it, because only by visiting pages that are inconsistent with the previous pages can a new group be formed (leaving those most recent pages behind).

- **Real user testing.** This system was tested with a model of real users over pages which have known properties. The next stage of testing will involve real users and a much broader set of pages with more variable qualities, such as with the general Web. Preliminary testing in this manner has yielded promising results. In more open testing, users would be able to rate the search results discovered and provide a qualitative score to both determine the real success of the search agents and to provide feedback for the system to choose which avenues of search are most fruitful.

REFERENCES

Asnicar, F. A., & Tasso, C. (1997, June 2-5). ifWeb: A prototype of user model-based intelligent agent for document filtering and navigation in the World Wide Web. In *Proceedings of the Workshop on Adaptive Systems and User Modeling on the World Wide Web, Sixth International Conference on User Modeling,* Chia Laguna, Sardina (pp. 3-12).

Balabanovic, M., & Shoham, Y. (1997). Combining content-based and collaborative recommendation. *Communications of the ACM, 40*(3), 66–72. doi:10.1145/245108.245124

Brusilovsky, P. (1996). Methods and techniques of adaptive hypermedia. *User Modeling and User-Adapted Interaction, 6*(2-3), 87–129. doi:10.1007/BF00143964

Chan, P. (1999, August 15). Constructing web user profiles: A non-invasive learning approach. In *Proceedings of the KDD-99 Workshop on Web Usage Analysis and User Profiling,* San Diego, CA (pp. 7-12).

Chen, C. C., & Chen, M. C. (2002). PVA: A self-adaptive personal view agent. *Journal of Intelligent Information Systems, 18*(2/3), 173–194. doi:10.1023/A:1013629527840

Cosley, D., Lawrence, S., & Pennock, D. M. (2002, August 20-23). REFEREE: An open framework for practical testing of recommender systems using researchindex. In *Proceedings of the 28th International Conference on Very Large Databases (VLDB 2002),* Hong Kong (pp. 35-46). VLDB Endowment.

De Bra, P., & Ruiter, J. P. (2001, October 23-27). AHA! Adaptive hypermedia for all. In *Proceedings of the 2001 WebNet Conference,* Orlando, FL (pp. 262-268). Association for the Advancement of Computing in Education.

Fink, J., Kobsa, A., & Nill, A. (1997). Adaptable and adaptive information access for all users, including the disabled and the elderly. In A. Jameson, C. Paris, & C. Tasso (Eds.), *User Modeling: Proceedings of the Sixth International Conference, UM97,* Vienna (pp. 171-173). New York: Springer.

Freitag, D., Joachims, T., & Mitchell, T. (1995, March). WebWatcher: A learning apprentice for the World Wide Web. *Working Notes of the AAAI Spring Symposium: Information Gathering form Heterogeneous, Distributed Environments,* Palo Alto, CA (pp. 6-12). AAAI Press.

Godoy, D., & Amandi, A. (2000, November 19-22). PersonalSearcher: An intelligent agent for searching web pages. In M. C. Monard & J. S. Sichman (Eds.), *Advances in Artificial Intelligence, IBERAMIA-SBIA 2000,* Atibaia, Brazil (LNAI 1952, pp. 43-52).

Godoy, D., & Amandi, A. (2002, September 9-13). *A user profiling architecture for textual-based agents.* Paper presented at the 4th Argentine Symposium on Artificial Intelligence (ASAI 2002) in the 31st International Conference on Computer Science and Operational Research (JAIIO 2002), Santa Fe, Argentina.

Joachims, T., Freitag, D., & Mitchell, T. (1997, August 23-29). WebWatcher: A tour guide for the World Wide Web. In *Proceedings of the 15th International Joint Conference on Artificial Intelligence,* Nagoya, Japan (pp. 770-775). Morgan Kaufmann.

Kleinberg, J. M. (1999). Authoritative sources in a hyperlinked environment. *Journal of the ACM, 46*(5), 604–632. doi:10.1145/324133.324140

Kobsa, A., Koenemann, J., & Pohl, W. (2001). Personalized hypermedia presentation techniques for improving online customer relationships. *The Knowledge Engineering Review, 16*(2), 111–155. doi:10.1017/S0269888901000108

Lieberman, H. (1995, August 20-25). Letizia: An agent that assists web browsing. In *Proceedings of the 14th International Joint Conference on Artificial Intelligence,* Montreal, Quebec, Canada (pp. 924-929), Morgan Kaufmann.

Lieberman, H., Van Dyke, N. W., & Vivacqua, A. S. (1999, January 5-8). Let's browse: A collaborative web browsing agent. In *Proceedings of the 1999 International Conference on Intelligent User Interfaces (IUI'99),* Los Angeles (pp. 65-68). ACM Publishing.

Mobasher, B., Dai, H., & Tao, M. (2002). Discovery and evaluation of aggregate usage profiles for web personalization. *Data Mining and Knowledge Discovery, 6*, 61–82. doi:10.1023/A:1013232803866

Pazzani, M. J., & Billsus, D. (1997). Learning and revising user profiles: The identification of interesting web sites. *Machine Learning, 27*(3), 313–331. doi:10.1023/A:1007369909943

Porter, M. (1980). An algorithm for suffix stripping. *Program, 14*(3), 130–137.

Schwab, I., Pohl, W., & Koychev, I. (2000, January 9-12). Learning to recommend from positive evidence. In *Proceedings of the 2000 International Conference on Intelligent User Interfaces,* New Orleans, LA (pp. 241-248). ACM Publishing.

YAHOO! (2004). *Yahoo! search engine.* Retrieved from http://www.yahoo.com

This work was previously published in the International Journal of Information Technology and Web Engineering 4(3), edited by Ghazi I. Alkhatib, and Ernesto Damiani, pp. 78-89, copyright 2009 by IGI Publishing (an imprint of IGI Global).

Chapter 12
Analyzing the Traffic Characteristics for Evaluating the Performance of Web Caching

G.P. Sajeev
Government Engineering College, India

M.P. Sebastian
National Institute of Technology, India

ABSTRACT

Web cache systems enhance Web services by reducing the client side latency. To deploy an effective Web cache, study about traffic characteristics is indispensable. Various reported results show the evidences of long range dependence (LRD) in the data stream and rank distribution of the documents in Web traffic. This chapter analyzes Web cache traffic properties such as LRD and rank distribution based on the traces collected from NLANR (National Laboratory of Applied Network Research) cache servers. Traces are processed to investigate the performance of Web cache servers and traffic patterns. Statistical tools are utilized to measure the strengths of the LRD and popularity. The Hurst parameter, which is a measure of the LRD is estimated using various statistical methods. It is observed that presence of LRD in the trace is feeble and has practically no influence on the Web cache performance.

INTRODUCTION

Web caching is emerged as a technique to leverage the quality of Web services (Barish & Obraczka, 2000). A proxy cache deployed near to a client serves the Web documents locally as shown in Figure 1. This increases the client side download speed and reduces the outborn traffic. An efficient proxy-cache server can deliver most of the requests from its local cache. The performance of such a service depends on the cache architecture, admission policy, replacement method and cache

DOI: 10.4018/978-1-60960-523-0.ch012

Figure 1. A proxy-cache server system

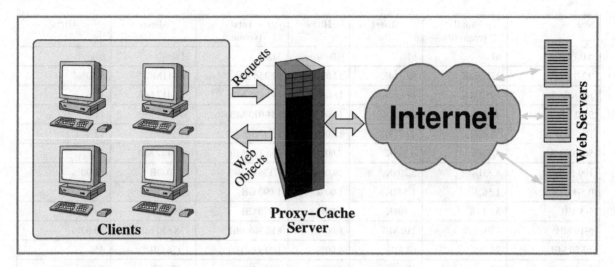

consistency. Handling the input traffic dynamics is the key aspect in a cache server's success.

In spite of the evolution of new caching schemes and algorithms, the performance of cache services never reached to the expected levels, as can be seen from Table 1, 2 and 3. Suitable setting of the cache performance parameters can provide

a solution to this problem. Hit ratio, byte-hit ratio, client side latency and network load reduction (server side and network) are some important cache performance parameters. These parameters can be estimated by analyzing the input traffic stream and Web proxy traces.

Table 1. Traces Used

Trace	Date	Number of requests	Hit Ratio	Zipf slope
NLANR-pa	1 'st Sep 2007	2,80,062	36%	0.72
NLANR-pa	1 'st Oct 2007	2,10,734	32%	0.76
NLANR-bo2	10'th Aug 2007	2,43,356	26%	0.69
NLANR-sj	9'th Jan 2007	5,44,356	20%	0.80
Internet Traffic Archive	23 'rd Jan 2005	28,338	48%	0.72

Table 2. Summary statistics of ircache.net on May 2007

Servers	sj.nlanr.net	uc.nlanr.net	bo2.nlanr.net	sd.nlanr.net	pa.nlanr.net	rtp.nlanr.net	ny.nlanr.net
HTTP Requests	252276	238156	114426	1093569	136211	1475734	269663
Hit rate (docs)	42%	31%	35%	8%	18%	18%	40%
MEAN Obj Size	10255	15722	18636	42719	11603	32801	12569
MB served (all)	2467	3571	2033	44552	1507	46164	3232
MB served cache	215	243	166	2651	67	2850	263
Percent Savings	9%	7%	8%	6%	5%	6%	8%

Table 3. Size Hit ratio performance sj.ircache.net Jan 2007

Size	Total (requests)	Misses	Hit%	Total (volume)	Misses	Hit%
0-0.1KB	61	61	0.00%	318 B	318B	0%
0.1-1.0KB	232.353K	58.344K	32.00%	97.356 MB	70.411MB	8.00%
1-5 KB	195.171K	174.626 K	11.00%	443.825 MB	393.417 MB	11%
5-10 KB	41.556K	35.611K	14.00%	284.013 MB	244.657 MB	14%
10-50KB	54.226K	47.719K	12.00%	1.147GB	1.010 GB	12%
50-100KB	6.794K	6.289K	7.00%	456.296 MB	423.437 MB	7%
100-500KB	8.531K	5.209K	39.00%	2.376 GB	1.010 GB	58.00%
0.5-1.0MB	1.562K	1.542K	1.00%	1.090 GB	1.075 GB	1.00%
1-5 MB	3.23 1K	3.198K	1.00%	6.970 GB	6.904 GB	1.00%
5-10 MB	120	110 MB	8.00%	818.308 MB	738.650 MB	10.00%
10-50 MB	71	68 MB	4.00%	1.219 GB	1.176 GB	4%
50-100MB	17	17	0.00%	1.339 GB	1.339 GB	0.00%
~100MB	11	11	0.00%	1.810 GB	1.810 GB	0%
Grand Total	544.370K	432.805K	20.00%	18.003 GB	1.851 GB	10%

A simple Web cache caches all cache-able objects, which are referenced through it. This decision is not influenced by the traffic pattern or by the physical location of the cache. Thus, the traditional caching algorithms normally fill cache with irrelevant pages. Cache itself may become a bottleneck for the end user when all his requests are routed through the cache. An effective cache system must terminate majority of the requests within it, thus reducing end-user latency and load on the network. In order to reap the full benefit of caching, a cache system must be able to cache and preserve the pages which are on demand (Jin & Bestavros, 2000). To fill the cache with relevant pages, the cache designer must study the request streams characteristics.

It has been reported (Breslau, Cao, Fan, Phillips, & Shenker, 1999, Krashakov, Teslyuk, & Shchur, 2006) that the nature of Web access follows Zipf-like power law (Zipf, 1929). The introduction of proxy-cache service between Web client and the Web server has not improved the situation. That is, though the Web traffic is routed through cache servers, the access nature of user community remains more or less unchanged. This finding helps to identify the objects which are on demand and popular for a user community. Based upon Zipf law, caching schemes are proposed for object replacement (Jin & Bestavros, 2000, Chen & Zhang, 2003) and admission control (Huang, Yang, & Lee, 2009).

Self-similar and long range dependence (LRD) properties in Web traffic came into the attention of researchers when it was discovered that Ethernet traffic exhibits these properties (Leland, Taqqu, Willinger, & Wilson, 1994). LRD is a significant property in optimizing buffer sizes, admission and congestion control in LAN traffic (Rezaul & Grout, 2007). Similar observations were made for Web traffic characteristics also (Crovella & Bestavros, 1996).

This paper focuses on studying the Web traffic characteristics and its impact on the Web cache parameters. The previous related works were either to search for a new characteristic or to improve the system using a known characteristic (Khayari, 2006). Our objective is to compare the *strengths* of these characteristics with real and synthetic traffic traces. Also, we intend to determine the influence of these characteristics on the Web cache performance parameters. First we check the traffic streams for its self-similar nature. If the traffic is self-similar, we measure the strength of LRD in terms of the Hurst parameter. Then, the experiments are carried out with the dataset of real traffic, to evaluate the performance parameters such as Hit Ratio (HR) and Byte Hit Ratio (BHR). A second round of experiments is done with the same dataset, but with induced LRD. Then the cache performances are compared. Similarly, measurements are carried out for the rank distribution. Further, we determine the effect of the rank distribution on cache performance. Thus, the main objective of this research is to find the weaknesses in the general characterization of the Web cache traffic, and its impact on the cache performance.

The remainder of the chapter is organized as follows. In the next section, we present the related works. The subsequent section narrates the basics of long range dependence and rank distribution. Then, the data analysis using the collected trace files is presented. This is followed by the details on simulation setup and results. The chapter is then concluded with some directions for future research.

RELATED WORKS

The properties like self-similarity, LRD and rank distribution were observed and reported in various domains and contexts by the researchers. G K Zipf (Zipf, 1929) observed rank distribution of words in English dictionary. The self-similarity was observed by Edwin Hurst in the flood levels of river Nile (Liu, Wang, & Qu, 2005). The rank distribution of Web objects has been reported in many publications. Bresalu (Breslau et al., 1999) is carried out an extensive trace analysis and observed that Web access nature follows a Zipf-like law. Dolgikh (Dolgikh & Sukhov, 2002) has done theoretical study of cache system based

up on Zipf-like law. Krashkov (Krashakov et al., 2006) observed that Web site popularity can be formulated using Zipf-like law. Mark E (Crovella & Bestavros, 1996) found that self similarity in HTTP traffic can be explained using Web document's size distribution. Stephan Dill (Dill et al.., 2002) discovered the Web's fractal behavior in several senses, scales and folds. His work revealed the feasibility of modeling the Web as a graph. A new classification algorithm is formulated in (Khayari, 2006) using the self-similarity and heavy-tail nature of the Web traffic. An extensive trace study has been done in (Cesar & Deni, 2007) to explore the self-similarity. The time domain analysis of Web traffic characteristics is carried out in (Bai & Williamson, 2004) and they have suggested that the approximate model to capture the properties of Web traffic is the *gamma* distribution. In (Callahan, Allman, & Paxson, 2010), the client and server behavior to Web objects and the connection characteristics are investigated.

LONG RANGE DEPENDENCE AND RANK DISTRIBUTION

This section reviews the fundamental principles of LRD and rank distribution. Kolmogorov first reported the self-similar process in 1941. Improvements in this were suggested by a number of researchers (Gong, Liu, Misra, & Towsley, 2005, Cesar & Deni, 2007, Pacheco & Roman, 2006, Crovella & Bestavros, 1996, Bai & Williamson, 2004).

Self-Similarity

A stochastic process is *self-similar*, if it is invariant in distribution of time and space. Consider a m-aggregated time series

$$X^{(m)} = \sum_m X_k^{(m)} k = 1, 2, 3, \dots \qquad (1)$$

That is, $X^{(m)}$ is obtained by summing the series $(X_k; k=1, 2, 3, ...)$ over non overlapping block of size m. Hurst parameter is a measure of self-similarity and LRD. The time series X is self-similar, if for all positive m, has the same distribution as X is rescaled by m^H. That is,

$$X_t = \frac{1}{m^H} \sum_{i=(t-1)m+1}^{tm} X_i \qquad (2)$$

The auto-correlation function (ACF) of X is

$$r(k) = \frac{E[X_t - \mu]E[X_{t+k} - \mu]}{\sigma^2} \qquad (3)$$

We say that, the series X has self-similarity, if $r(k)$ is the same for all $X(m)$. The series with self-similarity may exhibit long-range dependence when,

- The auto-correlation function (ACF) plot with respect to m will not decay rapidly.
- $r(k)$ follows a power law.
- The summation of auto-correlation function tends to infinity.

MEASURE OF SELF-SIMILARITY AND LRD

We consider seven standard methods to test self-similarity (Crovella & Bestavros, 1996, Leland et al., 1994). In that, five are graphical methods and two are of non-graphical type. We examine each of these methods in brief.

Absolute Value method: In this method, an aggregated series $X^{(m)}$ is defined, using different block sizes m. The log-log plot between the aggregation level and the absolute first moment of the aggregated series $X^{(m)}$ is a straight line with slope of $H-1$, if the data is long-range dependent.

Variance-time plot: This plot is between variance of $X^{(m)}$ and m on a log-log scale. The slope of the straight line is denoted as β. If β is greater than -1, then the data series posses LRD.

R/S Plot: The rescaled range of data series and R/S plot was developed by Edwin Hurst (Pacheco & Roman, 2006). He established that for many naturally occurring processes, the expected value of R/S, is proportional to n^H, where n is the size of the data set and H is the Hurst parameter. If H value is greater than 0.5, the data series is having long-term dependent structure.

Periodogram method: This method uses a frequency domain approach. The plot is between the power spectrum of the data set and the frequency. The slope of the straight line of the Peridogram plot is $\beta - 1 = 1 - 2H$, which is close to the origin.

Whittle estimator: This method also belongs to the frequency domain, and is based on the minimization of a likelihood function, which is applied to the Periodogram of the time series. It gives an estimation of H and produces the confidence interval. It does not produce a graphical output.

Variance of Residuals: A log-log plot of the aggregation level and the average of the variance of the residuals of the series is a straight line with slope of $2H$.

Abry-Veitch: Wavelets are used to estimate the Hurst exponent. The energy of the series in various scales is studied to provide an estimate.

Most of the earlier researchers (Gong et al., 2005, Cesar & Deni, 2007) used the terms self-similarity and LRD interchangeably. In (Pacheco & Roman, 2006), clear distinctions between these terms are explored. We assume similar meaning for both the terms and define a new terminology *strong-LRD* for describing the traffic nature.

Strong-LRD: A data series possesses strong-LRD if the *Hurst* parameter H takes a value close to 1. Precisely, *$0.75 < H < 1$*. Our definition is justified according to (Gong et al., 2005). When H *tends* to 1, the series becomes perfect self-similar.

Document Rank Distribution

The document distribution for request approximately follows a form of Zipf's law (Breslau et al., 1999, Krashakov et al., 2006, Serpanos, Karakostas, & Wolf, 2000) and is given by

$$P_k(\alpha, N) = \frac{\frac{1}{k^\alpha}}{H_N} \tag{4}$$

With

$$H_N = \sum_{k=1}^{N} \frac{1}{k^\alpha}$$

where P_k is the probability that k^{th} ranked document will be accessed from N documents under consideration, and $\alpha\alpha$ is some parameter between and 0 and 1. We assume that k is defined for $i=1, 2...N$. In other words, Zipf's law allows one to calculate the number of accesses to each object based on its popularity. Zip function is used to quantify the probability that access is made to the object O_k, where k is the rank of the object.

Let us have a closer examination of the Zipf law. We follow (Breslau et al., 1999, Serpanos et al., 2000, Krashakov et al., 2006) and use a simple form of Zipf law

$$P_i = \frac{A}{i^\alpha} \tag{5}$$

where P_i is the probability of accessing the ith popular object and A is a constant related to the number accesses to the highest ranked object. Intuitively, $A = P_1$ is the probability that most popular object will be requested. Since the sum of the probabilities is equal to 1,

$$\sum_{i=1}^{N} P_i = 1 \Rightarrow A \times H_N = 1 \tag{6}$$

Thus

$$A = \frac{1}{H_N} \approx \frac{1}{\ln N} \tag{7}$$

Where H_N is the Nth harmonic number which is approximated to ln N.

Now

$$P_i = \frac{A}{i^\alpha} = \frac{1}{H_N \times i^\alpha} \approx \frac{\ln N}{i^\alpha} \tag{8}$$

If the number of accesses N_A is directed towards the set of N objects, then the object O_i will be accessed $Pi \times N_A$ times. Then the number accesses towards k popular objects is given by

$$\sum_{i=1}^{k} = N_A \times \frac{H_k}{H_N} \tag{9}$$

Then the document hit ratio is computed as

$$h_d = \frac{N_A \times \frac{H_k}{H_N}}{N_A} = \frac{H_k}{H_N} \tag{10}$$

Also,

$$H_k = H_N \times h_d \approx \log k$$

Hence

$$k = e^{h_d \times H_N} \tag{11}$$

Thus, one computes, k, the number of popular objects required in the cache in order to achieve a hit ratio of out of N objects. In other words, the cache size can be determined for a given hit ratio.

SITE POPULARITY

According to Krashakov (Krashakov et al., 2006), the Web site accesses can also be modeled in the form of Zipf-like law with a modified rule (Zipf-Mandelbrot law). The problem with pure Zipf law is *trickle-down* effect (Doyle, Chase, Gadde, & Vahdat, 2002), (it will not hold true in tails or small rank region). The authors (Krashakov et al., 2006) proposed an offset parameter to correct this problem.

Now we extend this result to analyze the cache parameters with respect to the Web sites. Let there be M requests for Web sites. The probability that a Web site with rank ω will be accessed can be written in the form of Zipf law as

$$R_w = \frac{\Omega}{w^\alpha} \qquad (12)$$

where $R_{\omega\omega}$ is the number accesses towards ω^{th} popular site and $R\Omega$ is a parameter similar to A in equation (5). Extending equations (6) through (10), the Web site hit ratio is formulated as

$$h_w = \frac{H_w}{H_M} \qquad (13)$$

Also,

$$w = e^{h_w \times H_M} \qquad (14)$$

That is, for a given hit ratio h_ω, one can compute $\omega\omega$ popular Web sites pertaining to a user community. The parameter ω can be used for Web site mirroring and for maintaining DNS records (Krashakov et al., 2006).

Note that a *Web site hit* on the cache server does not necessarily be a *document hit*. It only implies some documents of the corresponding Web site is stored in the cache. Without loosing generality, we assume that the average number of documents in ω popular Web sites is μ. Then the total number of documents pertaining to ω Web site is $\omega\omega$ x μ. $\times \mu$

By combining equations (10) and (13), the aggregate hit ratio is computed as

$$h = \frac{H_k}{H_N} + \frac{H_w}{H_M} - (\frac{H_k}{H_N} \times \frac{H_w}{H_M}) \qquad (15)$$

Application of Zipf-like law yields a quantitative approximation regarding number of accesses towards Web objects and Web sites.

Data Collection and Analysis

We have collected traces, sanitized logs and summary statistics from NLANR caches (NLANR, 2007) during the period January 2005 to May 2008 and analyzed the traces for access behavior of users and Web cache performance. This collection enabled us to generate an enough workload for the simulation runs. To generate the synthetic work load, we used the same dataset. With help of software tools (Karagiannis, Faloutsos, & Molle, 2003, Markatchev & Williamson, 2004), LRD is induced in the dataset. This is for generating a workload which is independent of any process. Note that most of the simulation tools of cache systems generally use Autoregressive Integrated Moving Average (ARIMA) class of process to generate workload.

We present some of the traces and their characteristics. Table 1 depicts the trace, period and their properties. Table 2 is the performance summary of IR cache (NLANR, 2007) on a particular day, and Table 3 gives a detailed analysis of the trace. The maximum hits occur for the objects of size

Figure 2. Basic Characteristics of a sample trace

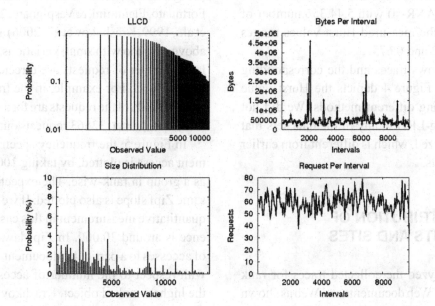

between 100 KB and 500 KB and larger objects are not often cached.

Figure 2 shows the basic characteristics of one sample trace. The *requests per interval* indicate that the cache server is loaded constantly as shown in Figure 2. The spikes in the *bytes per interval* plot and object size distribution in indicate that, a detailed check may be useful to measure the LRD factor in the trace. To know about the quantitative performance of Zipf-law (Krashakov et al.., 2006) for Web sites, we have enlisted the rank of a particular Web site for a period of one year, as shown in Table 5.

OBSERVATIONS ON SELF-SIMILARITY AND LRD

We have processed the data from the collected trace files, in number of ways by making use of various tools (R Development Core Team, 2008, Karagiannis, Faloutsos, & Molle, 2003, Markatchev & Williamson, 2004). Initially, we used the R language package (R Development Core Team, 2008) to know about the raw data

behavior. We have plotted ACF and R/S plots in Figure 3, and found that the behavior is not perfect self-similar, but *only self-similar*. Also the R/S diagram reveals the evidences of self-similarity. To measure the Hurst parameter, we used the *Selfis* tool (Karagiannis et al., 2003) and found that Hurst values are in the range of

Table 5. Summary statistics from ircache.nlanr.net, of Website frendster.com for a period of one year

Date	# of requests	Rank
10/09/05	22966	3
10/10/05	13591	5
12/11/05	20565	4
10/12/05	31254	2
08/01/06	29656	3
12/02/06	28184	12
10/03/06	23729	11
22/04/06	18838	7
22/05/06	not ranked	-
01/06/06	17473	12
01/07/06	56435	1
01/08/06	40372	5

0.312 to 0.572. For large trace file that we have analyzed (NLANR-sj) with 5,44,356 number of requests and the measured Hurst values ranges between 0.412 and 0.675.

Table 4 shows traces and the corresponding Hurst values. Figure 4 depicts the Hurst value estimation using different methods. We did not observe strong-LRD in any of the data sets that we have analyzed, which is different from earlier reported results.

RANK DISTRIBUTION OF DOCUMENTS AND SITES

We have analyzed the collected traces for rank distribution of Web documents and Web as shown in Figure 6. The observations by (Meiss, Menczer, Fortunato, Flammini, & Vespignani, 2008, Breslau et al.., 1999, Krashakov et al., 2006) are true in the above case too with small variations. Here a very large number of requests are directed towards a single object. For example, in the trace we have analyzed, 6% of the requests are for a single object (in sj.ircache.net, 32563 requests out of 544356).

In Figure 5, the frequency spectrum of document access is plotted, by taking 100 documents as a group in rank-wise. The expected values pf same Zipf slope is also plotted. If we consider the quantitative measurement in this case, the difference is around 30,000. In Zipf law, the number of accesses to a particular document is calculated with respect to the number of accesses towards the highest ranked object. Krashkov (Krashakov

Figure 3. LRD check using ACF and R/S plot

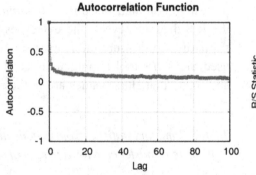
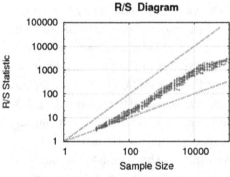

Table 4. Hurst value estimation using various methods

Estimation method	pa.nlanr.net(1)	pa.nlanr.net(2)	bo2.nlanr.net	sj.nlanr.net	Internet Traffic Archive
Variance	0.458	0.315	0.484	0.525	0.256
RS plot	0.458	0.498	0458	0.509	0.290
Absolute Moment	0.519	0.490	0.519	0.587	0.320
Variance of Residuals	0.312	0.134	0.302	0.412	0.297
Peridogram	0.564	0.474	0.564	0.625	0.319
Whittle	0.502	0.574	0.541	0.675	0.380
Abry-Veitch	0.572	0.500	0.522	0.636	0.382

Figure 4. Hurst value estimation using different methods

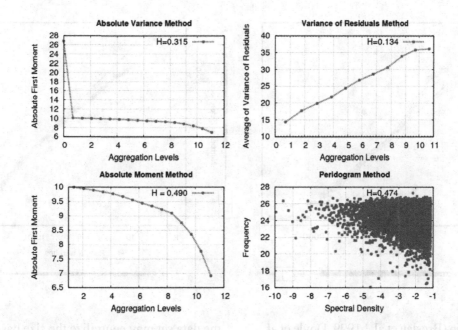

et al., 2006), proposed a method to fit the data to Zipf-plot (for Websites) by considering the data set as number of windows.

A fixed user community always tries to access a relatively small number of Web sites very frequently (of course during a period). Table 5 shows the summary statistics from IRCache (NLANR, 2007) of a particular Website for a period of one year.

Figure 5. Document access nature of bo2.nlanr.net

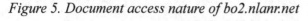

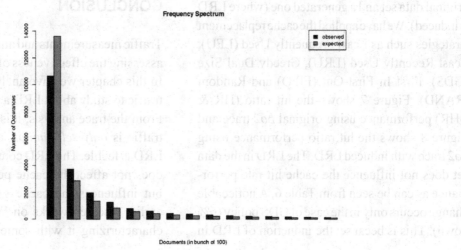

PERFORMANCE EVALUATION

Our simulations use NLANR traces and synthetic workload generated using WebTraf (Markatchev & Williamson, 2004). The simulations are carried out in NS2 and WebTraf environments. Trace analysis tools like *traceconv* (TraceGraph, 2005) are also used. Simulations were under different values of Zipf exponent, and varying cache size.

Figure 6. Rank distribution of document and Web site accesses

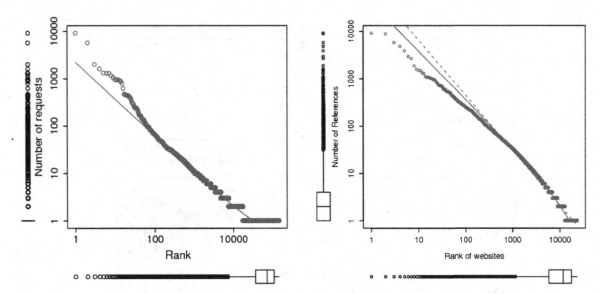

As reported in (Breslau et al.., 1999, Doyle et al.., 2002), a good approximation of Zipf law holds true for a larger sample size in the order of 10^5. We have taken sufficient number of references (20000 to 400000) in all the cases. For the real work load we have used the data set from NLANR traces (NLANR, 2007).

We have preprocessed the NLANR traces as described in (Cao & Irani, 2002). The NLANR traces contain IMS (if-modified-since), and non cache-able objects like *cgi-bin*. The preprocessor removes all such requests before generating the work load. Experiments are carried out using the original data set and a generated one (where LRD is induced). We have applied the cache replacement strategies such as Least Frequently Used (LFU), Least Recently Used (LRU), Greedy Dual Size (GDS), First In First Out (FIFO) and Random (RAND). Figure 7 shows the hit ratio (HR & BHR) performance using original *bo2* trace and Figure 8 shows the hit ratio performance using *bo2* trace with induced LRD. The LRD in the data set does not influence the cache hit rate performance as can be seen from Table 6. A noticeable change occurs only in the case of GDS policy (6% down). This is because; the induction of LRD in

the data set may neutralize the size based policy. Note that the LRD in the dataset offers uniform bursts in the traffic.

The effect of LRD on cache growth is as shwon in Figure 9. The traces used for the simulation are with equal length and varying Hurst value. It is observed that the cache is being filled at faster rate for a trace with a larger Hurst value. The effect of rank distribution on hit ratio is in Figure 10. A larger hit ratio is achieved using a synthetic work load, which follows perfect Zipf law.

CONCLUSION

Traffic measurements and analysis are needed for assessing the effectiveness of Web cache servers. In this chapter we have analyzed the Web cache traffic to study about LRD and rank distribution. From the trace analysis, it is found that the Web traffic is *only self-similar*, and the presence of LRD is feeble. The LRD component in the traffic does not affect the cache performance directly, but influences the cache growth. Most of the earlier research works on Web traffic were for characterizing it with some generic rules. Our

Figure 7. Hit ratio performance of original NLANR-bo2 trace with H=0.564

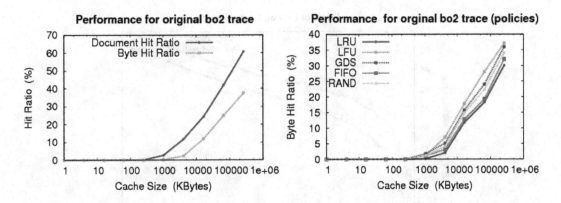

Figure 8. Hit ratio performance of shuffled NLANR-bo2 trace with H=0.864

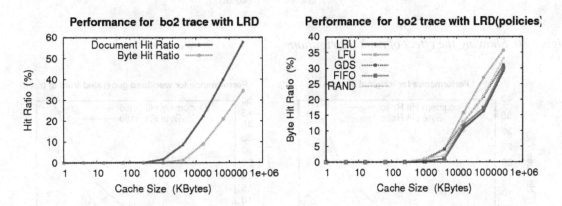

measurements have revealed that a considerable portion of the Web cache traffic is heterogeneous and follows no specific rules like the Zipf-law. Though a general characterization of the Web traffic yield simplified caching models, it may not give precise results.

Our results could be useful to optimize the cache framework. Simulation tools for Web cache systems generally use Autoregressive Integrated Moving Average (ARIMA) class of method to generate the synthetic workload. In the light of new evidences, we suggest Generalized Autoregressive Conditional Heteroskedasticity (GARCH) type of

Table 6. Performance comparison of different cache replacement policies on LRD

Policy	Original Trace	LRD induced trace
LRU	30%	29%
LFU	38%	37%
GDS	37%	31%
FIFO	30%	31%
Random	34%	32%

Figure 9. Showing the effect of LRD on cache growth

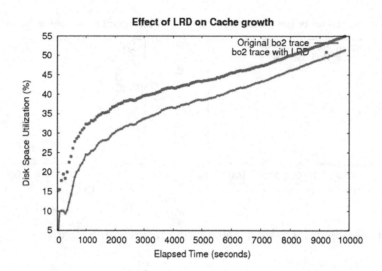

Figure 10. Showing the effect of rank distribution

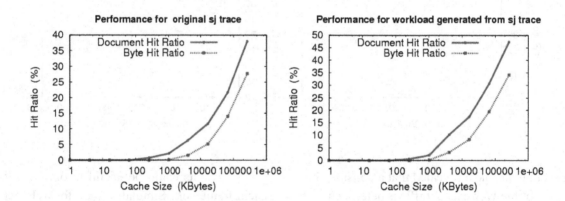

method, to represent the irregular components of the traffic. Building a cache framework considering this irregularity of the Web cache traffic is suggested as a topic for further research.

REFERENCES

Bai, G., & Williamson, C. (2004). Time-domain analysis of Web cache filters effects. *Performance Evaluation, 58*(5), 285–317. doi:10.1016/j.peva.2004.07.009

Barish, G., & Obraczka, K. (2000, May). World Wide Web caching trends and techniques. *IEEE Communications Magazine, 51*(6), 178–185. doi:10.1109/35.841844

Breslau, L., Cao, P., Fan, L., Phillips, G., & Shenker, S. (1999, Mar). Web caching and zipf-like distributions: evidence and implications. *INFOCOM '99. Eighteenth Annual Joint Conference of the IEEE Computer and Communications Societies. Proceedings. IEEE, 1*, 126-134 vol.1.

Callahan, T., Allman, M., & Paxson, V. (2010). A Longitudinal View of HTTP Traffic. In *Passive and active measurement* (pp. 222–231).

Cao, P., & Irani, S. (2002, May). Cost-aware www proxy caching algorithms. *IEEE Transactions on Computers, 51*(6), 193–206.

Cesar, R. P. J., & Deni, T. R. (2007). Local and cumulative analysis of self-similar traffic traces. In *Conielecomp '06: Proceedings of the 16th international conference on electronics, communications and computers* (p. 27-32). Washington, DC, USA: IEEE Computer Society.

Chen, X., & Zhang, X. (2003). *A popularity-based prediction model for web prefetching* (*Vol. 36*, pp. 63–70). Los Alamitos, CA, USA: IEEE Computer Society Press.

Crovella, M. E., & Bestavros, A. (1996). Self-similarity in world wide Web traffic: evidence and possible causes. In *Sigmetrics '96: Proceedings of the 1996 acm sigmetrics international conference on measurement and modeling of computer systems* (pp. 160–169). New York, NY, USA: ACM.

Dill, S., Kumar, R., McCurley, K., Rajagopalan, S., Sivakumar, D., & Tomkins, A. (2002). Self-similarity in the Web. *ACM Transactions on Internet Technology, 2*(3), 205–223. doi:10.1145/572326.572328

Dolgikh, D., & Sukhov, A. (2002). Parameters of cache systems based on a zipf-like distribution. *Elsevier Computer Networks, 37*, 711–716. doi:10.1016/S1389-1286(01)00243-2

Doyle, R. P., Chase, J. S., Gadde, S., & Vahdat, A. M. (2002). The trickle-down effect: Web caching and server request distribution. *Computer Communications, 25*, 345–356. doi:10.1016/S0140-3664(01)00406-6

Gong, W. B., Liu, Y., Misra, V., & Towsley, D. (2005). Self-similarity and long range dependence on the internet: a second look at the evidence, origins and implications. *Computer Networks, 48*(3), 377–399. doi:10.1016/j.comnet.2004.11.026

Huang, C., Yang, C., & Lee, C. (2009). Proxy Cache Admission and Replacement Policies for Layered Video Streaming. *Proceedings of the International Computer Symposium* (pp. 637–642). Tamkang University, Taiwan.

Jin, S., & Bestavros, A. (2000). Popularity-aware greedydual-size Web proxy caching algorithms. In *In proceedings of icdcs* (pp. 254–261).

Karagiannis, T., Faloutsos, M., & Molle, M. (2003). A user-friendly self-similarity analysis tool. *SIGCOMM Comput. Commun. Rev., 33*(3), 81–93. doi:10.1145/956993.957004

Khayari, R. E. A. (2006). Design and evaluation of Web proxies by leveraging self-similarity of Web traffic. *Computer Networks, 50*(12), 1952–1973. doi:10.1016/j.comnet.2005.10.003

Krashakov, S. A., Teslyuk, A. B., & Shchur, L. N. (2006). On the universality of rank distributions of Website popularity. *Computer Networks, 50*(11), 1769–1780. doi:10.1016/j.comnet.2005.07.009

Leland, W. E., Taqqu, M. S., Willinger, W., & Wilson, D. V. (1994). On the self-similar nature of ethernet traffic (extended version). *IEEE/ACM Transactions on Networking, 2*(1), 1–15. doi:10.1109/90.282603

Liu, S. G., Wang, P. J., & Qu, L. J. (2005, Aug.). Modeling and simulation of self-similar data traffic. *Machine Learning and Cybernetics, 2005. Proceedings of 2005 International Conference on, 7*, 3921-3925 Vol. 7.

Markatchev, N., & Williamson, C. (2004). Webtraff: A gui for Webproxy cache workload modelling and analysis. *Computer Communications*, 76–81.

Meiss, M. R., Menczer, F., Fortunato, S., Flammini, A., & Vespignani, A. (2008). Ranking Web sites with real user traffic. In *Wsdm '08: Proceedings of the international conference on Web search and Web data mining* (pp. 65–76). New York, NY, USA: ACM.

NLANR. (2007). Cache access logs[onlne] available. ftp://ircache.nlanr.net/Traces/.

Pacheco, J. C. R., & Roman, D. T. (2006). A tool for long-range dependent analysis via the r/s statistic. In *Cic '06: Proceedings of the 15th international conference on computing* (pp. 361–366). Washington, DC, USA: IEEE Computer Society.

R Development Core Team. (2008). R: A language and environment for statistical computing. Vienna, Austria: Rezaul, K. M., & Grout, V. (2007). An overview of long-range dependent network traffic engineering and analysis: characteristics, simulation, modelling and control. In *Valuetools '07: Proceedings of the 2nd international conference on performance evaluation methodologies and tools* (pp. 1–10). ICST, Brussels, Belgium, Belgium: ICST (Institute for Computer Sciences, Social-Informatics and Telecommunications Engineering).

Serpanos, D., Karakostas, G., & Wolf, W. (2000). Effective caching of Web objects using zipf's law. In *Multimedia and expo, 2000. icme 2000, ieee international conference* (Vol. 2, pp. 727–730).

TraceGraph. *(2005).* trace graph tool [onlne] available: http://www.tracegraph.com/ traceconverter.html.

Zipf, G. K. (1929). *Relativity frequency as a determinant of phonetic change* (Vol.XL).

Chapter 13
Increased Popularity through Compliance with Usability Guidelines in E-Learning Web Sites

Greg Scowen
ETH Zurich, Switzerland

Holger Regenbrecht
University of Otago, New Zealand

ABSTRACT

This paper identifies and measures correlations between compliance with usability guidelines and the popularity of a Web site. A sample of e-learning Web sites was reviewed and their usability scored using a Web-based evaluation system developed during the study. This usability score was then tested against five different ranking systems using Spearman's Rank correlation. The results of these tests show a strong correlation between compliance with usability guidelines and Web site popularity. The five ranking systems also showed positive correlations to each-other and to the usability of the sites. The conclusion drawn from these results is that compliance with usability guidelines could be a way to achieve higher Web site popularity and visitor numbers.

INTRODUCTION

We have often suggested to clients and students that usability is an essential part of any Web site development and that compliance to usability

DOI: 10.4018/978-1-60960-523-0.ch013

guidelines could be a pathway towards a more popular site. Yet many times these suggestions have been ignored, or in the least respondents have not considered usability studies to be important to their project. Due to a lack of previous research which examines the relationship between usability and popularity, convincing developers to invest resources into usability studies has been difficult. This research aims to answer the question: is there a positive relationship between compliance with usability guidelines and Web site popularity, and if so how strong and relevant is this relationship? Other questions addressed consider what usability guidelines should be adopted and how popularity can best be measured. The findings of this study are intended to create a foundation for further investigation into the effect of compliance with usability guidelines on Web site popularity.

The scope and objectives of this research are:

- To identify academically established—industry recognized Web site usability guidelines.
- To measure the compliance with these guidelines in e-learning Web sites. The population of this study has been narrowed down from all Web sites to e-learning Web sites, with the intention that the representation of the findings in one industry is transferable to others.
- To measure the correlation between compliance with usability guidelines and the popularity of a Web site. An assumption has been made that members of a group of Web sites within a particular educational subject area, that is, English or Math, have the same chance as each other of becoming popular.
- To identify and measure correlations between compliance with usability guidelines and five Web site ranking systems

The first section of this paper reviews previous literature surrounding the fields of usability and Web site popularity. The method section follows on from the literature review and provides a detailed description of how this research was conducted. This is followed by the results and conclusions sections which include a discussion about what the findings could signify and what work still needs to be done.

PREVIOUS USABILITY AND POPULARITY RESEARCH

Overview

Tools and methods that may be used to prove a correlation between usability and Web site popularity have been reviewed. The tools concerned include established Web site design usability guidelines and software for testing compliance to such guidelines. Suggested methods, as an alternative to tools, for testing compliance are also discussed and accompanied with a review of methods for measuring Web site popularity.

Usability

What is Usability?

Usability is a well established concept and is precisely defined by the widely accepted ISO9241 standard (Petrie & Kheir, 2007). Part 11 of ISO9241 defines usability as the effectiveness, efficiency and satisfaction with which specified users achieve specified goals in particular environments (ISO, 1998). In this context *effectiveness* refers to the accuracy and completeness of the tasks, *efficiency* considers the resources expended in completing the tasks, and satisfaction means the comfort and acceptability of the system to its users. Prior to the development and wide-spread acceptance of ISO9241, perhaps the most commonly cited definition of usability was that of Jakob Nielsen who broke usability into five areas: learnability, efficiency, memorability, errors, and satisfaction (1993).

It is important, for the purpose of this study, to clarify the separation between usability and accessibility. While there are many similarities between usability and accessibility guidelines, the two fields are not the same. However, accessibility could be considered a subset of usability, since usability implies accessibility (Brajnik, 2000). If a Web site is usable by all users then it must be accessible. Brajnik also shows that the contrary is not necessarily true, that is, problems that may affect the usability of a page may not affect the accessibility. Likewise, a paper produced in partnership with the National Cancer Institute makes an attempt, as the title suggests, at "Bridging the Gap: Between Accessibility and Usability" (Theofanos & Redish, 2003). Further reinforcing the subset theory, Theofanos and Redish note "meeting the required accessibility standards does not, however, necessarily mean that a Web site is usable for people with disabilities" (p. 38).

Established Web Site Usability Guidelines

The definitions for usability by ISO (1998) and Nielsen (1993) are also suitable for Web sites, in that a Web site is a form of system. Defining suitable guidelines, however, with which to achieve this usability is more difficult. Attempting to further define Web site usability and appropriate guidelines are subjects of ongoing research by a number of Web site usability organizations. This research and less formal sources can be easily found through common search engines. However, the quantity of material available only compounds the problem because much of the information is conflicting. In a 1997 report where he attempted to create a resource guide for Web site usability, Ohnemus (1997) produced a list of 8 guide books, 22 Web style guides, 8 accessibility guides, and a further 10 resources on usability. Furthermore, the World Wide Web Consortium (or W3C) also produced a set of guidelines that quickly gained acceptance. These guidelines were officially focused on accessibility, although the confusion of whether they were usability guidelines was even prevalent among the W3C members responsible for them (W3C, 2001).

The conflict between all of the available guidelines did not go unnoticed and in 2001, the National Cancer Institute started working on identifying research related to Web design and

usability. Their findings became the subject of panels at conferences (Koyani & Allison, 2003) and later developed into a set of 187 peer reviewed guidelines that are now published by the American Government for use in government Web sites (HHS, 2006). The effort made and resulting guidelines have been noted and praised:

Prescriptive guidance is often voluminous, vague, conflicting, or divorced from the context in which sites are being developed, thus making it difficult to apply. Many guidelines have not been validated empirically and there is little overlap across guideline sets. A noteworthy exception is the research-based guidelines that researchers at the National Cancer Institute developed (Ivory & Megraw, 2005).

Due to the general support and the nature of the continual redevelopment/refinement by the HHS, this study will be based on a selection of their guidelines. The next question to answer is how best to test for compliance to these guidelines.

Testing a Web Site's Compliance to the Guidelines

Normally a usability evaluation would be completed using one or both of two kinds of methods: usability inspection methods or user testing (Brajnik, 2000). An example of usability evaluation is Nielsen's heuristic evaluation (Nielsen & Mack, 1994) where a group of experts use a Web site and assign severity levels to usability issues. By contrast, a normally non-specialist and randomly sampled group of system users conduct user testing. These users are given instructions of tasks to complete on the Web site and are asked to note system functions that do not work or that they do not like (Instone, 1999). Both of these methods confirm the findings of Preece et al. that "evaluation is concerned with gathering data about the usability of a design or product by a specified group of users for a particular activity within a specified environment or work context" (Preece et al. cited in Spiliopoulou, 2000).

However, for this study we do not need to fully evaluate the usability of a Web site to show that the chosen guidelines have been complied with. To conduct either usability inspections or user testing for a large number of Web sites would also be beyond the scope of this study due to time restraints and the quantity of information required. Rather, each Web site will be tested against a checklist of items derived from the chosen guidelines. Such a checklist can be tested through the use of an automated tool or by manual observation.

Brajnik (2000) compiled a comprehensive table for the comparison of evaluation tool features and one tool, 'LIFT' (Usablenet, n.d.), stood out clearly above the rest, due to its coverage of more aspects of usability and extended features. When supplied a URL, the LIFT tool retrieves the text form of the Web site and analyses it according to various rules. These include, for example, checking for completeness of "Alt Tags" in images, use of Web safe colors, and the validity of HTML code. Unfortunately, the features measured by the LIFT tool were often inconsistent with the guidelines produced by the HHS. In fact, the majority of the items checked by automated tools seem to relate more to accessibility than usability as a whole. As previously discussed, merely meeting accessibility standards does not infer meeting usability standards. Wattenberg (2004) refers to LIFT and other tools from Brajnik's table as "automatic validation tools ... to help evaluate the accessibility levels of a completed Web site" (p. 14). He goes on to note that "these tools have also been found to bypass emerging technologies and miss important usability problems." Even when we only consider the automated tools as being accessibility measurement systems, Wattenberg points out that they cannot be considered efficient by discussing a study from Scotland where the potential to develop a single evaluative tool to help create accessible

Web sites was conducted. "The researchers did not find a single tool or process that would achieve these goals" (Wattenberg, 2004, p. 14).

With automated testing declared unsuitable, the remaining option for testing compliance to usability guidelines is to manually mark items off on a checklist. The use of this method has been validated by Keevil (1998) who defines a checklist as "a list of questions that require a yes or no answer" (p. 271), although he also offers an alternative of using scoring instead of yes/no options (p. 273). Preferring the "Yes or No" concept, Keevil goes on to explain how to create a checklist. His suggestion is to select measurable attributes that are based on usability research and then to write these down in a question format (p. 274). An example of a question that may be included on a checklist could be: "Is some form of notice given (e.g., breadcrumbs) to identify where on the site the user is?" In his summary, Keevil provides a brief list of advantages and disadvantages to using a checklist system. One noted advantage is that a "checklist is inexpensive and easy to implement" (p. 275). The major disadvantage is that a bias may be introduced by evaluator's interpretations of the guidelines. However, according to Keevil, this bias is overcome through the use of a "Yes or No" technique. Keevil's work has been a major contributor to the design of this study. For the evaluation of compliance to usability guidelines, a checklist with the "Yes or No" design will be used, with the addition of a 50% option. Where a guideline has been adhered to in part, but perhaps not in full or throughout all assessed parts of the system, then a 50% or "partially complied" grade will be given. Further to Keevil's support for the checklist evaluation system, Human Factors International—a large and experienced user-centered design group—have also touted the use of a similar checklist system called "Usability Scorecards" (Weinschenk, 2007).

Web Site Popularity

What is Web Site Popularity?

Unlike Web site usability, the definition of Web site popularity is not so clear. First, it is important to discuss the relationship between success and popularity. If popularity is taken to mean the state of being "liked or admired by many or by a particular group" (Oxford, n.d.) then success is not necessarily equal to popularity. Belanger et al. (2006) note that since success is goal-specific, it is defined differently depending on the needs of the business. For an online retailer, success may mean the percentage of visitors converted to buyers, or the degree of loyalty as shown by the number of return visitors (Schonberg, Cofino, Hoch, Podlaseck, & Spraragen, 2000). The quantity of site traffic is, however, still recognized as "… the predominant way of determining success from organizations' perspective" (Belanger et al., 2006). For the purposes of this study, we have defined Web site popularity based on the Oxford definition of popularity above: A popular Web site is one that is liked or admired by many people.

How a Web site becomes popular is the topic of much discussion. Adamic and Huberman (2001) report that Web site growth follows power laws, allowing for the growth of a Web site to be mathematically predictable: "The day to day fluctuations in the number of visitors to a site is proportional to the number of visitors the site receives on an average day" (p. 58). The visitors to a site are of two types; repeat visitors who in turn influence new visitors, and new visitors who have come through a referral or advertising. The more visitors a site has, the more referrals they get and the more advertising they can afford. This idea of growth infers that popular pages will always become more popular than less popular pages. Smaller Web sites do not have the same chance to grow. This theory is supported by Cho and Roy (2004) who report that popularity-based search engine rankings are biased against unknown pages: "When search engines constantly return popular pages at the top of their search results, more Web users will 'discover' and look at those pages, increasing their popularity even further" (p. 20-21). In this case, popular pages are those that have high visitor numbers, rather than inbound links as are used in this study. This finding is also echoed by Kavassalis, Lelis, Rafea, and Hardi who state that "…users are thus more likely to learn about popular pages than unpopular ones" (2004). The question should be asked, however, of how sites that are newer can have come to be much more popular than older sites. The power law theory of popularity does not take into account how a popular site became popular in the first place. An example to consider would be that of Google vs. Yahoo. For many years, Yahoo was a search engine that was widely known and used. Suddenly, in 1998, Google launched a similar service, albeit with a new approach and differing methods behind the system. Within a few years, Google had become the search engine of choice for more Internet users than the others. What caused this? Could it be that Google was more usable?

Another report from De Angeli, Sutcliffe, and Hartman (2006) explains how they conducted user testing on two Web sites with identical content but different navigational systems and layouts. One site had a traditional menu-driven layout; the other was a metaphor-based interactive and animated design. Their findings clearly showed that the different designs had more or less appeal and usability levels dependent on the age group of the users. Therefore, we also need to question what influence the age of Internet users has on Web site popularity. If the majority of Internet users fall into a certain age group, will a particular style of Web site also have an increased potential to become popular? With this question in mind, this study will use a sample of Web sites from the educational sector with the aim of limiting the potential age differential in users as much as possible.

Measuring Web Site Popularity

There are two common methods for measuring Web site popularity. One of these is to use a statistical program to count the number of visitors to the site and compare this with other sites. The alternative method mirrors the academic world (and as shown below the concept of Google PageRank) and is measured by counting the number of inbound links to a Web site, which are considered as referrals in support of a Web site.

Attempting to count the number of visitors to all Web sites is an impossible task. To do this, every Web site host in the whole world would need to submit their user data to one central location. This could be achieved through the use of automated software or by manual means, but overseeing such a task would require huge infrastructure and a lot of financial resources. This does not even take into consideration the ethical and business reasons that would stop a large portion of these hosts from sharing that information. This conundrum has resulted in various companies establishing services or tools that count traffic of competing Web sites. An example of a well-known traffic counting service is the Internet media and market research company The Nielsen Company and their "Nielsen Netratings" (n.d.). This company charges clients a fee for providing them with traffic statistics for their Web sites and those of their immediate competitors. Unfortunately, the fees involved are well beyond the budget afforded to this study. An alternative tool is available for free, that of Alexa.com (Alexa, 2007), a subsidiary of the Amazon Company that provides a downloadable tool-bar for Internet Explorer users. This toolbar offers search engine functionality and information about the sites that users are browsing. In the background it also records traffic information and saves this data to their Web site, which in turn reports the traffic rating of Web sites. Although this information sounds of promise to this study it not altogether helpful. This is because "Alexa's sample is known to be biased towards users of Microsoft

Windows, particularly those who use Microsoft Internet Explorer" (Sullivan & Matson, 2000, p. 141). Since users of other operating systems or browsers are not recorded, and traffic from all other Internet users is not counted, the resulting traffic statistics are not very helpful at all. With this limited scope in mind, the Alexa rating for sites will be reported in this study, but will not be the primary indicator of popularity.

Conversely, the concept of links toward a Web site being positive referrals to a site makes a lot of sense. Even when a Web site links to a site the owners do not necessarily like, they are still suggesting that other people look at it, so therefore it is a positive referral in at least one sense. Brin and Page understood this concept when they designed the search engine Google (1998). They created a system called PageRank, where links pointing to a page are accorded a quality status (depending on the pages they appear on) and counted. A page, therefore, has a calculated PageRank that is based on the number of links pointing to it and the quality of those links. Through PageRank, the position of a page in Google search engine results is decided. As with the Alexa rating, the PageRank of each site's main page will be recorded, however, for this study the popularity rating of each Web site will be assessed through the number of links (treated as referrals) located through three sources: Google, Yahoo, and Del.icio.us. Because Google's PageRank system puts Web sites and links through tough checks and removes spam content, the number of links in Google (Google link-count) will be the chief indicator of popularity in this study.

Yahoo and Del.icio.us have been selected as additional link-count sources due to their popularity and the availability of their statistics. Yahoo is a search engine that operates in a similar fashion to Google and will be used to reinforce the Google results. Del.icio.us (2007), on the other hand, considers the social aspect of the Web. The Del.icio.us site allows for Web users to create bookmark/favorite lists publicly, thus allowing for other users to discover sites based on what their peers like. Unlike the process used by Google's PageRank system, in thus study the quality of the sources of links will not be considered.

A Proposed Correlation between Usability and Web Site Popularity

The objective of this study is to show that a correlation exists between adherence to usability best practices and the popularity of a Web site. There are a few studies that propose a correlation between usability and popularity; however, none of these actually measure the existence of a relationship between the two or set out to evaluate this relationship.

One paper that suggests that usability is important to the popularity of a Web site contains comments that appear, unfortunately, to be based on the author's opinion rather than evidenced fact. In his paper "User Interface Directions for the Web," Jakob Nielsen brashly states:

"Unfortunately, it is common for sites to aim at being 'cool', 'sizzling', or even 'killers' rather than trying to do anything for their users.... Design Darwinism will tend to drive out the most flamboyant sites and concentrate traffic at sites that follow the usability principles" (Nielsen, 1999).

It is clear that when he made this statement, Nielsen had not taken into account sites that contain numerous usability issues yet remain largely popular. A modern-day example can be found at MySpace.com and when Nielsen wrote his report there were similar examples, including the MySpace of the 90's, geocities.com. There will always be exceptional Web sites that become popular regardless of their flaws. This is due to the overwhelming social drive behind the Web. As discussed by Malcolm Gladwell, there can become a point in the lifecycle of a product, service, or system where it can simply cross a threshold, tip, and spread like wildfire (2000). Other comments regarding the importance of usability to Web site growth seem to carry a little more credibility.

Weinschenk reminds developers, marketers, and technology managers that the key to success remains that a product or service is actually useful and usable (Weinschenk, 2007). This supports the theory that usable Web sites will be more popular than unusable Web sites. Lederer, Maupin, Sena, and Zhuang confirm that "use of Web sites is to some extent dependent on the usefulness of the information content and ease of using the site" (1998, p. 200). They go on to suggest that to encourage visitors to their sites, Web managers should focus on usability (p. 201).

A report by Sullivan and Matson, "Barriers to Use: Usability and Content Accessibility on the Web's Most Popular Sites" (2000) is one of the key resources used in the preparation of this study. Sullivan and Matson made an analysis of the Web's 50 most highly trafficked sites, as identified through the use of the previously discussed Alexa toolbar (p. 141). While the study claims to have assessed the usability of their sample sites, the tool used for this assessment was LIFT (p. 142), the same tool discussed above. As has been previously established though this review of literature, LIFT does not adequately assess usability, rather it focuses on accessibility issues. Therefore the results of this report pertaining to the usability of the sites reviewed are not particularly reliable. Sullivan and Matson have pointed out the bias of Alexa, but failed to acknowledge the unsuitability of the LIFT tool to usability analysis. Moreover, they claim that their findings "...suggest that a meaningful ordinal ranking of content accessibility... correlates significantly with the results of independent automated usability assessment procedures" (p. 139) based on the use of the LIFT tool. The relevance of their findings is diminished when the LIFT tool is inspected and shown to really assess accessibility rather than usability. Instead of assessing both usability and accessibility, Sullivan and Matson appear to have assessed accessibility twice with differing tools and have then shown a correlation between the consequential results. However, because accessibility is a subset of usability, it is true that when a site is made more accessible it is inevitably also made more usable to at least some users.

There are, however, some insightful remarks to be taken from Sullivan and Matson's work that have been considered in the design of this study. These include the review of the Alexa toolbar which has been used to help design what does and does not receive consideration for ranking popularity (p. 141) and the concept of treating the homepage as representative of the whole site (p. 141). They also conclude that although guidelines are widely available, publicized, and known about they appear to be largely ignored. This serves as confirmation of the researcher's beliefs and as motivation for this study. If it can be shown, as predicted, that compliance with usability guidelines correlates with Web site popularity perhaps more organizations will invest time and effort into this field.

Summary of Literature Review

Reviewing literature related to this study has answered many questions, but also created new questions that need answering. A gap in knowledge has been identified. Does compliance with usability guidelines correlate to increased Web site popularity? It is obvious that some researchers are hinting at this but there does not appear to be any previous study that attempts to answer that question.

The review has also helped to identify appropriate tools and methods for conducting such a study, while identifying others that are not so suitable. Through reading the research of others a clear definition of usability has been established and the definition of popularity has been refined and stated, in the least for how it is to be used for the purpose of this study.

Key contributors to the field have been identified and their findings taken into consideration. With this solid foundation to build upon, we conducted this study.

METHOD

The Sample: Web Sites for Review

How Sites Originally Identified

We have defined e-learning Web sites as sites that contain educational resources such as self-testing software, games, templates, lesson plans, and tutorials. This study will further minimize the population by including only sites that contain resources for the K-12 sector of the education industry (hereafter referred to as Educational Resource Sites). Dr. Keryn Pratt, the tutor of a University of Otago course called "ICT in Education" (EDUX317, 2007) supplied the sample. One of the assignments that students of this course complete involves identifying three educational resource Web sites in a subject area of their choosing, and then reviewing these Web sites. Dr. Pratt agreed to supply a list of more than 200 of these identified Web sites from her files. The list included Web sites from various subject areas and did not include information about the original students or their reviews. From this list, it was intended to create groups by subject of no less than 10 sites. However, following a selection according to the criteria below, only 32 sites in total were included in the study and only two groups identified.

Selection Criteria for Sites

In attempt to minimize as many external influences as possible, official Web sites of universities, government organizations, and schools were not included in the study. Because university Web sites are frequently visited by most students of that university, a larger institution would have a significantly higher visitor count. Government sponsored Web sites are often supported by large televised advertising campaigns, and furthermore some sites are a prescribed part of a curriculum, meaning that they are used regardless of their popularity or appeal.

This, essentially, leaves sites that are developed by independent companies or organizations and hobby groups to be considered. An example of a site that would be suitable could be a resource site developed by a nationwide astronomical club to help attract new members. The sites should all have content that is suitable for, or directed at, the K-12 sector of the education industry, meaning resources for primary and secondary education. All Web sites included in the study must have English as the main language of navigation and content to minimize the risk of the language of the intended audience acting as a compounding variable.

Other than this, the base criterion of selection was that the Web site was operational at the time of review.

Exceptions to Selection

One Web site that is provided by the University of Texas was included in the study. The "World Lecture Hall" site (http://web.austin.utexas.edu/wlh/) is a sub-site within the University's main Web site and is an open resource for any interested visitors. The homepage used for data purposes and review was a second level directory in the main site, so no data was inherited from the University Web site itself.

There were no exceptions on Web sites that were not included in the study.

Problems Encountered in Site Selection

Having checked through the original supplied list of 225 sites supplied, only 38 sites met the criteria for inclusion in the study. One group of 10 Web sites was identified that dealt with a diverse range of subject areas, and one other group of 7 Web sites that included resources for business education. The remaining sites formed groups of two

or three in more individual subject areas such as physical education or biology.

Due to the original Web site list being created by New Zealand Teaching students, a few sites included in the study are on New Zealand domains. These Web sites are inherently likely to have lower visitor numbers than those on international domains. However, without including New Zealand and United Kingdom sites there would not be a sufficient quantity of sites in the study.

Measuring Usability and Popularity

Choosing Usability Guidelines

Initially we were prepared to collate a selection of numerous governmental and industry produced guideline documents, and to then compare these, charting the guidelines that were consistently agreed upon. During the collation process, a guideline document was encountered that had been produced by the US Department of Health and Human Services (HHS, 2006). This guideline document consists of 209 usability guidelines that have been collated through the collaborative effort of 18 academics and industry professionals. The result is a reliable, quantified and peer reviewed set of guidelines that do not exist anywhere else (HHS, 2006). The discovery of this document provides a sound base for this study.

We narrowed down the 209 guidelines to a more manageable selection of points that could be tested. The HHS guideline document applies "Strength of Evidence" and "Relative Importance" scores to each guideline which helped in this process. "Strength of Evidence" has been determined by a panel of eight usability researchers, practitioners and authors, and considers how well established each guideline is in academia and industry. "Relative Importance" refers to how important each guideline is to the success of a Web site. This was determined by a panel of 16 reviewers, half of whom are usability experts, the others Web site developers. Because the testability of each guideline determined which ones could be used, this study included a broad range of both of these scores.

The first criterion for selecting a guideline for inclusion on this study was the ability to test conclusive compliance to the guideline visually by viewing a Web site. Subjective guidelines such as "Provide useful content" and development technique guidelines like "Establish user requirements" could therefore not be included.

A further criterion was the relative importance of a guideline. The HHS Guidelines "Relative Importance" scores fall between 1 and 5. For this study, only guidelines with a score of 3 or more were considered for selection. After identifying a set of 33 guidelines in the first selection process, a further five were removed according to the same criteria in a second round. This left a remaining set of 28 guidelines.

The Usability Score Concept

The selected guidelines had a range of relative importance scores associated with them, with 10 having a relative importance of 5, a further 16 with an importance of 4, and two with an importance of 3. From these relative importance rankings a 'Usability Score' was developed. If a Web site complied with all guidelines, the combined total of relative importance scores achieved would be 120. Assuming that compliance to more important guidelines makes a site more usable, we decided to measure the usability of a site based on this total, rather than based on a simple count of how many guidelines are complied. This 'Usability Score' was reported both as a total out of 120 and as a percentage.

Measures of Popularity

Five measurements of Web site popularity will be obtained during the data collection process. All of these will be reported in the results; however, the most importance will be placed on the

number of links pointing to the site as found on the Google search engine. Further link-count measures included are sourced from Yahoo and Del.icio.us. Both of these are included to further support the Google link-count and to identify if there are similarities between these three sources. Additionally, the Google PageRank and Alexa rating will be reported to identify if these have a correlation with usability, although neither can be relied upon as an indicator of popularity.

Conducting the Reviews

Method of Reviewing Sites

Early in the study it was determined that individually reviewing each Web site and entering responses into a document would be very time consuming. Potentially, this would also result in discrepancies due to the difference in dates when the sites are reviewed and the mood of the reviewer. Automated options were considered, however these were found to be lacking in either their abilities for testing the guidelines or their reliability.

To combat these problems, the first author designed a Web-based evaluation tool specifically for use in this study. Using HTML frames, PHP scripting, and a MySQL database, the tool would enable the site under review to be presented alongside review questions and buttons for navigating the review process. As each question is answered, the response is saved to a database and the next question appears on screen with a refreshed copy of the review-site's homepage. Following the 28 guideline questions, five further questions asking for the rankings of Google, Del.icio.us, Yahoo, and Alexa would be presented.

Creating the Review Software (WES)

Web site Evaluation System (WES) was created using simple HTML framing techniques. A Frameset was created with a narrow band across the top of the page where each guideline could be presented as a question, and the remainder of the browser window showed the site being reviewed. Adjacent to the question were four response options in the form of a radio-button group, and a button used for submitting the response and moving to the next question. All questions were written in a way that a "Yes" response equaled to compliance with the guidelines. A "No" response meant no compliance was visible. Furthermore, options were provided to indicate "partial compliance" with a guideline, or to "skip" the guideline if it wasn't applicable. Both of these options allocated a score of half the relative importance of the guideline considered. A guideline that might be skipped, for example, is "Label data entry fields consistently." If no forms were found on the site, this guideline was skipped and half points given to avoid inconsistencies in data.

The use of frames in this manner resulted that the site could be negotiated in the lower window of the browser without the question area being affected. This enabled the reviewer to locate instances of compliance to guidelines more efficiently. When a response was selected and the submit button clicked, the data was submitted via a script to a database and the next question would appear with a refreshed copy of the homepage of the review site presented. Because each response was directly submitted to the database, if a connection failure occurred, the review could be easily continued from the point of failure.

To assist in the retrieval of rankings from five different sources, five extra questions were presented following the 28 guideline questions. These questions asked for a textual input of the various ranks used in the study. To assist in answering these questions, a link was provided to a source for each ranking. These links took the URL of the site being reviewed as a variable and opened a new browser window where the required data was automatically shown. The same technique was used to obtain the download speed of sites for one of the guidelines.

Upon completion of all 33 questions, a "submit and review" button was provided. Upon clicking this, the scores were tallied, a usability score as a percentage was calculated, and all review data was presented on the screen. These reports would be printed for each Web site reviewed. The results of all site reviews were stored in the MySQL database and then exported to an Excel spreadsheet, and later to SPSS.

Gathering Data

All 38 sites were reviewed over a two-day period in August 2007. The first author was the only reviewer involved in the study and treated all sites with the same criteria for grading the compliance to guidelines. The review was conducted using Internet Explorer version 7 on a Windows Vista operating system. The screen resolution was 1280 x 800 in wide-screen format on a laptop PC. Horizontal scrolling measurements were based on a 1024px wide resolution. Download times were calculated by an automated third-party system and were measured against a benchmark of downloading the homepage on 56k modem in 10 seconds or less.

The number of incoming links on Google and Yahoo were based only on links from external sites where possible. Both the Google and Yahoo link counting techniques used did not count links from within the base site itself.

Data Analysis

Breaking the Sites into Subject Categories

To create meaningful data the sites reviewed were broken down into categories based on subject matter. Web sites that deal with a diverse range of subjects are inherently going to receive more visitors that a site that includes resources on Astronomy for example. Sites that included more than five subject areas were allocated as members of the "Diverse" category.

Measuring the Correlation

To measure the strength of a correlation between compliance with usability guidelines and Web site popularity, all data obtained through the review of sites was imported into SPSS for analysis.

The chosen method of measurement applied to this data was Spearman's Rank Correlation (Spearman, 1904). This method was chosen over the widely-known Pearson Product Moment method due to its suitability to non-linear, non-normal, ordinal data and also to ranked variables (McDonald, 2006). The number of links in Google, Yahoo, and Del.icio.us are non-normal in their distribution, and both Alexa and Google PageRank are ranks. The Alexa ranking system is a reverse order rank, so a correlation between the Alexa Rating and usability would be represented by a negative correlation coefficient.

Possible Factors that Skew Data

Some of the sites reviewed operated in a link-farm type manner, or were part of a network of sites that link to them exceedingly. A link-farm is a Web site that excessively trades links with other sites to artificially inflate their importance. Link-farms often contain little unique content and are more of a directory to other content.

Another external factor that may affect data is the location of the Web site, or its national centricity. Some sites reviewed are on the New Zealand domain (.co.nz) and are targeted at New Zealand students. Naturally, these sites don't attract as many visitors as a site on the .com domain which is international in its reach.

Subject area is also very relevant to the data. One site that scored very highly for usability was an Astronomy site. The popularity of the site was much lower than some other subject areas such as Internet, which is relative to the popularity of the

subject itself. This is why the final research data is broken into groups based on subject.

RESULTS

Compliance to Usability Guidelines

An objective of this study was to measure the compliance with usability guidelines within a group of e-learning Web sites. The results of the review of 28 selected guidelines over 38 Web sites is presented in Appendix Table 1.

Two of the tested usability guidelines were complied to most frequently: "Eliminate horizontal scrolling" and "use mixed-case for prose text." Both of these guidelines were complied with in 36 of the 38 sites reviewed. Horizontal scrolling was considered to be eliminated if no horizontal scrollbar was displayed when viewing the site at a resolution 1024 pixels wide. None of the reviewed Web sites completely failed to comply with the prose-text recommendations. The two sites that did not fully comply had some segments of prose-text that were capitalized, with the majority being correctly formatted.

The least frequently complied guideline was "Minimize page download times," which required that the homepage of the Web site being reviewed download in 10 seconds or less on a 56k modem. This was tested with the support of an external source; Only 5 of the 38 Web sites tested complied with the 10 second requirement. Because this guideline could only be complied with completely or not at all it was also the guideline most frequently not complied with, with 86.8% of sites failing to download in 10 seconds or less.

Of the 28 guidelines, the majority of these (23) were more often complied with than not. Four guidelines exhibited a greater degree of non-compliance, with the remaining guideline "Distinguish required and optional data entry fields" often not being applicable because of a lack of data entry forms on a site. In these cases it was scored as partially complied so as to not skew data.

The Correlation between Usability and Web Site Popularity

The main objective of this study was to measure the strength and significance of the correlation between compliance with usability guidelines and Web site popularity. Using Spearman's Rank method, the correlations between the Usability Score of each reviewed Web site and each of the five ranks that were included in the data collection process were measured. Appendix Table 2 shows the scores of the reviewed sites prior to testing for correlation.

As previously established, the most important measure of popularity for the purpose of this study is the number of inbound links to the Web site in Google. The other popularity measurements have been included to further support the findings. The first analysis measured the correlations across all 38 sites included in the study. The results are shown in Appendix Table 3.

When measuring the correlation between compliance to usability guidelines with the five ranking systems across all 48 Web sites a significant correlation is visible in all cases except for that of Del.icio.us online bookmarking. The correlation between Usability Score and links in Google is of medium strength (.594) and is significant at the 0.01 level (2-tailed). This is the strongest correlation between Usability Score and the ranking systems.

High correlations are also visible between the number of Google links and Google PageRank and Yahoo link-count (.797 and .792 respectively). Both of these correlations are also significant. Medium correlations between Google link-count and the Alexa rating and number of Del.icio.us bookmarks are also visible. Because the Alexa system ranks Web sites from 1, the most visited Web site on the net, to an infinite number, the least-visited, the correlation between Alexa and other scores appears negative.

To counter the affect that the subject matter of a Web sites being reviewed may have on its popularity, or potential reach, the sites were grouped by subject and the same tests were conducted on two of the groups. The larger of these groups was Web sites that contain educational resources for a diverse range of subjects. Appendix Table 4 presents the findings of tests on this group of 10 sites.

Again, the most significant and strongest correlation between Usability Score and a ranking system is that of Google link-count. Having narrowed down the sample to a group of sites with similar content, a very strong correlation becomes visible. Furthermore, despite the small sample size, this correlation coefficient of .855 is significant at the 0.01 level (2-tailed). Also visible in this smaller sample is a strong correlation (.830) between the Usability Score and Google PageRank. Other than a slight decrease in the correlation between Google link-count and Google PageRank and Yahoo link-count, the other correlations visible in this test are similar or even stronger than with the larger sample.

The same patterns emerge in the 3rd test, that of Web sites that provide educational resources for business courses. With a sample of just six sites, a significant correlation of .941 is found between compliance to usability guidelines and the number of links pointing to the site in Google. In this sample, strong correlations between the pairs Usability Score - Google PageRank and Google link-count - Google PageRank are also shown (Appendix Table 5). None of the six sites had any bookmarks on Del.icio.us, resulting in no correlation data being calculable.

All of the correlations visible in these three tests provide support for the hypothesis of this study, that compliance with usability guidelines has a positive effect on Web site popularity.

CONCLUSION

Observed Compliance with Usability Guidelines

Overall the 28 usability guidelines selected for the study are complied with more frequently than not. For the most part, it seems that usability is either being considered, or it is naturally occurring, in Web site development. However, simple guidelines which really seem fundamentally obvious in design are visibly ignored or forgotten in many cases. How can it be that over half of the sites reviewed had cluttered displays on some or all of their pages? Or that only 60.5% of sites display the majority of their content in high-contrast color combinations so that it can actually be read?

Some of the guidelines show such high levels of compliance that it can be suggested they are now common-sense Web site design rules. Only one Web site displayed a horizontal scrollbar, which indicates that the problem of horizontal scrolling has been almost eliminated from the Web. It appears that Web site developers have also achieved a greater command of English, in that prose text is nearly always formatted correctly in mixed-case.

Page download time remains as much of an issue today as it did 10 years ago. Less than 14% of the sites reviewed downloaded in less than 10 seconds of a 56k modem, leaving the remaining sites at risk of losing visitors. It is possible the developers of the slow sites have calculated that with the uptake of broadband technologies the risk of upsetting visitors is too minimal to be of concern. But this leaves all visitors on modem connections in an unfortunate predicament. Should these users be dictated to and forced into more expensive technology by Web developers?

Increased Popularity through Usability

All five of the ranking methods that data were collected for show positive correlations with compliance to usability guidelines. The main indicator of popularity in this study, the number of inbound links found in Google, consistently shows a strong to very strong correlation across all three tests. Breaking the Web sites down into groups based on the content subject achieved a stronger result. The lack of a more complete sample for this study creates the need for further studies of this nature to be completed. However, we are confident that the same results obtained now would be reflected in the results from these tests over a sample of any size.

We believe that the principle hypothesis of this study has been proven, that is; increased compliance with usability guidelines does have a correlation with increased popularity of a Web site. Moreover, this correlation is shown to be both very strong and significant. Causality cannot be implied by a correlation alone, however the indication is indeed that Web sites that comply with usability guidelines will also inherently be more accepted by users, and thus boast higher popularity.

More usable Web sites not only acquire a greater number of links from other Web sites, but they also achieve both a higher Google PageRank and are more popular according to the Alexa rating system. Perhaps, then, more focus might be given to usability as a means to achieving success in Web sites in the future. Further research of this nature is called for, to enhance and support the results obtained so far. If the results of this study can be confirmed, perhaps Web site usability consulting services will become as popular as search engine optimization has been in the last few years.

Ranking Systems

Although the review of literature suggests that the Alexa ranking system is biased and not a reliable indicator of Web site popularity, it is apparent that it is at least consistent with the other rankings used. In all cases, the Alexa rank showed the appropriate negative correlation with the other ranking systems and the Usability Score.

The lack of Del.icio.us bookmarks came as something of a surprise. A system suggested to have been an extremely popular method of sharing Web sites turned out to be disappointing. Only 5 of the sites reviewed had any bookmarks in the Del.icio.us system. The majority of these sites did also exhibit high counts of links on Google and Yahoo, but it still brings a few questions to mind. Is Del.icio.us as popular as rumors suggest? If it is, then what sort of elitism does a site need to achieve before it appears in Del.icio.us? Does the average internet user want to bookmark their favorite sites online, or do they even know they can? And finally, do users of Del.icio.us fall into any particular age or demographic that results in favoritism towards certain types of site? In our opinion, comparing the number of bookmarks in Del.icio.us is not a suitable way of determining popularity.

Google PageRank cannot be considered to be a measure of popularity, but it is intended to indicate quality in a site. Compliance with usability guidelines correlates to increased popularity but also that increased usability results in popularity among higher quality referrers.

The findings of the study show a strong and significant correlation between the quantities of links found on Google and Yahoo, suggesting that Yahoo link-count may also be a suitable indicator of popularity. Yahoo, however, whilst always showing a correlation between Usability Score and link-count, did not consistently show a significant correlation. The number of links on Yahoo was normally many times that of Google and often featured links from partner sites in a related network (link farms) or from within the site being explored. Where Google has clearly spent effort developing a system for scoring the quality of links (PageRank) and minimizing the quantity of spam links, Yahoo has failed. This has resulted in the quality of Yahoo link-count as an indicator of popularity being diminished.

Limitations of this Study

The principle limitation of this study is the quantity and quality of the sample. Future studies need to be conducted with a larger sample which has been more carefully sourced. Following the processing of the original sample, only 38 Web sites remained from an original count of over 200. This number of Web sites, while sufficient enough to establish results, did not constitute a coherent sample.

Furthermore, nine of the sites reviewed were location-centric, six to the UK and three to New Zealand. The New Zealand based sites, in particular, were outliers; often with a high Usability Score but a low popularity due to the limited size of their target audience. In future studies this issue should also be avoided through careful sampling.

Finally, the snapshot nature of this research is a possible limitation. What is considered vital to Web site success one year can change in the next. The correlation between usability and popularity can therefore also change at a rapid pace. Research of this nature should be made on a regular basis, perhaps annually, to determine if these results are indicative of the Internet industry through time, or just a one-off occurrence.

Discussion

This study shows that certain usability guidelines are complied with frequently, while others are almost completely ignored. What does this mean for usability practitioners? Is it possible that some of the guidelines published are too hard to implement, or that developers feel too limited by them? Should guidelines that have become common-sense be published at all?

Certainly the suggestion that increased compliance with usability guidelines has a strong relationship with increased Web site popularity is of importance to the Internet industry. Will further findings of this type result in a higher uptake of usability studies during Web site development? The implications of this finding for organizations developing Web sites is if they want to attract more visitors, then some effort could be well applied to usability awareness. For usability consulting companies, this research calls for more studies of a similar nature to help strengthen the industry and to build greater awareness of the importance of usability and possible benefits.

ACKNOWLEDGMENT

This paper is based on the first author's unpublished case study thesis in Information Science at the University of Otago. We would like to thank all our colleagues for their advice and, in particular, Colin Aldridge for his methodological guidance. Thanks to Keryn Pratt for providing the necessary e-learning resources and her help.

REFERENCES

W3C. (2001). *WCAG WG minutes 29 March 2001.* Retrieved July 20, 2007, from http://www.w3.org/ WAI/GL/ 2001/03/ 29-minutes.html

Adamic, L. A., & Huberman, B. A. (2001). The Web's hidden order. *Communications of the ACM, 44*(9), 55–60. doi:10.1145/383694.383707

Alexa. (2007). *Alexa the Web Information Company.* Retrieved May 7, 2007, from http://www. alexa.com

Belanger, F., Fan, W., Schaupp, C. L., Krishen, A., Everhart, J., & Poteet, D. (2006). Web site success metrics: Addressing the duality of goals. *Communications of the ACM, 49*(12), 114–116. doi:10.1145/1183236.1183256

Brajnik, G. (2000). *Automatic Web usability evaluation: What needs to be done?* Retrieved May 5, 2007, 2007, from http://www.dimi.uniud. it/~giorgio/ papers/ hfweb00.html

Brin, S., & Page, L. (1998, April 14-18). *The anatomy of a large-scale hypertextual Web search engine.* Paper presented at the International Conference on World Wide Web, Brisbane, Australia.

Cho, J., & Roy, S. (2004, May 17-20). Impact of search engines on page popularity. In *Proceedings of the 13th International Conference on World Wide Web,* New York (pp. 20-29). ACM Publishing.

De Angeli, A., Sutcliffe, A., & Hartmann, J. (2006, June 26-28). Interaction, usability and aesthetics: What influences users' preferences? In *Proceedings of the 6th ACM Conference on Designing Interactive Systems,* University Park, PA (pp. 271-280). ACM Publishing.

Del.icio.us. (2007). *del.icio.us.* Retrieved May 7, 2007, from http://del.icio.us/

Gladwell, M. (2000). *The tipping point: How little things can make a big difference.* New York: Time Warner Book Group.

Google. (2007). *Advanced Google search operators.* Retrieved May 7, 2007, from http://www. google.com/ intl/ en/help/ operators.html

HHS. (2006). *Research-based Web design & usability guidelines.* Retrieved March 13, 2007, from http://www.usability.gov/ pdfs/ guidelines.html

Instone, K. (1999). *How to test usability.* Retrieved from http://usableweb.com/ instone/ howtotest

ISO. (1998). *International Standard ISO 9241-11: Ergonomic requirements for office work with visual display terminals (VDTs) - part 11: Guidance on usability.* Retrieved March 13, 2007, from http://www.idemployee.id.tue.nl/ g.w.m.rauterberg/ lectures.html

Ivory, M. Y., & Megraw, R. (2005). Evolution of Web site design patterns. *ACM Transactions on Information Systems, 23*(4), 463–497. doi:10.1145/1095872.1095876

Kavassalis, P., Lelis, S., Rafea, M., & Haridi, S. (2004). What makes a Web site popular? *Communications of the ACM, 47*(2), 50–55. doi:10.1145/966389.966415

Keevil, B. (1998, September 24-26). Measuring the usability index of your Web site. In *Proceedings of the 16ᵗʰ Annual International Conference on Computer documentation,* Quebec City, Quebec, Canada (pp. 271-277). ACM Publishing.

Koyani, S., & Allison, S. (2003, April 5-10). Use of research-based guidelines in the development of Web sites. In *Extended Abstracts on Human Factors in Computing Systems: Proceedings of CHI '03,* Ft. Lauderdale, FL (pp. 696-697). ACM Publishing.

Lederer, A. L., Maupin, D. J., Sena, M. P., & Zhuang, Y. (1998, March 26-28). The role of ease of use, usefulness and attitude in the prediction of World Wide Web usage. In *Proceedings of the 1998 ACM SIGCPR Conference on Computer Personnel Research,* Boston (pp. 195-204). ACM Publishing.

McDonald, J. (2006). *Spearman's rank correlation.* Retrieved September 9, 2007, from http://www.udel.edu/ ~mcdonald/ statspearman.html

Nielsen, J. (1993). *Usability engineering.* San Diego, CA: Academic Press.

Nielsen, J. (1999). User interface directions for the Web. *Communications of the ACM, 42*(1), 65–72. doi:10.1145/291469.291470

Nielsen, J., & Mack, R. (1994). *Usability inspection methods.* New York: Wiley.

Ohnemus, K. R. (1997, October 19-22). Web style guides: Who, what, where. In *Proceedings of the 15ᵗʰ Annual International Conference on Computer Documentation,* Salt Lake City, UT (pp. 189-197). ACM Publishing.

Oxford. (n.d.). *Compact Oxford English dictionary (ask Oxford).* Retrieved July 08, 2007, from http://www.askoxford.com/ concise_oed/ popular?view=uk

Petrie, H., & Kheir, O. (2007, April 28-May 3). The relationship between accessibility and usability of Web sites. In *Proceedings of the SIGCHI Conference on Human Factors in Computing Systems (CHI 2007),* San Jose, CA (pp. 397-406). ACM Publishing.

Schonberg, E., Cofino, T., Hoch, R., Podlaseck, M., & Spraragen, S. L. (2000). Measuring success. *Communications of the ACM, 43*(8), 53–57. doi:10.1145/345124.345142

Spearman, C. (1904). The proof and measurement of association between two things. *The American Journal of Psychology, 15*(1), 72–101. doi:10.2307/1412159

Spiliopoulou, M. (2000). Web usage mining for Web site evaluation. *Communications of the ACM, 43*(8), 127–134. doi:10.1145/345124.345167

Sullivan, T., & Matson, R. (2000, November 16-17). Barriers to use: Usability and content accessibility on the Web's most popular sites. In *Proceedings on the 2000 Conference on Universal Usability,* Arlington, VA (pp. 139-144). ACM Publishing.

The Nielsen Company. (2007). *Nielsen netratings.* Retrieved July 9, 2007, from http://www.nielsennetratings.com

Theofanos, M. F., & Redish, J. (2003). Bridging the gap: Between accessibility and usability. [ACM]. *Interaction, 10*(6), 36–51. doi:10.1145/947226.947227

Usablenet. (n.d.). *LIFT online.* Retrieved April 12, 2007, from http://www.usablenet.com/ products_services /lift_online/ lift_online.html

Wattenberg, T. (2004). Beyond standards: Reaching usability goals through user participation. *SIGACCESS Accessability and Computing, 79,* 10–20. doi:10.1145/1040053.1040055

Weinschenk, S. (2007). *Trends in user-centred design* (White Paper). Fairfield, IA: Human Factors International.

Yahoo. (n.d.). *Yahoo site explorer*. Retrieved May 7, 2007, from http://siteexplorer.search.yahoo.com

APPENDIX

Table 1. Compliance to usability guidelines in 38 Web sites

#	Guideline	Complied		Partially Complied		Not Complied	
		#	%	#	%	#	%
1	Do not display unsolicited windows or graphics	33	86.8	4	10.5	1	2.6
2	Show all major options on the homepage	34	89.5	2	5.3	2	5.3
3	Avoid cluttered displays	16	42.1	8	21.1	14	36.8
4	Place important items consistently?	21	55.3	8	21.1	9	23.7
5	Eliminate horizontal scrolling	36	94.7	1	2.6	1	2.6
6	Use meaningful link labels	22	57.9	14	36.8	2	5.3
7	Distinguish required and optional data entry fields	10	26.3	16	42.1	12	31.6
8	Label pushbuttons clearly	18	47.4	17	44.7	3	7.9
9	Organise information clearly	26	68.4	9	23.7	3	7.9
10	Facilitate scanning	19	50.0	7	18.4	12	31.6
11	Ensure that images do not slow downloads	25	65.8	3	7.9	10	26.3
12	Include logos	31	81.6	4	10.5	3	7.9
13	Minimize page download times	5	13.2	0	0.0	33	86.8
14	Provide text equivalents for non-text elements	14	36.8	5	13.2	19	50.0
15	Provide a search option on every page	17	44.7	1	2.6	20	52.6
16	Communicate the websites value and purpose	20	52.6	12	31.6	6	15.8
17	Limit homepage length	19	50.0	2	5.3	17	44.7
18	Use bold text sparingly	27	71.1	3	7.9	8	21.1
19	Provide feedback on user's location	14	36.8	4	10.5	20	52.6
20	Provide descriptive page titles	16	42.1	9	23.7	13	34.2
21	Use descriptive headings liberally	19	50.0	13	34.2	6	15.8
22	Link to related content	32	84.2	3	7.9	3	7.9
23	Use text for links	26	68.4	11	28.9	1	2.6
24	Use black text on plain, high-contrast backgrounds	23	60.5	8	21.1	7	18.4
25	Use mixed-case for prose text	36	94.7	2	5.3	0	0.0
26	Ensure visual consistency	27	71.1	6	15.8	5	13.2

continued on following page

Table 1. continued

27	Format lists to ease scanning	26	68.4	4	10.5	8	21.1
28	Label data entry fields consistently	24	63.2	13	34.2	1	2.6
	Mean	23	59.8	7	17.8	9	22.5
	Median	23	59.8	6	15.8	7	18.4
	Maximum	36	94.7	17	44.7	33	86.8
	Minimum	5	13.2	0	0.0	0	0.0

Table 2. Review scores (by subject then usability score)

Site	Alexa Rating	PageRank	GoogleLinks	YahooLinks	Del.icio.us	Usability Score	Loc	Subject
022	2478826	5	15	659	0	107.5		Astronomy
036	338704	5	159	3768	6	96	NZ	Biology
028	235941	6	141	5833	0	92.5		Biology
027	70158	6	290	31151	644	66.5		Biology
038	85387	7	732	7355	0	116	UK	Business
034	0	3	5	167	0	87	NZ	Business
030	1126005	5	87	2136	0	83.5		Business
035	502470	4	56	2655	0	79		Business
033	168971	4	61	5834	0	68		Business
032	0	4	3	297	0	65.5		Business
029	5899631	0	0	147	0	63		Business
052	1325979	4	4	743	0	71		Classics
023	1360	8	38100	737123	12989	107		Diverse
014	306470	7	783	28677	0	105.5		Diverse
007	2360	7	614	1459	0	101		Diverse
024	42	7	1140	13340	0	98	UK	Diverse
019	23057	6	1720	59284	5	87.5		Diverse
001	117478	1	413	1942	0	83		Diverse
004	2184730	5	81	1708	0	81		Diverse
042	142425	5	136	9813	0	75.5	UK	Diverse
005	112354	5	104	1580	0	59.5	UK	Diverse
050	1026411	5	20	7180	0	58.5	UK	Diverse
017	229847	6	619	25517	0	99.5		English

continued on following page

Table 2. continued

031	877519	6	147	1033	0	66		Ethics
046	8601318	4	94	6918	0	60.5		Ethics
037	815276	6	320	322	0	88.5		History
053	175772	6	314	14499	0	75.5		History
039	605	8	5700	242450	31000	113.5		Internet
040	14542	7	5790	1071387	1629	94.5		Internet
048	399853	6	488	13606	0	75		PE
047	1455426	4	15	934	0	46.5		PE
049	5542429	5	43	1494	0	39		PE
043	91802	6	144	18972	0	101.5		Physics
041	397750	5	6	142	0	92.5	NZ	Physics
044	437826	7	276	6221	0	76		Physics
008	2230007	7	405	15821	0	65		Science
021	27148	6	992	50207	0	104		Technology
016	455728	5	679	8781	0	102	UK	Technology

Table 3. Spearman's rho Correlations (all sites)

		Alexa	PageRank	GoogleLinks	YahooLinks	Delicious	Usability Score
Alexa	Correlation Coefficient Sig. (2-tailed) N	1.000 . 38	-.379(*) .019 38	-.490(**) .002 38	-.392(*) .015 38	-.418(**) .009 38	-.456(**) .004 38
PageRank	Correlation Coefficient Sig. (2-tailed) N		1.000 . 38	.797(**) .000 38	.657(**) .000 38	.391(*) .015 38	.527(**) .001 38
GoogleLinks	Correlation Coefficient Sig. (2-tailed) N			1.000 . 38	.792(**) .000 38	.478(**) .002 38	.594(**) .000 38
YahooLinks	Correlation Coefficient Sig. (2-tailed) N				1.000 . 38	.530(*) .001 38	.366(*) .024 38
Delicious	Correlation Coefficient Sig. (2-tailed) N					1.000 . 38	.282 .086 38
Usability Score	Correlation Coefficient Sig. (2-tailed) N						1.000 . 38

*Correlation is significant at the 0.05 level (2-tailed)
**Correlation is significant at the 0.01 level (2-tailed)

Table 4. Spearman's rho Correlations (diverse subject sites)

		Alexa	PageRank	GoogleLinks	YahooLinks	Delicious	Usability Score
Alexa	Correlation Coefficient Sig. (2-tailed) N	1.000 . 10	-.608 .062 10	-.758(*) .011 10	-.261 .467 10	-.450 .192 10	-.552 .098 10
PageRank	Correlation Coefficient Sig. (2-tailed) N		1.000 . 10	.754(*) .012 10	.500 .141 10	.488 .152 10	.830(**) .003 10
GoogleLinks	Correlation Coefficient Sig. (2-tailed) N			1.000 . 10	.697(*) .025 10	.701(*) .024 10	**.855(**)** **.002** **10**
YahooLinks	Correlation Coefficient Sig. (2-tailed) N				1.000 . 10	.701(*) .024 10	.479 .162 10
Delicious	Correlation Coefficient Sig. (2-tailed) N					1.000 . 10	.467 .173 10
Usability Score	Correlation Coefficient Sig. (2-tailed) N						1.000 . 10

*Correlation is significant at the 0.05 level (2-tailed).
**Correlation is significant at the 0.01 level (2-tailed).

Table 5. Spearman's rho correlations (business subject sites)

		Alexa	PageRank	GoogleLinks	YahooLinks	Delicious	Usability Score
Alexa	Correlation Coefficient Sig. (2-tailed) N	1.000 . 6	-.395 .439 6	-.257 .623 6	-.429 .397 6	. . 6	-.200 .704 6
PageRank	Correlation Coefficient Sig. (2-tailed) N		1000 . 6	.941(**) .005 6	.698 .123 6	. . 6	.941(**) .005 6
GoogleLinks	Correlation Coefficient Sig. (2-tailed) N			1.000 . 6	.829(*) .042 6	. . 6	**.943(**)** **.005** **6**
YahooLinks	Correlation Coefficient Sig. (2-tailed) N				1.000 . 6	. . 6	.771 .072 6
Delicious	Correlation Coefficient Sig. (2-tailed) N					. . 6	. . 6
Usability Score	Correlation Coefficient Sig. (2-tailed) N						1.000 . 6

*Correlation is significant at the 0.05 level (2-tailed).
**Correlation is significant at the 0.01 level (2-tailed).

This work was previously published in the International Journal of Information Technology and Web Engineering 4(3), edited by Ghazi I. Alkhatib, and Ernesto Damiani, pp. 38-57, copyright 2009 by IGI Publishing (an imprint of IGI Global).

Chapter 14
Discovery and Mediation Approaches for Management of Net–Centric Web Services

Frederick Petry
Stennis Space Center, USA

David Aha
Naval Research Laboratory, USA

Roy Ladner
Stennis Space Center, USA

Bruce Lin
Stennis Space Center, USA

Kalyan Gupta
Knexus Research, USA

Richard Sween
Stennis Space Center, USA

Philip Moore
Knexus Research, USA

ABSTRACT

This paper describes an Integrated Web Services Brokering System (IWB) to support the automated discovery and application integration of Web Services. In contrast to more static broker approaches that deal with specific data servers, our approach creates a dynamic knowledge base from Web Service interface specifications. This assists with brokering of requests to multiple data providers even when those providers have not implemented a community standard interface or have implemented different versions of a community standard interface. A specific context we illustrate here is the domain of meteorological and oceanographic (MetOc) Web Services. Our approach includes the use of specific domain ontologies and has evaluated the use of case-based classification in the IWB to support automated Web Services discovery. It was also demonstrated that the mediation approach could be extended to OGC Web Coverage Services.

DOI: 10.4018/978-1-60960-523-0.ch014

INTRODUCTION

In an increasingly net-centric world, Web services and service oriented architectures usage has grown and become a standard for data usage (Erickson & Siau, 2010). Web Services are becoming the technology used to share data in many domains. Web Services technologies provide access to discoverable, self-describing services that conform to common standards (Papazoglou, 2007; Ratnasingam, 2010) Thus, this paradigm holds the promise of an automated capability to obtain and integrate data. While desirable, access and retrieval of data from heterogeneous sources in a distributed system such as the Internet pose many difficulties and require efficient means of discovery, mediation and transformation of requests and responses. Differences in schema and terminology prevent simple querying and retrieval of data. These functions require processes that enable identification of appropriate services, selection of a service provider of requested data, transformation of requests/responses, and invocation of the service interface (Bai et al., 2008; Boutrous et al., 2009; Deng et al., 2009). Service availability must also be resolved. There have been a variety of approaches developed for these functions, but primarily independently of each other and not fully automated, i.e., often requiring human intervention (Rama, 2007)

In this paper we describe the design of an integrated end-to-end brokering system that performs automated discovery, automated mediation and automated transformation of Web Services requests and responses. In contrast to more static approaches that deal with pre-selected data servers, our approach creates a dynamic knowledge base from Web Service interface specifications that are discovered on the fly. The dynamic knowledge base assists with mediating requests to data providers that have ad-hoc interfaces or differing versions of a community accepted interface.

Our design incorporates ontologies into the development of an Integrated Web Services Broker (IWB). This approach contrasts with developments that assume that shared ontologies have been adopted or published in order to support service discovery and integration. In addition to the use of ontologies we have evaluated classifier technology for the subtask of Web Services discovery. It has been noted that classifiers generalize well in sparse data, which is a characteristic of our Web Services application domain. Our use of classifiers in this manner does not require a formal domain definition nor does it require data providers to deploy any additional specialized ontological descriptions of their web service.

There are general characteristics that should be found in any environment in which an automated system will operate. First, the domain must be one in which human intervention is neither required nor desirable. Since we are considering a Web Services context, data providers must have adopted a text-based, structured Web Services interface. This interface should subscribe to Web Services standards of self-description. While the structural content of each Web Services interface may differ significantly, the domain should be one in which key terminology that may be found in any interface has common conceptual content and is well understood and bounded. In this operating environment, it is desirable to isolate potential data sources in advance as opposed to attempting to discover service availability and capability on demand.

These characteristics are broadly applicable and encompass many typical application areas, and in this paper we describe the design and development of the IWB relative to these characteristics. The steps and issues we will be describing are basically applicable to any Web Services brokering system. Here, we illustrate the design specifically for the application context in which we are developing this system, i.e., meteorological and oceanographic (MetOc) forms of data.

Figure 1. Illustrated Use of Web Services

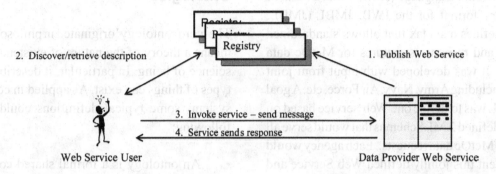

BACKGROUND

Web Services

Web Services provide data and services to users and applications over the Internet through a consistent set of standards and protocols. The most commonly used standards and protocols include, but are not necessarily limited to, the Extensible Markup Language (XML), Simple Object Access Protocol (SOAP), the Web Services Definition Language (WSDL) and Universal Discovery Description and Integration (UDDI) (Cerami, 2002).

XML is a language used to define data in a platform and programming language independent manner. XML has become one of the widely used standards in interoperable exchange of data on the Internet but does not define the semantics of the data it describes. Instead, the semantics of an XML document are defined by the applications that process them. XML Schemas define the structure or building blocks of an XML document. Some of these structures include the elements and attributes, the hierarchy and number of occurrences of elements, and data types, among others (Dick, 2000).

WSDL allows the creation of XML documents that define the "contract" for a web service. The "contract" details the acceptable requests that will be honored by the web service and the types of responses that will be generated. The "contract" also defines the XML messaging mechanism of the service. The messaging mechanism, for example, may be specified as SOAP. A web service describes its interface with a WSDL file and may be registered in a UDDI type registry. Interfaces defined in XML often identify SOAP as the required XML messaging protocol. SOAP allows for the exchange of information between computers regardless of platform or language.

A registry provides a way for data providers to advertise their Web Services and for consumers to find data providers and desired services (Figure 1). It is, of course, not necessary to register a web service. However, that would be similar to a business not listing its telephone number in a telephone directory. Not having a listing would make it more difficult for consumers to discover and utilize a web service. This advertisement of Web Services may or may not be desirable for net-centric operations in many application communities such as those found in many military operations (Ladner and Petry, 2005).

There are applications that provide services on the Web without using all components of the Web Services stack. These Web-based services employ diverse methods for discovery, description, messaging and transport. Within these Web-based services adherence to standards and protocols vary. There has been some work in applying soft computing techniques for discovery (Chao et al., 2005; Fenza et al. 2007; 2008; Li et al., 2009)

Since we are interested in querying MetOc data some of which is available from DoD, the Joint

MetOc Broker Language (JMBL) was a basis of the query format for the IWB. JMBL (JMBL, 2009) defines a syntax that allows standardized request and response structures for MetOc data queries. It was developed with input from joint forces including Army, Navy, Air Force, etc. A goal of JMBL was to define one Web Service based on jointly defined XML Schemas that would serve all types of MetOc data requests.. Each agency would implement this jointly defined Web Service and would therefore have interoperable implementations of the same Web Service.

The JMBL Web Service is defined by one WSDL file and several XML Schemas. These Schemas define the structure of requests that the JMBL Web Service will accept and the structure of responses that the JMBL Web Service will provide. The request and response Schemas include several other Schemas, which define global data types and structures. Figure 2 shows this conceptual organization. As shown in Figure 2, several of the global Schemas are included in other global Schemas. Schemas in Figure 2 are represented by "XSD".

Ontologies

The word 'ontology' originated in philosophy and means a theory of the nature of existence or the science of being. In particular, it describes what types of things can exist. As applied in computer systems some typical definitions could be the following:

- An ontology is a formal shared conceptualization of a particular domain of interest (Stojanovic et al., 2004)
- An ontology is an explicit specification of an abstract, simplified view of a world we desire to represent. (Holsapple & Joshi, 2002).

An ontology defines common words and concepts used in the description of an area of knowledge to share domain information for applications. An ontology is usually structured by including classes representing concepts, instances of classes and the relationships among them. Also included are their properties and functions or processes related to them.

Figure 2. Conceptual View of JMBL WSDL and Schemas

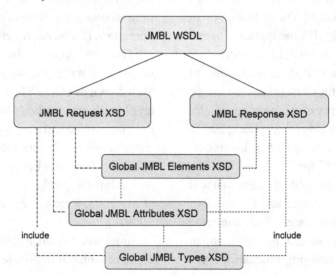

There are two approaches that can be taken to ontology development, top-down and bottom-up approaches. Many ontologies have been constructed by top-down iterative development. This falls in the same approach as the design of taxonomies and classifications by a specialization process. Bottom-up design techniques typically begin by specifying the list of primitive concepts and construction rules that define more complex concepts, i.e. a generalization process. In practice it is often a mix of these two approaches that are actually utilized. Building ontologies is typically difficult, time-consuming and expensive. This is especially so, if the goal is to construct an ontology that is rich and powerful enough to perform automated inferencing. Construction of such an ontology requires careful attention to detail and a strong ability to organize information meaningfully. It is often stated that ontology development is a craft rather than a science (der Vet & Mars, 1998).

Ontological frameworks for describing the semantics of data include such developments as the Resource Description Framework (RDF) and Web Ontology Language (OWL). RDF provides a flexible representation of information and a reliable means of supporting machine reasoning (Powers, 2003). OWL permits users to more fully describe the meanings of terms found in Web documents and to represent the relationships among these terms (Lacy, 2005). Numerous methodologies for engineering and maintaining domain ontologies have been reported (Cristani and Cuel, 2004; Corcho, et al., 2007). There are also editors that assist with ontology development, such as the open source editor Protégé. A Protégé extension supports OWL ontologies (Knublauch et al., 2004). Even with these tools, ontology development remains a time- and skill-intensive activity.

Utilization of ontologies as metadata for various data sources on the semantic web is of specific concern (Kim, 2002). Recent efforts to improve interoperability include Web Services

technologies such as WSDL and XML Schemas. While these provide structured content, the limited nature of the semantic description hinders interoperability. Ontologies are often considered to be the basis of semantic meaning for these sorts of documents. OWL-S has been developed to extend OWL to supply the constructs for defining an ontology of services that is intended to support automated Web Services discovery, invocation, and composition. This is accomplished in the OWL-S ontology through classes that describe what the service does (service profile), how to ask for the service, what happens when the service is carried out (service grounding), and how the service can be accessed (service model) (W3C Member Submission, 2004).

IWB ARCHITECTURE

This section describes many of the processes and architectural features of an automated brokering system. We will illustrate this for the specific instance of our prototype application context, the MetOc Web Services domain. Meteorological and oceanographic Web Services provide actual and forecast weather information to a variety of government and commercial entities and the public. The information they provide can vary considerably depending on their intended audiences. Consequently, for an end-user, selecting and interacting with suitable Web Service(s) poses a significant challenge.

IWB Functionality

We are designing the IWB to automatically discover MetOc Web Services and then to dynamically translate data and methods across them. The IWB's Web Services search and discovery function is illustrated in Figure 3. The IWB will search a variety of identified registries for MetOc Web Services using the search feature supplied

Figure 3. The IWB search and discovery function

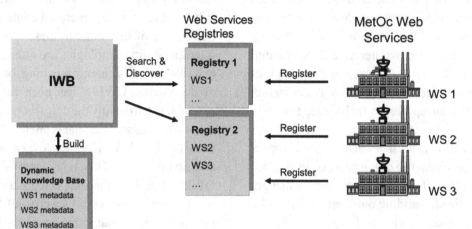

by that registry. This then enables the IWB to locate candidate sources to which requests may be brokered. Based on the characteristics of the Web Services it discovers, the IWB builds a dynamic knowledge base to support mediation.

This knowledge base allows the IWB to automatically translate user requests to differing Web Service interface specifications. For example, this shall assist with brokering requests to multiple MetOc data providers whose services may have implemented a) a community standard interface, b) an interface that is not a community standard, or c) an evolving version of a community standard interface. This approach contrasts with approaches that use pre-programmed solutions for pre-selected data servers. The IWB's mediation function is depicted in Figure 4. The client request is then dynamically translated and mediated to Web Services with differing WSDLs/Schemas.

IWB Processes

The high level processes at work in the IWB are Web Services discovery and mediation/transformation of user data requests. In this section we will describe the individual steps of each of these processes.

Web Services Discovery

To prepare for the web service discovery process (Adda, 2010), the IWB first loads the functional ontology. This ontology allows IWB to interpret terms found in WSDLs and schemas, as necessary, in order to build the Dynamic Knowledge Base.

The actual search function of the IWB entails a capability to search specific registries. Our approach is to query these registries for Web Services whose name or description contains relevant keywords. For example, a name/description keyword list might be {metoc, ocean, atmosphere, temperature, etc.}. The search will examine UDDI registries that may be applicable to this domain, as well as other known Web Services registries such as xmethods or Binding Point. Relevant WSDLs and corresponding schemas of identified Web Services are then downloaded.

The next step is the processing of the discovered WSDLs. This step involves the examination of each newly discovered WSDL and recording particular information about the web service to enable mediation. The WSDL is decomposed into a symbol table of its contents so that available methods and their inputs can be easily identified. We use terms found in these methods and their inputs to identify those methods that are most likely

Figure 4. The IWB dynamic mediation function

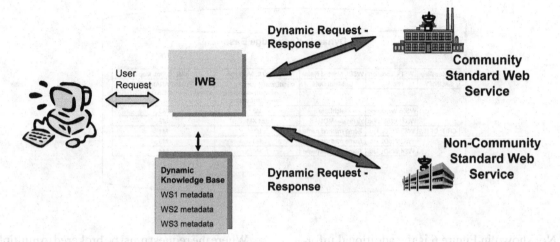

to be MetOc data relevant. Following this is the creation of a blank XML message conforming to the required input of each of the identified methods. Finally, the structure of this XML message is mapped to ontology concepts. That is, for each term in the blank XML message, we determine which concept in the ontology it is related to. This permits the content of a client request to the IWB to be mapped to the target blank XML structure.

Now it is possible for the IWB to add the newly found web service to its Dynamic Knowledge Base (DKB). The DKB provides a quick means of identifying Web Services that provide specific data and data types, and it is updated every time the IWB identifies a new web service or detects an update to a previously discovered web service. The records comprising the DKB are built as follows. For each MetOc parameter supplied by the identified WSDL data retrieval method, the following is performed:

a. Retrieve the concept from the ontology.
b. Complete the blank XML template with the parameter name ("sal", "depth" etc.). For this, we associate the term used by the web service with the concept from the ontology.
c. Create a web service method record including the method name, xml message and XML to Ontology map as shown in Figure 5.
d. Record the web service method record in the Dynamic Knowledge Base.

Next we discuss a typical example of the indexing required for the Dynamic Knowledge Base as shown in Figure 6. The index key is the domain concept relevant to the parameters the web service provides. These parameters are identified from terms found in the web service's WSDL and schema. For example, a web service, which contains oceanographic data such as "sea salinity" as an enumerated parameter, would be indexed by the concept "salinity."

Figure 5. Web Service Method Record

Web Service Method Record			
WSDL Location	WS Method Name	Blank XML Message	XML to Ontology Map

Figure 6. IWB Dynamic Knowledge Base

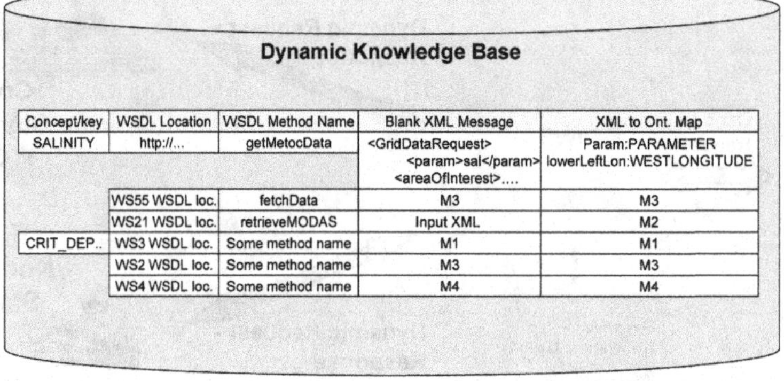

Concept/key	WSDL Location	WSDL Method Name	Blank XML Message	XML to Ont. Map
SALINITY	http://...	getMetocData	\<GridDataRequest\> \<param\>sal\</param\> \<areaOfInterest\>....	Param:PARAMETER lowerLeftLon:WESTLONGITUDE
	WS55 WSDL loc.	fetchData	M3	M3
	WS21 WSDL loc.	retrieveMODAS	Input XML	M2
CRIT_DEP..	WS3 WSDL loc.	Some method name	M1	M1
	WS2 WSDL loc.	Some method name	M3	M3
	WS4 WSDL loc.	Some method name	M4	M4

Not shown in Figure 6 is the additional information necessary to mediate user requests, including each element/attribute that the schema identifies as mandatory, the SOAP Action & Service endpoint, the location for which data is provided and the type of MetOc data provided (such as grids, observational data, imagery, etc.).

Web Service Mediation

We now describe the second high-level process of the IWB; namely, the mediation of user requests for data. This step includes the transformation of user requests and Web Services responses. The steps involved are:

1. Receive an XML formatted user request for data.
2. Decompose the user request to identify those XML tags that have associated values.
3. Locate the tag that corresponds to a "parameter" synonym. This tag identifies the data request using the end-user's terminology.
4. Query the ontology for the concept corresponding to the term provided by the user.
5. Query the Dynamic Knowledge Base by this concept to obtain all Web Services that provide data related to the concept.
6. Transform the user's request to target web service's request structure.

Where the request must be brokered to multiple Web Services, there may be multiple transformations. This step utilizes the XML template recorded during the discovery process. This transformation is illustrated below. Figure 7a shows a request received by the IWB and the ensuing transformed request to be submitted to a web service. Figure 7b further depicts the decomposed IWB request and the indexed web service request object. Transformation of the server response proceeds in a similar manner.

IWB High Level Architecture

Here we will describe in some detail the architecture that integrates the processes described in the previous section. The functional components of the IWB are shown in Figure 8. The IWB can begin mediating user requests once its Mapper component has discovered Web Services and begun populating the Dynamic Knowledge Base. Specifically, the Mapper takes as *input* (1) discovered Web Services interface specifications and (2) the MetOc ontology. It uses this information to build the Dynamic Knowledge Base, and it also assigns a qualitative and quantitative confidence score to each service.

After the IWB is initialized it is ready to process user requests to the appropriate web service or multiple services. The Mediator is the compo-

Figure 7. a) Request Transformation, b) Request Decomposition Example

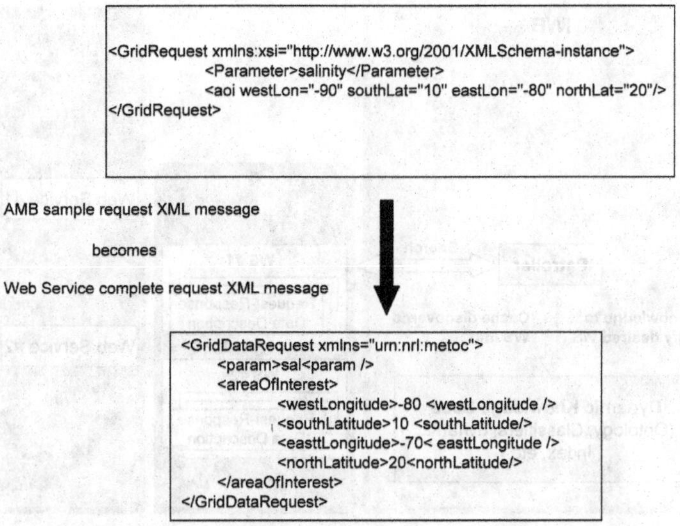

```
<GridRequest xmlns:xsi="http://www.w3.org/2001/XMLSchema-instance">
        <Parameter>salinity</Parameter>
        <aoi westLon="-90" southLat="10" eastLon="-80" northLat="20"/>
</GridRequest>
```

AMB sample request XML message

becomes

Web Service complete request XML message

```
<GridDataRequest xmlns="urn:nrl:metoc">
        <param>sal<param />
        <areaOfInterest>
                <westLongitude>-80 <westLongitude />
                <southLatitude>10 <southLatitude/>
                <easttLongitude>-70< easttLongitude />
                <northLatitude>20<northLatitude/>
        </areaOfInterest>
</GridDataRequest>
```

a

Decomposed User request

Concept	Request XML tag name	Request XML tag value	Attribute or element
PARAMETER	Parameter	salinity	element
WESTLONGITUDE	westLon	-80	attribute
SOUTHLATITUDE	southLat	10	attribute
EASTLONGITUDE.	eastLon	-70	attribute
NORTHLONGITUDE	northLat	20	attribute

becomes

XML to Ontology mapped request object

Concept	XML tag name	XML tag value	Attribute or element
PARAMETER	param	sal	element
WESTLONGITUDE	westLongitude		element
SOUTHLATITUDE	southLatitude		element
EASTLONGITUDE.	easttLongitude		element
NORTHLONGITUDE	northLat		element

b

nent of the IWB that provides the necessary transforms for this to occur. Clients submit data requests to the Mediator in an IWB XML format. The Mediator uses the previously created mappings to translate the client request into a candidate web service format specified in the Web Services Registry and submits the request to the web service provider. As the recipient web service sends the data response back to the Mediator, the web service response is transformed by the Mediator to the end-user format and forwards it to the IWB's Client. This is the inverse of the request mapping process.

Partial Matching in IWB

As discussed IWB performs two tasks: automated discovery and classification of web services that produce MetOc data, and syntax-independent consumption of this data by clients utilizing an ontology of domain information for identification of MetOc services. For instance, the ontology captures the top-level concept of a MetOc "Parameter." An instance of this class, such as "Sea Temperature" may have synonyms: "SeaTemp" and "TempSea". As a new web service is corralled by the IWB, its service description is broken into lexemes and matched to terms in the ontol-

Figure 8. a) IWB Architecture – Dynamic Discovery, b) IWB Architecture – Dynamic Mediation

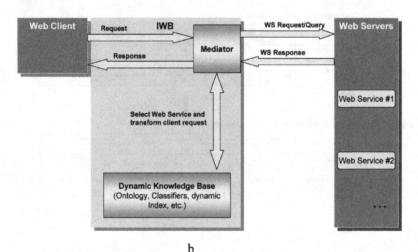

a

b

ogy. The ontology is manually constructed and maintained by domain experts, which results in a concise data model. However, small variations in a service description may thwart proper classification. For example, a service which offers a sea temperature parameter as "sTemp" may fail precise term matching, but there may be enough information to facilitate semi-automated ambiguity resolution. Another problem encountered while trying to index some web services was the non-uniformity of labeling and describing web

services. For any given concept in the ontology, there could be many different synonyms that mean the same thing. Some services were labeled with terms that were similar to concepts in the ontology, but not exact matches. One example is the term "temperature." Using just the term, it is unclear whether the web service provides air temperature, sea temperature, surface temperature, etc.

The IWB therefore employs a partial matching system to insulate the classification from unnecessary failure which generates a similarity measure to be used in resolving ambiguous cases. Many such metrics exist, such as the Levenshtein edit distance. The N-gram distance proves to be a fast method that performs well in the types of variations present in MetOc web service descriptions. The IWB will then both index the service with a recording of the similarity value and utilize a GUI to allow expert user guidance in the disambiguation as illustrated in Figure 9. Specifically, terms from a web service that were not exact matches for concepts in the ontology are evaluated as partial matches. The list of possible partial matches is returned to the IWB and a disambiguation window is then displayed on the IWB server monitor. This allows the user in charge of maintaining the IWB server to select which concept to index the web service under. In order to assist the user in deciding which concept fits the web service in question, links to the web service and WSDL are provided. If it is determined that the service is not a MetOc

Figure 9. Sample Disambiguation Window for Term "temperature"

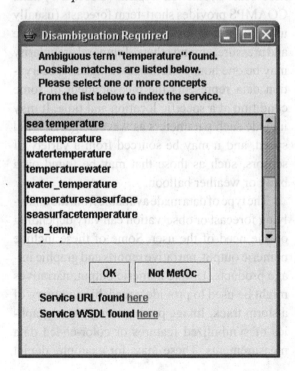

web service, the user may click Not MetOc, and the service will not be indexed.

IWB Mediation of OGC Web Coverage Services

The Open Geospatial Consortium (OGC) Web Coverage Services (WCS) also provides METOC data description and we have also extended the capability of the IWB to integrate data from WCS sites. WCS supports retrieval of geospatial data as "coverages" – that is, geospatial information representing space-varying phenomena. WCS structurally differs from World Wide Web Consortium (WC3) Web Services standards (e.g., WSDL) but does utilize formal XML structures to provide three operations: GetCapabilities, DescribeCoverage and GetCoverage. We have found these three sufficient to integrate data in this format

A demonstration of IWB for mediation OGC data was conducted at the NATO Underwater Research Center (NURC)) at La Spezia Italy. This demonstration was in coordination with NURC's Turkish Straits Survey (TSS) exercise. End-to-end data brokering from the Turkish Straits Survey (TSS) to data consumers at Naval Research Lab (NRL) was provided by effectively integrating a NURC WCS into the IWB, including index and data retrieval. Figure 10 illustrates the environment for the demonstration. In the figure TSS data from RV Alliance (remote sensed, in-situ, model output) is delivered to NURC Data Fusion group.. Data is then loaded into NURC OpenGeoserver, published as OGC layers/KML. IWB indexes these layers and can answer JMBL queries with WCS metadata

It should be noted that future OGC plans are to provide a web service capability for WCS similar to WC3 standards, which would facilitate use of IWB.

Figure 10. Turkish Straits Survey Environment

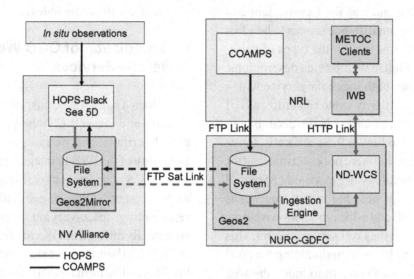

DEVELOPMENT OF METOC ONTOLOGY FOR IWB

As we have discussed, development of complex ontologies are difficult and time consuming. We describe in this section the data sources and data descriptions we have used in the development of a MetOc ontology and give an example of such an ontology. Finally we introduce the possible use of a classifier to complement the discovery process.

MetOc Data and Sources

In this section we describe some relevant MetOc data and its available sources. This overview describes a diverse mix of data that will be seen to present a number of troublesome issues for ontology development.

For the development of the IWB, we focus on forecasts and observations of ocean and atmospheric parameters. Parameters of interest include measures of phenomena such as wave height, wave period, sea temperature, air temperature, pressure, etc. This forecasted data is generally derived from numerical models, which predict the measurement of conditions either at specific locations or over broad areas. When area data is produced, it may be a uniform grid in either two or three dimensions. Additionally, the forecast may include such data for multiple time-steps, showing environmental change over time. Representative of the nature of this output is the Coupled Ocean/Atmosphere Mesoscale Prediction System (COAMPS) data. COAMPS provides short-term forecasts (usually up to 72 hours) for data such as air temperature and pressure, among others. Temporal granularity may be one hour increments or higher. Observation data represents the measurement of some condition at a specific location and time. It may include such parameters as wave height or wind speed, and it may be sourced from a variety of sensors, such as those that may be found on a buoy or weather balloon.

The type of data made available from the underlying forecast or observation can vary depending on the need of the user. Some of these include numeric output, narrative reports and graphic image products. Unlike numeric output, narratives might be used to provide a readable summary of a storm track. Image products may show graphics of symbolized features or color-coded data measurements. These may, for example, depict weather fronts or temperature variations on the ocean surface.

MetOc data is prepared and distributed by a number of government agencies and other sources. These include the Naval Oceanographic Office for ocean data and Fleet Numerical Meteorology and Oceanographic Center and the Air Force Weather Agency for atmospheric data. The National Oceanic and Atmospheric Administration (NOAA) and the National Data Buoy Center also provide such data for the atmosphere and ocean. NOAA, in particular, provides a wide range of data including weather information, ocean data on reefs, tides, currents, etc., real-time satellite imagery and data on large-scale climate conditions such as El Nino and global warning. The Argus Program includes seven stations around the world. These provide time exposure imagery that reveal sand bar movements. At some locations sensors record changing waves, winds, tides and currents on approximately an hourly basis. Many research facilities are also sources of oceanographic and atmospheric data. Some of these include Antarctic Cooperative Research Centre, the Center for Ocean Land Atmosphere Studies, Columbia University/ LDEO - International Research Institute, the Inte-

grated Global Ocean Services System Products, the National Center for Atmospheric Research, among others.

Lack of naming convention uniformity among models and data providers is a significant issue when dealing with data retrieval in a distributed system. For example, the parameter name "temperature" may be used by different data producers to describe two very different temperatures - sea temperature and air temperature. The meaning may be known by the nature of the data provider, from the data itself or from associated documentation. One data provider, for example, may be known to produce ocean data, supporting the conclusion that the data is sea temperature. In other cases, units of measure in the data set may be those customarily used to describe isobar levels, supporting the conclusion that the data is air temperature.

Discussion of the MetOc Ontology

The sample ontology in Figure 11 captures a portion of both MetOc domain terminology and potential data source terminology. Some of the MetOc terms are quite general such as *surface* and *subsurface* and some very specific such as

Figure 11. Sample of Part of MetOc Ontology

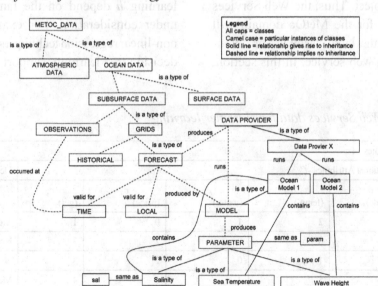

salinity. Other terms provide the descriptions of the data formats such as *grids* or *observations*. For the web service identification it may be also useful or necessary to have data providers described along with the forecast models. This is just a simple illustration of the complexity involved in the development of such an ontology.

Because of this complexity in the development of domain ontologies, we have evaluated the use of case-based classification for some IWB tasks. Specifically this is intended as a complement to ontologies to support the automated discovery process for meteorological and oceanographic Web Services in our application. Case-based reasoning (CBR) is a problem solving methodology that retrieves and reuses decisions from stored cases to solve new problems (Kolodner, 1992), and case-based classification focuses on applying CBR to supervised classification tasks (Osman et al., 2010).

CLASSIFIER APPROACH

Identifying whether a given web service supplies data for a particular domain can be framed as a classification or categorization task, which involves assigning one or more predefined labels to an unlabelled object. Thus, the Web Services identification task for the MetOc domain will involve assigning the label "MetOc" or "Non-MetOc" to a given web service. In this section,

we describe our approach, which uses nearest-neighbor or case-based classification. Finally, we evaluate our methodology using meteorological Web Services.

Overview of Classification Approaches

Our goal is to automatically build classifiers from example data, often termed *supervised learning.* To formally describe a supervised classifier learning approach, we first present the relevant notation. The example data required for classifier learning should be in a tabular format, where each row in the table is an object o and each column in table is an attribute a (see Table 1). Let O represent set of objects in the table and A represent the set of attributes (i.e., columns) in the table. Each cell in the table is the value v_{ij} of the attribute for a_j for a particular object o_i. We partition the attributes into two types: (1) *Conditional attributes* denoted by C, *which* are the object characteristics that provide information for classification and (2) *Decision attribute(s)* D, which are attributes whose values indicate the category that applies to an object.

Learning a classifier implies finding the function h that maps objects in O to decisions in D, that is, $h: O \rightarrow D$. The methods for estimating or learning h depend on the family of functions under consideration. For example, linear and non-linear regression techniques, neural networks, decision tree learning, support vector machines,

Table 1. Example Web Services data for classifier learning

		Attributes -A					
		Conditional Attributes -C					Decision Attribute D
		c_1 (zipcode)	c_2 (temp.)	c_3 (water)	c_4 (price)	c_5 (get)	d
O	o_1	3	2	1	0	1	Metoc
	o_2	1	0	0	2	3	Non-Metoc
	o_3	1	1	0	2	3	Non-Metoc
	o_4	2	1	4	1	4	Metoc

Figure 12. Web Service Classifier Training Process

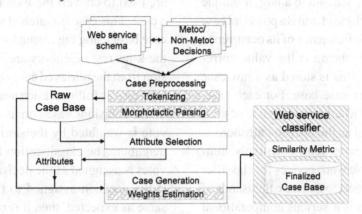

and nearest neighbor techniques are some of the methods used for building classifiers (Tan et Al., 2006). Different classifiers have various strengths and weaknesses depending on the nature and the amount of example data. Typically, most classifiers are hard to develop when the data has a large number of attributes (in thousands), missing values, and only a few example objects (< 100 per class). Many applications have such characteristics, especially those that deal with attributes that are textual in nature. Email classification and text categorization have attributes that run into 1000s (Gupta & Aha, 2004). For such applications, case-based or nearest-neighbor classification approaches have been shown to be effective.

Case-Based Classification

Case-based classification proceeds as follows. To classify a new object, the classification decision from previously classified objects is reused. Objects that have characteristics similar to the new object are called cases. Each object in the Table 1 is a case, and the list of objects in the table constitutes the casebase. To assess the similarity of one case with another, the classifier uses a similarity metric or a matching function such as the Euclidean distance metric used as a similarity function. The cases that are most similar to the unclassified object are called the nearest neighbors.

The decisions from the k nearest neighbors from the case base are used in assigning the class label to a new object. Training the classifier typically implies estimating the weights or parameters applicable to the similarity metric.

Web service classification in the MetOc application entails assigning one of the following two labels, "MetOc" or "non-MetOc", to a web service in question. The input to the classifier is a web service schema described using the WSDL and the output is an associated label. Prior to using the classifier, it must be trained on example cases as follows (see Figure 12):

1. *Case preprocessing*: For classification, each WSDL and its associated schema must be converted into a case with attributes and values. We treat all the element contents in a schema as a source of attributes. For example, an element in a schema may contain the text "waterTemperature." Alternatively, to reduce sparseness of cases, the element can be broken down by the tokenization process into constituent terms. So "waterTemperature" is broken into "water" and "temperature". Subsequently, the morphotactic parsing process further reduces words into their baseforms (Gupta & Aha, 2005). The word "producer" is reduced to its baseform "produce". This then has transformed

the web service schema to a bag of unique baseforms. Each baseform is a potential case attribute and the frequency of its occurrence in a particular schema is the value corresponding to it. This is stored as a raw case in a preliminary case base. For each case, the decision of whether it is MetOc or non-MetOc is added as the decision attribute.

2. *Attribute selection*: With potentially hundreds of example web services for classifier training, we expect to generate thousands of attributes. This is a serious computational challenge and can also adversely affect classification performance by introducing noisy and irrelevant attributes. For example, the attribute "http" may appear in all cases and provide no useful information to discriminate MetOc from non-MetOc web services. To counter this problem, we perform attribute selection, where a metric is used to select a subset of attributes with a potential to improve classification performance. Attribute selection metrics such as mutual information, information gain, document frequency (Yang and Pederson, 1997), and rough set methods can be used (Gupta et al., 2005) to select attributes. We apply the information gain metric to select attributes in the Web Services Classifier. In a following section we describe the rough set feature selection approach (Selvakuberan et al., 2010). in more detail.

3. *Case Generation*: After the attributes have been selected, each case must be indexed with the selected attributes and their corresponding weights must be computed. We use the information gain metric to calculate the weights applicable to the attributes. This outputs a classifier that includes the finalized cases and the similarity metric.

After training is complete, the classification of a new web service proceeds as follows. First, case preprocessing and case generation processes are used to convert the web service schema into a case. This case is matched with the cases in the case base using the learned similarity metric and the k-nearest neighbors are retrieved. The decision from the retrieved cases is then applied to the new case as follows. Each nearest neighbor votes on the decisions based on its classification. Each vote is weighted by the similarity of the voting neighbor. The classification label with the most votes is assigned as the decision to the new case. If the decision assigned to the new case is the same as expected, then it is counted as a correct classification or else a wrong classification. The classifier performance is measured by the percentage of cases classified correctly.

Rough Set Feature Selection

Rough set theory, introduced by Pawlak (Pawlak, 1984) is a technique for dealing with uncertainty and for identifying cause-effect relationships in databases as a form of database learning. Rough sets involve a universe of discussion U, which cannot be empty, and an indiscernability relation R, or equivalence relation. This relation then will determine $[x]_R$ which denotes the equivalence class of R containing x, for any element x of U,

Therefore, for any given approximation space defined on some universe U and having an equivalence relation R imposed upon it, U is partitioned into equivalence classes called elementary sets which may be used to define other sets in A. Let $X \subseteq U$. Then X can be specified by the following:

lower approximation of X in A is the set RX = {x $\in$ U | $[x]_R \subseteq$ X}

upper approximation of X in A is the set ¯RX = {x $\in$ U | $[x]_R \cap X \neq \varnothing$}.

Another way to describe the set approximations is as follows. Given the upper and lower approximations ¯RX and RX, of X a subset of U, the R-positive region of X is $POS_R(X)$ = RX, the

R-negative region of X is $NEG_R(X) = U - {}^-RX$ and the boundary or R-borderline region of X is $BN_R(X) = {}^-RX - RX$. X is called R-definable if and only if $RX = {}^-RX$ Otherwise, $RX \neq {}^-RX$ and X is rough with respect to R. In Figure 13 the universe U is partitioned into equivalence classes denoted by the squares. Those elements in the lower approximation of X, $POS_R(X)$, are denoted with the letter P and elements in the R-negative region by the letter N. All other classes belong to the boundary region of the upper approximation.

Now we will use these rough set concepts relative to cases and features (features) that describe a decision process in which we wish to account for indiscernibility of certain feature values. We want to automatically build classifiers from example data. The case data required for the development of the classifier learning can be illustrated in a table format, where the rows are n cases $c_1, c_2, ..., c_n$ and the columns are m features

$a_1, a_2, ..., a_m$. We must distinguish one specific feature or attribute: the class (or decision) feature a_d. The remaining m-1 features are the standard conditional data features used to predict the class of a case.

In general we wish to characterize the subset, $C' \subseteq C$, of cases that are indistinguishable with respect to certain features, $A' \subseteq A$. So the indiscernibility relation R specifies that a set of cases C' is indiscernible with respect to A', if for each $a_k \in A'$

$a_k(c_i) = a_k(c_j)$ for all $c_i, c_j \in C'$ ($i \neq j$)

We illustrate an approach based on rough sets using the cases shown in Table 2, which pertains to making decisions based on three features. This example illustrates possible conditions that might affect the choices of suitable sites for an amphibious landing operation. Examining the cases in

Figure 13. Example of a Rough Set X

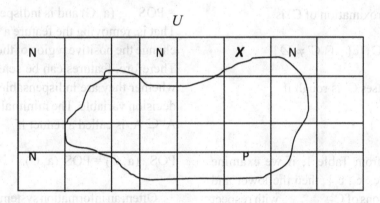

Table 2. A case base example for mission planning

Cases/ Features	a_1 = wave height	a_2 = current	a_3 = visibility	a_d = commit
c_1 = Site Alpha	2-3 ft.	strong	good	no-go
c_2 = Site Bravo	1-2 ft	moderate	excellent	go
c_3 = Site Charlie	2-3 ft.	strong	good	go
c_4 = Site Delta	2-3 ft	weak	poor	no-go
c_5 = Site Echo	1-2 ft	weak	good	yes
c_6 = Site Foxtrot	1-2 ft	weak	good	yes

Table 2, we see for example that cases c_1 and c_3 for sites Alpha and Charlie have identical values for all the features, and thus are indiscernible with respect to the three conditional features a_1, a_2, and a_3.

As we have discussed earlier, an indiscernibility relation R is an equivalence relation that partitions the set of cases into equivalence classes. Each equivalence class contains a set of indiscernible cases for the given set of features / attributes A'. This partitions C in general into several subsets of that are indiscernible. For example, from the mission planning table we obtain the partition of C as $\{\{ c_1, c_3 \}, \{ c_2 \}, \{ c_4 \}, \{ c_5, c_6 \}\}$ where A' = {wave height, current, visibility} and $C = \{c_1, c_2, c_3, c_4, c_5, c_6\}$.

The equivalence class of a case c_i with respect to selected features A' is denoted by $[c_i]_{A'}$. Then as we have defined above, for $C' \subseteq C$, the lower approximation of C' is

$$R_{A'}(C') = \{c \in C \mid [c]_{A'} \subseteq C'\}$$

and the upper approximation of C' is

$$\overline{R}_{A'}(C') = \{c \in C \mid [c]_{A'} \cap C' \neq \emptyset\}$$

So the set of cases C' is rough if

$$R_{A'}(C') \neq \overline{R}_{A'}(C')$$

For example, from Table 1, if we examine $C'_{\{commit = go\}} = \{c_2, c_3, c_5, c_6\}$, then the lower and upper approximations of $C'_{\{commit=go\}}$ with respect to all of the other features are

$$R_{A'}(C') = \{c_2, c_5, c_6\}$$

$$\overline{R}_{A'}(C') = \{c_1, c_2, c_3, c_5, c_6\}$$

Case c_1 is not included in the lower approximation because its equivalence class $\{c_1, c_3\}$ is not a subset of $C'_{\{commit=go\}}$. However, it is included in the upper approximation because its equivalence class has a non-empty intersection with $C'_{\{commit = go\}}$.

To lead into the consideration of a feature selection algorithm we must introduce the concept of the reduct based on the positive region. The positive region of a decision feature a_d with respect to $A' \subseteq A$ is defined as:

$$POS_{A'}(a_d, C) = \cup R_{A'}(C')$$

or the collection of the A'-lower approximations corresponding to all the equivalence classes of a_d. For example, the positive region of a_d {commit} with respect to A'={wave height, current, visibility}, where $R_{A'}(C')_{\{commit=no-go\}} = \{c_4\}$, is as follows:

$$POS_{A'}(a_d, C) = R_{A'}(C')_{\{commit = go\}} \cup R_{A'}(C')_{\{commit = no-go\}} = \{c_2, c_4, c_5, c_6\}$$

The positive region can be used to develop a measure of a feature's ability to contribute information for decision making. A feature $a* \in A'$ makes no contribution or is dispensable if $POS_{A'}(a_d, C) = POS_{A'-a*}(a_d, C)$ and is indispensable otherwise. That is, removing the feature a* from A' does not change the positive region of the decision feature. Therefore, features can be selected by checking whether they are indispensable with respect to a decision variable. The minimal set of features A', $A' \subseteq A$, is called a reduct if

$$POS_{A'}(a_d, C) = POS_A(a_d, C).$$

Often, an information system has more than one possible reduct. Generating a reduct of minimal length is a NP-hard problem. Therefore, in practice, algorithms have been developed to generate one "good" reduct. We used an adaptation of Johnson's reduct algorithm which sequentially selects features by finding those that are most discernible for a given decision feature (Gupta et al 2006). It computes a discernibility matrix M, where each cell m_{ij} of the matrix corresponding to cases c_i and c_j includes the conditional features in which

Table 3. Classifier Operational Performance

Registry Used	Non-MetOc	MetOc	Number False Positives	Number False Negatives	Accuracy	Recall
xmethods	368	16	10	0	97.40%	100.%
websrvicex	64	2	0	2	97.01%	50. %

the two cases' values differ. Formally, we define strict discernibility as:

$$m_{i,j} = \{\{\ f \in F_p : f(c_i) \neq f(c_j)\} \text{ for } f_d(c_i) \neq f_d(c_j), \text{ and } \varnothing \text{ otherwise }\}$$

Given such a matrix M, for each feature, the algorithm counts the number of cells in which it appears. The feature f_h with the highest number of entries is selected for addition to the reduct R. Then all the entries $m_{i,j}$ that contain f_h are removed and the next best feature is selected. This procedure is repeated until M is empty.

Classifier Evaluation

We have evaluated the Web Services Classifier with in-lab testing and operationally. For in-lab testing, a set of 64 web service schemas was obtained from the registries on the Web. Our meteorological subject matter expert classified 26 of these schemas as MetOc relevant. We followed the leave-one-out method of performance evaluation for the classifier. In the leave one out method, one case is taken out of the set as a test case and the remaining cases are used to train the classifier. The classification accuracy for the test case is recorded using the trained classifier. This process of training and classification is repeated for each case in the set to evaluate classification accuracy.

Using the above data and leave one out testing, we obtained a maximum classification accuracy for the Web Services Classifier of 93.75%. The number of nearest neighbors used for this classification was 5, and the number of attributes used in the process was 523, which reflected a

reduction from 1790 total possible attributes. The optimal parameters were obtained by a genetic algorithm that used the classification accuracy as its fitness function.

In addition to this in-lab testing, we have examined the operational performance of the classifier against two registries, xmethods and webservicex. These results are shown in Table 3. In this experiment, the number of total WSDLs in xmethods were 384 and in webservicex 66. The results showed that the classifier correctly classified 97.40% of the web services in xmethods and 97.01% of the web services in the webservicex registry as being MetOc or non-MetOc. A significant finding was that there were no false negatives for the xmethods registry and only two for the webservicex registry. This indicates that no substantial sources of MetOc data were overlooked by the classifier.

DISCUSSION AND CONCLUSION

There has been considerable research on ontologies to help resolve difficulties of sharing knowledge among various domains of interest. In some uses of ontologies by web services, data providers are assumed to deploy an ontological description of their web service to support automated discovery and integration by interested client applications (Paolucci et al., 2004).. The IWB approach of using a dynamic knowledge base does not require such ontological descriptions.

There has also been some research on Web Services Classification as a means of automating or semi-automating the annotation of Web Services with semantic meaning. That work has had as its focus the automatic generation of Web Services ontologies such as OWL-S (Heß and Kushmerick, 2003,2004). In contrast to the use of OWL-S, we have investigated the use of classifiers for Web Services discovery.

In this paper we have presented the general design principles of an Integrated Web Services Brokering System (IWB). The IWB embodies an end-to-end system that performs automated discovery, automated mediation and automated request/response transformation and is in the specific context of the domain of meteorological and oceanographic Web Services. While we utilize domain specific ontologies, we have also examined the feasibility of case-based classification to support automated Web Services discovery.

ACKNOWLEDGMENT

The authors would like to thank the Naval Research Laboratory's Base Program, Program Element No. 0602435N for sponsoring this research.

REFERENCES

W3C Member Submission (2004) OWL-S: Semantic Markup for Web Services, http://www.w3.org/Submission/OWL-S

Adda, M. (2010). A Pattern Language for Knowledge Discovery in a Semantic Web Context. *International Journal of Information Technology and Web Engineering*, 5(2), 16–31..doi:10.4018/jitwe.2010040102

Bai, X., & Lee, S. Tsai, W. & Chen, Y. (2008) Collaborative Web Services Monitoring with Active Service Broker. *Proceedings IEEE International Computer Software and Application Conference*, 84-91.

Boutrous, C., Couiliaby, D., Haddad, S., Melliti, T., Moreaux, P., & Rampacek, S. (2009). An Integrated Framework for Web Services Orchestration. *International Journal of Web Services Research*, 6(4), 1–29..doi:10.4018/jwsr.2009071301

Cerami, E. (2002). *Web Services Essentials*. Sebastopol, CA: O'Reilly and Associates.

Chao, K., Younas, M., Lo, C., & Tan, T. (2005) Fuzzy Matchmaking for Web Services, *Proc. 19th Int. Conf. on Advanced Information Networking and Applications, Vol 2*, Taiwan, 721-726.

Corcho, O., Fernandez-Lopez, M., & Gomez-Perez, A. (2007). Ontological Engineering: What are Ontolgoies and How can we Build Them? In J. Cardoso & I. G. I. Global (Eds.), *Semantic Web Services* (pp. 44–70). Hershey, PA. doi:10.4018/9781599040455.ch003

Cristani, M., & Cuel, R. (2004). A Survey on Ontology Creation Methodologies. *International Journal on Semantic Web and Information Systems*, 1(2), 49–69..doi:10.4018/jswis.2005040103

Deng, S., Wu, Z., Wu, J., Li, Y., & Yin, J. (2009). An Efficient Service Discovery Method and its Application. *International Journal of Web Services Research*, 6(4), 94–117..doi:10.4018/jwsr.2009071305

Dick, K. (2000). *XML: A Manager's Guide*. Reading, MA: Addison Wesley.

Erickson, J., & Siau, K. (2010). Web Services, Service-Oriented Computing, and Service-Oriented Architecture: Separating Hype from Reality. In Tatnall, A., & Global, I. G. I. (Eds.), *Web Technologies: Concepts* (pp. 1786–1798). Methodologies, Tools, and Applications.

Fenza, G., Loia, V., & Senatore, S. (2007) Improving Fuzzy Service Matchmaking through Concept Matching Discovery, *Proc. IEEE Int. Conf on Fuzzy Systems*, London UK, CD.

Fenza, G., Loia, V., & Senatore, S. (2008). A Hybrid Approach to Semantic Web Service Matching. *International Journal of Approximate Reasoning, 48*(3), 808–828..doi:10.1016/j.ijar.2008.01.005

Gupta, K., Aha, D., & Moore, P. (2006) Rough set feature selection algorithms for textual case-based classification, *Proc. of 8th European Conf. on Case-Based Reasoning*, Turkey, 153-57.

Gupta, K., Moore, P. G., Aha, D., & Pal, S. (2005) Rough-Set Feature Selection Methods for Case-Based Categorization of Text Documents. *Proc. 1st Int.Conference on Pattern Recognition and Machine Intelligence*, Kolkata, India, 792-798.

Gupta, K. M., & Aha, D. W. (2004) RuMoP: A Morphotactic Parser, *Proc. of the Int. Conference on Natural Language Processing*, Hyderabad, India, 280-284.

Heß, A., & Kushmerick, N. (2003) Learning to Attach Semantic Metadata to Web Services, *Proc. of the 2nd International Semantic Web Conference*, Sanibel Island Florida, 258-273. AAAI Spring Symp. Semantic Web Services

Heß, A., & Kushmerick, N. (2004) Machine Learning for Annotating Semantic Web Services, *Proceedings of the AAAI Spring Symp. Semantic Web Services*, 341-346.

Holsapple, C., & Joshi, K. (2002). A Collaborative Approach to Ontology Design. *Communications of the ACM, 45*(2), 42–47..doi:10.1145/503124.503147

JMBL. (2009) Joint METOC Public Data Administration Website. www.cffc.navy.mil/metoc/

Johnson, D. (1974). Approximation algorithms for combinatorial problems. *Journal of Computer and System Sciences, 9*, 256–278..doi:10.1016/S0022-0000(74)80044-9

Kim, H. (2002). Predicting How Ontologies for the Semantic Web Will Evolve. *Communications of the ACM, 45*(2), 48–54..doi:10.1145/503124.503148

Knublauch, H. Fergerson, F. Noy N.and Musen,M. (2004) The Protege OWL Plugin: An Open Development Environment for Semantic Web Applications. *Third International Conference on the Semantic Web (ISWC-2004)*, Hiroshima, Japan, 342-351.

Kolodner, J. (1992). An Introduction to Case-Based Reasoning. *Artificial Intelligence Review, 6*, 3–24..doi:10.1007/BF00155578

Lacy, L. (2005). *Owl: Representing Information Using the Web Ontology Language*. Trafford Publishing London UK.

Ladner, R., & Petry, F. (2005). *Net-Centric Approaches to Intelligence and National Security*. Kluwer Press. doi:10.1007/b137009

Li, M., Yu, B., Sahota, V., & Qi, M. (2009). Web Services Discovery wth Rough Sets. *International Journal of Web Services Research, 6*(1), 69–86..doi:10.4018/jswr.2009092104

Osman, T., Thakker, D., & Al-Dabass, D. (2010). In Tatnall, A., & Global, I. G. I. (Eds.), *Utilisation of Case-Based Reasoning for Semantic Web Services Composition. Web Technologies: Concepts* (pp. 604–622). Methodologies, Tools, and Applications.

Paolucci, M., Soudry, J., Srinivasan, N., & Sycara, K. (2004), A Broker for OWL-S Web services, *Proceedings of the AAAI Spring Symposium on Semantic Web Services*, 562-567.

Papazoglou, M. (2007). *Web Services: Principles and Technology*. Prentice Hall.

Pawlak, Z. (1984). Rough Sets. *International Journal of Man-Machine Studies, 21*, 127–134..doi:10.1016/S0020-7373(84)80062-0

Powers, S. (2003) *Practical RDF*, O'Reilly Media, Inc, Sebastopol, CA.

Rama, A. (2007). Semantic Web Services. In Cardoso, J., & Global, I. G. I. (Eds.), *Semantic Web Services* (pp. 191–216). Hershey, PA.

Ratnasingam, P. (2010). The Role of Web Services: A Balance Scorecard Perspective. In Tatnall, A., & Global, I. G. I. (Eds.), *Web Technologies: Concepts* (pp. 865–879). Methodologies, Tools, and Applications.

Selvakuberan, K., Devi, I., & Rajaram, R. (2010). Feature Selection for Web Page Classification. In Tatnall, A., & Global, I. G. I. (Eds.), *Web Technologies: Concepts* (pp. 1462–1477). Methodologies, Tools, and Applications.

Stojanovic, L. J. Schneider, A. Maedche, S. Libischer, R. Studer, T. Lumpp, A. Abecker, G. Breiter, J. Dinger. (2004). The Role of Ontologies in Autonomic Computing Systems. *IBM Systems Journal*, *43*(3), 598–616..doi:10.1147/sj.433.0598

Tan, P., Steinbach, M., & Kumar, V. (2006). *Introduction to Data Mining*. Boston, MA: Pearson Pub.

van der Vet, P N. Mars. (1998). Bottom-up Construction of Ontologies. *IEEE Transactions on Knowledge and Data Engineering*, *16*(4), 513–526..doi:10.1109/69.706054

Yang, Y., & Pederson, J. (1997). A comparative study of feature selection in text categorization. *Proceedings of the Fourteenth International Conference on Machine Learning*, Nashville, TN: Morgan Kaufmann, 412-420.

Section 4

Chapter 15

Measuring the Unmeasurable?
Eliciting Hard to Measure Information about the User Experience

Andrew Saxon
Birmingham City University, UK

Shane Walker
Birmingham City University, UK

David Prytherch
Birmingham City University, UK

ABSTRACT

This chapter focuses on the adoption and adaptation of methodologies drawn from research in psychology for the evaluation of user response as a manifestation of the mental processes of perception, cognition and emotion. We present robust alternative conceptualizations of evaluative methodologies, which allow the surfacing of views, feelings and opinions of individual users producing a richer, more informative texture for user centered evaluation of software. This differs from more usual user questionnaire systems such as the Questionnaire of User Interface Satisfaction (QUIS). We present two different example methodologies so that the reader can firstly, review the methods as a theoretical exercise and secondly, applying similar adaptation principles, derive methods appropriate to their own research or practical context.

INTRODUCTION

Viewed from a visual design perspective, there appears to be a lack of empirical research investigating the determinants of important aspects of user behaviour such as emotion and motivation,

and how an understanding of these may influence designers' decisions in the software evaluation process. The ubiquitous nature of information technology today means that the computer is no longer just a tool for those who are compelled to use it, or have to learn to use it, as was the case in the 1980s. Interfaces, in particular on the Internet, must appeal to a broad base of users with varying

DOI: 10.4018/978-1-60960-523-0.ch015

levels of skill and ability, and should work first time to ensure the user is not 'put off' the experience. Aesthetic considerations (often referred to as beauty) may also be considered significant in this context, (Hartmann, Sutcliffe & De Angeli, 2007) but have only attracted significant interest from researchers in the last few years. (Hassenzahl, 2008) Modern psychological theories on motivation that attempt to unify other existing theories (e.g. Ford, 1992) agree on a basic structure of component processes: goal directed activity, an individual's belief in their skills and the context within which they will work, and finally their emotions. This approach sits well with other theories of human motivation and personality (Ryan and Deci, 2000) currently cited in the HCI field.

Motivation is a rather abstract term that historically has challenged psychologists to provide satisfactory definitions. Unified theories that attempt to satisfactorily explain human motivation have been developed only relatively recently and research on motivation within HCI such as the Technology Acceptance Model, (TAM) (Davis, 1989) supports the argument that visual communication and functionality (perceived ease of use) influence users' motivation, and change user behaviour in a way that impacts on usability. Research has shown that highly motivated users experience less anxiety, have higher perceptions of self-efficacy and more positive attitudes towards the software. (Davis, ibid) The source and impact of generating positive attitudes in users is subject to ongoing debate. Norman (2004) suggests that attractive things generate positive moods that impact directly on improving thought processes and therefore task performance. Hassenzahl (2008) suggests the process is more complex, and that a clear link to task performance is not proven. However, there is agreement that aesthetics satisfies basic human needs and therefore can impact on motivation. (Tractinsky & Hassenzahl, 2005).

In order to assess how far visual design techniques applied to the user interface can harmonize with psychological needs for optimal performance on specific tasks and attainment of goals, we must base questions on a fundamental understanding of key influencing variables of the interaction process, together with a clear knowledge of their relative importance to the individual user. In perceptual terms, interactive computer systems are not just representations of knowledge, but interactive *experiences* that should seek to fully exploit the user's senses and emotions, developing new ways to deliver effective communication.

Variables during interaction that can influence user motivation lie in the gulf between executing the task and its evaluation. The users evaluate their goals, their own ability to attain them and the potential of the context, (in this case the computer system) to support them in this activity. Evaluation is on going as perception is regularly matched against expectation, with emotions playing a key role in this process leading to opportunities to evaluate the success of the interface. This gulf may be bridged by addressing issues from either direction, the computer or the user. The system designer can bridge such issues by creating interaction mechanisms that better match the psychological needs of the user as evidenced by the task model.

We present two different examples, describing tested methodologies for addressing these needs, though many other comparable adaptations of different domain methodologies might be similarly useful. (e.g. Greenberg, Fitzpatrick, Gutwin, & Kaplan, 2000; Hollan, Hutchins & Kirsh, 2000; Duric et al., 2002)

The first example is derived from Motivation Systems Theory (MST) (Ford, *op.cit.*) wherein components of human behaviour are modelled as simple behavioural processes. MST integrates the conceptual frameworks of 32 motivational theories around its core concepts and was also found to compare well with models and theories already used to describe user interaction in HCI.

The second example is derived from Kelly's (1955) Repertory Grid Technique. This method uses a highly qualitative approach to the surfacing of a user's experience using his/her own frame of reference. The technique is highly amenable to customization by the experimenter, to suit the particular needs of his/her investigation, and details on customization carried out by the authors are described.

In order to prove these derived methodologies, they were used as part of a suite of usability tests that were run on *Webomatic*, a website design application aimed at UK Small and Medium sized Enterprises (SMEs) which itself was one of the outcomes of an earlier European Regional Development Fund (ERDF) part-funded project to investigate the implications of design for e-commerce.

Technique 1: Motivation Systems Theory (MST)

MST is based on the Living Systems Framework (LSF) (Ford, 1987) which considers the person holistically on both a granular and global level, for example in considering goals, emotions, perceptions and actions. LSF also describes how the individual component processes work together to form organized patterns of behaviour. The LSF

breaks physical structure and organization of living systems into four sets of basic functions:

1. **Biological Functions:** Life sustaining biological processes, the functioning of the body.
2. **Transactional Functions:** Exchange processes vital for life (sensory-perceptual actions, body movement etc).
3. **Cognitive Functions:** Regulatory functions, evaluative thoughts.
4. **Arousal Functions:** Attention and consciousness arousal, emotional arousal.

A person's behaviour can be represented as an organised flow of complex patterns. The LSF uses the concept of a behaviour episode, which is based on the premise that the individual will undertake goal directed activity until one of the following occurs:

- The goal is accomplished
- The person is distracted and another goal takes precedence
- The goal is evaluated as unattainable

Figure 1. Chapter Structure

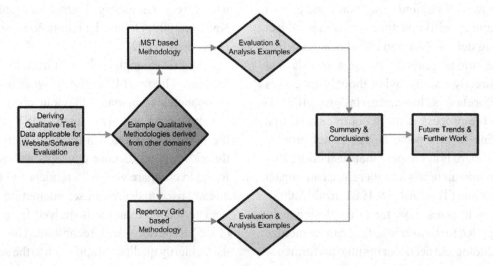

The behaviour episode is therefore organised by goals and context and the psychological constraints dictated by them.

The LSF integrates motivation with cognitive and arousal processes. MST emerged from an iterative process of integrating the basic framework provided by the LSF with concepts and data provided by existing work on motivation (both historical and contemporary). Motivation has often been considered a separate topic of research within the field of psychology leading to theories that cannot be compared. The theories and ideas have reached a level of maturity where referring to them to provide an extended view of the user can produce robust and enlightening findings. Unification and agreement of these processes has been found in psychology and HCI and this makes the study of users' motivation at the interface a more viable proposition, and arguably one that cannot be ignored. The importance of goals (intrinsic and extrinsic) and contexts for motivation highlighted by Ford *(op. cit.)* suggests there may be value in attempting to apply the motivational theory to HCI. Most behaviour is goal directed, and goals can be considered as needs which when satisfied, generate positive emotions that energize motivation. Ryan and Deci *(op. cit)* identify three basic needs, competence, autonomy and relatedness (energizing states) that need to be satisfied for an individual to thrive. An individual's personal goals illustrate the most distinctive characteristic of humans, the capability to use thought to construct models of action that can represent their past, present, and future activity and to then be able to utilise these to guide future decisions and behaviour. Designers may construct the conceptual design model for the interactive system through an understanding of the users' background experience, knowledge and expectations. Our expectations are initially fashioned by our prior experience however they are continually re-modelled during subsequent experiences.

MST attempts to represent three basic components of motivation. Firstly, the overall aim of the individual – what they are attempting to do. Secondly, what energises people and what does the opposite, and thirdly how people make decisions to continue or alternatively to give up. The theory describes the processes that guide these components: Goal setting activities will only be effective if (a) feedback is provided; the person/user must be able to evaluate any discrepancies between the current and desired consequences and (b) capability beliefs for realizing the desired consequences in the face of discouraging feedback. The person/user must have the skill (capability belief) and (c) a responsive and supporting environment (context belief) within which to attain their goals. Emotions play an evaluative and energizing role throughout these processes. The approach to the field of motivation taken by MST enables broader applications that are not possible with many other theories. Its unifying approach (32 other theories on motivation) and broad agreement with existing HCI models, e.g. TAM (Davis, *op.cit.*) makes it attractive for application to HCI, hence it was planned to adapt the model to analyze, measure and assess the role of motivation in the user experience at the software interface.

A novel qualitative user test based on MST was applied to twelve users whose roles had some involvement in web site design, content, construction and/or management. The descriptive terminology (for example, personal goals) used in MST required modification to improve semantic relevance to the HCI context. The application of the theory through the user tests provided a new 'lens' through which to view the users' experience and this proved to be an effective tool during the user tests to gauge motivational responses.

Data Analysis Methods

An assessment of the user's motivation prior to using the software will provide a point of reference so that assessments can be made whilst the software is being used, and post-use. This should provide a basis for determining the user's behavioural response and assist in the post-test interviews by suggesting lines for further investigation.

User's motivation assessment will require gathering information on the user's goals, emotions, and Personal Agency Beliefs (PABs) (Ford, *op. cit.*). Personal Agency Beliefs consist of context and (the user's) capability beliefs. This will be achieved primarily by the use of a questionnaire that specifically links design attributes of the software with the components of motivation (identified by Ford, *ibid.*). Figure 2 provides an example of how context beliefs can be applied to HCI and how they relate to usability principles. The objective of this method is to obtain a user profile of behavioural response accumulated qualitatively through the user's experience of the software. Motivational theory can identify major influences on the user, but cannot necessarily provide answers with regard to the exact causes of motivational change. Through observation, video recording, asking the user to think aloud, and using keyword selection techniques it is possible to attribute motivational patterns to the user's experience of the software. The tests are designed to capture a broad range of impacts on the user that stem from user goals and needs. A

specific focus is to elicit information about the user's response to the design of the software.

Pre-Test Stage

The pre-test questions provided a profile of the user, their background, previous experience, knowledge, psychological characteristics, attitudes and expectations before the test commenced. The task brief was set out as written text and was explained verbally to the user. After a demonstration of the software the user was asked to select from three keyword tables: emotions, aesthetics and usability. Following this a questionnaire was administered to assess the impact of the demonstration on the user.

During the Test

During the test, valuable data were obtained by combining traditional user observation techniques with MST. It was possible to elicit in-depth information on the user's behavioural response to the software during the test, indicating their progress towards conscious and unconscious goals, including an assessment of the user's own evaluative processes. To facilitate effective data

Figure 2. Example of how context beliefs can be applied to HCI and how they relate to usability principles

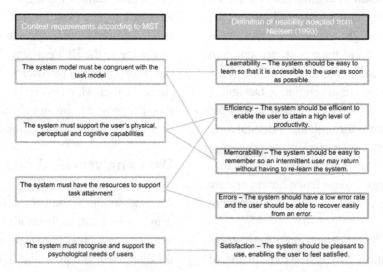

gathering during the tests, lookup tables (See Figure 3) with representative keywords were used. This minimised cognitive load by reducing time off task. The purpose of the tables was to gauge emotional response and the users' view on the aesthetics and usability of the software. Emotions, although subjective, are good indicators of the user's experience, because of their evaluative role. The user was encouraged to think aloud describing their experience as they used the software. Recording this additional qualitative data during the test provided insight into the users' selection of keywords in the event of any notable conscious emotions experienced during use of the software. Each conscious emotion event was recorded separately and a short one-page questionnaire was given at around the mid-point of task completion. These records could be reviewed together with video/audio recordings thus delivering a snapshot of the users' behavioural responses, underpinned by an assessment of their motivation over time. The technique further enhances other information gathered during observation for example, by 'think aloud', as the user selects descriptions that they feel fit their current experience and view of the software.

On screen activity was captured and was synchronised with a camera that directly faced the user and recorded facial expression throughout the test. This video showing users' interaction with the software proved invaluable for explaining behaviour and mapping the user's response to the software over time. Most importantly the videos captured the strength of the user's feeling

Figure 3. Example Keyword Selection table

Keyword Selection *For office use: ID*

Please choose keywords that describe your opinion of Webomatic. Complete Section 1 before moving on to Section 2

Section 1 **User Interface Aesthetics**

The user interface is... Please tick all that apply

Dull	Appealing	Plain	Fun
Stimulating	Unattractive	It's Okay	Dreary
Mediocre	Stylish	Average	Attractive
Beautiful	Conservative	Sterile	Commonplace
Ordinary	Entertaining	Annoying	Original
Conventional	Ugly	Amusing	Pleasant
Creative	Formal	Boring	Unique
Unappealing	Disorderly	Engaging	Mundane

Section 2 **Ease of Use / Usability**

When using Webomatic I consider it to be... Please tick all that apply

Predictable	Illogical	Manageable	Unusable
Inconsistent	Clear	Confusing	Satisfying
Intuitive	Unpredictable	Logical	Unsupportive
Frustrating	Controllable	Risky	Unintuitive
Tedious	Flexible	Unruly	Chaotic
Easy to use	Rigid	Encouraging	Simple
Useless	Surprising	Interesting	Uncontrollable
Consistent	Unsurprising	Usable	Unsafe
Difficult to use	Safe	Complicated	Supportive

as an issue or event occurred at the interface, and provided the opportunity to make observations on strengthening or waning emotions as interaction continued. These recordings allowed the opportunity for further analysis of users' responses by linking closely with data collected through the questionnaires.

Post-Test

The post-test stage commenced with the completion of the three keyword selection tables that were identical to those completed at the post-demon-

stration and during-use stages. A questionnaire was completed and a reflective interview was conducted. The questionnaire was composed of closed questions using Likert and semantic differential scales (Osgood, Suci, & Tannenbaum, 1971; Oppenheim, 1992; Robson, 1993). Questions at this stage were compared with questions at the pre-test stage so that it was possible to record and measure any shift in the user's responses as a result of using the software. A 'before and after' analysis was possible, including an explanation of the shift, if it occurred.

Figure 4. Example Emotion Keyword sheet

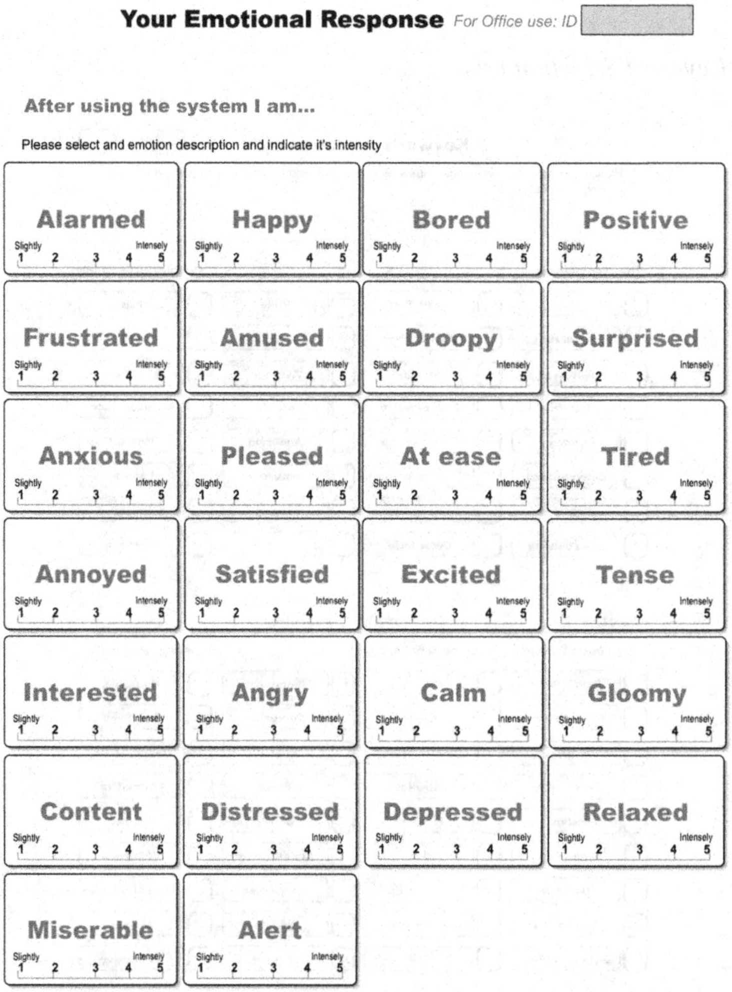

Your Emotional Response *For Office use: ID*

After using the system I am...

Please select and emotion description and indicate it's intensity

Alarmed	Happy	Bored	Positive
Slightly 1 2 3 4 5 Intensely	Slightly 1 2 3 4 5 Intensely	Slightly 1 2 3 4 5 Intensely	Slightly 1 2 3 4 5 Intensely
Frustrated	**Amused**	**Droopy**	**Surprised**
Slightly 1 2 3 4 5 Intensely	Slightly 1 2 3 4 5 Intensely	Slightly 1 2 3 4 5 Intensely	Slightly 1 2 3 4 5 Intensely
Anxious	**Pleased**	**At ease**	**Tired**
Slightly 1 2 3 4 5 Intensely	Slightly 1 2 3 4 5 Intensely	Slightly 1 2 3 4 5 Intensely	Slightly 1 2 3 4 5 Intensely
Annoyed	**Satisfied**	**Excited**	**Tense**
Slightly 1 2 3 4 5 Intensely	Slightly 1 2 3 4 5 Intensely	Slightly 1 2 3 4 5 Intensely	Slightly 1 2 3 4 5 Intensely
Interested	**Angry**	**Calm**	**Gloomy**
Slightly 1 2 3 4 5 Intensely	Slightly 1 2 3 4 5 Intensely	Slightly 1 2 3 4 5 Intensely	Slightly 1 2 3 4 5 Intensely
Content	**Distressed**	**Depressed**	**Relaxed**
Slightly 1 2 3 4 5 Intensely	Slightly 1 2 3 4 5 Intensely	Slightly 1 2 3 4 5 Intensely	Slightly 1 2 3 4 5 Intensely
Miserable	**Alert**		
Slightly 1 2 3 4 5 Intensely	Slightly 1 2 3 4 5 Intensely		

The aim of the post-test stage was to gather further qualitative data on the user's experience after completion of the task. This was an opportunity to obtain insights into particular events to which the user had reacted strongly. User reflection and explanation were valuable aids to the subsequent assessment of their experience. The method used was an exploratory interview, semi-structured by the use of a questionnaire. This gathered data to support an assessment of user motivation after the experience and in anticipation of further use of the software. In depth interview techniques (Oppenheim, *ibid.*) elicited information that indicated whether the user's goals had been accomplished and what types of goals they were, for example task goals, personal goals. Additionally this included an assessment of the user's context and capability beliefs (Ford, *op. cit.*) to detect any shift during the experience.

Summary of MST based tests

The techniques described for pre-test and during test phases collect information on the user's motivation and emotions as they happen. The post-test phase seeks to identify the significance of earlier findings, reinforcing them with qualitative data collected from the in-depth interview and establishes the impact of the software users' experience on their motivation. It also assesses the users' motivation with regard to future use of the software. A key requirement for the interview is to enhance the qualitative data gained from the questionnaires, confirm the user's responses and facilitate explorative open questioning on aspects of the experience that proved particularly interesting for different reasons. Another important role is to enable the user to reflect on their experience and to elicit their own opinions, which can then be compared with data collected during observation. This support for observational data will assist ranking of events that had a powerful motivational influence on the user, as conscious

evaluations that can be recalled later to give an indication of the impact on the user's experience.

Throughout the development of the tests, comparisons and checks were made to establish comparability and validity with other models used to evaluate computer user's behaviour (Venkatesh, 2000; Norman, Ortony, & Russell, 2003). Reference to HCI user satisfaction questionnaires helped to define the scope of the questions and were extended by this research through reference to MST and other relevant theories and models in the field of psychology/HCI (Venkatesh, ibid.; Norman et al, ibid.) to deliver a predictive and explanatory framework. The understanding of users' needs derived from this approach can have a direct impact on the design of the interface with new requirements for design solutions.

The tests showed that it was possible to gain valuable information about the user with implications for designers, particularly when tracking the user over time, highlighting the significance of each user interaction. The strengthening and waning of emotions was particularly evident and the results indicated that the opportunity to manage and capitalize on the interaction process is under-recognized. *Satisfaction* is simply one of a number of goals the user is striving for. An optimal user experience may be partly dependent on recognizing a broader range of goals and associated emotional response in the software design. For example, in a study of storytelling software (used in Museums) Hassenzahl & Ullrich (2007) found that this effect plays a central role in user experience, whether or not the user has a specific task or is just exploring the software.

Using MST for understanding and determining the strength of the users' response provided a robust framework that detected measurable shifts in the experience. These shifts indicated a link to the qualities of the software, highlighting virtues and shortfalls in the software design. The user tests established the importance of satisfying users' personal goals and additionally, this was recognized by the individuals as evidenced by user comments in interviews and questionnaires. This response depended to a large extent on successful use of the software, and also on qualities of the design and the users' experience.

Motivation embodies emotions and closer inspection of this readily observable aspect of the human response should inform an assessment of the software, providing valuable support to user surveys. Recognition of motivational aspects of the user response suggests the need to review information traditionally collected in user satisfaction surveys. Hassenzahl, (2008) suggests that User Experience is not well-defined within HCI, although he defines it as,

Momentary, primarily evaluative feeling (good-bad) while interacting with a product or service.

Stewart (2009) describes the revision to ISO 13407 (International Standard for Human-Centred Design) to incorporate the term user experience.

In the revised standard we define it as 'all aspects of the user's experience when interacting with the product, service, environment or facility' and we point out that 'it is a consequence of the presentation, functionality, system performance, interactive behaviour, and assistive capabilities of the interactive system. It includes all aspects of usability and desirability of a product, system or service from the user's perspective.

It is possible that the user's psychological needs have been generally under-recognized by the HCI community. This view is supported by research on user emotion undertaken at MIT and IBM (Picard & Wexelblat, 2002; Norman, Ortony, & Russell,, *op.cit.*; Bickmore and Picard, 2005).

Technique 2: Repertory Grid Technique

The Repertory Grid Technique was developed from Kelly's (1955) Personal Construct Theory. This theory had, at its starting point the belief that people are scientists. By this, it is meant that each

of us has constructed our own point of view about the world (a theory), our own opinions on what will happen in a given situation (a hypothesis) and that in our day-to-day behaviour, we continually test our views against our reality (we conduct experiments) and, based upon our day-to-day experiences (the experimental data,) we modify our world-view (our theory), forming new opinions on how the world works (a revised hypothesis).

According to Kelly (*ibid.*), as these constructs represent a set of individual qualitative judgments about the world, it is preferable to think of them as being scalar, having two contrasting poles. Kelly (*ibid.*) observed that our judgments are usually bipolar, rather than unipolar. The concept of *good* can only exist as the opposite of *bad;* the concept of *wet* can only exist as the opposite to *dry.* Therefore, when an individual offers a judgment, the question *'as opposed to what?'* needs always to be asked in order to further clarify the individual's meaning and the context. For example, the term *good* may mean *skilful* as opposed to *novice* when discussing sporting ability, or it may mean *virtuous* as opposed to *evil* when discussing the moral character of another individual. The exact meaning of a word in a given context cannot therefore be assumed. Even where the opposite pole is thought obvious by the experimenter, it should still be sought in order to eliminate observer bias. Repertory Grid Technique sets out to measure subjective aspects of a participant's experience using a highly qualitative approach whose methods are amenable to customization by the experimenter.

Adherents of the quantitative approach, upon recognizing that a user's subjective response to the software under evaluation can be an important aspect of evaluation, will often add a criterion that aims to deal with the subjective dimension of how much the user *liked* using the software. This is illustrated in Nielsen's (1993) model of the attributes of system acceptability, which explores and charts the notion of usability through consideration of such matters as: learnability, efficiency, memorability, user error-rate, and satisfaction. In so doing, they are acknowledging that no matter how well it performs in the other categories, if the software and its interface are not liked by the user, it may not actually be used much, and may even be discarded. On the World Wide Web, it is accepted that the competition is just one click away, so the importance of gaining a clear understanding of users' experience with web software cannot be overstated.

Data Analysis Methods

The application of Repertory Grid Technique requires the identification of a set of *elements*, or objects. These elements define the subject matter of the Repertory Grid interview. The interviewee is then asked to define some *constructs*, or attributes, to characterize the elements. These constructs are written down in a scalar, bipolar form, and each element is ranked along the bipolar scale. The *grid* or table is then created with the elements and constructs on its two axes, and the scores are entered at the element-construct intersections. The resulting grid is then available for analysis. This ability of Repertory Grid to help people articulate using their own range of convenience, *in their own terms,* that which they normally cannot coherently articulate, is of key importance as it is this facility that is used to help ascertain the particular quality of a specific user's experience.

Due to the widespread adoption of Repertory Grid outside of the particular domain for which it was originally devised it has been necessary to elaborate the technique for more applied uses. A selection of common elaborations, according to Fransella and Bannister (1977), would include: Grid (the original method); Rank Order Grid (which added rank ordering of elements to the Grid form); Ratings Grid (where each element is rated on a scale defined by the two construct poles) and the Implications Grid (which uses only one element, the self, concentrating on eliciting constructs relating to the self). This particular elaboration is designed to elicit tacit information

from users. The addition of Rank Order Grid and Ratings Grid also make this a methodology which can very effectively combine qualitative with quantitative data providing an exceptionally rich information source.

There are obvious similarities between Repertory Grid and Osgood's Semantic Differential (Snider & Osgood, 1969), the latter being based to some extent upon the former. The major difference between the two is that Osgood's Semantic Differential supplies the bipolar constructs for the interviewee to use, thereby forcing them to use the construct system labels of the questionnaire designer, whereas the Repertory Grid elicits the bipolar constructs, actively engaging the construct system of the interviewee. This ensures that the constructs used in the interview lie within the range of convenience of the interviewee.

Choosing Elements and Eliciting Constructs

Repertory Grid elements can be identified by several means, but Stewart and Stewart (1981) identify three main methods: the interviewer can provide them; or interviewees can be asked to think of a list of elements based upon a briefing which outlines what kinds of elements are sought; or the interviewer can supply a list of questions, the answers to which become the elements. Each of these methods has advantages and disadvantages.

Interviewer-provided elements can be closely targeted to the precise needs of the particular investigation by the interviewer, but can immediately introduce observer bias, in that the construct system of the interviewer (or questionnaire designer) is used as the basis for the interview, rather than the construct system of the interviewee.

Elements that are supplied free-form by the interviewee are, of course, making extensive use of the construct system of that interviewee, but the elements supplied may vary widely in relevance to the particular investigation at hand. The interviewee may supply elements that can seem irrelevant to the investigation. Stewart and Stewart (*ibid.*) point out that this technique will also introduce bias in the interviewee's choice of elements toward those with which he/she is familiar, and also toward those elements that are preferred by the interviewee.

Elements that are supplied by the interviewee in response to a pre-prepared list of questions appear to inhabit an optimal position. The pre-prepared list of questions will focus the interviewee's construing on the topic of the investigation, whilst the free-form nature of the interviewee's answers will extensively utilise the construct system of that interviewee. Observer bias is controlled due to the free-form nature of the resulting elements, and interviewee bias is controlled due to the strong focus provided by the need to work within the framework provided by the pre-prepared list of questions.

Eliciting Constructs

By far the most common method of construct elicitation is Kelly's (*op. cit.*) triadic method, where three elements are shown to the interviewee, who is then asked to specify some way in which two of these elements are alike and thereby different from the third. The reply, representing the *likeness* pole of the bipolar pair, is then recorded. Then, the interviewee is asked in what way the third element differs from the other two. This reply, representing the *contrast* pole in the bipolar pair is also recorded. The process is then repeated using as many triads of elements as the interviewer thinks appropriate.

Another less common, yet equally effective method according to Ryle and Lunghi (1970) is the dyadic method, where only two elements are shown to the interviewee, so that the two construct poles can be elicited more directly. The dyadic method is felt to be simpler in operation than the triadic method, without sacrificing either validity or reliability. Fransella and Bannister (*op. cit.*) note that the dyadic method is useful where constructs

that are already present in the interviewee's mind are to be elicited, noting that in such cases there is no reason for using the triadic method.

Epting, Suchman, & Nickeson (1971) the contrast pole during the Repertory Grid interview. These are called the *opposite method* and the *difference method*, the latter, over time, becoming the more popular of the two. Using the *difference method*, after the likeness pole has been identified, as stated above, the interviewee is asked to specify some way in which two of the elements in the triad are alike and thereby *different* from the third.

Using the *opposite method*, after the likeness pole has been identified, as stated above, the interviewee is asked to specify what he/she considers to be the *opposite* of the characteristic given for the likeness pole. Epting, Suchman, & Nickeson (*ibid.*) found that the *opposite method* produced a greater number of bipolar constructs than the *difference method* when using the Repertory Grid procedure.

Reliability and Validity

Fransella and Bannister (*op. cit.*) and Bannister and Fransella (1986) discuss the reliability and validity of Repertory Grid Technique, suggesting that the common experimental meaning attached to these terms needs a degree of contextualisation when applied to Repertory Grid.

Reliability

As Kelly (*op. cit.*) believed that living creatures were a form of motion, as opposed to being static objects, he envisaged that each of us is engaged in a constant and continuous re-evaluation and development of our personal construct systems. On this basis, it is highly likely that successive applications of Repertory Grid with the same interviewee over time would bring to light different results. This however, is not indicative of poor experimental reliability in the technique.

Yin (1994, p. 37) notes that the objective of reliability is: "…to be sure that if a later investigator followed the same procedures as described by an earlier investigator and conducted the same case study all over again, the later investigator should arrive at the same findings and conclusions." If such a 'later investigator' were to find the interviewee 'frozen in time' and therefore completely unchanged, then this would be the case.

However, Bannister and Fransella (*op. cit.*) posit that: as people may maintain or alter how they construe their world over time, the reliability of Repertory Grid arises from its ability to permit effective investigation of this very issue,

Validity

Validity in an experimental sense is described by Yin (*op. cit.*, p. 37) as: "[dealing] with the problem of knowing whether a study's findings are generalizable beyond the immediate case..."

This widely used definition of validity causes immediate problems when considering Repertory Grid Technique. Our construct systems are different each to another, and furthermore, they are differently and personally expressed, often using private language (made-up words) to describe aspects of the world. At face value then, Repertory Grid Technique has low validity in the traditional experimental sense, as it is unwise to attempt generalisation from existing data to other as-yet-unknown situations.

In rebuttal of this view, Fransella and Bannister (*op. cit.*) argue that Repertory Grid is not actually a test, but rather a format into which information can be put in order to find out if relationships exist within the data.

Applications of the Repertory Grid Technique to Software Evaluation

When considering Repertory Grid Technique as the vehicle for gathering qualitative assessments of the user experience, as opposed to quantitative

assessments of software usability, exemplars can be seen in the literature that demonstrate a precedent, and which may be shown to clarify the appropriateness of the theory for use in this context.

Baber (1996) provides an example of the use of Repertory Grid Theory in comparative product evaluation, suggesting that further use could be made of the technique in the early stages of product design, when compiling a list of desirable design characteristics. Baber (ibid., p. 164) also envisages its use

…as a means of defining users' conceptions of usability, perhaps through a comparison of a range of products which users are encouraged to consider in terms of functionality, ease of use, etc.

Boy (1997) presents the Group Elicitation Method (GEM), which seeks to overcome the problems experienced by different individuals when they are used as 'experts' on a product review panel. GEM has been used to facilitate the mutual understanding of terms and ideas among experts who have been gathered together in order to provide solutions to design or usability issues.

Much indebted to Personal Construct Theory, GEM acts as a decision support tool, producing clear and mutually understood outcomes. Boy (ibid., p. 33) states: "Although we have used GEM to design new systems, we have observed that it would be useful for evaluating existing systems and suggesting alternatives."

Both Baber (op. cit.) and Boy (op. cit.) appear to have recognised a symmetry between initial product design and user testing that deploys an individual's personal construct system as a kind of yardstick against which to evaluate a product, either at the beginning or at the end of the design process.

Verlinden and Coenders (2000, p. 143) describing their approach to the use of Repertory Grid for the evaluation of a website state: "Most usability techniques are quantitative and measure the performance, retrieval times, success times/

failure rates... Although [a quantitative method] might provide some information on experiences with respect to websites, it exposes a number of shortcomings."

Repertory Grid is offered as it "...facilitates an objective approach of capturing subjective aspects of web usability." (Verlinden & Coenders, ibid., p. 144)

The approach they use is comparative, but in this case the comparison is made between different pages of the website under evaluation, one against the other.

The experimental approach used by Verlinden and Coenders (ibid.) however can be criticised. One of the stated goals of the experimental approach was to exclude the observer's frame of reference and worldview from the evaluation. In the interests of speeding up construct elicitation and of streamlining the analysis stages of the Repertory Grid process, interviewees were asked to select any two from a list of three pre-prepared elements, each with pre-prepared bipolar constructs attached. Whilst taking less time and producing more uniform data, this short cut may have compromised the main strength of the Repertory Grid technique by introducing observer bias at crucial early stages.

Hassenzahl and Trautmann (2001, p. 167) set out to evaluate the "holistic overall impression [or] 'character' of a web site." This approach was chosen (rather than merely evaluating isolated aspects of the site, such as usability) on the basis that the overall "character [of a site] will have an impact on interpretation, acceptance and further interaction..."

The method used was to employ Repertory Grid Technique to enable interviewees to compare a new website design, created for a German online bank, with the old design, along with the other six prominent online banking sites available in Germany. The experiment produced useful data, enabling a comparative evaluation of the eight websites to be conducted, facilitating a view on the success of the new site design in terms of its users' experience. (Hassenzahl & Trautmann, ibid.)

Hassenzahl, Beu, & Burmester, (2001a) discuss the evolved needs of software product evaluation during the '00's, stating that the industry-wide focus on usability engineering over the last 30 years must now be extended to acknowledge contemporary users' needs. Citing 'joy of use' as an example, Hassenzahl et.al. (ibid.) argue that software possessing a high 'joy of use' factor tends to fare better with users on several levels, including: user acceptance and user satisfaction (Igbaria, Schiffman, & Wieckowski, 1994); sustained quality of performance when using 'joy of use' enabled software at the customer interface (Millard, Hole, & Crowle, 1999); enhanced ability to benefit from learning software (Draper, 1999); and overall amount of system usage together with system enjoyment (Mundorf, Westin, & Dholakia, 1993).

Hassenzahl et.al. *(op.cit.)*, recognising that hedonic qualities in software can, in some cases reduce software usability and utility, perform a selective review of existing measurement methods and tools. Repertory Grid is cited as a valuable tool in this regard. The method used presents interviewees with a randomly drawn triad from the software product set occupying the design space of interest to the evaluators. The interviewee is then asked the classic question: *in what way are two of these three products similar to each other, but different from the third?* In this way, the personal construct systems of the interviewees are used as a means of communicating responses to the products under evaluation.

Hassenzahl et.al. (*ibid.*, p. 5) explain thus:

For example, if you perceive two software products as being different, you might come up with the personal construct 'too colourful—looks good' to name the opposed extremes. On the one hand, this personal construct tells something about you, namely that too many colours disturb your sense of aesthetics. On the other hand, it also reveals information about the product's attributes.

Hassenzahl, Wessler, & Hamborg (2001b), seeking ways to better capture design requirements in the early stages of software design, introduce the Structured Hierarchical Interview for Requirement Analysis. (SHIRA).

A SHIRA interview aims to capture the interviewee's own point of view about desirable product qualities pertaining to a product under consideration *in his/her own terms* for later use in the design of the software. To this end, an open, non-directed approach is used in the interview. Data captured by a series of SHIRA interviews with different individuals can then be aggregated prior to use in the design stages of the product or system. To facilitate this use, the information gathering stage must also be highly structured.

As well as being useful in the early stages of designing, SHIRA has (as yet unexplored) potential for use as an evaluative tool. Hassenzahl, Beu, & Burmester, (*op. cit.*, p. 7) note that: "SHIRA is especially suited to gather information at early stages of the design process for interactive systems. However, it might also be possible to evaluate software at a later stage regarding how it fits the user's expectations."

Importantly, this technique avoids the need for the product or system under consideration to be viewed comparatively with other similar or competing systems. Instead, the experimenter takes a view of one product or system only at a time. Further, there appears to be a good 'fit' with the use of Personal Construct Theory in utilising an interviewee's own terms of reference in any evaluation.

Tan and Tung (2003) set out to investigate website designers' notions of what makes an 'effective' website. They used Repertory Grid Technique to ascertain a clear set of design principles, which were derived from constructs elicited from a panel of 20 designers, who evaluated six high-traffic websites. Tan and Tung (ibid., p. 65)

note that this approach helped to avoid the use of predetermined methods that may limit the scope of the study such as: " pre-structured questionnaires to collect data...[and]...scripted actions that govern the way participants walkthrough a website."

In a similar way to Boy *(op.cit.)* then, Tan and Tung *(op. cit.)* used Repertory Grid technique to achieve a consensus view drawn from expert consultations.

Fallman and Waterworth (2005) sought to couple Repertory Grid Technique to empirical data analysis methods in the evaluation of user experience and affective responses to artefacts. They used seven digital artefacts, including a digital camera, a PDA and a mobile phone. These artefacts were used as elements, and constructs were elicited from 18 participants. Although the focus of the work was on the use of empirical methods, the choice of such a wide variety of elements may have caused the elicitation process to be rather diffuse, as evidenced by the example constructs listed. This may have been exacerbated by the relatively short artefact familiarisation time provided to participants by the experimenters. However they conclude that as: "the data are meaningful to the participant, not to the experimenter... the data that is found within a participant's own repertory grid has not already been influenced by—i.e. interpreted in the light of—the researcher's pet theory." (Fallman & Waterworth, ibid., p. 4).

The preceding exemplars from Baber *(op.cit.)*, Boy *(op. cit.)*, Verlinden and Coenders *(op. cit)*, Hassenzahl and Trautmann *(op.cit.)* Hassenzahl, Wessler, & Hamborg. *(op.cit.)*, Hassenzahl, Beu, & Burmester *(op. cit.)* and Tan and Tung *(op. cit.)* demonstrate that Repertory Grid Technique may be used successfully in the evaluation of designed artefacts in general, and websites and software products in particular.

Repertory Grid Technique has been successfully used in the synchronisation or co-ordination of the efforts of 'experts' so that they can better contribute to a review panel during the design of a new IT system and to the creation of a consensus view on a design framework for business websites, as seen in Boy *(op. cit.)* and Tan and Tung *(op. cit.)* respectively, while Baber *(op. cit.)* has shown that the technique can be used for comparative product evaluation. Websites have been evaluated by taking a comparative view of the site under evaluation, either among its peers and competitors as seen in Hassenzahl and Trautmann *(op.cit.)* or by taking a comparative view within the different pages of the site itself as seen in Verlinden and Coenders *(op.cit.)*. Also, Hassenzahl, Beu, and Burmester *(op. cit.)* have proposed that a software product's user experience, and hedonic quality could be comparatively evaluated by using Repertory Grid to expose the product under evaluation to the personal construct system of individual users, and in a controlled, structured manner, to develop evaluative data. Fallman and Waterworth *(op. cit.)* have demonstrated an approach for the evaluation of the user experience of a small number of digital artefacts, and the subsequent statistical analysis of the data produced.

Applying the Repertory Grid Technique

As has been shown above, Repertory Grid Technique has strong possibilities for application where a comparative view is needed of how one software product fares against its competitors in the eyes of its users. Where a software product must be evaluated in a stand-alone manner however, a novel approach is needed. Optimally, the required approach retains the many advantages offered by Repertory Grid Technique, whilst facilitating the stand-alone evaluation of the software user experience.

Our approach is described below: In brief, we use an initial card-sorting activity to identify precise themes for enquiry, after which an individualised questionnaire is created that can later be used to evaluate the test software. This questionnaire is made up of themes that were identified by the participant as important to him/her self.

The specific questions used in the questionnaire were conceived and worded by the participant, thus ensuring that the terms of reference used fell within his/her range of convenience.

The specific method is explained below, step-by-step.

- Interviewees are sought from members of the target audience for the software under evaluation. The interviews are conducted singly. Interviewees are screened by questionnaire as to their IT skills.

- The interviewee is welcomed to the experimental venue. We use an office, provided with a round table, chairs, a desk and a computer connected to the Internet, running the software under evaluation. At the table, the interviewee is introduced to the aim and purpose of the experiment, and any initial questions are answered.

- A list of the software's design objectives is offered to the interviewee. These are written on index cards, one objective per card. The interviewee is asked to sort the cards, ranking them in order of importance according to his/her own opinion, by laying them out in a line on the table with 'most important' at one end and 'least important' at the other. Any questions asked by the interviewee are answered.

- The final card ranking arrived at by the interviewee is noted and recorded for future reference.

- The five cards ranked as most important are selected by the interviewer and the design objectives written on them are noted. These objectives correspond to the *elements* in a Repertory Grid interview.

- For each design objective (*element*), the interviewee is then asked to think of a characteristic that the software under evaluation would need, in order to fulfil that design objective in such a way that their experience of using the software would be positive. The resulting statement is written down on the Personal Statements Sheet form. Then the interviewee is asked to think of the opposite to the already stated characteristic, with the prompt "…as opposed to what?" This statement is also written down on the Personal Statements Sheet form. The two characteristics stated: one desirable, the other its opposite in the interviewee's own terms represent his/her personal construct relating to that design objective. The bipolar construct is written down as anchors, one at each end of a seven-point ratings scale.

- This step is repeated, to produce a total of three bipolar constructs for each of the five elements, making 15 in total. The interviewer must take great care to avoid influencing the interviewee's choice of words at all times. Careful use of repetition and reflecting during the interview will help the interviewee to state clearly what they mean, where difficulty is experienced.

- All 15 constructs are written out to create a personal Ratings Form, in effect, creating a 'blank' user experience questionnaire that is completely personalised to the interviewee, being based on elements, that he/she has chosen from a large pool of design objectives, using dyadic personal constructs elicited by the *opposite method* (discussed earlier) from these elements.

- The interviewer and the interviewee then move to the desk with the computer, where the interviewer briefly introduces the software under evaluation. Any questions asked are answered.

- Each interviewee is invited to use the software under evaluation to achieve the same real-world task. During the process, any questions asked are answered.

- When the interviewee states that he/she had finished, he/she is invited to complete the personal Ratings Form, scoring the software under evaluation against their previously elicited constructs.

- The interviewee is asked to share any other comments or views that have not been captured by the personal Ratings Form, and these are noted.

- The interviewee is thanked, and the experiment is concluded.

The data gathered are then ready for analysis. A Repertory Grid interview session as described above takes approximately two hours from beginning to end. We used 10 participants, each in a separate session. All interviews must be conducted in the same manner, preferably using the same venue.

Three methods are suggested for analysis of the data gathered, and these are described below:

Ranking of Design Objectives by Importance

As each participant had ranked all of the design objective cards in order of importance, the information may be tabulated in order to indicate an overall importance ranking as expressed by the whole group. This ranking may then be examined. On several occasions, this has produced surprising results where design objectives ranked 'most important' by the system designers were low-ranked by interviewees. The converse is also seen, where design objectives ranked 'least important' by the system designers were high-ranked by interviewees.

Tabulation of each participant's personal ratings with mean of overall scores for each participant

This method tabulates scores taken from the Personal Ratings Sheets drawn up for each participant. The five design objectives selected by the participant as most important (the Repertory Grid elements) and the scores for each of the three sets of paired, bipolar statements associated with each design objective (the Repertory Grid constructs) are presented, summed and a mean score is calculated. The data are thus readily available for an 'eyeball' test. Robson (1993), Clegg (1990), prior to further analysis.

Personal Ratings Sheet Discussion

Participants' Personal Ratings Sheets are reviewed and discussed. This discussion presents the individual subjective judgements made by each participant about their user experience of the software under review. Standard content analysis methods are useful here. Due to the Repertory Grid methodology used in the experiment, the judgements are stated using participants' own range of convenience and in their own terms of reference. These dimensions of judgement were hitherto hidden from view.

Summary of Repertory Grid Technique Applied to Software Evaluation

After all 15 personal constructs discussed above have been elicited, each participant is invited to use the software under review to perform the same real-world task. Once the participant has finished this task, he/she is invited to complete a Personal Ratings Sheet. This takes the form of a questionnaire, which uses the personal constructs elicited earlier in the session as questionnaire items. Each questionnaire item uses the personal construct 'likeness' and 'contrast' poles as anchors, separated by a seven-point ratings scale (1-7) with 7 representing greatest agreement with the 'likeness' pole and 1 representing greatest agreement with the 'contrast' pole.

The questionnaire items have therefore been elicited from the participant *before* using the software to perform any tasks. Participants must have no prior experience of using the software beforehand. Whilst participants are using the software, the experimenter transfers the personal constructs to the Personal Ratings Sheet, creating a questionnaire 'blank'. The questionnaire is administered *after* the user task is finished. Figures 5 and 6 show a blank Personal Statement Sheet (eliciting constructs) and a Personal Ratings sheet (post task questionnaire) used to elicit user data for analysis.

OVERALL SUMMARY AND CONCLUSIONS

Valuable data on the user experience is available if novel methods of investigation are applied. Many traditional HCI evaluation models have not been sufficiently sensitive to elicit data on user behaviour, which has significant implications for software design. However, the need to understand more about the covert judgments made by users is now critical for the success of software applications.

An important outcome has been the development of frameworks for surfacing these affective judgments in a structured manner. The two different techniques described here could be extended and applied to the design development of software capable of delivering a highly positive user experience.

The first technique showed that the design of the software does indeed influence the users' emotional response and motivation. An understanding of the relative importance of the differing and changing responses and how to address them in the design is derived from a theory of motivation that models this component of human behaviour as simple behavioural processes, (Ford, 1992) enabling the designer to attribute design features to components of motivated behaviour in the user. The MST – derived technique is compatible with current models and theories describing user interaction in HCI and this was an important reason for its selection.

The tests (pre, during and post test) revealed that tracking the user over time is valuable for gathering important information about the user's

Figure 5. Example blank Personal Statement Sheet (eliciting constructs)

changing experience, which is not captured by previous methodologies. This extends beyond evaluation at specific stages, since the user records their emotional response as soon as they experience it. This technique reveals some variability in users' experience and the way that consecutive good or bad experiences appear to have a cumulative effect in terms of users' overall rating.

Video of facial expressions showing users' interaction with the software proves invaluable for explaining behaviour and mapping the user's response to the software over time. Most importantly the videos capture the strength of the user's feeling as an issue or event occurs at the interface, providing the opportunity to make observations on strengthening or waning emotions as interaction continues. Keyword selection successfully assists the tracking of specific emotional responses and their intensity over time. This information can then be analysed alongside the video/audio recordings of interaction events and the transcripts from interview and questionnaire analysis.

The second technique, derived from Repertory Grid Technique, begins with an initial card sorting activity which helps participants settle into the session. As questions arise, they are answered, helping to relax participants further. The card sorts are normally completed with no problems, and the five cards ranked as 'most important' are reserved. The Repertory Grid 'elements' are therefore elicited with great ease.

Figure 6. Example Personal Ratings sheet (post task questionnaire)

Webomatic user experience survey
Personal Ratings Sheet

Now that you have finished making your website, please complete the evaluation form by circling the numbers which reflect your impressions about using Webomatic.

Form number ....

Attributes giving a **positive** experience...	...as opposed to...	...Attributes giving a **negative** experience
	7 6 5 4 3 2 1	
	7 6 5 4 3 2 1	
	7 6 5 4 3 2 1	
	7 6 5 4 3 2 1	
	7 6 5 4 3 2 1	
	7 6 5 4 3 2 1	
	7 6 5 4 3 2 1	
	7 6 5 4 3 2 1	

Completing the 'Personal Statements Sheet' form by taking each element and asking the question '…as opposed to what?' is very straightforward. In some cases long pauses occur while participants think through their answers. Timely follow up questions and focusing conversations may be needed in order to arrive at clear and unambiguous answers, taking great care at all times to avoid interviewer bias. Bipolar Repertory Grid construct elicitation requires deep thought on the part of the participant, but construction of the resulting Personal Ratings Form is very simple.

This form constitutes the 'blank' user experience questionnaire for that individual, ready for use.

After using the software under evaluation, the Personal Ratings Forms are normally completed with no difficulty by participants. Some previous participants have commented on the ease and smoothness of the experiment, and seemed pleasantly surprised at this.

Data collected are well structured, and easily accessible to later content analysis. The initial 'eyeball test' of the data immediately highlights areas of interest. The data are, as can be expected, very rich and highly value laden, but the values seen are those of the respective interviewees whose covert judgments regarding the software under evaluation have been surfaced and recorded. In the interests of bias free construct elicitation, the interviewer must use good active listening skills (Richardson, 2002) and must deliberately and repeatedly reflect back the participant's utterances, resisting the natural tendency to summarize them. This may need to be practiced beforehand in pilot sessions. Overall, the protocol is simple to deploy in the experimental setting.

Future Trends

The philosophy underlying these two methodologies is fundamentally concerned with eliminating interviewer bias to the greatest extent possible whilst focusing on the user's own perceptions in his/her own terms. This is not done reductively by iterating draft questionnaire items but constructively by simply asking users what is important to them. Qualitative methods as described, which produce "stackable" data for close analysis will change, due to the shift in emphasis, from merely measuring software usability to evaluating the quality and enjoyment of the software user's experience and will play an increasingly important role in software evaluation. (Blythe, Overbeeke, Monk, & Wright, 2004)

Further, whilst the prevailing view may be to discount less easily measurable aspects as not being worthwhile, these same less easily measured aspects will gradually take up centre stage in determining the value of software to its users.

The two approaches we have proposed, illuminating the general by close examination of the specific, (paraphrasing Denscombe, 2007) lend weight to theories of participatory design and amplify the user's voice in the software design cycle in ways that are authentic, genuine and transparent.

Work is now in progress on the development of a Qualitative User Experience Survey Tool (QUEST) which will be deeply rooted in our stated philosophy of "ask the user" and will incorporate key aspects of the two approaches described here.

REFERENCES

Baber, C. (1996). Repertory grid theory and its application to product evaluation. In Jordan, P., Thomas, B., Weerdmeester, B., & Mclelland, I. (Eds.), *Usability evaluation in industry* (pp. 157–165). London: Taylor and Francis.

Bannister, D., & Fransella, F. (1986). *Inquiring man: the psychology of personal constructs* (3rd ed.). London: Routledge.

Bickmore, T. W., & Picard, R. W. (2005). Establishing and maintaining long-term human-computer relationships. *ACM Transactions on Computer-Human Interaction*, 12(2), 293–327. doi:10.1145/1067860.1067867

Blythe, M., Overbeeke, K., Monk, A., & Wright, P. (Eds.). (2004). *Funology: From Usability to Enjoyment*. Springer.

Boy, G. (1997). The group elicitation method for participatory design and usability testing. *Interactions of the ACM*, 4(2).

Clegg, F. (1990). *Simple Statistics*. Cambridge: Cambridge University Press.

Davis, F. D. (1989). Perceived Usefulness, Perceived Ease of Use, and User Acceptance of Information Technology. *MIS Quart*, 13(3), 319–339. doi:10.2307/249008

Denscombe, M. (2007). *The Good Research Guide: For Small-scale Social Research Projects*. McGraw-Hill International.

Draper, S. W. (1999). Analysing fun as a candidate software requirement. *Personal and Ubiquitous Computing*, 3, 117–122. doi:10.1007/BF01305336

Duric, Z., Gray, W. D., Heishman, R., Li, F., Rosenfeld, A., & Schoelles, M. ... Wechsler, H. (2002). 'Integrating perceptual and cognitive modeling for adaptive and intelligent human-computer interaction. *Proceedings of the IEEE, 90*(7), 1272-1289.

Epting, F., Suchman, D., & Nickeson, C. (1971). An evaluation of elicitation procedures for personal constructs. *The British Journal of Psychology, 62*(4), 513–517.

Fallman, D., & Waterworth, J. A. (2005). *Dealing with User Experience and Affective Evaluation in HCI Design: A Repertory Grid Approach.* Paper presented at the CHI Workshop on Evaluating Affective Interfaces: Innovative Approaches.

Ford, D. H. (1987). *Humans as Self-Constructing Living Systems: A Developmental Theory of Behaviour and Personality.* Hillsdale, NJ: Erlbaum.

Ford, M. E. (1992). *Motivating Humans, Goals, Emotions and Personal Agency Beliefs.* Thousand Oaks, CA: Sage.

Fransella, F., & Bannister, D. (1977). *A manual for repertory grid technique.* London: Academic Press.

Greenberg, S., Fitzpatrick, G., Gutwin, C., & Kaplan, S. (2000). Adapting the locales framework for heuristic evaluation of groupware. [AJIS]. *Australasian Journal of Information Systems, 7*(2), 102–108.

Hartmann, J., Sutcliffe, A., & De Angeli, A. (2007). 'Investigating attractiveness in web user interfaces. Paper presented at the SIGCHI Conference on Human Factors in Computing Systems, San Jose, California.

Hassenzahl, M. (2008). Aesthetics in interactive products: Correlates and consequences of beauty. In Schifferstein, H. N., & Hekkert, P. (Eds.), *Product Experience* (pp. 287–302). Elsevier. doi:10.1016/B978-008045089-6.50014-9

Hassenzahl, M., Beu, A., & Burmester, M. (2001a). Engineering Joy. *IEEE Software, 18*(1). doi:10.1109/52.903170

Hassenzahl, M., & Trautmann, T. (2001). *Analysis of web sites with the repertory grid technique.* Paper presented at the CHI 2001: extended abstracts: interactive poster sessions, New York, N.Y.

Hassenzahl, M., & Ullrich, D. (2007). To do or not to do: Differences in user experience and retrospective judgments depending on the presence or absence of instrumental goals. *Interacting with Computers, 19*, 429–437. doi:10.1016/j.intcom.2007.05.001

Hassenzahl, M., Wessler, R., & Hamborg, K. (2001b). *Exploring and understanding product qualities that users desire.* Paper presented at the Joint AFIHM-BCS conference on Human-Computer Interaction IHM-HCI'2001, Toulouse, France.

Hollan, J., Hutchins, E., & Kirsh, D. (2000). Distributed Cognition: Toward a New Foundation for Human-Computer Interaction Research. *ACM Transactions on Computer-Human Interaction, 7*(2), 174–196. doi:10.1145/353485.353487

Igbaria, M., Schiffman, S., & Wieckowski, T. (1994). The respective roles of perceived usefulness and perceived fun in the acceptance of microcomputer technology. *Behaviour & Information Technology, 13*(6). doi:10.1080/01449299408914616

Kelly, G. (1955). *The psychology of personal constructs* (Vol. 1 & 2). New York, NY: Norton.

Millard, N., Hole, L., & Crowle, S. (1999). Smiling through: motivation at the user interface. In Bullinger, H.-J., & Ziegler, J. (Eds.), *Human-Computer Interaction Ergonomics and User Interfaces* (pp. 824–828). Mahwah, NJ, USA: Lawrence Erlbaum.

Mundorf, N., Westin, S., & Dholakia, N. (1993). Effects of hedonic components and user's gender on the acceptance of screen-based information services. *Behaviour & Information Technology, 12*(5), 293–303. doi:10.1080/01449299308924393

Nielsen, J. (1993). *Usability Engineering*. San Francisco: Morgan Kaufmann (Academic Press).

Norman, D. A. (2004). *Emotional design: Why we love (or hate) everyday things*. New York: Basic Books.

Norman, D. A., Ortony, A., & Russell, D. M. (2003). Affect and Machine Design: Lessons for the Development of Autonomous Machines. *IBM Systems Journal, 42*(1), 38–44. doi:10.1147/sj.421.0038

Oppenheim, A. N. (1992). *Questionnaire design, interviewing and attitude measurement* (2nd ed.). London: St Martins Press.

Osgood, C. E., Suci, G. J., & Tannenbaum, P. H. (1971). *The Measurement of Meaning*. London: University of Illinois Press.

Picard, R. W., & Wexelblat, A. (2002). *Future interfaces: social and emotional*. Paper presented at the CHI '02 Extended Abstracts on Human Factors in Computing Systems, Minneapolis, Minnesota, USA.

Richardson, J. T. E. (2002). *Handbook of Qualitative Research Methods for Psychology and the Social Sciences*. Oxford: BPS Blackwell Publishing.

Robson, C. (1993). *Real World Research*. Oxford: Blackwell.

Ryan, R. M., & Deci, E. L. (2000). Self-Determination Theory and the Facilitation of Intrinsic Motivation, Social Development, and Well-Being. *The American Psychologist, 55*, 68–78. doi:10.1037/0003-066X.55.1.68

Ryle, A., & Lunghi, M. (1970). The dyad grid: a modification of repertory grid technique. *The British Journal of Psychology*, 117.

Snider, J. G., & Osgood, C. E. (Eds.). (1969). *Semantic Differential Technique: A SourceBook*. Chicago: AldineTransaction.

Stewart, T. (2009). *Usability or User Experience - What's the difference?* [Online]. Available: http://www.system-concepts.com/articles/usability-articles/2008/usability-or-user-experience- whats-the-difference.html [Accessed 2010].

Stewart, V., & Stewart, A. (1981). *Business applications of the repertory grid*. Maidenhead, Berks.: McGraw-Hill.

Tan, F. B., & Tung, L. L. (2003). *Exploring website evaluation criteria using the repertory grid technique: A web designers' perspective*. Paper presented at the Second annual workshop on HCI research in MIS, Seattle: Washington.

Tractinsky, N. & Hassenzahl, M. (2005). Arguing for Aesthetics in Human-Computer Interaction. *i-com, 4*, 66-68.

Venkatesh, V. (2000). Determinants of Perceived Ease of Use: Integrating Control, Intrinsic Motivation, and Emotion into the Technology Acceptance Model. *Information Systems Research, 11*(4), 342–365. doi:10.1287/isre.11.4.342.11872

Verlinden, J., & Coenders, M. (2000). *Qualitative usability measurement of websites by employing the repertory grid technique*. Paper presented at the CHI 2000: extended abstracts, The Hague, The Netherlands.

Yin, R. (1994). *Case study research: design and methods*. London: Sage.(Stewart, 2009)

Chapter 16
A Conceptual Tool for Usability Problem Identification in Website Development

Mikael B. Skov
Aalborg University, Denmark

Jan Stage
Aalborg University, Denmark

ABSTRACT

Techniques and tools that enable website developers without formal training in human-computer inter-action to conduct their own usability evaluations would radically advance the integration of usability engineering in website development. This paper presents experiences from usability evaluations conducted by developers in an empirical study of means to support non-experts in identifying usability problems. A group of software developers who were novices in usability engineering analyzed a usability test session with the task of identifying usability problems experienced by the user. When doing this, they employed a simple one-page conceptual tool that supports identification of usability problems. The non-experts were able to conduct a well-organized usability evaluation and identify a reasonable amount of usability problems with a performance that was comparable to usability experts.

INTRODUCTION

Over the last decade, software usability as a discipline has made considerable progress. An important indicator of this is that more and more software organizations are beginning to take us-ability seriously as an important aspect of devel-

opment. Yet there are still significant obstacles to a full integration of usability engineering into software development (Bak et al., 2008). The average developer has not adopted this concern for usability, and usability specialists are not involved until late in development, when most substantial changes are too costly to implement (Anderson et al., 2001).

DOI: 10.4018/978-1-60960-523-0.ch016

There are several areas of software development where the limited integration of usability efforts is apparent. Development of sites for the World Wide Web is one such area. It is usually argued that the web is qualitatively different from conventional software systems. For the typical web application, the user group is more varied and fluent, and the application itself has a considerably shorter lifetime compared to other kinds of software. For development of web applications, the main difference compared to other applications is that it is done by a broad variety of companies, ranging from one or two person companies to large corporations, and many of the development companies, in particular the smaller ones, do not have any usability experts available. Budget constraints prohibit hiring specialists, and the development schedule does not leave time for usability testing and feedback to iterative design (Scholtz et al., 1998). Research indicates that work practices in website development seem to largely ignore the body of knowledge and experience that has been established in the disciplines of software engineering, human-computer interaction, and usability engineering (Sullivan & Matson, 2000). Conventional usability evaluation is expensive, time consuming and requires usability specialists. This is incompatible with web development, where many websites are designed and implemented in fast-paced projects by multidisciplinary teams that involve such diverse professions as information architects, Web developers, graphic designers, brand and content strategists, etc. Such teams are usually not familiar with established knowledge on human-computer interaction (Braiterman et al., 2000). The consequence of this is clear. A large number of websites have severe usability problems that prohibit effective and successful use (Spool et al., 1999). An investigation of usability through content accessibility found that 29 of 50 popular websites were either inaccessible or only partly accessible (Spool et al., 1999; Sullivan & Matson, 2000).

There are at least two ways of integrating usability expertise in website development projects. First, developers can adapt and use tailored usability heuristics in the evaluation and let these heuristics guide the usability work in the development team (Agarwal & Venkatesh, 2002; Sutcliffe, 2001). The practical implications of usability heuristics in software design have been discussed for several years, but traditional heuristics is not of focus in this paper. Secondly, the limited integration of usability in software development can be resolved by involving non-experts in the usability engineering activities. This could be accomplished by offering ordinary software developers means for creating usable websites and evaluating them in a systematic manner (Skov & Stage, 2001). This might bring usability into the earliest possible phases of software development where it could have most impact by improving initial design and eliminating rework. It would also solve a potential problem with availability of usability experts. The professional evaluator resource is very scarce, thus evaluating the usability of just a fraction of all new websites would be well beyond their capacity.

This paper presents an empirical study of a specific means to support non-experts in web usability in conducting a website usability evaluation. We have explored to what extent a simple one-page conceptual tool for usability problem identification can support and stimulate the analytical skills of novice usability evaluators. By doing this, we wish to explore whether people with a basic foundation in software engineering and programming through methodological support can build a capability to identify, describe and classify usability problems. The next section provides an overview of existing literature on identification of usability problems. The following section describes the design of an empirical study we have conducted in order to examine the usefulness of the usability problem identification tool we have developed for problem identification. Then the results of the empirical study are presented and discussed. Finally, we conclude on our study.

BACKGROUND

With the prevalent role of contemporary websites in today's societies, website usability has received increased attention over the last years and several textbooks on website usability has been published (Badre, 2002; Krug, 2000; Nielsen, 2000; Nielsen & Tahir, 2002). While such literature primarily focuses on specific elements of usability in websites, e.g. Nielsen and Tahir (2002) analyze 50 different websites on their usability; some references in the research literature provide methodological support of the usability evaluation process for websites. Primarily, some research attempts have proposed heuristics for website evaluation (Agarwal & Venkatesh, 2002; Sutcliffe, 2001). On the other hand, the more general literature on usability evaluation practices and means to support it is varied and rich. On the overall level, there are methods to support the whole process of a usability evaluation, e.g. (Rubin, 1994). The literature that compares usability evaluation methods also includes detailed descriptions of procedure for conducting evaluations, e.g. how to identify, group and merge lists of usability problems (Hornbæk & Frøkjær, 2004; Jeffries et al., 1991; Karat et al., 1992). All of this deals with user-based usability evaluation.

Heuristic methods for usability evaluation have been suggested as means to reduce the resources required to conduct a usability evaluation. In many cases, strong limitations in terms of development time effectively prohibits conventional usability testing as it is described in classical methods (Dumas & Redish, 1993; Fath et al., 1994; Nielsen, 1993; Nielsen et al., 1992; Rubin, 1994). Such evaluations are very time-consuming, and considerable costs arise when a large group of users is involved in a series of tests. Heuristic inspection evolved as an attempt to reduce these costs (Lavery et al., 1997; Nielsen, 1993; Nielsen

et al., 1992). The basic idea is that a group of usability experts evaluate an interface design by comparing it to a set of guidelines, called heuristics (Nielsen, 1992). The first heuristics consisted of nine principles (Lavery et al., 1997), which have been developed further over the last ten years. The literature on heuristic inspection also includes empirical studies of its capability for finding usability problems. The first studies indicated that the method was very effective (Agarwal & Venkatesh, 2002; Lavery et al., 1997; Nielsen, 1992; Nielsen et al., 1992). Other studies have produced less promising results as they conclude that a conventional user-based usability test yields similar or better results compared to inspection (Karat et al., 1992), and heuristic inspection tends to find many low-priority problems (Jeffries et al., 1991). But usability heuristics designated for website design and evaluation have been proposed and successfully adapted in some research studies (Agarwal & Venkatesh, 2002; Sutcliffe, 2001). Finally, the basic idea in heuristic evaluation is also the key characteristic of the usability evaluation method called MOT, where five metaphors of human thinking are used as a basis for evaluation (Hornbæk & Frøkjær, 2004).

There is also research that describes how usability experts actually conduct evaluations. It has been established that expert evaluators find different usability problems. This has been denoted as the evaluator effect (Hertzum & Jacobsen, 2001; Jacobseb et al., 1998). There is a remarkable difference both in the number of problems and the specific problems they find. The strength is that if we introduce more evaluators, we find more problems. The weakness is that it seems random and difficult to trust.

Changes in software development with new development approaches such as open source development, global software development and outsourcing are challenging conventional usability evaluation practices. With outsourcing and global software development, developers, evaluators and users are distributed across multiple organizations and time zones. This also characterizes several website development projects and makes conventional user-based usability testing considerably more complex and challenging (Murphy et al., 2004). This makes remote usability testing increasingly important as an alternative to conventional usability testing (Andreasen et al., 2007). Remote usability testing denotes a situation where "the evaluators are separated in space and/or time from users" (Castillo et al., 1998). The first methods for remote usability testing emerged about ten years ago. At that time, some empirical studies were conducted that showed results comparable to conventional methods (Hartson et al., 1998). A very interesting method was based on the idea that users should report the critical incidents they experienced while using the system (Hartson et al., 1996; Hartson et al., 1998). A recent study of remote usability evaluation methods concluded that users report significantly fewer problems compared to a classical usability evaluation but the method imposes considerably less effort on the evaluators (Andreasen et al., 2007; Bak et al., 2009).

A related line of research has inquired into the ability of novice usability evaluators to identify usability problems. Based on a comparison with experts it is concluded that novice evaluators can quickly learn to plan and conduct user-based usability evaluations and to write up the related reports. However, when it comes to identification, description and categorization of usability problems, they perform at a significantly lower level than expert evaluators (Skov & Stage, 2001, 2004).

The amount of research on user-based usability evaluation conducted by novices is very limited. We have only been able to find one reference where novices conducted the evaluation, and this was heuristic evaluation and not user-based (Slavkovic & Cross, 1999). An effort with training focused on transfer of developers' skills in design of user interfaces from one technology to another (Nielsen et al., 1992).

These streams of research emphasize a need for methodological support to novice or non-expert usability evaluators in identifying usability problems. They also illustrate that the literature is limited in this area.

CONCEPTUAL TOOL FOR USABILITY PROBLEM IDENTIFICATION

During a series of courses on usability testing for under-graduate students, we discovered a clear fundamental need for support on usability problem identification for novice usability evaluators. Especially, we found that even though test participants experienced usability problems, novice evaluators were incapable of identifying and classifying such problems (Skov & Stage, 2001). As a solution, we came up with the idea of the usability problem identification tool (see Table 1).

The basic idea in the usability problem identification tool is that it provides a conceptual or overall interpretation of what constitutes a problem. Inspired by previous research (Molich, 2000; Nielsen, 1993; Rubin, 1994) and our own practical experiences with usability test teaching, we identified four overall categories of usability problems as experienced by users:

1. Slowed down
2. Understanding
3. Frustration
4. Test monitor intervention.

These four episodes often reveal some sort of usability problem. 1) The first category includes problems where the test participant is being slowed down relatively to normal speed. Several usability problems denotes and describes some sort of users being slowed down while interacting with a website. Thus, they are not able to complete assigned tasks in an efficient manner. 2) The second category of problems deals with

Table 1. Usability problem identification tool

	Slowed down *relative to normal work speed*	Understanding	Frustration	Test monitor intervention
Critical	Hindered in solving the task	Does not understand how information in the system can be used for solving a task. Repeats the same information in different parts of the system.		Receives substantial assistance (could not have solved the task without it).
Serious	Delayed for several seconds	Does not understand how a specific functionality operates or is activated. Cannot explain the functioning of the system.	Is clearly annoyed by something that cannot be done or remembered or something illogical that you must do. Believes he has damaged something.	Receives a hint.
Cosmetic	Delayed for a few seconds	Does actions without being able to explain why (you just have to do it).		Is asked a question that makes him come up with the solution

users' understanding of the website. Often users find it difficult to understand how website are constructed, what functionality the website offers, and how information is organized in the website. 3) The third category describes problems related to the user's level of frustration. This is a classical metric in usability evaluation studies where researchers focus on the user frustration as an indicator of website usability. Users may (or may not) show their frustration during a usability test session, however if they do so, it is often due to interaction problems with the interface. 4) The fourth category shows problems where the test monitor has intervened or helped the test participant in order to complete the assigned tasks. A good acting test monitor will intervene (and only intervene) if the participant experience severe problems in task completion.

On the other dimension, we distinguish between three severities of problem namely critica problem, serious problems, and cosmetic problems – inspired by previous research (Molich, 2000).

EMPIRICAL STUDY

We have conducted an empirical study with a usability problem identification tool that is intended to support novice or non-expert evaluators in identifying usability problems in a user-based evaluation. The purpose of the empirical study was to examine whether this tool was useful for such inexperienced evaluators.

Setting: The empirical study was conducted in relation to a course that one of the authors of this paper was teaching. The course was an introduction to design and implementation of user interfaces. It consisted of the following three modules:

A. Introduction to human computer interaction and a method for user interaction design
B. Implementation of user interfaces in Java
C. Usability evaluation of interactive systems

Each module consisted of five class meetings with a two-hour lecture and an equal amount of time for exercises. The experiment was part of the last module (module C). The content of that module was a presentation of the activities of a usability evaluation and techniques that are relevant in each activity. The main literature was (Preece et al., 2002) supplemented with selected articles. The five lectures of this module had the following contents:

1. The purpose of a usability evaluation, the concept of usability and overview of the activities involved in a usability evaluation
2. Basic decisions, field versus lab, the test monitor role and the test report
3. Creation of test context, tasks assignments, conducting the test and the think-aloud technique
4. Interpretation of data, the ISO definition, task load, identification of usability problems, exercises in identification and categorization of usability problems
5. Presentation of experiences from our evaluation, heuristic evaluation, comparison with think-aloud and training of novices in usability evaluation

Subjects: The participants in the experiment were 24 undergraduate second-year students in computer science. They had a basic qualification in programming and software engineering. They were offered to participate in this experiment as a voluntary exercise, and they were promised feedback on their products.

Usability problem identification tool: The empirical study involved a one-page usability problem identification tool that the authors had developed during earlier usability evaluations, see Table 1. The authors also used this tool in their own data analysis.

Experimental procedure: The empirical study was conducted between lecture 3 and 4. The stu-dents were only told in advance that there would be an exercise about usability problems, but no details were given. The empirical study lasted for three and a half hour. All students came into the class at 8:30. They were handed a CD-ROM with the same recording of a usability test session and a few practical guidelines for carrying out the exercise. The test session was app. 30 minutes. The students also received the usability problem identification tool they were asked to use, cf. Table 1. The recording was of a user that solved a series of tasks on a website for a large furniture store. The think-aloud technique was used. The empirical study ended at noon when they delivered their problem lists and diaries by email.

The students were asked to work individually on the task. They would see the recording and note down usability problems as they occurred. In doing so, they were encouraged to use the usability problem identification tool. Thus the tool gave a practical definition of usability problems, and it was supposed to be used in the detailed analysis. For each usability problem they identified, they were also asked to record in the diary if they used the tool and which field in the table the problem was related to.

Data collection: The main result was the problem list from each student. In addition, they were asked to maintain a diary with reasons why they decided that something was a usability problem and why they categorized it at a certain level. In this paper, we only deal with the problem lists.

Data analysis: The two authors of this paper analysed the recording independently of each other and produced an individual problem list where each problem was described as illustrated in Table 2. The first column contains the unique number

Table 2. Example of a usability problem

No.	Window	Description	Severity
13	Product page	Does not know how to buy the article that is described in the page; is uncertain about the procedure to buy an article on-line	Serious

Table 3. Mean numbers of identified problems and non-problems.

	Problems	Non-Problems	Sum
Tool Participants (N=24)	8.00 (4.63)	2.95 (2.87)	10.39 (5.83)

of the problem. The second column specifies the window or screen where the problem occurred. The third column contains the description of the way the user experiences the problem. In the individual problem lists, each evaluator also made a severity assessment for each usability problem. This was expressed on a three-point scale, e.g. cosmetic, serious, or critical (Molich, 2000). The individual problem lists from the two authors were merged through negotiation into one overall list of usability problems. The resulting problem list was the basis for evaluating the problem lists produced by the participants in the experiment. Thus the problem list from each student was compared to the authors' joint problem list.

Validity: The specific conditions of this study limit its validity in a number of ways. First, the students participated in the empirical study on a voluntary basis receiving no immediate credit for their participation. Thus, motivation and stress factors could prove important. This implies that students did not have the same kinds of incentives for conducting the usability test sessions as people in a professional usability laboratory. Secondly, the demographics of the test subjects are not varied with respect to age and education. Most subjects were students of approximately 22 years of age with approximately the same school background and recently started on a computer science education.

RESULTS

This section presents the key results from our empirical study. First, we present the problem identification by the 24 participants and compare

their reporting with the usability experts. Second, we analyze the identified problems according to their categorization as done by the participants.

Identifying and Reporting Usability Problems

The participants identified very different numbers of usability problems. This is illustrated by two participants reporting no usability problems while one participant identified and reported 18 different usability problems. On average, the participants identified 8.00 usability problems (SD=4.63). This is illustrated in Table 3. The high variety in numbers of reported problems suggests strong presence of the evaluator effect. Therefore, the usability problem identification tool did not in itself remove this effect and indicates that some participants only marginally used the tool.

From our data it seemed from the reporting of usability problems that our participants could be divided into three different groups regarding numbers of reported problems. The first group reported no or very few problems (0-3), the second group reported up to ten problems (4-10), and the third group reported more than ten problems (>10). Six participants belonged to the first group, and 11 participants belonged to the second group, while seven participants belonged to the third group. Interestingly, we saw a gap between participants from the first group compared to the second group as the "best" participants in group one identified three problems whereas none in the second group reported less than seven problems

As stated earlier and further illustrated above, novice evaluators often find it difficult just to see and identify usability problems. Additionally, they

Table 4. Total numbers of identified problems for the two approaches.

	Usability Experts (N=2)	Participants (N=24)	Sum (N=26)
Critical	2	2	2
Serious	19	16	19
Cosmetic	17	12	18
Total	38	28	39

are typically faced with challenges when trying to describe (or illustrate) identified problems. Several participants reported issues from the usability test as problems but it was impossible for us to figure out or extract the actual problem from the descriptions. We denote such issues as non-problems (see Table 3). In several cases, these issues were even described in a non-problematic way (e.g. as a positive or neutral feature of the tested system). The participants reported on average 2.95 non-problems (SD=2.87). Again, the numbers of reported non-problems were very diverse between participants having some participants reporting zero non-problems while one participant reported 10 non-problems.

Having discussed numbers of problems identified per participant, we will now outline the reporting of problems for all participants as one group. Two usability experts also conducted a video analysis of the test session and reported usability problems. We will in the following compare the participants in the experiment with these usability experts.

The 24 participants together identified and reported a total of 28 different usability problems. Thus on one hand, they were not able to identify all known problems as reported by the usability experts, but they were able to report on a substantial amount of these problems (72%). When looking at problem severity, we found that the participants were able to identify many of the more severe problems. As a group, they identified 86% of the most severe problems (critical and serious problems) where they identified both

critical problems and 16 out of the 19 serious problems. On the other hand, they reported on the identification of 12 cosmetic problems out of a total of 18 problems. One participant identified a usability problem not identified or reported by any of the two usability experts. In summary, the participants as a group were able to identify most severe problems as reported by the usability experts while they missed some cosmetic problems in their reporting. (see Table 4)

Considering numbers of participants reporting the 28 problems, further analysis show that problem severity had an impact on identification and reporting. Thus, the more severe a problem was the higher the chance of identification and reporting. On average, the critical problems were reported by 67% of the participants. The two critical problems were reported by 18 participants respectively 14 participants. The same figures are considerably lower for the serious and cosmetic problems. In fact, our analysis show that a critical usability problem was significantly more likely to be reported by a participant than a serious or a cosmetic usability problem according to two-tailed Chi-square tests ($\chi^2[1]=47.691$, p=0.0001; $\chi^2[1]=66.012$, p=0.0001). However, we only discovered a tendency towards a serious problem being more likely to be reported than a cosmetic problem, but this finding was not significant ($\chi^2[1]=3.725$, p=0.0536). Summarized, it appeared that severity had considerable impact on identification as severe problems were more likely to be reported.

Categorization of Usability Problems

As an integrated part of the usability problem identification tool, problems should be categorized according to severity. The usability problem identification tool integrates three levels of severity namely critical, serious, and cosmetic problems (see Table 1). The categorization was characterized by some diversity but also by agreement between the participants. All problems had been categorized according to severity by the two usability experts.

The two problems categorized as critical by the usability experts were identified by 18 respectively 14 participants out of the total number of 24 participants (as discussed previously). However, the two problems were categorized very differently by the participants. The first critical problem (reported by 18) was unanimously categorized as critical by all participants who identified it. This particular problem is that the test subject was unable to complete a purchase on the website. Interestingly, the second critical usability problem was categorized rather differently, where only one participant categorized it as critical, and nine participants categorized it as serious, while four categorized it as cosmetic. This problem is subtle as it reflects how the test subject understands interface elements which make her navigate wrongly. The problem was categorized as critical by both of the usability experts as it delayed her task completion for several minutes. Either the participants did not see this long delay or they disagreed that she was delayed this long. This is not clear from the descriptions, but their reporting typically lacked information on task delay in this situation. This was quite the opposite for the other problem where she failed to complete the task and the delay was obvious.

The remaining 26 serious and cosmetic problems were categorized quite differently by the participants compared the categorization made by the usability experts. Three problems received all three categorizations ranging from critical to cosmetic, but most problems were categorized

as either serious or cosmetic. Also, five problems received unanimously categorizations by the participants. Summarized, our analysis of usability problem categorization confirms that this is a highly difficult and challenging task. Furthermore, it seems that individual differences between evaluators are very prominent.

DISCUSSION

Our aim with the usability problem identification tool is to provide software designers and programmers support in constructing more usable interfaces. Thus, we strive to contribute to the body of knowledge within discount usability evaluation by integrating the activities of usability testing into the knowledge of the software developer. In addition, we are interested in providing software projects that are distributed physically with tools or techniques that can support remote usability testing. Inspired by previous research on usability evaluation and particularly on the challenges related to usability problem identification, we developed a usability problem identification tool for use in user-based usability evaluations. The tool is supposed to support evaluators during video analysis of user interaction with a computerized system by emphasizing different levels of problems and modes of experiencing problems. We evaluated the usability problem identification tool in an experiment with 24 participants. All participants had only introductory knowledge of human-computer interaction issues and no specific training in analysis of usability test sessions.

Our empirical study shows that the participants were able to identify and report many of the more severe problems from the test session. Two critical problems were identified by more than half of the participants; in fact, one critical problem was discovered by 75% of the participants. Several participants used and applied the tool in the identification of the problems and tried to express the problems in terms of the different suggested modes. Especially user delay was commonly used in the reporting. Not surprisingly, less severe problems were not identified to the same extent as the critical problems. More of these problems were only reported by one or two participants, while only four problems were reported by at least ten participants. No problem was reported by all participants partly as a consequence of the fact that two participants reported no usability problems at all.

Promoting remote or distance usability testing conducted by the users themselves require some sort of framework to guide the testing or the analysis. As a group, somewhat surprisingly the participants performed well by identifying a substantial amount of the usability problems. In fact, the most severe problems namely the critical and serious problems were identified almost completely by the group taken as a whole.

A major challenge in usability problem identification and categorization is the so-called evaluator effect. Previous studies have found that the evaluator effect is challenging in user-based usability evaluations such as think-aloud tests as evaluators identify substantial amounts of unique problems (Hertzum & Jacobsen, 2001; Jacobsen et al., 1998). Furthermore, evaluators also suffer from the fact that they identify very few common problems. Our results seem to confirm the evaluator effect as our participants identified several unique problems. This is not surprising. At this stage, we cannot conclude whether the tool addressed or solved some of the inherent problems of the evaluator effect, but we can see that participants in several cases used the tool actively in their descriptions. But further studies are needed to confirm or reject the effects of different evaluators.

Categorization of usability problems is very difficult and challenging. This was confirmed in our experiment. It seemed that the tool only marginally supported the categorization. The tool was designed to integrate key aspects of severity by illustrating different modes of usability problems

for different severity ratings. In certain situations, it seemed to help the participants in understanding the situation and therefore more easily being able to categorize the observed problem. As an example, most participants actively used the tool in the categorization of one of the critical problems. However, several problems were categorized rather differently by the participants sometimes reflecting differences in the assessed scope of the problem.

We have only involved novice evaluators as participants in our study, just like the studies in (Hornbæk & Frøkjær, 2004). Studies involving expert evaluators tend to identify more and different kinds of problems (Nielsen, 1992). However, to compensate against this potential problem, we measured the participants' performance against experienced usability evaluators. The participants taken together identified a significant proportion of the problems identified by the experts.

FURTHER DEVELOPMENT

The conceptual tool for usability problem identification used in the empirical study reported above has been developed through introspective observation of our own problem identification and categorization process in other usability evaluations. In addition, certain parts are still vaguely defined.

The conceptual tool is similarities to a checklist. In other domains, there is a considerable confidence in the use of checklists. Schamel (2008) present the history behind introduction of checklists in aviation. Hales and Provonost (2006) describes a checklist as a list of action items or criteria that are arranged in a systematic manner, which allow the user to record the presence/absence of the individual items listed to ensure that all of them are considered or completed. They emphasize that the objectives of a checklist may be to support memory recall, standardization and regulation of processes or methodologies. They present an overview of the use of checklists in the areas of aviation, product manufacturing, healthcare and critical care.

Hales et al. (2008) have conducted a systematic study of literature on checklist. They provide a categorization of different checklists with examples from medicine. Some of these categories are clearly relevant for usability evaluation. The tool we have presented in this paper resembles what they call a Diagnostic checklist or a Criteria of merit checklist. They also provide guidelines for development of checklists. This could be a useful basis for enhancing our conceptual identification tool.

Verdaasdonk et al. (2008) argue that the use of checklists is a promising strategy for improving patient safety in all types of surgical processes. They present requirements and guidelines for implementation of checklists for surgical processes. Helander (2006) describes checklists in relation to HCI. He emphasizes the checklist as a memory aid that can be used to support systematic assessment of ergonomics in a workplace.

All of these examples deal with checklists for professionals. Our conceptual tool can be considered as a simple checklist. It has been shown that a usability problem identification tool like the one presented in this paper combined with education provides solid support to problem identification and categorization (Skov & Stage, 2005). The results presented in this paper show that even without prior formal training in usability engineering, the tool provides some assistance. However, the results also indicate that the tool should be improved. Other researchers in the HCI area have worked with description of usability problems from a usability problem identification platform (Cockton et al., 2004; Lavery et al., 1997). It may be possible to combine this with the guidelines for developing checklist in order to create an enhanced usability problem identification tool.

CONCLUSION

This paper has presented results from an empirical study of a conceptual tool to support identification of usability problems as part of a usability evaluation. The non-expert participants in the study found on average 8 usability problems, but with substantial differences between them. Two usability experts found 38 problems. Compared to this, the performance of the participants is limited. On the other hand, the 24 participants together identified 72% of the problems found by the experts; and the non-experts found nearly all critical and serious problems. This is very interesting given that the time spent by the experts on data analysis of the problem lists produced by the participants was very limited. This indicates that even with a very limited expert effort you are able to get a large proportion of the severe problems provided that you involve a group of participants that is larger than what we normally are used to. This gives a reason to be optimistic about the ideas of having developers report usability problems.

The idea of this approach is to reduce the expert efforts needed to conduct usability testing. This is consistent with the ideas behind heuristic inspection and other walkthrough techniques. On a more general level, it would be interesting to identify other potential areas for reducing effort.

These conclusions are based on a single experiment with 24 participants. Unfortunately, there are very few results in the literature to compare with. Therefore, it would be interesting to repeat the empirical study. The usability problem identification tool could also be developed further, especially in order to support categorization of usability problems.

ACKNOWLEDGMENT

The work behind this paper received financial support from the Danish Research Agency (grant no. 2106-04-0022 and no. 2106-08-0011). We would especially like to thank all the participating test subjects. Finally, we want to thank the anonymous reviewers for comments on earlier drafts of this paper.

REFERENCES

Agarwal, R., & Venkatesh, V. (2002). Assessing a Firm's Web Presence: A Heuristic Evaluation Procedure for the Measurement of Usability. *Information Systems Research, 13*(2), 168–186. doi:10.1287/isre.13.2.168.84

Anderson, J., Fleek, F., Garrity, K., & Drake, F. (2001). Integrating Usability Techniques into Software Development. *IEEE Software, 18*(1), 46–53. doi:10.1109/52.903166

Andreasen, M. S., Nielsen, H. V., Schrøder, S. O., & Stage, J. (2006). Usability in open source software development: Opinions and practice. *Information Technology and Control, 35A*(3), 303–312.

Andreasen, M. S., Nielsen, H. V., Schrøder, S. O., & Stage, J. (2007). What Happened to Remote Usability Testing? An Empirical Study of Three Methods. In *Proceedings of CHI 2007*. New York: ACM Press.

Badre, A. N. (2002). *Shaping Web Usability – Interaction Design in Context*. Boston: Addison-Wesley.

Bak, J. O., Nguyen, K., Risgaard, P., & Stage, J. (2008) Obstacles to Usability Evaluation in Practice: A Survey of Software Organizations. In *Proceedings of NordiCHI 2008*. New York: ACM Press.

Benson, C., Muller-Prove, M., & Mzourek, J. (2004). Professional usability in open source projects: Gnome, openoffice.org, netbeans. In *Proceedings of CHI 2004* (pp. 1083-1084). New York: ACM Press.

Braiterman, J., Verhage, S., & Choo, R. (2000). Designing with Users in Internet Time. *Interaction, 7*(5), 23–27. doi:10.1145/345242.345253

Bruun, A., Gull, P., Hofmeister, L., & Stage, J. (2009). Let your users do the testing: A comparison of three remote asynchronous usability testing methods. In *Proceedings of CHI 2009*. New York: ACM Press.

Castillo, J. C., Hartson, H. R., & Hix, D. (1998). Remote usability evaluation: Can users report their own critical incidents? In *Proceedings of CHI 1998* (pp. 253-254). New York: ACM Press.

Cockton, G., Woolrych, A., & Hindmarch, M. (2004). Reconditioned Merchandise: Extended Structured Report Formats in Usability Inspection. In *CHI 2004 Extended Abstracts*, (pp. 1433-1436). New York: ACM Press.

Dempsey, B. J., Weiss, D., Jones, P., & Greenberg, J. (2002). Who is an open source software developer? *Communications of the ACM, 45*(2), 67–72. doi:10.1145/503124.503125

Dumas, J. S., & Redish, J. C. (1993). *A practical guide to usability testing*. Norwood, NJ: Ablex Publishing.

Fath, J. L., Mann, T. L., & Holzman, T. G. (1994). A Practical Guide to Using Software Usability Labs: Lessons Learned at IBM. *Behaviour & Information Technology, 13*(1-2), 25–35.

Frishberg, N., Dirks, A. M., Benson, C., Nickell, S., & Smith, S. (2002). Getting to know you: Open source development meets usability. In *Proceedings of CHI 2002* (pp. 932-933). New York: ACM Press.

Hales, B. M., & Provonost, P. J. (2006). The checklist. A tool for error management and performance improvement. *Journal of Critical Care, 21*, 231–235. doi:10.1016/j.jcrc.2006.06.002

Hales, B. M., Terblanche, M., Fowler, R., & Sibbald, W. (2008). Development of medical checklists for improved quality of patient care. *International Journal for Quality in Health Care*, *20*(1), 22–30. doi:10.1093/intqhc/mzm062

Hartson, H. R., & Castillo, J. C. (1998). Remote evaluation for post-deployment usability improvement. In *Proceedings of AVI 1998* (pp. 22-29). New York: ACM Press.

Hartson, H. R., Castillo, J. C., Kelso, J., & Neale, W. C. (1996). Remote evaluation: The network as an extension of the usability laboratory. In *Proceedings of CHI 1996* (pp. 228-235). New York: ACM Press.

Helander, M. (2006). *A Guide to Human Factors and Ergonomics* (2nd ed.). Boca Raton, FL: CRC Press.

Hertzum, M., & Jacobsen, N. E. (2001). The evaluator effect: A chilling fact about us-ability evaluation methods. *International Journal of Human-Computer Interaction*, *13*(4), 421–443. doi:10.1207/S15327590IJHC1304_05

Hornbæk, K., & Frøkjær, E. (2004). Usability Inspection by Metaphors of Human Thinking Compared to Heuristic Evaluation. *International Journal of Human-Computer Interaction*, *17*(3), 357–374. doi:10.1207/s15327590ijhc1703_4

ISO 9241-11. (1997). *Ergonomic Requirements for Office Work with Visual Display Terminals (VDTs)* (Part 11: Guidance on usability). ISO.

Jacobsen, N. E., Hertzum, M., & John, B. E. (1998). The Evaluator Effect in Usability Tests. In *Proc. CHI'98*. New York: ACM Press

Jeffries, R., Miller, J. R., Wharton, C., & Uyeda, K. M. (1991). User Interface Evaluation in the Real World: A Comparison of Four Techniques. In *Proceedings of CHI '91* (pp. 119-124). New York: ACM Press.

Karat, C.-M., Campbell, R., & Fiegel, T. (1992). Comparison of Empirical Testing and Walkthrough Methods in User Interface Evaluation. In *Proceedings of CHI '92* (pp. 397-404). New York: ACM Press

Krug, S. (2000) *Don't Make Me Think – A Common Sense Approach to Web Usability*. Circle.com Library, USA

Lavery, D., Cockton, G., & Atkinson, M. P. (1997). Comparison of Evaluation Methods Using Structured Usability Problem Reports. *Behaviour & Information Technology*, *16*(4), 246–266. doi:10.1080/014492997119824

Molich, R. (2000). *User-Friendly Web Design*. Copenhagen, Denmark: Ingeniøren Books.

Murphy, J., Howard, S., Kjeldskov, K., & Goschnick, S. (2004). Location, location, location: Challenges of outsourced usability evaluation. In *Proceedings of the Workshop on Improving the Interplay between Usability Evaluation and User Interface Design, NordiCHI 2004*, Aalborg University, Department of Computer Science, HCI-Lab Report no. 2004/2 (pp. 12-15).

Nielsen, J. (1992). Finding Usability Problems through Heuristic Evaluation. In *Proceedings of CHI '92* (pp. 373-380). New York: ACM Press.

Nielsen, J. (1993). *Usability Engineering*. San Francisco: Morgan Kaufmann Publishers.

Nielsen, J. (2000). *Designing Web Usability*. New York: New Riders Publishing.

Nielsen, J., Bush, R. M., Dayton, T., Mond, N. E., Muller, M. J., & Root, R. W. (1992). Teaching experienced developers to design graphical user interfaces. In *Proceedings of CHI 1992* (pp. 557-564). New York: ACM Press.

Nielsen, J., & Tahir, M. (2002). *Homepage Usability – 50 Websites Deconstructed*. New York: New Riders Publishing.

Preece, J., Rogers, Y., & Sharp, H. (2002). *Interaction Design: Beyond Human-Computer Interaction*. New York: John Wiley & Sons.

Rohn, J. A. (1994). The Usability Engineering Laboratories at Sun Microsystems. *Behaviour & Information Technology*, *13*(1-2), 25–35. doi:10.1080/01449299408914581

Rubin, J. (1994). *Handbook of Usability Testing: How to plan, design and conduct effective tests*. New York: John Wiley & Sons.

Schamel, J. (2008). *How the pilot's checklist came about*. Retrieved from http://www.atchistory.org/History/ checklst.htm

Scholtz, J., Laskowski, S., & Downey, L. (1998). Developing Usability Tools and Techniques for Designing and Testing Web Sites. In *Proceedings of the 4th Conference on Human Factors & the Web*. AT&T.

Skov, M. B., & Stage, J. (2001). A Simple Approach to Web-Site Usability Testing. In *Proceedings of 1st International Conference on Universal Access in Human-Computer Interaction* (pp. 737-741). Mahwah, NJ: Lawrence-Erlbaum.

Skov, M. B., & Stage, J. (2004) Integrating Usability Design and Evaluation: Training Novice Evaluators in Usability Testing. In K. Hornbæk & J. Stage (Eds.), *Proceedings of the Workshop on Improving the Interplay between Usability Evaluation and User Interface Design, NordiCHI 2004* (pp. 31-35), Aalborg University, Department of Computer Science, HCI-Lab Report no. 2004/2.

Skov, M. B., & Stage, J. (2005) Supporting Problem Identification in Usability Evaluations. In *Proceedings of the Australian Computer-Human Interaction Conference 2005 (OzCHI'05)*. New York: ACM Press.

Slavkovic, A., & Cross, K. (1999). Novice heuristic evaluations of a complex interface. In *Proceedings of CHI 1999* (pp. 304-305). New York: ACM Press.

Spool, J. M., Scanlon, T., Schroeder, W., Snyder, C., & DeAngelo, T. (1999). *Web Site Usability – A Designer's Guide*. San Francisco: Morgan Kaufmann Publishers.

Sullivan, T., & Matson, R. (2000, November 16-17). Barriers to Use: Usability and Content Accessibility on the Web's Most Popular Sites. In *Proceedings of Conference on Universal Usability* (pp. 139-144). New York: ACM.

Sutcliffe, A. (2001). Heuristic Evaluation of Website Attractiveness and Usability. *Interactive Systems: Design, Specification, and Verification* (LNCS 2220, pp. 183-198).

Verdaasdonk, E. G. G., Stassen, L. P. S., Widhiasmara, P. P., & Dankelman, J. (2008). Requirements for the design and implementation of checklists for surgical processes. *Surgical Endoscopy*.

Chapter 17
A Framework for Early Usability Integration in Web Applications Development Process

Daniela M. Andrei
Babes-Bolyai University, Romania

Adriana M. Guran
Babes-Bolyai University, Romania

ABSTRACT

Developing usable products becomes more and more important for software developers. Developing web applications it's more challenging than developing desktop applications due to the various users that will interact with the final product. Satisfying users' expectations becomes a very difficult task, as usability proves to be a very complex goal to achieve in the context of increased productivity targets in software engineering process. The present chapter focuses on the idea of rethinking the concept of usability moving from the traditional view of usability expressed in the internal characteristics of the product towards usability understood as deriving from the quality of interactions between humans, their work and the web design product. Usability is not only an add-on or a final result in the design process but it is embedded as a main concern within the design process itself. In order to build usable products, a great attention should be oriented to users and their needs, and this can be a very challenging task for software developer teams. In this chapter we will describe an interdisciplinary approach, based on applying social sciences techniques and methods that can be helpful in overcoming the difficulties in understanding the users. We will provide a short description of the proposed methods, a guide in applying these methods and a framework that integrates each of the proposed methods into the corresponding step of the web product development life cycle. The chapter ends with the presentation of two case studies showing the applicability of the proposed solution in real design contexts.

DOI: 10.4018/978-1-60960-523-0.ch017

INTRODUCTION

Usability, user interface, and interaction design are among the group of essential, but unfortunately overlooked, skills that all software developers require, yet few seem to have. Surveys show that over 50% of the design and programming effort on projects is devoted to the user interface (Myers & Rosson 1992). Tools developed by the HCI community can dramatically decrease costs and increase productivity. Studies have shown that applying usability engineering in software projects generates savings attributed to decreased task time, fewer errors, greatly reduced user disruption, reduced burden on support staff, elimination of training, and avoidance of changes in software after release. By estimating all the costs associated with usability engineering, another study found that the benefits can be up to 5000 times the cost (Nielsen & Landauer, 1993).

Usability has become a topic of great interest to researchers in the field of human computer interaction and interaction design due to an increasingly strong connection between usability and the overall success of a given product, be it an object, software or a website (Kuniavsky, 2003; Nielsen, 1993; Norman, 2002). Although researchers agree that usability does not, in itself guarantee the success of such a product (Kuniavsky, 2003; Norman, 2002), they also underline the fact that the lack of usability and a low quality user experience may contribute substantially to the failure of a product or design (Kuniavsky, 2003; Norman, 2002). Together with a substantially grown interest in usability, even though the subject did not represent the focus of design process in its starting years (Norman, 2002; Jordan, 2002) a certain trend in the conceptualization of usability can be observed as the traditionally accepted view of usability is moving towards an integrated perspective in which usability is not just an end goal or attribute of the final product but is also represented by the quality of user experience it enables. Moreover, the maturation of this concept is seen in terms of quality in software, quality in interaction and quality in value (Law, Hvannberg, & Cockton, 2008), a perspective which clearly passes over the traditional view of usability as a validating measure for the design product (Dumas & Redish, 1999).

Taking into account this shift in conceptualization, our approach is organized around the idea of rethinking the concept of usability and building a usability framework that naturally integrates usability artifacts into the software development process. This means moving from the traditional view of usability expressed in the internal characteristics of the product towards usability understood as deriving from the quality of interactions between humans, their work and the web design product (van Welie, 2001) or, in other words, from the better understanding of the user experience (Kuniavsky, 2003). More and more researchers argue that a user-centered approach or interactive design is the kind of approach that can support this conceptualization of usability (Benyon, Turner & Turner, 2005; Kuniavsky, 2003; van Welie, 2001; Brink, Gergle & Wood, 2002). As a result, usability becomes a permanent concern for researchers and designers. Moreover, designing for usability starts precisely from the first stage of web design: user needs analysis.

Still, there is a lack of theoretical foundations to guide software developers in practicing usability engineering. The process of software development becomes more and more related to the clients (users), such that a singular approach, coming from software developers teams is not sufficient in the complex task of understanding what the users really need. As the interaction design literature shows, there is a need of a multidisciplinary approach. In this paper we propose a solution (framework) of integrating the techniques provided by social sciences into the software development life cycle in order to continuously involve users into the design process and, by this way, to achieve usability.

Although there are some proposals of frameworks having the goal of assuring the usability of the designed products, most of the approaches are oriented towards specific categories of software products (King, 2004; Koua, MacEachren, & Kraak, 2006; Chang & Bourguet, 2008; Sarnikar & Murphy, 2009). What can be also observed is the fact that most of these approaches focus on usability evaluation, rather than usability engineering. In King, Ma, Zaphiris, Petrie, & Hamilton, (2004) some of the qualitative and quantitative methods are mentioned, but they are used only for usability evaluation, in the final stage of product development. There are no generally accepted recommendations regarding the way these tools can be used in usability assessment, most of the times being considered auxiliary tools to user testing. In their paper, Koua et al. (2006) present a usability framework for geovisualization environments. The framework is reduced to a usability testing that focuses only on the effectiveness of design, neglecting the other fundamental dimensions of usability, like satisfaction or efficiency. The techniques mentioned in the paper refer to usability inspection and cognitive walkthroughs, thus addressing only the evaluation aspect of usability. Sarnikar & Murphy (2009) propose a usability framework having the goal of identifying, classifying and prioritizing errors in the context of healthcare information technologies. These approaches, based on usability testing, can be rather integrated in the maintenance phase of the software development life cycle, and less into the design or development phase. As Cato (2001) argues, these types of approaches focus on correcting all the things that should have been right in the first place, wasting resources.

Another common characteristic of these frameworks is the fact that they most frequently rely on usability questionnaires and tests in order to assess and ensure usability. Such a trend has been also underlined by recent literature reviews (van Velsen, van der Geest, Klaassen, & Steehouder, 2008). Even more recently proposed frameworks approach usability rather as an attribute of the final product, not a feature that must be carefully considered even from the early steps in the design process.

Our goal is to provide a general framework that involves usability related activities starting from the first insights in the problem domain and ending with the final product delivery. The difference between our approach and the existing ones is that we are focusing on ensuring usability during the entire life cycle of the product, and not solely on usability evaluation. Moreover, we provide operational methods for software development teams to communicate with their users and really get to know their needs, and the suggested approach can be used during both design and evaluation phases of web design.

To summarize, the main advantages of the framework we are proposing is the fact that it takes usability into consideration starting from the very first steps of the design life cycle. Moreover, it is based upon a multidisciplinary approach of design and provides operational methods in usability engineering. Last but not least, it can serve as a structured and general methodology both for designing and evaluating web interaction.

The paper is structured as follows: in the first section we will provide a short background on the trends and movements in research and software design methods and the way usability is/should be incorporated. Aligned to these research trends, this paper argues that instead of usability testing, which has been the focus of the majority of the publications in this field, researchers and designers should be primarily interested in usability building even from the beginning of the process by assuring the fact that their design will address the real and important needs and problems of future users. This goal cannot be achieved without a deep and accurate understanding of people, their world and their activities, their needs, problems or aspirations. This may appear very daunting to a software designer who has no training in research involving people, but can be very natural to a social scientist who has been trained in using all social research methods. We will argue that both in the traditional perspective on usability but even more now, social research techniques are becoming essential in ensuring a good design (and therefore usable products) and that all known techniques can be used as tools to help us in attaining this goal (Dumas & Redish, 1999). As a result, in this paper we are going to shortly present the social research tools (or methods) that can be used during the first step of user-centered design in order to provide a deep and thorough understanding of the users, their needs, desires or problems, an understanding that will constitute the basis for usability building throughout the design process (Brink, Gergle & Wood, 2002). Some of the most popular methods are presented together with their relevance and applicability into this field. The fundamental ideas related to usability engineering regarded from the two perspectives, user experience specialists and software developers, are merged in the proposed framework that has the goal of providing a systematic and interdisciplinary approach in building usable products. The final part of this paper will be dedicated to the illustration of the way in which these methods have been used in our research and the benefits they generated for the further stages of the design process.

BACKGROUND

The history of usability research in the field of interactive systems design is rich and very interesting ranging from a point when it was barely acknowledged as relevant (Kuniavsky, 2003; Norman, 2002) to a stage when usability became a business in itself (Rubin, 1994) and finally to the present day when even the term usability seems unable to encompass the developments regarding this concept and new concepts like user experience are taking over (Law et al., 2008). The transformations in the concerns for usability followed an ascending pattern but there are still

authors arguing that we are not in the right place with the implementation of usability principles (Kuniavsky, 2003) or that there are very deep differences in usability practices between different organizations, some still at the beginnings of usability evaluation while other are influencing the development in this field (Rosenbaum, 2008).

The development of usability research in the field of web design started, just as in any other design fields, from a complete unawareness of its importance (Kuniavsky, 2003). Kuniavsky (2003) underlines the fact that in the beginnings, web designers were more concerned with being the first ones on a certain market and with marketing and branding issues. The user was not important as there was no budget for such research. Things changed dramatically as technology developed and interactive systems (websites included) started being available to more people. The same reason for ignoring the user up to that point, the financial profit, became the reason for an increased attention being given to usability aspects as usability started being seen as a competitive advantage (Baven, 2008; Kuniavsky, 2003). This increased attention led to the structuring of the research in this field. A structured body of research on the topic of usability was becoming visible. The characteristic of this development is the fact that usability research was still somehow technology-oriented. As a result, the traditional view of usability that became most popular among developers refers to the attributes of the interface that ease the use of product for its users (Bevan, 2008). This traditional view on usability can be seen by analyzing some of the most well-known definitions of usability which all refer to internal characteristics of technology. For example, Nielsen (1993) defines usability in terms of system attributes: learnability, efficiency, memorability, errors and satisfaction. Dix et al. (2004) describe usability in terms of learnability, flexibility and robustness which are primarily identified in the product and the features that enhance these properties. A short critical overview of these definitions can indicate that even during this prolific period in usability research most of the focus was on technology and not on people, or on users. Also, most of these conceptualizations reflect the efforts to develop standardized tools for measuring usability, and indeed, they are most suited for this purpose (Nielsen, 1993). The problem with this perspective on usability is neither the internal consistency of its elements nor the fact that it is not correctly defined, but the fact that the success of any product does not rely solely on usability and usability is not just an end product of the design process. Constraints coming from users are representing only one source of constraints for the success of a product and especially web design product usability is seen more as the balancing of different and often conflicting constraints (Kuniavsky, 2003; Norman, 2002).

The view on usability started to change when another popular usability definition was proposed. Usability was thought to represent the measure in which specified users can use a product to achieve certain goals with effectiveness, efficiency and satisfaction (ISO, 1998). The change of focus is clear as the new definition doesn't rely anymore on the characteristics of the product but on the results of using the product. The characteristics the definition underlines (efficiency, effectiveness and satisfaction) refer as much to the product as to all the other elements of the system: users, their task and the environment in which they are performing their task (Bevan, 2008). This view on usability is more suitable to the present research and practice as it can more easily address business goals: efficiency, effectiveness and satisfaction are directly related to profitability (Bevan, 2005). With this definition, usability started to be seen from the inside-out and focus changed from technology characteristics to the ability of meeting the users' goals and needs (Bevan 2008). On the other hand, we must point out that a similar argument can be found in other classical work in the field. For example, Norman (2002) argues that usability is the result of balancing the needs of all stakeholders in the product development so the new focus is not

entirely new but a returning to the essence of the concept. This returning is supported by the main challenges that the human computer interaction community is continually acknowledging. This community is focusing more and more not only on the way users are best supported by technology to meet their needs and goals, but also on the way users play a role in shaping the development of future designs. Other concerns are represented by the way user requirements are embodied in design products and also the support and measurement of the quality in use when nonfunctional attributes are also taken into account (Law, Hvannberg & Cockton, 2008) The present understanding of usability has reinforced the interest in the quality of interactions between humans, their work and the web design product (van Welie, 2001) or, in other words, in a better understanding of the user experience (Kuniavsky, 2003).

This trend is even more visible when we take into consideration web-design because in this context customers have a greater power. If the traditional view set the usability experience after buying the product, on the web this situation is reversed: users can experience usability right from the beginning, before committing to any website and certainly before buying something (Nielsen, 2000). That is why a better understanding of user experience and usability has become central to the field of web design.

The Evolution of Usability Reflected in the Evolution of Design Models

These movements in the way researchers and designers think about usability have a correspondence in the way the design process has been remodeled over the years. The traditional way of thinking about usability is compatible to the traditional waterfall-model or corporation edict type of design process in which usability is taken into consideration only at the end of the design process when the product is already finished and launched on the market. The problem with this kind of design process is the fact that it does not afford for the early identification of possible design problems and, as a result, the balancing of different needs and constraints that creates a good user experience is very difficult.

The alternative that developed to overcome the shortcomings of this design process was the iterative design. The underlying assumption of iterative development was the fact that it is practically impossible to create perfect solutions from the beginning, so we need several design cycle in which to alternate activities such as problem description, creating solutions and evaluating those solutions against problems described previously. This design method was more suitable for addressing the new perspective on usability as it is flexible and adaptable enough to incorporate different types of constraints that determine usability. The only weak point of it was the fact that, in its initial form, the iterative design process did not make the involvement of users necessary in the design process (Kuniavsky, 2003). Indeed, we can develop an iterative design process without talking to any end user at any stage if we assume that we already know everything there is to know about the user and the product. Starting from the middle of the '80s many researchers have argued that it is not sufficient to provide users with a formal role within a technically dominated design process and Hirscheim (1985) considers that successful system design is primarily an exercise in organizational change and, as such, user-dominated socio-technical design methods should be employed.

As seductive as this assumption appears to be, the present orientation in design is based exactly on the observation that designers are not users, do not resemble the final user and cannot fully understand the user's needs and problems (Benyon et al., 2005; Kuniavsky, 2003; Norman, 2002). This is the argument that makes it necessary that end users be involved in the design process even from the very early stages and most of the literature argues the importance of user-centered

design (Jokela, 2008, Brink et al., 2002; Rubin, 1994; van Welie, 2001). User-centered design principles include early and continuous contact with users, quantitative usability criteria and evaluations, and iterative design (Keinonen, 2008). The main characteristic of this design process is the fact that users become partners in the design and are involved at every design stage. Most of all, the user-centered design contributes to the shift in user interest from the end of the design process to the beginnings. If the traditional design processes started with the specification of requirements for the new product, user-centered design places the needs analysis as the first phase in the design process and further retains the adaptability and flexibility of iterative design (Jokela, 2008; Benyon et al, 2005; Brink et al, 2002; Rubin, 1994). Moreover, researchers now agree that usability engineering has become more and more iterative, involving users throughout the design process (Dumas & Redish, 1999) and that usability should be followed throughout the entire design process (Brink et al., 2002).

Despite what the researchers have found, the technically dominated approach is still preferred in software design and development, although new design methods have been developed. Nowadays, Agile development is becoming increasingly mainstream, but the fit between user experience and the Agile development process is problematic, even though the philosophies of User Experience designers and Agile software designers both emphasize iterative refinement and learning from users (Ambler, 20007). Agile development does not address usability and it is not yet clear how usability can be integrated into the process without sacrificing the advantages of agile development (Constantine, 2001). This gap occurs because there is a lack of understanding of usability engineering among software developers that still ignore the users' needs. Although usability is considered as a major quality of software products, the Agile software development community and the user experience community encounter difficulties in integrating both approaches into the development life cycle. As some authors argue, there is a need of improved interaction design skills within the programming community (Cooper, 2004; Ambler, 2007). Proposals regarding the incorporation of usability activities during Agile development are still reduced to usability testing and acceptance testing (Ambler, 2007), but as Jokela and Abrahamsson (2004) state, an essential step is for agile software development practitioners to accept that good usability of an end product can be ensured only by systematic usability engineering activities during the development iterations.

Most researchers stress the need for a user-centered approach to design but very few of them offer operational design models that could inform practice. Even the ISO 13407 standards regarding user-centered design seem to offer only general principles that are not bound to specific phases in the development cycle (Jokela, 2008). Regarding the development cycle, a review of existing models shows us that, with some differences in terminology and organization, all existing models of user centered design include a requirement analysis stage (or user analysis), conceptual design, prototype design and evaluation (mockups, prototypes, simulations), implementation and evaluation at every of these stages (Jokela, 2008; Brink et al, 2002; van der Veer, 1999; van Welie, 2001, Rubin, 1994). In a more simplified form, the core of these models is represented by a reiterative cycle of understanding the context of use, uncovering the user needs, developing design solutions and evaluating them against context and user requirements (Jokela, 2008, Benyon et al, 2005).

Although most of these authors agree that the main characteristics of user centered design are the importance given to an early involvement of users into the design process and the importance given to the first stages of the design model, they rarely include specifications for how to conduct the first stage of user need analysis within the model itself. We conducted a review of existing models of user centered design focusing mostly on the first stage of user needs analysis. The synthesis of these models (Jokela, 2008; Benyon et al, 2005; Pitariu, 2003; Brink et al, 2002) allowed us to articulate our own approach towards user need analysis which we have used in our research projects. The approach is presented in Figure 1 and it represents a systematization of existing models and guidelines on user-needs analysis in user centered design.

Qualitative vs. Quantitative Methods

These changes in the design process also generated modifications in the way usability was measured and the aspects that were measured. If the traditional usability concept generated well standardized measurement tools focused on the internal dimensions of the construct itself, user-centered design in its early focus on user needs and tasks created a need to develop and use less standardized methods that enable us to have a better understanding of people, their activities, the context in which these activities take place, and their needs and values that could affect the design at every stage. A move from validating products toward understanding user experience and behavior can be identified in the research literature.

We can observe that the paradigm change in design is accompanied by a pressure of paradigm change in evaluation methodology. Signs of this paradigm change are highlighted in present literature, many researchers indicating a growing importance given to qualitative methods and to contextual, field research (Rosenbaum, 2008). A closer analysis of the scientific paradigms which fundament quantitative and qualitative methodology will support a better understanding of this growing emphasis on the qualitative.

Usually, quantitative methodology is associated with a positivist paradigm, which is the dominant paradigm in science. This paradigm is based on the ontological position that there is a single, absolute, true, objective and independent reality

Figure 1. Our approach to user-needs analysis based on existing models

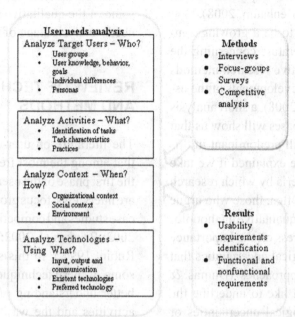

which can be known using objective analysis and the tools of logical reasoning (Hatch & Yanow, 2008). The focus is on exact measures that could offer the researcher true and unbiased description of the reality. As a result, the preferred methodology is the quantitative one.

Qualitative methodology is associated to an interpretive or constructivist paradigm which assumes that reality does not exist independently outside of the human being. Reality is permanently constructed out of internal and external resources and the focus changes from true description of reality to different interpretations and meanings that constitute reality (Hatch & Cunliffe, 2006). As a result, researchers should not focus on discovering true facts of reality, but on understanding people, the way they interpret experience and the processes of meaning-making that contribute to reality building. The knowledge resulted in this paradigm will never constitute universal, abstract theories, but will allow for a deeper understanding of a given phenomenon in a given context and for explanations of specific situations. As a result, this knowledge should be judged in terms of its

trustworthiness, credibility, transferability and confirmability (Denzin & Lincoln, 2005). As we can see, these evaluation criteria for qualitative research are concerned more with the applicability and credibility of results and less with internal and external validity.

A short analysis of the arguments given in the previous part of this paper shows us that such a paradigm shift from positivism to constructivism can be mirrored in the historical evolution of the usability research literature and practice. The beginnings of this field were marked by positivist and quantitative approaches in an effort to justify the concept (usability) and to contribute to a mature science. But the later growing emphasis on user involvement in the design process and formative usability evaluation changed the focus toward a deeper understanding of users and their needs. More and more researchers and practitioners consider that the value of usability evaluation is in diagnosing problems and not in validating products (Dumas & Redish, 1999). This emphasis marks the shift towards an interpretive/constructivist paradigm in human computer interaction which is also illustrated by a greater importance given to qualitative methods (Rosenbaum, 2008).

Although there seems to be a growing consensus in the research literature concerning the appropriateness of qualitative research methods in the present and future developments of the usability field (Rosenbaum, 2008), a short analysis of some well-known databases will show us that quantitative studies are still predominant in this field. This situation can be explained if we take into consideration the criteria by which research is judged and evaluated. Often, those who argue on the importance of using qualitative methodologies are also those who stress on the importance of solving the methodological uncertainties that accompany qualitative approaches (Dumas & Redish, 1999). We would like to underline the fact that these methodological uncertainties or flaws are identified only when we are judging qualitative approaches by the same criteria we use to evaluate quantitative research. Given the different paradigm, qualitative research is based on different ontological and epistemic assumptions and therefore it has specific criteria against which it should be evaluated (Denzin & Lincoln, 2005). If we take these criteria into consideration, there should be no uncertainties related to the use of qualitative data in usability research and especially in user need analysis.

The characteristics of qualitative research make it very useful at this stage of user needs analysis and the literature shows indeed that qualitative methods are most indicated here as we are trying to better understand people and their experiences. The main characteristics are the descriptive nature of these methods, their interdisciplinary character and lack of formalizations which make it very accessible to researchers in different domains (Van Maanen, 1998). All these characteristics make qualitative research very suitable in this first stage of user-centered design when the focus is on a deep understanding of people.

In the following section we will briefly describe some of the qualitative methods used in the user needs analysis stage of user-centered design.

REVIEW OF TECHNIQUES AND METHODS

The literature on user-centered research shows that among the most frequently used methods in the first phase of the user-centered design process are interviews, focus groups, user diaries, surveys, case studies and competitive analysis (Kuniavsky, 2003; Brink et al, 2002; Dumas & Redish, 1999; Rubin, 1994,). In this section we will focus on some of these techniques that, by allowing for a better understanding of people, their goals and activities and the way they relate to them, can support a design for usability even from the start of the design process. The selection we have made does not illustrate all the social qualitative research techniques that could possibly inform the user needs analysis but are among the most popular techniques in user research and qualitative psychological research. Also, we will be able to draw some insights into the way we used them in two of our projects.

The user needs analysis is focused on acquiring a deep and accurate understanding of the people who will be involved in using the final web design product, the activities that the design will support, the context in which these activities will be performed as well as all the complex interactions between these elements. This deep understanding is crucial for the next stage of requirements development for the product which will be designed (Benyon et al., 2005). Moreover, we cannot consider this phase to be over when the design process begins and the first steps in design work are done. The user need analysis, requirements development, design process and evaluation are very tightly interrelated and constitute a permanent iterative process (Jokela, 2008; Benyon et al., 2005, Brink et al, 2002; Kuniavsky, 2003).

In conclusion, user needs analysis aims at getting to know the people, what they want, what they do, what problems they frequently encounter in their area of activity and how they might want to do things in order to help designers create a more usable and enjoyable product. The translation of these findings into requirements for a new design is not so straightforward and will often have to go back into the user research process to be validated.

As we have described earlier, the user research in the early stages of the design process can seem a very complex and difficult job (even more so for a designer not trained in this kind of research). The most common techniques imply observing people, interviewing them, organizing focus groups, in short, a qualitative, in depth approach to people involved and their needs, aspirations, experiences and problems. At the beginning, before any idea of the product is put forward, the user research has to stay less structured and qualitative in essence. At more advanced stages other more structured techniques such as the structured interview or surveys can be used.

Interviews

Interviews are one of the most used research methods in social sciences and one of the best suited to gain a thorough understanding of peoples' wants and needs. Interviews can also provide a very flexible structure that can allow us to address multiple categories of stakeholders involved in the design process.

There are several types of interviews ranging from very structured interviews to unstructured ones. The structured interview closely resembles a survey as the researcher develops a fixed number of questions prior to the research. Those questions will be addressed in exactly the same way to every participant. Moreover, most of the time there are preset answers from which people have to choose. This type of interview can be very useful when the researcher needs to verify things but will become inappropriate when the focus is

the in-depth understanding of people's needs and wishes as the high level of structure will not allow for unexpected responses and insights to arise.

Another type of interview is the unstructured interview which is, as its name suggests, completely dependent on what happens and develops during the interview itself. The researcher will not structure anything before the interview and will have no preset topic agenda besides the general topic of the project which is the focus of research. This type of interview can be very useful in projects which are less specified, for which there is very little information or when there is a great concern for putting aside the designer's preset solutions or preconceptions about the project.

Most of the time in user needs analysis and user research we will use semi-structured interviews. This type of interview is somewhere in-between the other two types being a degree more structured than the unstructured interview but still allowing for a great deal of unexpected, new information or insights to arise. The researcher will prepare in advance some questions or topics he/she will want to discuss during the interview, but the way in which these are brought into discussion is very flexible. Also, if new, unaccounted aspects arise during the interview, these can be further analyzed and included among the topics of interest. This form of open interview can be demanding for the researcher but it can produce a lot of valuable data to inform the design. More on how to prepare and conduct interviews can be found in King (2004).

When to use Interviews

Most of qualitative research methods are in a way or another based on some form of interview, that is why interviews are so present in mostly all the stages of web design process. They are suited to address the first stage of user needs analysis and at this stage we will most probably use less structured or even unstructured interviews in order to uncover underlying experiences, beliefs and values. Interviewing is also present in later stages of development when it is more probable to use more structured interviews as we are trying to find out specific information and reactions to the design we have proposed. Besides the enormous advantages provided by this methods, we must also be careful to the problems that can arise during interviews and that can affect the results. We will have to remember that people do not always tell what they really believe but maybe the interpretation of this phenomenon could become relevant for our research project. Moreover, they can sometimes answer a completely different question than the one addressed. The researcher must very careful observe and assess these things in order to overcome this type of situation. As a result the data obtained using an interview is strongly dependent on the interviewer skills and mastery of the technique which is gained through exercising.

Focus Groups

Focus groups are related to interviews in the sense that they are more or less structured group interviews. Focus groups are a form of qualitative research based on creating a group interactive setting where people can be asked about their attitudes and feelings towards an idea, a product or a service. Also people are allowed to talk with each other, to question or develop each others' statements. The reason why focus groups can represent a valuable tool in this design phase is the fact that they are appropriate methods to gain access to people's needs, experiences, wishes and priorities. Although focus groups are most often associated with marketing research, they have been adapted to include social science research (Marshall & Rossman, 2006). As a social science research tool they are often very suitable for the study of people in their natural setting even more if they are used together with participant observation in order to elicit unexpected thoughts and issues for further exploration (Morgan, Krueger & King, 1998). As a result, the relevance of focus

groups for the field of user research comes from both lines of research: focus on the product or service (marketing) or focus on understanding people, their attitudes and needs (social research). Due to its wide applicability in several stages of design, focus groups are one of the oldest methods of user research (Kuniavsky, 2003).

Literature on qualitative methods shows that focus groups have a high apparent validity (the result are trusted, believable, as it is very easy to see how people came to those results) and that they are also a very easy to learn and inexpensive method (Marshall & Rossman, 2006). There are also some shortcomings associated with this method and the first one relates to the power dynamics in group interaction that can affect the results obtained. The researcher will have to pay a great deal of attention to these aspects and be prepared to facilitate the interaction very well. Also, the researcher usually has less control over the interviewees during this kind of approach and unwanted discussions can take a part of the interviewing time. The groups can vary a great deal or can be more difficult to be assembled. At last, the method requires us to set up special rooms with highly trained observers or recording solutions in order to make the most of the data (Marshall & Rossman, 2006).

A focus group consists in a series of group discussions which are moderated by the researcher or collaborator according to a preset agenda. The focus of the entire interaction between the moderator and the group is to facilitate a group climate that will support opinion and feeling sharing among the participants. This method is appropriate both for a stage in which there is yet no idea regarding the final product and the main concern is the understanding of people's needs, problems, priorities and way of thinking and also for the stage in which some requirements are already translated into features and we need people to assess this translation or to prioritize these features.

When to use Focus Groups

As we have already underlined, focus groups can be used at various stages in usability building and usability assessment. Their use can be seen at the very beginning of the design process where, together with contextual inquiry and task analysis can build a very detailed picture of how people are behaving right now and of their perceptions regarding important issues. At this stage, focus groups can be used as a method for analyzing the competition also. This use of the method can bring information related to the problems that our product is designed to solve, the reasons why it can be a more valuable resource than other similar products and the features that consumers perceive to be critical in the competition. All this information will enable us to set up requirements and features for our product that will be closer to what people want and value, and save a lot of resources from the beginning.

Focus groups can be also used at a later moment in the development cycle in order to identify and prioritize features or even in order to create or develop new features (Kuniavsky, 2003). They can also be used in the redesign process in order to improve present designs.

We also have to point out some instances in which this method is not suitable. We will not use focus groups as a usability assessment technique to generalize all the findings to a larger population or to justify a position or to prove a point (Kuniavsky, 2003).

Surveys

Even though very often surveys are considered to be mostly quantitative research, opposite to the qualitative research methods presented so far, we have to keep in mind that surveys are nothing more than very structured interviews: a very structured way of asking questions that enables us to address a large group of people and record their answers. The fact that the questions are always the same for everybody and that even responses can be given in a very structured format (multiple choice questions, checklists, Likert scales) allows the researcher to use statistical tools to examine the characteristics of the targeted population. On the other hand, the survey being rooted in qualitative research can still contain open ended questions where people are allowed to tell you what they want to communicate in the form they choose and these questions represent often valuable and rich information. The problem with open questions is that most often people have a very low response rate to them (Nielsen, 1993)

The types of information that can be obtained using surveys cover the characteristics of users groups and eventually, the identification of several user subgroups. We can also use surveys to find out which of the features of the product are more appealing or more important for the targeted users, the information and features that people look for in our product, problems that people have encountered while using our site or similar websites, the level of user satisfaction, suggestions for improvement and so on.

As we can see, most of this information relates to a stage where we have already designed a product and we want to test it or when we want to redesign our products. But surveys can be also used in the first stages of user needs analysis when the focus is on ensuring and building usability not on assessing it. At this stage surveys can be very useful to test and prioritize findings from earlier qualitative, in depth research. For example, insights and ideas obtained using a focus group can be tested to check if the value, needs and characteristics of the users identified using the focus-group results can also be met within a larger population. The survey results will enable us to see which of the developed requirements are the most important for the general population and should become priorities in the development process and which of the requirements developed so far are less relevant for further stages in design. The survey at this stage will also be very useful in helping us identify different groups of users for which the needs and preferences hierarchy is different and need to be addressed differently in the design process.

As we can seen surveys can be used at any design stage, ranging from the very first stage of user needs analysis, through the stage of the current design evaluation in order to begin a new design cycle and up to the last stage when, after releasing the product, we can use surveys to check if our design meets the user's needs and to identify possible improvements for the future.

When to Use Surveys

As we have already underlined, surveys are used when we want to test the preferences and needs of a broader population about a product or a potential product. As it involves a greater effort in planning and design and as it requires a higher level of standardization (Kuniavsky, 2003) it is recommended to be used in design stages when in-depth information is not needed so much. As a result, we will use surveys when passing from the user needs analysis towards requirement specification in order to structure and prioritize the findings from interviews, observations and other less structured methods. Also, surveys can be very effectively used in testing preliminary ideas and designs as well as assessing the characteristics of the final product.

A FRAMEWORK FOR INTEGRATING SOCIAL SCIENCES TOOLS IN USER CENTERED DESIGN

In the previous section we have made a concise presentation of the methods from the social sciences that can be effectively used in user-centered design process. Although we have previously mentioned that one of the principles of user-centered design is quantitative usability measurement and evaluation, we suggest an improved approach by

adjusting it with the advantages of qualitative methods. In the following, we will provide a synthesis of the usage of each of the methods and the motivation for using it during the design of a web product (see Table 1). We have to underline the fact that the proposed approach addresses the usability from the very first steps in the design process, it is not restricted to the evaluation step in the design life cycle, carefully monitoring usability artifacts during each step, and provides an operational design model for those interested in practicing usability engineering, and not just/ alongside usability evaluation (see Figure 2).

As it can be observed, these methods can be used during each step of the design process, but the most complex step, when the benefits of using these methods are maximized, is the user needs analysis step, when one can take advantage of using exploratory methods in order to gather as much information as possible about the prospective users, and after that, the information can be validated, or the findings can be prioritized using more structured methods as surveys or focus-groups.

CASE STUDIES: USER NEEDS ANALYSIS FROM OUR OWN RESEARCH PROJECTS

The Development of a Website Pattern

The results of this project have been presented in Onaca, Tarta, & Pitariu (2006), so here we will not emphasize them or the pattern proposed but the methodology we used to formulate this pattern. The illustration of this methodology is rather outside the main line of argument used here as we have focused mainly on user need identification for building a usable website within a user-centered design approach. The investigation we will present here was focused on proposing a design pattern for theatre and opera websites but the approach

Table 1. An overview of the framework

Design step/method	Motivation
User needs analysis	
Observation	To get information about people's observable actions and the work environment
Unstructured interviews	To explore underlying experiences, beliefs and values
Focus-groups	To elicit unexpected thoughts and issues for further exploration
Surveys	To identify groups of users, to prioritize findings from the qualitative methods
Requirements	
Focus-group	To gain access to people priorities and wishes
Surveys	To find out which of the features are more important
Conceptual design	
Interviews	To derive design ideas or to test design ideas
Focus groups	To assess the translation of requirements in features and to prioritize the identified features
Prototyping	
Structured interviews	To find specific information/reactions to the proposed design
Focus-groups	To identify new features
Surveys	To identify which product features are more appealing
Evaluation	
Structured interviews	To evaluate the effectiveness of the system, intention to use and perceived usefulness
Surveys	To find the problems user encountered using the product, to assess user satisfaction

was still user-centered and the final focus was on advancing a design solution that would enhance the usability and acceptability of such websites. Therefore, we consider that this project constitutes an illustrative example of user needs analysis in the service of usability.

Van Welie & Traetteberg (2000) argue that the main concern in developing patterns should be on improving usability as many of the problems designers have during the design process and that are addressed in user interface design have no connection and produce no benefit for the end user. Researchers in UID underline the fact that developing a pattern in this field is not an easy task and the structure of such a pattern is different from an architectural pattern. One of the most important features of an UID pattern is that it is best suited to describe usability related problems (van Welie, Van der Veer & Eliens, 2000) so the

development of a pattern should benefit from an increased attention paid to users and their needs.

User Needs Analysis

The research undertaken at this stage represented an exploratory study that aimed at identifying the categories of users, what are their usual actions related to a theatre/opera house, in what context do they perform those actions, what type of information they are using to perform those actions and what are the technologies they currently use or would like to use in the future.

The initial method we have used consisted in a semi-structured interview in which we have tried to cover all the above related aspects. We have started the interview without any references to theatre/opera houses websites and asked people to refer to their experiences going to the theatre/

Figure 2. A diagrammatic representation of the framework

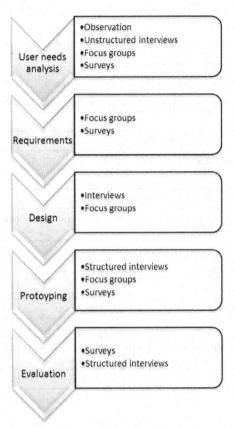

(artists, critics, people who collaborate with the theatre/opera). We have also discovered a wide range of activities related to the theatre, starting from the usual activity of play/show attendance to other activities such as discussing and debating different performances, planning events (including photo shoots, galas, weddings) into the theatre building and also looking for job opportunities. The existent technologies used for accomplishing these activities have constituted a good indicator regarding possible opportunities and constraints to every theatre/opera house website.

In a second phase, we have directed our interview analysis towards prioritizing the needs of users in terms of actions and information which should be provided. A better way to do achieve this was considered to be the development of an exploratory survey based on the qualitative data obtained in interviews.

The dimensions we identified analyzing the interviews were mapped into the main features of some well-known theatre/opera websites and the main dimensions of the questionnaire were established:

1. Access/information about theatre's services
2. Communication, interaction, opinions exchange
3. Tourist information
4. Information about theatre's staff
5. Information about historical evolution of the theatre
6. Information about theatre's management
7. Information about present and future projects

For each of these dimensions a group of five experts generated items based on the initial qualitative data. Those items entered then in a procedure of redistribution on each dimension and only those items that met at least 70 percent in rating agreement were kept. In the end, a number of 43 items have been included in the questionnaire. Each item was rated on a 5 steps Likert scale ranging from completely useless to very useful information.

opera, their interests and needs in different aspects of the cultural life, the way they decide on what play/show to attend, difficulties that they have encountered in attending a play/show, details regarding the context of these activities. When the use of a website was mentioned, we used more in-depth questions related to their experience using different websites. The results of the interviews showed us that there were some aspects worth being taken into consideration as the social-nature of the attendance planning and also of the social-nature of experiencing the artistic act.

The analysis of the interviews focused on identifying specific user categories with specific goals and interests and here we have been able to take into consideration some categories which have been purely included in previous designs

The questionnaire, designed in English, was administered to a non-random sample using an interactive web application. The sample included 112 volunteer participants. Their average age was 27.54 and 49.1% were men and 50.9% were women. Participants came from various countries: 67% Romania, 12% Netherlands, 8% Spain, 1.8% Switzerland, 1.8% Poland, 3.6% USA, 0.9% France, 0.9% Leetonia, 0.9% Indonesia, 0.9% Germany, 0.9% Austria, 0.9% Republic of Moldavia). Also, regarding their occupations, the distribution of the sample was: 0.9% pilot, 0.9% account manager, 2.7% actor/actress, 0.9% sales representatives, 30.4% students, 4.5% high school teachers, 13.4% university teachers, 31.3% IT, 0.9% retired, 10.7% psychologists, 1.8% MD doctors, 1.8% administration personnel.

Participants filled in the questionnaire voluntarily. The instructions that preceded the questionnaire were the following:

This questionnaire is designed to assess the most relevant types of information and actions that a theatre/opera website should provide. Please read carefully the statements and choose the answer that fits you best. There is no right or wrong answer and data collected through this survey are confidential and will be used only for academic purposes.

All fields are required and for every question you should choose only one answer.

A Short Description of Our Results

An important step in our analysis was represented by the descriptive results for each of the 7 dimensions in order to determine which categories of information and actions are perceived to be the most useful (most compatible to the user's needs) and should be included in a theatre/opera website.

Our data indicated that this information and these actions refer to a functional dimension – granting access to performances, theatre's pro-

gram, the price of tickets and having the option of booking them online, of checking the available seats, of accessing specialized information about shows, information about theatre's location, watching fragments of present and past performances and getting information about the author, cast, plot of the plays, about present and future projects, prizes and providing them with contact data and the possibility of searching the website. As a result we are suggesting that these information categories should be the main elements of the homepage when designing a website for a theatre/opera house and users should be able to access them rapidly, performing very few actions.

As we have already mentioned, this state of facts might be related to the fact that most of our sample used in the survey belonged to the audience category. If we question a different category of people connected to the theatre/opera world, like actors/actresses, critics, theatre specialists, people from show business, events organizers, the information considered to be most relevant might be different, as previous suggested by interviews. In order to verify this assumption we need to further investigate the differences between user categories regarding their needs. If such differences are found we will be able to propose the design of websites which can adapt to the needs of different types of users.

Although at the beginning of the investigation we started with the assumption that there are different categories of people who might be interested in having information about theatre/opera houses and accessing this information on a website, we defined their interests and actions, our sample didn't comprise people from all these categories. As a result, the fact that our investigation indicated the information and actions related to the audience category to be the most relevant was not a surprise. A future direction of our investigation consists in analyzing the informational needs of people belonging to other categories of users.

As a result, we can observe that the richness of our initial qualitative data has been partly lost in our effort of standardization. On the other hand, it is exactly this initial qualitative data that can indicate to us the *way* the informational need should be embedded in the design (for example it is not enough to provide the possibility of buying tickets, this process of buying must be accompanied by expert advices and commentaries on the performance to match the experience of buying tickets directly from the theatre's representative which can always inform you on the recent events related to the play and the cast). Also, these initial qualitative data made us aware that we must take into consideration different categories of people with different goals, different context in which people come into contact with theatres/opera houses. Although our effort of prioritizing needs excluded most of these categories, we are now aware of the fact that our solution serves only a specific goal and that future efforts should be directed towards the inclusion of other identified categories.

As a result, the pattern we proposed at the end of our project, based on these results is mainly suited for those situations when the main goal of the theatre/opera is to inform and attract the audience using their websites and also to facilitate the access of the audience to performances by allowing specific actions to be carried on their websites. For more complex objectives like facilitating the contact with suppliers, contractors, people from show business or organizers etc., a further investigation is necessary in order to identify these needs.

User Needs Analysis for Developing an Intelligent Web Assistant

The second project we analyze here which is to illustrate the usefulness of the techniques presented for user needs research refers to creating an intelligent web assistant for career-related decision making. The detailed results are presented in Onaca & Guran (2008) and here we will insist on the way we have used the methodology described

above for analyzing our possible users' needs. The project began when the university decided to award a research grant for creating an intelligent web assistant to help future students make their decision regarding which faculty to enroll to. The grant was awarded to a designer's team assisted by a psychologist and a human computer interaction expert. The idea the management had in mind was to deliver a webpage were high school graduates could test their abilities and compare their own profile to the profiles most suitable for different professions. Then, they should have the opportunity to find out which faculty can educate them for that profession and gather relevant information about that faculty. Moreover, the assistant had to be able to learn from past interactions and associate profiles with most requested information categories in order to personalize interaction.

The way the project was formulated followed a very traditional corporate edict (Kuniavsky, 2003) design process. Regardless of the very articulated request, we have managed to convince the research and design team to take into account a user-centered approach arguing that a great deal of effort and money could be spent with little results if we do not find first who are the people this product will address and which are their real needs. So, the first step taken was an extensive user-need analysis using several techniques from contextual inquiry to extensive interviews, focus-groups and survey. The results were partially contradictory to the initial request but very informing for the future steps of the project. For orienting this step we used the framework depicted in Figure 1 and analyzed the people who could become interested users, the activities that characterize the decision making process, the context in which these activities take place and what technology is now used or is considered to be best suited to support these activities.

The methodology we used was somehow unusual as we have decided to teach master students user-centered design by involving them as research teams in the project. We have formed 7 research teams all having no idea related to the way the project was initially formulated to prevent biases towards confirming the initial management idea. All the groups had the same research questions: *How do people choose the faculty they attend in our university* and *How do they perceive the idea of an assistant to help them make that decision.* More operational objectives included identifying the possible users, identifying specific actions, identifying the action sequence in this kind of decision making, identifying their difficulties and needs, their opinion and values related to this decision and all the contextual factors that come in at certain moments, and last but not least, how the process could be improved and by what type of technology.

The methods each group used were mostly qualitative but every group was gradually oriented to focus on a different aspect than the others in order to gain access to very diverse information (some focused on certain user category, some focused on gaining a deep understanding related to the process, some focused on structuring the initial qualitative data using surveys). The methods used were semi structured interviews, focus-groups, content analysis of educational forums and surveys.

All the methods used have been shaped by the initial operational objectives described earlier. We have instructed students to develop their methods focusing on people and the way they perceive this process of deciding the future of their education. That is why interviews and focus-groups have been designed to elicit personal concerns and difficulties related to the decision-making process and did not directly focus on the sequences of this process which is are not very easy to overtly explain without a process of post-decision justification. As a result participants in interviews were asked to reflect upon the process of choosing their faculty specialization (be it situated in the present for some or in the past for others). Main directions followed concerning the process itself, how they have come to the decision, what emotions ac-

companied this process, who were the people they discussed these issues with, who did they trust for advice in this process and why, difficulties they had encountered on the way, how would they do things differently. Follow-up questions directed the discussion towards the main categories of information described in Figure 1.

We will not insist here on the methodology or exact results but we want to emphasize the importance of knowledge gathered during this phase of user needs analysis and the way it affected the project. The total number of participants involved in this research was 189 ranging from high school students, to undergraduate students, graduates, master students and other people involved in this process of decision making (high school head teachers and counselors, parents, teachers).

A Short Description of our Results

The results: during the process we have identified several user categories which seemed very interested in tools to improve the process of decision making besides the initial one which was considered to be high school students. Moreover, we have identified that the most interested categories were not these students, but working people interested in continuing their education (and having less time to find information and compare it) and counselors and teachers who are often asked to assist their students in the decision making. Also, we have discovered that many of the undergraduate students or graduates were also possible users as they were very interested in following a Masters Program (or a second specialization) and needed support in identifying the best alternative.

Based on data gathered from interviews, we have been able to group characteristics and needs in 4 typologies: independent (they take decisions independently and only need information in order to make their mind), decided (the decision is already taken, the main needs involve support for implementing it), undecided (they can not decide between alternatives and the assistance needed consists in comparing and integrating information about alternatives and about self) and influenced (can change decisions depending on the others and the main needs refer to integrating information about self and finding social support for certain alternatives).

The results also lead us towards the design of a decision making process in this field of university program enrollment. The designed followed a model of rational decision supported by literature in the field of career management (Lemeni & Miclea, 2004). While building on this model we have realized that the information about their own abilities profile and the degree of fit with the profiles of the profession was only one information element needed in order to form and evaluate alternatives. Information regarding workforce, economical development in the area and economical perspectives were also highly invoked. Moreover, users did not want to have only the possibility of finding out this information but also the possibility to compare information using given or their own criteria.

Another surprising result was related to the implementation stage of the decision making process. Most of the users wanted to be assisted not only during the first phases of the decision making (as the project was formulated at the beginning) but also (and mostly) at the final stage of decision implementation. As a result, needs uncovered in this area were related to administrative details regarding admission procedures, automating some of these procedures, providing informational and social support for an easier and quicker adaptation to the new status and roles. The most surprising thing was that the needs of people related to this final stage were higher than the ones related to the earlier stages.

The last result that affected a lot the next stage was the fact that the decisions of Romanian people regarding their own educational career have a highly social character and are emotionally loaded. Very often people who participated in the research would envision the assistant as a human expert providing personalized interaction and social and emotional support and they would very seldom think of technology supported assistance. That is why in the further development of requirements we had to take into account the fact that future features of the web assistant will have to support this kind of personalized interaction, expert advice and social support networks. Most probably if we hadn't taken into account this issue the final acceptance of our product would have been seriously endangered.

CONCLUSION

By these two final examples we have tried to illustrate both the "how" and the "why" aspects of using methodologies from social sciences in analyzing user needs for the development of successful and more usable designs.

With our first example we have tried to underline the process of creating and using a survey and the way we can correlate two different methods in the same research (interview and survey). In the second example we chose not to focus on the way we used the qualitative methodology but on the benefits we can obtain by focusing the entire initial research on discovering important user categories, their characteristics and needs.

The procedures and results which we have underlined come to complete the extensive literature body which is currently supporting the very early involvement of users into the design process in order to improve the outcome both in usability and acceptance as well as in their financial success. After all, the success of a product is determined by the degree in which it is needed and desired by the users, and the degree in which it can satisfy their needs and can be easily used by them (Kuniavsky, 2003). These are the characteristics of a web design product that can create its competitive advantage over other similar products. If by usability we understand a good design, then usability becomes critical for the success of a product. Designing for usability starts from the very first steps of understanding the users, their problems and needs in order to address them at further stages of development.

A last observation that can be made is the fact that the methods and tools discussed here represent only a small part of all social-research methods that can be used in user research. We chose to present only this three methods because they are the most popular and used methods in this field. Moreover, it is important to underline the fact that all methods of social research can become relevant and useful for user research but not everybody is prepared to properly and usefully design and conduct this kind of research. The results obtained from qualitative research depend a great deal on the researcher's training and expertise in using specific techniques and results analysis. As we have shown, many researchers still have difficulties in using qualitative methods mostly due to the fact that they are used to evaluate research depending on positivist criteria of internal and external validity. We wish to reemphasize here the fact that our results taken from the two projects do not represent universal truths and should not be judged in terms of their generalizability. They represent the level of understanding we have reached in relation to our targeted users and the specific problems we have addressed. They are useful and relevant to this given situation and we do not make (nor wish to make) any statement related to their value for other situations or design problems. On the other hand, the part that can be useful in other similar situations is the approach to user needs analysis which may end in different results every time but every time these results will be able to inform and direct future stages in design and ensure a more usable product. That is why we have to support more actively the importance of interdisciplinary design teams that could help us overcome the complexities involved in user-centered design and ensure the quality and success of the final design products. Our first attempts in doing so resulted in the usability framework that we have presented in this chapter. We intend to further develop our work in the direction of integrating approaches from usability engineering and software engineering in a manner that proves to be easy to understand and use for both communities.

ACKNOWLEDGMENT

The present chapter is an extended version of the original paper, Pitariu, H. D., Andrei, D.M., & Guran, A.M. (2009). Social research methods used in moving the traditional usability approach towards a user-centered design approach, *Journal of Information Technology and Web Engineering*, *4*(4). Unfortunatelly, Prof. Pitariu passed away on March 25th 2010 after a lifetime dedicated to psychology research and practice.

REFERENCES

Ambler, S. W. (2007). Tailoring Usability into Agile Software Development Projects. In Law, E. L.-C., Hvannberg, E., & Cockton, G. (Eds.), *Maturing Usability: Quality in Software, Interaction and Value, Human-Computer Interaction Series* (pp. 75–95). London: Springer-Verlag Limited.

Benyon, D., Turner, P., & Turner, S. (2005). *Designing Interactive Systems, People, Activities, Context and Technology*. Edinburgh: Addison-Wesley.

Bevan, N. (2005). Cost benefits framework and case studies. In Bias, R. G., & Mayhew, D. G. (Eds.), *Cost-Justifying Usability: An update for the internet age*. San Francisco: Morgan Kaufmann. doi:10.1016/B978-012095811-5/50020-1

Bevan, N. (2008). A framework for selecting the most appropriate usability measures. In *COST 294-MAUSE Workshop: Critiquing Automated Usability Evaluation Methods*. March.

Brinck, T., Gergle, D., & Wood, S. D. (2002). *Usability for the Web: Designing Web Sites that Work*. San Francisco: Morgan Kaufmann.

Cato, J. (2001). *User-centered Web design*. London: Addison-Wesley.

Chang, J., & Bourguet, M. (2008). Usability framework for the design and evaluation of multimodal interaction. In *Proceedings of the 22nd British HCI Group Annual Conference on People and Computers: Culture, Creativity, interaction* (pp. 123-126) Liverpool, UK: British Computer Society Conference on Human-Computer Interaction.

Constantine, L. (2001). Process Agility and Software Usability. *Software Development 9*(5). Retrieved June 12th, 2010, from http://www.foruse.com/Files/ Papers/agiledesign.pdf.

Cooper, A. (2004). *The Inmates Are Running the Asylum: Why High-Tech Products Drive Us Crazy and How to Restore the Sanity*. Indianapolis: SAMS Publishing.

Dawson, J. W. (2006). *A holistic usability framework for distributed simulation systems*. Unpublished PhD thesis. Orlando: University of Central Florida.

Denzin, N. K., & Lincoln, Y. S. (2005). The discipline and practice of qualitative research. In: N.K., Denzin, & Y. S., Lincoln (Eds.) *The SAGE handbook of qualitative research*, 3rd Edition. London: Sage.

Dix, A., Finlay, J. E., Abowd, G. D., & Beale, R. (2004). *Human-Computer Interaction*. Upper Saddle River, NJ: Pearson Education.

Dumas, J. S., & Redish, J. C. (1999). *A Practical Guide to Usability Testing*. Bristol, UK: Intellect Books.

Glosiene, A., & Manzhukh, Z. (2005). Towards a usability framework for memory institutions. *New Library World, 106*(7/8), 303–319. doi:10.1108/03074800510608620

Gould, J. D., & Lewis, C. (1985). Design for usability: Key principles and what designers think. *Communications of the ACM, 28*(3), 360–411. doi:10.1145/3166.3170

Hatch, M. J., & Cunliffe, A. L. (2006). *Organization Theory. Modern, Symbolic, and Postmodern Perspectives* (2nd ed.). Oxford, UK: Oxford University Press.

Hatch, M. J., & Yanow, D. (2008). Methodology by Metaphor: Ways of Seeing in Painting and Research. *Organization Science, 29*(1), 23–44. doi:10.1177/0170840607086635

Hirscheim, R. (1985). *Office automation: a social and organisational perspective*. Chichester, UK: Wiley.

ISO 9241-11 (1998). *Ergonomic requirements for office work with visual display terminals* (VDTs), (Part 11: Guidance on usability). New York: ISO

Jokela, T. (2008). Characterizations, Requirements, and Activities of User-Centered Design—the KESSU 2.2Model. IN: E. L-C., Law, E.T., Hvannberg, & G., Cockton (Eds). *Maturing Usability. Quality in interaction, software and value*. London: Springer-Verlag Limited.

Jokela, T., & Abrahamsson, P. (2004). Usability Assessment of an Extreme Programming Project: Close Co-operation with the Customer Does Not Equal Good Usability. In *Product Focused Software Process Improvement: 5th International Conference, PROFES 2004 Proceedings* (pp. 393–407). Berlin: Springer-Verlag.

Jordan, P. W. (2002). *An Introduction To Usability*. London: Taylor and Francis.

Karat, C. M. (1990). Cost-benefit analysis of usability engineering techniques. In *Proceedings of the Human Factors Society 34th Annual Meeting* (Vol 2), (pp. 839-843), Orlando, FL.

Keinonen, T. (2008). User-centered design and fundamental need. In *Proceedings of the 5th Nordic Conference on Human-Computer interaction: Building Bridges* (pp. 211-219), Lund, Sweden.

King, N. (2004). Using interviews in Qualitative Research . In *C., Cassell, & G., Symon, Essential Guide to Qualitative Methods in Organizational Research*. Thousand Oaks, CA: Sage Publications.

King, N., Ma, T. H.-Y., Zaphiris, P., Petrie, H., & Hamilton, F. (2004). An incremental usability and accessibility evaluation framework for digital libraries . In Brophy, P., Fisher, S., & Craven, J. (Eds.), *Libraries without walls 5: The distributed delivery of library and information services* (pp. 123–131). London, UK: Facet.

Koua, E., MacEachren, A. M., & Kraak, M. (2006). Evaluating the usability of visualization methods in an exploratory geovisualization environment. *International Journal of Geographical Information Science, 20*(4), 425–448. doi:10.1080/13658810600607550

Kuniavsky, M. (2003). *Observing the user experience. A practitioner's guide to user research.* San Francisco: Elsevier.

Law, E. L.-C., Hvannberg, E. T., & Cockton, G. (2008). A Green Paper on Usability Maturation In E. L-C., Law, E.T., Hvannberg, & G., Cockton (Eds). *Maturing Usability. Quality in interaction, software and value.* London: Springer-Verlag Limited.

Lemeni, G., & Miclea, M. (2004). *Consiliere şi orientare. Ghid de educaţie pentru carieră.* Cluj-Napoca: Editura ASCR.

Marshall, C., & Rossman, G. B. (2006). *Designing Qualitative Research* (3rd ed.). London: Sage.

Morgan, D. L., Krueger, R. A., & King, J. A. (1998). *Focus Group Kit.* London: Sage.

Myers, B. A., & Rosson, M. B. (1992). Survey on user interface programming. In Proceedings *of SIGCHI'92: Human Factors in Computing Systems* (pp. 195-202), Monterey, CA: ACM.

Nielsen, J. (1993). *Usability Engineering. San Francisco: Morgan Kaufmann, Elsevier. Norman, D.A. (2002). The design of every day things.* New York: Basic Books.

Nielsen, J., & Landauer, T. K. (1993). A mathematical model of the finding of usability problems. In *Proceedings INTERCHI'93: Human Factors in Computing Systems* (pp. 206-213), Amsterdam, NL.

Onacă (Andrei). D.M., & Guran, A.M. (2008). A User-centred approach in developing an intelligent web assistant for supporting career related decision making. In *Proceedings of* the *Romanian Computer Human Interaction Conference.* Bucureşti: Matrix Rom, Onacă (Andrei), D.M., Tarţa, A.M., & Pitariu, H.D. (2006). The development of a theatre/opera website pattern based on a user need assessment approach, *Psihologia Resurselor Umane, 4*(1).

Pitariu, H.D. (2003). The influence of personality traits upon human computer interaction. *Cognition, Brain, Behavior, 7*(3).

Rosenbaum, S. (2008). The Future of Usability Evaluation: Increasing Impact on Value . In Law, E. L.-C., Hvannberg, E., & Cockton, G. (Eds.), *Maturing Usability: Quality in Software, Interaction and Value, Human-Computer Interaction Series* (pp. 75–95). London: Springer-Verlag Limited.

Rubin, J. (1994). *Handbook of usability testing. How to plan, design and conduct effective tests.* Montreal, Canada: John Wiley and Sons.

Sarnikar, S., & Murphy, M. (2009). A Usability Analysis Framework for Healthcare Information Technology. *Sprouts: Working Papers on Information Systems, 9*(62). Retrieved on July 10th 2010 from http://sprouts.aisnet.org/9-62.

van Maanen, J. (1998). *Qualitative studies of organizations. The Administrative Science Quarterly, Series in Organization Theory and Behaviour*. London: Sage Publications.

van Velsen, L., Van der Geest, T., Klaassen, R., & Steehouder, M. (2008). User-centered evaluation of adaptive and adaptable systems: a literature review. *The Knowledge Engineering Review, 23*(3), 261–281. doi:10.1017/S0269888908001379

van Welie, M. (2001). *Task-Based user interface design*. Amsterdam: SIKS.van Welie, M., Traetteberg, H., (2000). Interaction Patterns in User Interfaces, In *7th Pattern Languages of Programs Conference*, 13-16 August, Allerton Park Monticello, Illinois. Retrieved June 20, 2005, from http://www.welie.com/about.html.

van Welie, M., van der Veer, G. C., & Eliëns, A. (2000). Patterns as Tools for User Interface Design, In *International Workshop on Tools for Working with Guidelines*, (pp. 313-324) October 7-8, Biarritz, France. Retrieved June 17, 2005, from http://www.welie.com/about.html

Chapter 18
Integrating Accessibility Evaluation into Web Engineering Processes

Christopher Power
University of York, UK

André Pimenta Freire
University of York, UK

Helen Petrie
University of York, UK

ABSTRACT

This chapter presents methodologies and techniques for performing accessibility evaluations on web applications. These methodologies are discussed in the context of performing them within a web engineering process, be it a traditional, unified or agile process. In this chapter the case is made that website commissioners and web engineers cannot afford to overlook accessible practices as they risk alienating an increasingly large user base who may require accessible web features.

INTRODUCTION

Accessibility is becoming a required feature of web applications for commerce, health care and government. For website commissioners and engineers who are unfamiliar with it, accessibility can be a word that conjures up spectres of legal obligations, litigation and increased costs in development. For those who are familiar with the technical side of accessibility, images of

long documents of guidelines, regulations and criticisms of both are come to mind. Finally, for people with disabilities, accessibility can inspire either dread, due to the current state-of-the-art in accessibility in web technology, or hope, for the future of web applications, or both.

Faced with all of these views, what are web engineers to do? Many want to make their applications available to as many people as possible; however, just as many have thrown up their hands in dismay at the current perceived state of accessibility, and the seeming impenetrability of the

DOI: 10.4018/978-1-60960-523-0.ch018

process. These web engineers often take the road of conformance with guidelines and checklists, a route that does not necessarily guarantee accessibility (DRC, 2004). While this is often the route that leads to the largest acceptance within an organization, there are larger implications to the website engineer of which they should be aware. An inaccessible website has the potential to alienate a large audience that the organization could reach to offer their products and services. As a result, managers, designers and developers all must be concerned about accessibility itself, not just guideline conformance.

The goal of this chapter is to present the concept of accessibility and what it means to the web engineer. In particular, it will focus on the development and evaluation of web applications for accessibility, ensuring that the largest number of people of the web audience can use them.

This chapter will present the relationship between usability, a concept well understood by the web engineering community, and accessibility. It will discuss how these two concepts interact, and how they are achieving the same end goal: allowing users to use web applications.

In the sections following, the authors have chosen to ignore conventional wisdom regarding discussing web problems via guidelines, checkpoints and specific technologies. Instead, the focus is placed on the users and their interactions with web applications. After all, technology continues to change, but humans change very slowly, and the challenges and issues associated with accessibility will remain long after the current crop of web technologies is gone.

The chapter will present different types of evaluation available to the web engineer: expert inspection, automatic tools and user evaluation. An analysis of where these evaluation processes can be applied in web engineering processes is discussed as well as structured unified processes and flexible agile processes.

BACKGROUND

In order to understand the techniques discussed later in this chapter, it is important to understand what accessibility is and why it is important. This chapter presents several different views of accessibility. This is followed by a discussion regarding why accessibility is a factor that must be considered by the web engineer and website commissioners. Hereafter, a *web site* consists of many interconnected *web pages* all belonging to the same domain address. Further, a *web application* is a website that has interactive components for completing complex tasks.

The Accessible Web vs. the Usable Web vs. Using the Web

With web engineering being focused on the design and development of both content and structure in websites, it is perhaps unsurprising that usability is well represented in the web engineering literature and in experience reports (Mariage & Vanderdonckt, 2005; Martens, 2003; Agarwal, 2002; Becker, 2002; Palmer, 2002; Ivory & Hearst, 2001).

In general, it is reasonable to say that the web engineering community has taken on board the concept of usability, addressing different aspects of effectiveness, efficiency and satisfaction[1] (Shneiderman, 1998). In comparison, the uptake of accessible design and evaluation slow to come into common practice. In some cases, this is a result of the definition of accessibility being unclear and at times contradictory, making it difficult for web engineering teams to adopt a culture of accessibility. Petrie and Kheir (2007) provide an extensive discussion of these definitions a portion of which is included here for completeness.

In this chapter, *technical accessibility* refers to the checking of features of a website for conformance against a set of guidelines specifying what is and what is not accessible to people with disabilities (Petrie and Kheir, 2007). The guidelines typically used for such evaluations are the Web Content Accessibility Guidelines (WCAG) (Chisholm, 1999; Caldwell *et al.*, 2008) from the Web Accessibility Initiative (WAI) of the World Wide Web Consortium (W3C). Indeed, it is often the case that legislation or company policies are based on this view of accessibility.

Unfortunately, it has been demonstrated that accessibility is not so simple. Indeed, the extensive study performed for the Disability Rights Commission in the UK (2004) concluded that there was no relationship between technical accessibility and the success of users with disabilities in achieving their goals on a particular website. Clearly a more user-based definition is required to truly capture the essence of what it means for a website to be accessible.

There have been several attempts to define what accessibility means to the user, from Shneiderman's (2000, 2003) *universal usability* which presents accessibility as a precursor to usability; to Thatcher *et al.* (2003) who defines accessibility as being a disjoint subset of problems of people with disabilities from mainstream users. Unfortunately, neither of these definitions appears to be sufficient to describe the issues encountered by people with disabilities on the web. Petrie and Kheir (2007) demonstrated that there is a common subset of problems that are shared between web users with disabilities and mainstream users, as well as those that are disjoint between the two groups. It is also the case that there is evidence that certain types of usability problems are amplified for people with disabilities (Harrison and Petrie, 2006; Petrie, King and Hamilton, 2005; DRC, 2004), with this research showing a "usability bonus", where websites become more usable for all users due to good accessibility practices. Clearly, the issue about what is or is not accessible is not as clear as the technical accessibility enthusiasts would have us believe.

For purposes of this chapter, the authors adopt the term *accessibility* to mean that people with disabilities and other user groups such as older adults are able to successfully perceive, understand and interact with websites and web applications[2].

Modern Web Audiences Impact on Website Use

There is a segment of the design and development community that contends that there are not enough users that would benefit from accessible practices to warrant their inclusion in development cycles. In this section, the case will be made that there are too many web users in the broader audience who can be reached through accessible practices to ignore.

A report prepared for the Royal National Institute of Blind People (RNIB) by the University of York (Kennaugh and Petrie, 2006) discusses the demographics of the UK population of potential users of interactive online services. In that report, calculations of potential market sizes were derived from estimates of the number of people in the overall population of the UK who fall into one of two broad categories of people who can benefit from accessible applications. The first, core group of users consists of those who are: over 75; people with severe visual disabilities; people with profound hearing loss; people with severe dyslexia; people aged 16-74 with dementia and people aged 16-74 with the tremor related illness of Parkinson's. This core group is estimated to be approximately 7,797,000 people.

A further secondary group of approximately 13,382,000 users was also identified as people whose lives would benefit from the provision of accessible digital applications. This user group consists of those people who have: mild to moderate hearing loss; learning difficulties; mild dyslexia; arthritis aged 16-74 of 75; and people with low literacy.

Certainly, it would not be expected that all individuals in these user groups would adopt accessible digital services through either television or the web; however, if only 10% of the potential users gain access to digital services on the web, this could mean millions of additional users.

In an online marketplace that is largely usage-based for generating revenue, driven by funding through online advertising, these numbers cannot be overlooked for much longer. With the overall average population age increasing, we are moving into a crucial phase where the majority of people using the internet will experience some mild to moderate accessibility problems, these numbers are expected to increase over time.

Companies, web commissioners and web engineers have a unique opportunity to integrate accessibility and evaluation practices into their businesses now, before the massive shift in population demographics occurs.

Accessible Practices for Modern Web Applications

In the last decade the web has changed from a source of information for a small audience, to a necessity for a business, education and leisure. In the same way that the audiences of the web have evolved, so has the content with which they interact. Text and static pictures have been augmented with multimedia, animation and interactive components. This section explores some of the features that make up the modern web and discusses some of the accessibility issues that can arise due to them. As there are several good resources on implementation of accessible designs (Thatcher *et al.*, 2003), and as accessibility needs often do not change as the underlying web technology evolves, the web features are discussed from the user centric point of view, with examples of current technology provided, where appropriate, that both satisfies users and WCAG 2.0.

Text

Text is still perhaps the most common form of information available on the web. Text is still the main medium of presentation, with a marked increase recently in participatory web communities such as blogs and wikis. This is fortunate, as text is relatively easy to transform from symbols into synthetic speech, thus solving many of the perceptual problems associated with graphics and other types of media that occur for people with visual disabilities or people with specific learning difficulties; however, this does not mean that text is always accessible to users.

For example, the use of text decoration, such as bold, italics or font colour, needs to be implemented in such a way that screen readers[3] and other assistive technologies can determine that it is in fact intended for emphasis. In current technology this means using (X)HTML elements such as *strong* and *em(phasis)* in combination with cascading style sheets to provide access to the semantic information to both mainstream users and people with visual disabilities.

Text size remains a problem for many users, and thus in browser options are often used to view text. However, if implemented incorrectly, this resizing can be a disaster! For example, Figure 1 demonstrates that text can be rendered unreadable in large font if a fixed spacing layout is used.

A further example, which often affects mainstream users as well as older adults or people with specific learning difficulties, is the use of large blocks of complicated text that are difficult to parse (Kurniawan, 2003). Smaller, more organized, sections of text, or simpler text can be easier to perceive and understand for many users.

Images

On the web, the use of images varies between *informative* and *decorative*. *Informative images* are those that contain information critical to undertaking tasks on a given website. These could be graphics that provide instruction, or those that require direct interaction from the user (such a graphic links).

One group that is severely affected by images on websites are people with visual disabilities, who

Figure 1. An example of a website created with fixed spacing of (X)HTML div elements resulting in poor rendering of enlarged text

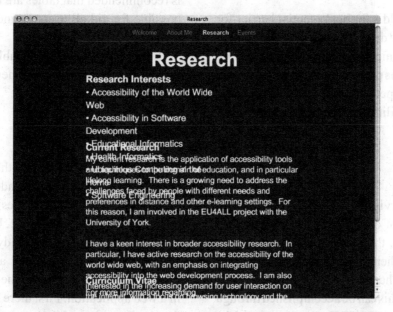

require alternative text on informative images to describe the contents of images for interpretation and understanding of their contents. Indeed, this is perhaps the most studied issue in regards to accessibility, with several studies citing serious problems with the lack of alternative text for informative images on websites (DRC, 2004; Harrison and Petrie, 2006).

In comparison, *decorative images* are those that provide no direct information to the user about the contents or use of the web page and as a result do not need to be voiced. In current practice, this means that alternative text attributes in (X)HTML should be included with empty character strings. This will result in most screen readers skipping over the image.

Beyond this, forced direct manipulation of very large images or very small images can cause accessibility issues for anyone with tremor or dexterity disabilities including older adult users and users with physical disabilities.

Multimedia

Multimedia, which can include audio content or video content, provides interesting challenges in accessibility. There are not only the challenges in making sure that the content is accessible, but also the media players and other technology (e.g. Flash, SCORM players) that are used to deliver the content must themselves be accessible. While this chapter is primarily concerned with the aspects of the web engineering process (i.e. content, structure etc.), it is worth noting that in the procurement process for a multimedia player, a web engineer should place accessibility in its requirements.

For audio content, it is essential that text equivalents in the form of either captioning or a transcript be provided. This is similar for audio tracks in a video. When using the transcript, people with certain specific learning difficulties can be further supported by using time dependent highlighting, with text being highlighted during relevant points in the video. On the other hand, some sign-language using people who are deaf would prefer captioning be done with sign-language (Fels *et al.*, 2004; Petrie, Weber and Fisher, 2005).

Video does add a further potential barrier for people with visual disabilities as the visual content must also be augmented with audio description. These descriptions provide information regarding the activities happening in the video for a person with visual disabilities (Petrie, Weber and Fisher, 2005).

Tables

When presented visually, tables can provide an efficient means of organizing and viewing data. In audio formats, this form of data presentation can be arduous when it is linearized without audio cues about table headings and table columns. In current practice this can be accomplished through the *TH* element in (X)HTML. Further, use of the caption and summary attributes of tables can help orient all users to the purpose of the table(s) and information about the contents, respectively.

In other cases, where tables are more complex, sophisticated reading strategies may be required to make sense of the data through audio. Many of these types of strategies, and a more in-depth discussion of the impact of linearization of tables for people with visual disabilities can be found in

the work by Yesilada *et al.* (2004). In general, it is recommended that tables are kept as simple as possible for aid all users in understanding their contents.

In regards to the use of tables for layout on websites: a developer should never use tables for layout on websites[4].

Links

Links would seem like an easy thing to get right on web pages. By adding a web address, some text, or a graphic, a designer provides a user with a way to navigate to a new web page. Unfortunately, in addition to the problems already associated with text and graphics mentioned above, there is a need to be careful regarding the labeling of links in a web application. First there is the problem of the sheer number of links on a web page. If the complete list of links is overly long, it is difficult to navigate for all users[5]. Further, if these links are not labeled appropriately, with meaningful identifiers, they will be impossible to interpret in a list of links such as those used by screen reader users. Consider the following screenshot of such a links list from the phone sales page on a major UK phone company's website. (see Figure 2)

Figure 2. Screen shot of a screen reader style links list for the website of a UK based mobile phone company

As can be seen, there were (at least) four phones on the page being viewed, with links to select a specific phone, or links to the details regarding a phone. However, it is impossible to tell from this listing *what* phone would be viewed when a link is followed.

This type of problem of overloading of link text is not unique to the audio browsing user. Mainstream users can run into similar problems if links are not sufficiently distinguished from one another either explicitly through their labels, or implicitly by the context in which they are used.

Headings

Even the earliest markup languages included heading elements for indicating divisions in a web document. However, as technology evolved, it became easier to add visual emphasis to words to indicate sections of the website. Unfortunately, this visual information is often not implemented in such a way that it can be detected by assistive technologies such as screen readers. In order to make a website easy to navigate for someone using such technology, the developer should use appropriate markup, such as the heading elements (e.g. *H1*, *H2*) available in (X)HTML. Proper indication of headings, in both visual and screen reader detectable markup has been shown to increase performance for both mainstream users and users who are blind (Watanabe, 2007).

Forms

The possibility of including forms to provide features in websites was provided in early versions of the HTML, and has played a key role for the implementation of interaction in the web. Although forms have been widely used since early applications were available, many web systems still have many inaccessible forms.

When designing a form, a web designer or developer must ensure that the form is accessible through keyboard and mouse input, with *onfocus* events replacing *onclick*. Further, proper association between fields and their *label* elements such that the two are linked is also important. This will allow screen readers users to detect the labels associated with one or more fields; however, it will also benefit mouse users as they can click on the associated label to select the field. In this way, web engineers can use graphical positioning as they wish without concern that the labels will become disassociated with their appropriate fields.

ACCESSIBILITY EVALUATION TECHNIQUES

The techniques presented above provide web engineers with practical advice regarding how to build accessible websites. However, without proper evaluation techniques it is impossible for web engineers to know whether or not they have been successful in providing accessible designs and implementations. In this section, techniques for evaluating web accessibility are presented.

Throughout this section examples are provided from accessibility evaluations performed on a number of UK museum websites by the authoring team during a recent contract[6].

Conformance Evaluations and Accessibility Evaluations

As was mentioned previously, the evaluation of a web page, website or web application for its conformance to the Web Content Accessibility Guidelines (WCAG) is one measure of the accessibility of a website. *Conformance evaluation* consists of checking the features of a website as to whether they satisfy aspects of accessibility that are specified in WCAG. For web engineers who are familiar with accessibility, this is the most common type of evaluation done due to the influence that WCAG has had on the legal and political landscape.

The first version of WCAG (Chisholm, 1999) was produced by the Web Accessibility Initiative (WAI) of the World Wide Web Consortium (W3C) as a recommendation for practice on the web. The primary goal of these guidelines was to increase awareness of accessibility as well as to provide best practices for developers to help them make the web available to all users. The first version of the guidelines had 14 guidelines with 65 checkpoints. Each checkpoint had a *Priority* from 1 to 3 that indicated its importance to making the website accessible to user groups. If a website met all Priority 1 checkpoints it was said to meet *Level A* conformance. Further, if a website met all Priority 1 and 2 checkpoints, it was conformant to *Level AA*. Finally meeting all of the checkpoints meant that a website was conformant to *Level AAA*.

In December, 2008 the second version of WCAG was released. This substantial update included a reorganization of the guidelines. In WCAG 2.0 there are four guiding principles, specifically that a website should be: perceivable to the senses of the user, operable by the user, understandable to the user, and robust in that it can function when used with a variety of technologies. Within these four principles are 12 guidelines, within which there are success criteria (SC). Each SC has a priority attached to it, where priorities are now A, AA, AAA. As a result, conformance levels of A, AA, and AAA are met by meeting all guidelines of the same priority and lower.

A *conformance evaluation* can be undertaken through *conformance tests* conducted via *automated evaluation tools* and *inspection methods*. When such an evaluation is undertaken, the evaluator goes through each guideline checking the features of a website against the criteria of that guideline[7]. Some of these criteria, such as the presence or absence of alternative text, can be checked with an automatic evaluation tool. In other cases, such as criteria relating to the clarity of the contents of the alternative text, the evaluation can only be conducted using human judgment.

Further information regarding conformance tests is contained in the following sections. However, while conformance evaluations are perhaps the most common evaluations conducted in industry, it is unclear that conformance to WCAG leads to an accessible website. Indeed, there is evidence from the DRC report that there is no relation between WCAG 1.0 and user reported problems on websites. As a result, the following sections also provide information regarding evaluation methodologies that are not based on guideline conformance checking.

Automated Evaluation

Automated evaluation for the verification of accessibility issues provides an efficient way of checking a subset of WCAG and are heavily used by practitioners (Ivory, 2003). This broad use of automated evaluation tools has resulted in a wide range of tools, including the previously widely used *Bobby*, *Wave*[8], *Hera* (Benavidez et. al, 2006), *Imergo* (Mohamad et. al 2004) and many others. All of these tools provide similar functionality through the processing of the markup of web pages.

First, these tools can check the validity of (X) HTML mark-up and the use of style sheets. This can include checking features such as the correct nesting of elements in tables and headers, and proper use of other W3C recommended technologies. This first step helps ensure that a web page can be read by assistive technologies.

Beyond the technical tests regarding the technology, automated testing can check things that are, in general, deterministic. They can check the presence or absence of features, such as alternative text attributes and headings, or can check values against known standards, such as values for colour contrast. The results of all these tests are usually presented to the user in the form of a report that details problem areas of the web page(s) for the developer.

Figure 3. A summary document provided by the automated evaluation tool HERA

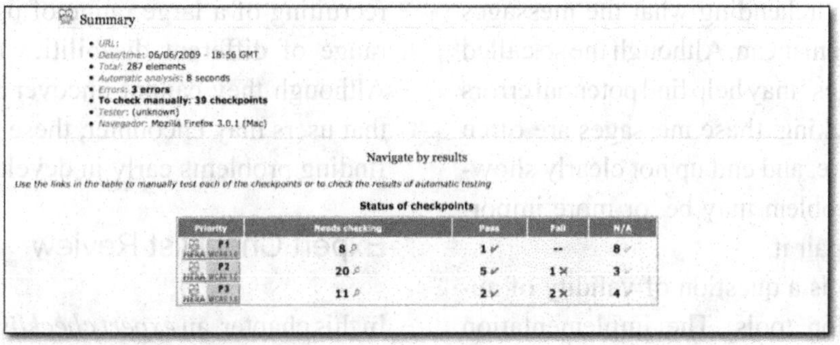

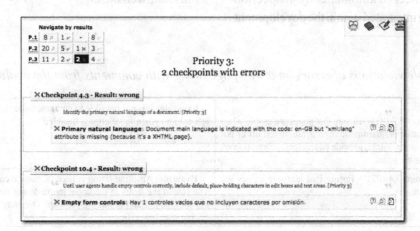

However, in context of an evaluation, it is important to highlight that automated evaluation tools are very limited in their capabilities. Although they may help a lot to identify problems that otherwise would very tedious to test, there is only a small number of WCAG guidelines that can be tested automatically. For WCAG 1.0 checkpoints, the Unified Web Evaluation Methodology (UWEM) (WAB Cluster, 2007) defines a set of methods and accessibility test cases. From the 108 test cases listed at UWEM for the WCAG 1.0 checkpoints only 26 of the tests (less than 20%) can be checked with an automatic tool. Although many of these automatable tests may help considerably to reduce time and effort spent in evaluation, it is clear that, even for evaluation based on checkpoints review, relying exclusively on automated tools covers only a very limited number of problems users may encounter. As an example, consider the use of text alternatives for images. Although it is possible for an automatic tool to identify whether an image element has an *alt* attribute, the tool cannot identify if the text contained within that attribute describes the image appropriately.

Figure 3 presents summary outputs from one such automatic evaluation tool HERA[9], which displays the errors and warnings on a particular web page. Further to this, Figure 4 displays an expanded view of the Priority 3 errors, with a description of the checkpoint violated and the location in the code of the violation.

Understanding the outcomes of an automated evaluation tool is also frequently a challenge to evaluators and developers (Choi et. al, 2006).

Figure 4. An expanded view of the accessibility errors for Priority 3 checkpoints

Even experienced evaluators very often face problems in comprehending what the messages provided from them mean. Although the so called "warning messages" may help find potential errors in a manual checking, these messages are often vague and obscure, and end up not clearly showing where the problem may be, or more importantly, how to repair it.

Finally, there is a question of validity of automatic evaluation tools. The implementation of the checking algorithms varies substantially between different tools, and validation tests for the tools are often not available. This can lead to inaccuracies in checks, such as those found by Brajnik (2004) where he identifies reporting errors in various tools.

The proper use of automated evaluation tools can be an asset to the web engineering team. However, evaluators should bear in mind not only the advantages of such tools, but their severe limitations to broadly cover all possible accessibility problems. Performing expert evaluations and user tests are essential for creating accessible websites.

Inspection Methods

Along with tests with automated evaluation tools, *inspection methods* by expert evaluators play an important role in the evaluation process of web applications. The use of inspection methods is important to help finding barriers in web resources that cannot be checked automatically. Inspection methods may be integrated within the development cycles of web projects, as they do not demand the recruiting of a large range of users with a wide range of different disabilities and restrictions. Although they cannot uncover all the problems that users may encounter, these tests are good at finding problems early in development.

Expert Checklist Review

In this chapter, an *expert checklist review* refers to the inspection method where a human checks the conformance of a website against a set of guidelines such as WCAG. Expert checklist reviews can be difficult for non-experienced evaluators, as the checkpoints are usually related to issues that cannot be automatically checked require in-depth knowledge of accessibility. Additionally, the guidelines and checkpoints may not always be clear and easy to understand and may cause confusion even to experienced evaluators (Colwell and Petrie, 1998). As a result, training and experience are needed to be able to do these checklists well.

With this in mind, if a web engineering team wishes to achieve conformance of their website to WCAG, or another set of guidelines, it is essential that they perform a checklist review as some problems can only be detected through human inspection.

As an example, Table 1 presents two violations that were discovered through an expert conformance review of one of the mentioned UK museum websites.

Table 1. Example violations of errors on a web page along with comments from the evaluator.

Violation: Checkpoint 6.3 (P1) – Ensure that pages are usable when scripts, applets, or other programmatic objects are turned off or not supported. If this is not possible, provide equivalent information on an alternative accessible page.	**Example:** It is not possible to navigate through the objects in the left column when JavaScript is disabled.
Violation: Checkpoint 3.4 (P2) – Ensure that text size values are relative than absolute.	**Example:** Absolute sizing is used in many elements in the CSS. The size of the items in the upper menu do not resize when changing the size preferences in the browser. This may be a problem for people with low vision.

Barriers Walkthrough

The Barriers Walkthrough method (Brajnik, 2006) was inspired in the use of usability heuristics to perform walkthrough evaluations. The method is based on the concept of detection of *barriers* for users with different types of disabilities.

The method adopts the concept of an *accessibility barrier* as "any condition that hinders the user's progress towards the achievement of a goal" (Brajnik, 2006). The method provides evaluators with a list of possible barriers, which are described according to 1) the types of users and types of disabilities that may be affected, 2) the type of assistive technology being used, 3) the *failure mode* (activity or task that may be impacted by the barrier) and 4) the consequences of the occurrence of the barrier. The list of barriers to be used with the method is classified according to groups of users separated by types of disabilities.

With a pre-defined list of barriers defined by the method, the evaluation process involves four steps:

1) Define the relevant user categories;
2) Define the user goals to be analysed with the correspondent pages to be tested and scenarios to be considered;
3) Check the relevant barriers (according to the user categories defined) in the selected web pages;
4) Assign a severity level for each of the occurrence of a barrier.

In two experiments (Brajnik, 2006, 2008), a comparison between the checklist review and barriers walkthrough method showed the latter to be better in several aspects. The barriers walkthrough showed to be more precise (problems found are more prone to be true problems), to produce to a smaller number of reports of false problems and to be better to identify more severe problems.

However, according to the second experiment comparing the methods (Brajnik, 2008), barriers

walkthrough had low reliability between evaluators, as independent evaluators tend to produce different results. In particular, the barriers list provides a level of understanding to the evaluator as to what each of the barrier means, which could be advantageous for raising knowledge of accessibility in engineering teams. This is similar to other evaluation methods, and implies that more than one evaluator is required when using this method.

User Evaluation

In order to ensure that an application is accessible, the "gold standard" for evaluation is the *user evaluation*. In this section, the steps to preparing a typical user evaluation are discussed (Monk *et al.*, 1993, Stanton *et al.*, 2005) along with advice from the authors regarding minimum numbers of users to engage based on experience in evaluating websites for accessibility.

User Recruitment

One key aspect to user evaluation is recruiting people who are representative of those who are likely to use the web application. For purposes of evaluation, many web engineers will select people who surround them; in particular, people within the office or within the business. However, one of the key problems with this type of recruitment is that the participants such as these will bring biases to the table. These internal users share a common vocabulary and set of knowledge with the engineer that users do not have available. This type of bias can cause simple errors that would otherwise be revealed to go undetected as the internal participants rely on their own experiences and knowledge to compensate for errors.

Instead of this type of internal recruitment, it is critical that a target population of users be identified. This target audience should be people who will use the web application, but are separate from the development team. Similarly, if there are particular types of errors that are attempting to be detected, such as accessibility errors, then it is important that users who are likely to encounter these errors be engaged in evaluation. Indeed, it is only through users experiencing the web application through their own user agents and assistive technologies that the engineering team can truly understand accessibility errors.

Again, due to the daunting nature of having to recruit from such a large and varied population, evaluation may be bypassed entirely by a team. However, recent results, such as in the study conducted by the Disability Rights Commission (2004), showed that there was a large overlap between disability groups in terms of accessibility problems. While it is advisable to have as many people as possible evaluate a web application, *a minimal set* of 5 people from each of the following groups will reveal *some* of the critical accessibility errors:

- People who are blind and use a screen reader,
- People who have low-vision and use a screen magnifier,
- People who have severe dyslexia,
- People who have upper body physical disabilities and
- Mainstream users with no identified disability as a control group.

While this set is not complete, notably missing people with hearing disabilities, it does account for individuals who will encounter many of the most common accessibility errors on web applications. Of course, it would be preferable to have people with hearing disabilities in the user group, and to have as many people as can be recruited participate in the evaluation.

Task Preparation

It is insufficient to seat a participant in front of a website or web application and ask them to "play around" on it. For proper data collection, and for proper identification of errors in the web application, it is necessary for the evaluator to prepare tasks in advance for people to complete. These tasks should be representative of the types of things that users are likely to do on the website, and should provide coverage of critical tasks.

When preparing tasks, it is essential that all members of the design team be involved so that the aspects of the web application (e.g. the web store, the contact information) that are most important to the stakeholders be evaluated. Once the critical tasks have been identified, broader tasks that are complex (such as a multi-page shopping page) may need to be broken down into sub-tasks and detailed instructions prepared for the participants. These tasks should be written in the users' language, not business terms, and they should be piloted with a few users to ensure that they are understandable. Finally, task length needs to be estimated to ensure that users are not conducting overly long evaluations[10]. An example of tasks that were created for the UK museum websites is presented in Table 2.

From these initial pilot tests, the evaluators can check to ensure that the data they are receiving makes sense as per what they are trying to find out about the web application. A simple

Table 2. Tasks used to evaluate a set of museum websites.

1. What time is the museum open on Sundays?
2. Are all floors of the museum accessible via a lift?
3. What will you find in the Wilkinson Collection?
4. Find the page to join the mailing list for the museum. Fill in the form, but only submit it if you actually do want to join the mailing list!
5. How much is a copy of "Getting Better: Stories from the History of Medicine" from the Museum shop?

example is: if the evaluator is concerned about the time to completion of a task, a time record should be kept[11].

Running the Evaluation

When running an evaluation, the participant should be brought in at a time convenient for both the evaluator and the participant. They should be made comfortable[12] and given the opportunity to read a briefing form regarding the evaluation. This form should inform the participants what they will be doing, how they will be compensated, how their information will be used and what the risks to them, if any, are expected. This form should not provide detailed information about what the evaluation is attempting to uncover, as that may influence the participant. Finally, the participant should be informed that they may leave the evaluation at any point.

When the participant begins the tasks, the evaluator should record any issues they may encounter. The participant should be encouraged to voice their thoughts about what they are doing and why they are doing it, and in particular what problems they are encountering, in what is termed a "think-aloud protocol". This protocol will allow the evaluator to determine when problems occur, and provide an opportunity for questions to be asked. One possible way to record errors encountered is with a description of the magnitude of the problem encountered as per Nielsen's ratings (Nielsen & Mack, 1994):

- **Cosmetic:** a small problem that does not hinder the task
- **Minor:** a small problem that hinders the task, but the participant can continue
- **Major:** a large problem that hinders the task and the participant has difficulty recovering, but could complete the task if needed
- **Catastrophic:** a large problem that hinders the task to the point that the partici-

pant would give up if it was encountered in the real world

When the tasks are completed, the participant should be provided with a debriefing form. This form should provide more detail about what the participant has completed and provide them with contact information if they have any further questions.

Summarize Results

It is beyond the scope of this chapter to discuss detailed techniques for qualitative and quantitative data analysis. However, the collection of comments and the magnitude rankings from the participants can be summarized to provide feedback to the web engineering team. This summarization should provide:

- An overall description of what types of participants were recruited,
- A description of the tasks undertaken by the evaluation team,
- A general statement about the web application in terms of what was evaluated (e.g. accessibility, usability etc.),
- A detailed list of problems encountered by participants, with magnitude ratings averaged.

With this information the web engineering team can move into revision of their web application.

FUTURE TRENDS: INTEGRATING EVALUATION

The rapid growth of the number of web applications produced has motivated the specification of a number of approaches to make the development of such systems more disciplined. In the context of the Software Engineering discipline, the different aspects attributed to the development of web applications and websites have motivated the establishment of a special set of techniques and methods, which are the body of the Web Engineering discipline (Ginige & Murugesan, 2001). However, despite this rapid growth, evaluation of a website or web application is seldom mentioned as a concern.

In this section, the open question regarding where accessibility evaluation fits in existing Web Engineering and Software Engineering approaches is explored. Existing approaches are analysed in regards to their features, their proposed phases and the methodologies that are typically applied. Currently, there are no major case studies available discussing the success of integrating accessibility practices into any of the processes mentioned in this section. As such, the authors do not prescribe adopting any particular approach discussed in this section and instead opt to present possible places where accessibility could be integrated into each approach.

Web Engineering Processes

According to Deshpande *et al.* (2002), Web Engineering is regarded as "the systematic, structured and quantifiable application of methodological proposals to the development, evaluation and maintenance of web applications". Accordingly, a Web Engineering approach or method should provide basis for a solid process from requirements to evaluation for websites and web applications.

As a basis for this discussion, consider that Pressman (2005) defines that Web Engineering processes should involve activities covering Formulation, Planning, Analysis, Design (Architecture, Navigation and Interface), Generation, Testing and Evaluation. Although many of the existing methods provide good resources for some of these tasks, they do not provide enough guidance for all activities involved in the development cycle (Escalona *et al.*, 2007) (Domingues *et al.*, 2008), and the activities related to testing and evaluation are particularly pointed out as being

poorly addressed by current methods (Domingues *et al.*, 2008).

Early Web Engineering methods were mainly concerned with modelling issues. For example, the HDM (Hypermedia Design Model) (Garzotto *et al.*, 1993) presented an approach for modelling hypermedia applications by extending the entity-relationship model from database design. According to an analysis performed by Escalona *et al.* (2007), subsequent methods later extended methodological coverage to include implementation and page generation issues. These methods include: RMM (Relationship Management Method) (Isakowitz et. al, 1995), OOHDM (Object Oriented Hypermedia Design Method) (Schwabe & Rossi, 1998) and the WSDM (Website Design Method) (Troyer & Leune, 1998).

Besides the strong emphasis on modelling, the evolution of new methods has brought the inclusion of new tools and methods of the Web Engineering development life cycle. Languages such as WebML (Web Modelling Language) (Ceri *et al.*, 2000) and methods like OO-H (Object-Oriented Hypermedia Method) (Gómez *et al.*, 2001), have also included activities related to analysis and refinement of web application architectures. The methods W2000 (Baresi et. al, 2001) and UWE (UML-Based Web Engineering) (Koch, 2001) each include activities for analysis, design and implementation and also provide resources to help the activities for requirements elicitation.

However, while many of the above methods cover the development aspects of Pressman's description, they still fail to provide a solid foundation on which to perform testing and evaluation. Even the methods that do provide some sort of high-level guidance for testing are restricted to code testing issues (Domingues et. al, 2008). Evaluation with users and evaluation of accessibility issues seems to be absent from most of the methods. As a result, the current Web Engineering methodologies will need substantial extension to encompass and address accessible development.

Figure 5. An idealized version of the UP lifecycle including the 6 disciplines of business modeling, requirements, analysis and design, implementation, test and deployment

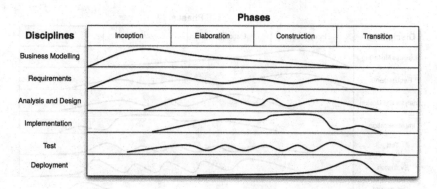

Evaluation in Unified Processes for Web Engineering

For comparison to Web Engineering processes, the Unified Processes (UP) are examined here regarding their potential to have accessibility evaluations integrated into them.

Unified Processes provide a structure for managing both the risks incurred by a web engineering project and for addressing key issues such as requirements and testing. UPs can be adopted either formally through the use of particular techniques such as Use Cases and UML, as recommended by the Rational Unified Process (RUP) (Kruchten, 2003), or through a set of development principles as is seen in the Open Unified Process (OpenUP) initiatives of the open source development community (Borg *et al.*, 2007).

Unified Processes focus on disciplines that consist of three key components: roles, work products and tasks. The roles that can be adopted within a project are key to understanding responsibility and accountability for particular tasks. Work products are the outputs of any particular task. There are several standard disciplines that are adopted in UP: business modeling, requirements, analysis and design, implementation, testing (code verification) all as core tasks, and deployment, management

and maintenance practices as additional tasks (Kroll & Kruchten, 2003).

Figure 5 depicts an idealized version of UP (adapted from Kruchten, 2003). Each track in the diagram represents the amount of team activity along the vertical axis, with one track per discipline. The horizontal axis represents the timeline of a project, with a website or web application moving four different phases. Inception focuses on the gathering and analysis of basic business case and capability that will be provided by the web application. Elaboration allows designers and developers to move initial designs and use cases into more detailed designs and prototypes. Construction focuses on the building of complex, hi-fidelity prototypes and then Transition moves the web application into a production ready state for deployment.

One approach to including accessibility evaluations would be to include accessibility professionals on the team who provide detailed evaluation reports as their only work products. These team members would review the outputs of other disciplines for accessibility concerns. This approach is depicted in Figure 6, where evaluation could be considered its own discipline, which has a flow similar to testing, where after initial elaboration there is a crucial evaluation of prototypes before entering into major implemen-

Figure 6. An idealized version of UP where evaluation has been added as a discipline to be managed in the project

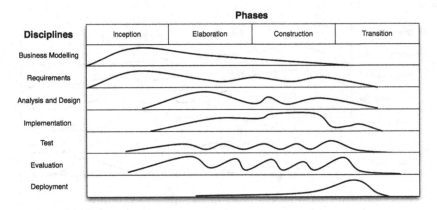

tation details. An iteration of construction would be followed by a period of code verification and then accessibility evaluation. Finally, it would be necessary to have a large integrated user evaluation just before deploying the software to end users, in the first transition period. This project configuration matches well with the existing work in the literature on the Usability Engineering Lifecycle where emphasis is placed on design and evaluation of prototypes in iterative stages (Nielsen & Mack, 1994; Lif & Goransson, 2007).

In contrast, if each team member is familiar with accessibility evaluation practices, evaluations could be integrated into each of the design and implementation iterations. An idealization of this situation is presented in Figure 7. As can be seen, concerns about accessibility could also be integrated into the requirements phase, with careful review of the users and their needs and preferences being considered early in the project.

While this chapter focuses on primarily accessibility evaluation in the unified processes, it is perfectly reasonable that evaluation of other aspects such as usability or user experience could be integrated in a similar way to the two described project configurations.

Figure 7. An idealized version of evaluation being included across disciplines in a project

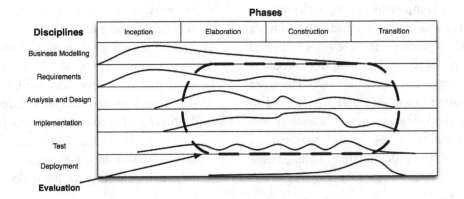

Evaluation in Agile Processes for Web Engineering

In comparison to the heavy-weight processes associated with UP, the proponents of Agile Processes (AP) to software emphasize the need for flexibility when working in environments with volatile requirements. With the emphasis largely being on the process for producing software artifacts, agility has come to be embraced by people in various sectors, including business processes, management and production lines. All of these areas have taken on board aspects of the Agile Manifesto (Beck *et al.*, 2001), usually focusing on the fast turn around of prototypes and End-User engagement. One critical point is that the focus of AP is on the products being produced, not the process and roles that produce them.

Web engineering has long discussed the importance of such flexibility due to the very nature of web applications. With the need to flexibly build the software, infrastructure, information structure and the actual content, often centered on the needs of a particular business or domain model, makes web engineering projects perfect candidates for an AP (McDonald & Welland, 2004). Indeed, McDonald and Welland (2004) provide an overview of different Agile approaches in commercial web engineering systems, in which they identified 7 key characteristics that must be met by Agile Web Engineering (AWE) processes. Among these key characteristics, are:

- Evaluation with End-Users
- Rigorous validation testing against requirements

While the former encompasses the broader functional aspects of consulting End-Users on domain specific issues, such as business rules, there are examples where this includes evaluation of the usability aspect (Haire *et al.*, 2001). As such, the case certainly can be made that accessibility evaluation can be integrated seamlessly into AP.

Further, the second characteristic emphasizes the importance of validation of user requirements for web applications. For accessibility to properly integrated into development approaches, it is essential that it become a fundamental aspect of requirements work, focusing on the needs of the users, and then on the systems to address them.

User-Centred Design (UCD) methodologies in AP have been introduced in several different places by usability researchers and practitioners with no overarching vision of where these methodologies fit into AP emerging. Beyer *et al.* describe several different challenges with UCD in AP (Beyer *et al.*, 2004) and indirectly suggest that an ethnographic observation of users in context can provide much needed insights into user needs. Memmel *et al.* (2007) demonstrate in their work how AP can incorporate into Universal Access Design for older adults with rapid prototyping. Similarly, Meszaros and Aston (2006) provide an experience report on incorporating UCD and in particular evaluations through paper prototyping into an AP. Further work is presented regarding requirements acquisition for UCD in the paper by Duchting *et al.* (2007) where they observe neither Extreme Programming or Scrum based processes have sufficient focus on evaluation of usability principles. However, they also point to these AP as having the opportunity of exploiting the close ties between the development and design activities for purposes of delivering a high-quality, evaluated product. In the following, a selection of APs are presented with an examination of their key concepts and a discussion of how these concepts can be leveraged for evaluation of web applications.

Feature Driven Development (FDD) (Palmer & Felsing, 2002) presents a process that organizes development of web (and other) applications by feature. It concentrates on the identification of key features, and then the team focuses on designing and building a particular feature (or small set of features). FDD is unique in agile approaches in that it has a comprehensive management focus at the beginning of the process that allows designers and developers to focus on particular aspects of the software that is of particular concern. One challenge for accessibility proponents, much like the challenges faced by usability proponents, is to move accessibility requirements to be one of these chief concerns (Ambler, 2008).

The focus of FDD on fast turnaround teams for individual features provides a unique synergy with the above evaluation methodology in that accessibility can be addressed in each step in the FDD model for each individual feature. This provides for the opportunity to isolate particular pieces of an application and perform accessibility evaluations on it before integration. This results in a much smaller set of accessibility issues at integration time with, in theory, only transitions between features needing to be checked for accessibility requirements. All of the types of accessibility evaluations can rigorously applied to each feature in the FDD process, with the advantage that user evaluations for individual features will lessen the time commitment for each individual participant at any given time. However, due to the need to conduct user evaluations on the smaller components and then, most importantly, at integration, there are challenges that must be addressed in recruitment and retention of users for testing.

The Dynamic Systems Development Method (DSDM) being one of the oldest of the APs has some of the highest uptake in industry, and thus has some of the best understood processes (Stapleton, 2003). With DSDM, the project begins with an understanding of the domain in which the application is to be built, with a focus on understanding the feasibility and business cases for the application being developed. DSDM provides three broad states that a prototype moves through. The Functional Model Iteration focuses on the rapid development of prototypes for review, after which the prototype can evolve in the Design and Build state in which the prototype is evaluated iteratively by users. Finally, in the Implementation state the prototype is transferred from development to production, with users being trained in its operation.

Certainly DSDM contains many of the broad aspects of evaluation model above, and the basic principles of understanding the needs of the users, conducting prototype design development and then evaluation. Indeed, it perhaps embodies best the ideals behind user involvement and evaluation, introducing users and their input in the process from the beginning. Indeed, this is supported by the large number of developers who concern themselves with usability aspects of their software (Bygstad *et al.*, 2007).

For purposes of accessibility testing, there are more difficult challenges that need to be managed in comparison to FDD. In DSDM, the entire system is being developed in a sequence of small, fast iterations. This results in relying more heavily on automated and expert testing as having users test an entire large application at each iteration is likely infeasible.

Extreme Programming (XP) (Beck, 2000) is inherently centered on the development of software (and thus web) artifacts. A combination of practices, such as pair programming, refactoring and the use of metaphors for development are used in short cycles of iterative development. With XP being one of the most well-known APs it is natural to ask: where in this development centric process the evaluation model presented fit?

There are several practices within XP that could be exploited for purposes of including all aspects of the evaluation methodology above. Certainly, there is a case to be made that users are represented and understood through the use of user written *User Stories* detailing how the application should behave in real-world environments. Much like FDD, these User Stories drive the development, allowing users and develops to select functionality that will be developed in the next iteration of development. Further, user stories mesh nicely with many well-known scenario based design techniques used in UCD (Wolkerstorfer *et al.*, 2008). The engineering systems with minimal design, foregoing the inclusion of future extension, and a practice of refactoring to keep functionality sets relatively small and fit-to-purpose certainly indicate that evaluation of prototypes with a critical eye is already being done in this AP. Finally, the necessity of keeping short releases of small chunks of functionality seems to blend the advantages of FDD with some of the process advantages of DSDM for purposes of evaluation.

When looking at accessibility, it is clear that automated testing is an option for XP teams. With the heavy emphasis in XP that is placed on the output of working code, it is natural, and indeed within the philosophy of many APs, for developers to use automated tools to produce reports on accessibility. However, the responsibility of interpretation of these reports and the impact of such analysis is unclear as the role responsible for such analysis is not clear in XP. Certainly there are places where expert evaluation and user evaluation of accessibility could be integrated into an XP environment, but whether this is in scope of XP, where the focus is code artifacts, also remains unclear. Finally, the key XP practice of adopting coding standards for a given application is very attractive in web application development; however, for accessibility professionals this raises the concern of developers slavishly following coding guidelines for conformance, which is insufficient for access, as opposed to being focused on the outcomes for the user.

When looking at Agile Processes, there is a lot of potential for integrating accessibility and other types of UCD criteria into the processes. Indeed, there is a great deal of interest from the UCD community in the increased presence of users and their needs into APs. However, there are several reports of challenges that have yet to be addressed in agile environments. There have been experience reports of developer dominance, where developers override the judgment and expertise of other types of analysts (Gerber *et al.*, 2007). Given the challenges already faced in getting accessibility concerns into development environments, this is very concerning. Further, there are reports of coding standards being poorly adopted, which is

of concern when considering the technical accessibility of a website (Tingling & Saeed, 2007). Finally, the role of interface design and evaluation in APs is relatively poorly understood, with only a moderate amount of work investigating these crucial aspects of software design (Ferreira *et al.*, 2007; Lee, 2007; Obendorf & Finck, 2008; Wolkerstorfer *et al.*, 2008).

CONCLUSION

In this chapter, the authors have presented an overview of accessibility evaluation and its role in the web engineering process.

It has presented a view of accessibility from the point of view of the users and their goals, and what challenges they are presented with when interacting with web applications. These challenges were related to the technologies through which the user interacts with as well as the types of content present in web applications. A case has been made that users that encounter accessibility issues on websites, be they people with disabilities or older adults, represent a large market that is going to become more important in the knowledge economy.

This chapter has presented the major types of accessibility evaluation that are available to web designers/developers. The evaluation techniques, whether they involve expert inspections, automated evaluation tools or users evaluations all provide the opportunity to identify accessibility issues that may arise after a website or web application is deployed.

Finally, the chapter presented an analysis of the current state of web engineering and software engineering processes regarding evaluation. This analysis has produced a list of opportunities for web engineers as to how to integrate accessibility evaluations into existing processes in order to ensure that web pages, websites and web applications are created that everyone can use, independent of user preferences for access.

REFERENCES

Agarwal, R., & Venkatesh, V. (2002). Assessing a Firm's Web Presence: A Heuristic Evaluation Procedure for the Measurement of Usability. *Information Systems Research, 13*(2), 168–186. doi:10.1287/isre.13.2.168.84

Ambler, S. W. (2008). Tailoring Usability into Agile Software Development Projects. In *Maturing Usability* (pp. 75-95). Berlin: Springer.

Baresi, L., Garzotto, F., & Paolini, P. (2001). Extending UML for modeling Web applications. In *Proceedings of the 34th Annual Hawaii International Conference on System Sciences* (pp. 1285-1294).

Beck, K. (2000). *Extreme Programming Explained--Embrace Change*. Reading, MA: Addison-Wesley.

Beck, K., Beedle, M., van Bennekum, A., Cockburn, A., & Cunningham, W. (2001). *Manifesto for agile software development: Agile Manifesto Website*. Retrieved 01/2009 from http://agile-manifesto.org/

Becker, S. A. (2002). An Exploratory Study on Web Usability and the Internationalizational of US E-Businesses. *Journal of Electronic Commerce Research, 3*(4), 265–278.

Benavídez, C., Fuertes, J. L., Gutiérrez, E., & Martínez, L. (2006). Semi-Automatic Evaluation of Web Accessibility with HERA 2.0. In *Proceedings of the 10th International Conference on Computers Helping People with Special Needs (ICCHP 2006)* (pp. 199-106). Berlin: Springer.

Beyer, H., Holtzblatt, K., & Baker, L. (2004). An Agile Customer-Centered Method: Rapid Contextual Design. In *Extreme Programming and Agile Methods - XP/Agile Universe 2004. Proceedings,* (pp. 50-59). Berlin: Springer.

Borg, A., Sandahl, K., & Patel, M. (2007). Extending the OpenUP/Basic Requirements Discipline to Specify Capacity Requirements. In *15th IEEE Internationalm, Requirements Engineering Conference, 2007 (RE '07), Proceedings*. Washington, DC: IEEE.

Brajnik, G. (2004). Comparing accessibility evaluation tools: a method for tool effectiveness. *Univers. Access Inf. Soc., 3*(3), 252–263. doi:10.1007/s10209-004-0105-y

Brajnik, G. (2006). Web Accessibility Testing: When the Method Is the Culprit. In *Proceedings of 10th International Conference on Computers Helping People with Special Needs* (pp. 156-163). Berlin: Springer.

Brajnik, G. (2008). A comparative test of web accessibility evaluation methods. In *Assets '08: Proceedings of the 10th international ACM SIGACCESS conference on Computers and accessibility* (pp. 113-120). Berlin: ACM.

Bygstad, B., Ghinea, G., & Brevik, E. (2007). Systems Development Methods and Usability in Norway: An Industrial Perspective. In *Usability and Internationalization. HCI and Culture. Proceedings,* (pp. 258-266). Berlin: Springer.

Caldwell, B., Cooper, M., Reid, L. G., & Vanderheiden, G. (2008). *Web content accessibility guidelines 2.0*: World Wide Web Consortium. Retrieved June, 2009 from http://www.w3.org/TR/ WCAG20/

Ceri, S., Fraternali, P., & Bongio, A. (2000). Web Modeling Language (WebML): a modeling language for designing Web sites. *Computer Networks, 33*(1-6), 137 - 157.

Chisholm, W., Vanderheiden, G., & Jacobs, I. (1999). *Web content accessibility guidelines 1.0: World Wide Web Consortium*. Retrieved June, 2009 from http://www.w3.org/ TR/ WCAG10/

Choi, Y. S., Yi, J. S., Law, C. M., & Jacko, J. A. (2006). Are universal design resources designed for designers? In *Assets '06: Proceedings of the 8th international ACM SIGACCESS conference on Computers and accessibility* (pp. 87-94). New York: ACM.

Cluster, W. A. B. (2007). *Unified Web Evaluation Methodology (UWEM 1.2)*. Retrieved 01/2009 from www.w3c.org

Deshpande, Y., Murugesan, S., Ginige, A., Hansen, S., Schwabe, D., & Gaedke, M. (2002). Web Engineering. *Journal of Web Engineering, 1*(1), 3–17.

Disability Rights Commission. (2004). *The Web: access and inclusion for disabled people*. London: The Stationery Office.

Dix, A., Finlay, J. E., Abowd, G. D., & Beale, R. (2003). *Human-Computer Interaction* (3rd ed.). Upper Saddle River, NJ: Prentice Hall.

Domingues, A. L. S., Bianchini, S. L., Re, R., & Ferrari, R. G. (2008). A Comparison Study of Web Development Methods. In *Proceedings of the 34th Latin-American Conference on Informatics* (pp. 10).

Düchting, M., Zimmermann, D., & Nebe, K. (2007). Incorporating User Centered Requirement Engineering into Agile Software Development. In *Human-Computer Interaction. Interaction Design and Usability. Proceedings.* (pp. 58-67). Springer.

Escalona, M. J., & Torres, J., Mejĺas, M., GutiÈrrez, J. J., & Villadiego, D. (2007). The treatment of navigation in web engineering. *Advances in Engineering Software, 38*(4), 267–282. doi:10.1016/j.advengsoft.2006.07.006

Fels, D. I., Richards, J., Hardman, J., Soudian, S., & Silverman, C. (2004). American sign language of the web. In *CHI '04 Extended Abstracts on Human Factors in Computing Systems* CHI '04 (pp. 1111-1114). New York: ACM.

Ferreira, J., Noble, J., & Biddle, R. (2007). Agile Development Iterations and UI Design. In *Proceedings AGILE Conference,* (pp. 50-58). Washington, DC: IEEE.

Freire, A. P., Goularte, R., & de Mattos Fortes, R. P. (2007). Techniques for developing more accessible web applications: a survey towards a process classification. In *SIGDOC '07: Proceedings of the 25th annual ACM international conference on Design of communication* (pp. 162-169). New York: ACM.

Freire, A. P., Russo, C. M., & Fortes, R. P. M. (2008). A survey on the accessibility awareness of people involved in web development projects in Brazil. In *W4A '08: Proceedings of the 2008 international cross-disciplinary conference on Web accessibility (W4A)* (pp. 87-96). New York: ACM.

Garzotto, F., Paolini, P., & Schwabe, D. (1993). HDM--a model-based approach to hypertext application design. *ACM Transactions on Information Systems, 11*(1), 1–26. doi:10.1145/151480.151483

Gerber, A., Van Der Merwe, A., & Alberts, R. (2007). Practical implications of rapid development methodologies. In *Proceedings Computer Science and Information Technology Education Conference.*

Ginige, A., & Murugesan, S. (2001). Web engineering: an introduction. *Multimedia, IEEE, 8*(1), 14–18. doi:10.1109/93.923949

Ginige, A., & Murugesan, S. (2001). Guest Editors' Introduction: Web Engineering - An Introduction. *IEEE MultiMedia, 8*(1), 14–18. doi:10.1109/93.923949

Gómez, J., Cachero, C., & Pastor, O. (2001). Conceptual Modeling of Device-Independent Web Applications. *IEEE MultiMedia, 8*(2), 26–39. doi:10.1109/93.917969

Haire, B., Henderson-Sellers, B., & D., a. L. (2001). Supporting web development in the OPEN process: additional tasks. In *Proceedings COMPSAC'2001: International Computer Software and Applications Conference.* New York: ACM.

Harrison, C., & H., P. (2006). Impact of usability and accessibility problems in e-commerce and e-government websites. In *Proceedings HCI 2006.* (Vol. 1). London: British Computer Society.

Hesse, W. (2003). Dinosaur meets Archaeopteryx? or: Is there an alternative for Rational's Unified Process? *Software and Systems Modeling, Springer, 2*(4), 240–247. doi:10.1007/s10270-003-0033-y

Isakowitz, T. a., Stohr, E. A., & Balasubramanian, P. (1995). RMM: a methodology for structured hypermedia design. *Communications of the ACM, 38*(8), 34–44. doi:10.1145/208344.208346

Ivory, M. Y. (2003). *Automated Web Site Evaluation: Researchers and Practitioners Perspectives.* Amsterdam: Kluwer Academic Publishers.

Ivory, M. Y., & Hearst, M. A. (2001). The state of the art in automating usability evaluation of user interfaces. *ACM Computing Surveys, 33*(4), 470–516. doi:10.1145/503112.503114

Kennaugh, P., & Petrie, H. (2006). *Enhanced Access to Television (EAT): humanITy.*

Koch, N. (2001). *Software engineering for adaptive hypermedia applications.* Munich, Germany: Uni-Druck Publishing Company.

Koch, N., & Kraus, A. (2003). Towards a Common Metamodel for the Development of Web Applications. In *Web Engineering* (pp. 419-422). Berlin: Springer.

Kroll, P., & Kruchten, P. (2003). *The Rational Unified Process Made Easy: A Practitioner's Guide to the RUP.* Reading, MA: Addison-Wesley.

Kruchten, P. (2003). *The Rational Unified Process: An Introduction.* Reading, MA: Addison-Wesley.

Kurniawan, S. H. (2003). Aging. In *Web Accessibility: A foundation for research* (pp.47-58). Berlin: Springer

Lazar, J., Dudley-Sponaugle, A., & Greenidge, K. (2004). Improving Web Accessibility: A Study of Webmaster Perceptions. *Computers in Human Behavior, 20*(2), 269–288. doi:10.1016/j.chb.2003.10.018

Lee, J. C., & McCrickard, D. S. (2007). Towards Extreme(ly) Usable Software: Exploring Tensions Between Usability and Agile Software Development. In *Proceedings AGILE Conference,* (pp. 59-71). Berlin: IEEE.

Lif, M., & Goransson, B. (2007). Usability Design: A New Rational Unified Process Discipline. In *Proceedings Human-Computer Interaction; INTERACT 2007,* (pp. 714-715). New York: ACM.

Mariage, C., & Vanderdonckt, J. (2005). Creating Contextualised Usability Guides for Web Sites Design and Evaluation. *Computer-Aided Design of User Interfaces, IV,* 147–158. doi:10.1007/1-4020-3304-4_12

Martens, A. (2003). Usability of Web Services. *International Conference on Web Information Systems Engineering Workshops,* (pp. 182-190). Washington, DC: IEEE.

McDonald, A., & Welland, R. (2004). Evaluation of Commercial Web Engineering Processes. In *Web Engineering* (pp. 166-170). Berlin: Springer.

Memmel, T., Reiterer, H., & Holzinger, A. (2007). Agile Methods and Visual Specification in Software Development: A Chance to Ensure Universal Access. In *Proceedings of Universal Access in Human Computer Interaction Coping with Diversity.* (pp. 453-462). Berlin: Springer.

Meszaros, G., & Aston, J. (2006). Adding usability testing to an agile project. In *Proceedings of Agile Conference, 2006*. Washington, DC: IEEE.

Mohamad, Y., Stegemann, D., Koch, J., & Velasco, C. A. (2004). imergo: Supporting Accessibility and Web Standards to Meet the Needs of the Industry via Process-Oriented Software Tools. In *Proceedings of the 9th International Conference on Computers Helping People With Special Needs (ICCHP 2004)*, (pp. 310-316). Berlin: Springer.

Monk, A., Wright, P., Haber, J., & Davenport, L. (1993). *Improving your human-computer interface: a practical technique*. Bath, UK: Redwood Books.

Motschnig-Pitrik, R. (2002). Employing the Unified Process for Developing a Web-Based Application - A Case-Study. In *Practical Aspects of Knowledge Management: 4th International Conference, PAKM 2002 Vienna, Austria, December 2-3, 2002, Proceedings*, (pp. 97-113). Berlin: Springer.

Ncube, C., Lockerbie, J., & Maiden, N. A. M. (2007). Automatically Generating Requirements from \it * Models: Experiences with a Complex Airport Operations System. In *Proceedings REFSQ*, (pp. 33-47).

Nielsen, J., & Mack, R. (1994). Usability Inspection Methods (pp. 448p). New York, NY.

Obendorf, H., & Finck, M. (2008). Scenario-based usability engineering techniques in agile development processes. In *CHI '08: CHI '08 extended abstracts on Human factors in computing systems* (pp. 2159-2166). New York: ACM.

Paddison, C., & Englefield, P. (2004). Applying heuristics to accessibility inspections. *Interacting with Computers, 16*(3), 507–521. doi:10.1016/j.intcom.2004.04.007

Palmer, J. W. (2002). Web site usability, design, and performance metrics. *Information Systems Research, 13*(2), 151–167. doi:10.1287/isre.13.2.151.88

Palmer, S. R., & Felsing, J. M. (2002). *A Practical Guide to Feature-Driven Development*. Upper Saddle River, NJ: Prentice Hall PTR.

Petrie, H., Hamilton, F., King, N., & Pavan, P. (2006). Remote usability evaluations with disabled people. In *CHI '06: Proceedings of the SIGCHI conference on Human Factors in computing systems* (pp. 1133-1141). New York: ACM.

Petrie, H., & Kheir, O. (2007). The relationship between accessibility and usability of websites. In *CHI '07: Proceedings of the SIGCHI conference on Human factors in computing systems* (pp. 397-406). New York: ACM.

Petrie, H., King, N., & Hamilton, F. (2005). *Accessibility of museum, library and archive websites: the MLA audit*. Retrieved 01/2009 from http://www.mla.gov.uk/ webdav/ harmonise?Page/ @id=73&Document/ @id=23090&Section%5B@stateId_eq _left_hand_root %5D/ @id=4302

Petrie, H., Weber, G., & Fisher, W. (2005). Personalization, interaction and navigation in rich multimedia documents for print disabled users. In *IBM Systems Journal*. Armonk NY: IBM.

Pressman, R. (2006). *Software Engineering: A Practitioner's Approach* (6th ed.). New York: McGraw-Hill.

San Murugesan, Y. D., Hansen, S., & Ginige, A. (2001). Web Engineering: A New Discipline for Development of Web-Based Systems. In *Web Engineering Managing Diversity and Complexity of Web Application Development*, (LNCS Vol. 2016, pp. 3-13). Berlin: Springer.

Schwabe, D., & Rossi, G. (1998). An object oriented approach to web-based applications design. *Theory and Practice of Object Systems, 4*(4), 207–225. doi:10.1002/(SICI)1096-9942(1998)4:4<207::AID-TAPO2>3.0.CO;2-2

Shneiderman, B. (1998). *Designing the User Interface*. Reading, MA: Addison-Wesley.

Shneiderman, B. (2000). Universal usability. *Communications of the ACM, 43*(5), 85–91. doi:10.1145/332833.332843

Shneiderman, B. (2003). Promoting universal usability with multi-layer interface design. In *Proceedings of the 2003 Conference on Universal Usability (CUU 2003)*. New York: ACM.

Soares, K., & Furtado, E. (2003). RUPi - A Unified Process that Integrates Human-Computer Interaction and Software Engineering. In *Workshop Bridging the Gap Between Software-Engineering and Human-Computer Interaction at ICSE 2003, Proceedings*, (pp. 41-48).

Sousa, K., & Furtado, E. (2005). A Unified Process Supported by a Framework for the Semi-Automatic Generation of Multi-Context UIs. In *12th International Workshop on Design, Proceedings*.

Sousa, K., Mendonça, H., & Vanderdonckt, J. (2007). Towards Method Engineering of Model-Driven User Interface Development. In *Task Models and Diagrams for User Interface Design* (pp. 112-125). Berlin: Springer.

Stanton, N. A., Salmon, P. M., Walker, G. H., Baber, C., & Jenkins, D. P. (2005). *Human Factors Methods: A Practical Guide for Engineering and Design*. London: Ashgate.

Stapleton, J. (2003). *DSDM: Business Focused Development* (2nd ed.). Harlow, UK.: Addison-Wesley.

Thatcher, J., Waddell, C. D., Henry, S. L., Swierenga, S., Urban, M. D., Burks, M., et al. (2003). *Constructing accessible web sites*. San Francisco: glasshaus.

Tingling, P., & Saeed, A. (2007). Extreme Programming in Action: A Longitudinal Case Study. In *Human-Computer Interaction. Interaction Design and Usability, Proceedings*, (pp. 242-251).

Troyer, O. M. F. D., & Leune, C. J. (1998). WSDM: a user centered design method for Web sites. *Computer Networks and ISDN Systems, 30*(1-7), 85 - 94.

Watanabe, T. (2007). Experimental evaluation of usability and accessibility of heading elements. In *Proceedings of International Cross-Disciplinary Conference on Web Accessibility (W4A)* (pp. 157-164). New York: ACM Press.

Wolkerstorfer, P., Tscheligi, M., Sefelin, R., Milchrahm, H., Hussain, Z., Lechner, M., et al. (2008). Probing an agile usability process. In *CHI '08: Extended abstracts on Human factors in computing systems Proceedings*, (pp. 2151-2158). New York: ACM.

Yesilada, Y., Stevens, R., Goble, C. A., & Hussein, S. (2004). Rendering tables in audio: the interaction of structure and reading styles. In *Proceedings of the ACM SIGACCESS Conference on Computers and Accessibility (ASSETS)*, (pp. 16-23). Berlin: Springer.

ENDNOTES

[1] The authors acknowledge that even though the community may have taken on board the concept of usability it is often the case that usability is not achieved in websites.

[3] Screen readers are assistive technology software that transform text, controls and other aspects of the screen into audio.

4   The authors recommend the website http:// shouldiusetablesforlayout.com/ which has a discussion on this topic.

5   During preparation of this chapter the authors checked one UK mobile phone company website and found over 100 links on the home page.

6   These evaluations were completed using WCAG 1.0 guidelines.

7   Checkpoints in WCAG 1.0, Success Criteria in WCAG 2.0.

8   Available at http://wave.webaim.org, last access on June 1, 2009

9   http://www.sidar.org/hera/index.php.en, last access on June 1, 2009

10 The authors strive for keeping evaluations for each participant under 1 hour for the completion of all tasks. Experience has shown that beyond this will affect the concentration level of the participant.

11 Sadly, the authors have seen this particular error in several evaluation protocols that have already been completed testing with their users with no time data being recorded.

12 Comfortable within reason; some older books comment that participants should be offered a cigarette. The authors find a cup of tea is often sufficient.

This work was previously published in the International Journal of Information Technology and Web Engineering 4(4), edited by Ghazi I. Alkhatib, and Ernesto Damiani, pp. 54-77, copyright 2009 by IGI Publishing (an imprint of IGI Global).

Chapter 19
VoiceWeb:
Spoken Dialogue Interfaces and Usability

Dimitris Spiliotopoulos
University of Athens, Greece

Georgios Kouroupetroglou
University of Athens, Greece

Pepi Stavropoulou
University of Athens, Greece

ABSTRACT

This chapter presents the state-of-the-art in usability issues and methodologies for VoiceWeb interfaces. It undertakes a theoretical perspective to the usability methodology and provides a framework description for creating and testing usable content and applications for conversational interfaces. The methodologies and their uses are discussed as well as certain technical issues that are of specific importance for each type of system. Moreover, it discusses the hands-on approaches for applying usability methodologies in a spoken dialogue web application environment, including methodological and design issues, resource management, implementation using existing technologies for usability evaluation in several stages of the design and deployment. Finally, the challenging usability issues and parameters of the emerging advanced speech-enabled web interfaces are presented.

INTRODUCTION

Research in human-computer interaction aims at gaining an in depth understanding of the nature and principles governing the interactive communication between humans and machines, so that this understanding may be utilized in the development of universally usable and useful interfaces that address and adapt to user rather than system needs. In this line of thought enabling the use of various modalities like speech, gestures, haptics and graphical displays as input and output to such systems should enhance naturalness and ease of use.

At the same time, advances in web technologies over the past years have significantly increased the range of practical applications suited for such multimodal interaction. With high speed inter-

DOI: 10.4018/978-1-60960-523-0.ch019

net availability providing access to demanding multimodal services to all homes, a lot of people can now benefit from real-time services ranging from voice banking to online socialising and e-commerce. While most high-level services are provided solely through web pages and the traditional mouse and keyboard interface, there are, nevertheless, providers who have begun deploying spoken dialogue interfaces to new or existing web applications, acknowledging the fact that spoken dialogue is now widely considered to comprise a significant aspect of multimodal human-machine interaction and a means to increased customer satisfaction and naturalness of information access.

As with all human-computer interfaces, spoken dialogue interfaces are built with the target user in mind. Thorough requirements analysis and efficient design methodology are imperative in their case as well, especially if one takes into account the capabilities and limitations of current speech understanding technologies that should be compensated for in order to reach industrial standards. Not all technologies involved in the development process are of the same maturity and/or standardisation, and there is only a limited number of platforms available for building such systems. Thus, given the range, variability and complexity of the actual business cases it is obvious that the enabling technologies may produce working systems of variable usefulness due to design and/or implementation limitations. In addition, the use of a transient medium such as speech as the main input and output mode substantially differentiates spoken dialogue interfaces from traditional graphical user interfaces (GUIs) and web interfaces. Therefore, even though core usability principles may in general apply, there are particular to the development of speech based web interfaces considerations, principles, guidelines and techniques that simply render the direct translation of a non-speech user interface into a speech-based interface infelicitous. Indeed spoken dialogue far more enhances naturalness in comparison to using forms and buttons on a traditional

web interface. However, is the user satisfaction similarly improved? Does the performance of the resulting application meet the user requirements? How is usability ensured by design and verified by evaluation in a spoken dialogue web interface?

This chapter discusses the background of speech-based human-computer interaction and elaborates on the spoken dialog interfaces and the ways they differ from traditional web interfaces. It explores what usability is and how it is ensured for natural spoken dialogue interaction interface design and implementation. Finally, it presents key methodologies for usability testing of spoken dialogue web interfaces and discusses some of the challenges posed by the use of speech as the main modality in light of a speech-enabled complex application.

INTERACTING VIA SPOKEN DIALOGUE

The term usability has been used for many years to denote that an application or interface is *user friendly, easy-to-use*. It applies to most interfaces, including web interfaces and more importantly speech-based web interfaces, and it can be assessed on both full system level and individual modules and processes level. Therefore, in order to evaluate usability it is important to first understand the design requirements and the architecture of such interfaces. In the following sections we describe the main interaction frameworks that the architecture of most speech enabled applications falls into.

Multimodal Interaction Framework

A general framework (Larson et al., 2003) for the description and discussion of multimodal interaction on the web is developed by the World Wide Web Consortium (W3C). It describes the input and output modes that can be used in a relational abstractive architecture that includes all component types required for the interaction.

Figure 1. Non-speech based interface

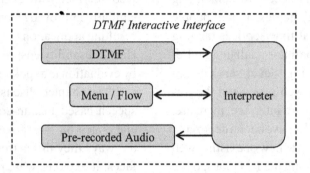

In such framework, an application may handle several requests through one or more input modes and respond accordingly. The user may use their input options to make a request for an archive retrieval, the system may respond by either requesting an explicit verification or present all options from the retrieval function, the user may specify or select their preference, allowing the application to present the information. More information on multimodal dialogue can be found in the latest literature (Kuppevelt et al., 2005; Wahlster, 2006).

Non-Speech Based Interaction: DTMF Interactive Systems

DTMF-based interactive systems are widely used for many applications, either web-based or telephone based. The main modalities used on such systems are audio, typing, and point-and-click. Speech is usually pre-recorded since all states of the dialogue are predetermined. The flow is state-based, usually a tree structure flow with options presented to the user at each step. Figure 1 shows the typical design of a non-speech interface where a menu-driven interactive system uses DTMF as input from a series of available choices and responds using predetermined recorded audio.

Such systems may alternatively present the information visually on a screen, thus using the visual modality as well, if the application and design permits.

Speech-Based Interaction Framework

The use of speech as input/output for interaction requires a spoken language oriented framework that adequately describes the system processes. W3C has defined the Speech Interface Framework to represent the typical components of a speech-enabled web application (Larson, 2000). A general depiction of a Spoken Dialogue Interface is shown in Figure 2.

A generic dialogue system comprises of the following basic modules:

- The Automatic Speech Recognition (ASR) module that converts user's spoken input into a text string. In addition, a DTMF rec-

Figure 2. Spoken dialog interface

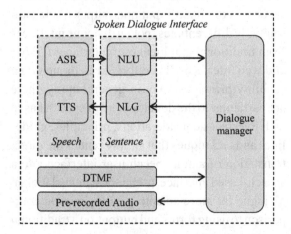

ognizer may be used to allow for DTMF input as well.

- The Natural Language Understanding (NLU) module that interprets the text string passed by the speech recognizer, assigning it an appropriate semantic value.

- The Dialogue Manager (DM), the core of the dialogue system and probably the most complicated component. It handles the conversation flow, evaluating the input and creating the output. In order to do that, it first evaluates and if necessary disambiguates the NLU input based on knowledge about general conversation principles as well as specific conversation context (dialog state and history, task, domain and user information), and then proceeds to create a specific dialog strategy in order to respond. Accordingly, it updates the state of the dialog (or belief state), formulates a dialog plan and employs the necessary dialog actions in order to fulfil the plan. The DM further accesses and utilizes all external knowledge resources, such as back-end databases and world knowledge.

- The Natural Language Generator (NLG) that formulates the actual system prompts, converting the DM output from abstract communicative acts into a well formed written utterance.

- The Text to Speech Synthesizer (TTS) that converts the text passed by the NLG to speech and/or audio. Natural Language Generators are typically coupled with TTS synthesizers but they can also be coupled with Concept-to-Speech (Pan & McKeown, 1997) or Document-to-Audio (Xydas et al., 2004) synthesizers that make use of appropriate linguistic markup and document meta-information in order to manipulate the utterance prosody and achieve increased naturalness and legibility of synthetic speech. Alternatively, in simpler systems, pre-recorded prompts may be used

instead. In that case the DM substitutes for the NLG and the TtS forming the output by registering all text prompts and correlating them with prerecorded audio files.

The technologies used for each component may differ depending on the type of the spoken dialogue interface at hand. Following McTear (2004) there are three basic types of spoken dialogue interfaces based on their design and dialogue management techniques involved:

i. State based directed dialogue systems, DTMF replacements
ii. Frame based directed dialogue systems
iii. Agent based, natural language mixed-initiative conversational systems

State-based directed dialogue systems are the very basic menu-driven interfaces where a static tree-based layout is presented to the user. The user may respond with yes/no answers or a limited set of in domain phrases/commands and navigate through the menu options. Such systems are not very efficient nor user-friendly, as the user has to spend precious time going through various levels of menus and listening to every option, in order to complete an often simple task. The main advantage is that they are very robust, posing low recognition and understanding challenges.

Frame-based systems use more advanced techniques in order to accommodate a more natural interaction with the user. The menus may be dynamic, have confirmation and disambiguation prompts as well as more elaborate vocabulary. Furthermore they can support limited mixed initiative dialogue strategies, as they can handle overspecification; that is the user can provide more items of information than those requested by the system at each dialogue turn. Still, user input needs to be properly restricted so that it can be handled by the grammar. On the upside, the small grammars keep the system relatively robust. Such systems are the most commonly used on the market today, providing an industry feasible trade-off between efficiency and robustness.

Agent-based systems are used for large scale applications. These systems are targeted for user satisfaction and naturalness. The users may respond to natural open ended "how may I help you" system prompts with equally natural replies. The utterances may be long, complex and exhibit great variety. The dialogue is dynamic and the demand for successful ASR and NLU is high. Statistical or machine learning methods may be used for interpretation or/and dialogue management as well. The dialogue management is primarily plan-based, the system creating tasks and plans of actions to fulfil. The users expect high-level natural interaction, a very important element to factorise in usability parameterisation.

More on speech-based systems and speech-based interaction enabling technologies can be found in respective textbooks (Dybkjær et al., 2007; Dybkjær & Minker, 2008; Tatham & Morton, 2005, Bernsen et al., 1998; Jurafsky & Martin, 2000; Huang et al., 2001; McTear, 2004).

Voice Browsers

In Robin & Larson (1999) a voice browser is broadly defined as "a device which interprets a voice markup language and generates a dialog with voice output and possibly other output modalities and/or voice input and possibly other modalities". Voice browsers are, by design, single-initiative (system or even user-directed) dialogue applications with a very limited domain and limited dialogue strategy, where dialogue management complexity is not a demand. They are meant to provide the means to browse information and navigate web documents. In our analysis, voice browsers can be considered as a subset of the spoken dialogue web interface description. In this respect, the usability requirements and evaluation methods for spoken dialog web interfaces discussed later in this chapter also apply to voice browsers.

SPOKEN DIALOGUE CHARACTERISTICS

Before entering the usability realm, it is important to first take a look at the inherent characteristics of speech and spoken dialogue in particular as the main interaction modality, since they affect principal design and usability aspects of speech based interfaces compared to non-speech web interfaces. As the underlying philosophy of the web interface designer is directly dependent on the mode of communication, the same service would be designed and implemented in much different way if the hosting platform was a traditional point-and-click web interface than a speech-based one.

First of all, the transient, ephemeral nature of speech along with human cognitive limitations place constraints on the speech output, the amount of information that may be presented to the user and the application structure in general. Non-speech web interfaces, on the other hand, utilize vision and space, and can present a large amount of information that can be easily and quickly processed by the user. Visual menus, which exploit recognition rather than recall, may include up to ten choices per level (Galitz, 2007), while in the case of spoken menus a breadth of three or four information items is recommended (Cohen et al, 2004). As a result, more steps and longer time are often required for speech-based interface users to complete their task. Nor navigating these menus is such a simple task when vision, space and feedback on navigation history are not available. Thus, it comes as no surprise that it is traditional web interfaces – as opposed to speech based ones – that are so strongly menu oriented and information rich. While menus and lists may be a very efficient and useful tool for the former, menu navigation in the case of the latter may result in a significant decrease in efficiency and user satisfaction.

In addition, complex prototypically visual structures such as data tables or nested bulletin are particularly difficult to effectively communicate through speech. Prosody manipulation and use of earcons can improve the "intelligent" acoustic rendition of such structures, as it has been shown by Spiliotopoulos et al (2009a).

Prosody in general is a significant dimension of spoken language that can be utilized to convey discourse and information structure, turn taking protocol, speech act type or even emotions. Final lowering of the fundamental frequency (f0) of the utterance may denote declaration instead of question, high f0 boundaries have been characterized as turn yielding, increase in duration often correlates with emphasis, while rapid changes in intensity may suggest anger. As a result, when prosody is properly manipulated, processing speed increases, comprehension is facilitated and the interaction as a whole becomes more engaging.

Another aspect particularly important to spoken dialogue compared to non speech modalities is grounding. Grounding is the establishment of common ground among the interlocutors. The term refers to the goal and process of achieving mutual understanding within the dialogue and acknowledging this understanding, thus making the other participant confident of the progress made to fulfil the dialogue's goal. In traditional web interfaces the stable visual representation provides the user with the interaction context aiding memory and providing instant feedback on system's actions. Speech based interfaces, in contrast, lack the underlying visual cues and so the system needs to both acknowledge its understanding and remind the users of the interaction point they are at. Yankelovich et al (1995) note that users are often confused when the system does not explicitly acknowledge shared understanding.

Furthermore, several considerations should be addressed with regards to the technology behind speech based interfaces. When building a speech-based human-computer interaction system, certain basic modules must be present. The Dialogue Manager is responsible for the system behavior, control and strategy. The ASR and NLU recognize the spoken input and identify semantic values. The language generator and TtS or the prerecorded audio generator provides the system response. The performance of the particular modules is an indication of usability issues. The ASR accuracy and the lack of language understanding due to dysfluencies, out-of-grammar utterances or ambiguity hinder the spoken dialogue. Moreover, the lack of pragmatic competence of the dialogue manager (compared to the human brain) and the response generation modules sometimes overcomplicate the dialogue and frustrate the user. In the case of graphical interfaces, on the contrary, mouse or keypad input interpretation is more or less error free, and the rest of the components are missing.

Still there are significant advantages to the speech modality. Firstly, speech is an indispensable part of a design for all approach to user interfaces, providing an accessible alternative medium to a number of users such as people with print disability (people with partial or total vision loss, cognitive limitations or limited dexterity) or the elderly. Speech based interfaces can overcome the physical barriers that apply to graphical interfaces making it possible to browse the web, access information and use any application from any telephone anytime and anywhere. Speech is ideal for hands/eyes busy situations such as equipment repairing or driving, or as a browsing alternative on small mobile phone screens. As part of a multimodal interface, it provides users with additional control over the way they interact with the system and express their intent.

Moreover, for several tasks speech is the most efficient medium. People speak at least three times faster than they type (Karat et al., 1999), and multiple actions on a visual display can be performed with a single spoken command. Finally, speech is a more natural means of communication and the one that people are more experienced with. First we learn to talk, and then we learn to read, write or type. Speech based interfaces accommodate conversational behaviour learnt implicitly at a very young age. Graphical interfaces, on the other hand, often resort to use of arbitrary symbols that users are not familiarized with.

All the above considerations affect key usability parameters, some of which are particular to speech based interfaces. For example, low speech recognition and interpretation success rate considerably undermine the user experience (Kamm & Walker, 1997). Voice output quality, feedback adequacy and quick recovery from misrecognitions are only some of the usability aspects that are especially important for speech-based interfaces. Similarly, testing methodology issues may vary.

SPEECH-BASED INTERFACES AND USABILITY

As already mentioned, usability is a broad term that refers to various types of interfaces including graphical web interfaces and speech based web interfaces, denoting that the interface is u*ser-friendly*, *easy-to-use*. Usability is measured according to the attributes that describe it, as explained below (Rubin & Chisnell, 2008):

- Usefulness – measures the level of *task enablement* of the application. As a side result it determines the *will* of the user to actually use it for the purpose it was designed for.
- Efficiency – assesses the *speed, accuracy* and *completeness* of the tasks or a user's goal. This is particularly useful for evaluating an interface sub-system since the tasks may be broken down in order to evaluate each module separately.
- Effectiveness – quantifies the system *behaviour*. It is a user-centric measure that calculates whether the system behaves the way the users expect it to. It also rates the system according to the level of *effort* required by the user to achieve certain goals and respective *difficulty*.

- Learnability – it extends the effectiveness of the system or application by evaluating the user's effort required to do specific tasks over several repetitions or time for training and expertise. It is a key measure of user experience since most users expect to be able to use an interface effortlessly after a period of use.
- Satisfaction – it is a subjective set of parameters that the users are asked to estimate and rank. It encompasses the user overall *opinion* about an application based on whether the product meets their *needs* and performs *adequately*.
- Accessibility – in the strict sense, it is not part of the usability description. As a starting point, it is a totally different approach on system design. Accessibility is about access to content, information, and products by everyone, including people with disability. *Design-for-all* is a term that denotes that an application is designed in such way so that everyone can use it to full extent (Stephanidis, 2001). An accessible web site should be implemented according to specification in order to enable voice browsers to navigate through all available information. An accessible web interface should allow for everyone to use. A blind user, for instance, could use certain modalities for input but the system should never respond by non-accessibly visual content (Freitas & Kouroupetroglou, 2008). Accessibility is a very important and broad discipline with many design and implementation parameters. It can be thought as an extension of the aforementioned usability attributes to the universal user. Universal Accessibility (Stephanidis, 2009) strives to use most modalities in order to make the web content available to everyone. Speech and audio interfaces are used for improved accessibility (Fellbaum & Kouroupetroglou, 2008; Duarte & Carriço, 2008). For example,

spoken dialogue systems are considered as key technological factors for the universal accessibility strategies of public terminals, information kiosks and Automated Teller Machines (ATMs) (Kouroupetroglou, 2009). It is mentioned here for completeness; however, it is out of the scope of this chapter.

Interaction Design Lifecycle (Interfaces) and Usability

The basic interaction design process is epitomized by the main activities that are followed for almost every product. There are five activities in the lifecycle of a speech interface (Sharp et al., 2007):

- Requirements specification and initial planning
- Design
- Implementation and testing
- Deployment
- Evaluation

In terms of usability there are three key characteristics pertaining to user involvement in the interaction design process (Sharp et al., 2007):

- User involvement should take place throughout all five stages.
- The usability requirements, goals and evaluation parameters should be set at the start of the development
- Iteration through the four stages is inevitable and, therefore, should be included in the initial planning.

Figure 3 shows how usability generally integrates with the development of a speech-based dialogue interface.

As mentioned in a previous section, spoken dialogue interfaces may be of three basic types (repeated here for ease of presentation):

- State based directed dialog systems, DTMF replacements
- Frame based directed dialog systems
- Agent based, natural language mixed-initiative conversational systems

As each type differs with regards to the level of complexity and sophistication, it becomes clear that each type entails particular usability expectations, and is expected to excel in certain aspects. Table 1 illustrates how usability is taken

Figure 3. Typical interface lifecycle of a speech-based dialogue system

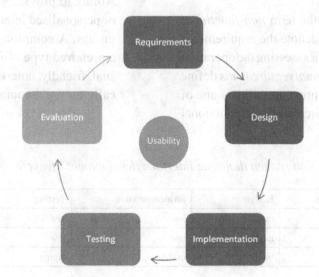

into account in each stage of the product lifecycle depending on the type of speech-based application (Spiliotopoulos & Kouroupetroglou, 2010).

The development of such applications is an iterative process, as mentioned before. Based on our-own experience from our involvement through the development and testing of a number of nationwide-size spoken dialogue business applications, we can declare that practitioners in industrial settings agree that usability parameters, as well as testing, are also part of the iterative process (Kouroupetroglou & Spiliotopoulos, 2009). Agent-based systems possess the highest potential for usability integration. In that respect, the remainder of this chapter refers mostly to agent-based systems and less to the other two. These days, such systems are the centre of the attention by researchers, developers and customers alike, focusing on advanced voice interaction and high user satisfaction. The use of natural voice response (regarding both wording and prosody) and the natural dialogue flow constitute the state-of-the-art in spoken dialogue interfaces. The web provides the means for the application deployment and the system-world communication, aiming to provide stability and vast amount of available information.

Typical Requirements for Real-Life Spoken Dialogue Interfaces

In systems engineering the term *non-functional requirements* is used to denote the requirements that specify the criteria for assessing the operation of a system, while *functional requirements* define the behaviour. In this context, usability is one of the major functional requirements. Non-functional requirements do not encompass usability per se, however they are effective constraints on the design of the system and may indirectly affect the user experience.

Before the start of the design phase, there are certain accustomed typical requirements pertaining to the areas that the design should focus, i.e. the actual issues that the spoken dialogue system is asked to realize or abide with. Some of them are specifically usability-oriented while others are domain-dependent or generic system-oriented. These typical requirements for voiceweb interfaces are:

- User satisfaction – Users that should be satisfied or very satisfied either as stand-alone users or comparing their input from using an earlier interface.
- Quality of service offering – improvement on the quality of the way the requested services/tasks are presented. For example, a large DTMF tree-based dialogue may require the user to navigate through several menu layers to achieve their goal, while a natural language dialogue may identify the initial user request and retrieve the requested service right at the start.
- State-of-the art solution – The system should deploy cutting edge technology.
- Ability to provide customised behavioural or personalised interaction for specific user groups. A common example is the use of a preferred type of interaction (formal, casual, friendly, entertaining, etc.) set specifically for the domain.

Table 1. Usability impact on spoken dialogue interface development lifecycle

Type	Requirements	Design	Implementation	Testing	Evaluation
a	low	medium	low	low	low
b	medium	medium	low	low	medium
c	high	high	medium	high	high

- Complete access to all services or business units that are supported. By design, the system should be able to provide the users the same high quality interaction for all services that the interface is used for.
- Reliability – extends to the system providing the intended functions continuously without failing.
- Continuity of processing – including problem recovery. In this case a natural language interface should cater for the interaction when a system problem occurs.
- Auditability – ensuring the transparency of the system providing supporting evidence to trace processing of data.
- Performance requirements describe the capacity of the system to perform certain functions or process certain volume of transactions within a prescribed time.
- Usability-related factors that the operator of a spoken dialogue interface may find prudent to stress upon to the designer.

These requirements are usually followed by a list of mandatory *acceptance tests* that the final system should pass before it is deployed to the web. The format imposed for the acceptance tests is generally comprised of *key performance indicators* (KPIs) for ASR and TtS success. These should be developed by the designer and be available on production to use also for tuning purposes. Furthermore, acceptance tests include task completion evaluation for all requested tasks that are to be tested.

For average size/complexity spoken dialogue interfaces, a magnitude of 10-15 trialists should be sufficient for the acceptance tests. There are two main areas that the tests are carried out in:

A. *Functional assessment* of the system respective modules and functions such as accuracy of information relayed to the user, start/end of dialogue or sub-dialogue flow, service/information provision accuracy, and so on.

B. *User Experience assessment* in terms of
  B.1 quality issues
      B.1.1 speech or dialogue pause length between activities such as voice request, system search, information retrieval, information relay/output, and prompt delays between responses
      B.1.2 output voice (natural or synthetic) consistency and naturalness for all stages of dialogue as well as in special cases where critical information or explicit help is required
      B.1.3 choice of presenting output voice, clear and non-breaking, during loudspeaker mode or in noisy environments
      B.1.4 correct pronunciation and focus placement in sentences
  B.2 user interaction
      B.2.1 ease of use, navigation through the interface
      B.2.2 instructions and help prompt quality
      B.2.3 smart recovery from misinterpretations or misrecognitions
      B.2.4 disambiguation and confirmation function performance
      B.2.5 dialogue flow cohesion
      B.2.6 overall satisfaction.

Since all this information is available to the designer beforehand, it can be put to good use especially during the design. Most of these requirements are the constraints set by the operator so that the design should be built around them. A good design should take those into account in order for the final system to pass the acceptance test assessments.

USABILITY EVALUATION FOR SPEECH-BASED SYSTEMS

Usability evaluation can be formative or summative and thus it can be performed either during or at the end (or near the end) of the development cycle. The methodologies that can be used for that differ in their scope, their main difference being that, when a product is finished (or nearly finished), *usability testing* serves for fine-tuning certain parameters and adjusting others to fit the target user better. During the design phase, usability evaluation methods can be used to probe the basic design choices, the general scope and respective task analysis of a web interface. Some of the most common factors to think about when designing a usability study are:

- Simulate environment conditions closely similar to the real world application use.
- Make sure the usability evaluation participants belong to the target user group
- Make sure the user testers test all parameters you want to measure
- Consider onsite or remote evaluation.

These factors are referenced later in this section.

Methodologies

Usability evaluation for speech-based web interfaces is carried upon certain evaluation methods and approaches on the specific modules and processes that comprise each application. Each approach measures different parameters and goals and can be applied at different stages in the product lifecycle. They all have the same main objective, to evaluate usability for a system, sub-system or module. However, each approach targets specific parameters for evaluation. The main two usability evaluation classes for spoken dialogue systems include the Wizard-of-Oz (WOZ) formative testing (Harris, 2005) and the summative usability testing.

The Wizard-of-Oz Formative Evaluation

It is a common formative approach that can be used not only for speech-based dialogue systems but for most web applications. It allows for usability testing during the early stages by using a human to simulate a fully working system. In the case of speech-based dialog systems, the human "wizard" performs the speech recognition, natural language understanding, dialog management and output generation. The WOZ approach is primarily used during the initial design phase to test the proposed dialogue flow design and the user response to information presentation parameterisation. Main advantages of the approach are listed below (Cohen et al., 2004; Harris, 2005):

- Early testing – it can be performed in the early stages in order to test and formulate the design parameters as early in the product lifecycle as possible. That way design shortcomings that would be costly to fix later in the product's lifecycle are avoided.
- System updates – the system, being a mock-up, can be updated effortlessly to accommodate for changes imposed from the input from the test subjects, making it easier to re-test the updated system in the next usability evaluation session.
- Language resources - Grammar coverage for the speech recognition (ASR) and respective machine learning approaches for interpretation (NLU) are always low when testing a non-finalised product, and as such they may hinder the usability evaluation. However, the use of the human usability expert eliminates such handicap. Moreover, problems such as integration bugs that may arise later in the development are eliminated in the case of the mock-up.
- Significant information can be gathered about the vocabulary and the syntax used, the users' attitudes and mental model of the task. The dialogues collected can also

be utilized as initial training corpus for the implementation of the ASR and NLU components.

On the other hand, the WOZ approach faces certain drawbacks that are inherent to user-testing in general:

- Unrealistic system use conditions – as test participants are not motivated in the same way as real users are, and are often not representative of the end user population. Earlier studies (Turunen et al., 2006; Ai et al., 2007) have shown that there are differences between usability testing and actual use conditions; differences refer to the use of barge-in, explicit help requests, significant silence timeouts, speech recognizer rejection rates and dialog duration among others. For WOZ testing in particular, the realistic aspect is further compromised, as speech recognition and language interpretation errors are difficult to simulate and not taken into account.
- User bias – the language used to describe the tasks to be performed inevitably influences the participants' choice of vocabulary and utterance structure, and so the utility and reliability of elicited language patterns and behaviour are undermined.
- Resources consumed – setting up a WOZ experiment requires people and time, as well as tools that can be costly to develop (Jankelovich, interview in Weinschenk, 2000)

There are two requirements for successful usability testing, the design of the tasks and the selection and training of participants. The participants must be representative of the end-user population, taking into account age, demographics, education. Other criteria may be set depending on the actual application domain, for example users of a specific web site. Moreover, novice and expert users can be recruited in order to provide the means of applying the system design to the worst-case (low experience level) and best-case (high experience level) population.

The participants are required to complete a number of tasks that are carefully selected to test the system. In a dialogue system the primary concern to evaluate is the dialogue flow. Two sets of scenarios should be designed, one asking the participants to perform specific actions or pursue predetermined goals using scenarios and another asking for uncontrolled access of the system pursuing goals of their own choice. The controlled predetermined scenarios are used to evaluate the behaviour of the participants against the expected behaviour of the designer, exposing possible flaws of the design. The uncontrolled interaction is used to evaluate the generic performance of the participants revealing the basic faults of the design, such as non-obvious availability of *help* function or *ambiguous* interaction responses from the system.

The results of the WOZ tests are both from the user subjective feedback and the examination of the objective performance measures. The performance measures include:

- task completion – whether the participants completed the specified tasks that were set within the scenarios successfully,
- efficiency – whether the participants chose the most direct route to the goal, using the predetermined scenario feedback to compare against the optimal path for the same scenario that was expected by the designer,
- dialogue flow – how the participants chose to interact with the system,, the number of times the help was requested and how informative it was, as well as the number of times disambiguation, confirmation and error recovery sub-dialogs were enabled.

The subjective input of the participants is recorded through questionnaires that the participants fill in after each task completion as well as at the end of the evaluation. The questions are used to assess the user experience asking about complexity, effort required, efficiency, linguistic clarity, simplicity, predictability, accuracy, suitable tempo, consistency, precision, forgiveness, responsiveness (see Ward & Tsukahara, 2003), appropriateness, overall impression and acceptance of the system either regarding particular tasks or the full system (Weinschenk & Barker, 2000). The participants are usually asked to mark their level of their agreement to the questions through a 1 to 5 or 1 to 7 scales (for example, 1 being "totally disagree" and 7 "totally agree" and the rest in between), commonly known as Likert scales.

The data are analysed and problems are prioritized in terms of type, severity, and frequency. The subjective feedback also indicates behavioural flaws in the design. Both results enable the designer to take certain action to fix or eliminate those flaws from the design and proceed to implementation.

The Summative Usability Testing of Voice Web Systems

At the end of the implementation, pre-final versions of the system should be tested by potential users in order to evaluate the usability. Usability testing at this stage is not much different to WOZ in terms of planning. But now there is no human actor (wizard) but the full system interaction with the user. This means that the ASR, context interpretation and generation, and TtS are now part of the usability metrics.

At this stage, the usability tests play a much more pivotal role since the development of the system is near completion. There are three distinct purposes for usability testing of a working system: the *development*, *testing* and *tuning*. During the development the users test a nearly finished product, during testing a finished product, and during tuning a finished and already deployed product. Regardless of purpose, the tests focus

on all aspects that the WOZ handled as well as several aspects that the WOZ ignored:

- Grammar testing
- Interpretation testing
- Dialogue management/flow
- System response adequacy
- Output speech quality.

For spoken dialogue interfaces, the following 15 objective (both quantitative and qualitative) and subjective usability evaluation criteria have been proposed (Dybkjær & Bernsen 2000):

1. Modality appropriateness.
2. Input recognition adequacy.
3. Naturalness of user speech relative to the task(s) including coverage of user vocabulary and grammar.
4. Output voice quality.
5. Output phrasing adequacy.
6. Feedback adequacy.
7. Adequacy of dialogue initiative relative to the task(s).
8. Naturalness of the dialogue structure relative to the task(s).
9. Sufficiency of task and domain coverage.
10. Sufficiency of the system's reasoning capabilities.
11. Sufficiency of interaction guidance (information about system capabilities, limitations and operations).
12. Error handling adequacy.
13. Sufficiency of adaptation to user differences.
14. Number of interaction problems (Bernsen et al. 1998).
15. User satisfaction.

Bernsen & Dybkjær (2000) have have proposed the use of the *evaluation templates*, i.e. "models of what the developer needs to know in order to apply an evaluation criterion to a particular property of a Spoken Language Dialogue System or component", in their methodology as best practice guides. Later, they formed a set of guidelines for up-to-date spoken dialogue design, implementation and testing, covering seven major aspects: informativeness, truth and evidence, relevance, manner, partner asymmetry, background knowledge, repair and clarification (Bernsen & Dybkjær, 2004). These aspects can be used as the basis for usability testing strategies and for evaluation frameworks (Dybkjær & Bernsen, 2001; Dybkjær et al., 2004). One of them is the PARADISE evaluation framework (Walker et al., 1998; Hajdinjak & Mihelic, 2006) with general models developed for it (Walker et al., 2000).

As with WOZ, usability testing needs participants. The recruitment procedure is pretty much the same as described earlier in WOZ, with a few additional parameters. The participants use the real system, which means that, at this stage, functional parameters in speech recognition and speech synthesis should be tested, measured and decided upon. As mentioned above there is extensive work on the comparison of usability evaluation feedback between in-house recruited participants versus real users indicating substantial differences. Moreover, parameter measurements in speech recognition rejection, choice of interaction ending, help and repeat requests, user interruptions and silence timeouts, show that there users behave differently in the first month of their interaction. After that, the users become accustomed to the system, experienced and their behaviour becomes more or less stabilised (Turunen et al., 2006).

Kamm et al. (1998) stress the importance of a successful quick tutorial on the users before using a speech-based application. They show that the initial user experience can be ensured when the first-time users are trained on the use of the system. The user satisfaction and the system performance were significantly improved in this case. Also, there is significant differentiation between onsite and remote evaluation. Participants recruited for onsite evaluation know that they are required to evaluate the system and may behave unexpectedly or even use extreme caution when using the system, a behavior much dissimilar to that of real users.

Apart from task completion and dialogue flow, depending on the domain, as a general rule, functional measurements should be recorded for at least the following indicative parameters:

- Average call duration
- Peaks and valleys of usage per hour per day
- Successful speech recognitions
- Misrecognitions
- No-inputs
- Timeouts
- Rejections
- Early hang-ups
- Successful interpretations
- Failed interpretations (no-matches)
- Successful repairs
- Failed repairs.

Performance metrics may be derived by calculating parameters such as the number of user and system turns, elapsed time, number of help requests, number of timeout prompts, mean ASR accuracy and number of speech recognition rejections (Kamm & Walker, 1997; Kamm et al., 1999). Generally, the above parameters can indicate functional problems with the application and the degree that each of those affects the user experience (Walker et al., 1999). Furthermore, the data can be automatically processed using appropriate methods (Hartikainen et al., 2004), used to train models for evaluation-based problem prediction that leads to an adaptive spoken dialogue interface (Litman et al., 1998; Litman & Pan, 2002).

The user subjective feedback is also very important at this stage. It illustrates the user experience as perceived by the user (to be compared with automatically-derived user experience level form the performance metrics analysis) and stresses the points where the users were not satisfied. By analysing the questionnaires down to the usability factors (Larsen, 2003) the designer can even, to an extent, predict the quality and usability of spoken dialogue services (Moller et al. 2006; 2008).

Usability Challenges for Advanced Speech-Enabled Web Interfaces

VoiceWeb may include non-speech enabled interfaces for certain tasks that are simple and linear. The aim for choosing such approach is robustness. Lee & Lai (2005) have made a comparative study on the use of speech-enabled versus DTMF approaches and reported on usability issues. The scope was limiting enough to implement via a DTMF system. The results showed that for the specific tasks the effectiveness and efficiency (summative evaluation) of the DTMF system were clearly much higher than the speech-enabled one for all but the sole most complex task. That task required longer communication between the user and the system, which in effect favoured the spoken dialogue. The users, however, in their formative evaluation clearly preferred the speech modality and the respective system, in terms of naturalness, ease-of-use, and overall satisfaction. That was also the case for the usability evaluation comparison between a DTMF and a speech-enabled interface for a large customer care domain. The complexity of the domain showed the clear advantage of the spoken dialogue system in terms of system and dialogue/task level criteria such as usefulness, efficiency, naturalness, user satisfaction, system behaviour, interaction flow and initiative, etc. (Spiliotopoulos et al., 2009b)

The above study illustrates and proves the need for speech-enabled communication for all but the very simple tasks. Earlier studies (Delogu et al., 1998) have indicated that the usability evaluation methodologies should be adapted to the specific complexity of each approach or system that is evaluated, while others provided extensive sets of objective and subjective measures that can be applied for specific measurements for usability evaluation of spoken dialogue systems (Larsen, 2003).

This brings the topic to a new level, the determination of how a web interface can best cope with the speech modality depending on the complexity of the tasks and the type of information that must be communicated. In terms of application domain and requirements, there are two major types of applications:

i.   *The standard, widely-used speech based applications,* such as call centres, customer care automated spoken dialogue systems.

ii.   *The complex, speech-enabled approaches for interfacing composite information that requires intense navigation and/or delicate communication sub-tasks.* Such approaches can be used when a system must present many pieces of compound information to the user according to the user feedback, and re-adjust, interrupt and re-focus the search or delivery of information as needed.

The latter presents a challenge when trying to render complex information to the speech modality. For example, rendering the data and their respective relations from a normal table structure to speech is a very hard task that requires extensive manipulation of factors such as prosody or auditory markers (Spiliotopoulos et al. 2010). Moreover, the requirements of the spoken output and the ability of the system to confirm that the user understood the spoken output (confirmation, disambiguation) are quite different and much more demanding. The NLG and TTS components required for such tasks are more refined and include both grammars and adaptive statistical approaches, as do the NLU and Dialogue Management. There are certain semantic relations, sometimes in the form of meta-information that must be relayed to the user in order to make the output understandable.

All these considerations must unavoidably be integrated to the usability evaluation for such systems. The suitable usability evaluation criteria based on their significance throughout the development lifecycle process are denoted below:

A. Output quality

    A.1 Dialogue-related TTS utterances – statement, confirmation, disambiguation

    A.2 Content sentence generation – NLG

    A.3 Quality of TTS – prosody, clarity of information provision

B. Spoken Input

    B.1 User input handling – NLU

    B.2 Dialogue management decisions based on successful NLU

C. System parameters

    C.1 Response time

    C.2 Coherence and continuation of information

    C.3 Low deviation of the mean number of turns needed for task completion

    C.4 Number and type of misrecognition or rejections of user input

D. Task completion

    D.1 Percentage of task completion

    D.2 Analysis of incomplete tasks by examining the process and identifying the parameters from groups 1, 2 and 3.

The key to evaluating such systems is the determination of how each criteria and respective parameters affect the system efficiency and user acceptance. In order to do that a combined method of WOZ testing and early system parameterization can successfully formulate particular performance metrics bases for the later testing and evaluation.

CONCLUSION

Advances in speech processing, natural language understanding and web technologies have allowed the development of useful, universally usable and user friendly speech enabled web interfaces. Utilizing the speech modality for web applications can increase naturalness, efficiency and user satisfaction, provided that usability issues and parameters are taken into consideration and usability evaluation is integrated throughout the interface's lifecycle. In this regard, this chapter outlined the different types of speech based interaction and the ways in which speech based interfaces differ from traditional point-and-click web interfaces posing particular usability challenges. It presented usability evaluation methods and approaches focusing on usability frameworks primarily targeted for speech-based web interfaces. Furthermore, usability challenges presented by complex speech based applications in terms of output – as in the case of data tables rendition – or high NLU demands were discussed. Such issues are important to factorize in usability evaluation to ensure the development of high quality applications.

In general, it is important that usability testing is employed in all steps of the process, from design to deployment and maintenance, and users' input is accordingly taken into account. First, the designer utilizes user feedback to formulate an interface that provides all the requested functionality in a user-friendly, user-tested and approved manner. Throughout the implementation phase the system is put to test and design choices are further validated. Once the system is finished or nearly finished, specified functional tests are performed and usability evaluation assures that requirements are met. Finally, the already deployed system is re-evaluated for quality assuring or updating purposes. For the latter a WOZ-like evaluation can be used that enables the developers to intervene during the interaction and try out alternative flows and presentation modes. In short, building a speech-based interface is an ongoing, iterative test and development process with more general as well as particular to the speech modality usability objectives, methods and approaches. The development of and abiding by advanced usability standards becomes even more imperative, as web interfaces become more sophisticated allowing for more flexible and natural spoken language input and output.

ACKNOWLEDGMENT

The work described in this chapter has been funded by the Special Account for Research Grants of the National and Kapodistrian University of Athens under the KAPODISTRIAS program.

REFERENCES

Ai, H., Raux, A., Bohus, D., Eskenazi, M., & Litman, D. (2007). Comparing spoken dialog corpora collected with recruited subjects versus real users. In Proc. of the 8th SIGdial workshop on Discourse and Dialogue, pp. 124–131.

Bernsen, N. O., Dybkjaer, H., & Dybkjaer, L. (1998). *Designing Interactive Speech Systems: From First Ideas to User Testing*. New York: Springer-Verlag.

Bernsen, N. O., & Dybkjær, L. (2000). A Methodology for Evaluating Spoken Language Dialogue Systems and Their Components. In Proc. 2nd International Conference on Language Resources & Evaluation - LREC 2000, pp.183-188.

Bernsen, N. O., & Dybkjær, L. (2004). Building Usable Spoken Dialogue Systems: Some Approaches. *Sprache und Datenverarbeitung, 28*(2), 111–131.

Cohen, M., Giancola, J. P., & Balogh, J. (2004). *Voice User Interface Design*. Boston, MA: Addison-Wesley Professional.

Delogu, C., Di Carlo, A., Rottundi, P., & Sartori, D. (1998). Usability evaluation of IVR systems with DTMF and ASR, 5th International Conference on Spoken Language Processing, paper 0320, Australia, 1998.

Duarte, C., & Carriço, L. (2008). Audio Interfaces for Improved Accessibility. In Pinder, S. (Ed.), *Advances in Human Computer Interaction* (pp. 121–142). Vienna, Austria: I-Tech Education and Publishing.

Dybkjær, L., & Bernsen, N. O. (2000). Usability Issues in Spoken Language Dialogue Systems. *Natural Language Engineering, 6*(3-4), 243–272. doi:10.1017/S1351324900002461

Dybkjær, L., & Bernsen, N. O. (2001). Usability Evaluation in Spoken Language Dialogue Systems. In. Proc.ACL Workshop on Evaluation Methodologies for Language and Dialogue Systems, pp.9-18.

Dybkjær, L., Bernsen, N. O., & Minker, W. (2004). Evaluation and Usability of Multimodal Spoken Language Dialogue Systems. *Speech Communication, 43*(1-2), 33–54. doi:10.1016/j.specom.2004.02.001

Dybkjær, L., Hemsen, H., & Minker, W. (Eds.). (2007). *Evaluation of Text and Speech Systems*. Berlin, Heidelberg: Springer-Verlag. doi:10.1007/978-1-4020-5817-2

Dybkjær, L., & Minker, W. (Eds.). (2008). *Recent Trends in Discourse and Dialogue*. Berlin, Heidelberg: Springer-Verlag. doi:10.1007/978-1-4020-6821-8

Fellbaum, K., & Kouroupetroglou, G. (2008). Principles of Electronic Speech Processing with Applications for People with Disabilities. *Technology and Disability, 20*(2), 55–85.

Freitas, D., & Kouroupetroglou, G. (2008). Speech Technologies for Blind and Low Vision Persons. *Technology and Disability, 20*(2), 135–156.

Galitz, W. O. (2007). *The Essential Guide to User Interface Design*. Wiley Publishing, Inc.

Hajdinjak, M., & Mihelic, F. (2006). The PARADISE evaluation framework: Issues and findings. *Computational Linguistics, 32*(2), 263–272. doi:10.1162/coli.2006.32.2.263

Harris, R. A. (2005). *Voice Interaction Design: Crafting the New Conversational Speech Systems*. San Francisco: Morgan Kaufmann.

Hartikainen, M., Salonen, E.-P., & Turunen, M. (2004). Subjective Evaluation of Spoken Dialogue Systems Using SERVQUAL Method. In Proc. 8th International Conference on Spoken Language Processing - ICSLP, pp. 2273-2276.

Huang, X., Acero, A., & Hon, H.-W. (2001). *Spoken Language Processing: A Guide to Theory, Algorithm and System Development.* New Jersey: Prentice Hall PTR.

Jurafsky, D., & Martin, J. H. (2008). *Speech and Language Processing. An Introduction to Natrural Language Processing, Computational Linguistics, and Speech Recognition.* New Jersey: Prentice-Hall.

Kamm, C. A., Litman, D. J., & Walker, M. A. (1998). From novice to expert: The effect of tutorials on user expertise with spoken dialogue systems. In Proc. 5th International Conference on Spoken Language Processing - ICSLP.

Kamm, C. A., & Walker, M. A. (1997). Design and Evaluation of Spoken Dialogue Systems. In Proc. IEEE Workshop on Automatic Speech Recognition and Understanding, pp. 14–17.

Kamm, C. A., Walker, M. A., & Litman, D. J. (1999). Evaluating spoken language systems. In Proc. Applied Voice Input/Output Society Conference - AVIOS, pp. 187–197.

Karat, C. M., Halverson, C., Horn, D., & Karat, J. (1999). Patterns of entry and correction in large vocabulary continuous speech recognition systems. ACM Conference on Human Factors in Computing Systems. Pittsburgh, PA.

Kouroupetroglou, G. (2009). Universal Access in Public Terminals: Information Kiosks and Automated Teller Machines (ATMs). In Stephanidis, C. (Ed.), *The Universal Access Handbook* (pp. 761–780). Boca Raton, Florida: CRC Press. doi:10.1201/9781420064995-c48

Kouroupetroglou, G., & Spiliotopoulos, D. (2009). Usability Methodologies for Real-Life Voice User Interfaces. *International Journal of Information Technology and Web Engineering, 4*(4), 78–94. doi:10.4018/jitwe.2009100105

Larsen, L. B. (2003). Issues in the Evaluation of Spoken Dialogue Systems using Objective and Subjective Measures. In Proc. 8th IEEE Workshop on Automatic Speech Recognition and Understanding -ASRU, pp. 209-214.

Larsen, L. B. (2003). On the Usability of Spoken Dialogue Systems. PhD Thesis, Aalborg University.

Larson, J. A. (2000). Introduction and Overview of W3C Speech Interface Framework, Retrieved August 2, 2009, from http://www.w3.org/ TR/voice-intro/

Larson, J. A., Raman, T. V., & Raggett, D. (2003). W3C Multimodal Interaction Framework, Retrieved August 2, 2009, from http://www.w3.org/TR/mmi-framework/

Lee, K. M., & Lai, J. (2005). Speech Versus Touch: A Comparative Study of the Use of Speech and DTMF Keypad for Navigation. [Lawrence Erlbaum Associates.]. *International Journal of Human-Computer Interaction, 19*(3), 343–360. doi:10.1207/s15327590ijhc1903_4

Litman, D. J., & Pan, S. (2002). Designing and evaluating an adaptive spoken dialogue system. *User Modeling and User-Adapted Interaction, 12*(2-3), 111–137. doi:10.1023/A:1015036910358

Litman, D. J., Pan, S., & Walker, M. A. (1998). Evaluating Response Strategies in a Web-Based Spoken Dialogue Agent. In Proc. 36th Annual Meeting of the Association for Computational Linguistics and 17th International Conf. on Computational Linguistics (ACL/COLING), pp.780–786.

McTear, M. F. (2004). *Spoken Dialogue Technology: Towards the Conversational User Interface.* London: Springer-Verlag.

Moller, S., Engelbrecht, K., & Schleicher, R. (2008). Predicting the quality and usability of spoken dialogue services. *Speech Communication, 50*(8-9), 730–744. doi:10.1016/j.specom.2008.03.001

Moller, S., Englert, R., Engelbrecht, K., Hafner, V., Jameson, A., Oulasvirta, A., et al. (2006). MeMo: Towards Automatic Usability Evaluation of Spoken Dialogue Services by User Error Simulations. In Proc. 9th International Conference on Spoken Language Processing - ICSLP, pp. 1786-1789.

Pan, S., & McKeown, K. (1997). Integrating language generation with speech synthesis in a concept to speech system. In Proceedings of ACL/EACL'97 Concept to Speech Workshop, Madrid, Spain.

Robin, M., & Larson, J. (1999). Voice Browsers: An introduction and glossary for the requirement drafts. W3C Working Draft, December 1999

Rubin, J., & Chisnell, D. (2008). *Handbook of Usability Testing: Howto Plan, Design, and Conduct Effective Tests.* Indianapolis, Indiana: Wiley Publishing, Inc.

Sharp, H., Rogers, Y., & Preece, J. (2007). *Interaction Design: Beyond Human-Computer Interaction.* West Sussex, England: John Wiley & Sons, Inc.

Spiliotopoulos, D., & Kouroupetroglou, G. (2009). *Usability Methodologies for Spoken Dialogue Web Interfaces. Chapter in the book: Integrating Usability Engineering for Designing the Web Experience: Methodologies and Principles, 2009, Information Science Reference Press.* Pennsylvania, USA: IGI Global.

Spiliotopoulos, D., Stavropoulou, P., & Kouroupetroglou, G. (2009a). *Acoustic Rendering of Data Tables using Earcons and Prosody for Document Accessibility. Lecture Notes on Artificial Intelligence 5616* (pp. 587–596). Universal Access in HCI, Springer Berlin Heidelberg.

Spiliotopoulos, D., Stavropoulou, P., & Kouroupetroglou, G. (2009b). *Spoken Dialogue Interfaces: Integrating Usability. Lecture Notes in Computer Science 5889* (pp. 484–499). HCI and Usability for e-Inclusion, Springer Berlin Heidelberg.

Spiliotopoulos, D., Xydas, G., Kouroupetroglou, G., Argyropoulos, V., & Ikospentaki, K. (2010, June). Auditory Universal Accessibility of Data Tables using Naturally Derived Prosody Specification. [Springer Berlin Heidelberg.]. *Univ. Access Inf. Soc., 9*(2), 169–183. doi:10.1007/s10209-009-0165-0

Stephanidis, C. (Ed.). (2001). *User Interfaces for All: Concepts, Methods and Tools.* Mahwah, New Jersey: Lawrence Erlbaum Associates.

Stephanidis, C. (Ed.). (2009). *The Universal Access Handbook.* Boca Raton, Florida: CRC Press.

Tatham, M., & Morton, K. (2005). *Developments in Speech Synthesis.* West Sussex, England: John Wiley & Sons, Inc.doi:10.1002/0470012609

Turunen, M., Hakulinen, J., & Kainulainen, A. (2006). Evaluation of a Spoken Dialogue System with Usability Tests and Long-term Pilot Studies: Similarities and Differences. In Proc. 9th International Conference on Spoken Language Processing - INTERSPEECH pp. 1057-1060.

van Kuppevelt, J., Dybkjær, L., & Bernsen, N. O. (Eds.). (2005). *Advances in natural multimodal dialogue.* Dordrecht, The Netherlands: Springer. doi:10.1007/1-4020-3933-6

Wahlster, W. (Ed.). (2006). *SmartKom: Foundations of Multimodal Dialogue Systems*. Berlin, Heidelberg: Springer-Verlag. doi:10.1007/3-540-36678-4

Walker, M. A., Borland, J., & Kamm, C. A. (1999). The utility of elapsed time as a usability metric for spoken dialogue systems. In Proc. IEEE Automatic Speech Recognition and Understanding Workshop - ASRU, pp. 317–320.

Walker, M. A., Kamm, C. A., & Litman, D. J. (2000). Towards developing general models of usability with PARADISE. *Natural Language Engineering*, *6*(3-4), 363–377. doi:10.1017/S1351324900002503

Walker, M. A., Litman, D. J., Kamm, C. A., & Abella, A. (1998). Evaluating spoken dialogue agents with PARADISE: Two case studies. *Computer Speech & Language*, *12*(3), 317–347. doi:10.1006/csla.1998.0110

Ward, N., & Tsukahara, W. (2003). A Study in Responsiveness in Spoken Dialog. *International Journal of Human-Computer Studies*, *59*, 603–630. doi:10.1016/S1071-5819(03)00085-5

Weinschenk, S., & Barker, D. T. (2000). *Designing effective speech interfaces*. New York: John Wiley & Sons, Inc.

Xydas, G., Argyropoulos, V., Karakosta, T., & Kouroupetroglou, G. (2004). An Open Platform for Conducting Psycho-Acoustic Experiments in the Auditory Representation of Web Documents, Proc. of the Conf. ACOUSTICS 2004, 27-28 Sept. 2004, Thessalonica, pp. 157-164

Yankelovich, N., Levow, G. A., & Marx, M. (1995). *Designing Speech Acts: Issues in speech user interfaces. Human Factors in Computing Systems* (pp. 369–376). Denver: Association of Computing Machinery.

Compilation of References

Adamic, L. A., & Huberman, B. A. (2001). The Web's hidden order. *Communications of the ACM, 44*(9), 55–60. doi:10.1145/383694.383707

Adda, M. (2010). A Pattern Language for Knowledge Discovery in a Semantic Web Context. *International Journal of Information Technology and Web Engineering, 5*(2), 16–31..doi:10.4018/jitwe.2010040102

Adomavicius, G., Sankaranarayanan, R., Sen, S., & Tuzhilin, A. (2005). Incorporating contextual information in recommender systems using a multidimensional approach. *ACM Transactions on Information Systems, 23*, 103–145. doi:10.1145/1055709.1055714

Adomavicius, G., & Tuzhilin, A. (2005). Towards the Next Generation of Recommender Systems: A Survey of the State-of-the-Art and Possible Extensions. *IEEE Transactions on Knowledge and Data Engineering, 17*(6). doi:10.1109/TKDE.2005.99

Adomavicius, G., & Tuzhilin, A. (2010). Context-Aware Recommender Systems. In Ricci, F., Rokach, L., Shapira, B., & Kantor, P. B. (Eds.), *Recommender Systems Handbook: A Complete Guide for Research Scientists and Practitioners*. Berlin, Heidelberg: Springer.

Agarwal, R., & Venkatesh, V. (2002). Assessing a Firm's Web Presence: A Heuristic Evaluation Procedure for the Measurement of Usability. *Information Systems Research, 13*(2), 168–186. doi:10.1287/isre.13.2.168.84

Ai, H., Raux, A., Bohus, D., Eskenazi, M., & Litman, D. (2007). Comparing spoken dialog corpora collected with recruited subjects versus real users. In Proc. of the 8th SIGdial workshop on Discourse and Dialogue, pp. 124–131.

Alexa. (2007). *Alexa the Web Information Company*. Retrieved May 7, 2007, from http://www.alexa.com

Alonso, G., Günthör, R., Kamath, M., Agrawal, D., El Abbadi, A., & Mohan, C. (1996). Exotica/FMDC: A Workflow management System for Mobile and Disconnected Clients. *Distributed and Parallel Databases, 4*(3), 229–247. doi:10.1007/BF00140951

Ambler, S. W. (2007). Tailoring Usability into Agile Software Development Projects. In Law, E. L.-C., Hvannberg, E., & Cockton, G. (Eds.), *Maturing Usability: Quality in Software, Interaction and Value, Human-Computer Interaction Series* (pp. 75–95). London: Springer-Verlag Limited.

Anand, S. S., & Mobasher, B. (2005). Intelligent techniques for web personalization. *Proceedings of the 2nd Workshop on Intelligent Techniques in Web Personalization (ITWP 2003)*, Springer LNAI 3169, Acapulco, Mexico.

Anderson, J., Fleek, F., Garrity, K., & Drake, F. (2001). Integrating Usability Techniques into Software Development. *IEEE Software, 18*(1), 46–53. doi:10.1109/52.903166

Andreasen, M. S., Nielsen, H. V., Schrøder, S. O., & Stage, J. (2006). Usability in open source software development: Opinions and practice. *Information Technology and Control, 35A*(3), 303–312.

Andreasen, M. S., Nielsen, H. V., Schrøder, S. O., & Stage, J. (2007). What Happened to Remote Usability Testing? An Empirical Study of Three Methods. In *Proceedings of CHI 2007*. New York: ACM Press.

Artail, H., Safa, H., Mershad, K., Abou-Atme, Z., & Sulieman, N. (2008). COACS: A Cooperative and Adaptive Caching System for MANETs. *IEEE Transactions on Mobile Computing, 7*(8), 961–977. doi:10.1109/TMC.2008.18

Atluri, V., & Huang, W. (1996). An Authorization Model for Workflows. Proceedings of the 4th European Symposium on Research in Computer Security (ESORICS), London, U.K. (pp. 44-64). Berlin, Germany: Springer.

Baber, C. (1996). Repertory grid theory and its application to product evaluation. In Jordan, P., Thomas, B., Weerdmeester, B., & Mclelland, I. (Eds.), *Usability evaluation in industry* (pp. 157–165). London: Taylor and Francis.

Badre, A. N. (2002). *Shaping Web Usability – Interaction Design in Context*. Boston: Addison-Wesley.

Bai, G., & Williamson, C. (2004). Time-domain analysis of Web cache filters effects. *Performance Evaluation, 58*(5), 285–317. doi:10.1016/j.peva.2004.07.009

Bai, X., & Lee, S. Tsai, W. & Chen, Y. (2008) Collaborative Web Services Monitoring with Active Service Broker. *Proceedings IEEE International Computer Software and Application Conference,* 84-91.

Bak, J. O., Nguyen, K., Risgaard, P., & Stage, J. (2008) Obstacles to Usability Evaluation in Practice: A Survey of Software Organizations. In *Proceedings of NordiCHI 2008*. New York: ACM Press.

Baldauf, M., Dustdar, S., & Rosenberg, F. (2007). A survey on context-aware systems. *In Ad Hoc and Ubiquitous Computing,* Vol. 2, 263-277.

Balfanz, D., Smetters, D. K., Stewart, P., & Wong, H. C. (2002). Talking to strangers: authentification in ad-hoc wireless networks. Proceedings of the Network and Distributed System Security Symposium.

Bannister, D., & Fransella, F. (1986). *Inquiring man: the psychology of personal constructs* (3rd ed.). London: Routledge.

Baresi, L., Garzotto, F., & Paolini, P. (2001). Extending UML for modeling Web applications. In *Proceedings of the 34th Annual Hawaii International Conference on System Sciences* (pp. 1285-1294).

Barish, G., & Obraczka, K. (2000). World Wide Web caching trends and techniques. *IEEE Communications Magazine, 51*(6), 178–185. doi:10.1109/35.841844

Baumeister, H., Koch, N., Kosiuczenko, P., & Wirsing, M. (2003). *Extending Activity Diagrams to Model Mobile Systems. Proceedings of NetObjectDays 2002 (NOD), revised papers, Erfurt, Germany* (pp. 278–293). Berlin, Germany: Springer.

Beck, K. (2000). *Extreme Programming Explained-- Embrace Change*. Reading, MA: Addison-Wesley.

Beck, K., Beedle, M., van Bennekum, A., Cockburn, A., & Cunningham, W. (2001). *Manifesto for agile software development: Agile Manifesto Website*. Retrieved 01/2009 from http://agilemanifesto.org/

Becker, C., & Dürr, F. (2005). On Location Models for Ubiquitous Computing. *Personal and Ubiquitous Computing, 9*(1), 20–31. doi:10.1007/s00779-004-0270-2

Becker, S. A. (2002). An Exploratory Study on Web Usability and the Internationalizational of US E-Businesses. *Journal of Electronic Commerce Research, 3*(4), 265–278.

Belanger, F., Fan, W., Schaupp, C. L., Krishen, A., Everhart, J., & Poteet, D. (2006). Web site success metrics: Addressing the duality of goals. *Communications of the ACM, 49*(12), 114–116. doi:10.1145/1183236.1183256

Bell, D. E., & LaPadula, J. (1976). *Secure Computer System: Unified Exposition and Multics Interpretation. Technical Report of MITRE Corporation*. Bradford, MA, USA: MITRE Corporation.

Bell, D. E. (2005). Looking back at the Bell-LaPadula Model. *Proceedings of the 21st Annual Computer Security Applications Conference (ACSAC 2005)*, Tucson, USA (pp. 337-351). Los Alamitos, USA: IEEE Computer Society.

Benantar, M. (2006). *Access Control Systems. Security, Identity Management and Trust Models*. New York, USA et al.: Springer.

Benavídez, C., Fuertes, J. L., Gutiérrez, E., & Martínez, L. (2006). Semi-Automatic Evaluation of Web Accessibility with HERA 2.0. In *Proceedings of the 10th International Conference on Computers Helping People with Special Needs (ICCHP 2006)* (pp. 199-106). Berlin: Springer.

Benson, C., Muller-Prove, M., & Mzourek, J. (2004). Professional usability in open source projects: Gnome, openoffice.org, netbeans. In *Proceedings of CHI 2004* (pp. 1083-1084). New York: ACM Press.

Benyon, D., Turner, P., & Turner, S. (2005). *Designing Interactive Systems, People, Activities, Context and Technology*. Edinburgh: Addison-Wesley.

Bernsen, N. O., Dybkjaer, H., & Dybkjaer, L. (1998). *Designing Interactive Speech Systems: From First Ideas to User Testing*. New York: Springer-Verlag.

Bernsen, N. O., & Dybkjær, L. (2004). Building Usable Spoken Dialogue Systems: Some Approaches. *Sprache und Datenverarbeitung, 28*(2), 111–131.

Bernsen, N. O., & Dybkjær, L. (2000). A Methodology for Evaluating Spoken Language Dialogue Systems and Their Components. In Proc. 2nd International Conference on Language Resources & Evaluation - LREC 2000, pp.183-188.

Bertino, E., Ferrari, E., & Atluri, V. (1999). The Specification and Enforcement of Authorization Constraints in Workflow Management Systems. ACM Transactions on Information and System Security. 2(1), 1999, 65-104.

Bevan, N. (2005). Cost benefits framework and case studies. In Bias, R. G., & Mayhew, D. G. (Eds.), *Cost-Justifying Usability: An update for the internet age*. San Francisco: Morgan Kaufmann. doi:10.1016/B978-012095811-5/50020-1

Bevan, N. (2008). A framework for selecting the most appropriate usability measures. In *COST 294-MAUSE Workshop: Critiquing Automated Usability Evaluation Methods*. March.

Beyer, H., Holtzblatt, K., & Baker, L. (2004). An Agile Customer-Centered Method: Rapid Contextual Design. In *Extreme Programming and Agile Methods - XP/Agile Universe 2004. Proceedings,* (pp. 50-59). Berlin: Springer.

Bickmore, T. W., & Picard, R. W. (2005). Establishing and maintaining long-term human-computer relationships. *ACM Transactions on Computer-Human Interaction, 12*(2), 293–327. doi:10.1145/1067860.1067867

Blythe, M., Overbeeke, K., Monk, A., & Wright, P. (Eds.). (2004). *Funology: From Usability to Enjoyment*. Springer.

Borg, A., Sandahl, K., & Patel, M. (2007). Extending the OpenUP/Basic Requirements Discipline to Specify Capacity Requirements. In *15th IEEE Internationalm, Requirements Engineering Conference, 2007 (RE '07), Proceedings*. Washington, DC: IEEE.

Boutrous, C., Couiliaby, D., Haddad, S., Melliti, T., Moreaux, P., & Rampacek, S. (2009). An Integrated Framework for Web Services Orchestration. *International Journal of Web Services Research, 6*(4), 1–29.. doi:10.4018/jwsr.2009071301

Boy, G. (1997). The group elicitation method for participatory design and usability testing. *Interactions of the ACM, 4*(2).

Braiterman, J., Verhage, S., & Choo, R. (2000). Designing with Users in Internet Time. *Interaction, 7*(5), 23–27. doi:10.1145/345242.345253

Brajnik, G. (2004). Comparing accessibility evaluation tools: a method for tool effectiveness. *Univers. Access Inf. Soc., 3*(3), 252–263. doi:10.1007/s10209-004-0105-y

Brajnik, G. (2000). *Automatic Web usability evaluation: What needs to be done?* Retrieved May 5, 2007, 2007, from http://www.dimi.uniud.it/~giorgio/papers/hfweb00.html

Brajnik, G. (2006). Web Accessibility Testing: When the Method Is the Culprit. In *Proceedings of 10th International Conference on Computers Helping People with Special Needs* (pp. 156-163). Berlin: Springer.

Brajnik, G. (2008). A comparative test of web accessibility evaluation methods. In *Assets '08: Proceedings of the 10th international ACM SIGACCESS conference on Computers and accessibility* (pp. 113-120). Berlin: ACM.

Breslau, L., Cao, P., Fan, L., Phillips, G., & Shenker, S. (1999, March). Web caching and zipf-like distributions: Evidence and implications. In *Proceedings of the 18th Annual Joint Conference of the IEEE Computer and Communications Societies (INFOCOM 1999)*, New York (Vol. 1, pp. 126-134). Washington, DC: IEEE Computer Society.

Brin, S., & Page, L. (1998, April 14-18). *The anatomy of a large-scale hypertextual Web search engine*. Paper presented at the International Conference on World Wide Web, Brisbane, Australia.

Brinck, T., Gergle, D., & Wood, S. D. (2002). *Usability for the Web: Designing Web Sites that Work*. San Francisco: Morgan Kaufmann.

Broch, J., Maltz, D. A., Johnson, D. B., Hu, Y.-C., & Jetcheva, J. (1998). A performance comparison of multi-hop wireless ad hoc network routing protocols. Proceedings of the 4th annual ACM / IEEE international conference on Mobile computing and networking, ACM Press, Dallas, Texas, United States, 85-97.

Bruun, A., Gull, P., Hofmeister, L., & Stage, J. (2009). Let your users do the testing: A comparison of three remote asynchronous usability testing methods. In *Proceedings of CHI 2009*. New York: ACM Press.

Burggraf, D. S. (2006). Geographic Markup Language. *Data Science Journal, 5*, 187–204. doi:10.2481/dsj.5.178

Burke, R. (2002). Hybrid recommender systems: Survey and experiments. *User Modeling and User-Adapted Interaction, 12*, 331–370. doi:10.1023/A:1021240730564

Bussler, C. (1995). Access Control in Workflow-Management Systems. *Post-Workshop Proceedings of IT-Sicherheit*, Vienna, Austria, (pp. 165-179). Munich, Germany: Oldenbourg-Verlag.

Bygstad, B., Ghinea, G., & Brevik, E. (2007). Systems Development Methods and Usability in Norway: An Industrial Perspective. In *Usability and Internationalization. HCI and Culture. Proceedings,* (pp. 258-266). Berlin: Springer.

Caldwell, B., Cooper, M., Reid, L. G., & Vanderheiden, G. (2008). *Web content accessibility guidelines 2.0*: World Wide Web Consortium. Retrieved June, 2009 from http://www.w3.org/ TR/ WCAG20/

Callahan, T., Allman, M., & Paxson, V. (2010). A Longitudinal View of HTTP Traffic. In *Passive and active measurement* (pp. 222–231).

Cao, P., & Irani, S. (2002). Cost-aware www proxy caching algorithms. *IEEE Transactions on Computers, 51*(6), 193–206.

Castillo, J. C., Hartson, H. R., & Hix, D. (1998). Remote usability evaluation: Can users report their own critical incidents? In *Proceedings of CHI 1998* (pp. 253-254). New York: ACM Press.

Cato, J. (2001). *User-centered Web design*. London: Addison-Wesley.

Cerami, E. (2002). *Web Services Essentials*. Sebastopol, CA: O'Reilly and Associates.

Ceri, S., Fraternali, P., & Bongio, A. (2000). Web Modeling Language (WebML): a modeling language for designing Web sites. *Computer Networks, 33*(1-6), 137 - 157.

Cesar, R. P. J., & Deni, T. R. (2007). Local and cumulative analysis of self-similar traffic traces. In *Conielecomp '06: Proceedings of the 16th international conference on electronics, communications and computers* (p. 27-32). Washington, DC, USA: IEEE Computer Society.

Chandran, S. M., & Joshi, J. B. D. (2005). LoT-RBAC: A Location and Time-Based RBAC Model. *Proceedings of the 6th International Conference on Web Information Systems Engineering (WISE '05)*. New York, USA (pp. 361-375), Berlin, Germany: Springer.

Chang, J., & Bourguet, M. (2008). Usability framework for the design and evaluation of multimodal interaction. In *Proceedings of the 22nd British HCI Group Annual Conference on People and Computers: Culture, Creativity, interaction* (pp. 123-126) Liverpool, UK: British Computer Society Conference on Human-Computer Interaction.

Chao, K., Younas, M., Lo, C., & Tan, T. (2005) Fuzzy Matchmaking for Web Services, *Proc. 19th Int. Conf. on Advanced Information Networking and Applications, Vol 2*, Taiwan, 721-726.

Chen, X., & Zhang, X. (2003). *A popularity-based prediction model for web prefetching* (*Vol. 36*, pp. 63–70). Los Alamitos, CA, USA: IEEE Computer Society Press.

Chen, A. (2005). Context-aware collaborative filtering system: predicting the user's preferences in ubiquitous computing. *Proceedings of the 1st International Workshop Location- and Context-Awareness (LoCA 2005)*, Springer LNCS 3479, Oberpfaffenhofen, Germany.

Chin, K.-W., Judge, J., Williams, A., & Kermode, R. (2002). Implementation experience with MANET routing protocols. *SIGCOMM Comput. Commun. Rev, 32*(5), 49–59. doi:10.1145/774749.774758

Chisholm, W., Vanderheiden, G., & Jacobs, I. (1999). *Web content accessibility guidelines 1.0: World Wide Web Consortium.* Retrieved June, 2009 from http://www.w3.org/ TR/ WCAG10/

Chlamtac, I., Conti, M., & Liu, J. J.-N. (2003). Mobile ad hoc networking: imperatives and challenges. *Ad Hoc Networks, 1*(1), 13–64. doi:10.1016/S1570-8705(03)00013-1

Cho, J., & Roy, S. (2004, May 17-20). Impact of search engines on page popularity. In *Proceedings of the 13ᵗʰ International Conference on World Wide Web,* New York (pp. 20-29). ACM Publishing.

Choi, Y. S., Yi, J. S., Law, C. M., & Jacko, J. A. (2006). Are universal design resources designed for designers? In *Assets '06: Proceedings of the 8th international ACM SIGACCESS conference on Computers and accessibility* (pp. 87-94). New York: ACM.

Clegg, F. (1990). *Simple Statistics.* Cambridge: Cambridge University Press.

Cluster, W. A. B. (2007). *Unified Web Evaluation Methodology (UWEM 1.2).* Retrieved 01/2009 from www.w3c.org

Cockton, G., Woolrych, A., & Hindmarch, M. (2004). Reconditioned Merchandise: Extended Structured Report Formats in Usability Inspection. In *CHI 2004 Extended Abstracts,* (pp. 1433-1436). New York: ACM Press.

Codd, E. (1970). A relational model for large shared data banks. *CACM, 13,* 6.

Codd, E. (1972). *Further normalization of the data base relational model. Data Base Systems.* Prentice Hall.

Cohen, M., Giancola, J. P., & Balogh, J. (2004). *Voice User Interface Design.* Boston, MA: Addison-Wesley Professional.

Constantine, L. (2001). Process Agility and Software Usability. *Software Development 9*(5). Retrieved June 12th, 2010, from http://www.foruse.com/Files/ Papers/agiledesign.pdf.

Cooper, A. (2004). *The Inmates Are Running the Asylum: Why High-Tech Products Drive Us Crazy and How to Restore the Sanity.* Indianapolis: SAMS Publishing.

Corcho, O., Fernandez-Lopez, M., & Gomez-Perez, A. (2007). Ontological Engineering: What are Ontolgoies and How can we Build Them? In J. Cardoso & I. G. I. Global (Eds.), *Semantic Web Services* (pp. 44–70). Hershey, PA. doi:10.4018/9781599040455.ch003

Cristani, M., & Cuel, R. (2004). A Survey on Ontology Creation Methodologies. *International Journal on Semantic Web and Information Systems, 1*(2), 49–69.. doi:10.4018/jswis.2005040103

Crovella, M. E., & Bestavros, A. (1996). Self-similarity in world wide Web traffic: evidence and possible causes. In *Sigmetrics '96: Proceedings of the 1996 acm sigmetrics international conference on measurement and modeling of computer systems* (pp. 160–169). New York, NY, USA: ACM.

Damiani, M. L., Bertino, E., & Perlasca, P. (2007). Data Security in Location-Aware Applications: An Approach Based on RBAC. *International Journal of Information and Computer Security., 1*(1/2), 5–38. doi:10.1504/IJICS.2007.012243

Davis, F. D. (1989). Perceived Usefulness, Perceived Ease of Use, and User Acceptance of Information Technology. *MIS Quart, 13*(3), 319–339. doi:10.2307/249008

Davis, J., Sow, D., Bourges-Waldegg, D., Guo, C., Hoertnagl, C., Stolze, M., et al. (2006). Supporting Mobile Business Workflow with Commune. Proceedings of the 7ᵗʰ IEEE Workshop on Mobile Computing System & Applications (WMCSA), Washington, DC, USA, (pp. 10-18). Los Alamitos, USA: IEEE Computer Society.

Dawson, J. W. (2006). *A holistic usability framework for distributed simulation systems.* Unpublished PhD thesis. Orlando: University of Central Florida.

De Angeli, A., Sutcliffe, A., & Hartmann, J. (2006, June 26-28). Interaction, usability and aesthetics: What influences users' preferences? In *Proceedings of the 6ᵗʰ ACM Conference on Designing Interactive Systems,* University Park, PA (pp. 271-280). ACM Publishing.

Decker, M. (2009b). Location-Aware Access Control: An Overview. In *Proceedings of Informatics 2009 – Special Session on Wireless Applications and Computing (WAC '09), Carvoeiro, Portugal* (pp. 75–82). Lisbon, Portugal: IADIS.

Decker, M. (2008a). An Access-Control Model for Mobile Computing with Spatial Constraints - Location-aware Role-based Access Control with a Method for Consistency Checks. *Proceedings of the International Conference on e-Business (ICE-B 2008)*, Porto, Portugal (pp. 185-190), Sétubal, Portugal: INSTICC Press.

Decker, M. (2008d). Location Privacy — An Overview. *Proceedings of the International Conference on Mobile Business (ICMB 08)*, Barcelona, Spain. Los Alamitos, USA: IEEE Computer Society.

Decker, M. (2009a). Prevention of Location-Spoofing. A Survey on Different Methods to Prevent the Manipulation of Locating-Technologies. *Proceedings of the International Conference on e-Business (ICE-B)*. Milan, Italy (pp. 109-114). Sétubal, Portugal: INSTICC Press.

Decker, M. (2009c). Modelling Location-Aware Access Control Constraints for Mobile Workflows with UML Activity Diagrams. *The Third International Conference on Mobile Ubiquitous Computing, Systems, Services and Technologies (UbiComm 2009)*, Sliema, Malta (pp. 263-268). Los Alamitos, USA: IEEE Computer Society.

Decker, M. (2009c). Mandatory and Location-Aware Access Control for Relational Databases. *Proceedings of the International Conference on Communication Infrastructure, Systems and Applications in Europe (EuropeComm 2009)*, London, U.K. (pp. 217-228). Berlin, Germany: Springer.

Decker, M., Che, H., Oberweis, A., Stürzel, P., & Vogel, M. (2010). Modeling Mobile Workflows with BPMN. *Proceedings of the Ninth International Conference on Mobile Business (ICMB 2010)/Ninth Global Mobility Roundtable (GMR 2010)*, Athens, Greece (pp. 272-279). Los Alamitos, USA: IEEE Computer Society.

Del.icio.us. (2007). *del.icio.us*. Retrieved May 7, 2007, from http://del.icio.us/

Delogu, C., Di Carlo, A., Rottundi, P., & Sartori, D. (1998). Usability evaluation of IVR systems with DTMF and ASR, 5th International Conference on Spoken Language Processing, paper 0320, Australia,1998.

Dempsey, B. J., Weiss, D., Jones, P., & Greenberg, J. (2002). Who is an open source software developer? *Communications of the ACM, 45*(2), 67–72. doi:10.1145/503124.503125

Deng, S., Wu, Z., Wu, J., Li, Y., & Yin, J. (2009). An Efficient Service Discovery Method and its Application. *International Journal of Web Services Research, 6*(4), 94–117..doi:10.4018/jwsr.2009071305

Denning, D., & MacDoran, P. (1996). Location-Based Authentication: Grounding Cyberspace for Better Security. *Computer Fraud & Security,*(2): 12–16. doi:10.1016/S1361-3723(97)82613-9

Denning, D. E., & Denning, P. J. (1979). Data Security. *ACM Computing Surveys, 11*(3), 227–249. doi:10.1145/356778.356782

Denscombe, M. (2007). *The Good Research Guide: For Small-scale Social Research Projects*. McGraw-Hill International.

Denzin, N. K., & Lincoln, Y. S. (2005).The discipline and practice of qualitative research. In: N.K., Denzin, & Y. S., Lincoln (Eds.) *The SAGE handbook of qualitative research*, 3rd Edition. London: Sage.

Deshpande, Y., Murugesan, S., Ginige, A., Hansen, S., Schwabe, D., & Gaedke, M. (2002). Web Engineering. *Journal of Web Engineering, 1*(1), 3–17.

Dey, A. K., Salber, D., & Abowd, G. D. (2001). A conceptual framework and a toolkit for supporting the rapid prototyping of context-aware-applications. *Human-Computer Interaction, 16*, 97–166. doi:10.1207/S15327051HCI16234_02

Dick, K. (2000). *XML: A Manager's Guide*. Reading, MA: Addison Wesley.

Dill, S., Kumar, R., McCurley, K., Rajagopalan, S., Sivakumar, D., & Tomkins, A. (2002). Self-similarity in the Web. *ACM Transactions on Internet Technology, 2*(3), 205–223. doi:10.1145/572326.572328

Disability Rights Commission. (2004). *The Web: access and inclusion for disabled people*. London: The Stationery Office.

Dix, A., Finlay, J. E., Abowd, G. D., & Beale, R. (2003). *Human-Computer Interaction* (3rd ed.). Upper Saddle River, NJ: Prentice Hall.

Dolgikh, D., & Sukhov, A. (2002). Parameters of cache systems based on a zipf-like distribution. *Elsevier Computer Networks, 37*, 711–716. doi:10.1016/S1389-1286(01)00243-2

Domingos, H., Martins, J. L., Preguica, N., & Duarte, S. M. (1999). A Workflow-Architecture to Manage Mobile Collaborative Work. *Proceedings of Encontro Portugues de Computacao Movel (EPCM '99)*, Tomar, Portugal.

Domingues, A. L. S., Bianchini, S. L., Re, R., & Ferrari, R. G. (2008). A Comparison Study of Web Development Methods. In *Proceedings of the 34th Latin-American Conference on Informatics* (pp. 10).

Dourish, P. (2003). What we talk about when we talk about context. *Personal and Ubiquitous Computing, 8*(1), 19–30. doi:10.1007/s00779-003-0253-8

Doyle, R. P., Chase, J. S., Gadde, S., & Vahdat, A. M. (2002). The trickle-down effect: Web caching and server request distribution. *Computer Communications, 25*, 345–356. doi:10.1016/S0140-3664(01)00406-6

Draper, S. W. (1999). Analysing fun as a candidate software requirement. *Personal and Ubiquitous Computing, 3*, 117–122. doi:10.1007/BF01305336

Duarte, C., & Carriço, L. (2008). Audio Interfaces for Improved Accessibility. In Pinder, S. (Ed.), *Advances in Human Computer Interaction* (pp. 121–142). Vienna, Austria: I-Tech Education and Publishing.

Düchting, M., Zimmermann, D., & Nebe, K. (2007). Incorporating User Centered Requirement Engineering into Agile Software Development. In *Human-Computer Interaction. Interaction Design and Usability. Proceedings.* (pp. 58-67). Springer.

Dumas, J. S., & Redish, J. C. (1999). *A Practical Guide to Usability Testing.* Bristol, UK: Intellect Books.

Duric, Z., Gray, W. D., Heishman, R., Li, F., Rosenfeld, A., & Schoelles, M. ... Wechsler, H. (2002). 'Integrating perceptual and cognitive modeling for adaptive and intelligent human-computer interaction. *Proceedings of the IEEE, 90*(7), 1272-1289.

Dybkjær, L., & Bernsen, N. O. (2000). Usability Issues in Spoken Language Dialogue Systems. *Natural Language Engineering, 6*(3-4), 243–272. doi:10.1017/S1351324900002461

Dybkjær, L., Bernsen, N. O., & Minker, W. (2004). Evaluation and Usability of Multimodal Spoken Language Dialogue Systems. *Speech Communication, 43*(1-2), 33–54. doi:10.1016/j.specom.2004.02.001

Dybkjær, L., Hemsen, H., & Minker, W. (Eds.). (2007). *Evaluation of Text and Speech Systems.* Berlin, Heidelberg: Springer-Verlag. doi:10.1007/978-1-4020-5817-2

Dybkjær, L., & Minker, W. (Eds.). (2008). *Recent Trends in Discourse and Dialogue.* Berlin, Heidelberg: Springer-Verlag. doi:10.1007/978-1-4020-6821-8

Dybkjær, L., & Bernsen, N. O. (2001). Usability Evaluation in Spoken Language Dialogue Systems. In. Proc. ACL Workshop on Evaluation Methodologies for Language and Dialogue Systems, pp.9-18.

Earp, R., & Bagui, S. (2000). Oracle's joins. *Oracle Internals, 2*(3), 6–14.

Ebner, G., Köhler, T., Lattemann, C., Preissl, B., & Rentmeister, J. (2004). *Rahmenbedingungen für eine Breitbandoffensive in Deutschland, Research study for Deutsche Telekom AG.* DIW-Berlin.

Eigner, R., & Linsmeier, W. (2006). Design criteria for wireless payment applications in vehicular ad-hoc networks. *Proceedings of the IADIS International Conference e-Commerce*, Barcelona, Spain.

Elmasri, R., & Navathe, S. B. (2007). *Fundamentals of Database Systems.* Boston, MA: Pearson Education.

Epting, F., Suchman, D., & Nickeson, C. (1971). An evaluation of elicitation procedures for personal constructs. *The British Journal of Psychology, 62*(4), 513–517.

Erickson, J., & Siau, K. (2010). Web Services, Service-Oriented Computing, and Service-Oriented Architecture: Separating Hype from Reality. In Tatnall, A., & Global, I. G. I. (Eds.), *Web Technologies: Concepts* (pp. 1786–1798). Methodologies, Tools, and Applications.

Erl, T. (2006). *Service-oriented architecture: concepts, technology, and design.* Upper Saddle River, NJ, USA: Prentice Hall PTR.

Ernest-Jones, T. (2006). Pinning down a security policy for mobile data. *Network Security,* (6): 8–12. doi:10.1016/S1353-4858(06)70399-3

Escalona, M. J., & Torres, J., Mejìas, M., GutiÈrrez, J. J., & Villadiego, D. (2007). The treatment of navigation in web engineering. *Advances in Engineering Software*, *38*(4), 267–282. doi:10.1016/j.advengsoft.2006.07.006

Fallman, D., & Waterworth, J. A. (2005). *Dealing with User Experience and Affective Evaluation in HCI Design: A Repertory Grid Approach*. Paper presented at the CHI Workshop on Evaluating Affective Interfaces: Innovative Approaches.

Fath, J. L., Mann, T. L., & Holzman, T. G. (1994). A Practical Guide to Using Software Usability Labs: Lessons Learned at IBM. *Behaviour & Information Technology*, *13*(1-2), 25–35.

Fellbaum, K., & Kouroupetroglou, G. (2008). Principles of Electronic Speech Processing with Applications for People with Disabilities. *Technology and Disability*, *20*(2), 55–85.

Fels, D. I., Richards, J., Hardman, J., Soudian, S., & Silverman, C. (2004). American sign language of the web. In *CHI '04 Extended Abstracts on Human Factors in Computing Systems* CHI '04 (pp. 1111-1114). New York: ACM.

Fenza, G., Loia, V., & Senatore, S. (2008). A Hybrid Approach to Semantic Web Service Matching. *International Journal of Approximate Reasoning*, *48*(3), 808–828.. doi:10.1016/j.ijar.2008.01.005

Fenza, G., Loia, V., & Senatore, S. (2007) Improving Fuzzy Service Matchmaking through Concept Matching Discovery, *Proc. IEEE Int. Conf on Fuzzy Systems*, London UK, CD.

Ferraiolo, D. F., Kuhn, D. R., & Chandramouli, R. (2007). *Role-Based Access Control* (2nd ed.). Boston, USA: Artech House.

Ferreira, J., Noble, J., & Biddle, R. (2007). Agile Development Iterations and UI Design. In *Proceedings AGILE Conference,* (pp. 50-58). Washington, DC: IEEE.

Florescu, D., Grunhagen, A., & Kossmann, D. (2003). XL: A platform for web services. Proceedings of First Biennial Conference on Innovative Data Systems Research (CIDR).

Ford, D. H. (1987). *Humans as Self-Constructing Living Systems: A Developmental Theory of Behaviour and Personality*. Hillsdale, NJ: Erlbaum.

Ford, M. E. (1992). *Motivating Humans, Goals, Emotions and Personal Agency Beliefs*. Thousand Oaks, CA: Sage.

Fransella, F., & Bannister, D. (1977). *A manual for repertory grid technique*. London: Academic Press.

Franz, W., Eberhardt, R., & Luckenbach, T. (2001). FleetNet - Internet on the Road. Proceedings of the 8th World Congress on Intelligent Transportation Systems, ITS 2001, Sydney, Australia.

Freire, A. P., Goularte, R., & de Mattos Fortes, R. P. (2007). Techniques for developing more accessible web applications: a survey towards a process classification. In *SIGDOC '07: Proceedings of the 25th annual ACM international conference on Design of communication* (pp. 162-169). New York: ACM.

Freire, A. P., Russo, C. M., & Fortes, R. P. M. (2008). A survey on the accessibility awareness of people involved in web development projects in Brazil. In *W4A '08: Proceedings of the 2008 international cross-disciplinary conference on Web accessibility (W4A)* (pp. 87-96). New York: ACM.

Freitas, D., & Kouroupetroglou, G. (2008). Speech Technologies for Blind and Low Vision Persons. *Technology and Disability*, *20*(2), 135–156.

Frey, P., Gonclaves, R., Kersten, M., & Teubner, J. (2009). Spinning relations: High-speed networks for distributed join processing. Proceedings of the 5th International Workshop on Data Management on New Hardware (DaMon 2009), 27-33.

Frishberg, N., Dirks, A. M., Benson, C., Nickell, S., & Smith, S. (2002). Getting to know you: Open source development meets usability. In *Proceedings of CHI 2002* (pp. 932-933). New York: ACM Press.

Fuchß, C., Stieglitz, S., & Hillmann, O. (2006). Ad-hoc Messaging Network in a Mobile Environment. Proceedings of the International Conference of Internet Technology and Secured Transactions, London.

Galitz, W. O. (2007). *The Essential Guide to User Interface Design*. Wiley Publishing, Inc.

Garzotto, F., Paolini, P., & Schwabe, D. (1993). HDM--a model-based approach to hypertext application design. *ACM Transactions on Information Systems*, *11*(1), 1–26. doi:10.1145/151480.151483

Gerber, A., Van Der Merwe, A., & Alberts, R. (2007). Practical implications of rapid development methodologies. In *Proceedings Computer Science and Information Technology Education Conference*.

Ginige, A., & Murugesan, S. (2001). Web engineering: an introduction. *Multimedia, IEEE, 8*(1), 14–18. doi:10.1109/93.923949

Ginige, A., & Murugesan, S. (2001). Guest Editors' Introduction: Web Engineering - An Introduction. *IEEE MultiMedia, 8*(1), 14–18. doi:10.1109/93.923949

Gladwell, M. (2000). *The tipping point: How little things can make a big difference*. New York: Time Warner Book Group.

Glosiene, A., & Manzhukh, Z. (2005). Towards a usability framework for memory institutions. *New Library World, 106*(7/8), 303–319. doi:10.1108/03074800510608620

Gómez, J., Cachero, C., & Pastor, O. (2001). Conceptual Modeling of Device-Independent Web Applications. *IEEE MultiMedia, 8*(2), 26–39. doi:10.1109/93.917969

Gong, W. B., Liu, Y., Misra, V., & Towsley, D. (2005). Self-similarity and long range dependence on the internet: a second look at the evidence, origins and implications. *Computer Networks, 48*(3), 377–399. doi:10.1016/j.comnet.2004.11.026

Gong, W. B., Liu, Y., Misra, V., & Towsley, D. (2005). Self-similarity and long range dependence on the internet: a second look at the evidence, origins and implications. *Computer Networks, 48*(3), 377–399. doi:10.1016/j.comnet.2004.11.026

Google. (2007). *Advanced Google search operators*. Retrieved May 7, 2007, from http://www.google.com/intl/ en/help/ operators.html

Gould, J. D., & Lewis, C. (1985). Design for usability: Key principles and what designers think. *Communications of the ACM, 28*(3), 360–411. doi:10.1145/3166.3170

Greenberg, S., Fitzpatrick, G., Gutwin, C., & Kaplan, S. (2000). Adapting the locales framework for heuristic evaluation of groupware. [AJIS]. *Australasian Journal of Information Systems, 7*(2), 102–108.

Gupta, K. M., & Aha, D. W. (2004) RuMoP: A Morphotactic Parser, *Proc. of the Int. Conference on Natural Language Processing*, Hyderabad, India, 280-284.

Gupta, K., Aha, D., & Moore, P. (2006) Rough set feature selection algorithms for textual case-based classification, *Proc. of 8th European Conf. on Case-Based Reasoning*, Turkey, 153-57.

Gupta, K., Moore, P. G., Aha, D., & Pal, S. (2005) Rough-Set Feature Selection Methods for Case-Based Categorization of Text Documents. *Proc. 1st Int.Conference on Pattern Recognition and Machine Intelligence*, Kolkata, India, 792-798.

Haas, Z. J., Pearlman, M. R., & Samar, P. (2003). *The Zone Routing Protocol (ZRP) for Ad Hoc Networks*. IETF.

Hackmann, G., Haitjema, M., Gill, C., & Roman, G.-C. (2006). Sliver: A BPEL Workflow Process Execution Engine for Mobile Devices. *Proceedings of the 4th International Conference on Service Oriented Computing (ICSOC 2006)*, Chicago, IL, USA (pp. 503-508). Berlin, Germany: Springer.

Haire, B., Henderson-Sellers, B., & D., a. L. (2001). Supporting web development in the OPEN process: additional tasks. In *Proceedings COMPSAC'2001: International Computer Software and Applications Conference*. New York: ACM.

Haiyun, L., Zerfos, P., Jiejun, K., Songwu, L., & Lixia, Z. (2002). Self-securing ad hoc wireless networks. Proceedings of the 7th International Symposion on Computers and Communications, 567-574.

Hajdinjak, M., & Mihelic, F. (2006). The PARADISE evaluation framework: Issues and findings. *Computational Linguistics, 32*(2), 263–272. doi:10.1162/coli.2006.32.2.263

Hales, B. M., & Provonost, P. J. (2006). The checklist. A tool for error management and performance improvement. *Journal of Critical Care, 21*, 231–235. doi:10.1016/j.jcrc.2006.06.002

Hales, B. M., Terblanche, M., Fowler, R., & Sibbald, W. (2008). Development of medical checklists for improved quality of patient care. *International Journal for Quality in Health Care, 20*(1), 22–30. doi:10.1093/intqhc/mzm062

Handy, M., & Timmermann, D. (2006). Time-Slot-Based Analysis of Bluetooth Energy Consumption for Page and Inquiry States. Proceedings of the 9th Euromicro Conference on Digital System Design (DSD 2006), 65-66.

Hansen, F., & Oleshchuk, V. (2003). SRBAC: A Spatial Role-Based Access Control Model for Mobile Systems. *Proceedings of the 7th Nordic Workshop on Secure IT Systems (NORDSEC '03).* Gjovik, Norway (pp. 129-141). Trondheim, Norway: NTNU.

Harris, R. A. (2005). *Voice Interaction Design: Crafting the New Conversational Speech Systems.* San Francisco: Morgan Kaufmann.

Harrison, C., & H., P. (2006). Impact of usability and accessibility problems in e-commerce and e-government websites. In *Proceedings HCI 2006.* (Vol. 1). London: British Computer Society.

Hartikainen, M., Salonen, E.-P., & Turunen, M. (2004). Subjective Evaluation of Spoken Dialogue Systems Using SERVQUAL Method. In Proc. 8th International Conference on Spoken Language Processing - ICSLP, pp. 2273-2276.

Hartmann, J., Sutcliffe, A., & De Angeli, A. (2007). *'Investigating attractiveness in web user interfaces.* Paper presented at the SIGCHI Conference on Human Factors in Computing Systems, San Jose, California.

Hartson, H. R., & Castillo, J. C. (1998). Remote evaluation for post-deployment usability improvement. In *Proceedings of AVI 1998* (pp. 22-29). New York: ACM Press.

Hartson, H. R., Castillo, J. C., Kelso, J., & Neale, W. C. (1996). Remote evaluation: The network as an extension of the usability laboratory. In *Proceedings of CHI 1996* (pp. 228-235). New York: ACM Press.

Hassenzahl, M., Beu, A., & Burmester, M. (2001a). Engineering Joy. *IEEE Software, 18*(1). doi:10.1109/52.903170

Hassenzahl, M., & Ullrich, D. (2007). To do or not to do: Differences in user experience and retrospective judgments depending on the presence or absence of instrumental goals. *Interacting with Computers, 19,* 429–437. doi:10.1016/j.intcom.2007.05.001

Hassenzahl, M. (2008). Aesthetics in interactive products: Correlates and consequences of beauty. In Schifferstein, H. N., & Hekkert, P. (Eds.), *Product Experience* (pp. 287–302). Elsevier. doi:10.1016/B978-008045089-6.50014-9

Hassenzahl, M., & Trautmann, T. (2001). *Analysis of web sites with the repertory grid technique.* Paper presented at the CHI 2001: extended abstracts: interactive poster sessions, New York, N.Y.

Hassenzahl, M., Wessler, R., & Hamborg, K. (2001b). *Exploring and understanding product qualities that users desire.* Paper presented at the Joint AFIHM-BCS conference on Human-Computer Interaction IHM-HCI'2001, Toulouse, France.

Hatch, M. J., & Cunliffe, A. L. (2006). *Organization Theory. Modern, Symbolic, and Postmodern Perspectives* (2nd ed.). Oxford, UK: Oxford University Press.

Hatch, M. J., & Yanow, D. (2008). Methodology by Metaphor: Ways of Seeing in Painting and Research. *Organization Science, 29*(1), 23–44. doi:10.1177/0170840607086635

Helander, M. (2006). *A Guide to Human Factors and Ergonomics* (2nd ed.). Boca Raton, FL: CRC Press.

Herlocker, J., Konstan, J. A., Terveen, L. G., & Riedl, J. T. (2004). Evaluating collaborative filtering recommender systems. *ACM Transactions on Information Systems, 22,* 5–53. doi:10.1145/963770.963772

Herlocker, J. L., Konstan, J. A., Borchers, A., & Riedl, J. (1999). An algorithmic framework for performing collaborative filtering. *Proceedings of the 22nd Annual international ACM SIGIR Conference on Research and Development in information Retrieval,* Berkeley, CA.

Hertzum, M., & Jacobsen, N. E. (2001). The evaluator effect: A chilling fact about us-ability evaluation methods. *International Journal of Human-Computer Interaction, 13*(4), 421–443. doi:10.1207/S15327590IJHC1304_05

Heß, A., & Kushmerick, N. (2003) Learning to Attach Semantic Metadata to Web Services, *Proc. of the 2nd International Semantic Web Conference,* Sanibel Island Florida, 258-273. AAAI Spring Symp. Semantic Web Services

Heß, A., & Kushmerick, N. (2004) Machine Learning for Annotating Semantic Web Services, *Proceedings of the AAAI Spring Symp. Semantic Web Services*, 341-346.

Hesse, W. (2003). Dinosaur meets Archaeopteryx? or: Is there an alternative for Rational's Unified Process? *Software and Systems Modeling, Springer, 2*(4), 240–247. doi:10.1007/s10270-003-0033-y

Hewett, R., & Kijsanayothin, P. (2009). Location Contexts in Role-based Security Policy Enforcement. *Proceedings of the 2009 International Conference on Security and Management*. Las Vegas, USA (pp. 13-16). Las Vegas, USA: CSREA Press.

HHS. (2006). *Research-based Web design & usability guidelines*. Retrieved March 13, 2007, from http://www.usability.gov/ pdfs/ guidelines.html

Hightower, J., & Boriello, G. (2001). Location Systems for Ubiquitous Computing. *IEEE Computer, 34*(8), 57–66.

Hirscheim, R. (1985). *Office automation: a social and organisational perspective*. Chichester, UK: Wiley.

Hollan, J., Hutchins, E., & Kirsh, D. (2000). Distributed Cognition: Toward a New Foundation for Human-Computer Interaction Research. *ACM Transactions on Computer-Human Interaction, 7*(2), 174–196. doi:10.1145/353485.353487

Holsapple, C., & Joshi, K. (2002). A Collaborative Approach to Ontology Design. *Communications of the ACM, 45*(2), 42–47..doi:10.1145/503124.503147

Hornbæk, K., & Frøkjær, E. (2004). Usability Inspection by Metaphors of Human Thinking Compared to Heuristic Evaluation. *International Journal of Human-Computer Interaction, 17*(3), 357–374. doi:10.1207/s15327590ijhc1703_4

Horvitz, E., Koch, P., & Subramani, M. (2007). Mobile opportunistic planning: Methods and models. *Proceedings of the 11th Conference on User Modeling (UM 2007)*, Springer LNCS 4511, Corfu, Greece.

Huang, X., Acero, A., & Hon, H.-W. (2001). *Spoken Language Processing: A Guide to Theory, Algorithm and System Development*. New Jersey: Prentice Hall PTR.

Huang, C., Yang, C., & Lee, C. (2009). Proxy Cache Admission and Replacement Policies for Layered Video Streaming. *Proceedings of the International Computer Symposium* (pp. 637–642). Tamkang University, Taiwan.

Huopaniemi, J., Patel, M., Riggs, R., Taivalsaari, A., Uotila, A., & Peursem, J. v. (2003). *Programming Wireless Devices with Java (TM)*. Platform Addison Wesley Professional.

Igbaria, M., Schiffman, S., & Wieckowski, T. (1994). The respective roles of perceived usefulness and perceived fun in the acceptance of microcomputer technology. *Behaviour & Information Technology, 13*(6). doi:10.1080/01449299408914616

Instone, K. (1999). *How to test usability*. Retrieved from http://usableweb.com/ instone/ howtotest

Isakowitz, T. a., Stohr, E. A., & Balasubramanian, P. (1995). RMM: a methodology for structured hypermedia design. *Communications of the ACM, 38*(8), 34–44. doi:10.1145/208344.208346

ISO 9241-11 (1998). *Ergonomic requirements for office work with visual display terminals* (VDTs), (Part 11: Guidance on usability). New York: ISO

ISO 9241-11. (1997). *Ergonomic Requirements for Office Work with Visual Display Terminals (VDTs)* (Part 11: Guidance on usability). ISO.

ISO. (1998). *International Standard ISO 9241-11: Ergonomic requirements for office work with visual display terminals (VDTs) - part 11: Guidance on usability*. Retrieved March 13, 2007, from http://www.idemployee.id.tue.nl/ g.w.m.rauterberg/ lectures.html

Ivory, M. Y., & Megraw, R. (2005). Evolution of Web site design patterns. *ACM Transactions on Information Systems, 23*(4), 463–497. doi:10.1145/1095872.1095876

Ivory, M. Y., & Hearst, M. A. (2001). The state of the art in automating usability evaluation of user interfaces. *ACM Computing Surveys, 33*(4), 470–516. doi:10.1145/503112.503114

Ivory, M. Y. (2003). *Automated Web Site Evaluation: Researchers and Practitioners Perspectives*. Amsterdam: Kluwer Academic Publishers.

Jacobsen, N. E., Hertzum, M., & John, B. E. (1998). The Evaluator Effect in Usability Tests. In *Proc. CHI '98.* New York: ACM Press

Jeffries, R., Miller, J. R., Wharton, C., & Uyeda, K. M. (1991). User Interface Evaluation in the Real World: A Comparison of Four Techniques. In *Proceedings of CHI '91* (pp. 119-124). New York: ACM Press.

Jin, S., & Bestavros, A. (2000, April 10-13). Popularity-aware greedydual-size Web proxy caching algorithms. In *In Proceedings of International Conference on Distributed Computing Systems (ICDCS),* Taipei, Taiwan (pp. 254-261).

Jing, J., Huff, K., Hurwitz, B., Sinha, H., Robinson, B., & Feblowitz, M. (2000). WHAM. Supporting Mobile Workforce and Applications in Workflow Environments. Proceedings of 10th International Workshop on Research Issues in Data Engineering (RIDE), San Diego, California, USA (pp. 31-38). Los Alamitos, USA: IEEE Computer Society.

JMBL. (2009) Joint METOC Public Data Administration Website. www.cffc.navy.mil/metoc/

Johnson, D. (1974). Approximation algorithms for combinatorial problems. *Journal of Computer and System Sciences, 9,* 256–278..doi:10.1016/S0022-0000(74)80044-9

Jokela, T. (2008). Characterizations, Requirements, and Activities of User-Centered Design—the KESSU 2.2Model. IN: E. L-C., Law, E.T., Hvannberg, & G., Cockton (Eds). *Maturing Usability. Quality in interaction, software and value.* London: Springer-Verlag Limited.

Jokela, T., & Abrahamsson, P. (2004*).* Usability Assessment of an Extreme Programming Project: Close Co-operation with the Customer Does Not Equal Good Usability. In *Product Focused Software Process Improvement: 5th International Conference, PROFES 2004 Proceedings* (pp. 393–407). Berlin: Springer-Verlag.

Jordan, P. W. (2002). *An Introduction To Usability.* London: Taylor and Francis.

Jurafsky, D., & Martin, J. H. (2008). *Speech and Language Processing. An Introduction to Natrural Language Processing, Computational Linguistics, and Speech Recognition.* New Jersey: Prentice-Hall.

Kamm, C. A., & Walker, M. A. (1997). Design and Evaluation of Spoken Dialogue Systems. In Proc. IEEE Workshop on Automatic Speech Recognition and Understanding, pp. 14–17.

Kamm, C.A., Litman, D. J., & Walker, M.A. (1998). From novice to expert: The effect of tutorials on user expertise with spoken dialogue systems. In Proc. 5th International Conference on Spoken Language Processing - ICSLP.

Kamm, C. A., Walker, M. A., & Litman, D. J. (1999). Evaluating spoken language systems. In Proc. Applied Voice Input/Output Society Conference - AVIOS, pp. 187–197.

Karagiannis, T., Faloutsos, M., & Molle, M. (2003). A user-friendly self-similarity analysis tool. *SIGCOMM Computer Communication Review, 33*(3), 81–93. doi:10.1145/956993.957004

Karat, C. M. (1990). Cost-benefit analysis of usability engineering techniques. In *Proceedings of the Human Factors Society 34th Annual Meeting* (Vol 2), (pp. 839-843), Orlando, FL.

Karat, C.M., Halverson, C., Horn, D., & Karat, J. (1999). Patterns of entry and correction in large vocabulary continuous speech recognition systems. ACM Conference on Human Factors in Computing Systems. Pittsburgh, PA.

Karat, C.-M., Campbell, R., & Fiegel, T. (1992). Comparison of Empirical Testing and Walk-through Methods in User Interface Evaluation. In *Proceedings of CHI '92* (pp. 397-404). New York: ACM Press

Kavassalis, P., Lelis, S., Rafea, M., & Haridi, S. (2004). What makes a Web site popular? *Communications of the ACM, 47*(2), 50–55. doi:10.1145/966389.966415

Keevil, B. (1998, September 24-26). Measuring the usability index of your Web site. In *Proceedings of the 16th Annual International Conference on Computer documentation,* Quebec City, Quebec, Canada (pp. 271-277). ACM Publishing.

Keinonen, T. (2008). User-centered design and fundamental need. In *Proceedings of the 5th Nordic Conference on Human-Computer interaction: Building Bridges* (pp. 211-219), Lund, Sweden.

Kelly, G. (1955). *The psychology of personal constructs* (Vol. 1 & 2). New York, NY: Norton.

Kennaugh, P., & Petrie, H. (2006). *Enhanced Access to Television (EAT): humanITy.*

Khayari, R. E. A. (2006). Design and evaluation of Web proxies by leveraging self-similarity of Web traffic. *Computer Networks, 50*(12), 1952–1973. doi:10.1016/j.comnet.2005.10.003

Kim, W., Reiner, D. S., & Batory, D. S. (1985). *Query Processing in Database System.* New York: Springer-Verlag.

Kim, H. (2002). Predicting How Ontologies for the Semantic Web Will Evolve. *Communications of the ACM, 45*(2), 48–54..doi:10.1145/503124.503148

King, N. (2004). Using interviews in Qualitative Research. In *C., Cassell, & G., Symon, Essential Guide to Qualitative Methods in Organizational Research.* Thousand Oaks, CA: Sage Publications.

King, N., Ma, T. H.-Y., Zaphiris, P., Petrie, H., & Hamilton, F. (2004). An incremental usability and accessibility evaluation framework for digital libraries. In Brophy, P., Fisher, S., & Craven, J. (Eds.), *Libraries without walls 5: The distributed delivery of library and information services* (pp. 123–131). London, UK: Facet.

Knublauch, H. Fergerson, F. Noy N.and Musen,M. (2004) The Protege OWL Plugin: An Open Development Environment for Semantic Web Applications. *Third International Conference on the Semantic Web (ISWC-2004),* Hiroshima, Japan, 342-351.

Kobsa, A. (2007). Privacy-Enhanced Personalization. *Communications of the ACM, 50*(8), 24–33. doi:10.1145/1278201.1278202

Koch, N. (2001). *Software engineering for adaptive hypermedia applications.* Munich, Germany: Uni-Druck Publishing Company.

Koch, N., & Kraus, A. (2003). Towards a Common Metamodel for the Development of Web Applications. In *Web Engineering* (pp. 419-422). Berlin: Springer.

Kolodner, J. (1992). An Introduction to Case-Based Reasoning. *Artificial Intelligence Review, 6,* 3–24.. doi:10.1007/BF00155578

Koua, E., MacEachren, A. M., & Kraak, M. (2006). Evaluating the usability of visualization methods in an exploratory geovisualization environment. *International Journal of Geographical Information Science, 20*(4), 425–448. doi:10.1080/13658810600607550

Kouroupetroglou, G., & Spiliotopoulos, D. (2009). Usability Methodologies for Real-Life Voice User Interfaces. *International Journal of Information Technology and Web Engineering, 4*(4), 78–94. doi:10.4018/jitwe.2009100105

Kouroupetroglou, G. (2009). Universal Access in Public Terminals: Information Kiosks and Automated Teller Machines (ATMs). In Stephanidis, C. (Ed.), *The Universal Access Handbook* (pp. 761–780). Boca Raton, Florida: CRC Press. doi:10.1201/9781420064995-c48

Koyani, S., & Allison, S. (2003, April 5-10). Use of research-based guidelines in the development of Web sites. In *Extended Abstracts on Human Factors in Computing Systems: Proceedings of CHI '03,* Ft. Lauderdale, FL (pp. 696-697). ACM Publishing.

Krashakov, S. A., Teslyuk, A. B., & Shchur, L. N. (2006). On the universality of rank distributions of Website popularity. *Computer Networks, 50*(11), 1769–1780. doi:10.1016/j.comnet.2005.07.009

Kroll, P., & Kruchten, P. (2003). *The Rational Unified Process Made Easy: A Practitioner's Guide to the RUP.* Reading, MA: Addison-Wesley.

Kruchten, P. (2003). *The Rational Unified Process: An Introduction.* Reading, MA: Addison-Wesley.

Krug, S. (2000) *Don't Make Me Think – A Common Sense Approach to Web Usability.* Circle.com Library, USA

Kumar, M., & Newman, R. E. (2006). STRBAC — An Approach Towards Spatio-Temporal Role-Based Access Control. *Proceedings of the Conference on Communication, Network, and Information Security (CNIS)* (pp. 150-155). Calgary, AB, Canada: ACTA Press.

Kuniavsky, M. (2003). *Observing the user experience. A practitioner's guide to user research.* San Francisco: Elsevier.

Küpper, A. (2007). *Location-based Services. Fundamentals and Operation (reprint).* Chichester, U.K.: Wiley & Sons.

Kurniawan, S. H. (2003). Aging. In *Web Accessibility: A foundation for research* (pp.47-58). Berlin: Springer

Lacy, L. (2005). *Owl: Representing Information Using the Web Ontology Language*. Trafford Publishing London UK.

Ladner, R., & Petry, F. (2005). *Net-Centric Approaches to Intelligence and National Security*. Kluwer Press. doi:10.1007/b137009

Lampson, B. (1974). Protection. *Operating Systems Review, 8*(1), 18–24. doi:10.1145/775265.775268

Larsen, L. B. (2003). Issues in the Evaluation of Spoken Dialogue Systems using Objective and Subjective Measures. In Proc. 8th IEEE Workshop on Automatic Speech Recognition and Understanding -ASRU, pp. 209-214.

Larsen, L. B. (2003). On the Usability of Spoken Dialogue Systems. PhD Thesis, Aalborg University.

Larson, J. A. (2000). Introduction and Overview of W3C Speech Interface Framework, Retrieved August 2, 2009, from http://www.w3.org/ TR/voice-intro/

Larson, J. A., Raman, T. V., & Raggett, D. (2003). W3C Multimodal Interaction Framework, Retrieved August 2, 2009, from http://www.w3.org/ TR/mmi-framework/

Lattemann, C., & Stieglitz, S. (2007). Online Communities for Customer Relationship Management on Financial Stock Markets - A Case Study from a German Stock Exchange, Proceedings of Americas Conference on Information Systems (AMCIS 2007), Colorado, USA.

Lavery, D., Cockton, G., & Atkinson, M. P. (1997). Comparison of Evaluation Methods Using Structured Usability Problem Reports. *Behaviour & Information Technology, 16*(4), 246–266. doi:10.1080/014492997119824

Law, E. L.-C., Hvannberg, E. T., & Cockton, G. (2008). A Green Paper on Usability Maturation In E. L-C., Law, E.T., Hvannberg, & G., Cockton (Eds). *Maturing Usability. Quality in interaction, software and value*. London: Springer-Verlag Limited.

Lazar, J., Dudley-Sponaugle, A., & Greenidge, K. (2004). Improving Web Accessibility: A Study of Webmaster Perceptions. *Computers in Human Behavior, 20*(2), 269–288. doi:10.1016/j.chb.2003.10.018

Lederer, A. L., Maupin, D. J., Sena, M. P., & Zhuang, Y. (1998, March 26-28). The role of ease of use, usefulness and attitude in the prediction of World Wide Web usage. In *Proceedings of the 1998 ACM SIGCPR Conference on Computer Personnel Research,* Boston (pp. 195-204). ACM Publishing.

Lee, K. M., & Lai, J. (2005). Speech Versus Touch: A Comparative Study of the Use of Speech and DTMF Keypad for Navigation. [Lawrence Erlbaum Associates.]. *International Journal of Human-Computer Interaction, 19*(3), 343–360. doi:10.1207/s15327590ijhc1903_4

Lee, J. C., & McCrickard, D. S. (2007). Towards Extreme(ly) Usable Software: Exploring Tensions Between Usability and Agile Software Development. In *Proceedings AGILE Conference,* (pp. 59-71). Berlin: IEEE.

Leland, W. E., Taqqu, M. S., Willinger, W., & Wilson, D. V. (1994). On the self-similar nature of ethernet traffic (extended version). *IEEE/ACM Transactions on Networking, 2*(1), 1–15. doi:10.1109/90.282603

Leland, W. E., Taqqu, M. S., Willinger, W., & Wilson, D. V. (1994). On the self-similar nature of ethernet traffic (extended version). *IEEE/ACM Transactions on Networking, 2*(1), 1-15.

Lemeni, G., & Miclea, M. (2004). *Consiliere şi orientare. Ghid de educaţie pentru carieră*. Cluj-Napoca: Editura ASCR.

Lemire, D., & Maclachlan, A. (2005). Slope one predictors for online rating-based collaborative filtering. *Proceedings of the SIAM Conference on Data Mining (SDM 2005)*, Newport Beach, USA.

Leopold, M., Dydensborg, M. B., & Bonnet, P. (2003). Bluetooth and sensor networks: a reality check. Proceedings of the 1st international conference on Embedded networked sensor systems.

Li, M., Yu, B., Sahota, V., & Qi, M. (2009). Web Services Discovery wth Rough Sets. *International Journal of Web Services Research, 6*(1), 69–86..doi:10.4018/jswr.2009092104

Lif, M., & Goransson, B. (2007). Usability Design: A New Rational Unified Process Discipline. In *Proceedings Human-Computer Interaction; INTERACT 2007,* (pp. 714-715). New York: ACM.

Linsky, J. (2001). Bluetooth and power consumption: issues and answers. *R.F. Design*, 74–95.

Litman, D. J., & Pan, S. (2002). Designing and evaluating an adaptive spoken dialogue system. *User Modeling and User-Adapted Interaction*, *12*(2-3), 111–137. doi:10.1023/A:1015036910358

Litman, D. J., Pan, S., & Walker, M. A. (1998). Evaluating Response Strategies in a Web-Based Spoken Dialogue Agent. In Proc. 36th Annual Meeting of the Association for Computational Linguistics and 17th International Conf. on Computational Linguistics (ACL/COLING), pp.780–786.

Liu, S. G., Wang, P. J., & Qu, L. J. (2005, August 18-21). Modeling and simulation of self-similar data traffic. In *Proceedings of 2005 International Conference on Machine Learning and Cybernetics*, Guangzhou, China (Vol. 7, pp. 3921-3925). Washington, DC: IEEE Computer Society.

Macker, J. P., & Corson, M. S. (1998). Mobile ad hoc networking and the IETF. *ACM Mobile Computing and Communications Review*, *2*(1), 9–14. doi:10.1145/584007.584015

Mariage, C., & Vanderdonckt, J. (2005). Creating Contextualised Usability Guides for Web Sites Design and Evaluation. *Computer-Aided Design of User Interfaces*, *IV*, 147–158. doi:10.1007/1-4020-3304-4_12

Markatchev, N., & Williamson, C. (2004). Webtraff: A gui for Webproxy cache workload modelling and analysis. *Computer Communications*, 76–81.

Marshall, C., & Rossman, G. B. (2006). *Designing Qualitative Research* (3rd ed.). London: Sage.

Martens, A. (2003). Usability of Web Services. *International Conference on Web Information Systems Engineering Workshops,* (pp. 182-190). Washington, DC: IEEE.

McDonald, A., & Welland, R. (2004). Evaluation of Commercial Web Engineering Processes. In *Web Engineering* (pp. 166-170). Berlin: Springer.

McDonald, J. (2006). *Spearman's rank correlation*. Retrieved September 9, 2007, from http://www.udel.edu/~mcdonald/ statspearman.html

McTear, M. F. (2004). *Spoken Dialogue Technology: Towards the Conversational User Interface*. London: Springer-Verlag.

Meiss, M. R., Menczer, F., Fortunato, S., Flammini, A., & Vespignani, A. (2008). Ranking Web sites with real user traffic. In *Wsdm '08: Proceedings of the international conference on Web search and Web data mining* (pp. 65–76). New York, NY, USA: ACM.

Memmel, T., Reiterer, H., & Holzinger, A. (2007). Agile Methods and Visual Specification in Software Development: A Chance to Ensure Universal Access. In *Proceedings of Universal Access in Human Computer Interaction Coping with Diversity.* (pp. 453-462). Berlin: Springer.

Meszaros, G., & Aston, J. (2006). Adding usability testing to an agile project. In *Proceedings of Agile Conference, 2006.* Washington, DC: IEEE.

Michael, L., Nejdl, W., Papapetrou, O., & Siberski, W. (2007). Improving distributed join efficiency with extended bloom filter operation. 21st International Conference on Advanced Networking and Applications.

Michiardi, P., & Molva, R. (2001). CORE: A Collaborative Reputation Mechanism to enforce node cooperation in Mobile Ad hoc Networks, IFIP Conference Proceedings, Vol. 228, 107-121.

Millard, N., Hole, L., & Crowle, S. (1999). Smiling through: motivation at the user interface. In Bullinger, H.-J., & Ziegler, J. (Eds.), *Human-Computer Interaction Ergonomics and User Interfaces* (pp. 824–828). Mahwah, NJ, USA: Lawrence Erlbaum.

Miller, B. N., Konstan, J. A., & Riedl, J. T. (2004). PocketLens: Toward a Personal Recommender System. *ACM Transactions on Information Systems*, *22*(3), 437–476. doi:10.1145/1010614.1010618

Mishra, P., & Eich, M. H. (1992). Join processing in relational databases. *ACM Computing Surveys*, *24*(1), 63–113. doi:10.1145/128762.128764

Moegele, K. (2010). *Evaluating the Recommendation Quality of a Mobile Recommender System*. Munich, Germany: Guided Research, Institut fuer Informatik, Technische Universitaet Muenchen.

Mohamad, Y., Stegemann, D., Koch, J., & Velasco, C. A. (2004). imergo: Supporting Accessibility and Web Standards to Meet the Needs of the Industry via Process-Oriented Software Tools. In *Proceedings of the 9th International Conference on Computers Helping People With Special Needs (ICCHP 2004)*, (pp. 310-316). Berlin: Springer.

Molich, R. (2000). *User-Friendly Web Design*. Copenhagen, Denmark: Ingeniøren Books.

Moller, S., Engelbrecht, K., & Schleicher, R. (2008). Predicting the quality and usability of spoken dialogue services. *Speech Communication*, *50*(8-9), 730–744. doi:10.1016/j.specom.2008.03.001

Moller, S., Englert, R., Engelbrecht, K., Hafner, V., Jameson, A., Oulasvirta, A., et al. (2006). MeMo: Towards Automatic Usability Evaluation of Spoken Dialogue Services by User Error Simulations. In Proc. 9th International Conference on Spoken Language Processing - ICSLP, pp. 1786-1789.

Monk, A., Wright, P., Haber, J., & Davenport, L. (1993). *Improving your human-computer interface: a practical technique*. Bath, UK: Redwood Books.

Morgan, D. L., Krueger, R. A., & King, J. A. (1998). *Focus Group Kit*. London: Sage.

Motschnig-Pitrik, R. (2002). Employing the Unified Process for Developing a Web-Based Application - A Case-Study. In *Practical Aspects of Knowledge Management: 4th International Conference, PAKM 2002 Vienna, Austria, December 2-3, 2002, Proceedings*, (pp. 97-113). Berlin: Springer.

Mundorf, N., Westin, S., & Dholakia, N. (1993). Effects of hedonic components and user's gender on the acceptance of screen-based information services. *Behaviour & Information Technology*, *12*(5), 293–303. doi:10.1080/01449299308924393

Mundt, T. (2006). Two Methods of Authenticated Positioning. Proceedings of the International Workshop on Quality of Service & Security for Wireless and Mobile Networks (Q2S Winet). Terromolinos, Spain (pp. 25-32). Boston, MA, USA: ACM Press.

Murphy, J., Howard, S., Kjeldskov, K., & Goschnick, S. (2004). Location, location, location: Challenges of outsourced usability evaluation. In *Proceedings of the Workshop on Improving the Interplay between Usability Evaluation and User Interface Design, NordiCHI 2004*, Aalborg University, Department of Computer Science, HCI-Lab Report no. 2004/2 (pp. 12-15).

Myers, B. A., & Rosson, M. B. (1992). Survey on user interface programming. In Proceedings *of SIGCHI '92: Human Factors in Computing Systems* (pp. 195-202), Monterey, CA: ACM.

Ncube, C., Lockerbie, J., & Maiden, N. A. M. (2007). Automatically Generating Requirements from \it * Models: Experiences with a Complex Airport Operations System. In *Proceedings REFSQ*, (pp. 33-47).

Ni, S.-Y., Tseng, Y.-C., Chen, Y.-S., & Sheu, J.-P. (1999). The broadcast storm problem in a mobile ad hoc network. Proceedings of the 5th annual ACM/IEEE international conference on Mobile computing and networking, ACM Press, Seattle, Washington, USA, 151-162.

Nielsen, J. (1999). User interface directions for the Web. *Communications of the ACM*, *42*(1), 65–72. doi:10.1145/291469.291470

Nielsen, J. (1992). Finding Usability Problems through Heuristic Evaluation. In *Proceedings of CHI '92* (pp. 373-380). New York: ACM Press.

Nielsen, J. (1993). *Usability Engineering*. San Francisco: Morgan Kaufmann Publishers.

Nielsen, J. (2000). *Designing Web Usability*. New York: New Riders Publishing.

Nielsen, J., & Landauer, T. K. (1993). A mathematical model of the finding of usability problems. In *Proceedings INTERCHI '93: Human Factors in Computing Systems* (pp. 206-213), Amsterdam, NL.

Nielsen, J., & Mack, R. (1994). Usability Inspection Methods (pp. 448p). New York, NY.

Nielsen, J., & Tahir, M. (2002). *Homepage Usability – 50 Websites Deconstructed*. New York: New Riders Publishing.

Nielsen, J., Bush, R. M., Dayton, T., Mond, N. E., Muller, M. J., & Root, R. W. (1992). Teaching experienced developers to design graphical user interfaces. In *Proceedings of CHI 1992* (pp. 557-564). New York: ACM Press.

Nissanka, B. Priyantha, N.B., Chakraborty, A., Balakrishnan, H. (2000). The Cricket location-support system. Proceedings of the 6th Annual International Conference on Mobile Computing and Networking (MobiCom 2000), Boston, MA, USA (pp. 32-43). Boston, MA, USA: ACM Press.

NLANR. (2007). *Cache access logs*. Retrieved from ftp://ircache.nlanr.net/Traces/

Norman, D. A. (2004). *Emotional design: Why we love (or hate) everyday things*. New York: Basic Books.

Norman, D. A., Ortony, A., & Russell, D. M. (2003). Affect and Machine Design: Lessons for the Development of Autonomous Machines. *IBM Systems Journal, 42*(1), 38–44. doi:10.1147/sj.421.0038

Obendorf, H., & Finck, M. (2008). Scenario-based usability engineering techniques in agile development processes. In *CHI '08: CHI '08 extended abstracts on Human factors in computing systems* (pp. 2159-2166). New York: ACM.

Oberweis, A. (2005). Person-to-Application Processes. Workflow-Management (Chapter 2). In M. Dumas, W. v.d. Aalst, & A. Hofstede (Eds.), *Process-Aware Information Systems — Bridging People and Software Through Process Technology* (pp. 21-36). Hoboken, USA: Wiley Interscience.

Ogata, H., & Yano, Y. (2000). Supporting Knowledge Awareness for Ubiquitous CSCL. *E-learning*, 2362–2369.

Ohnemus, K. R. (1997, October 19-22). Web style guides: Who, what, where. In *Proceedings of the 15th Annual International Conference on Computer Documentation*, Salt Lake City, UT (pp. 189-197). ACM Publishing.

Onacă (Andrei). D.M., & Guran, A.M. (2008). A User-centred approach in developing an intelligent web assistant for supporting career related decision making. In *Proceedings of* the *Romanian Computer Human Interaction Conference*. Bucureşti: Matrix Rom, Onacă (Andrei), D.M., Tarţa, A.M., & Pitariu, H.D. (2006). The development of a theatre/opera website pattern based on a user need assessment approach, *Psihologia Resurselor Umane, 4*(1).

Oppenheim, A. N. (1992). *Questionnaire design, interviewing and attitude measurement* (2nd ed.). London: St Martins Press.

Osgood, C. E., Suci, G. J., & Tannenbaum, P. H. (1971). *The Measurement of Meaning*. London: University of Illinois Press.

Osman, T., Thakker, D., & Al-Dabass, D. (2010). In Tatnall, A., & Global, I. G. I. (Eds.), *Utilisation of Case-Based Reasoning for Semantic Web Services Composition. Web Technologies: Concepts* (pp. 604–622). Methodologies, Tools, and Applications.

Ouzzani, M., & Bouguettaya. (2004). A. Efficient access to web services. *IEEE Internet Computing, 8*(2), 34–44. doi:10.1109/MIC.2004.1273484

Oxford. (n.d.). *Compact Oxford English dictionary (ask Oxford)*. Retrieved July 08, 2007, from http://www.ask-oxford.com/ concise_oed/ popular?view=uk

Pacheco, J. C. R., & Roman, D. T. (2006, November). A tool for long-range dependent analysis via the r/s statistic. In *Proceedings of the 15th International Conference on Computing (CIC '06)*, Mexico City, Mexico (pp. 361-366). Washington, DC: IEEE Computer Society.

Paddison, C., & Englefield, P. (2004). Applying heuristics to accessibility inspections. *Interacting with Computers, 16*(3), 507–521. doi:10.1016/j.intcom.2004.04.007

Pajunen, L., & Chande, S. (2007). Developing Workflow Engine for Mobile Devices. *Proceedings of the 11th IEEE International Enterprise Distributed Object Computing Conference (EDOC 2007)*, Annapolis, Maryland, USA (pp. 279-286). Los Alamitos, USA: IEEE Computer Society.

Palmer, J. W. (2002). Web site usability, design, and performance metrics. *Information Systems Research, 13*(2), 151–167. doi:10.1287/isre.13.2.151.88

Palmer, S. R., & Felsing, J. M. (2002). *A Practical Guide to Feature-Driven Development*. Upper Saddle River, NJ: Prentice Hall PTR.

Pan, S., & McKeown, K. (1997). Integrating language generation with speech synthesis in a concept to speech system. In Proceedings of ACL/EACL'97 Concept to Speech Workshop, Madrid, Spain.

Paolucci, M., Soudry, J., Srinivasan, N., & Sycara, K. (2004), A Broker for OWL-S Web services, *Proceedings of the AAAI Spring Symposium on Semantic Web Services,* 562-567.

Papazoglou, M. (2007). *Web Services: Principles and Technology.* Prentice Hall.

Pawlak, Z. (1984). Rough Sets. *International Journal of Man-Machine Studies, 21,* 127–134..doi:10.1016/S0020-7373(84)80062-0

Pei, G., Gerla, M., & Chen, T.-W. (2000). Fisheye state routing: a routing scheme for ad hoc wireless networks. Proceedings of the IEEE Internations Conference on Communications, 70-74.

Perrizo, W., Lin, J. Y. Y., & Hoffman, W. (1989). Algorithms for distributed query processing in broadcast local area networks. *IEEE Transactions on Knowledge and Data Engineering, 1*(2), 215–225. doi:10.1109/69.87961

Peterson, J. L. (1977). Petri Nets. *ACM Computing Surveys, 9*(3), 223–252. doi:10.1145/356698.356702

Petrie, H., & Kheir, O. (2007, April 28-May 3). The relationship between accessibility and usability of Web sites. In *Proceedings of the SIGCHI Conference on Human Factors in Computing Systems (CHI 2007),* San Jose, CA (pp. 397-406). ACM Publishing.

Petrie, H., Hamilton, F., King, N., & Pavan, P. (2006). Remote usability evaluations with disabled people. In *CHI '06: Proceedings of the SIGCHI conference on Human Factors in computing systems* (pp. 1133-1141). New York: ACM.

Petrie, H., King, N., & Hamilton, F. (2005). *Accessibility of museum, library and archive websites: the MLA audit.* Retrieved 01/2009 from http://www.mla.gov.uk/ webdav/ harmonise?Page/ @id=73&Document/ @id=23090&Section%5B @stateId_eq _left_hand_root %5D/ @id=4302

Petrie, H., Weber, G., & Fisher, W. (2005). Personalization, interaction and navigation in rich multimedia documents for print disabled users. In *IBM Systems Journal.* Armonk NY: IBM.

Picard, R. W., & Wexelblat, A. (2002). *Future interfaces: social and emotional.* Paper presented at the CHI '02 Extended Abstracts on Human Factors in Computing Systems, Minneapolis, Minnesota, USA.

Pirzada, A. A., & McDonald, C. (2004). Establishing trust in pure ad-hoc networks. Proceedings of the 27th conference on Australian computer science, 26.

Pitariu, H.D. (2003). The influence of personality traits upon human computer interaction. *Cognition, Brain, Behavior, 7*(3).

Powers, S. (2003) *Practical RDF,* O'Reilly Media, Inc, Sebastopol, CA.

Preece, J., Rogers, Y., & Sharp, H. (2002). *Interaction Design: Beyond Human-Computer Interaction.* New York: John Wiley & Sons.

Pressman, R. (2006). *Software Engineering: A Practitioner's Approach* (6th ed.). New York: McGraw-Hill.

R Development Core Team. (2008). *R: A language and environment for statistical computing.* Retrieved from http://cran.r-project.org/ doc/ manuals/ refman.pdf

Rama, A. (2007). Semantic Web Services. In Cardoso, J., & Global, I. G. I. (Eds.), *Semantic Web Services* (pp. 191–216). Hershey, PA.

Ramesh, S., Papapetrou, O., & Siberski, W. (2008). Optimizing distributed joins with bloom filters. *Lecture Notes in Computer Science, 5375,* 145–156. doi:10.1007/978-3-540-89737-8_15

Rao, S., & March, S. T. (2004). Optimizing distributed join queries: A genetic algorithm approach. *Annals of Operations Research, 71*(0), 199–228.

Ratnasingam, P. (2010). The Role of Web Services: A Balance Scorecard Perspective. In Tatnall, A., & Global, I. G. I. (Eds.), *Web Technologies: Concepts* (pp. 865–879). Methodologies, Tools, and Applications.

Ray, I., & Kumar, M. (2006). Towards a Location-based Mandatory Access Control Model. *Computers & Security, 25*(1), 36–44. doi:10.1016/j.cose.2005.06.007

Ray, I., Kumar, M., & Yu, L. (2006). LRBAC: A Location-Aware Role-Based Access Control Model. *Proceedings of the Second International Conference on Information Systems Security (ICISS '06)*, Kolkata, India (pp. 147-161). Berlin, Germany: Springer.

Resende, L., & Feng, R. (2007). Handling heterogeneous data sources in a SOA environment with Service Data Objects (SDO). SIGMOD'07, Beijing, China.

Rezaul, K. M., & Grout, V. (2007, October 23-25). An overview of long-range dependent network traffic engineering and analysis: characteristics, simulation, modelling and control. In *Proceedings of the 2nd International Conference on Performance Evaluation Methodologies and Tools,* Nantes, France (pp. 1-10). Brussels, Belgium: Institute for Computer Sciences, Social-Informatics and Telecommunications Engineering.

Ricci, F. (2010). (to appear). Mobile Recommender Systems. *International Journal of Information Technology and Tourism.*

Richardson, J. T. E. (2002). *Handbook of Qualitative Research Methods for Psychology and the Social Sciences.* Oxford: BPS Blackwell Publishing.

Robin, M., & Larson, J. (1999). Voice Browsers: An introduction and glossary for the requirement drafts. W3C Working Draft, December 1999

Robson, C. (1993). *Real World Research.* Oxford: Blackwell.

Rohn, J. A. (1994). The Usability Engineering Laboratories at Sun Microsystems. *Behaviour & Information Technology, 13*(1-2), 25–35. doi:10.1080/01449299408914581

Rosenbaum, S. (2008). The Future of Usability Evaluation: Increasing Impact on Value. In Law, E. L.-C., Hvannberg, E., & Cockton, G. (Eds.), *Maturing Usability: Quality in Software, Interaction and Value, Human-Computer Interaction Series* (pp. 75–95). London: Springer-Verlag Limited.

Royer, E. M., & Toh, C.-K. (1999). *A Review of Current Routing Protocols for Ad Hoc Mobile Wireless Networks.* IEEE Personal Communications.

Rubin, J., & Chisnell, D. (2008). *Handbook of Usability Testing: How to Plan, Design, and Conduct Effective Tests.* Indianapolis, Indiana: Wiley Publishing, Inc.

Rubin, J. (1994). *Handbook of Usability Testing: How to plan, design and conduct effective tests.* New York: John Wiley & Sons.

Ryan, R. M., & Deci, E. L. (2000). Self-Determination Theory and the Facilitation of Intrinsic Motivation, Social Development, and Well-Being. *The American Psychologist, 55*, 68–78. doi:10.1037/0003-066X.55.1.68

Ryle, A., & Lunghi, M. (1970). The dyad grid: a modification of repertory grid technique. *The British Journal of Psychology*, 117.

San Murugesan, Y. D., Hansen, S., & Ginige, A. (2001). Web Engineering: A New Discipline for Development of Web-Based Systems. In *Web Engineering Managing Diversity and Complexity of Web Application Development,* (LNCS Vol. 2016, pp. 3-13). Berlin: Springer.

Sandhu, R. (1991). Separation of Duties in Computerized Information Systems. *Database Security IV: Status and Prospects - Results of the IFIP WG 11.3 Workshop on Database Security*, Halifax, U.K. (pp. 179-189). Amsterdam, Netherlands: North-Holland Publishing.

Sarnikar, S., & Murphy, M. (2009). A Usability Analysis Framework for Healthcare Information Technology. *Sprouts: Working Papers on Information Systems, 9*(62). Retrieved on July 10th 2010 from http://sprouts.aisnet.org/9-62.

Sastry, N., Shankar, U., & Wagner, D. (2003). Secure Verification of Location Claims. *Proceedings of the Conference on Wireless Security (WiSe)*, San Diego, California, USA (pp. 1-10). Boston, MA, USA: ACM Press.

Sauermann, L., et al. (2006). Semantic Desktop 2.0: The Gnowsis Experience. *Proceedings 5th International Semantic Web Conference*, Springer LNCS 4273.

Schamel, J. (2008). *How the pilot's checklist came about.* Retrieved from http://www.atchistory.org/ History/checklst.htm

Scheuermann, P., & Chong, E. I. (1995). Distributed join processing using bipartite graphs. Proceedings of the 15th International Conference on Distributed Computing Systems, 385.

Scholtz, J., Laskowski, S., & Downey, L. (1998). Developing Usability Tools and Techniques for Designing and Testing Web Sites. In *Proceedings of the 4th Conference on Human Factors & the Web*. AT&T.

Schonberg, E., Cofino, T., Hoch, R., Podlaseck, M., & Spraragen, S. L. (2000). Measuring success. *Communications of the ACM, 43*(8), 53–57. doi:10.1145/345124.345142

Schwabe, D., & Rossi, G. (1998). An object oriented approach to web-based applications design. *Theory and Practice of Object Systems, 4*(4), 207–225. doi:10.1002/(SICI)1096-9942(1998)4:4<207::AID-TAPO2>3.0.CO;2-2

Segev, A. (1986). Optimization of join operations in horizontally partitioned database systems. *ACM Transactions on Database Systems, 11*(1), 48–80. doi:10.1145/5236.5241

Selvakuberan, K., Devi, I., & Rajaram, R. (2010). Feature Selection for Web Page Classification. In Tatnall, A., & Global, I. G. I. (Eds.), *Web Technologies: Concepts* (pp. 1462–1477). Methodologies, Tools, and Applications.

Serpanos, D., Karakostas, G., & Wolf, W. (2000, July 30-August 2). Effective caching of Web objects using zipf's law. In *IEEE International Conference on Multimedia and Expo 2000 (ICME 2000)*, New York (Vol. 2, pp. 727-730). Washington, DC: IEEE Computer Society.

Serpanos, D., Karakostas, G., & Wolf, W. (2000). Effective caching of Web objects using zipf's law. In *Multimedia and expo, 2000. icme 2000, ieee international conference* (Vol. 2, pp. 727–730).

Sharp, H., Rogers, Y., & Preece, J. (2007). *Interaction Design: Beyond Human-Computer Interaction*. West Sussex, England: John Wiley & Sons, Inc.

Shneiderman, B. (2000). Universal usability. *Communications of the ACM, 43*(5), 85–91. doi:10.1145/332833.332843

Shneiderman, B. (1998). *Designing the User Interface*. Reading, MA: Addison-Wesley.

Shneiderman, B. (2003). Promoting universal usability with multi-layer interface design. In *Proceedings of the 2003 Conference on Universal Usability (CUU 2003)*. New York: ACM.

Skov, M. B., & Stage, J. (2001). A Simple Approach to Web-Site Usability Testing. In *Proceedings of 1st International Conference on Universal Access in Human-Computer Interaction* (pp. 737-741). Mahwah, NJ: Lawrence-Erlbaum.

Skov, M. B., & Stage, J. (2004) Integrating Usability Design and Evaluation: Training Novice Evaluators in Usability Testing. In K. Hornbæk & J. Stage (Eds.), *Proceedings of the Workshop on Improving the Interplay between Usability Evaluation and User Interface Design, NordiCHI 2004* (pp. 31-35), Aalborg University, Department of Computer Science, HCI-Lab Report no. 2004/2.

Skov, M. B., & Stage, J. (2005) Supporting Problem Identification in Usability Evaluations. In *Proceedings of the Australian Computer-Human Interaction Conference 2005 (OzCHI'05)*. New York: ACM Press.

Slavkovic, A., & Cross, K. (1999). Novice heuristic evaluations of a complex interface. In *Proceedings of CHI 1999* (pp. 304-305). New York: ACM Press.

Snider, J. G., & Osgood, C. E. (Eds.). (1969). *Semantic Differential Technique: A SourceBook*. Chicago: AldineTransaction.

Soares, K., & Furtado, E. (2003). RUPi - A Unified Process that Integrates Human-Computer Interaction and Software Engineering. In *Workshop Bridging the Gap Between Software-Engineering and Human-Computer Interaction at ICSE 2003, Proceedings,* (pp. 41-48).

Sousa, K., & Furtado, E. (2005). A Unified Process Supported by a Framework for the Semi-Automatic Generation of Multi-Context UIs. In *12th International Workshop on Design, Proceedings.*

Sousa, K., Mendonça, H., & Vanderdonckt, J. (2007). Towards Method Engineering of Model-Driven User Interface Development. In *Task Models and Diagrams for User Interface Design* (pp. 112-125). Berlin: Springer.

Spearman, C. (1904). The proof and measurement of association between two things. *The American Journal of Psychology, 15*(1), 72–101. doi:10.2307/1412159

Spiliopoulou, M. (2000). Web usage mining for Web site evaluation. *Communications of the ACM, 43*(8), 127–134. doi:10.1145/345124.345167

Spiliotopoulos, D., & Kouroupetroglou, G. (2009). *Usability Methodologies for Spoken Dialogue Web Interfaces. Chapter in the book: Integrating Usability Engineering for Designing the Web Experience: Methodologies and Principles, 2009, Information Science Reference Press.* Pennsylvania, USA: IGI Global.

Spiliotopoulos, D., Stavropoulou, P., & Kouroupetroglou, G. (2009a). *Acoustic Rendering of Data Tables using Earcons and Prosody for Document Accessibility. Lecture Notes on Artificial Intelligence 5616* (pp. 587–596). Universal Access in HCI, Springer Berlin Heidelberg.

Spiliotopoulos, D., Stavropoulou, P., & Kouroupetroglou, G. (2009b). *Spoken Dialogue Interfaces: Integrating Usability. Lecture Notes in Computer Science 5889* (pp. 484–499). HCI and Usability for e-Inclusion, Springer Berlin Heidelberg.

Spiliotopoulos, D., Xydas, G., Kouroupetroglou, G., Argyropoulos, V., & Ikospentaki, K. (2010, June). Auditory Universal Accessibility of Data Tables using Naturally Derived Prosody Specification. [Springer Berlin Heidelberg.]. *Univ. Access Inf. Soc., 9*(2), 169–183. doi:10.1007/s10209-009-0165-0

Spool, J. M., Scanlon, T., Schroeder, W., Snyder, C., & DeAngelo, T. (1999). *Web Site Usability – A Designer's Guide.* San Francisco: Morgan Kaufmann Publishers.

Srivastava, U., Munagala, K., Widom, J., & Motwani, R. (2006). Query optimization over web services. VLDB '06, Seoul Korea.

Stanton, N. A., Salmon, P. M., Walker, G. H., Baber, C., & Jenkins, D. P. (2005). *Human Factors Methods: A Practical Guide for Engineering and Design.* London: Ashgate.

Stapleton, J. (2003). *DSDM: Business Focused Development* (2nd ed.). Harlow, UK.: Addison-Wesley.

Stephanidis, C. (Ed.). (2001). *User Interfaces for All: Concepts, Methods and Tools.* Mahwah, New Jersey: Lawrence Erlbaum Associates.

Stephanidis, C. (Ed.). (2009). *The Universal Access Handbook.* Boca Raton, Florida: CRC Press.

Stewart, T. (2009). *Usability or User Experience - What's the difference?* [Online]. Available: http://www.system-concepts.com/ articles/usability-articles/2008/usability-or-user-experience- whats-the-difference.html [Accessed 2010].

Stewart, V., & Stewart, A. (1981). *Business applications of the repertory grid.* Maidenhead, Berks.: McGraw-Hill.

Stieglitz, S. (2008). *Steuerung Virtueller Communities.* Wiesbaden: Gabler.

Stieglitz, S., Fuchß, C., Hillmann, O., & Lattemann, C. (2007). Mobile Learning by Using Ad Hoc Messaging Network. Proceedings of the International Conference on Interactive Mobile and Computer Aided Learning, Amman, Jordan.

Stojanovic, L. J. Schneider, A. Maedche, S.Libischer, R. Studer, T. Lumpp, A. Abecker, G.Breiter, J. Dinger. (2004). The Role of Ontologies in Autonomic Computing Systems. *IBM Systems Journal, 43*(3), 598–616.. doi:10.1147/sj.433.0598

Stormer, H., & Knorr, K. (2001). PDA- and Agent-based Execution of Workflow Tasks. Proceedings of Informatik 2001, Vienna, Austria, (pp. 968-973). Bonn, Germany: Gesellschaft für Informatik (GI).

Strang, T., & Linnhoff-Popien, C. (2004). A Context Modeling Survey, *Proceedings UbiComp 1st International Workshop on Advanced Context Modelling, Reasoning and Management,* Nottingham, UK.

Sullivan, T., & Matson, R. (2000, November 16-17). Barriers to Use: Usability and Content Accessibility on the Web's Most Popular Sites. In *Proceedings of Conference on Universal Usability* (pp. 139-144). New York: ACM.

Sutcliffe, A. (2001). Heuristic Evaluation of Website Attractiveness and Usability. *Interactive Systems: Design, Specification, and Verification* (LNCS 2220, pp. 183-198).

Swami, A., & Gupta, A. (1988). Optimizing large join query. Proceedings of SIGMOD, 8-17.

Tan, P., Steinbach, M., & Kumar, V. (2006). *Introduction to Data Mining.* Boston, MA: Pearson Pub.

Tan, F. B., & Tung, L. L. (2003). *Exploring website evaluation criteria using the repertory grid technique: A web designers' perspective.* Paper presented at the Second annual workshop on HCI research in MIS, Seattle: Washington.

Tatham, M., & Morton, K. (2005). *Developments in Speech Synthesis.* West Sussex, England: John Wiley & Sons, Inc.doi:10.1002/0470012609

Thatcher, J., Waddell, C. D., Henry, S. L., Swierenga, S., Urban, M. D., Burks, M., et al. (2003). *Constructing accessible web sites.* San Francisco: glasshaus.

The Nielsen Company. (2007). *Nielsen netratings.* Retrieved July 9, 2007, from http://www.nielsennetratings.com

Theofanos, M. F., & Redish, J. (2003). Bridging the gap: Between accessibility and usability. [ACM]. *Interaction, 10*(6), 36–51. doi:10.1145/947226.947227

Tingling, P., & Saeed, A. (2007). Extreme Programming in Action: A Longitudinal Case Study. In *Human-Computer Interaction. Interaction Design and Usability, Proceedings,* (pp. 242-251).

TraceGraph. (2005). *Trace graph tool.* Retrieved from http://www.tracegraph.com/ traceconverter.html

Tractinsky, N. & Hassenzahl, M. (2005). Arguing for Aesthetics in Human-Computer Interaction. *i-com, 4,* 66-68.

Troyer, O. M. F. D., & Leune, C. J. (1998). WSDM: a user centered design method for Web sites. *Computer Networks and ISDN Systems, 30*(1-7), 85 - 94.

Tscherning, H., Mathiassen, L. (2010). Early Adoption of Mobile Devices: A Social Network Perspective, Journal of Information Technology Theory and Application (JITTA). 11(1), Article 3.

Turunen, M., Hakulinen, J., & Kainulainen, A. (2006). Evaluation of a Spoken Dialogue System with Usability Tests and Long-term Pilot Studies: Similarities and Differences. In Proc. 9th International Conference on Spoken Language Processing - INTERSPEECH pp. 1057-1060.

Usablenet. (n.d.). *LIFT online.* Retrieved April 12, 2007, from http://www.usablenet.com/ products_services / lift_online/ lift_online.html

van der Vet, P N. Mars. (1998). Bottom-up Construction of Ontologies. *IEEE Transactions on Knowledge and Data Engineering, 16*(4), 513–526..doi:10.1109/69.706054

van Kuppevelt, J., Dybkjær, L., & Bernsen, N. O. (Eds.). (2005). *Advances in natural multimodal dialogue.* Dordrecht, The Netherlands: Springer. doi:10.1007/1-4020-3933-6

van Maanen, J. (1998). *Qualitative studies of organizations. The Administrative Science Quarterly, Series in Organization Theory and Behaviour.* London: Sage Publications.

van Velsen, L., Van der Geest, T., Klaassen, R., & Steehouder, M. (2008). User-centered evaluation of adaptive and adaptable systems: a literature review. *The Knowledge Engineering Review, 23*(3), 261–281. doi:10.1017/S0269888908001379

van Welie, M., van der Veer, G. C., & Eliëns, A. (2000). Patterns as Tools for User Interface Design, In *International Workshop on Tools for Working with Guidelines,* (pp. 313-324) October 7-8, Biarritz, France. Retrieved June 17, 2005, from http://www.welie.com/about.html

Venkatesh, V. (2000). Determinants of Perceived Ease of Use: Integrating Control, Intrinsic Motivation, and Emotion into the Technology Acceptance Model. *Information Systems Research, 11*(4), 342–365. doi:10.1287/isre.11.4.342.11872

Verdaasdonk, E. G. G., Stassen, L. P. S., Widhiasmara, P. P., & Dankelman, J. (2008). Requirements for the design and implementation of checklists for surgical processes. *Surgical Endoscopy.*

Verlinden, J., & Coenders, M. (2000). *Qualitative usability measurement of websites by employing the repertory grid technique.* Paper presented at the CHI 2000: extended abstracts, The Hague, The Netherlands.

W3C (2004). *Composite Capability/ Preference Profiles (CC/PP),* W3C Recommendation January 2004, Retrieved November 02, 2008, from http://www.w3.org/TR/ CCPP-struct-vocab/.

W3C Member Submission (2004) OWL-S: Semantic Markup for Web Services, http://www.w3.org/Submission/OWL-S

W3C. (2001). W*CAG WG minutes 29 March 2001*. Retrieved July 20, 2007, from http://www.w3.org/ WAI/ GL/ 2001/03/ 29-minutes.html

Wahlster, W. (Ed.). (2006). *SmartKom: Foundations of Multimodal Dialogue Systems*. Berlin, Heidelberg: Springer-Verlag. doi:10.1007/3-540-36678-4

Wainer, J., Barthelmess, P., & Kumar, A. (2003). W-RBAC —A Workflow Security Model Incorporating Controlled Overriding of Constraints. *International Journal of Cooperative Information Systems, 12*(4), 455–485. doi:10.1142/ S0218843003000814

Walker, M. A., Kamm, C. A., & Litman, D. J. (2000). Towards developing general models of usability with PARADISE. *Natural Language Engineering, 6*(3-4), 363–377. doi:10.1017/S1351324900002503

Walker, M. A., Litman, D. J., Kamm, C. A., & Abella, A. (1998). Evaluating spoken dialogue agents with PARADISE: Two case studies. *Computer Speech & Language, 12*(3), 317–347. doi:10.1006/csla.1998.0110

Walker, M. A., Borland, J., & Kamm, C. A. (1999). The utility of elapsed time as a usability metric for spoken dialogue systems. In Proc. IEEE Automatic Speech Recognition and Understanding Workshop - ASRU, pp. 317–320.

Wallbaum, M., & Diepolder, S. (2005). Benchmarking Wireless LAN Location Systems. *Proceedings of the Second IEEE International Workshop on Mobile Commerce and Services (WMCS '05)*, Munich, Germany (pp. 42-51). Los Alamitos, USA: IEEE Computer Society.

Wang, K., & Li, B. (2002). Efficient and Guaranteed Service Coverage in Partionable Mobile Ad-hoc Networks. IEEE INFOCOM, 1089-1098.

Want, R., Hopper, A., Falcao, M., & Gibbons, J. (1992). The active badge location system. [TOIS]. *ACM Transactions on Information Systems, 19*(1), 91–102. doi:10.1145/128756.128759

Ward, N., & Tsukahara, W. (2003). A Study in Responsiveness in Spoken Dialog. *International Journal of Human-Computer Studies, 59*, 603–630. doi:10.1016/ S1071-5819(03)00085-5

Watanabe, T. (2007). Experimental evaluation of usability and accessibility of heading elements. In *Proceedings of International Cross-Disciplinary Conference on Web Accessibility (W4A)* (pp. 157-164). New York: ACM Press.

Wattenberg, T. (2004). Beyond standards: Reaching usability goals through user participation. *SIGACCESS Accessability and Computing, 79*, 10–20. doi:10.1145/1040053.1040055

Weinschenk, S., & Barker, D. T. (2000). *Designing effective speech interfaces*. New York: John Wiley & Sons, Inc.

Weinschenk, S. (2007). *Trends in user-centred design* (White Paper). Fairfield, IA: Human Factors International.

Witt, U. (1997). "Lock-in" vs. "critical masses" - Industrial change under network externalities. *International Journal of Industrial Organization, 15*(6), 753–773. doi:10.1016/ S0167-7187(97)00010-6

Woerndl, W., & Schlichter, J. (2008). Contextualized Recommender Systems: Data Model and Recommendation Process. In Pazos-Arias, J., Delgado Kloos, C., & Lopez Nores, M. (Eds.), *Personalization of Interactive Multimedia Services: A Research and Development Perspective*. Hauppauge, NY: Nova Publishers.

Woerndl, W., & Eigner, R. (2007). Context-aware, collaborative applications for inter-networked cars. *Proceedings of the 5th IEEE International Workshop on Distributed and Mobile Collaboration (DMC 2007)*, Paris, France, IEEE.

Woerndl, W., & Groh, G. (2007). Utilizing physical and social context to improve recommender systems. *Proceedings of the IEEE Workshop on Web Personalization and Recommender Systems (WPRS), International Conference on Web Intelligence (WI 2007)*, Silicon Valley, USA, IEEE.

Woerndl, W., & Hristov, A. (2009). Recommending Resources in Mobile Personal Information Management. *Proc. Third International Conference on Digital Society (ICDS2009)*, Cancun, Mexico.

Woerndl, W., & Woehrl, M. (2008), SeMoDesk: Towards a Mobile Semantic Desktop. *Proceedings Personal Information Management (PIM) Workshop*, CHI 2008 Conference, Florence, Italy.

Woerndl, W., Schueller, C., & Wojtech, R. (2007). A Hybrid Recommender System for Context-aware Recommendations of Mobile Applications. *Proceedings IEEE 3rd International Workshop on Web Personalisation, Recommender Systems and Intelligent User Interfaces (WPRSIUI'07)*, Istanbul, Turkey.

Wolkerstorfer, P., Tscheligi, M., Sefelin, R., Milchrahm, H., Hussain, Z., Lechner, M., et al. (2008). Probing an agile usability process. In *CHI '08: Extended abstracts on Human factors in computing systems Proceedings*, (pp. 2151-2158). New York: ACM.

Woo, S.-C. M., & Singh, S. (2001). Scalable routing protocol for ad hoc networks. *Wireless Networks, 7*(5), 513–529. doi:10.1023/A:1016726711167

Xiaoyan, H., Kaixin, X., & Gerla, M. (2002). Scalable routing protocols for mobile ad hoc networks. *Network IEEE, 16*(4), 11–21. doi:10.1109/MNET.2002.1020231

Xu, K., Hong, X., & Gerla, M. (2003). Landmark routing in ad hoc networks with mobile backbones. *Journal of Parallel and Distributed Computing, 63*(2), 110–122. doi:10.1016/S0743-7315(02)00058-8

Xydas, G., Argyropoulos, V., Karakosta, T., & Kouroupetroglou, G. (2004). An Open Platform for Conducting Psycho-Acoustic Experiments in the Auditory Representation of Web Documents, Proc. of the Conf. ACOUSTICS 2004, 27-28 Sept. 2004, Thessalonica, pp. 157-164

Yahoo. (n.d.). *Yahoo site explorer*. Retrieved May 7, 2007, from http://siteexplorer.search.yahoo.com

Yang, Y., & Pederson, J. (1997). A comparative study of feature selection in text categorization. *Proceedings of the Fourteenth International Conference on Machine Learning*, Nashville, TN: Morgan Kaufmann, 412-420.

Yankelovich, N., Levow, G. A., & Marx, M. (1995). *Designing Speech Acts: Issues in speech user interfaces. Human Factors in Computing Systems* (pp. 369–376). Denver: Association of Computing Machinery.

Yesilada, Y., Stevens, R., Goble, C. A., & Hussein, S. (2004). Rendering tables in audio: the interaction of structure and reading styles. In *Proceedings of the ACM SIGACCESS Conference on Computers and Accessibility (ASSETS)*, (pp. 16-23). Berlin: Springer.

Yin, R. (1994). *Case study research: design and methods*. London: Sage.(Stewart, 2009)

Yoo, H., & Lafortune, S. (1989). An intelligent search method for query optimization by semi-joins. *IEEE Transactions on Knowledge and Data Engineering, 1*(2), 226–237. doi:10.1109/69.87962

Yu, C. T., Guh, K. C., Zhang, W., Templeton, M., Brill, D., & Chen, A. L. P. (1987). Algorithms to process distributed queries in fast local networks. *IEEE Transactions on Computers, C-36*, 10, 1153–1164. doi:10.1109/TC.1987.1676856

Yu, C. T., Chang, C. C., Templeton, M., Brill, D., & Lund E. (1985). Query processing in a fragmented relational database system: Mermaid. IEEE Trans. Software Eng. SE-11 8, 795-810.

Yu-Chee, T., Sze-Yao, N., Yuh-Shyan, C., & Jang-Ping, S. (2002). The Broadcast Storm Problem in a Mobile Ad Hoc Network. *Wireless Networks, 8*(2-3), 153–167.

Zhao, H., Xia, C. H., Liu, Z., & Towsley, D. (2010). *Distributed resource allocation for synchronous fork and join processing networks*. SIGMETRICS.

Zhen, B., Park, J., & Kim, Y. (2003). Scatternet formation of Bluetooth ad networks. Proceedings of the 36th Annual Hawaii International Conference on System Sciences, Hawaii, USA.

Zipf, G. K. (1929). Relativity frequency as a determinant of phonetic change. *Harvard Studies in Classical Philology*, XL.

About the Contributors

Ghazi Alkhatib is an assistant professor of software engineering at the College of Computer Science and Information Technology, Applied Science University (Amman, Jordan). In 1984, he obtained his Doctor of Business Administration from Mississippi State University in information systems with minors in computer science and accounting. Since then, he has been engaged in teaching, consulting, training, and research in the area of computer information systems in the US and gulf countries. In addition to his research interests in databases and systems analysis and design, he has published several articles and presented many papers in regional and international conferences on software processes, knowledge management, e-business, Web services, and agent software, workflow, and portal/grid computing integration with Web services.

* * *

David W. Aha supervises the Adaptive Systems Section (Code 5514) within NRL's Navy Center for Applied Research in Artificial Intelligence. His projects, whose foci vary from automated maritime threat analysis to goal formulation in continuous planning environments, involve the development of decision aids for DoD and other sponsors. His research interests include case-based reasoning, mixed-initiative reasoning, machine learning (i.e., collective classification), and related topics. He founded the UCI Repository of Machine Learning Databases, and has received three Best Paper awards. David has (co-)organized 18 international events, (co-)edited three special journal issues on AI topics, serves on the editorial boards for three journals and annually on several conference PCs., and was a AAAI Councilor.

Daniela Andrei is an assistant professor at the Faculty of Psychology and Education Sciences, Babes-Bolyai University, Cluj-Napoca, Romania. She is a licensed psychologist and holds a Master degree in Human Resources Management and Marketing. She has participated in several international training programs in the field of human-computer interaction and interaction design and recently became involved in COST Action IC0904 on the Integration of Trans-sectorial IT Design and Evaluation. Her current research focuses on integrating the use social sciences methods in interactive systems design, implementation of interactive systems in organizations, compatibility between interactive systems' design and organizational culture.

Sikha Bagui is an Associate Professor in the Department of Computer Science at the University of West Florida, Pensacola, Florida. She has authored several books on database and SQL, and her areas of research are database and database design, data mining, pattern recognition, and statistical computing.

Michele Brocco received his bachelor and master degree in computer science from the Technische Universitaet Muenchen (TUM), Germany in 2005 and 2007 respectively. In his master thesis he designed and implemented the context-aware gas station recommender system described in this paper. Since 2007, he is a doctoral researcher at the chair for Applied Informatics / Cooperative Systems at TUM. At present time he is working on projects concerned with the design and development of intelligent IT-support systems tailored for Open Innovation processes funded by the German Ministry of Research and Education (BMBF). These support systems include for example trend spotting services and services to improve awareness in terms of fame and reputation as well as skill management and creativity support systems. His current research focus is on the analysis and development of algorithmic team composition and team recommendation approaches within large-scale communities such as networks of innovators or large enterprises.

Michael Decker studied industrial engineering with focus on computer science and operations research at the University of Karlsruhe (TH) in Germany. Directly after receiving his diploma he joined the research group "Mobile Business" at the Institute of Applied Informatics and Formal Description Methods (AIFB) at this University's faculty for economics. Meanwhile, the University of Karlsruhe became part of the Karlsruhe Institute of Technology (KIT). The research group concentrates on specific problems for small and medium-sized enterprises (SME) when employing mobile technologies, e.g., when developing mobile applications for customers or for the support of internal business processes. Another focus of research is the employment of tamper-resistant smartcards to tackle mobile-specific security issues. Mr. Decker's main research topic is the modeling of access control policies which are process-aware and regard the user's current location. From January till August 2010 Mr. Decker also stayed as guest researcher at the "School of Software" at the "Beijing Institute of Technology" (BIT) in China.

Robert Eigner graduated from Technische Universitaet Muenchen (TUM) with a diploma in computer science and then started working as a research assistant at the chair for Applied Informatics / Cooperative Systems (Prof. Dr. J. Schlichter). Together with other German universities and major car manufacturers, he was engaged in the national research project Networks-on-Wheels where he focused on mobile context-aware applications based on car-to-car-networking. The project aimed at specifying and standardising a communication system for transmission of sensor data und further information (e.g. hazard warnings) between vehicles based on standard WLAN technologies, which was demonstrated in a reference implementation. Based on the work in this project, he pursued his research on context-modeling in vehicular ad-hoc networks using semantic web technologies; a field, in which he (co-)authored several papers and for which he finally received his PhD degree from TUM in 2010.

Christoph Fuchß is founder and CEO of Virtimo Webbased Applications, a company that offers consulting services in the field of business process management (BPM), application integration and mobile networks. He holds a master degree in Information Science from the University of Potsdam and studied IT at the universities of Paderborn, Berlin and Potsdam. Beside the scientific research commitment within his company towards BPM and collaboration, he published several articles on mobile ad-hoc messaging in international journals. Before entering the field of BPM consulting he worked as a research engineer on telemedicine at the academic medical center of Charité Berlin. In this position he was engaged in research on mobile network communication and developed the theoretical background of AMNETs.

E. George Dharma Prakash Raj received his M.Sc,MPhil and PhD degrees in Computer Science from Bharathidasan University in 1990, 1998 and 2008 respectively. He is currently working as a Lecturer in the Department of Computer Science, Bharathidasan University, Tiruchirapalli, India. He has published several research papers in various International/National Journals and Conference proceedings. His main Research Interest is in Computer Networking, with an emphasis on Quality of Service Routing and Congestion Control. He is in the Editorial Board of various International Journals. He is also a Full time member of Indian Association of Research in Computing Science (IARCS) of Tata Institute of Fundamental Research Mumbai.

Ali Ghorbani has held a variety of positions in academia for the past 29 years including heading up project and research groups and as department chair, director of computing services, director of extended learning and as assistant dean. He received his PhD and MasterÕs in Computer Science from the University of New Brunswick, and the George Washington University, Washington D.C., USA, respectively. Dr. Ghorbani currently serves as Dean of the Faculty of Computer Science. He holds UNB Research Scholar position. His current research focus is Web Intelligence, Network & Information Security, Complex Adaptive Systems, and Critical Infrastructure Protection. He authored more than 220 reports and research papers in journals and conference proceedings and has edited 8 volumes. He served as General Chair and Program Chair/co-Chair for 7 International Conferences, and organized over 10 International Workshops. Dr. Ghorbani is the founding Director of Information Security Centre of Excellence at UNB. He is also the coordinator of the Privacy, Security and Trust (PST) network at UNB. Dr. Ghorbani is the co-Editor-In-Chief of Computational Intelligence, an international journal, and associate editor of the International Journal of Information Technology and Web Engineering and the ISC journal of Information Security.

Kalyan Moy Gupta, is the founder and president of Knexus Research Corporation, a company dedicated to providing intelligent system research services to the government and industry. His research interests span various artificial intelligence (AI) topics such as knowledge representation and discovery, machine learning, relational inference, automated knowledge brokering, natural language understanding, information and knowledge extraction and ontologies. Products of his research are deployed in information extraction companies such as Cymfony, decision support applications company such as CDM Technologies, and in manufacturing & services companies such as DuPont, Bombardier Aerospace, and Honeywell Systems. He has authored four U.S. patents, and has published over 4 dozen articles in journals and peer reviewed conferences on various AI topics. He obtained his PhD in business administration from McMaster University, Canada, in 1996.

Adriana-Mihaela Guran is lecturer at the Department of Computer Science of the Faculty of Mathematics and Computer Science, Babeş-Bolyai University of Cluj-Napoca (Romania). She holds a bachelor's degree in computer science and a master's degree in computer science (both from the University of Cluj-Napoca). She has a PhD focusing on ergonomic modeling of user interfaces obtained from the same university. Her current research focuses on integrating social sciences methods in interactive systems design, automatic usability evaluation methods, and intelligent interfaces.

Mark Kilfoil received Master's Degree in computer science from The University of New Brunswick, Canada, in 2004, and is currently pursuing his PhD degree. He is a founding member of the Intelligent and Adaptive Systems Research Group at UNB. His current research interests include multi-agent negotiation, adaptive web systems, mobile agents and information management and filtering technologies.

Georgios Kouroupetroglou holds a B.Sc. in Physics and a Ph.D. in Communications and Signal Processing. He is the Director of the Speech and Accessibility Laboratory, Department of Informatics and Telecommunications, University of Athens and Head of the e-Accessibility Unit for Students with Disabilities. His research interests focuses on the area of Speech Communication, Voice Technologies and Computer Accessibility, as parts of the major domain of Human-Computer Interaction. Currently he is also involved in the research domains on Document Accessibility, Augmentative and Alternative Communication and Emotional Computer Interaction. Professor G. Kouroupetroglou has actively participated as in more than 52 European Union and National funded research projects, and he served as scientific coordinator among the 34 of them. He has been reviewer or evaluator and member of working groups and/or technical panels of numerous European Union's projects and programs.

Roy Ladner is the director of the Data Architecture and Administration Division at the Naval Meteorology and Oceanography Command. He serves as staff lead and directs technical, programmatic and administrative aspects of the data and information life cycle to support all METOC and geospatial information and services information requirements for the Naval METOC Command. Ladner also performs as the agent for the Command's Navy-wide role as the functional data manager for the METOC/GI&S functional area and serves as co-lead for METOC data and information standardization across the Department of Defense.

Bruce Lin is a computer scientist employed by the Naval Research Lab at Stennis Space Center. Lin conducts research and software development for the Marine Geosciences Division specializing in image analysis, machine learning, and geospatial web services. He is also a PhD candidate in computer science at Louisiana State University completing his dissertation research in computer-aided cancer diagnosis.

Adam Loggins, MS, University of West Florida, Pensacola, Florida. Mr. Loggins is an Engineering Scientist Associate at The Applied Research Laboratories, The University of Texas at Austin. His main interests are in databases, networks and artificial intelligence.

Perfecto Mariño received the Ph.D. degree in Telecommunications Engineering from the Polytechnic University of Madrid (Spain) in 1984. From 1978 to 1993 he was Associate Professor in the Electronic Technology Department (University of Vigo, Spain). In 1988 he was Visiting scientist in the Computer Science Department of Carnegie Mellon University (Pittsburgh, USA). Since 1993 he has been a Full Professor in the Electronic Technology Department (University of Vigo, Spain).

Drakoulis Martakos is an associate professor and head of the Sector of Computer Systems and Applications at the Department of Informatics and Telecommunications of the National and Kapodistrian University of Athens, Greece. He is also director of the Information Systems Laboratory (ISLab) Research Group within the department. Professor Martakos is a consultant to public and private organizations, a project leader in numerous national and international projects and the author or co-author of more than 70 scientific publications and a number of technical reports and studies.

Philip Moore is a senior software engineer with Knexus Research Corporation, where he researches and develops distributed intelligent systems applications. His research interests include human-computer interaction, artificial intelligence in gaming, and empirical evaluation of intelligent systems. He currently specializes in large- scale integrations of knowledge discovery and gaming systems. He has published in journals such as Soft Computing, the Journal of Chemical Physics, Journal of Metals and the Journal of Materials Engineering and Performance, as well as in peer-reviewed conference proceedings. His accomplishments include Best Paper and Best Video awards from AI conferences and developing a distributed question-answering application server for Intelligence Analysts which was demonstrated for the U.S. Congress. He received his BS in computer science from the University of Maryland in 2002.

Santiago Otero received the M.S. degree in telecommunications engineering from the University of Vigo, Vigo, Spain, in 2003. Currently, he is a researcher with the Digital Communications Division, Electronic Technology Department, University of Vigo. e-mail: jsotero@uvigo.es.

G.P. Sajeev is now a Ph.D. candidate at National Institute of Technology Calicut (NITC). He received M.Tech degree in computer science and engineering from NITC in March 2000. He is the faculty member of Govt Engineering College Kozhikode, Inida. His research interests include web cache systems, p2p networking, traffic measurement and modeling and web server acceleration.

Fernando Pérez Fontán obtained his degree in Telecommunications Engineering in 1982 from the Technical University of Madrid and his PhD in 1992 from the same university. After working in industry since 1984 he became an assistant professor at the University of Vigo in 1988. In 1993 he became a senior lecturer (associate professor) and in 1999 he became a full professor at the Signal Theory and Communications Department of the University of Vigo. He lectures in Radiocommunication Systems, especially in terrestrial fixed and mobile system related topics. He is the author of a number of books and journal papers and has been the leader in a number of projects funded by public and private entities. He has participated in several ESA projects as the University of Vigo leader dealing with propagation effects on GNSS2, Galileo and land mobile satellite systems. In the frame of these contracts, statistical and deterministic propagation tools were developed. One such deterministic tool is based on ray-tracing and UTD techniques, which was successfully used within those contracts. He participates in ITU-RWG3 on Propagation modeling, where he has contributed with two models to the current ITU-R Recommendation 681 on land mobile satellite propagation. He has been Management Committee Member of EU' COST 255 and 280, and currently participates with the same status in COST 297. He is also a participant in EU's Network of Excellence SatNex on Satellite Communication Systems. Currently he participates as the University of Vigo leader in EU Project ANASTASIA where he studies interference effects on aeronautical navigation systems and channel effects on aeronautical satellite communication systems. He is also currently working on a contract with AENA, the Spanish national aeronautical authority, where multipath effects on ILS and VOR navigation systems are being studied using the ray-tracing tools mentioned above.

André P. Freire is a researcher at the University of York. His research interests are related to techniques and methods to help in the inclusive design and evaluation of web systems. In his previous research projects at the University of São Paulo, he conducted research on the awareness of web developers in Brazil regarding web accessibility. He has also conducted wide studies on the accessibility of governmental web sites at Brazil over time. His current work is focused on the investigation of issues regarding the impact of the involvement of users with disabilities on quantitative metrics in the accessibility evaluation of web sites.

M.P. Sebastian received his Bachelors degree in Electronics & Communication Engineering from Kerala University, Trivandrum and Masters degree in Computer Science & Engineering from Indian Institute of Science, Bangalore. He received his PhD also from the Indian Institute of Science, Bangalore. Prior to joining IIM Kozhikode as Professor, he served at National Institute of Technology Calicut as Professor & Head of the Department of Computer Science & Engineering and as Chairman of Information Technology & Communication Centre. He served in Space Applications Centre (ISRO), Ahmedabad and Bharat Electronics Ltd., Bangalore also for short durations. His areas of teaching/ research interest include Cloud Computing, Enterprise Resource Computing, Information Security Management, Networks Management and Software Project Management, and have published many research papers. He is on the editorial board of many journals and is a reviewer of international journals including IEEE Transactions on Vehicular Technology, Wiley InterScience Journal on Wireless Communications and Mobile Computing, IEE Proceedings Computers and Digital Techniques, Optics Letters, and International Journal of Modelling and Simulation.

Panagiota Papadopoulou is currently a research associate at the Department of Informatics, University of Athens. She holds a B.Sc (Hons) from the Department of Informatics, University of Athens, an MSc with distinction in Distributed and Multimedia Information Systems from Heriot-Watt University, U.K. and a PhD from the Department of Informatics, University of Athens. She has worked as a visiting professor at the University of Athens, University of Pireaus and the University of Peloponnese. Dr. Papadopoulou has also actively participated in a number of European Community and National research projects. Her current research interests focus on web-based information systems, interface design and online trust.

Helen Petrie is Head of the HCI Group as a Professor of Human-Computer Interaction in the Department of Computer Science. She has been involved in many research projects on the design and evaluation of technology for disabled and elderly people, including 12 EU-funded projects; for the EU-funded MultiReader Project she was Project Leader. She led the team that conducted the largest and most comprehensive study of web site accessibility for the Disability Rights Commission of Great Britain and the same team conducted a similar study of web accessibility for the UK Council of Museums, Libraries and Archives (MLA). She also led the academic work on the UK funded VISTA Project on the accessibility of digital television which won the Royal Television Society Award for Technical Innovation in 2003. She is on the board of a number of academic journals, is a Lay Advisor to the Royal College of Ophthalmologists and is a trustee of the Foundation for Assistive Technology (FAST).

Frederick Petry received a PhD in computer and information science from The Ohio State University. He has been on the computer science faculty of the University of Alabama in Huntsville, Ohio State University, Tulane University, and is currently a computer scientist at the Naval Research Laboratory. His research interests include representation of imprecision via fuzzy sets and rough sets in databases, GIS and other information systems, and Semantic Web technology. Petry has over 350 scientific publications including 135 journal articles/book chapters and 8 books written or edited. He is an IEEE fellow, a fellow of the International Fuzzy Systems Association and a distinguished scientist of the ACM.

Christopher Power is a Research Fellow in the University of York HCI Group. Coming from a software engineering background, he has participated in multiple research projects relating to web accessibility, specifically working on the development of test methodologies for web accessibility. Further, he has worked in the management of requirements for people with disabilities in the creation of websites and in the establishing the accessibility of web authoring tools.

SinthuJanita Prakash received her M.C.A degree from Bharathidasan University in 1996 and M.Phil degree in Computer Science from Mother Teresa University, India in 2001. She is pursuing her PhD in Computer Science in the area of QoS related Congestion Control Algorithms She is currently working as Head, Department Of Information Technology at Cauvery College for Women, Tiruchirapalli, India. She has attended several seminars and conferences and has presented and published research papers in various International National conference proceedings. Her area of Interest is Quality of Service in Computer Networking and Wireless Communication.

David Prytherch is Senior Research Fellow in Haptics and Computer Interface Design working in User-lab, a dedicated research and development lab in User Centred Design, Human Computer Interaction and Haptics. Prior to this, he had 30 years professional experience as a freelance glass engraver/sculptor and is a Fellow of the Guild of Glass Engravers. Research interests include Haptic (tacit) learning and teaching, the role of haptics in skill development, particularly in the arts, haptic implications in activity satisfaction and motivation, and issues surrounding tool use and material embodiment, particularly with regard to computer interface systems. A particular interest lies in the development of inclusive interface systems that facilitate transparent access to creative processes for people with disabilities.

Kasmir Raja received his M.Sc Degree and Ph.D degree in Physics from University of Madras in 1969 and 1979 respectively and M.Phil degree in Computer Science from Bharathidasan University in 1995.He is currently working as Dean Research, SRM University, Kattankulathur, Chennai, India. He has published several research papers in various International / National Journals and Conference proceedings.His areas of Interest are Parallel Processing, Digital Image Processing, Artificial Neural Networks, Quality of Service in Computer Networks and Knowledge Engineering.

Holger Regenbrecht is a Senior Lecturer at the department of Information Science at Otago University. His research interests include Human-Computer Interaction (HCI), (collaborative) Augmented Reality, 3D teleconferencing, psychological aspects of Mixed Reality, and three-dimensional user interfaces (3DUI). He is a member of IEEE, ACM, and igroup.org and serves as a reviewer and auditor for several conferences and institutions

Hassenet Slimani received her engineering degree and her master's degree in computer science from the Faculty of Sciences of Tunis (University of Tunis Elmanar) in 2003 and 2005 respectively. She is currently pursuing a PhD in mobile query processing in spatiotemporal databases.

Andy Saxon is Director of e-Learning at Birmingham City University's Institute of Art and Design, and a University Senior Learning and Teaching Fellow. His research interests lie in the application of arts-based models of designing to software user interface development, the evaluation of the software user interface and user experience design for software. The main focus of this work has been toward web and multimedia software. He is also involved in the development of e-learning initiatives within the Institute's Learning and Teaching Centre, which he leads. These include the design and evaluation of reusable learning objects, and research into e-pedagogies for art and design. He supervises Doctoral and Masters' students in the School of Visual Communication, where he is also Head of Research.

Greg Scowen received his bachelor's degree in information science from the University of Otago in 2006 and completed post-graduate research studies at the University of Otago in 2007. He is currently working as a software engineer/web developer at the Swiss Federal Institute of Technology (ETH) in Zürich, developing advanced web applications for the library. His research interest areas include usability, web development, and e-learning.

Mikael B. Skov is an associate professor at the HCI Lab, Department of Computer Science, Aalborg University, Denmark. Mikael completed his PhD in 2002 at Aalborg University on design of interactive narratives. He teaches general human-computer interaction to undergraduate computer science and informatics students as well as advanced human-computer interaction to graduate students. Mikael has supervised more than 25 Masters students on various topics within interaction design or human-computer interaction. His research interests are human-computer interaction and interaction design especially within mobile, pervasive, and ubiquitous computing. Mikael is currently involved in a major research project on improving web portal usability in close collaboration with several industry partners.

Dimitris Spiliotopoulos is currently a member of the Speech and Accessibility Laboratory of the Department of Informatics and Telecommunications, the National and Kapodistrian University of Athens, Greece. His research focuses on natural language engineering, speech processing, text/document analysis, intonation, natural language generation, spoken dialogue systems, universal accessibility, design-for-all, text-to-speech, document-to-audio, speech acoustics and evaluation. Academic studies include a PhD in Language Technology, a MPhil in Computation, a MA in Linguistics, and a BSc in Computation. He is a member of the IEEE Signal Processing Society, ISCA and the ACL. He has participated in several national and international research projects and his work has been published in international journals, books and conferences.

Tasos Spiliotopoulos is a researcher at the Department of Informatics and Telecommunications, National and Kapodistrian University of Athens, Greece. As a member of the Information Systems Laboratory Research Group since 2000 he has participated in numerous EU and national research projects. His current research focuses on human-computer interaction, computer systems usability, the social web and online security and privacy.

Jan Stage is full professor at the HCI Lab, Department of Computer Science, Aalborg University, Denmark. Jan holds a PhD in computer science from University of Oslo. His current research interests are in usability evaluation and user interaction design, with emphasis on reduction on the effort needed to conduct usability evaluations. He has published several journal and conference articles in these topics as well as in information system development and methods for software development. Jan teaches human-computer interaction and usability engineering to undergraduate, graduate and PhD students in computer science, informatics and information technology. He is also conduction training and consulting in software companies. Jan is currently involved in a major research project on improving web portal usability in close collaboration with several industry partners.

Pepi Stavropoulou holds a first degree in Linguistics and an MSc in Speech and Language Processing. Her main research interests include spoken dialogue systems, usability and design-for-all, prosody and the interface between prosody and pragmatics. She is a member of the Speech and Accessibility Laboratory of the Department of Informatics and Telecommunications at the University of Athens and has participated in several research and industry projects. She is currently undertaking her PhD on the relationship between Prosody and Information Structure and the utilization of this relationship for improving synthetic speech output in spoken dialogue interfaces.

Stefan Stieglitz is assistant professor of communication and collaboration management at the institute of information systems at the University of Muenster. He is founder of the Competence Center Smarter Work at the European Research Center for Information Systems (ERCIS). Furthermore, he is teacher at the School of Design Thinking at the Hasso-Plattner Institute. He formerly held positions as project manager in the financial industry and in the Internet economy. His research focuses on economic, social, and technological aspects of collaboration software. Of particular interest in his work is to learn more about the usage of technology based social networks in companies. Additionally, he is engaged in the field of unified communication & collaboration. Dr. Stieglitz studied business economics at the universities of Cologne, Paderborn, and Potsdam. He published several articles in reputable international journals. He is also a reviewer for international journals and conferences in the field of information systems.

Richard Sween is a STEP student employee at the Naval Research Lab, Stennis Space Center. He has worked on development of the Integrated Web Broker and participated in a demonstration of its capabilities at the NATO Undersea Research Center, La Spezia Italy, during the Turkish Straits Exercise. He is currently developing a Universal Core (UCore) based system for request/ response of MetOc data to be demonstrated during the 2010 Trident Warrior exercise in San Diego, CA. He is pursuing a BSc in computer science at Mississippi State University.

Shane Walker is Director of Knowledge Transfer Partnerships at Birmingham City University's Institute of Art and Design. This role determines current opportunities to develop capability and identify barriers to growth faced by creative industries in the West Midlands region and beyond. As a member of the University's Human Computer Interaction Design Research Group his research centres on the role of the users' motivation and emotion in software user interface evaluation and user experience design for software.

Wolfgang Woerndl obtained diploma degrees in both computer science and business administration at Technische Universitaet Muenchen (TUM) and Fernuniversitaet Hagen. After working in the industry for several years, he returned to Technische Universitaet Muenchen as a doctoral candidate and completed his dissertation on privacy in decentralized user profile management in 2003. Since then, he is a senior researcher and lecturer at the chair for Applied Informatics / Cooperative Systems at TUM. Given lectures and other courses include topics like distributed applications, computer-supported cooperative work, distributed problem solving and context-aware computing. His current research focuses on user modeling, personalization and recommender systems in a mobile environment. The goal of one current project is to apply different kind of context-aware recommender systems in various mobile scenarios. In addition, he investigates how to assist the user by services that are tailored towards her context and observed behaviour. Other past and present research interests include privacy enhancing technologies, personal information management and semantic web technologies.

Miguel Ángel Domínguez, Telecommunications Engineer from the University of Vigo (Spain, 1993). Received his doctorate in Telecommunications Engineering from the University of Vigo (Spain, 2000). Full Professor in the Electronic Technology Department (University of Vigo, Spain). Researcher of Digital Communications Division from the Electronic Technology Department (University of Vigo, Spain). Member of IEEE. e-mail: mdgomez@uvigo.es.

Faïza Najjar is an assistant professor at the National School of Computer Science and Engineering in Manouba (Tunisia). She received her PhD in Computer Science from the University of Tunis El-Manar, Tunisia, in June 1999. In 2003, she conducted a post-doctorate work on mobile computing and databases in the department of Computer Science and Engineering at SMU (Dallas-TX). Dr Najjar's current research interests are in pervasive and mobile computing and especially location based services.

Index